A2 PSYCHOLOGY

To Christine, Fleur, William,
and Juliet, with love

A2 PSYCHOLOGY

Key Topics

SECOND EDITION

Michael W. Eysenck

Psychology Press
Taylor & Francis Group

HOVE AND NEW YORK

First edition published 2003

Second edition published 2006 by Psychology Press Ltd
27 Church Road, Hove, East Sussex, BN3 2FA

http://www.psypress.co.uk
http://www.a-levelpsychology.co.uk

Simultaneously published in the USA and Canada by Taylor & Francis Inc
270 Madison Ave, New York, NY 10016

Psychology Press is part of the Taylor & Francis Group, an Informa business

British Library Cataloguing in Publication Data
A catalogue record for this book is available from the British Library

ISBN13: 978-1-84169-619-5
ISBN10: 1-84169-619-6

Cover design by Richard Massing
Typeset in India by Newgen Imaging Systems (P) Ltd
Printed and bound in Slovenia

CONTENTS

ABOUT THE AUTHOR

Michael W. Eysenck is one of the best-known British psychologists. He is Professor of Psychology and former Head of the Department of Psychology at Royal Holloway University of London, which is one of the leading departments in the United Kingdom. His academic interests lie mainly in cognitive psychology, with much of his research focusing on the role of cognitive factors in anxiety in normal and clinical populations.

He is an author of many titles, and his previous textbooks published by Psychology Press include *Psychology for A2 Level* (2001), *Psychology for AS Level, Third Edition* (2005), *Psychology: An International Perspective* (2004), *Psychology: A Student's Handbook* (2000), *Cognitive Psychology: A Student's Handbook, Fifth Edition* (2005, with Mark Keane), *Simply Psychology, Second Edition* (2002), *Perspectives on Psychology* (1994), *Individual Differences: Normal and Abnormal* (1994), and *Principles of Cognitive Psychology, Second Edition* (2001). He has also written the research monographs *Anxiety and Cognition: A Unified Theory* (1997), and *Anxiety: The Cognitive Perspective* (1992), along with the popular title *Happiness: Facts and Myths* (1990). He is also a keen supporter of Crystal Palace football club.

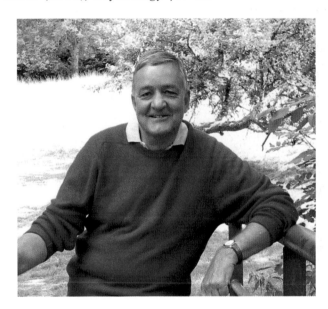

PREPARING FOR THE A2 EXAM

A2 Psychology overview p.3
- How does A2 differ from AS?
- Which options have I got?
- What do the units comprise?

How can I study more effectively? p.5
- How can I become more organised?
- What study strategies will be helpful?

How can I do well in the examination? p.6
- How can I revise effectively?
- What skills will I need for AO1 and AO2?
- How can I prepare for my examination essays?
- How can I write effective essays?
- How will I be assessed?
- Which strategies improve exam success and decrease stress?

Preparing for the A2 Exam

By Clare Charles

Head of Social Sciences & Psychology, North Leamington School, Leamington Spa

A2 PSYCHOLOGY OVERVIEW

You've coped with the demands of AS, well done. So now for A2. As you can see, the AQA A2 level examination consists of three papers: Unit 4 (the options paper, three questions to answer in 1½ hours); Unit 5 (the synoptic paper, three questions to answer in 2 hours); Unit 6 (coursework).

THREE MODULES

Unit 4	Unit 5	Unit 6
The options paper	**The synoptic paper**	**Coursework**
30% of A2 mark	40% of A2 mark	30% of A2 mark
1½ hours	2 hours	
30 minutes per question	40 minutes per question	
3 × 24-mark essays	2 × 30-mark essays and 1 structured question on the approaches	

Halve the percentages to get the total A level marks at A2, as your total A level grade comprises 50% AS and 50% A2.

How Does A2 Differ from AS?

The type of exam question
- Essays rather than structured answers except for the approaches question.

The ratio of AO1 to AO2 is now 50:50
- Not 60:40 as at AS and so you need more analysis and evaluation than at AS.
- Your answer needs to show an equal balance of knowledge and understanding and analysis and evaluation.

The emphasis on synopticity
- The difference in the number of essay marks between Units 4 and 5 is due to synoptic assessment.
- Synopticity is not that different from AO2 skills, e.g., methodological criticisms, using counterperspectives. So there is no need to see this as something new, you probably already have synoptic skills.

EXAM HINT

The minimum you must study is three topics from Unit 4, one topic from individual differences on Unit 5, three issues or three debates on Unit 5, and the approaches on Unit 5.

Options rather than compulsory content

- So choice, self-responsibility, and independence are required, rather than prescription! You can choose which topics to cover with your teacher's approval, and you have a choice over which content you revise as this depends on what you want to put into your essay.

The Options

The A2 course consists of options particularly on Unit 4, the options paper, and to a lesser extent on Unit 5, the synoptic paper. So the good news is you do not have to study all the elements of the A2 course. This textbook includes the topics most commonly taught at A2 according to our research—questionnaires were sent to teachers in schools and sixth form colleges all over the UK asking them which topics they taught, to find out which ones were the most popular. The results showed that some topics were widely taught and others were avoided; *A2 Psychology: Key Topics* reflects these findings and covers the topics that are liked best. There is still scope for choice as we include:

- Twice as many topics as you need for the Unit 4 options exam paper.
- The majority of the Unit 5 synoptic exam paper topics.
- Full coverage of the Unit 6 compulsory coursework section.
- The topics chosen span the six main areas in Psychology (Social, Physiological, Cognitive, Developmental, Comparative, and Individual Differences).

The end result is a smaller and less expensive textbook. We still encourage you to read around your chosen optional topics by referring to our main textbook, *Psychology for A2 Level* (M.W. Eysenck), which covers the complete course and that we hope you will find in your school or college library.

The Exam Units

Here we give a list of the topics available in this book. This selection is based on the findings of the survey on popular A2 choices. Compare this with the specification; if you prefer an option that is not available here, check the Psychology Press website for the further options available there (this is given at the end of this chapter).

EXAM HINT

The options paper (PYA4)—30 minutes = approximately 600 words, so six paragraphs of 100 words or four paragraphs of 150 words are needed.

EXAM HINT

The question numbers refer to the exam papers. It a good idea to make a mental note of these so that you can immediately turn to the questions you will be answering in the exam.

Unit 4 The options paper (PYA4)

- Social relationships, Q2
- Pro- and anti-social behaviour, Q3
- Biological rhythms, sleep, and dreaming, Q5
- Cognitive development, Q10
- Social and personality development, Q11
- Evolutionary explanations of human behaviour, Q15

One question is guaranteed per option. You need to have covered a minimum of three options for the Unit 4 exam paper, but may choose to do more than this to give you a choice of questions. As you can see, there is plenty of choice as we have provided six topics and you only have to answer questions on three of these.

Unit 5 The synoptic paper (PYA5)

- Psychopathology, Q2
- Treating mental disorders, Q3
- Issues: Gender bias; Cultural bias; Ethical issues; The use of non-human animals in psychological research, Q4 and Q5
- Debates: Free will and determinism; Reductionism; Psychology as science; Nature–nurture, Q6 and Q7
- Approaches/perspectives, Q8

For Unit 5 you may choose to do Psychopathology or Treating Mental Disorders or both (or Issues in classification and diagnosis, which is available on the Psychology Press website); Issues or Debates or both, and the Approaches are compulsory.

Unit 6 Coursework

You are required to conduct one piece of coursework, and write a report of your study. This is discussed fully in Chapters 13–14 of this book.

To achieve highly at A2 you need to further develop your study and revision skills and know how to do well in the examination. This can be achieved by knowing the skills and content required, knowing how you will be assessed, knowing how to write a good essay to tight time limits (30 or 40 minutes), and having an effective exam strategy. Each of these will now be considered.

> **EXAM HINT**
>
> The synoptic paper (PYA5)—40 minutes = approximately 800 words, so eight paragraphs of 100 words are needed.

> Synopticity is defined as an understanding of the breadth of theoretical and methodological approaches in psychology, which are the common threads that run across the specification.

> **INDEPENDENT STUDY IDEA**
>
> Throughout the book, coloured boxes, like this one, provide "Independent Study Ideas" at relevant places in the text. You may find that these suggestions help you to think of possible coursework projects, using research or content from the chapter that interested you as a starting-off point. Please remember that you should check the AQA A coursework guidelines carefully to make sure that your chosen coursework project meets all the ethical requirements. If in doubt, check with your teacher.

HOW CAN I STUDY MORE EFFECTIVELY?

Organisation

You need to devise a study and ultimately a revision programme of your own. Being realistic you will need to take regular breaks, but 3 days off study or revision in a row is too long! So plan a timetable that allows for sufficient study/revision and relaxation. Whilst a lot of study/revision is always optimal all study/revision is desirable, unless it's too much. In the exam you will have no distractions, simply pen and paper. Context-dependent memory suggests we remember best in the same situation we learned the information. So try to match your study/revision environment to exam conditions.

   You also need to keep your notes organised. So invest in a folder and organise it into the A2 topics you will cover during the course. Include at least one plastic wallet per topic where you can place all of the essays you complete on that topic.

Reinforcement

Also, plan the rewards. Reinforcement is very important—this may be as simple as a coffee break, a favourite TV programme, or a night out away from it all. But remember not to take too much time off from your study/revision programme!

Throughout the book the red boxes, like this one, give cross-references to *Revise A2 Psychology: Key Topics* by Diana Dwyer and Clare Charles (the revision guide)

See page 2 of the revision guide for an overview of A2 psychology.

Use of Resources

Be aware of the range of resources available, e.g., the revision guide and A2 Online (http://www.a-levelpsychology.co.uk/online/), that accompany this textbook. Decide what you find most useful—essay plans, chapter summaries, diagrams—and incorporate these into your own notes. Also use newspapers, magazines, journals, and other psychology texts.

Frequent Review

When asked, A2 students identify this as a key target for A2 so you may have thought of this already.

Self-assess What You Know and Prioritise What You Don't Know in Your Revision

You will probably know the grade you are aiming for at the end of A2. So as you complete each sub-section of a topic self-assess your knowledge. Is it in line with the grade you are aiming for? You may have had work assessed by your teacher—this will also help you decide if you are working at the right standard. If not, revise what is below standard first and then move on to the topics you have a better grasp of.

Understand Rather Than Memorise

When one is stressed, as is sometimes the case in the exam room, it is harder to recall material that has been learned in a rote fashion and it is easier to recall things that you understand well. So avoid just learning the facts parrot fashion. Instead you should focus on a more complete *understanding* of what it all means.

Cognition

There is a lot to be learned from positive and negative thinking. First of all, do not think negatively, the time to worry about failure to achieve desired grades is if it happens! Sportspeople say preparing for the worst often leads to exactly that happening. So remember the self-fulfilling prophecy: positive thinking = success.

AO1 is assessment objective 1: *knowledge and understanding* of psychological principles, theories, concepts, studies, methods, perspectives, and applications.

AO2 is assessment objective 2: *analyse and evaluate* psychological theories, concepts, studies, methods, principles, perspectives, and applications.

HOW CAN I DO WELL IN THE EXAMINATION?

To maximise your achievement you need to be knowledgeable and you need to be able to apply your knowledge effectively. So consider the following:

- Know how to revise well
- Know the AO1 and AO2 skills you will be examined on
- Prepare for the essays you might be asked to write
- Know how you will be assessed.
- Know how to write good essays
- Have an exam strategy
- Control your stress levels.

How Can I Revise Effectively?

The three key strategies of organisation, repetition, and making information meaningful improve memory, so bear this in mind during your revision programme. Also consider what has worked for you up to now and what hasn't, if appropriate.

Think about how you learn and revise best and add any further strategies that work for you onto the list below—and *use them*!

- Know what you need to know
- Work on good time management
- Do not revise passively—be active
- Make reading meaningful
- Use essay plans to create your own model answers
- Use your own words
- Plan so the content you learn is enough but not too much
- Practise writing essays
- Use your knowledge of stress management
- Use your knowledge of memory
- Create your own exam for practice
- Use a variety of revision methods
- Prioritise key points
- Reinforcement
- Don't give up.

See page 4 of the revision guide for a list of revision "Do's and Don'ts".

See pages 4–5 of the revision guide for further details on these revision tips.

What Skills Will I Need for AO1 and AO2?

AO1 and AO2 skills

As you are no doubt well aware from AS, assessment objective 1 (AO1) requires knowledge and understanding, and assessment objective 2 (AO2) requires analysis and evaluation.

A common error is for candidates to focus on content rather than skills. Yes, you are being assessed on your knowledge, but you are also being assessed on how you use this knowledge. On all questions there are an equal number of marks for each skill (12 marks each on Unit 4 and 15 marks each on Unit 5).

The AO1 part of the question usually begins with the injunction "describe" or "outline" and the AO2 part of the question usually begins with one of the following injunctions: "evaluate", "assess", "criticise", "critically analyse", or "critically assess". Or the exam question could begin with one of these: "discuss", "critically consider", "compare and contrast", or "distinguish between", which are terms for both AO1 and AO2.

The remainder of the question will then specify what you need to apply the injunctions to: psychological theories, terminology, concepts, studies, methods, perspectives, or applications.

If the question asks for research, theories and/or studies could be used. If the question includes a quote you must reference it, so comment on it in your introduction and conclusion.

EXAM HINT

Know the specification well, both what is required of you in terms of skills (AO1, AO2, synopticity) and content. In the exam *you need to know two theories in depth and to be able to use others as support or counterperspectives.* Thus, it is advisable to base your study and revision on this.

The A2 specification contains all of the possible exam questions so you can now work out the range of potential exam questions for the options you are studying by combining the following question stems with the content identified on the specification.

Outline and evaluate . . .
Describe and assess . . .
Discuss . . .
Critically consider . . .

I won't go on as I'm sure you can now add to this list yourself, using the box on page 8.

See page 7 of the revision guide for a summary of how to gain and lose AO1 and AO2 marks.

Terms used in A2 examination questions

The following glossary clarifies commonly used terms used in recent examinations and to be used in the future.

Each injunction or key command, is intended to prompt candidates to respond in such a way as to demonstrate the skills outlined in the assessment of the A2 Level specification.

AO1 terms

Describe, outline, explain, define require the candidate to supply evidence of assessment objective 1 (AO1).

Note that in addition:

Outline involves a summary description only (more breadth than detail/depth).

Define requires the candidate to state what is meant by a particular term.

AO2 terms

Evaluate, assess, analyse, to what extent require the candidate to supply evidence of assessment objective 2 (AO2). Analysis and evaluation should be informed and demonstrate an awareness of both strengths and limitations as far as possible.

AO1 and AO2 terms

Discuss, critically consider, compare and contrast require the candidate both to describe (AO1) and evaluate (AO2) by reference to different if not contrasting points of view. Questions may instruct the candidate to discuss with reference to particular criteria, for example, by the use of the phrase "...in terms of...".

When *compare and contrast* is used in an examination question a candidate can either:

• demonstrate knowledge and understanding of the stipulated topic areas (AO1) and then consider similarities and differences between the stipulated topic areas (AO2).

or

• demonstrate knowledge and understanding of similarities and differences between the stipulated topic areas (AO1) and then evaluate these similarities and differences (AO2).

Other terms

Evidence	Material from studies or theories that may be used in support or contradiction of an argument or theory.
Findings	The outcome or product of research.
Research	The process of gaining knowledge through the examination of data derived empirically or theoretically.
Study	An investigation providing evidence which may be empirical or non-empirical (such as meta-analysis).
Theory	A (usually) complex set of interrelated ideas/assumptions/principles intended to explain or account for certain observed phenomena.
Model	An explanation which is less complex/elaborate than a theory.
Applications	Actual or possible ways of using psychological knowledge in an applied/practical setting.

Preparing For Your Examination Essays

The list of potential essays is finite and so with thorough preparation you can prepare for all eventualities—even your least favourite questions, as it's best not to leave these out! This means your success is down to you and how well prepared you are to answer the range of possible exam questions. You should aim to have a portfolio of essays per topic that covers all of the main types of essay question for that topic.

Creating a list of potential essays

The box on the following page is an example of the type of essay list you need to construct for all the topics covered, and details of how many marks would be awarded for AO1 and AO2.

Psychopathology: Schizophrenia
1. Outline the clinical characteristics of schizophrenia. (10 AO1 marks)
2. Describe one biological explanation of schizophrenia and evaluate, including the evidence on which it is based. (30 full marks, divided as 15 AO1 marks and 15 AO2 marks)
3. Outline and evaluate two or more psychological explanations of schizophrenia. (30 full marks, divided as 15 AO1 marks and 15 AO2 marks)
4. Compare and contrast two explanations of schizophrenia. (30 full marks, divided as 15 AO1 marks and 15 AO2 marks)

Psychopathology: Depression
1. Outline the clinical characteristics of depression. (10 AO1 marks)
2. Discuss biological explanations for depression, including the evidence on which they are based. (30 full marks, divided as 15 AO1 marks and 15 AO2 marks)
3. Describe and evaluate the evidence on which one psychological explanation of depression is based. (30 full marks, divided as 15 AO1 marks and 15 AO2 marks)
4. Compare and contrast two explanations of depression. (30 full marks, divided as 15 AO1 marks and 15 AO2 marks)

Psychopathology: Anxiety
1. Outline the clinical characteristics of any one anxiety disorder. (10 AO1 marks)
2. Critically consider biological explanations of any one anxiety disorder. (30 full marks, divided as 15 AO1 marks and 15 AO2 marks)
3. Discuss two or more psychological explanations of any one anxiety disorder. (30 full marks, divided as 15 AO1 marks and 15 AO2 marks)
4. Compare and contrast two explanations of one anxiety disorder. (30 full marks, divided as 15 AO1 marks and 15 AO2 marks)

AO1 and AO2 assessment

To achieve highly it is important to develop *précis*. This is the ability to write concisely and so summarise information succinctly. This will improve your AO1 and AO2 performance, as it's important to condense description and evaluation in order to cover sufficient content in the tight time limits of 30 or 40 minutes. The best way to practise this is to focus on always using your own words when noting content and write only as much as *you* could realistically include in an essay in timed conditions.

The approaches question is quite distinct from the essay questions and will be considered in detail in Chapter 12. However, the suggestions on how to write effective AO1 and AO2 are relevant, as is précis, so although the structure of the question is different the skills you need to bring to it are the same.

Synopticity

Synopticity means having an overarching knowledge and critical understanding of fundamental psychological content, in particular methodologies and the different approaches/perspectives.

Synoptic rules
1. Know the range of methodological criticisms and how to integrate them into your answer.
2. Identify perspectives and evaluate them using the alternative perspectives, and conclude that a multiple perspective (e.g., diathesis–stress) is often optimal.

How Can I Write Effective Essays?

Ensure that essay practice is a weekly part of your studies, that you have prepared an essay answer for the various possible exam questions, and be very familiar with the mark schemes that will be used to assess your answers.

Do you remember SQ3R? Survey, question, read, recite, and review. Think about applying this to your studies.

A useful strategy is to know what conclusion you are heading towards and what you need to write about in each paragraph to get there. Practise, practise, practise as part of your study. We will consider how to answer essay questions in general and then look in particular at the synoptic issue in the section below.

Some tips on essay writing

You know a good essay when you read one! Perhaps you have been supplied with model answers in class and so can tell when an essay is really good. But how do you make yours equally so? Many problems crop up in examination answers again and again. Here are some tips on how to avoid the most common difficulties.

Lack of knowledge

Clearly there is no way that you can achieve a good examination mark without the necessary knowledge. So study consistently throughout your course. Test yourself in timed conditions without your notes so that you are learning the material as you go. Do not leave it until the month before the exam!

Effective use of knowledge

When marking an examination answer, it often appears that candidates might have knowledge of relevant research and/or ideas, but simply have either (1) not actually identified the content, (2) failed to make the content clear enough, or (3) not gone into enough depth to attract credit. We will consider this in more depth in the exam technique section later in the chapter.

Anecdotal material

It is tempting to include material such as "My own experience is . . . " when writing your examination answer. It is likely that your teacher will have used such anecdotes in class to help make the material more understandable and the lessons more lively, but in the examination you will only be credited for *psychologically informed* answers.

Answer the question that is set

It would be lovely if the questions in the examination were totally open-ended; if, for example, the question for the pro- and anti-social part of the specification was "Write an essay on pro- and anti-social behaviour." The difficulty with this approach would be that it would not discriminate very well between candidates. Everyone would get good marks if they knew what the question was going to be and could prepare their answer. So instead there is more than just one essay question per topic, which means you can only be awarded marks for your ability to answer the question set and not the question you would have liked to answer—no matter how good your other answer may be. So do not follow the "here's one I prepared earlier" approach. Although you should prepare for the range of possible questions, do be ready to adapt the material you have learnt to the question set on the day.

Deconstruct the question

To deconstruct a question you need to be familiar with the AQA A "injunctions" that tell you what to do. The most important ones are set out in the box on page 8.

When you open the examination paper, circle the questions that you might possibly answer, or those you must answer if you studied the minimum number of topics, and then in each one underline the key words. This will inform you

EXAM HINT

The exam questions often stipulate that you must discuss one or two theories. If just one is asked for you must select a theory that you can write about at length and in depth, so be selective. If two theories are asked for then you should present one of these in some depth and the other in slightly less detail.

whether AO1 or AO2 is being required and in what proportions. What you need to be aware of is that the question may be in two parts, where part (a) usually requires AO1 content and part (b) mainly AO2. The marks may be spread equally, so 12:12 or 15:15, or unevenly, e.g., (a) = 6 and (b) = 18 on Unit 4 and (a) = 10 and (b) = 20 on Unit 5. Or the question may be just that, one question, where the AO1 to AO2 ratio is always a 50:50 split. On the two-part questions part (a) is usually AO1 and then part (b) will consist of the remaining AO1 marks and all of the AO2.

Organise your answer

There is credit to be gained from an organised and well-constructed answer. Think about the organisation before you begin writing, i.e., *plan*. The easiest way to do this is to make a list of everything that comes into your head that would be relevant to the question. This then provides a useful check list—important points can be remembered and then forgotten in the space of writing an essay! Then number the points in order of how they should fit into paragraphs. Hence, your essay will demonstrate *structure* rather than a meandering flow. Of course more ideas may come to you as you go along, so do include them, but hopefully you will be so well prepared that relevant content will be listed from the outset.

This approach should also prevent you writing "everything you know" about a topic in the hope that something will get credit. If the examiner has to do the work in organising your material, then he or she should get the credit, not you. The ability to be selective is a higher order skill and one that you should demonstrate in order to get good marks.

Make sure your essay covers both assessment objectives

On all questions there are an equal number of marks for each skill (12 marks each on Unit 4 and 15 marks each on Unit 5). The key consideration then in terms of covering both assessment objectives is that there must be a 50:50 balance.

If you are asked to describe research studies, you may evaluate them using theories—this is a way of assessing how we can make sense of the research data, and of considering what is implied by the findings. You may also evaluate research studies with considerations about the methodology and/or ethics in so far as the ethics challenge the findings of the study. Don't overlook points of positive evaluation.

If you are asked to describe theories, you may evaluate them by contrasting them with other theories. Do not simply *describe* another theory but use the other theory as a means of criticism. You may also evaluate a theory by looking at implications and/or applications, and by describing research studies that support or challenge the theory.

Depth and breadth

An excellent answer manages to combine both depth and breadth. That means being able to cover sufficient breadth of ideas while also leaving sufficient time for detail (depth). It is not easy to achieve a good balance between these, but you must bear the trade-off in mind—if you try to cover too much material you will not be able to give enough detail. Therefore you must be selective in the

> **EXAM HINT**
>
> If you are asked to describe and evaluate one or two theories, be very careful how you bring in any further theories. They can only be used as counterperspectives so simply identifying one as a counterperspective and then describing it is not good enough. You must compare it to the theory/theories you've selected as your main content in a sustained manner, e.g., what insights are offered by the counterperspective that are ignored by the other theory/theories? Do the theories have similarities or differences in terms of strengths and weaknesses?

arguments, theories, and/or studies you describe and leave time to elaborate the ones you do include.

One issue to note, in relation to detail, is the question of names and dates. You do not have to know the names and dates of researchers but if you do, it helps in three ways. First, it adds a sense of detail to your essay. Second, it helps the examiner identify the particular study or theory you are discussing. Third, it should assist your recall. A name acts like a cue to access an area of memory.

Does your answer have MERIT?

When discussing research studies, use this mnemonic to check your answer is evaluative.

- **M**ethodological criticisms—Include criticisms of the research methods, design of the research, and sample, all of which have implications for reliability and validity.
- **E**thics—Do the ends justify the means? Much research has ethical implications so consider whether it should have passed the cost–benefit analysis.
- **R**eal-life validity, explanatory power, and applications—Don't forget that the main point of studies is to produce findings that support or contradict ideas and theories. Before looking at limitations of studies, make it clear that you *understand* the implications of findings for theories. How well does the theory/explanation/research relate to and explain real-life phenomenon? I.e., is it psychologically real? If so can the information be used in a positive way, i.e., applications? If not the theory/explanation/research may lack value and explanatory power.
- **I**ndividual, social, and cultural variation—Has such variation been accounted for? Are explanations culturally relative or universal? If cultural relativism has not been acknowledged the research may be ethnocentric. Remember to some extent all research is a product of the time and context when it was carried out and so contextualise the research and assess whether it is era-dependent and context-bound. Consider the consequences in terms of ecological (if you can't generalise the research to another context), population (if you can't generalise the research to other populations), and temporal validity (if you can't generalise the research to more current time periods).
- **T**heoretical—Reductionism and determinism can be used to evaluate most theories. Nature/nurture can also be used to assess theoretical perspectives. Don't forget to show that you *understand* why reductionism or nature/nurture might be relevant to the question you are answering. Use counterperspectives as evaluation and conclude that a multiple perspective is usually optimal.

How do I write effective AO1?

It is a common misconception that marks are given only for the number of points presented in an answer. This kind of "shopping list" approach does not attract high marks. You must communicate understanding and interpretation. You can demonstrate that you understand the relevance of the material by adding a sentence like "This shows that . . . " or "One can conclude . . . ".

Other useful tips
Show a clear focus on the question

- Use link sentences.

Be selective

- Only the most relevant content to the question should be included.

Plan so your answer has structure

- An essay plan will enable you to know what is going in each paragraph and the conclusion so that your answer has structure.

Try to provide depth and breadth

- It is better to give fewer studies/theories/explanations and so be able to go into some detail on those you do cover than include too many with too brief and superficial a description.
- The examiner knows the time constraints and that there must be a trade-off between depth and breadth, but you should aim to achieve both by writing about either one or two things in depth and then anything else more superficially.

Try to provide synopticity

- This can be achieved by identifying methodological approaches, criticisms, and using counterperspectives.

How do I write effective AO2?
Evaluation
Evaluation can be achieved through:

- The use of research studies to provide support for an argument
- Providing commentary on research studies, which challenges the findings because of flawed methodology or assumptions
- Presenting alternative theories as a contrasting viewpoint
- Suggesting useful applications
- Considering implications, and/or strengths and weaknesses.

Useful phrases in essays to introduce AO2
    So we can see that . . .
    This would imply . . .
    This suggests that . . .
    One consequence would be . . .
    One advantage of this is . . .
    An alternative explanation could be . . .
    Therefore we can conclude . . .
    This evidence provides support/contradicts the theory that . . .

> **EXAM HINT**
> Evaluation is not a "shopping list" of criticisms! A "shopping list" will achieve minimal marks in the exam. So make sure your AO2 content is a more sophisticated commentary. If you use points such as "lacks ecological validity", or "it is reductionistic", show that you understand *why* the comment is relevant to the study/theory, i.e., *contextualise* your material. A few points showing good understanding will earn more marks than a longer list of points not contextualised or elaborated. Further aspects of commentary are interpretation, analysis, evaluation, and conclusions.

EXAM HINT
There are many sources of AO2 and much of this is generalisable, i.e., can be used in different essays. So it's a good idea to create your own AO2 revision sheet of criticisms with elaboration and commentary. Also include some useful AO2 phrases as suggested in the text.

Not everyone reacts the same way, for example . . .
There may be cultural variations . . .
This has been applied to . . .
There are methodological weaknesses in this research as . . .
This study lacked internal/external validity because . . .
The strengths of this research . . .
There are ethical issues that must be considered . . .

How Will I be Assessed?

In order to do well in the examination, it is important to know how your essays will be marked.

Types of essay question

In the A2 examination you have two kinds of essay questions:

- Unit 4: each to be answered in 30 minutes and marked out of 24, i.e., 12 AO1 and 12 AO2 marks.
- Unit 5: each to be answered in 40 minutes and marked out of 30, with the addition of synoptic criteria, i.e., 15 AO1 and 15 AO2 marks.

Psychology A level essays are not marked as right or wrong. There is no "correct" answer. The criteria that are used for assessment have already been mentioned: detail, structure, knowledge, understanding, psychological information, effective use of material, and so on. The examiner reads the essay and then decides which descriptor in the marking allocation best fits the essay.

The options paper

The marking allocation for AQA A Unit 4 is summarised in the table opposite. This table indicates the descriptors for each skill and therefore what you are aiming for:

- AO1: descriptions that are accurate, with evidence of depth and breadth, and are well-structured.
- AO2: a commentary that is informed and coherently elaborated, with arguments that are well-selected and effectively used.

Examiners, when marking, bear in mind the fact that the essay is written by a notional 18-year-old in 30 minutes.

The synoptic paper

Unit 5 is slightly different from Unit 4. You have a longer time (40 minutes) to answer each question and each question is worth more marks (and the whole paper is worth more towards your final A level mark). The reason the questions and paper are worth more is because this paper assesses your understanding of psychology as a whole, as distinct from your knowledge of particular areas.

Synopticity can be defined as: "the ability to demonstrate an understanding and critical appreciation of the breadth of theoretical and methodological

In the same way that there are no right answers for students, there are no "right" or "wrong" theories. Freud, Piaget, and Broadbent, for example, did not get it wrong. Their theories continue to be highly influential even though some elements have been criticised.

KEY TERMS
Throughout the book we provide "Key Term" definitions in purple boxes in the margins. Unlike in the AS level exam, you will *not* be directly examined on key term definitions as the A2 level exam is essay based; however, you may find the definitions are helpful as background to clarify and highlight the material..

The Marking Allocation for AQA Specification A

For Unit 4 assessment objective 1 (AO1)

Band	Marks	Content	Detail and accuracy	Organisation and structure	Breadth and depth
3 (Top)	12–11	Substantial	Accurate and well-detailed	Coherent	Substantial evidence of both, and balance achieved
3 (Bottom)	10–9	Slightly limited	Accurate and reasonably detailed	Coherent	Evidence of both, but imbalanced
2 (Top)	8–7	Limited	Generally accurate and reasonably detailed	Reasonably constructed	Increasing evidence of breadth and/or depth
2 (Bottom)	6–5	Basic	Generally accurate, lacks detail	Reasonably constructed	Some evidence of breadth and/or depth
1 (Top)	4–3	Rudimentary	Sometimes flawed	Sometimes focused	
1 (Bottom)	2–0	Just discernible	Weak/muddled/inaccurate	Wholly/mainly irrelevant	

For Unit 4 assessment objective 2 (AO2)

Band	Marks	Evaluation is	Selection and elaboration	Use of material
3 (Top)	12–11	Thorough	Appropriate selection and coherent elaboration	Highly effective
3 (Bottom)	10–9	Slightly limited	Appropriate selection and elaboration	Effective
2 (Top)	8–7	Limited	Reasonable elaboration	Reasonably effective
2 (Bottom)	6–5	Basic	Some evidence of elaboration	Restricted
1 (Top)	4–3	Superficial and rudimentary	No evidence of elaboration	Not effective
1 (Bottom)	2–0	Muddled and incomplete	Wholly or mainly irrelevant	

For Unit 5 assessment objective 1 (AO1)

Band	Marks	Content	Detail and accuracy	Organisation and structure	Breadth/depth of content and synoptic possibilities
5	15–13	Substantial	Accurate and well-detailed	Coherent	Substantial evidence of both
4	12–10	Slightly limited	Accurate and reasonably detailed	Coherent	Evidence of both
3	9–7	Limited	Generally accurate and reasonably detailed	Reasonably constructed	Some evidence of both
2	6–4	Basic	Lacking detail	Sometimes focused	Little evidence
1	3–0	Just discernible	Weak/muddled/inaccurate	Wholly/mainly irrelevant	Little or no evidence

For Unit 5 assessment objective 2 (AO2)

Band	Marks	Evaluation is	Selection and elaboration	Use of material and synoptic possibilities
5	15–13	Thorough	Appropriate selection and coherent elaboration	Highly effective
4	12–10	Slightly limited	Appropriate selection and elaboration	Effective
3	9–7	Limited	Reasonable elaboration	Reasonably effective
2	6–4	Basic	Some evidence of elaboration	Restricted
1	3–0	Weak, muddled, and incomplete	Wholly/mainly irrelevant	Not effective

approaches in psychology." Why is synopticity so important? The essence of studying A level Psychology is to gain an appreciation of psychology. This is not the same as learning about why people remember and forget or what factors contribute to an emotional experience. These are all areas of psychology. The intention is that you will develop informed opinions about the breadth of theoretical and methodological approaches in psychology. Therefore, the synoptic paper is the last one you take in which you can demonstrate your knowledge on these overarching topics.

The mark scheme for this paper is the same as the others, except that there are five bands instead of three, and there is a synoptic criterion. In order to receive maximum marks your answer needs to fulfil these criteria:

- AO1: psychological content is *accurate* and *well-detailed* at the level of knowledge, description, and understanding. The organisation and structure is *coherent*. There is *substantial evidence of breadth and depth* and a *balance* between them is *achieved*. There is *clear* evidence of a range of different theoretical and/or methodological approaches relevant to the question.
- AO2: psychological content is *informed* and *thorough* in terms of analysis, evaluation, and interpretation of relevant psychological theories, concepts, evidence, or applications. Material has been used in a *highly effective* manner and shows evidence of *appropriate selection* and *coherent elaboration*. There is *clear* commentary on the different theoretical and/or methodological approaches used in the answer.

> See pages 8–10 of the revision guide for a summary of the different approaches to help achieve synopticity.

The marking allocation for Unit 5 is summarised in the table on page 15.

FOR UNIT 5—THE APPROACHES QUESTION

Marks

Part (a)	Content	Accuracy	Engagement
6–5	Reasonably thorough	Accurate	Coherent
4–3	Limited	Generally accurate	Reasonable
2–1	Basic	Sometimes flawed/inaccurate	Muddled
0			No engagement

Part (b)	Commentary	Use of material	Engagement
6–5	Reasonably thorough	Effective	Coherent
4–3	Limited	Reasonably effective	Reasonable
2–1	Basic	Restricted	Muddled
0			No engagement

Part (c)	Commentary	Plausibility	Engagement
6–5	Reasonably thorough	Appropriate	Coherent
4–3	Limited	Reasonably appropriate	Reasonable
2–1	Basic	Largely inappropriate	Muddled
0			No engagement

Part (d)	Commentary	Use of material	Engagement
6–5	Reasonably thorough	Effective	Coherent
4–3	Limited	Reasonably effective	Reasonable
2–1	Basic	Restricted	Muddled
0			No engagement

> **EXAM HINT**
>
> Many students find the approaches question particularly hard. We have provided several worked examples in Appendix B at the back of this book to help you get to grips with this part of the exam paper.

Exam Strategy

"Rules of the game"

The questions in AQA A examinations follow certain rules:

- Only injunctions from the glossary of terms are used.
- AO1 and AO2 are equally balanced in every question (except section C, Approaches, in Unit 5).
- Candidates are guaranteed one question from each subsection of the specification. In the cases of Issues and Debates there are two questions from these subsections.
- Questions are set from the specification. Make sure you have a copy so that you are familiar with the terms that are used. Anything given as "e.g." is only an example. No question would specifically refer to this. Anything given as "including" is a part of the specification and may be specifically named in a question.
- If a quotation is used in a question, there may be a specific instruction for it to be addressed. You will lose marks in such cases if you do not address the quotation.
- Numbers are specified where appropriate.
- Singular and plural are specified. Make sure you write about studies or factors if that is in the question.

The numbers game

This can be a very useful strategy so do give it some thought. Essentially it's a quick framework on how to organise your time and the amount written in the exam. These figures would need to be amended slightly for questions in two parts.

TIME CALCULATIONS			
	Time per essay	Approx. number of words	Number of paragraphs
Unit 4	30 minutes	600 words: AO1 = 300 words in 15 minutes AO2 = 300 words in 15 minutes	6 paragraphs: 3 AO1 and 3 AO2 Approximately 5 minutes per paragraph
Unit 5	40 minutes	800 words: AO1 = 400 AO2 = 400	8 paragraphs: 4 AO1 and 4 AO2 Approximately 5 minutes per paragraph

In the examination room

Here are some strategies to employ.

Answer the question

It sounds obvious but yet it's not always done.

EXAM HINT

Do not cross out your essay plan as it will be marked if your essay is incomplete—it will be looked at more favourably having been compiled from the outset rather than simply giving a list of points at the end when you are running out of time.

1. Check the injunctions to see whether AO1, AO2, or both are required.
2. If the question says "including" you must write about whatever is specified. If it says "e.g." you can choose alternative content if you prefer.
3. Cover two or more explanations of theories if the question includes "explanations", "theories", or "two or more".
4. If there is a quote, use it.
5. Leave spaces between paragraphs so that you can expand on your link sentences if you have time or feel you need to change them as you go along.

The way to make it clear to the examiner that you are answering the question is to use link sentences, i.e., rephrase the words of the question and make a mini-conclusion, one per paragraph so that it's clear whatever you've written about in that paragraph is relevant to the question. This is a good check for you as well because if you can't make a link sentence then chances are the material isn't relevant!

Be selective
You can only write a limited amount in 30 (Unit 4) or 40 (Unit 5) minutes.

1. The content you select must be the most relevant possible!
2. Don't go into lengthy descriptions containing an unnecessary amount of detail—this will reduce the time you have for more relevant material. For example, when describing a piece of research, give the findings and conclusions only—the aims and procedures are too much detail.
3. Having selected the most relevant material describe and evaluate two areas in detail to achieve depth, and write about alternative content superficially so that your answer shows a wider understanding and so achieves breadth.

Be informed
Make sure your use of material does you justice—the point is to show how much you have learned in psychology. To do this, AO1 must be accurate and detailed and AO2 must make effective use of research evidence.

Essay plans
These should be in memory of course as a result of planning in revision (see above)!

1. In the exam use the first minute allocated to an essay to plan your response. Write the numbers 1–6 (Unit 4) or 1–8 (Unit 5) along one line and underneath briefly note what will go into each paragraph. One word will do, as you do need to move quickly on to writing your essay.
2. Leave space so that you can add in anything else that occurs as you write the essay. The stress of exams can affect memory so if you think of something really good for paragraph 5 or the conclusion add it to the plan in case you forget it by the time you get to that paragraph.
3. Don't cross the plan out—this can only be credited if it's not crossed out so tick items if you like to check off what you've done.

Be balanced
AO1 and AO2 achieve equal marks.

> **EXAM HINT**
> Note the mnemonic ECR: explain, conclude, relate. Ensure you do this with a number of evaluation points per essay.

1. Make sure that AO1 and AO2 are balanced at the planning stage.
2. Provide evidence for and against to achieve balance.
3. Give positive and negative evaluation.

Time management

Manage your time in the exam very carefully, on Unit 4 you have 30 minutes per question, on Unit 5 you have 40 minutes per question. Resist the urge to spend a disproportionate amount of time on your first essay, because you could make it really good with 10 more minutes. It is far better to have three very good answers, than one brilliant and two average ones!

Don't just state, elaborate!

To achieve at grade C or above your answer cannot be superficial, which often occurs when criticisms are simply stated—it's easy to say a study lacks ecological validity, or is reductionist, deterministic, etc. You could simply learn a list of AO2 phrases and hardly know what they mean! So, unsurprisingly, stating criticisms achieves few marks. To go beyond mere statement you need to provide commentary:

> **Useful phrases in essays**
>
> So we can see that . . .
>
> This would imply . . .
>
> One consequence would be . . .
>
> One advantage of this is . . .
>
> An alternative explanation could be . . .
>
> Therefore . . .
>
> Not everyone reacts the same way, for example . . .
>
> There may be cultural variations . . .
>
> This has been applied to . . . .

1. Explain what the criticism means.
2. Conclude: make a conclusion by assessing the consequences of the criticism, e.g., if the research lacks validity then this reduces its value and so it does not provide strong support for ___ theory, which may reduce its explanatory power.
3. Relate this conclusion back to the question, i.e., write a link sentence (see above), e.g., if the question had asked you to assess the contribution of ___ explanations, and you have reached the above conclusion then you can say, "The theory lacks empirical support as the validity of the research evidence can be questioned and so there is a need for further research to substantiate the explanation. This means although it may appear to make sense we cannot fully accept the insights the explanation provides and so it lacks explanatory power. Furthermore, this explanation takes only one perspective, whereas a multi-perspective best accounts for ___."

Note in the example above the use of "and so" and "This means". There are many useful phrases, such as the examples in the box above, that you can use to ensure your answer does contain commentary and does link back to the question.

Cope with Exam Stress

Here is a topic that you have already studied: stress. What can psychological research tell us about coping with stress in an examination?

- Catharsis: before the examination go for a run or some other form of physical exercise to relieve pent-up feelings of stress.

> **EXAM HINT**
>
> Whilst it's very easy to contextualise the theories and research in terms of your own experience, this is not relevant material for an essay. Marks are gained for informed answers and so make relevant use of psychological research and theory, *not* anecdotal material.

A sample essay with examiner's comments

The essay below is a student answer to the question "Describe and evaluate research into factors involved in biological rhythms". (24 marks)

The sentences that are highlighted have been credited as AO2. Examiner's comments have been inserted in brackets.

There are many bodily rhythms. Circannual rhythms last a cycle of a year. Examples of this are migrations of birds and animals, and the mating cycles of animals. This can be shown to be due to environmental factors because birds and animals move towards warmth and food supplies. [First factor identified.] *In humans there is a condition known as Seasonal Affective Disorder which is also circannual. It can lead to periods of depression in winter months and can be seen as psychological because the bad winter weather makes people feel depressed. It is also physiological because it has been shown that the absence of sunshine leads to a lower production of melatonin, which makes us feel less happy.* [SAD explained in terms of both psychological and physiological factors. Nice balance and reasonable detail. Good to see use of technical terms.]

Infradian rhythms last over 24 hours, for example the menstrual cycle of women, which lasts 28 days. The physiological effects of the menstrual cycle can be dizziness, and abdominal pains a few days before menstruation. *This suggests that it is biological factors that are involved in the bodily rhythm of menstruation.* [Interpretation of evidence offered.] *However, there are also psychological effects such as mood swings and irritability.* [Contrasting viewpoint. Could be credited as AO1 but presented in an evaluative sense.] *This shows that both physiological and psychological factors are involved in infradian bodily rhythms.* [Interpretation and commentary.] [The second paragraph offers a discussion of the factors that might contribute to the menstrual cycle, an example of a second biological rhythm.]

Circadian rhythms last for 24 hours. Some people have been shown to be "morning" or "evening" types, that is they reach their physical and psychological peak in the morning or evening. There is physiological evidence for this, as people's hormone levels rise and fall through the day, giving rise to changes in mood and aptitude. It is also possible that changes in daylight through the day can affect the person's physiological and psychological state. [Factor explained for circadian rhythm—some people are naturally one type or the other. Could be more explicit and detailed, e.g., what hormone levels rise? But reasonable.] *Research also shows, however, that there are psychological factors which influence whether a person is a "morning" or "evening" type.* [Presented as contrasting view.] A person's aptitude through the day may influence whether or not they feel better able to do things in the morning or evening, whatever their personal experience and routine is. [Relevance not entirely clear. In what way is aptitude a biological rhythm? Is the candidate trying to say that aptitude is an alternative explanation? This material has not been effectively used.]

Nocturnal rhythms are those which occur at night, that is sleep cycles. [Fourth biological rhythm.] Sleep is a very physical state and much research has been conducted into whether the purpose of sleep is for physiological or psychological repair. One theory namely the "Restoration and Repair theory" states that sleep cycles are necessary for the synthesis of neurochemicals which are used up during the body's daytime functioning. [The candidate appears to be forgetting the title of the essay and writing about the functions of sleep rather than the factors that govern the cycle.] However more research has been done to disprove this theory, because although we need sleep (lack of sleep leads to dizziness and irritability), when we lose sleep we don't need to catch up on all we've lost. *So this shows that the nocturnal body rhythms and sleep cycles are influenced by physiological factors.* [Some attempt to make sense of the material in this paragraph, though better evidence might have been used to identify the physiological factors involved in sleep.]

There are also theories which say that we need sleep for psychological health. [Presenting an alternative view to the previous paragraph.] Freud believed that we sleep in order to dream, and our dreams are a disguised form of our repressed sexual anxieties and desires. This is supported because our dreams do seem to have meaning but many researchers do not believe that our anxiety and conflict need to be sexual. *This indicates that our nocturnal bodily rhythms are also psychological.* [Interpretation.]

Sleep cycles follow a pattern which includes five stages, and although they vary in length of time for each person, these are necessary stages that a person needs to follow. [Relevance not clear, detracts from selectivity and organisation. Would have been better omitted.]

Both physiological and psychological factors are involved in bodily rhythms, and this has been shown by research. [Commentary on whole essay but not of great value. Next sentence is more useful.] *It is not clear whether physiological or psychological factors are more important. It is probable that both have a part to play in the function of bodily rhythms. Some researchers tend towards the belief that physiological, psychological, and environmental factors are involved in bodily rhythms. This can be seen in Seasonal Affective Disorder where, environmentally, the lack of pleasant weather is a factor, as is the physical lack of melatonin from the sun, and so is the psychological belief that there is nothing to look forward to.* [Repetition of earlier material. In a well-organised essay this would have been saved to use here as an example of interaction between physiological, psychological, and environmental factors.] *This is shown in the treatment, which is exposure to more sunshine or extra strong light, though sufferers can be given counselling as well.* [Nice additional point of evaluation in terms of how the knowledge could be applied.]

[Incidentally, the word length of this essay is 664 words, which is a good length essay to be able to write in 30 minutes.]

In determining the mark for this essay, the examiner must ask a number of questions.

AO1: Is it accurate? Yes reasonably. Is it detailed? Again, reasonably. The content may be best described as slightly limited. What about the coherence and structure? Parts could have been omitted but there is a good structure, moving clearly through different biological rhythms. Is there a balance between breadth and depth? The candidate has covered a good range of bodily rhythms and research, and balanced this with a reasonable amount of detail.

Mark for AO1 = band 2 top, 8

Psychological content is *limited*, although *accurate* and *reasonably detailed* at the level of knowledge, description, and understanding. The answer is *reasonably constructed* in terms of its description of research and there is *some evidence of breadth and/or depth*.

The temptation is to go up to band 3 bottom because the essay is slightly limited, rather than limited, but it could not be described as "well-detailed".

AO2: Is the commentary informed? There is some evidence of identifiable research but it tends to be vague. The commentary mainly relies on interpretation rather than any challenge to the data. Contrasting viewpoints are presented but this is repetitive: there are physiological factors and then there are also psychological factors. Is it coherently elaborated? In general it is coherent and points are elaborated. Is the material used effectively? In general yes, but not always. The AO2 material is less effective than the AO1 skills.

Mark for AO2 = band 2 bottom, 6

Evaluation of research is *reasonable* but *limited* in terms of relevant concepts, evidence, or applications. The material is used in a *reasonably effective* manner and shows *some* evidence of *elaboration*.

For 7 marks the AO2 material would need to be "slightly limited", "effectively used", and "coherently elaborated". All of these criteria are nearly met, but not quite.

A total of 14 marks would be equivalent to a Grade C.

- Increase your sense of control by the use of positive self-statements: "I have spent as much time as I could revising."
- Avoid repression (a form of ego defence) by acknowledging your feelings of worry.
- Calm yourself by using some form of relaxation. During the examination have short breaks and think about nice things.
- Social support: think about people who give you comfort.
- Write essay plans in the examinations to organise your thoughts and reduce any anxiety you might have about not being able to answer the question.

Stress is a normal reaction, but having covered this topic you should be aware of the negative effects, e.g., unpleasant physiological arousal, emotional (over)reactions, and possibly exhaustion! This links to cognition because of course stress is determined by self-perception. Does this sound familiar: "I don't know enough, I'm going to fail, I'll never manage to revise enough!" This is the normal reaction to imminent exams. However, it is positive thinking that predicts success. Therefore, catastrophising (negative thoughts), often accompanied by procrastination ("I'll start revising tomorrow"), only distracts you from the task in hand!

Examiner's viewpoint

Over the years of these examinations candidates have shown consistent weaknesses. Some, like not knowing any psychology, cannot be solved by reading this chapter. Others can lead to many otherwise good candidates not achieving the marks they deserve, and some of these weaknesses are easily remedied.

Not answering the question

Read the question carefully, and do what it says. Don't rely on heavily pre-prepared essays *unless* they match the question exactly. Examiners mark *relevant* answers, not just anything vaguely in the right area. If the question asks for *explanations*, don't focus on *studies*, and vice versa. Know the difference between studies *investigating* cultural and gender differences, and studies or theories that *are* gender or culturally biased. Be clear between examples of ethical issues and examples of *ways of coping* with ethical issues. A few minutes at the start carefully reading the questions really pays off.

Not accessing AO2 marks

AO1 and AO2 marks are balanced in Units 4 and 5 so you need to produce more AO2 material than in the AS papers. Don't just rely on criticising individual studies. Show that you *understand* the significance of findings and how they relate to theories and explanations. If you refer to ecological validity, reductionism, cultural relativism, etc., show *why* they are relevant to this particular study and what the implications are. A few points done well and *contextualised* will earn more AO2 marks than a long list of brief statements. For many questions a paragraph at the end summarising the overall picture can be credited as relevant high level commentary.

Missing out on synopticity

Questions on Unit 5 automatically bring out synopticity if you answer them well. Make sure you remind yourself of what you learned for Unit 4 and even for the AS papers. Unit 4 material is very relevant to issues and debates. Bring in examples from different areas of psychology, and even from AS topics such as obedience, models of abnormality, and deprivation. Show that you are aware of the *breadth* of psychology, and the fact that in many areas there are alternative and competing theories and explanations.

Keeping a focus in the approaches question

This is the hardest question in Units 4 and 5. There are three key weaknesses:

1. Students do not *contextualise* their material, i.e., they have a good grasp of psychodynamic or behavioural explanations but do not apply them effectively to the particular scenario in the question. Give specific examples of how repression or positive reinforcement, for example, might explain the behaviour.
2. Students describe investigations that are not *practical* or *ethical*, and so do not earn marks. You do not have to be completely original; most studies are very straightforward, so try to base yours on ones you have read about. It sometimes helps to use coursework headings to organise your material.
3. Students describe studies that are not *directly relevant* to the scenario, e.g., a general demonstration of the principles of conditioning.

Timing

Always aim to complete three questions. Even if a favourite topic comes up, don't spend more time on it than the others. It is an unspoken law of examinations that the first few marks are easier to get than the last few, so always make a reasonable attempt at all the questions.

FURTHER READING

The topics in this chapter are covered in greater depth by P. Humphreys (2001) *Exam success in AQA A psychology* (London: Routledge). The classic book to read as an introduction to psychology is G.A. Miller (1966) *Psychology: The science of mental life* (Harmondsworth, UK: Penguin), which covers the history of psychology and describes some of the main figures. Two interesting case histories are discussed at length in the following books, giving an in-depth knowledge of many issues in psychology such as ethics and research, privation, language acquisition, gender development, and nature and nurture: the case of Genie is reported by R. Rymer (1993) *Genie: Escape from a silent childhood* (London: Michael Joseph), and an account of the twin boy who lost his penis as the result of a botched circumcision and spent his early life as a girl is given by J. Colapinto (2000) *As nature made him* (London: Quartet Books).

WEBSITES

www.aqa.org.uk
Access to the AQA A specifications for psychology, and other information from the examination board.

www.a-levelpsychology.co.uk
Psychology Press site with useful exam material and book details. Psychology Press is the largest publisher of psychology books in the UK. You can also access *A-Level Psychology Online*, a web-based eLearning resource for A-Level Psychology students.

SOCIAL PSYCHOLOGY

Attraction and the Formation of Relationships p.25
• The matching hypothesis says that we are attracted to people who have a similar level of attraction to our own. Is this true?
• Do we form relationships because they are rewarding?
• Why might relationships be adaptive?

Love and the Breakdown of Relationships p.48
• If a person feels that their partner is getting more out of the relationship, is he or she likely to end it?
• What happens when relationships break down?
• What is love?

Cultural and Sub-cultural Differences in Relationships p.58
• How do Western and non-Western relationships differ?
• Are gay and lesbian relationships different from heterosexual ones?
• What can psychologists tell us about relationships on the internet?

Relationships

This chapter looks at various aspects of interpersonal relationships: how they begin and end, and how culture and sub-culture also play a part in this process.

ATTRACTION AND THE FORMATION OF RELATIONSHIPS

There are several types of interpersonal relationships, ranging from romantic relationships to casual friendships in the workplace. However, we will focus mostly on the formation of romantic relationships as this has been the topic most investigated by psychologists.

Explanations of Interpersonal Attraction

Why are you attracted to one person rather than another? Numerous factors are involved in the formation of interpersonal relationships. It is not possible to consider all the relevant factors here. What has been done instead is to focus on six of the main ones: physical attractiveness, proximity, familiarity, attitude similarity, demographic similarity, and similarity in personality.

In general terms, the above factors are important because they influence the *rewards* we are likely to receive from another person (see later discussion of reinforcement theory). For example, we live in a society that values physical attractiveness, and so it enhances our status (i.e., is rewarding) to form a relationship with someone who is high in physical attractiveness. It is usually more rewarding to form a relationship with someone who is similar to us in attitudes, personality, and so on rather than dissimilar because they are more likely to want to do the things we personally find rewarding. Another point is that if everyone likes people who are similar to themselves, we have more chance of being liked by someone else who is similar to us rather than dissimilar!

Physical attractiveness

The first thing we generally notice when meeting a stranger is their physical appearance. This includes how they are dressed and whether they are clean or dirty, and it often includes an assessment of their physical attractiveness. People tend to agree with each other about whether someone is physically attractive. Women whose faces resemble those of young children are often perceived as attractive. For example, photographs of females with relatively large and widely separated eyes, a small nose, and a small chin are regarded as more attractive. However, wide cheekbones and narrow cheeks are also seen as attractive (Cunningham, 1986), and these features are not usually found in young children.

Cunningham also studied physical attractiveness in males. Men having features such as a square jaw, small eyes, and thin lips were regarded as attractive by women. These features can be regarded as indicating maturity, as they are rarely found in children.

Natalie Portman (top left) fits Cunningham's "attractive female" characteristics—note how her features are similar to the little girl's (top right). Johnny Depp (bottom left), however, looks very different from the little boy (bottom right).

Can you think of any famous people who are considered attractive, but who do not meet Cunningham's attractiveness criteria?

KEY TERMS

Halo effect: the tendency for one outstanding trait to unduly influence an overall impression.

Matching hypothesis: the notion that we are attracted to those who are about as physically attractive as we are.

Evidence that physically attractive people are thought of as being generally attractive was reported by Brigham (1971). Males and females both argued that physically attractive individuals are poised, sociable, interesting, independent, exciting, and sexually warm. This is called the **halo effect**, the tendency for the total impression formed to be unduly influenced by one outstanding trait.

The matching hypothesis

The **matching hypothesis** proposes that we don't seek the most physically attractive person but that we are attracted to individuals who match us in terms of physical attraction. This compromise is necessary because of a fear of rejection (a more attractive person might reject your advances) and/or to achieve a balance between partners. However, matching doesn't necessarily *only* involve physical attraction. For example, it is reasonable to argue that the actress Marilyn Monroe and the playwright Arthur Miller were well matched because she was very physically attractive and he was very intelligent.

Walster et al. (1966) tested the matching hypothesis by asking students to rate partners who had been randomly selected in terms of their interpersonal attraction, see the Key Study below. This study did *not* find that attraction was related to matching. The students preferred partners who were more physically attractive, not someone matching with their own attractiveness. This makes sense if we assume that we are initially attracted to those who are beautiful or handsome before we consider the realities of whether they are likely to be attracted to us!

Subsequent studies have found support for the matching hypothesis. Walster and Walster (1969) did a repeat of the original computer dance but this time the students had met beforehand and this probably meant that they had more time to think about the qualities they were looking for in a partner. As predicted by the matching hypothesis, students expressed the most liking for those who were at the same level of physical attractiveness as themselves.

Murstein (1972) obtained further support for the matching hypothesis. The physical attractiveness of engaged couples and those going out together was

KEY STUDY
Testing the matching hypothesis

Walster et al. (1966) advertised a "computer dance" for students during fresher's week at college. The first 376 male and 376 female volunteers were allowed in at $1.00 each. When the students arrived to sign up for the dance, four independent judges assessed each student's physical attractiveness as a measure of social desirability The participants were seated upstairs and asked to fill in a lengthy questionnaire, ostensibly for use in the computer pairing. In fact the questionnaire was used to provide data about similarity and the pairing was done randomly (except that no man was assigned to a taller woman). The dance was held two days later, before which the students were given their dates' names. During the dance, participants were asked to complete a questionnaire about the dance and their dates. The more physically attractive students were liked more by their partners than were the less attractive students, a finding that does not support the matching hypothesis.

Physical attractiveness proved to be the most important factor in liking, above such qualities as intelligence and personality. Liking was not affected by how attracted the other person felt towards the participant. Physical attractiveness was also the best predictor of the likelihood that they would see each other again, though it assumed less importance. Other factors such as intelligence and personality may not have emerged as important factors in determining liking because the students had only spent a very limited amount of time together.

Key study evaluation
The computer dance was not a very realistic test of the matching hypothesis because dates were assigned, and assessments were made before any rejection could have taken place. The interaction was very brief and therefore interpersonal assessments had to be based on superficial characteristics. It is also possible that the measure of physical attractiveness was not reliable. Finally, we should remember that the participants were students and therefore the findings may only apply to a youthful population who are not making long-term romantic choices.

When Walster et al. asked the students 6 months later whether they had dated their partners since the dance, they found that partners were more likely to have dated if they were similar in physical attractiveness than if they were dissimilar. This more realistic assessment does support the matching hypothesis.

Discussion points
1. Does the matching hypothesis seem correct in your experience?
2. Why does physical attractiveness play such an important part in dating behaviour and in relationships?

EXAM HINT

In the A2 exam you will not be directly examined on Key Studies, as you were in the AS exam, but you will have to draw from the content of the Key Studies in your essay answers.

judged from photographs. There was a definite tendency for the two people in each couple to be similar in terms of physical attractiveness.

Evaluation

Physical attractiveness is of importance in influencing initial attraction for other people. However, some people are much more affected by physical attractiveness than others. Towhey (1979) asked males and females how much they thought they would like a person whose photograph they had seen, and about whom they had read biographical information. The judgements of those scoring high on the Macho Scale (dealing with sexist attitudes, stereotypes, and behaviour) were much influenced by physical attractiveness, whereas those scoring low on the Macho Scale almost ignored physical attractiveness as a factor.

Is physical attractiveness mainly of importance only in the early stages of a relationship? The answer seems to be "no". For example, Murstein and Christy (1976) reported that married couples were significantly more similar than dating couples in physical attractiveness.

The matching hypothesis has been extended to suggest that couples can achieve a match in ways other than physical attractiveness, for example, a good-looking woman may be attracted to a man who lacks *physical* attractiveness but possesses other highly attractive features, such as intelligence or wealth. You can probably think of examples of famous couples whose attractive features are very different from each other.

Is physical attractiveness universal? Langlois et al. (2000) reported evidence suggesting it is. Participants in numerous different countries were asked to evaluate facial attractiveness, and there was a high level of agreement across cultures. However, there is disagreement so far as preferred female body size preference is concerned. Slim women were preferred to heavy women in most Western cultures, but the opposite was the case in cultures in which the food supply was moderately or very unreliable (Anderson et al., 1992).

The matching hypothesis predicts a match that is not necessarily based on looks alone. In fact, physical attractiveness can be matched with intelligence, as in the case of Marilyn Monroe and Arthur Miller.

INDEPENDENT STUDY IDEA: THE MATCHING HYPOTHESIS

Is the matching hypothesis true? We could investigate this by using wedding photos in a local paper. Cut each of the photos so that the brides and bridegrooms are separated. Ask participants to rate each photo for attractiveness on a scale of 1–10. To half the participants, show all the male photos first then the female and to the other half, present the female then the male.

An alternative but similar procedure would be to give all the male photos at once to each participant and ask them to place them in order from most to least attractive and use these ranks for your score. Do the same for the females. This second version avoids the possibility that you get a lot of "medium" scores (scores bunched around 5 or 6) for all the photos and that there are few low scores because participants don't want to appear unkind!

Again, some counterbalancing is necessary: half the participants do males first then females and the other half do it the other way around. If you want to be very fussy, you could get some participants to rank from least to most attractive whilst others rank from most to least. Just make sure your scoring is consistent, for example, you use a score of 1 for the least attractive and 10 for the most attractive for both males and females.

This is a correlational design: you are seeing if there is a positive relationship (correlation, association) between female ratings and male ratings for each married couple. The hypothesis is directional (one-tailed) because you expect, on the basis of previous research, that the more attractive one person is, the more attractive will be their partner.

Proximity

Proximity or nearness is an important factor in determining our choice of friends. Strong evidence for this was obtained by Festinger, Schachter, and Back (1950). They studied married graduate students who had been assigned randomly to flats in 17 different two-storey buildings. It was found that about two-thirds of their closest friends lived in the same building. Festinger et al. found that close friends who lived in the same building were twice as likely to be living on the same floor as the other floor. If you live on the same floor as someone, you are likely to bump into each other more frequently than if you are on different floors. This study suggests that such increased contact increases the likelihood that relationships form.

Friendships arise and are maintained between people who live close to each other, and who enjoy similar leisure pursuits.

The importance of proximity extends to romantic relationships leading to marriage. Bossard (1932) looked at 5000 marriage licences in Philadelphia. He found there was a clear tendency for those getting married to live close to each other. However, this may be less true today, because people are generally more mobile and travel much more than was the case in the 1930s. Having said that, it is still the case that you have to meet someone before forming a relationship, such as by going to the same college or the same swimming club, and frequency of contact is a starting point. Even internet relationships are formed through a kind of proximity.

Friendships and relationships are more common between individuals living close to each other, but so are antagonistic relationships. Ebbesen, Kjos, and Konecni (1976) found that most of the enemies of residents in apartment blocks in California also lived close by.

? Does the concept of proximity apply to your friends?

Evaluation

It is fairly obvious that proximity will be an important factor in the formation of relationships because proximity determines who you are likely to meet. Kerckhoff and Davis (1962) used the term "filter" to describe how superficial traits are used in the initial selection of friends or partners.

INDEPENDENT STUDY IDEA: PROXIMITY

Is the distance you live from someone still a major determinant of relationship formation? People used to marry those people who lived near them, but is this still the case? You could see if this trend is changing now that there is much greater mobility. Will there be a difference between older and younger married/cohabiting couples in this respect? Use two groups of participants who differ in age: for example, married or cohabiting couples over 50 (who have been married for 20 years or more) with couples under 30 who have been together for at least 2 years (these numbers are arbitrary but the older couples must have been together for some considerable time as we are interested in changes over time). Ask each couple where each originated from (where they were brought up during their teenage years) and work out the distance between the two places for each couple. Is there a difference between the two age groups (think about the design and level of measurement to decide the statistical test to use).

You could also consider whether a confounding variable is social class. Those who are from middle class and/or well-educated backgrounds are more likely to move around than those from working class and/or less well educated backgrounds.

Familiarity

Familiarity is another factor that influences interpersonal attraction. This was shown in a study by Moreland and Beach (1992). They carried out a study in which four women attended varying numbers of lectures given on a large lecture course at a college. The women sat quietly and didn't interact directly with any of the students. When the lecture course had finished, students on the course rated the women who were more familiar to them because they had attended many lectures as more interesting, warm, intelligent, and attractive than the women who had not attended many lectures. In addition, the students thought they would like better the women they had seen more often than the others.

Evaluation

Familiarity influences interpersonal attraction, and of course it is never sufficient on its own. There is a well-known saying, "Familiarity breeds contempt", and I am sure there are some people you know who are so unpleasant that you found yourself liking them *less* as you became more familiar with them. In spite of that, there is a general tendency to prefer people we know already to complete strangers.

Attitude similarity

One of the factors determining interpersonal attraction is attitude similarity. Newcomb (1961) paid students to take part in his study. Initially information was obtained about the beliefs and attitudes of students. He then used this information to assign students to rooms. Some students were given a room with someone of similar attitudes, whereas others were paired with someone having very different attitudes. Friendships were much more likely to develop between students who shared the same beliefs and attitudes than between those who did not (58% and 25%, respectively).

Byrne, London, and Griffitt (1968) found that attitude similarity had much more of an effect on interpersonal attraction when the attitudes were of importance to the individual. They arranged matters so that the other person seemed to have similar attitudes to the participants on either 75% or 25% of the topics. This was done by deliberately providing fake information about the other person. It was only when similarity was related to the topics of most importance to the participants that it affected attraction.

Evaluation

Werner and Parmalee (1979) argued that it was not attitude similarity as such that was important. They found that similarity in preference for leisure activities (which is related to attitude similarity) was more important for friendship than was attitude similarity. According to Werner and Parmalee (p.62), "those who play together, stay together."

Demographic similarity

Several studies have considered the effects of demographic variables (e.g., age, sex, social class). It has nearly always been found that those who have similar demographic characteristics are more likely to become friends. For example, Kandel (1978) asked students in secondary school to identify their best friend among the other students. These best friends tended to be of the same age, religion, sex, social class, and ethnic background as the students who nominated them.

? Do you think that preferring similar leisure activities is important in intimate relationships?

Similarity in personality

Reasonable similarity in physical attractiveness, attitudes, and demographic variables is found in friends, engaged couples, and married couples. What about similarity in personality? One possibility is that people who have similar personalities are most likely to become involved with each other ("Birds of a feather flock together"). Another possibility is that dissimilar people are most likely to become friends or to marry ("Opposites attract"). Winch (1958) argued for the latter possibility. He claimed that married couples will be happy if they each have complementary needs. For example, if a domineering person marries someone who is submissive, this may allow both of them to fulfil their needs.

Winch found that married couples different in personality were happier than those who were similar. However, most of the evidence indicates that similarity of personality *is* important, and that people tend to be intimately involved with those who are like themselves. Burgess and Wallin (1953) obtained detailed information from 1000 engaged couples, including information about 42 personality characteristics. There was no evidence for the notion that opposites attract. There was significant within-couple similarity for 14 personality characteristics (e.g., feelings easily hurt, leader of social events).

Evaluation of the six factors

There is much evidence that the formation of interpersonal relationships depends to a large extent on several kinds of similarity. Why is similarity so important? Rubin (1973) suggested various answers. First, if we like those who are similar to us, there is a reasonable chance that they will like us. Second, communication is easier with people who are similar. Third, similar others may confirm the rightness of our attitudes and beliefs. Fourth, it makes sense that if we like ourselves, then we should also like others who resemble us. Fifth, people who are similar to us are likely to enjoy the same activities. As mentioned earlier, someone who is similar to us is likely to be more rewarding than someone who is dissimilar.

Much research in this area is rather artificial (or even very artificial!). For example, the importance of physical attractiveness has sometimes been assessed by showing participants photographs of people they have never met, and asking them to indicate how much they would like to go out with them. Of course, physical attractiveness is going to have an enormous influence on the results when no other relevant information is available. Interpersonal relationships are formed over time as two people begin to know each other better, but the processes involved have rarely been studied in the laboratory.

A further limitation of most research is that individual differences have been largely ignored. Some people attach more importance than others to similarity of physical attractiveness, attitudes, and so on, but very little is known about this.

Considering the factors involved in the formation of relationships, what type of person are you likely to form a successful relationship with? Would it be someone like yourself or not?

Attraction and the Formation of Relationships

Psychologists are interested in formulating theoretical accounts of behaviour, on the basis of research evidence. We have reviewed some of the findings about the factors involved in interpersonal attraction. The next step is to consider how these can be woven into a coherent theory.

One major issue, for any theory, is its ability to account for the enormous diversity of interpersonal relationships between people. For example, it is important to distinguish between romantic relationships, same-sex friendships, opposite-sex friendships, interpersonal relationships in the workplace, and so on. It is obvious from experience that the processes involved in relationship formation differ considerably from one type of interpersonal relationship to another. It is hard to handle such diversity within a single theory. Many theorists have not been as careful as they might have been in indicating the type or types of interpersonal relationship to which their theory is most applicable. In addition they have ignored cultural and sub-cultural diversity, topics which are considered in the final Section of this chapter.

There are *two* other factors to consider in relation to any theory of interpersonal attraction and relationship formation. First of all, we have already noted the difficulties associated with research in this area. Studying social and interpersonal relationships is a nightmare for experimental psychologists because it is almost impossible for the researcher to *control* any of the important factors that influence the formation, maintenance, and dissolution of relationships except in highly artificial situations. Another problem is that one of the key features of nearly all interpersonal relationships is that they *change* over time. In order to understand these changes, we need to focus on the *processes* involved. However, these processes typically occur over long periods of time, and are very hard to observe experimentally. Therefore theories of interpersonal attraction and the formation of relationships may be rather poorly supported by research evidence.

> **EXAM HINT**
>
> The content in this section falls into two areas:
> - Research studies relating to interpersonal attraction, including evolutionary explanations, the matching hypothesis, and the factors in interpersonal attraction.
> - Theories of formation, such as reward/need satisfaction and economic theories.
>
> Make sure you can clearly distinguish between the initial attraction (interpersonal attraction) and what comes after (formation of relationships).

Evolutionary explanations

One way of considering social relationships is in **evolutionary** or **sociobiological** terms. The central idea is that the behaviours we observe around us must be **adaptive**, otherwise individuals possessing those characteristics would not have lived long enough to pass on those characteristics to their offspring. An adaptive behaviour is one that promotes the survival of the individual *and* results in successful reproduction. Therefore behaviours that are related to successful relationship formation leading to reproduction will be likely. If you're not successful at this your genes will die out!

One of the implications of the evolutionary approach is that males and females should both seek sexual partners who are most likely to produce healthy children. This could explain why physically healthy partners are generally preferred to unhealthy ones. Men may tend to prefer women who are younger than themselves because younger women are more likely to be fertile (Buss, 1989). There is a detailed discussion of this theory and the research evidence in Chapter 7, Evolutionary Explanations of Human Behaviour.

Further support for the evolutionary approach was reported by Langlois, Roggman, and Musselman (1994) and Henderson and Anglin (2003). Langlois et al. found that male and female faces based on averaging across many faces were

> **KEY TERMS**
>
> **Evolutionary:** following the theory of evolution, that certain behaviours are adaptive otherwise they would not have survived the process of natural selection.
>
> **Sociobiological:** an approach to explaining social behaviour in terms of evolutionary processes; with special emphasis on the gene as the unit for natural selection.
>
> **Adaptive:** the extent to which a behaviour increases the reproductive potential of an individual and survival of its genes.

regarded as more attractive than the individual faces from which they were constructed. Averaged faces are more symmetrical than individual faces, and symmetry is associated with good health. The link between facial attractiveness and health was shown clearly by Henderson and Anglin. High-school students in the 1920s whose photographs were rated as high in facial attractiveness lived significantly longer on average than those whose photographs were rated as low in facial attractiveness.

In interesting recent research, Elisabeth Cornwell and colleagues at St. Andrews (http://calvin.st-andrews.ac.uk) studied the effects of pheromones (chemical signals that travel between people) on sexual attraction. They found that some men preferred female sex pheromones to male ones whereas other men didn't. Men who preferred female sex pheromones also preferred women having feminised faces, whereas men preferring male sex pheromones preferred women having masculinised faces. According to evolutionary psychologists, the finding that smell is important as well as looks may be due to the long-term nature of many human relationships—this makes it important that *all* the available information is taken into account when choosing someone to marry.

The evolutionary approach has been extended to account for the close relationships often found within families. One way in which an individual can help to ensure the survival of his/her genes is by protecting relatives so they will be able to reproduce. For example, children share 50% of their genes with each of their parents. As a result, there are strong evolutionary reasons why parents should devote considerable efforts to looking after their children. The same considerations apply to our relationships with other relatives, with the level of involvement being determined by the genetic similarity. The term **kin selection** is used to describe the notion that survival of an individual's genes is ensured by helping the survival of close relatives (see pages 96–97).

Some evidence is consistent with the evolutionary approach. Fellner and Marshall (1981) found that 86% of people were willing to be a kidney donor for their children, 67% would do the same for their parents, and 50% would be a kidney donor for their siblings.

Parents invest a lot of time and resources in their children, which may be explained by biological theories of relationships—the parents' chances of passing on their genes are improved if they can help their children to survive and succeed.

Evaluation

Evolutionary theories of relationships help to account for the special nature of the relationships within families, and especially for the enormous amounts of time and resources that most parents devote to their children. However, such theories do not explain most relationships. For example, the notion that romantic relationships have reproduction as their primary goal does not apply to homosexual relationships, or to heterosexual relationships in which there is no intention to have children.

The evolutionary approach is of value in explaining why some faces are more attractive than ones. More specifically, people having more attractive faces tend to be healthier and to live longer than those who don't, which seems unfair on those who aren't lucky enough to have attractive faces!

The greatest limitation of evolutionary theories is that they focus on sexual relationships and ignore

> **KEY TERM**
>
> **Kin selection:** the view that the process of natural selection functions at the level of an individual's genes and thus any behaviour that promotes the survival and reproduction of all "kin" (genetic relatives) will also be selected.

Sociobiologists believe that the appeal of an older man may lie in his superior potential as a provider.

non-sexual relationships and friendships with non-relatives. It is hard for such theories to explain why women love their best friend as much as their lover, and like their best friend more (Sternberg & Grajek, 1984). In general terms, evolutionary theories are inadequate to account for interpersonal relationships.

Relative age: The sociobiological approach

In spite of various cultural differences in standards of physical attractiveness, there are also some important similarities. Buss (1989) studied 37 cultures around the world, and found that men in all of these cultures preferred women younger than themselves, and women preferred men older than themselves in all cultures except Spain. Buss also found that the personal qualities of kindness and intelligence were regarded as important in virtually all of the cultures he studied.

There are various possible reasons why men prefer younger women, and women prefer older men. One approach has been put forward by **sociobiologists**, who try to explain human social behaviour in terms of genetic and biological factors. According to sociobiologists (e.g., Buss, 1989), what men and women find attractive in the opposite sex are those features that maximise the probability of producing offspring and so allow their genes to carry over into the next generation. Younger women are preferred to older ones because older women are less likely to be able to have children. In similar fashion, women prefer older men because they are more likely to be able to provide adequately for the needs of their offspring.

Evaluation

The evolutionary or sociobiological approach is inadequate. First, evolutionary psychologists and sociobiologists don't provide an explanation of why men and women in nearly all cultures regard kindness and intelligence as being more important than age. Second, the factors determining the choice of marriage partner differ considerably from one culture to another. Evolutionary psychologists and sociobiologists consistently underestimate the importance of cultural factors in their explanations of social behaviour.

Howard, Blumstein, and Schwartz (1987) tried to explain the preference of men for younger women and of women for older men in social and cultural terms. According to them, women have historically had much lower social status than men. Women who wish to enhance their social status have usually had to do this by marrying an older man of high status. As women were unable to offer high social status because of the structure of society, they needed to offer youth and physical attractiveness instead. Of course, there have been important changes in society in recent years. Far more women than ever before have full-time jobs, and are financially independent from men. It follows from the sociocultural theory of Howard et al. that the preference of women for older, high-status men may change as a result. Time will tell.

Reward/need satisfaction

Reinforcement and need satisfaction theory is based on the notion that a key reason why we form friendships and relationships is because of the rewards or reinforcements that we receive from others. These rewards often consist of

KEY TERM

Sociobiologists: scientists who argue that the roots of social behaviour are to be found in biological and genetic factors.

approval, smiling, and so on. Foa and Foa (1975) argued that the rewards provided by other people can also include sex, status, love, help, money, and agreement with our opinions. These things may be rewarding because they meet our various social needs. For example, obtaining the approval of others satisfies our need for self-esteem, being comforted satisfies our dependency needs, controlling others meets our needs for dominance, and making love satisfies our sex needs (Argyle, 1988).

Byrne (1971) argued that classical conditioning also plays an important role in determining the effects of reinforcement on interpersonal attraction. According to classical conditioning theory, *any* background neutral stimuli associated with reward will come to produce positive feelings. This idea comes from Pavlov's research in which dogs that learned to associate a tone with the presentation of food salivated when the tone was presented. A study on humans was reported by Griffit and Guay (1969). They had someone give a reward or a punishment to several participants in the presence of an uninvolved bystander. The bystander was liked more by participants who were rewarded than by those who were punished.

As Skinner and others discovered many years ago, humans and animals are very responsive to rewards and punishments. Rats will press energetically on a lever if lever pressing is sometimes followed by food reward, but will stop pressing if lever pressing is followed by punishment (e.g., electric shock). In similar fashion, we typically decide to spend more time with people who provide us with rewards but as little time as possible with people who punish us.

Research support

Veitch and Griffitt (1976) tested the reinforcement affect model by arranging for single participants to wait in an experimenter's office while the experimenter went on an errand. The radio was left on with music playing and, in the time alone, the participant (a student) heard two news broadcasts. They contained either good or bad news. When the experimenter returned the participant was asked to fill in a "Feelings Scale" (to assess their emotional state) and to read a questionnaire supposedly filled in by another student. It was filled in to be either in close agreement or disagreement with attitudes previously expressed by the participant in an earlier questionnaire that had been done in class. The participant filled in an "Interpersonal Judgement Scale" to rate the supposed other student. The participants exposed to the "good" news reported significantly more positive feelings than those who listened to the "bad" news. In addition, "good news" participants felt significantly more attracted to the hypothetical other student. The effect was stronger where attitudes were more similar, though it occurred where attitudes were dissimilar. This supports the idea that positive feelings increase the possibilities of interpersonal attraction but note the artificiality of asking people to rate the attractiveness of someone they have never met!

Other research has supported this study, for example, Rabbie and Horowitz (1960) found that strangers expressed greater liking for each other when they were successful in a game-like task than when unsuccessful. However, Duck (1992) criticises these studies because they rely on the rather artificial "bogus stranger" method. There is no actual stranger but only one that is imagined and this may not elicit realistic responses.

? List the needs that are being met in the following types of relationship: best friend, parent with child, lover.

? What psychological harm may have been caused in this experiment?

Evaluation

We are more attracted to those who provide us with reinforcement than those who do not. For example, individuals who are high on rewardingness (i.e., friendly, co-operative, smiling, warm) are consistently liked more than individuals who are low on rewardingness (Argyle, 1988). However, reinforcement theory doesn't provide an adequate account of interpersonal attraction for various reasons. First, the theory is more relevant to the very earliest stages of attraction than to attraction within an ongoing friendship or relationship. Second, as Argyle pointed out, reinforcement has not been shown to be of much importance in determining the strength of the relationship between parents and their children.

Third, reinforcement theory assumes that people are totally selfish, and only concerned about the rewards they receive. In fact, people are often concerned about other people, and about the rewards that they provide for other people. Fourth, whether or not reinforcement increases interpersonal attraction depends to a large extent on the *context* in which the reinforcement is provided. For example, the need for sexual satisfaction can be fulfilled by a prostitute, but this doesn't mean that men who resort to prostitutes become attracted to them as people.

Fifth, reinforcement and need satisfaction theories are of more relevance to the **individualistic** societies of the Western world than to the **collectivistic** societies of the non-Western world (this is discussed further later). More speculatively, these theories may tend to be more applicable to men than to women. In many cultures, there is more emphasis on females than on males learning to be attentive to the needs of others (Lott, 1994).

Economic theories: Exchange and equity

An "economic theory" is one that expresses relationships in terms of some distribution of resources or trading of one thing for another.

Social exchange theory

Social exchange theory (e.g., Thibaut & Kelley, 1959) is similar to reinforcement theory. However, it is more specifically relevant to interpersonal attraction and provides a more plausible account. It is assumed that everyone tries to maximise the rewards (e.g., affection; attention) they obtain from a relationship, and to minimise the costs (e.g., devoting time and effort to the other person; coping with the other person's emotional problems). Thus, we focus on the cost–reward ratio—liking is determined by what is will cost to be reinforced or rewarded by the other person. For example, if you have a friend in constant need of support and encouragement, he/she needs to provide you with plenty of rewards to make up for all the costs if the friendship is to flourish! It is also assumed that if a relationship is to continue, people expect the other person to reward them as much as they reward the other person.

Thibaut and Kelley argued that long-term friendships and relationships go through four stages:

SAMPLING
The costs and rewards of associating with others are explored

BARGAINING
A process of negotiation in which rewards and costs are agreed

COMMITMENT
Exchange of rewards and acceptance of costs stabilises. Greater focus on the relationship itself

INSTITUTIONALISATION
Norms and expectations are firmly established

Additional assumptions are sometimes included in social exchange theory. For example, how satisfied individuals are with the rewards and costs of a relationship

? Based on reinforcement theory, how would you advise someone to behave to make a good impression on, or be liked by, someone they have never met before?

? What rewards and costs are associated with the following relationships: best friend, parent with child, lover?

KEY TERMS

Individualistic: a type of culture that emphasises individuality, individual needs, and independence. People tend to live in small nuclear families.
Collectivistic: a type of culture where individuals share tasks, belongings, and income. The people may live in large family groups and value interdependence.

will depend on what they have come to expect from previous relationships. In other words, they have a **comparison level** (CL) (Thibaut & Kelley, 1959), representing the outcomes they believe they deserve on the basis of past experiences—so if in the past they have had very poor relationships they may expect very little from subsequent ones. In addition, their level of satisfaction will depend on the rewards (e.g., affection, sex) and costs (e.g., arguments, loss of control) that would be involved if they formed a relationship with someone else; this is known as the "comparison level for alternatives" (CLalt). All of this makes sense—if you are a very attractive and popular person, you can afford to be very choosy in your friendships and relationships.

Sharing domestic chores may be a result of negotiation in an equitable relationship, in which each partner feels the other takes their share of responsibilities.

Equity theory

Some theorists (e.g., Hatfield, Utne, & Traupmann, 1979) have extended social exchange theory to include more of an emphasis on fairness or equity. According to equity theory, people expect to receive rewards from a relationship proportional to the rewards they provide for the other person. However, imbalance can be tolerated if the two people involved in a relationship accept the situation. Walster, Walster, and Berscheid (1978) expressed the main assumptions of equity theory as follows:

1. Individuals try to maximise the rewards they receive and minimise the costs.
2. There is negotiation to produce fairness; for example, one partner may do the shopping every week to compensate for going out to play sport twice a week.
3. If the relationship is unfair or inequitable, it produces distress, especially in the disadvantaged person.
4. The disadvantaged person will try hard to make the relationship more equitable, particularly when it is very inequitable. If that can't be achieved, the disadvantaged person is likely to leave the relationship.

Research evidence

Hatfield et al. (1979) asked newlyweds to indicate the extent to which they felt they were receiving more or less than they should in view of their contributions to the marriage. They also indicated their level of contentment, happiness, anger, and guilt. The under-benefited had the lowest level of overall satisfaction with their marriage, and tended to experience anger. The over-benefited came next (they tended to feel guilty), and those who perceived their marriage as equitable had the highest level of satisfaction. Men who were over-benefited were almost as satisfied as those in an equitable marriage, but over-benefited women were much less satisfied than women with equal benefit (Argyle, 1988).

The finding that those who perceive their marriages as equitable are happiest, and those who perceive themselves as under-benefited are least happy, was replicated by Buunk and VanYperen (1991). However, these findings applied only to those individuals high in exchange orientation (i.e., expecting rewards given by one person in a relationship to be followed immediately by rewards given by the other person). Those low in exchange orientation had fairly high marriage satisfaction regardless of whether they were over-benefited, under-benefited, or receiving equal benefit. (See the Key Study on pages 38–39 for a discussion of communal and exchange couples.)

[?] What could be the cause of gender differences, such as the one between over-benefited males and over-benefited females?

KEY TERM

Comparison level: the outcomes that people think they deserve from a relationship on the basis of past experience.

Evaluation

Equity theory seems more plausible than social exchange theory. It takes more account of the rewards and costs of the other person as well as of the individual himself/herself. The most obvious criticism of both approaches is that they assume people are very selfish and self-centred in their friendships and relationships. This assumption may possess some validity in an individualist society such as that of the United States, but is less likely to apply to collectivist societies. Evidence of cultural differences was reported by Gergen, Morse, and Gergen (1980). European students were found to prefer equality in their relationships, with an equal distribution of rewards. In contrast, American students tended to favour equity, based on a constant ratio of rewards to inputs.

One of the more obvious predictions from equity theory is that the future quality of equitable relationships should be greater than that of inequitable ones. However, there is often no association between equity and future quality (see Buunk, 1996).

Much of the research in this area has not proved very informative. Some of the reasons for this were identified by Argyle (1988, p.224):

> [Exchange] theory has led mainly to very artificial experiments . . . Research on real-life relationships has been hampered by the difficulty of scaling rewards.

What is the difference between equity and equality?

Notions of exchange and equity are more important between casual acquaintances than they are between people who are close friends or emotionally involved with each other. Happily married couples do not focus on issues of exchange or equity. Murstein, MacDonald, and Cerreto (1977) found that marital adjustment was significantly poorer in those married couples who were concerned about exchange and equity than in those couples who were not. Furthermore there are differences in the behaviour of communal and exchange relationships, as discussed in the Key Study below.

KEY STUDY
Communal and exchange relationships

Several theorists have doubted whether intimate relationships can be understood properly in terms of traditional theories. For example, Clark and Mills (1979) argued that there are two major kinds of relationships:

- *Communal relationships*: the main focus is on giving the other person what he or she needs; these relationships typically involve close friends or family members.
- *Exchange relationships*: the main focus is on the notion that what one puts into the relationship should balance what one receives; these relationships usually involve acquaintances or strangers.

According to Clark and Mills, most romantic relationships are not based on the principle of exchange. Those involved in such relationships are much more concerned about being able to meet the needs of the other person than about exchange or reciprocity.

Clark (1984) presented evidence consistent with this proposed distinction between communal and exchange relationships. Male students located sequences of numbers in a matrix with someone called Paula. Each student was told that he and Paula would receive a joint payment based on their performance, and they must decide how much each of them received. Some participants were told that Paula was single and was taking part in the experiment to make friends. The others were told that Paula was married, and that her husband was going to pick her up. Clark predicted that the former participants would tend to think in terms of a possible communal relationship with Paula, whereas the latter participants would expect an exchange relationship.

The participants found that Paula had already circled some sequences of numbers with a felt-tip pen. What was of interest was whether the participants used a pen of a different colour. It was argued that students looking for an exchange relationship would do so, because it would allow them to be paid on the basis of their contribution. In contrast, those seeking a communal relationship should use a pen of the same colour, because they were mainly concerned about their combined efforts. The findings were as predicted. About 90% of those students who thought Paula was married used a felt-tip pen of a different colour, compared with only 10% of those who thought she was single. Clark also found that pairs of friends were less likely than pairs of strangers to use different-coloured pens.

Fiske (1993) extended the line of theorising proposed by Clark and Mills. According to him, there are four types of relationship:

* *Exchange*: based on reciprocity.
* *Communal*: based on catering for the other person's needs.
* *Equality matching*: based on ensuring that everyone receives the same; for example, giving all of the children in a family an ice cream of the same size.
* *Authority*: based on the notion that one person's orders are obeyed by others.

Discussion points
1. Does the study by Clark and Mills really show that there is a distinction between exchange and communal relationships?
2. Have social psychologists focused too much on exchange relationships and not enough on communal relationships?

> **?** Assessing attitudes through the use of coloured felt-tip pens is quite ingenious, but how valid do you think it is?

Maintenance of Relationships

Self-disclosure
Sternberg (1986) identified intimacy as a key component of both liking and loving. **Self-disclosure**, which involves revealing personal and sensitive information about oneself to another person, is of fundamental importance in developing and maintaining intimacy. According to Altman and Taylor's (1973) **social penetration theory**, the development of a relationship involves increased self-disclosure on both sides. People who have just met tend to follow the **norm of self-disclosure reciprocity**, according to which they match the level of self-disclosure of the other person. According to Altman and Taylor, the move towards revealing more about oneself should not be done too rapidly, because the other person may feel threatened.

> **?** Why is self-disclosure risky in a new relationship?

> **?** Think of a time when you were getting to know someone better. What did you spend your time doing? Could it be described as mutual self-disclosure?

Depenetration
As a relationship develops, there is less adherence to the norm of self-disclosure reciprocity. In an intimate relationship, the other person is most likely to respond to hearing sensitive personal information by offering support and understanding rather than by engaging in self-disclosure (Archer, 1979). Problems in maintaining a relationship are associated with what Altman and Taylor (1973) called depenetration. **Depenetration** involves abandoning the habit of intimate self-disclosure to the other person across a wide range of topics. It takes two main forms. One form is simply

> **KEY TERMS**
> **Self-disclosure:** revealing personal information about oneself to someone else.
> **Social penetration theory:** the theory that the development of a relationship involves increasing self-disclosure on both sides.
> **Norm of self-disclosure reciprocity:** the expectation that friends usually match how much they disclose about themselves, gradually increasing how much they mutually reveal.
> **Depenetration:** deliberately reducing the amount of self-disclosure to someone else.

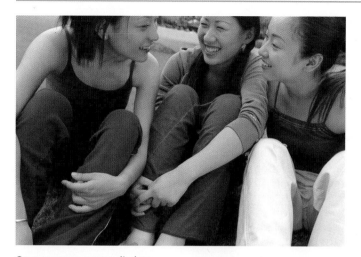

On average, women disclose more personal and sensitive information about themselves to same-sex friends than men do (Dindia & Allen, 1992).

refusing to reveal intimate information to the other person. The other form is talking intimately about only a few topics; these topics are chosen to hurt the other person, and usually involve strong negative feelings (Tolstedt & Stokes, 1984).

Gender differences

It is often argued that women have higher levels of self-disclosure in their various relationships than do men. The relevant evidence from 205 studies was reviewed by Dindia and Allen (1992). On average, women self-disclose more than men with their romantic partners of the opposite sex and with their same-sex friends. However, there was no difference between men and women in their self-disclosure levels to male friends. Most of the sex differences in self-disclosure were not large, but the differences didn't seem to have become smaller over the previous 30 years or so.

INDEPENDENT STUDY IDEA: GENDER DIFFERENCES

Are there significant differences in women and men in terms of same-sex friendships? One way of investigating this is via a confidential questionnaire. What you wish to ascertain is whether men are more likely to have "side-by-side" relationships and women "face-to-face" ones. The questionnaire should therefore contain items that measure both of these types of relationships. One way of doing this is to ask participants to think of a person they consider to be their "best" (or closest) same-sex friend and ask them to complete a check box of things they do with them, perhaps putting them in order of importance. Items can be divided into activities that would constitute "side-by-side" (such as sharing sporting interests) and "face-to-face" (such as discussing problems, including intimate ones). Then compare the female with the male responses on each of these two sets of activities. Note that you don't need any names on the questionnaires at all, simply the sex of the participant (and their age might add a valuable extra variable that may be relevant in your discussion). Pilot your first attempt at a questionnaire to see if it needs refinement (for example, you may need to ask how many times a month on average some activity is shared, rather than just whether or not it occurs). As far as analysis is concerned, you may have ordinal data or nominal data, depending on how you score the questionnaire, and you need a test of difference for independent groups.

Commitment

Commitment, in the sense of a determination to continue the relationship, increases over time. What are the factors leading to the growth of commitment? Rusbult (1980) put forward an investment model, in which she identified three key factors:

1. *Satisfaction*: the rewards provided by the relationship.
2. *Perceived quality of alternatives*: individuals will be more committed to a relationship if there are no other attractive options.
3. *Investment size*: the more time, effort, money, and so on invested in the relationship, the greater will be the commitment.

Lund (1985) found that the level of commitment depended more on investment size than on satisfaction or rewards. Michaels, Acock, and Edwards (1986) found that commitment to a relationship was stronger when the outcomes received exceeded those anticipated in alternative relationships than when they were smaller. They also found that the extent to which the relationship was equitable did not predict commitment.

Limitations

There are two limitations with Rusbult's approach. First, the three factors she identifies are not truly independent of each other. For example, individuals very satisfied with a relationship are more likely to have a large investment in it. Second, most of the research has focused on short-term rather than long-term relationships (Buunk, 1996).

Maintenance and repair strategies

Dindia and Baxter (1987) carried out a thorough study of the strategies used by married couples to maintain their marriages. They found evidence for 49 such strategies, which could be divided into maintenance strategies and repair strategies. Maintenance strategies mostly involved joint activities such as going for walks together or talking about the events of the day, and occurred because they were pleasurable. In contrast, repair strategies involved discussing issues or making difficult decisions, and occurred because there were problems within the relationship.

Dindia and Baxter found differences between those who had been married for only a short period of time, and those who had been married much longer. Newlyweds tended to make more use of maintenance strategies than the long-term married, but the reasons for this are not clear. The positive view is that maintenance strategies are less necessary when two people know each other very well. The negative view is that those who have been married for a long time simply take each other for granted and put less effort into everyday joint activities.

Rusbult, Zembrodt, and Iwaniszek (1986) identified four strategies that people use to deal with conflicts in relationships. Each strategy is active or passive, and constructive or destructive.

- *Voice* is the active, constructive strategy, in which people discuss their problems and seek answers to the relationship difficulties.
- *Loyalty* is the passive, constructive strategy, in which people wait and hope that the situation will improve.
- *Neglect* is a passive and destructive strategy, in which individuals ignore their partners or spend less time with them.
- Finally, there is *exit*. This is an active and destructive strategy involving individuals deciding to abandon the relationship.

What determines the choice of strategy? Rusbult et al. studied lesbian, gay, and heterosexual couples. Individuals with high psychological femininity (warmth, intimacy; concern with interpersonal relations) were much more likely to react constructively to relationship problems than were those with high masculinity (aggressiveness, independence, assertiveness).

VOICE	Active	Constructive	Discuss problems and seek answers	High psychological femininity
LOYALTY	Passive	Constructive	Wait and hope things improve	
NEGLECT	Passive	Destructive	Ignore partner and spend less time with them	High psychological masculinity
EXIT	Active	Destructive	Individual decides to abandon relationship	

A stage theory of maintenance

Levinger (1980) proposed that, over time, a relationship becomes progressively more intimate. The five stages in his ABCDE model are:

A: Acquaintance. A relationship starts with mutual attraction. We examined possible factors for this in the last Unit, such as attractiveness and proximity. In some relationships this stage may last indefinitely.

B: Build-up. As a couple engage in self-disclosure they become increasingly interdependent. At this stage participants may be evaluating rewards and costs.

C: Continuation. The relationship, if continuing, becomes consolidated. Partners may make some kind of long-term commitment such as becoming engaged or married, or buying a house together. Their lives become enmeshed by meeting each other's friends and families, and sharing routines and pastimes.

D: Deterioration. Not all relationships reach this stage but for those that do the causes may be an imbalance of costs and rewards, or a high number of risk factors. These are discussed later in this Unit.

E: Ending. Deterioration may lead to the end.

A Acquaintance	Relationship starts with mutual attraction
B Build-up	Couple engage in self-disclosure and become increasingly interdependent
C Continuation	Couple's lives become enmeshed and the relationship becomes consolidated
D Deterioration	Relationship may deteriorate due to an imbalance of costs and rewards, or a high number of risk factors
E Ending	Deterioration may lead the couple to end the relationship

The greatest strength of Levinger's model is that it emphasises the notion that relationships and close friendships change in predictable ways over time. However, Levinger regards the sequence of stages of a relationship as occurring in a fixed order, and so focuses on the similarities among relationships. In fact, there are large differences among couples in the progress of their relationships (Brehm, 1992). As a result, it may be preferable to think in terms of flexible phases rather than fixed stages (Brehm, 1992). Levinger's model provides some answers to *what* and *when* questions, telling us what happens during the course of a relationship and when different stages occur. However, it has little to say about *why* questions: Why do relationships go through this set of fixed stages? Why do relationships initially improve over time and then deteriorate?

This model can provide a useful framework for presenting the facts described in this Section.

[?] Do all relationships go through all of Levinger's five stages?

Relationship rules

In order to maintain a relationship successfully (whether a romantic relationship, friendship, or whatever), it is necessary for both of the people involved to keep to certain informal relationship rules ("behaviour which it is believed ought or ought not to be performed in each relationship", Argyle, 1988, p.233). Argyle and Henderson (1984) argued that there are four criteria by means of which friendship rules can be identified:

- There should be general agreement that the behaviour indicated in the rule is relevant to friendship.
- The rule should not be applied in the same way to current and former friends.
- Failure to stick to the rule should tend to lead to the abandonment of the friendship.
- The rule should identify some of the ways in which people's behaviour towards close friends and acquaintances differs.

Argyle and Henderson applied these four criteria to a study of friendship rules in England, Italy, Hong Kong, and Japan. They found there were six rules of major importance to friendships in all four countries. These were:

1. Trust and confide in the other person.
2. Show emotional support.

3. Share news of success.
4. Strive to make the friend happy when with him/her.
5. Volunteer help in time of need.
6. Stand up for a friend in his/her absence.

? Can you think of any other rules that operate in your relationships?

Argyle et al. (1986) found there were some interesting cultural differences in the importance attached to certain rules. For example, participants in Hong Kong and Japan were more likely than those in Britain or in Italy to support rules such as obeying superiors, preserving group harmony, and avoiding loss of face.

Cognitive factors

Duck and Pond (1989) noted that the key factor about routines or habitual patterns of interactions in relationships is the way that partners talk to one another in and about their interactions: relationships are *not* a string of routines but the cognitions (thoughts) that surround them. Murray and Holmes (1993) argued that an important way in which individuals maintain relationships is by means of "storytelling", in which the partner's faults are regarded as favourably as possible. Their research is described in the Key Study below. Fincham and Bradbury (1993) argued that the kinds of attributions that married people make about their spouse have an effect on how successfully the marriage is maintained. Husbands and wives who attributed their partner's negative behaviour to *internal* characteristics (e.g., personality) were more dissatisfied with the marriage 1 year later than were those who attributed it to external factors (e.g., hard work, worries about the family).

KEY STUDY
Cognitive factors in maintenance

Murray and Holmes (1993) argued that an important way in which individuals maintain relationships is by means of storytelling, in which the partner's faults are regarded as favourably as possible. This storytelling occurs even in unpromising circumstances. Murray and Holmes studied individuals who claimed that their relationships involved little conflict, and that conflict is harmful to intimacy. Some of them were then informed that there is strong evidence that conflict is beneficial to the development of intimacy. Finally, the participants were asked to write narratives describing the development of intimacy in their relationship.

What happened? The participants who had been told that conflict is advantageous were much more likely to write narratives in which they argued that conflicts and disagreements were valuable. For example, one participant wrote, "I feel he is facilitating our growth by increasingly being able to tell me when he disagrees with my opinions in all areas", and another wrote, "We've had only three disagreements . . . we were able to get to the root of the problem, talk it out, and we

What do you think is likely to happen if you tell yourself a story about your partner that emphasises their faults?

managed to emerge from it closer than before." Murray and Holmes (p.719) concluded as follows:

> We suspect that individuals' continued confidence in their partners . . . depends on their continued struggle to weave stories that depict potential faults in their partners in the best possible light.

Key study evaluation
The research by Murray and Holmes is important, because most previous researchers had ignored the role of storytelling in maintaining relationships. However, we need to know more of the factors determining when those involved in relationships will make use of storytelling. There is also the issue of whether the participants really believed what they were writing, rather than simply expressing views that they thought the experimenter wanted them to express.

Discussion points
1. What do you think of the storytelling approach to understanding the maintenance of relationships?
2. Are people aware that they are constructing stories about their partner?

Theories of Maintenance and Dissolution in Relationships

Earlier in the chapter we considered various theories accounting for the formation of relationships. These same theories can be related to maintenance (or its opposite, dissolution).

Social exchange theory
Levinger (1976) argued that the chances of a marriage surviving depend on three factors:

1. The attractions of the relationship, such as emotional security and sexual satisfaction.
2. The barriers to leaving the marriage, such as social and financial pressures.
3. The presence of attractive alternatives, such as a more desirable partner.

Divorce is most likely when the marriage has few attractions, there are only weak barriers to leaving the relationship, and there are very attractive alternatives. This is similar to Thibaut and Kelley's (1959) concept of a "comparison level for alternatives" (CLalt). When this is higher than the comparison level (CL) then we are motivated to leave a relationship.

Evaluation

How do these theories of maintenance and dissolution differ from models of dissolution described on pages 51–52?

One of the advantages of Levinger's social exchange theory is that it helps to explain why marital dissatisfaction doesn't strongly predict subsequent divorce (Karney & Bradbury, 1995). For example, married couples who are dissatisfied may not divorce because there are strong barriers to leaving the marriage and no attractive alternatives. The greatest disadvantage of Levinger's social exchange theory is that it doesn't explain the processes that cause initially successful marriages to become unsuccessful.

Vulnerability–stress–adaptation model

Karney and Bradbury (1995) put forward a vulnerability–stress–adaptation model of marriage. According to this model, three major factors determine marital quality and stability or duration:

1. Enduring vulnerabilities: these include high neuroticism (a personality dimension concerned with anxiety and depression) and an unhappy childhood.
2. Stressful events: these include short- and long-lasting life events such as illness, unemployment, and poverty.
3. Adaptive processes: these include constructive and destructive coping strategies to resolve difficulties.

```
Stressful event  →  Stretches couple's
                    capacity to adapt
        ↑                  ↓
Lack of adaptation
perpetuates or worsens
the original stress
```

According to Karney and Bradbury (1995), some couples who have enduring vulnerabilities can become stuck in this vicious cycle.

A key assumption of the model is that the three factors all affect each other. The use of adaptive processes is influenced by enduring vulnerabilities and by stressful events. For example, married individuals high on neuroticism or whose parents divorced tend to have relatively poor adaptive processes, and the stress created by unemployment is associated with more negative and less constructive interactions with spouses (Aubry, Tefft, & Kingsbury, 1990). In addition, enduring vulnerabilities can play a role in creating stressful events. For example, individuals who are very depressed often create stressful conditions in their lives (Hammen, 1991). Adaptive processes can also create stressful conditions. For example, clinically depressed individuals whose spouses were very critical were more likely to suffer relapses than were individuals with less critical spouses (Hooley, Orley, & Teasdale, 1986).

According to the vulnerability–stress–adaptation model (Karney & Bradbury, 1995, p.24), one way in which a marriage can disintegrate is through the following vicious cycle:

(a) stressful events challenge a couple's capacity to adapt, (b) which contributes to the perpetuation or worsening of those events, (c) which in turn further challenge and perhaps overwhelm their capacity to adapt.

This vicious cycle is most likely to occur in couples having enduring vulnerabilities.

Evaluation

As we saw earlier, numerous factors are associated with the maintenance or dissolution of marriages. One of the strengths of the vulnerability–stress–adaptation model is the way in which most of these factors can be related directly to the three broad variables of enduring vulnerabilities, stress, and adaptive processes. Another strength of the model is that it shows how these three variables can interact in different ways to reduce marital quality.

The greatest limitation of the vulnerability–stress–adaptation model is its emphasis on marital quality or satisfaction as the major determinant of marital stability. As Levinger (1976) argued, factors *external* to the marriage also affect marital stability. These factors include the barriers to leaving the relationship and the presence of attractive alternatives.

Depressed individuals are likely to create stressful situations in their lives, affecting their relationship with their partner.

SECTION SUMMARY
Attraction and the Formation of Relationships

Explanations of interpersonal attraction

❖ Certain factors explain why we form relationships with one person rather than another: physical attraction, proximity, familiarity, and similarity.

Physical attraction

❖ Generalised to other attractive characteristics (the halo effect).
❖ The matching hypothesis:

— We are attracted to those who match our own physical attraction.
— Support for this hypothesis has been obtained in studies of initial attraction and in married couples.

❖ Some people may be more influenced by physical attractiveness than others.
❖ Matching can be achieved through other attractive characteristics beyond good looks.

Proximity

❖ May be physical or psychological.
❖ Increased contact has been shown to increase the likelihood of friendships and romantic relationships—and also of antagonistic relationships.

Familiarity

❖ We have a general preference for the known over the unknown, and this explains why familiarity makes a difference.
❖ However, familiarity doesn't always lead to increased attraction!

Similarity

❖ Attitude similarity: This can increase attraction when the attitudes are of importance to the individual. However similarity in leisure activities has been found to be more important for attraction than attitude similarity.
❖ Demographic similarity: Those who are similar in demographic variables (e.g., age, sex, social class) are more likely to become friends.
❖ Personality similarity: People having similar personalities are also most likely to become involved with each other. Evidence that opposites attract each other was not supported by subsequent research.
❖ Similarity is probably important for various reasons. Liking for a similar person is likely to be reciprocated, communication is easier, and it confirms our attitudes. If one likes oneself then one should like someone similar, and partners can share activities. However much of the research is artificial and largely correlational. It tends to ignore individual differences.

Theories of attraction and the formation of relationships

❖ Theories of attraction and the formation of relationships offer an account of research evidence, though this is flawed because of its artificial nature.

Evolutionary theories

❖ Based on the idea that behaviours that promote reproduction are naturally selected.
❖ Symmetrical faces are associated with good health so there is a link between facial attractiveness and health.
❖ Family relationships can also be explained in terms of kin selection. However, many sexual relationships cannot be explained this way.

❖ The sociobiological approach:

— Men and women should seek partners who will produce healthy offspring who can be cared for.
— According to Buss (1989), men tend to prefer younger women as they are more fertile and women tend to prefer older men as they have more resources.

❖ Evaluation: This approach is inadequate and underestimates the importance of other factors.

❖ Reward/Need Satisfaction Theory:

— We are attracted to people who provide us with rewards (e.g., help, money, respect, status, sex, and love) but we dislike those who punish us.
— Neutral stimuli associated with reward come to produce positive feelings.

❖ Evaluation:

— This approach is of most relevance to the initial stages of attraction.
— It assumes that people are very selfish, and it ignores the context in which reinforcement is provided.
— This explanation is more relevant to individualist societies.

❖ Economic theories suggest that relationships involve some kind of trade.

Economic theories

❖ Social Exchange Theory:

— People try to maximise the rewards and minimise the costs of interpersonal relationships.
— Satisfaction can be expressed in terms of comparison levels as well as a comparison level for alternatives.

❖ Equity theory

— An extension of social exchange theory emphasising fairness (equity). People expect to receive rewards from a relationship proportional to the rewards they provide for the other person.
— Equity was found to be associated with happiness in relationships, though this may apply only to exchange couples rather than communal couples.

❖ Evaluation:

— Equity theory is more plausible than social exchange theory, because it takes more account of the other person's rewards and costs.
— Both approaches apply more to individualist cultures.
— We would expect to find an association between equity and future quality of a relationship, but research hasn't supported this.
— Exchange and equity may be more important in casual relationships; in fact marital adjustment may be poorer in exchange couples.

❖ Self-disclosure: Social penetration theory suggests that relationships develop as a result of mutual self-disclosure but this lessens in time as each partner listens to self-disclosures rather than responding with self-disclosure.

Maintenance of relationships

❖ Depenetration involves abandoning disclosure. Women self-disclose more to women than men.

Commitment

❖ Commitment can be explained by the investment model:

— Satisfaction
— Perceived quality of alternatives
— Investment size.

❖ All three factors are interrelated, which lessens the predictive value of the factors.

Maintenance strategies

❖ Many relationships are sustained by maintenance strategies particularly during the early stages.
❖ There are strategies that people use to deal with conflicts in relationships (voice, loyalty, neglect, and exit).
❖ Informal relationship rules are important for maintenance. There are six key friendship rules:

— Trust the other person
— Show emotional support
— Share news of success
— Strive to make the friend happy
— Offer help in time of need
— Stand up for a friend in his/her absence.

❖ Cultural similarities and differences have been found when looking at these friendship rules.
❖ Cognitive factors are also importance in maintenance such as "storytelling" and attributions made about one's partner's behaviour.

Theories of maintenance in relationships

❖ According to Levinger (1976), the chances of a marriage surviving depend on:

— The attractions of the relationship
— The barriers to leaving the marriage
— The presence of attractive alternatives (e.g., a more desirable partner).

See also pages 16–25 of the revision guide.

❖ The vulnerability–stress–adaptation model suggests that all factors (vulnerability, stress, adaptation) affect each other and may result in a vicious cycle leading to breakdown.

LOVE AND THE BREAKDOWN OF RELATIONSHIPS

Psychological Explanations of Love

They say that love is what makes the world go round. It certainly is of critical importance in terms of emotional development. In your AS level studies, you reviewed theories of attachment, in particular Bowlby's view that secure early attachments lead to healthy adult relationships. Hazan and Shaver's (1987) "Love Quiz" (see pages 50–51) demonstrated this link. They also found that adults whose childhood attachments with their parents were *not* secure tended to experience problems in their subsequent adult relationships.

What is love? It is an intense feeling of deep affection for another. Psychologists distinguish between liking and loving, and between different kinds of love, most importantly companionate and romantic (passionate) love.

Sternberg's triangular theory

Sternberg (1986) developed a **triangular theory of love**. According to this theory, love consists of three components: intimacy, passion, and decision/commitment. Sternberg defined them as follows:

> *The intimacy component refers to feelings of closeness, connectedness, and bondedness in loving relationships . . . The passion component refers to the drives that lead to romance, physical attraction, sexual consummation, and related phenomena in loving relationships. The decision/commitment component refers to, in the short term, the decision that one loves someone else, and in the long term, the commitment to maintain that love.*

The relative importance of these three components differs between short-term and long-term relationships. The passion component is usually the most important in short-term relationships, with the decision/ commitment component being the least important. In long-term relationships, on the other hand, the intimacy component is the most important, and the passion component is the least important.

Sternberg (1998) developed some of these ideas. He argued that the three components differ in several ways from each other. For example, intimacy and commitment are usually fairly stable in close relationships, whereas passion is relatively unstable and can fluctuate considerably. We have a reasonable ability to control our level of commitment, whereas intimacy is hard to control and passion is even harder to control in a deliberate way.

Sternberg argued that there are several kinds of love, consisting of different combinations of the three components. Some of the main kinds of love are as follows:

1. Liking or friendship: this involves intimacy but not passion or commitment.
2. Romantic love: this involves intimacy and passion, but not commitment.
3. Companionate love: this involves intimacy and commitment, but not passion.
4. Empty love: this involves commitment, but not passion or intimacy.
5. Fatuous love: this involves commitment and passion, but not intimacy.
6. Infatuated love: this involves passion but not intimacy or commitment.
7. Consummate love: this is the strongest form of love, because it involves all three components (commitment, passion, and intimacy).

KEY TERM

Triangular theory of love: Sternberg's theory that love has three components: intimacy, passion, and decision/commitment.

Who do you love?

Who do we tend to love and like the most? Sternberg and Grajek (1984) found that men generally love and like their lover more than their mother, father, sibling closest in age, or their best friend. Women also loved and liked their lover and best friend more than their mother, father, or sibling closest in age. However, women differed from men in that they loved their lover and their best friend of the same sex equally, but liked their best friend more than their lover.

Sternberg and Grajek also found that the amount of love that someone has for one member of their family predicts the amount of love they will have for the other members. For example, people who love their father very much also tend to have high levels of love for their mother and sibling closest in age. However, the amount of love that someone has for their lover or best friend is not predictable from the amount of love they feel for members of their own family.

Evaluation

It is possible to use this theory to analyse a relationship and perceive similarities and differences between partners. This may help to sensitise partners to changes they might make in order to make the relationship more satisfactory.

One disadvantage is that some of the components are rather vague. For example, the decision/commitment variable doesn't specify on what basis an individual actually decides to love another person.

Liking and loving

The best-known attempt to distinguish between liking and loving was made by Rubin (1970), who put forward the Rubin Love Scale and the Rubin Liking Scale. The items on the love scale measure three main factors: (1) desire to help the other person; (2) dependent needs of the other person; and (3) feelings of exclusiveness and absorption. In contrast, the items on the liking scale measure respect for the other person's abilities and similarity of the other person in terms of his/her attitudes and other characteristics.

Rubin's love and liking scales are highly correlated with each other. Sternberg and Grajek (1984) found that liking and loving scores for a lover correlated +0.72, and these scores correlated +0.66 for best friend, +0.73 for one's mother, and +0.81 for one's father. These high correlations mean that Rubin's scales do not discriminate very well between liking and loving.

Rubin did find that women tended to like the men more than the men liked the women. Men tended to love in the context of a sexual relationship whereas women experienced intimacy and attachment in a wider variety of relationships.

The kind of lover you are may be related to the kind of attachment you had as an infant.

KEY STUDY
The love quiz

Could it be that early attachment type can be used to explain later styles of adult romantic love? Hazan and Shaver (1987) proposed that the reason adults experience different kinds of romantic relationships is because of their different experiences as infants. To test this hypothesis they devised a "love quiz", a questionnaire that could assess an individual's style of love as well as their attachment type. The quiz consisted of two components:

- A measure of attachment style. A simple adjective checklist of childhood relationships with parents, and parents' relationships with each other.
- The love experience questionnaire which assessed individuals' beliefs about romantic love, such as whether it lasted for ever, whether it was easy to find, how much trust there was in a romantic relationship, and so on.

The love quiz was printed in the *Rocky Mountain News*, a local newspaper, and readers were asked to send in their responses. The researchers analysed the first 620 replies received, from people aged from 14 to 82. Hazan and Shaver used the answers (1) to classify respondents as secure, ambivalent, or avoidant "types" based on their description of their childhood experiences, and (2) to classify them on their adult style of romantic love. They found a consistent relationship between attachment "type" and adult style of love:

- Secure types described their love experiences as happy, friendly, and trusting. They emphasised being able to accept their partner regardless of any faults and their relationships tended to be more enduring.

- Anxious ambivalent types experienced love as involving obsession, a desire for reciprocation, emotional highs and lows, and extreme sexual attraction and jealousy. They worried that their partners didn't really love them or might abandon them.
- Avoidant lovers typically feared intimacy, emotional highs and lows, and jealousy. They believed that they did not need love to be happy.

These attachment "types" are based on research by Ainsworth et al. (1978) in the Strange Situation, as discussed in your AS studies.

Discussion points
1. Can you think of another way of explaining the correlation between attachment type and later love relationships?
2. What ethical issues are raised by this research?

Romantic and companionate love

Berscheid and Walster (1978) distinguished between liking, companionate love, and romantic or passionate love. Companionate love is on a continuum with liking—liking that involves more depth of feeling and involvement than simply liking an acquaintance. Romantic love is entirely different. Companionate love develops through mutual rewards, familiarity, steady and positive emotions, and tends to deepen over time, whereas passionate love is based on intense emotions that often become diluted over time, novelty, and a mixture of emotions (joy and anxiety, excitement and deep despair).

? Which kind of love is likely to be involved in marriage or long-term relationships?

Explanations and Research Studies Relating to the Breakdown of Relationships

There are many reasons why relationships come to an end. The reasons that are important in any one case depend on the particular circumstances in which the people concerned find themselves, and on their particular characteristics. Some relationship break-ups are accompanied by bitter recrimination and even violence, whereas others are handled in a more "civilised" way. In spite of these differences, it has been argued that similar processes tend to be involved in the dissolution of all relationships.

Stage models

One approach is to consider the stages of relationship as a means of explaining how relationships break down. An alternative would be to list "risk factors", i.e., those factors that are likely to trigger dissolution.

Lee's stage model

According to Lee (1984), the break-up of relationships should be regarded as a process taking place over a period of time rather than as a single event. More specifically, he argued that there are five stages involved in the process:

1. *Dissatisfaction*: one or both of the partners realise that there are real problems within the relationship.
2. *Exposure*: the problems identified in the dissatisfaction stage are brought out into the open.

EXAM HINT
You can use the theories covered under formation/maintenance, e.g., reward/need satisfaction and economic theories to explain relationship breakdown, but do fully relate them to relationship breakdown to ensure content is relevant.

3. *Negotiation*: there is much discussion about the issues raised during the exposure stage.
4. *Resolution attempts*: both partners try to find ways of solving the problems discussed in the negotiation stage.
5. *Termination*: if the resolution attempts are unsuccessful, then the relationship comes to an end.

How does this model compare with Levinger's ABCDE model (on page 42)?

Lee identified these five stages on the basis of a study of over 100 premarital romantic break-ups. The exposure and negotiation stages tended to be the most intense and exhausting stages in the break-up. One of the key findings was that it tended to be those relationships that had been the strongest in which it took the longest time to work through the five stages of dissolution. This makes sense: the more valuable a relationship has been, the harder (and longer) it is worth fighting for its continuation.

Duck's phase model

Duck (1982) put forward a somewhat similar stage model of the break-up of relationships. He identified four phases or stages of break-up, where each phase is triggered by a threshold:

What is the difference between a "model" and a "theory"? If you were asked a question about "theories of relationships", do you think you could include these models?

1. Threshold: "I can't stand this any more". *Intrapsychic phase*: this involves thinking about the negative aspects of one's partner and of the relationship, but not discussing these thoughts with him or her. It corresponds roughly to Lee's dissatisfaction stage.
2. Threshold: "I'd be justified in withdrawing". *Dyadic phase*: this phase involves confronting the partner with the negative thoughts from the intrapsychic stage, and trying to sort out the various problems. It corresponds to Lee's stages of exposure, negotiation, and resolution attempts.
3. Threshold: "I mean it". *Social phase*: this phase involves deciding what to do now that the relationship is effectively over; it includes thinking of face-saving accounts of what has happened. It corresponds roughly to Lee's termination stage.
4. Threshold: "It's now inevitable". *Grave-dressing phase*: this phase focuses on communicating a socially acceptable account of the end of the relationship. It is an important phase in terms of preparing the people involved for future relationships.

Comparing the two models

There are some important differences between Lee's stage model and Duck's phase model. Lee's version focuses mainly on the various processes involved when there is still some hope that the relationship can be saved, whereas Duck's model focuses more on the processes involved after it is clear that the relationship is at an end. It is probable that a six- or seven-stage model incorporating all of the processes identified in the two models would provide a more adequate account of relationship break-ups than either model on its own.

Both models have some useful practical implications. They can be used to identify the stage of breakdown and suggest appropriate ways to attempt to repair the relationship. The models also suggest how, once a relationship has broken down, couples may deal with the end in order to be ready to start afresh in new relationships. Duck (1994), for example, suggested that couples in the intrapsychic phase should aim to re-establish liking for their partner by focusing on the positive aspects of their relationship rather than the tendency in this phase to focus on the negative.

Neither model explains why relationships break down but merely focuses on the sequence of likely events. We will consider some explanations next.

Risk factors

Duck (1992) also considered the findings from longitudinal studies. He identified several factors that seem to make relationships more fragile and liable to dissolution. It is possible to distinguish between *internal* factors (e.g., the personalities of the two people) and *external* factors (e.g., one partner moves to another part of the country; the appearance of a rival; job loss). Duck suggested that these could be classified as predisposing and precipitating factors.

Predisposing personal factors (internal)

As one gets to know a partner better, one also becomes more aware of their personal characteristics, some of which will be distasteful. For example, your partner may leave dirty clothes lying around or like to eat food with lashings of garlic. For some people such characteristics may trigger the dissolution of the relationship.

There are other personal factors that may be important. Partners' interests or attitudes may change and the things that once held you together now no longer do so. If hobbies change, you may find yourselves spending less time together. Pre-existing differences, such as having different religious or educational backgrounds, may come to be significant. During the initial phases of the relationship one might overlook such differences but they may become progressively more significant.

Not surprisingly, personality is an important factor in determining whether a relationship will last or suffer breakdown. We saw earlier that divorce is more likely when one or both of the marriage partners are high in neuroticism. Another important aspect of personality is agreeableness—individuals high in agreeableness are co-operative, supportive, and non-confrontational in their dealings with other people. As you would expect, relationships involving people high in agreeableness are freer of conflict and more long-lasting than ones in which those involved are low in agreeableness (Graziano, Jensen-Campbell, & Hair, 1996).

Marriages where partners come from very different backgrounds in terms of culture, race, or religion are less stable than those where partners come from similar backgrounds. Marriages between partners from lower socio-economic groups and/or lower education levels are more likely to end in divorce. This suggests that these factors predispose the relationship to break down.

Marriages in which the partners are very young (e.g., teenagers) are less likely to last than marriages in which the partners are older. There are likely to be several reasons why age is a factor. Younger people tend to be less mature, they have not yet developed their adult personality, and they are less likely to have either a steady income or full-time employment.

A further personal factor is the inability to conduct a relationship. This may be due to having poor role models (parents who were divorced or who argued all the time) or the fact that one partner has poor social skills.

Precipitating factors (external)

In contrast, Duck identified other factors that are external and that may precipitate breakdown. For example, deception, boredom, relocation, conflict, or a better alternative are all factors that may herald the beginning of the end.

Jealousy and infidelity. One especially important factor in the dissolution of a relationship is jealousy. It is triggered by a real or imagined rival, and is a surprisingly common emotion. Eysenck (1990) discussed a study in which 63% of male students and 51% of female students admitted that they were currently jealous.

What factors produce jealousy? Buss et al. (1992) asked students whether they would experience greater distress in response to sexual or to emotional infidelity. Among male students, 60% reported greater distress over a partner's sexual infidelity. In contrast, 83% of the female students said they would be more distressed by emotional infidelity.

The destructive power of jealousy was emphasised by Buss et al.:

The more insecure you are, the more you will be jealous. "Jealousy", says Abraham Maslow, "practically always breeds further rejection and deeper insecurity". . . . It is never, then, a function of love but of our insecurities and dependencies. It is the fear of a loss of love and it destroys that very love.

Buss et al. may have over-stated their case, but there is some truth in their assertions. Jealousy is typically related to strong feelings of dependence and insecurity about the relationship (Salovey, 1991). It also has the negative effect of reducing the jealous person's level of self-esteem (Mathes, Adams, & Davies, 1985).

Jealousy may be caused by a real rival, but can be just as painful when the jealous partner imagines that he or she has competition.

Evaluation

We start with a general observation. It is difficult to study the breakdown of relationships for various reasons. Couples going through the misery of a relationship breakdown may well not feel inclined to talk about their personal lives in detail with researchers whom they don't know well. In addition, the individuals concerned may be under considerable emotional stress and may find it hard to give an accurate (and unbiased!) account of the factors responsible for the breakdown of their relationship.

There is also the problem of deciding what has caused what. For example, a relationship may apparently break down because of infidelity. However, the infidelity in turn may reflect pre-existing problems and unhappiness within the relationship.

The factors identified by Duck tell only part of the story. There are successful and stable marriages in which the partners possess all of the vulnerability factors, and there are partners having none of these factors who nevertheless have short-lived marriages. Some of these factors may be more complex than they appear to be. For example, consider the fact that couples with lower educational levels are more likely to divorce. What is important is not really the educational level itself, but rather the reduced prospects of owning their own home and having reasonable full-time jobs, which follow from the low level of education.

It is important to note that the data from most longitudinal studies are limited. For example, 75% of the samples used in the longitudinal studies reviewed by Karney and Bradbury (1995) consisted mainly of middle-class white couples. Karney and Bradbury (p.17) identified other limitations:

> *Nearly half of the studies lack the power to detect small effects, even though the effects in question are likely to be small in many cases. Data have been drawn almost exclusively from self-report surveys and interviews, whereas alternative means of gathering data have yet to be exploited.*

Sex differences

A further factor is gender difference. Women are more likely than men to end heterosexual relationships, and initiate about two-thirds of divorce proceedings in many Western countries. This may occur in part because women increasingly believe they have every right to focus on their own needs. Carmichael (1983) gave young Australian men and women the following statement: "People should consider needs of spouse and children as more important than their own." Only 57% of women agreed with that statement compared to 78% of men.

In general, the partner who initiates the break-up is the one who is less distressed by the ending. However, this tendency is much stronger in men than in women (Franzoi, 1996). Why is this so? According to Franzoi, control and power are more associated with the traditional male role than with the traditional female role. As a result, men find it very hard to cope when their partner renders them powerless and out of control by ending the relationship.

KEY STUDY
A longitudinal study of marital problems and subsequent divorce

Amato and Rogers (1997) published the results of a study conducted between 1980 and 1992. They investigated the extent to which reports of marital problems in 1980 predicted divorce in the following 12 years. In 1980, telephone interviewers used random-digit dialling to locate a national sample of 2033 married persons aged 55 years and under. Of those contacted, 78% completed the full interview. The analysis was based on individuals for whom information on marital status existed at two or more points in time (that is, 86% of the original 1980 sample). Wives were more likely to report their marital problems than husbands—this was not because husbands had fewer problems but because they tended not to report them.

The main factors that were found to predict divorce were infidelity, spending money foolishly, drinking or drug use or both, jealousy, moodiness, and irritating habits.

Discussion points
1. What theoretical framework might be useful in explaining these findings?
2. How could such evidence be put to practical use?

Cultural differences

There has been a substantial increase in recent decades in the percentage of marriages in the Western world ending in divorce. It is often assumed that increased wealth (especially among women) has made it easier for divorced people to manage financially and is responsible for much of the increase in the divorce rate. However, it is interesting to note that this trend to higher divorce rates is not universal, meaning that we need to consider cultural differences. Hirschman and Teerawichitchainan (2003) considered divorce rates in Indonesia, Malaysia, and Thailand. Over the past 25 years, the divorce rate in these countries has declined from an average of about 20% to only 12% in spite of growing affluence. The factors mostly responsible for this decline were as follows: increased education for women, later age at marriage, and more choice over marriage partner.

The postmodern approach

Those who favour the postmodern approach (e.g., Wood & Duck, 1995) doubt the value of most research on interpersonal relationships. According to the postmodern approach, relationships need to be considered in terms of the context or environment in which they occur. There are various ways in which the available evidence can be interpreted, and it is hard or impossible to establish that one interpretation is preferable to any other.

Social purpose

Lalljee (1981) put forward related ideas. According to him, we need to consider the underlying social purposes of the explanations that people provide for their behaviour. For example, when two people divorce, they typically explain the disintegration of their marriage in different terms. Each of them tends to suggest that it was the unreasonable behaviour of the other person that led to divorce. In view of people's need to justify their own behaviour to other people, it becomes very difficult to establish the truth. The postmodernists go further, and claim that there is no single "truth" that can be discovered. In the study discussed earlier, Murray and Holmes (1993) showed that storytelling about one's relationship can easily be altered to accommodate awkward facts. This suggests that the truth is a flexible notion.

Discourse analysis

Many postmodernists argue that progress can be made in understanding interpersonal relationships by making use of discourse analysis. **Discourse analysis** involves qualitative analysis of people's written or spoken communications; these are often taped under fairly natural conditions. An interesting example of discourse analysis is contained in the work of Gavey (1992). She studied the sexual behaviour of six women who had been forced to have sex. Here is part of what one of the women had to say:

He kept saying, just, just let me do this or just let me do that and that will be all. And this could go on for an hour . . . So after maybe an hour of me saying "no", and him saying "oh, come on, come on", I'd finally think, "Oh my God . . . for a few hours' rest, peace and quiet, I may as well".

This example shows that discourse analysis can provide striking evidence about the nature of relationships. However, Gavey and others who have used discourse analysis have often obtained evidence from only a small number of participants. This raises the issue of whether the findings obtained can be generalised to larger populations. There are also issues concerning the validity of the procedure. For example, we might expect someone to describe their sexual experiences rather differently to their partner, to a close friend, to an acquaintance, and to a stranger.

KEY TERM

Discourse analysis: qualitative analysis of spoken and written communications produced in fairly natural conditions; usually based on tape recordings.

SECTION SUMMARY
Love and the Breakdown of Relationships

❖ Love consists of three components:

   — Intimacy: Most important in the long term
   — Passion: Most important in the short term
   — Decision/commitment.

❖ The three components combine to produce: liking, romantic love, companionate love, empty love, fatuous love, infatuated love, and consummate love.

❖ The three components can be used to analyse a relationship; however, some of the components are rather vague.

Sternberg's triangular theory

❖ Rubin measured liking and love and found a high association. However:

   — Women tended to like men more than men liked women.
   — Men tended to love in the context of a sexual relationship.

❖ We can distinguish between liking, companionate love, and romantic or passionate love. Companionate love is like a very strong form of liking.

Liking and loving

❖ The final stage of a relationship is dissolution. One approach to understanding dissolution is through stage models:

❖ Lee's stage model:

   — Lee identified five stages in the break-up of premarital relationships: dissatisfaction, exposure, negotiation, resolution attempts, and termination.
   — The exposure and negotiation stages are the most intense and exhausting ones.

❖ Duck's phase model: Duck identified four phases: intrapsychic, dyadic, social, and grave-dressing.

❖ Comparing the two models:

   — Lee's model focuses on the processes before break-up becomes inevitable.
   — The two models could be combined.
   — Both models have some useful practical implications but neither offers an explanation of *why* some relationships dissolve.

Why do relationships come to an end?

❖ We can distinguish between:

   — Predisposing risk factors: distasteful habits, changes in interests, coming from different backgrounds, being young.
   — Precipitating risk factors: deception, relocation, conflict. Jealousy and infidelity are especially strong precipitating factors.

❖ The concept of risk factors is an over-simplification because many relationships are maintained despite such factors.

❖ There are also sex differences and cultural differences. Divorce has increased in most Western cultures in recent decades but has actually declined in several countries in Southeast Asia.

Risk factors that can lead to relationship breakdown

See also pages 26–31 of the revision guide.

CULTURAL AND SUB-CULTURAL DIFFERENCES IN RELATIONSHIPS

Most research on interpersonal relationships has been carried out in Western cultures, especially those of the United States and United Kingdom. The research has also been limited by its focus on heterosexual relationships at the expense of homosexual ones, and on voluntary relationships rather than obligatory ones. According to postmodern theorists, these limitations are very important. They argue that behaviour and communication need to be understood within the context in which they occur, and this context clearly differs considerably from one culture to another, and across different types of relationship. The crucial point here was made by Moghaddam, Taylor, and Wright (1993):

> *The cultural differences in interpersonal relationships remind us that scientists, like everyone else, are socialised within a given culture ... The cultural values and environmental conditions in North America have led Northern American social psychologists to be primarily concerned with first-time acquaintances, friendships, and intimate relationships.*

? What sort of methodological and ethical problems are associated with research into sexual behaviour?

We can readily accept that there are large differences in interpersonal relationships between cultures. However, there have also been substantial changes in such relationships within many cultures over the centuries. An American doctor, Celia Mosher, asked her middle-class female patients questions about their sexual lives during the latter part of the nineteenth century. Those who were born in the middle of the century described sex as necessary for reproduction, but did not regard it as pleasurable. Those who were born later in the century, described sex in much more positive terms, and saw sex as closely linked to passionate love (Westen, 1996).

It is important not to regard some types of relationships as better or worse than others. The relationships that individuals form depend on their personal needs and attitudes, the cultural context in which they live, and so on. As far as we can judge, all the various types of relationships are often very satisfying to the individuals concerned, and that is what matters.

Goodwin (1995) argued that a key difference between most Western societies and most Eastern societies is that the former tend to be individualistic, whereas the latter tend to be collectivistic. In other words, it is expected in Western societies (especially the United States) that individuals will make their own decisions and take responsibility for their own lives. In Eastern societies, in contrast, it is expected that individuals will regard themselves mainly as part of family and social groups, and that their decisions will be influenced strongly by their obligations to other people. This difference in attitude was summed up by Hsu (1981): "An American asks 'How does my heart feel?' A Chinese asks 'What will other people say?'." As a result, those in individualist Western societies tend to stress the personality of a potential spouse, whereas those in collectivist Eastern societies favour arranged marriages based on social status.

? Which of Hsu's questions would you consider first when meeting a potential partner? Are they equally important or not?

Types of Love

Romantic love

Evidence on love and marriage from India, Pakistan, Thailand, Mexico, Brazil, Hong Kong, the Philippines, Australia, Japan, England, and the United States was reported by Levine et al. (1995). Their key finding was that there was correlation of +0.56 between a society's individualism and the perceived necessity of love for the establishment of a marriage. In other words, there was a fairly strong tendency for members of individualist societies to regard love as more important for marriage than did members of collectivist societies.

Friendships

There is one other important difference between individualist and collectivist societies, which applies to friendships. As Goodwin (1995) pointed out, people in collectivist societies tend to have fewer but closer friendships than do people in individualist societies. For example, Salamon (1977) studied friendship in Japan and in West Germany. Japanese friendships were much more likely to be ones in which there were no barriers between the friends, so that very personal information could be discussed freely. This is known as the "*shin yin*" relationship.

Voluntary and involuntary relationships

In most non-Western cultures, marriages tend to be arranged rather than based on romantic love. Some of the cultural differences in attitudes towards romantic love were studied by Shaver, Wu, and Schwartz (1991). Most Chinese people associate romantic love with sorrow, pain, and unfulfilled affection. In the eyes of Chinese people, the Western view that marriage should be based on romantic love is regarded as unrealistically optimistic.

Evidence from 42 hunter-gatherer societies around the world was reported by Harris (1995; cited in Westen, 1996). There was evidence of romantic love in 26 of these societies. However, only six gave individuals complete freedom of choice of marriage partner, with all the others having arranged marriages or at least giving parents the right of veto.

Are arranged marriages happier or less happy than love marriages? Most of the available evidence indicates that the average level of marital satisfaction is about the same. Yelsma and Athappily (1988) compared Indian arranged marriages with Indian and North American love marriages. In most respects, there were no differences between the two kinds of marriages. Gupta and Singh (1982) compared arranged marriages and love marriages in India. Initially, those in arranged marriages rated their love for each as lower than did those in love marriages. However, as time went by, this trend was reversed.

The distinction between individualist and collectivist societies should not be taken too far. Even in societies in which arranged marriages are not the norm, there is often some restricted element of choice of marriage partner. In individualist societies, parents often strive to influence the marriage choice of their children.

In many non-Western cultures, arranged marriages are the norm. Evidence suggests that the average level of marital satisfaction is the same in both arranged marriages and those that are not arranged.

Permanent and impermanent relationships

The duration of relationships varies considerably between cultures. In some countries divorce is much less tolerated. For example, in China divorce is regarded as shameful and the divorce rate is less than 4% of married couples (Goodwin, 1999) whereas in the United States about 40–50% are divorced (US Bureau of Census, 1992).

Simmel (1971) claims that divorce is higher in individualistic societies because the philosophy is that one should constantly seek the ideal partner. People in individualistic societies are also more reliant on their one partner, rather than on a network of relationships within a community. This individualist/collectivist difference was illustrated in a study of Jewish families in New York (Brodbar-Nemzer, 1986). Over 4000 households were interviewed. Some were more traditionally Jewish—they attended synagogue regularly, had close friends who were Jewish, belonged to Jewish organisations, and contributed to Jewish charities. These families were examples of collectivist sub-cultures, as distinct from those Jewish families who classed themselves as Jewish but were more representative of individualist society. The former group had greater marital stability.

It is often assumed that divorce is much more common nowadays than it used to be in nearly every culture. However, as we saw earlier, that is by no means the case. Hirschman and Teerawichitchainan (2003) found that some of the countries in Southeast Asia (Indonesia, Malaysia, and Thailand) are exceptions to that trend. Indeed, the divorce rate across these three countries has almost halved in recent decades and in Malaysia it has actually more than halved. Later age at marriage and more years of education are two of the factors that have enabled these Southeast Asian cultures to go against the trend elsewhere of ever-increasing divorce rates.

Hirschman and Teerawichitchainan (2003) also carried out more detailed analyses on their data. They found that the Muslim populations of Indonesia, Malaysia, and Thailand all had much higher divorce rates than other groups within those countries. There is a relatively high level of tolerance for divorce among Muslim groups in Southeast Asia, and divorced Muslim women in that area have reasonable post-divorce opportunities.

Evaluation of cross-cultural research

There are several reasons for conducting cross-cultural research—that is, research that looks at the customs and practices of different countries and makes comparisons with our own cultural norms. First of all, such research can tell us about what might be universal in human behaviour. If the same behaviours are observed in many different cultures, all of which have different ways of socialising children, then the behaviour may be due to innate (universal) factors rather than learning. The second reason for conducting cross-cultural research is that it offers us insights into our own behaviour, insights that we may not otherwise be aware of. Perhaps that is the appeal of watching programmes on the television that show foreign lands and different people.

There are some major weaknesses to cross-cultural research. First of all, any sample of a group of people may well be biased and therefore we may be mistaken in thinking that the observations made of one group of people are representative of that culture. Second, where the observations are made by an outsider, that person's own culture will bias how they interpret the data they observe. Finally, the psychological tools that are used to measure people, such as IQ tests and questionnaires about relationships, are designed in one particular culture and based on assumptions of that culture. They may not have any meaning in another culture.

Therefore cross-cultural research has the potential to be highly informative about human behaviour, but also has many important weaknesses.

Monogamy and polygamy

A further apparent cultural difference exists in terms of the kinds of marriages that are acceptable. In some societies it is the norm for one man to have two or more wives. This is a form of polygamy called **polygyny**. There is also serial polygyny, where a male bonds with one female for a while and then moves on to another. Humans are usually regarded as a monogamous by nature (pairs bond once during their lifetime); however, studies across different cultures show that in fact humans tend towards polygyny (see pie chart on page 309).

The arguments in favour of polygyny are also sociobiological. It is claimed that males benefit from impregnating many women because this maximises the number of their offspring, especially in a situation where there is plenty of shared care on offer, as in a harem. The women benefit because they gain a man with resources—a man who can attract a harem must have resources. Such a man will either have power or good looks, and in either case the woman's offspring may inherit such characteristics. If the offspring are sons, they may have greater reproductive success, which ensures the continuance of the mother's genes as well (this is called the **sexy sons hypothesis**), so both partners benefit from polygyny.

These sociobiological accounts are described in greater detail in Chapter 7, Evolutionary Explanations of Human Behaviour.

"Under-studied" relationships
Under-studied relationships provide us with further information about sub-cultural differences. The term "under-studied" is used to refer to the fact that certain relationships have been relatively under-studied, partly because of their newness and/or fairly recent acceptability.

Gay and lesbian relationships
Most of the research on romantic relationships has concentrated exclusively on heterosexual couples. However, there are millions of people in the world who are involved in homosexual relationships, and such relationships are increasingly being studied.

Misconceptions. There are many misconceptions about homosexual relationships, and it is sometimes assumed that such relationships are very different from heterosexual ones. This is not, in fact, the case. As Bee pointed out:

> *Gay partnerships are more like heterosexual relationships than they are different. The urge to form a single, central, committed attachment in early adult life is present in all of us, gay or straight.*

It has often been assumed that homosexual relationships tend to be short-lived and unsatisfactory. In fact, it seems that about 50% of gay men and perhaps 65% of lesbians are in a steady relationship at any one time (Peplau, 1991). Kurdek and Schmitt (1986) measured love for their partner and liking for their partner in married, heterosexual cohabiting, gay, and lesbian couples. The mean level of love was

EXAM HINT

If you are asked to consider the extent to which relationships differ across cultures, try to provide evidence both for and against this statement. There are more arguments for differences, so think about how you will organise this section. For example, you could structure the material into six areas: individualistic and collectivist cultures, voluntary and involuntary relationships, permanent and impermanent relationships, romantic relationships, friendships, and family relationships. Do make sure you provide some arguments against, such as differences may be magnified by ethnocentric research and consider how the weaknesses of cross-cultural research may have reduced the validity of research.

? Why has psychological research mainly focused on heterosexual couples?

KEY TERMS

Polygyny: a mating system in which a male mates with several females, but females usually mate with only one male; parental care is usually provided by the female.
Sexy sons hypothesis: the notion that females mate with the most attractive males so that their own sons will inherit these characteristics and thus be attractive to other females. Related to the runaway process.

In 1996, 175 gay and lesbian couples took part in a formal domestic partners ceremony in San Francisco, similar to the conventional marriage ceremony.

high in all four types of couple, and did not differ significantly among them. The mean level of liking for their partner was also fairly high in all types of couple, but it was somewhat lower for heterosexual cohabiting couples than for any of the other couples.

The assumption that homosexual and heterosexual relationships are basically similar was described by Kitzinger and Coyle (1995) as **liberal humanism**. This approach was a move forward from the view that gays and lesbians are inferior to heterosexuals, and promoted the notion that they should be regarded as individuals rather than as members of a group defined by sexual orientation. In addition, this approach argues that homosexuality is as natural, normal, and generally healthy as heterosexuality. It sounds like a reasonable approach; however, it continues to equate homosexual relationships with heterosexual ones. As a result, it ignores the particular difficulties that gays and lesbians have to contend with in terms of the prejudices of society, and runs the risk of treating differences in characteristics of homosexual relationships from heterosexual ones as indicating "problems" in homosexual relationships.

Similarities and differences between homosexual and heterosexual relationships

As the liberal humanistic view implies, there are some important similarities between homosexual and heterosexual relationships. For example, both types of relationships are more long-lasting when the partners have similar backgrounds and are comparably committed to the relationship (Peplau, 1991). In addition, satisfaction with both homosexual and heterosexual relationships depends on a relatively high level of rewards and a low level of costs (Kurdek, 1994). Finally, it has been found that about 70% of gays, lesbians, and heterosexuals are satisfied with the sexual activity they have with their partners (Blumstein & Schwartz, 1983).

In spite of some similarities, the liberal humanistic view that homosexual relationships closely resemble heterosexual ones is an over-simplification. Homosexual couples are more likely than heterosexual ones to have additional sexual partners outside the relationship. Among couples together for more than 10 years, 22% of wives, 30% of husbands, 43% of lesbians, and 94% of gay men reported having had sex with at least one person other than their partner (Blumstein & Schwartz, 1983).

A major difference between homosexual and heterosexual relationships is that more importance is attached to equality of status and power in homosexual relationships. A lack of power equality was found to be a factor in the ending of lesbian and gay relationships but not of heterosexual marriages (Blumstein & Schwartz, 1983).

Another difference is that homosexuals have to contend with the hostility of society. As Kitzinger and Coyle (1995, p.67) pointed out:

Lesbian and gay couples are struggling to build and to maintain relationships in the context of a society that often deni+es their existence, condemns their sexuality, penalises their partnership and derides their love for each other.

? **What cross-cultural differences might you expect to find in homosexual relationships?**

KEY TERM

Liberal humanism: the view that all people, e.g., gays, lesbians, and heterosexuals, are equal and the ways they conduct relationships are basically similar.

As a result, cohabitation is less common in homosexual relationships than heterosexual ones. However, Harry (1983) reported that 50% of gay relationships involved cohabitation as did 75% of lesbian relationships.

Finally, heterosexual married couples typically stay together for longer than any type of unmarried couple, including gay or lesbian couples. One reason for this is undoubtedly that there is more social, cultural, and religious support for married couples than for unmarried ones.

> **EXAM HINT**
> The essay question will ask you to consider how homosexual relationships differ from heterosexual relationships, but not the causes of homosexuality. This is an interesting area but you will not be examined directly on it, so instead focus on how relevant the research you have covered under formation/maintenance/breakdown is to homosexual relationships. Bring in AO2 by assessing the weaknesses of past research, commenting on the differences, and evaluating the research on homosexual relationships.

Evaluation

One justification for psychological research is that it enables us to better understand our own behaviour. If you are a heterosexual reader then the earlier Sections on relationships may have appealed to you because you used them to understand and explain the relationships in which you have been involved. The same is true for homosexual individuals who have an equal interest in knowing about and understanding homosexual relationships, and this alone justifies such research. Note that much research on homosexual relationships *only* considers gay and lesbians couples who are cohabiting—this approach fails to consider the numerous homosexual couples who choose not to cohabit. Clearly there is a lot of such research remaining to be done before we can understand homosexual relationships.

A second reason for conducting research is for the purpose of real-world application and the HIV crisis provided just such a scenario. In order to plan effective prevention and treatment campaigns it was necessary to have accurate information about the sexual relationships between homosexual men.

? What sort of practical problems might prevent homosexual couples from cohabiting?

Mediated friendships

This is clearly a fascinating new area of research for social psychologists, where they can even conduct their studies through participant observation and online questionnaires! There are two main areas here. First, there are "electronic" relationships meaning all interpersonal contacts through the medium of the internet. The three main sources of internet contact are e-mail, usenets, and chat rooms. Second, there are friendships involving use of mobile phones. They can be used either to talk directly with someone else or text messages can be sent.

? What particular ethical problems may arise from conducting online research (e.g., informed consent)?

E-mail

E-mail, or electronic mail, is a way of writing a message and sending it via the internet to another person's electronic post-box, where it awaits collection by the recipient. This means one can collect an e-mail anywhere one has access to a computer.

How does e-mail differ from other forms of communication? Prior to the age of electronic methods, communication was either face to face (corporeal), or phone to phone (voice only), or the written word on paper ("snail" mail). When we speak with someone face to face there are a host of channels through which we are communicating aside from the actual words. In fact the nonverbal signals or **paralanguage** may be more important than the words themselves, for example

> **KEY TERM**
> **Paralanguage:** nonverbal signals, e.g., body language, eye contact.

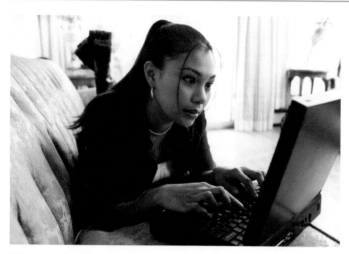

Many people use e-mail as a way of making and maintaining contact with friends and acquaintances.

? Nonverbal signals in face-to-face encounters are hard to control. Try making yourself look someone in the eye as you speak with them. What did you feel about doing this?

body posture and eye gaze express liking for someone else. On the telephone some of these nonverbal signals are still there, such as pauses and tone of voice. In letters, all such signals have been removed or, if they are included, it is done deliberately. The reason why nonverbal signals tend to have so much power is that many of them are not under conscious control. Certainly some people are able to monitor the way they present themselves and can learn to control nonverbal cues that indicate, for example, uncertainty or dishonesty. But most people don't and therefore we use nonverbal signals as a means of knowing what someone really means, especially the emotional content of their message.

For business contacts the lack of paralanguage would appear to make e-mail an ideal form of communication, though there is the difficulty of misunderstandings. You may think you've expressed yourself clearly but another person may take a different meaning from your words. Had the words been spoken, you might have accompanied them with subtle cues that aided interpretation and would probably pick up on any misinterpretation so that it could be explained and the true meaning made clear.

For more personal contacts, a new vocabulary and form of language is growing both on e-mail and in chat rooms to communicate nonverbal information. Language and paralanguage are used as a means of creating a social group identity, for example your accent and dialect identify you as a group member and indicate your desire to belong to that group. This is true of internet communication. Using accepted abbreviations (such as LOL for laughing out loud) and symbols (such as emoticons and smileys) shows others that you are "one of them". As you may have discovered for yourself, it can be potentially embarrassing if any of your highly personal emails are seen by the wrong people!

Usenets

"Usenet" is an umbrella term for more than 14,000 forums or newsgroups, each related to a specific topic. It is an ongoing discussion that you can join and leave and come back to any time you like. You just read what's been posted, post your comment or response, and come back and see what others had to say. Each usenet has a common focus, which might be an interest in sleep research or UFOs, or you might have a disorder such as depression or Parkinson's disease; the list is endless.

There are various counselling and diagnostic services on the net for addressing problems ranging from poor self-esteem and stressful relationships to addictions. Bloom (1998) points to the wide number of serious ethical concerns raised by this. For example, these include confidentiality, validity of data delivered via computer networks, misuse of computer applications by counsellors, lack of counsellor awareness of location-specific factors, and credentialing.

Another kind of usegroup is MUDs. MUD stands for Multi-User Dungeon or Dimension, a usually text-based multi-user simulation environment. Some are purely for fun and flirting, others are used for serious software development, or education purposes. A significant feature of most MUDs is that users can create things that stay after they leave and which other users can interact with in their absence, thus allowing a world to be built gradually and collectively. One user described his MUD experience thus:

> *I don't care how much people say they are, muds are not just games, they are *real*!!! My mud friends are my best friends, they're the people who like me most in the entire world. Maybe the only people who do . . . They are my family, they are not just some dumb game . . .*

There are adventure MUDs and social MUDs. JennyMUSH is an example of the latter. It was set up as a virtual help centre for people who have experienced sexual assault or abuse. The founder was a psychology student whose field of interest was the treatment of survivors of assault and abuse. However, JennyMUSH is an example of the difficulties of policing usegroups (see the box below).

Are the relationships developed in these usegroups shallow, impersonal, and hostile, or are they capable of liberating interpersonal relations from the confines of physical locality and creating opportunities for new, but genuine personal relationships and communities? Parks and Floyd (1996) investigated this by interviewing 176 members of internet newsgroups and their contributors, of whom 61% reported forming a new personal relationship via a newsgroup. Predictors of whether an individual formed such a relationship were frequency and duration of newsgroup participation. Online relationships often reached high levels of relational development and broadened to include interaction in other channels and settings: 98% communicated by direct e-mail; one third telephoned each other; and 28% used the postal system. Furthermore, one third of the newsgroup members who reported a personal relationship met each other in person.

JennyMUSH: A case of internet abuse

JennyMUSH was set up as a virtual help centre for people who have experienced sexual assault or abuse. The administrator, or "God", was a psychology student with a research interest in this field, and whose university fully supported the JennyMUSH project. Such official support ensures some degree of security for users of the system, but was unable to prevent a single user from being able to subvert the delicate social balance of the system by using both technical and social means to enact anonymously what amounted to virtual rape.

    Two weeks after being assigned a character, a user of the system used the MUD's commands to transform him or herself into a virtual manifestation of every other user's fears. This user changed "her" initial virtual gender to male, "his" virtual name to "Daddy", and then used the special "shout" command to send messages to every other user connected to the MUD. He described virtual assaults in graphic and violent terms. At the time at which this began, none of the MUD's administrators, or Wizards, were connected to the system, a fact that may well have been taken into account by the user. For almost half an hour, the user continued to send obscene messages to others. During that time, some of his victims logged out of the system, taking the simplest course to nullify the attack. Those users who did not log off moved their "virtual personae" (i.e., their electronic selves) to the same place (electronically speaking) as that of their attacker. Many pleaded with him to stop, many threatened him, but they were powerless to prevent his attacks. At the end of that half hour, one of the Wizards connected to the system. He found twelve users connected to the system, all congregated in one place. On transporting himself to that place, he found eleven of those users being obscenely taunted by the twelfth. Quickly realising what was going on, the Wizard took a kind of vengeance on the erring user that is only possible in virtual reality. He took control of the user's virtual manifestation, took away from him the ability to communicate, changed his name to "Vermin" and changed his description to the following: "This is the lowest scum, the most pathetic dismal object which a human being can become."
From Reid (1999).

There is no reason to suppose that internet relationships aren't governed by the same factors as offline ones. The Key Study by McKenna and Yael (1999) below compares internet and face-to-face meetings. In the case of the internet, proximity is determined by frequency of meeting (as mentioned on page 65) rather than face-to-face encounters. Hultin (1993, cited in Dwyer, 2001) found that initially people in usegroups sought out similar individuals, for example in terms of ethnic origin.

However, like in offline relationships, if significant differences in attitudes and interests were discovered then gradually the exchanges became shorter and less frequent until communication ceased altogether. Cooper and Sportolari (1997) point out that computer-mediated relating reduces the role that physical attributes play in the development of attraction, and enhances other factors such as proximity, rapport, similarity, and mutual self-disclosure, thus promoting erotic connections that stem from emotional intimacy rather than lustful attraction. It allows adult (and teen) men and women more freedom to deviate from typically constraining gender roles that are often automatically activated in face-to-face interactions, which may be a positive consequence. However, online relating can lead to destructive results when people act on, or compulsively overindulge in, a speeded-up, eroticised pseudo-intimacy. We will consider such erotic relationships next.

KEY STUDY
The computers that bind: Relationship formation on the internet

McKenna and Yael (1999) conducted a series of studies focusing on the formation and development of relationships between people who met initially on the internet. The research focuses on the personality factors that predispose some people to seek out friends and romantic partners on the internet; the speed with which these relationships develop; the similarities and the differences between internet relationship formation and traditional or "offline" relationship development; and the consequences of internet relationships for the individuals' real life. Four different methodologies were used for data collection: participant observation, in-depth interviews, a survey conducted with nearly 600 newsgroup users, and two laboratory experiments.

In terms of the first aim McKenna and Yael found that individuals who are socially anxious and lonely are more likely to form intimate relationships with others via the internet. Individuals who feel that they are able to express their "real self" on the internet are more likely to subsequently arrange to speak with or meet partners offline.

Results of the two laboratory experiments reveal that individuals like one another better if they first meet via the internet than if the first meeting takes place face to face. It is also shown that people tend to present and effectively convey a more idealised version of themselves in internet meetings than they do in face-to-face meetings. The survey and laboratory findings confirm the reports of the majority of those interviewed that internet relationships form more easily and then develop more quickly than traditional relationships, and end up becoming just as real. It appears that people tend, ultimately, to make their internet friends and romantic partners part of their actual, physical, day-to-day social worlds.

Discussion points
1. What is "participant observation" and what limitations are associated with this research method?
2. Why might individuals like each other better if they met on the internet than if they met face to face?

Chat rooms

A chat room is actually a channel over which people can meet and exchange messages in real time. The word "room" is used to promote the metaphor that you are actually speaking with someone as if in the same room. For some people it has the significant advantage that you can be anonymous. This can have various effects. Turkle (1995) noted that:

> *When people adopt an online persona . . . Some feel an uncomfortable sense of fragmentation, some a sense of relief. Some sense the possibilities for self-discovery, even self-transformation.*

Chats can take place among a large group, or individuals can go off on their own for private chats. Much of the focus is ultimately on romantic relationships and erotic encounters. Branwyn (1993) quoted by Deuel (1996) explains that "Compu-sex enthusiasts say it's the ultimate safe sex for the 1990s, with no exchange of bodily fluids, no loud smoke-filled clubs, and no morning after."

The technology associated with chat rooms has developed in recent years. For example, it is sometimes possible to send graphics and attachments or to hear speech. About 25% of American and Australian internet users report having visited chat rooms, meaning that literally millions of people have experience of them.

Cyberaffairs

A romantic or sexual relationship that is initiated through contact on the net is called a "cyberaffair". Griffiths (1999) suggests that there three types of cyberaffair. First, there are relationships between two people who meet on the internet and develop an erotic dialogue purely for sexual arousal. Such individuals may have real-life partners and the cyberaffair may be brief. Second, there are relationships that are more emotional than sexual, and which lead to offline contact, as described in the "Love at first byte" Case Study overleaf. The third kind of cyberaffair is where two people meet offline but maintain their relationship almost exclusively online, possibly because of geographical distance. These people may only meet occasionally but may talk on the internet daily.

Why are such relationships potentially seductive and addictive? Griffiths (2000) offers the following explanations. The internet is easy to access from home or work. It is becoming quite affordable and has always offered anonymity. For some people it offers an emotional and mental escape from real life, and this is especially true for individuals who are shy or feel trapped in unhappy relationships. It is also true for individuals who work long hours and have little opportunity for social life. The key features have been summed up variously as the Triple A Engine (access, affordability, and anonymity) or ACE Model (anonymity, convenience, and escape) (Cooper, 1998; Young, 1999).

Problems with electronic affairs. There are two major drawbacks. First, as we have seen, some individuals may well masquerade as something they are not. The potential havoc this can cause and the persistent sense of mistrust that this engenders in computer-mediated relationships means that many people cannot relax. However, the potential for being something you are not is not necessarily all bad. It might be an interesting experience to try out being a man or being a member of a minority ethnic group to see how others behave towards you.

> **?** To what extent do you think that self-disclosure forms part of internet relationships? What other explanations for formation, maintenance, and dissolution are equally as relevant in internet relationships as in face-to-face encounters?

CASE STUDY: LOVE AT FIRST BYTE

It's a new take on the age-old story. Boy meets girl—but in cyberspace. They make small talk via their computers and find they have lots in common. After months of wishing, wondering and long-distance message-sending, they finally meet face to face. And then, to put the virtual icing on the cake, they fall in love and decide to get married.

On 24 August 1996, John Herbert, 23, of Hertfordshire, and Heather Waller, 25, resident of Buffalo, New York State, will walk down the aisle. So far as written records show, John and Heather are the first people to have conducted a successful courtship by computer.

While agreeing that their romance is hardly Mills and Boon material, John and Heather both maintain that their path to true love was not the soulless, automated journey some people make it out to be.

"For a start, there's a lot of mistrust around on the Web," says John, who had his fingers burnt once before when it turned out that the person with whom he had been conducting an online flirtation was in fact a man pretending to be a woman. "You often get blokes chatting you up just for a laugh," he says, grimacing. "That was why I was so pleased when Heather actually phoned me up. It was reassuring to know that she really was a woman."

Indeed, far from seeing their coming-together as some kind of impersonal, electronic process, both John and Heather view it as a traditional, almost Victorian, romance: a union of souls first, bodies later. There is even a literary dimension, of sorts, in the way they developed their relationship through the written word. "Not many people realise it, but there is quite an art to expressing your feelings on the internet," says John. The other person gets it straight away. "It's not like talking on the telephone, either. The good part is that there's less financial pressure, because the internet costs only around 85p an hour, so you don't have this feeling that you're burning money.

"The not-so-good part is that when you're on the phone, you can hear the subtleties of expression in the other person's voice. On the internet, you can mean one thing, but the words you actually write can come across as meaning something else."

To cope with this, John has adopted a whole lexicon of symbol and speech patterns which are designed to invest messages with a kind of emotional sub-text. Sarcasm, for example, can read rather coldly, which is why he uses the symbol ;-) (look at it sideways) to show a smiling face winking. Similarly >:-o denotes horned devilment, while :-! conveys tight-lipped frustration and a suppressed swear-word. In addition, he employs a bizarre kind of third-person commentary—e.g., "observes John quizzically", or "shrugs John grumpily"—in order to invest the written word with the right tone.

John and Heather met on the Monochrome system, devised by "Absolute Zero" (aka Dave Brownley), who reserves the right to banish those miscreants who misuse it. John and Heather are now both "staff" members, which means it is their (unpaid) job to patrol given sectors of Monochrome, trimming overlong or out-of-date files and "slapping" users who resort to bad language or tasteless jokes.

Adapted from an article by Christopher Middleton in the *Telegraph* on 10 May 1996.

However, encouraging such practice, even with the aim of reducing sexism and racism, might be viewed as ethically unsound.

The second major drawback is that internet relationships encourage vulnerable individuals to be seduced emotionally and sexually, and may replace real-life relationships, which are ultimately more complex and satisfying. Many people do actually end up having a real-time relationship with friends they have met on the net but this is not true of everyone. According to Cooper (2000), about 10 million Americans a month access one of the main "adult" web sites. It is estimated that perhaps 15% of those who do so are suffering from cybersex addiction and have significant problems with their sexual behaviour. Those addicted to cybersex or cyberaffairs often lose their self-esteem as a result, and are at greater risk of divorce as a result of their addiction (Cooper, 2000).

One shouldn't forget that many of the problems inherent in internet relationships have always been with us. The telephone was and is used for erotic conversations with strangers. Letters have been used as a means for communicating with penpals, again leading in some cases to marriage as well as life-long friendships. These forms of communication permit anonymity and escape but they lack the immediacy and ease of access that is now available for many people on the internet.

Mobile phone conversations

As we all know, there has been a dramatic increase in the use of mobile phones to keep in touch with other people. Much of the time, men and women use mobile phones in order to gossip. According to Fox (2005), 33% of men engage in mobile gossip every day or nearly every day compared to 26% of women. The sexes are also similar in that about 65% of mobile conversation time for both men and women is devoted to social topics, especially personal relationships. However, there is one important difference between the sexes: when men talk about social relationships, they spend two thirds of the time focusing on their own relationships, whereas women devote only one third of the time to their own relationships.

Why do we use mobile phones so much? Most people say they use them to keep in touch, to gossip, and for social chatting. Fox (2005) quotes the views of one female mobile phone user:

> Mobiles allow you to keep up with the smallest details of what's going on in people's lives, and that's what makes you feel close to them. It allows you to maintain that relationship or friendship.

The importance of mobile phone conversations can be seen when the unthinkable happens and someone steals your phone. According to one young woman, "Having your phone stolen turns your whole world upside down—without my phone, I feel left out of my social group" (Fox, 2005).

In sum, mobile phones provide a very versatile and easy way of maintaining a large network of friendships. It is no exaggeration to say that mobile phones have greatly added to the social lives of millions of people and will continue to do so off into the future.

Short message service (SMS): Texting

Of course, mobile phones can be used for texting purposes as well as to have phone conversations. Texting is especially useful if you haven't got the money for lengthy mobile phone conversations or you feel you haven't got enough to say to justify a phone call. The obvious disadvantage of texting is that you can only communicate a limited amount of information—if you really want people to know a number of interesting things that have been happening to you, then texting is probably not the answer!

According to Fox (2005), a preference for texting over mobile phone calls is greatest among those in the 16–24 age group. In this group, 41% generally use texting rather than voice calls, with a further 45% using both texting and voice calls.

Texting provides an excellent way of maintaining contact with a wide circle of friends. In the words of one young woman:

> We haven't got loads of time to be keeping in contact with people, but just to be able to send that one message to someone is really nice. It means they know they're being thought about—and it's lovely when you get one.
>
> *(Fox, 2005)*

Women use texting more than men. However, men are more likely than women to use texting as a way of avoiding talking on their mobile phone through shyness or laziness. As one teenage boy expressed it,

> I never used to call my friends, or only just to arrange to meet, just practical things, but we text a lot—it's cheap, right, but there's also that you have time to think what you want to say.
>
> *(Fox, 2005)*

In sum, texting is a cheap and rapid way of keeping in touch with everyone you know. However, since you aren't interacting directly with the other person, and

> **EXAM HINT**
>
> In an essay on mediated relationships think about the recentness of such research and use this as the source of AO2, e.g., limited evidence, restricted samples, use of case studies, validity of data gathered over the internet, temporal validity, as technology will continue to change. Assess how, if at all, these weaknesses differ from face-to-face research.

since you can only send fairly short messages, it is clearly limited if you have lots of important things to communicate.

> **INDEPENDENT STUDY IDEA: TEXT MESSAGING—GENDER AND AGE DIFFERENCES**
> A very simple study would be to compare people in the 17–25 age group on how many texts they send in, say, a week (ask them to keep a record as guessing could be inaccurate) and compare that with people in the 30–38 year range (obviously you could choose your own age ranges). A likely finding is that young people use texting more than older ones, but unless you have previous research evidence for this, use a non-directional hypothesis. You could also look at how much time these two age groups actually spoke on the phone—findings may not be in the same direction—generally the 30–38 year group may have more money to spend on mobile calls. All the more interesting if you don't know the direction of the hypothesis.
> With respect to gender, as reported in this chapter, women use texting more than men do, so you could easily investigate this gender difference in a group of participants.

SECTION SUMMARY
Cultural and Sub-cultural Differences in Relationships

Individualism vs. collectivism

❖ It is important to study other cultures and sub-cultures, to broaden our understanding of relationships.

❖ One way that Western and non-Western cultures vary is in terms of individualism versus collectivism:

— Individualist Western societies: stress the personality of a potential spouse, romantic love, voluntary marriages, the quest for an ideal partner, and the reasonableness of divorce.
— Collectivist Eastern societies: favour arranged marriages based on social status, having fewer but closer friendships, and being less tolerant of divorce. Arranged marriages appear to have high levels of satisfaction and people in collectivist cultures see romantic relationships as unrealistically optimistic.

Monogamy and polygamy

❖ Polygyny is found in most societies.

❖ It benefits the males because they maximise their reproduction and it benefits the women because their men have power and good looks, characteristics that may be passed on to their sons and maximise the continuation of the mother's genetic line (sexy sons hypothesis).

Gay and lesbian relationships

❖ Certain relationships have been relatively understudied such as gay and lesbian relationships.

❖ There are many misconceptions, for example that homosexual relationships are short-lived and lacking love.

❖ The liberal humanistic view is that gay partnerships are more like heterosexual relationships than they are different, though there are differences. For example:

— Homosexual couples are more likely to have additional sexual partners and to place greater importance on equality of status and power.
— Homosexual couples also have to contend with the hostility of society.
— Heterosexual marriages may be more long-lasting because of the social and cultural support for such unions.

❖ Mediated friendships are a fast-growing area of research. They are divided into two main areas:

— Electronic friendships based on internet contact (email, usenets, chat rooms)
— Friendships involving mobile phones (talking directly, texting).

Mediated friendships

❖ E-mail communication differs from other forms of communication:

— It lacks nonverbal signals (paralanguage), but these are important because they are not under conscious control and communicate important emotional information.
— Abbreviations and symbols are used to create a group identity in the absence of language or dialect.

E-mail

❖ Usenets are communication channels where groups can meet to discuss specific topics, exchange information, or offer help and advice.
❖ Such groups are open to abuse either from individuals offering help who are not qualified to do so, or from anti-social individuals who take advantage of the medium.
❖ Many people derive great satisfaction from usegroups but it has been questioned whether such relationships are shallow or genuine. Research suggests that many relationships formed in this way lead on to more personal contact.

Usenets

❖ Chat rooms are a particular kind of usenet for more personal relationships, such as cyberaffairs.
❖ Such affairs may be just for eroticism, though some lead on to real-time romantic encounters. Others use the medium to continue real-time relationships when face-to-face contact is not possible.
❖ The appealing nature of such relationships can be explained, for example in terms of the ACE Model (anonymity, convenience, and escape).
❖ The danger is that affairs may be founded on untruths and vulnerable individuals may be seduced emotionally and sexually.
❖ Cyber relationships may replace real-life relationships which are ultimately more complex and satisfying. Many of these same issues have existed before, for example with penpals.

Chat rooms

❖ Mobile phones are used by millions of people (especially the young) to maintain good contact with their entire social group. They are used extensively for gossiping and for social chatting.
❖ Mobile phones are very versatile and can be used almost anywhere at almost any time.
❖ Short message service (SMS) or texting offers a cheap and effective way of keeping in touch with one's friends. Its disadvantages are that you lose the direct contact of a phone conversation and you can only send fairly short messages.

Mobile phone conversations

See also pages 32–38 of the revision guide.

FURTHER READING

The topics in this chapter are covered in greater depth by D. Dwyer (2001) *Relationships (2nd Edn.)* (London: Routledge), written specifically for the AQA A specification. Interpersonal relationships are discussed in an accessible way by N. Hayes (1993) *Principles of social psychology* (Hove, UK: Psychology Press) and also in Chapter 13 of M.A. Hogg & G.M. Vaughan (2002) *Social psychology (3rd Edn)* (Harlow: Prentice Hall). R. Goodwin (1999) *Personal relationships across cultures* (London: Routledge) looks at cultural and sub-cultural variation, and, for electronic relationships, you might look at P. Wallace (1999) *The psychology of the internet* (Cambridge University Press), which is written in a lively and amusing style.

EXAMPLE EXAMINATION QUESTIONS

You should spend 30 minutes on each of the questions below, which aim to test the material in this chapter.

1. (a) Describe **two** research studies relating to interpersonal attraction. (12 marks)
   (b) Evaluate these studies with reference to theories of interpersonal attraction. (12 marks)
2. (a) Describe **one or more** theories on the formation and/or maintenance of relationships. (12 marks)
   (b) Evaluate **one** of the theories described in part (a) in terms of research findings and/or alternative theories. (12 marks)
3. Describe and evaluate psychological theories on the formation and/or maintenance of relationships. (24 marks)
4. Critically consider **two** psychological explanations of love. (24 marks)
5. (a) Outline **two** theories of the formation and/or maintenance of interpersonal relationships. (12 marks)
   (b) Assess these theories in terms of their relevance to Western and non-Western cultures. (12 marks)
6. "Psychological research into relationships has tended to focus on romantic heterosexual relationships and ignored all the many other relationships between people, such as friendship and homosexual relationships, as well as those conducted over long distance such as 'electronic' friendships. There is no doubt that this is changing".
   Discuss research into "under-studied" relationships. (24 marks)

Examination Tips

Question 1. Note the word "describe" rather than "outline" for part (a), which means detail is important. When describing studies you can use the same guidelines as for AS level: write something about the aims, procedures, findings, and conclusions. Do *not* offer any evaluation of the studies as part (a) is AO1 alone and evaluation will receive no credit and cannot be exported to part (b). You must restrict your description to two studies. In part (b) you may refer to any relevant research studies and draw general conclusions about interpersonal attraction. Part of assessing the value of such studies could include a consideration of the validity of the research—if the methodology is flawed then the study cannot inform us much.

Question 2. Part (a) needs enough material for 12 AO1 marks so you will do better describing two or three theories rather than just one (unless you know it in great detail). Examiners will apply a depth/breadth trade-off in marking; more theories, less detail required. Although not essential, examiners will be impressed if you can link a theory to either formation or maintenance, but you can use theories from either or both areas. Part (b) requires you to evaluate one of the theories from (a). Research support is an effective way of doing this. If you use alternative theories, keep focusing on your target theory rather than evaluating each one in turn; is it better at explaining different types of relationship, or cultural differences, etc.?

Question 3.   This is a straightforward question requiring you to describe at least two theories on the formation/maintenance of relationships. Accessing the full range of AO1 marks will be easier if you describe at least three theories. Evaluation may involve looking at the implications of the theories, at research evidence (but don't forget you are evaluating the theories, not the studies, so don't waste time focusing on particular studies; emphasise findings and conclusions), issues of cultural and/or individual variation, and any general commentary that informs us about the value of the theories.

Question 4.   It is helpful, when "critically considering" a topic, to include both strengths and weaknesses. The question requires two explanations only, but if you wish to refer to others then ensure that they are explicitly presented as a form of evaluation. Make sure you give a full 15 minutes to evaluation otherwise you are sacrificing important marks.

Question 5.   The term "outline" means that you should present your chosen theories as a summary description only. You have no more than 15 minutes to do this so don't lose marks by providing too much detail for one theory and failing to attract many marks for your second theory. In part (b) you are not required to describe research into other cultures but to assess the extent to which the theory presented in part (a) can explain behaviour in all cultures. You may make reference to research studies but must use this material *effectively* to construct an overall argument.

Question 6.   In this question you are not required to address the quotation but it is there to encourage you to consider various "under-studied" relationships. "Research" may include theories and/or research studies.

WEBSITES

http://www.socialpsychology.org/social.htm#interpersonal
   Links about interpersonal relationships.
http://www.units.muohio.edu/~psybersite/attraction/
   Article and links about physical attraction.
http://www.mexconnect.com/mex_/culxcomp.html
   Interesting summary of cultural differences between Mexicans and their neighbours in North America.

SOCIAL PSYCHOLOGY

Pro- and Anti-social Behaviour

This chapter focuses on behaviour such as aggression and altruism. Why do some people behave aggressively whereas others do not? We examine social psychological and sociobiological approaches.

NATURE AND CAUSES OF AGGRESSION

Aggression involves hurting others on purpose. It has been defined as "any form of behaviour directed towards the goal of harming or injuring another living being who is motivated to avoid such treatment" (Baron & Richardson, 1993). The hurting has to be deliberate. For example, someone who slips on the ice and crashes into someone by accident would not be regarded as behaving aggressively.

Psychologists have identified different types of aggression, for example, person-oriented and instrumental aggression. **Person-oriented aggression** is designed to hurt someone else, and so causing harm is the main goal. In contrast, **instrumental aggression** has as its main goal obtaining some desired reward (e.g., an attractive toy), with aggressive behaviour being used to obtain the reward.

There is also a distinction between proactive and reactive aggression. **Proactive aggression** is aggressive behaviour that is initiated by the individual to achieve some desired outcome (e.g., gaining possession of an object). **Reactive aggression** is an individual's reaction to someone else's aggression.

It is important to note that aggressive behaviour need not involve fighting or other forms of physical attack. Of course, very young children often resort to physical attacks. However, by the age of 4 or 5, children usually have a good command of language, and they make much use of teasing and other forms of verbal aggression. In the research discussed later, aggression is assessed in several ways, such as aggressive play behaviour, willingness to give electric shocks to someone else, and punching and hitting a doll. The key measurement problem is that aggression involves the *intent* to harm someone or something, and it is often hard to know whether participants intended to cause harm.

> **KEY TERMS**
> **Person-oriented aggression:** aggression that has as its main goal harming another person.
> **Instrumental aggression:** harming another person in order to achieve some desired goal.
> **Proactive aggression:** aggressive behaviour that is initiated by the individual in order to achieve some goal.
> **Reactive aggression:** aggressive behaviour that is produced in response to someone else's aggressive behaviour.

The main goal of the aggression in this picture is to obtain a "reward" by stealing the bag, rather than to hurt someone. This is an example of instrumental aggression.

Social Psychological Theories of Aggression

Social learning theory

One of the most influential theories of aggression is that of **social learning** put forward by Albert Bandura (e.g., 1973). According to this approach, most behaviour (including aggressive behaviour) is learned. In the words of Bandura (1973):

The specific forms that aggressive behaviour takes, the frequency with which it is displayed, and the specific targets selected for attack are largely determined by social learning factors.

These three elements of social learning were demonstrated in Bandura's research with children and the Bobo doll (see the Key Study below). In this study it was found that exposure to an aggressive model led to imitation of specific acts, generally increased levels of aggression, and aggression was directed at the same target (Bobo doll).

KEY STUDY
The social learning of aggression

Bandura, Ross, and Ross (1961) carried out a classic study on observational learning or modelling, demonstrating that aggression can be learned via social interactions (i.e., social learning). Young children watched as an adult behaved aggressively towards a Bobo doll. The adult punched the doll and hit it with a hammer. After 10 minutes the children were moved to another room where there were some toys, including a hammer and a Bobo doll. The children had to walk some distance before they got to the room. This was done to create a sense of frustration. Once in the room, they were watched through a one-way mirror and rated for their aggression. The children who had watched a model behaving aggressively were more violent and imitated exactly some of the behaviours they had observed, as compared with children who either had seen no model or watched an adult (model) behaving in a non-aggressive manner.

Bandura (1965) carried out another study on aggressive behaviour towards the Bobo doll. One group of children simply saw a film of an adult model kicking and punching the Bobo doll. A second group saw the same aggressive behaviour performed by the adult model, but this time the model was rewarded by another

Adult "models" and children attack the Bobo doll.

adult for his aggressive behaviour by being given sweets and a drink. A third group saw the same aggressive behaviour, but the model was punished by another adult, who warned him not to be aggressive in future.

Children who had seen the model rewarded, and those who had seen the model neither rewarded nor punished, behaved much more aggressively towards the Bobo doll than did those who had seen the model punished. It could be argued that the children who had seen the model being punished remembered less about the model's behaviour than did the other groups of children. However, this was shown not to be the case by Bandura. All the children were rewarded for imitating as much of the model's aggressive behaviour as they could remember. All three groups showed the same good ability to reproduce the model's aggressive behaviour. Thus, the children in all three groups showed comparable levels of observational learning, but those who had seen the model punished were least likely to *apply* this learning to their own behaviour.

Key study evaluation

Bandura exaggerated the extent to which children imitate the behaviour of models. Children are very likely to imitate aggressive behaviour towards a doll, but they are much less likely to imitate aggressive behaviour towards another child. Bandura consistently failed to distinguish between real aggression and playfighting, and it is likely that much of the aggressive behaviour observed by Bandura was only playfighting (Durkin, 1995). The Bobo doll is of interest to young children, because it has a weighted base and so bounces back up when it is knocked down. Its novelty value is important in determining its effectiveness. Cumberbatch (1990) reported that children who were unfamiliar with the doll were five times more likely to imitate aggressive behaviour against it than were children who had played with it before.

Finally, there is the problem of **demand characteristics**. These are the cues used by participants to work out what a study is about. In an experiment, participants try to guess what it is they should be doing. This leads them to search for cues which might help them and they use these cues, or demand characteristics, to direct their behaviour. Because experiments aim to have the same conditions for all participants, all participants will be using the same cues and therefore they all end up behaving in ways that are predictable from the set up of the experiment. As Durkin (1995, p.406) pointed out:

> *Where else in life does a 5-year-old find a powerful adult actually showing you how to knock hell out of a dummy and then giving you the opportunity to try it out yourself?*

The Bobo doll experiment provided cues that "invited" the participants to behave in certain predictable ways.

Discussion points
1. How might the frustration–aggression hypothesis explain these findings?
2. How important do you think observational learning is with respect to producing aggressive behaviour?

[?] Considering the points made in the evaluation of Bandura's work, what conclusions can be reached from this study in terms of aggression?

Direct and indirect reinforcement

The essence of social learning theory is that new behaviours are learned indirectly as well as through direct reinforcement (traditional learning theory: classical and operant conditioning). Indirect reinforcement (vicarious reinforcement) results in observational learning. **Vicarious reinforcement** occurs when another person is observed to be rewarded for certain actions and this makes it more likely that an observer will imitate the actions. The imitator is not likely to repeat the behaviour immediately but may, at an appropriate time in the future, reproduce the behaviour. Thus it is said that **observational learning** has taken place and the behaviour may be imitated or **modelled** at a later date. This means that a model must be stored internally, and implies the involvement of cognitive processes.

KEY TERMS

Demand Characteristics: features of an experimental situation used by participants to work out what is expected of them and to behave as they think they are expected to.

Vicarious reinforcement: the concept in social learning theory that reinforcement can be received indirectly, by observing another person being reinforced.

Observational learning: a form of learning based on imitating or copying the behaviour of others.

Modelled: learning behaviour through observation and imitation.

Identify the three different ways that aggression can be learned.

This is a departure from traditional learning theory, which rejects the involvement of any cognitive factors in learning.

When aggression is imitated

Individuals are more likely to imitate another's behaviour if:

- The model is similar to themselves, such as being the same gender or similar in age.
- The model is perceived as having desirable characteristics or is admired, as in the case of a rock star or an impressive teacher.
- The individual has low self-esteem.
- The individual is highly dependent on others.
- Reinforcement is direct. Children respond most to direct reward, next to seeing a model in action, and least to a filmed model, especially a cartoon character (Bandura, Ross, & Ross, 1963).

Vicarious punishment may also occur, leading to a reduced response. For example, if you see someone else being told off for teasing, then you are less likely to do it. In addition social modelling may reduce the likelihood of a response because a different response has been strengthened. This was demonstrated in a study by Walters and Thomas (1963) who recruited participants for a study on the effects of punishment on learning. The participants worked in pairs, one was supposedly learning a task (this person was actually a confederate of the experimenters). The "true" participant was told to give the learner a shock following each error that was made. After each error, the participant was given the opportunity to select the level of shock to use for the next trial. Prior to the experiment all participants had been shown a film. Those participants who watched a violent scene were found to select higher shock intensities than those who watched a nonviolent movie scene.

This is an example of **disinhibition**. The participants observed socially unacceptable behaviour in the film and this *weakened* the pro-social behaviours they had previously learned. In other words their tendency to behave pro-socially was disinhibited or unlearned as a result of modelling. This concept of disinhibition is discussed again later when considering the effects of the media.

Can you think of an occasion when your own behaviour has been disinhibited?

More research evidence

The development of aggression. Probably the most important social models for a child are his or her parents. Patterson, DeBaryshe, and Ramsey (1989) looked at the factors in a child's home environment that might be related to the development of aggression. The researchers compared families having at least one highly aggressive child with other families of the same size and socio-economic status who had no problem children. Assessments were made through questionnaires and interviews with children, parents, peers, and teachers, as well as home observations. The key feature of certain families was a "coercive home environment" where little affection was shown, and family members were constantly struggling with each other and using aggressive tactics to cope. Parents rarely used social reinforcement or approval as a means of behaviour control. Instead they used physical punishment, nagging, shouting, and teasing. The children in such families were typically manipulative and difficult to discipline.

KEY TERM

Disinhibition: loss of inhibitions.

Patterson et al. suggested that the coercive home environment may create aggressiveness in three main ways. First, harsh discipline and lack of supervision results in disrupted bonding between parent and child, and lack of identification. Second, the parental behaviours provoked aggressiveness in the children. Finally, the children learned to behave aggressively through modelling; they observed that aggression was a means of resolving disputes. This analysis has useful practical application. It is possible that the way to reduce aggressiveness is to teach parents alternative skills, and give anti-social children social skills training (see page 411).

Video games and aggression.   Some research has considered the relationship between video games and aggression. According to social learning theory, children should copy the aggressive behaviour they observe in such games. The findings are mixed. For example, Cooper and Mackie (1986) observed the free play of 9- and 10-year-old children after they had played aggressive video games—aggressive behaviour increased only in girls. In another study, aggression levels did increase in 7- to 8-year-olds (Irwin & Gross, 1995). Griffiths (1997) discussed research on video games and aggressive behaviour. He concluded that increased aggression occurs most often in younger children and rarely in teenagers. Van Schie and Wiegman (1997) found in a large sample of children that the amount of time spent playing video games was *not* related to the amount of aggressive behaviour observed subsequently. However, children who spent time playing video games were less likely to behave in positive and helpful ways.

Anderson and Bushman (2001) considered findings from numerous studies on violent video games. They found that playing violent video games had several undesirable effects. More specifically, these video games increased aggressive thoughts, increased physiological arousal, produced aggressive emotions, and led to aggressive behaviour. It is very worrying that violent video games seem to have so many negative effects.

There are limitations with many of the studies. First, most of the studies have looked only at short-term effects, whereas it is more important to consider possible long-term effects. Griffiths and Hunt (1995) did this, and found that older children who played video games reported higher levels of aggression (note that the aggressive behaviour may be the cause rather than the effect of the video-game playing). Second, most researchers have only observed children's free play activity after playing video games, so we don't know much about the effects of these games in other situations. Third, there are obvious ethical reasons why researchers can't deliberately expose children to violent video games. Indeed, the American Psychological Association, in a 2005 press release, called for a significant reduction in the levels of aggression in video games (http://www.apa.org/releases/videoviolence05.html).

Cross-cultural evidence.   Finally, we might consider cross-cultural evidence. If aggression is due to social learning then we would expect the different practices in different cultures to produce variations in levels of aggression. Some of the best-known work on cross-cultural differences in aggression is that of the anthropologist Margaret Mead (1935). She compared three New Guinea tribes living fairly close to each other. In one tribe (the Mundugumor), both men and women were very aggressive and quarrelsome in their behaviour. At times, the Mundugumor had been cannibals who killed outsiders in order to eat them. In a second tribe (the Arapesh),

It is easy to dismiss the features listed here as not being present in your home environment—at least one of them probably is.

Does cross-cultural evidence suggest that aggression is learned, or not?

both men and women were non-aggressive and co-operative in their treatment of each other and their children. When they were invaded, the Arapesh would hide in inaccessible parts of their territory rather than fight the invader. In the third tribe (the Tchambuli), the men carved and painted, and indulged themselves with elaborate hairdos, whereas the women were relatively aggressive.

It is probable that Mead exaggerated the extent of the gender differences, for example even in the Tchambuli tribe it was the men who did most of the fighting in time of war. The fact that the men were *relatively* more aggressive in each society suggests that some aspects of aggression are biologically determined; but the fact that some societies are more aggressive than others supports the role of social learning in aggression.

Evaluation

Bandura's social learning approach is an important one. Much aggressive behaviour is learned, and observational learning or modelling is often involved. It has been found that children who watch violent programmes on television are more likely to behave in an aggressive way. These studies (discussed later) are consistent with social learning theory.

Social learning theory can account for cultural and individual variation; it can also explain why we behave aggressively in some situations and not others. When we are rewarded or reinforced for behaving aggressively this is related to specific situations. In other situations we might find that the same behaviour is not rewarded. For example, a child might find it a useful strategy to shout at a friend in the playground, but the same behaviour used in class would be sharply discouraged. The child learns when aggression is appropriate and when it is not. This is called **context-dependent learning**.

In spite of the successes of social learning theory, there are reasons for arguing that Bandura's approach is limited in scope. Aggressive behaviour does not depend only on observational learning. The cross-cultural evidence demonstrated that aspects of aggression are innate. Twin studies have also provided evidence of the importance of genetic factors. For example, McGue, Brown, and Lykken (1992) obtained scores on the aggression scale of the Multi-Dimensional Personality Questionnaire from 54 pairs of identical twins and 79 pairs of fraternal twins. The scores correlated +0.43 for identical twins and +0.30 for fraternal twins. The fact that the correlation was higher for identical twins suggested that genetic factors were of some importance, though it is possible that the twins reared together had learned aggression in their homes.

Frustration–aggression hypothesis

Think of occasions when you have behaved aggressively. Many of them probably involved frustrating situations. Dollard et al. (1939) argued in their **frustration–aggression hypothesis** that there are close links between frustration and aggression. In the words of Miller (1941, pp.337–338)

> *the occurrence of aggression always presupposes frustration . . . Frustration produces instigations to a number of different types of responses, one of which is an instigation to some form of aggression.*

This approach is of relevance to various broad themes in social psychology. For example, the frustration–aggression hypothesis may help to explain some

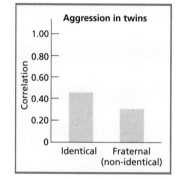

Aggression in twins

Correlation

1.00
0.80
0.60
0.40
0.20
0

Identical   Fraternal
(non-identical)

KEY TERMS

Context-dependent learning: Recall is better when it occurs in the same context as original learning. May result in learning that some behaviours are appropriate in some contexts and not in others.

Frustration–aggression hypothesis: a social-psychological explanation for aggressive behaviour that states that frustration always leads to aggression and aggression is always caused by frustration.

prejudiced behaviour against minority groups. Individuals or groups who feel frustrated because they suffer from unemployment and/or poverty may become so frustrated that they start behaving aggressively towards other individuals or groups.

? What types of situation do you find frustrating?

Research evidence

Evidence supporting the frustration–aggression hypothesis was reported by Doob and Sears (1939). Participants imagined how they would feel in each of 16 frustrating situations. In one situation, the participants imagined they were waiting for a bus, but the bus driver went past without stopping. Most participants reported that they would feel angry in each of the frustrating situations. Of course, anger does not always turn into aggression.

? In what other ways do people respond to frustration?

Real-life evidence supporting the frustration–aggression hypothesis was reported by Catalano, Novaco, and McConnell (1997) in San Francisco. Small increases in job losses (a cause of frustration) were associated with an increase in violence (aggression).

Justified and unjustified frustration.   Most of the evidence indicates that the frustration–aggression hypothesis is oversimplified. For example, Pastore (1952) argued that it is important to distinguish between justified and unjustified frustration. According to him, it is mainly unjustified frustration that produces anger and aggression. Doob and Sears (1939) found strong support for the frustration–aggression hypothesis because their situations involved unjustified frustration. Accordingly, Pastore produced different versions of the situations used by Doob and Sears involving justified frustration. For example, the situation with the non-stopping bus was rewritten to indicate that the bus was out of service. As predicted, Pastore found that justified frustration led to much lower levels of anger than did unjustified frustration.

Situational factors.   Evidence that aggressive behaviour doesn't always stem from frustration was reported by Zimbardo (1973). In his Stanford prison experiment (which was covered in your AS studies), the mock prisoners did less and less to frustrate the wishes of the mock warders. However, the mock warders behaved in an increasingly aggressive way towards them. In times of war, soldiers often behave aggressively towards the enemy because they are ordered to do so rather than because they are frustrated.

? What would happen to soldiers if they did not behave aggressively?

Berkowitz (1968) believed that the presence of guns could stimulate aggressive behaviour.

Environmental cues.   Berkowitz and LePage (1967) argued that aggressive behaviour does not depend only on frustration. The presence in the environment of aggressive cues also plays a part in making people behave aggressively, and this notion was tested by Berkowitz and LePage. Male university students received electric shocks from another student, who was a confederate working for the experimenter. They were then given the chance to give electric shocks to the confederate. In one condition, a revolver and a shotgun were close to the shock machine. In another condition, nothing was placed nearby.

The presence of the guns increased the average number of shocks that were given from 4.67 to 6.07. This is known as the **weapons effect**. According to Berkowitz (1968, p.22):

> *Guns not only permit violence, they can stimulate it as well. The finger pulls the trigger, but the trigger may also be pulling the finger.*

We need to consider a potential problem with the interpretation of the weapons effect. The presence of the guns may lead participants to assume that the experimenter wants them to behave in an aggressive way. If so, then only those participants who were suspicious of the experimenter's intentions would show the weapons effect. In fact, the evidence indicates that suspicious participants do *not* show the weapons effect. This suggests that Berkowitz's interpretation of the weapons effect is probably correct.

Cognitive-neoassociation. Berkowitz (1989) revised the frustration–aggression hypothesis in his cognitive-neoassociationistic approach. He argued that an aversive or unpleasant event causes negative affect or emotion (e.g., anxiety, anger). This negative affect activates tendencies towards aggression and towards flight. The behaviour we actually display depends on our interpretation of the situation. Suppose someone knocks into you as you are walking along the pavement. This may cause negative feelings and a tendency towards behaving in an aggressive way. However, if you realise that it was a blind person who knocked into you, your aggressive tendencies are likely to be replaced by feelings of guilt.

According to Berkowitz's (1989) theory, a frustrating situation is one example (but not the only one) of an aversive event. In similar fashion, behaving in an aggressive way is only one of several ways of responding to frustration. This theory is vaguer than the original frustration–aggression hypothesis. However, it is more reasonable than the frustration–aggression hypothesis, and more in line with the available evidence.

Excitation-transfer theory

It may be preferable to describe aggression as the consequence of a generally increased level of arousal or excitation. Zillmann (e.g., 1979) developed an excitation-transfer theory, according to which arousal caused by one stimulus can be transferred and added to the arousal produced by a second stimulus. What is important in determining the emotional reaction to the second stimulus is the way in which the transferred arousal is *interpreted*. For example, suppose that someone insults you on a very hot day. You might normally ignore the insult. However, because the hot weather has made you more aroused, you may become very aggressive. According to the theory, however, this should *only* happen if you attribute your aroused state to being insulted rather than to the temperature.

The notion that the interpretation given to one's arousal level is important resembles the theoretical approach of Schachter and Singer (1962) in their cognitive labelling theory of emotion. More generally, social psychologists increasingly recognise that the ways in which we behave in social situations depend on how we interpret our social world, especially the actions of those with whom we interact. Thus, we can only understand social behaviour by considering the ways in which we interpret internal (e.g., arousal) and external sources of information.

? How might you use this quote to argue against those Americans who believe in the right of every individual to bear arms?

? Could the demand characteristics of Berkowitz's laboratory situation have led participants to guess the true purpose of the study?

KEY TERM

Weapons effect: an increase in aggressive behaviour caused by the mere sight of weapons (e.g., guns).

The best way to see what is involved in excitation-transfer theory is to consider an experimental example of excitation transfer. In a study by Zillmann, Johnson, and Day (1974), male participants were provoked by a confederate of the experimenter. Half of the participants rested for 6 minutes and then pedalled on a cycling machine for 90 seconds, whereas the other half pedalled first and then rested. Immediately afterwards, all of the participants had the chance to choose the level of shock to be given to the person who had provoked them.

What do you think happened? Zillmann et al. predicted that participants who had just finished cycling would attribute their arousal to the cycling, and so would not behave aggressively towards their provoker. In contrast, those who had just rested for 6 minutes would attribute their arousal to the provocation, and so would behave aggressively by delivering a strong electric shock. The results were in line with these predictions.

Evaluation

Unexplained arousal can lead to increased anger and aggression in the way predicted by excitation-transfer theory. However, the theory is rather limited. In real life, we generally know *why* we are aroused, and the theory does not apply to such situations.

Deindividuation

Deindividuation refers to the loss of a sense of personal identity that can occur when we are, for example, in a crowd or wearing a mask. One explanation offered for unruly mob behaviour is that the loss of identity that occurs when you are part of a crowd means that individuals feel less constrained by norms of social behaviour, and more able to behave in an anti-social way. This may help to explain why some petrol stations (e.g., in Brighton) refuse to serve people wearing "hoodies".

In Zimbardo's (1973) prison study the guards were deindividuated because they wore uniforms and were given reflective sunglasses. However the prisoners also wore uniforms and were further deindividuated by having stockings on their heads and being referred to by a number rather than their name. The prisoners didn't behave aggressively but they did conform to the role of being a prisoner (i.e., they were very obedient). This suggests that deindividuation results in high levels of conformity but not necessarily aggression, as the prison guards were also conforming to a role.

Postmes and Spears (1998) considered the findings from 60 studies on group and crowd behaviour. Manipulations designed to produce deindividuation (e.g., anonymity, large groups) were only weakly associated with aggressive or anti-social behaviour. Their key discovery was that deindividuation increased

> **Relative deprivation theory**
>
> This theory can explain both aggressive and prejudiced behaviour. The basic principle is that a sense of having less than one feels entitled to leads to aggression. One's feelings of deprivation are judged in terms of what other people might be perceived to have, i.e., deprivation is relative to the state of others. A sense of relative deprivation exacerbates pre-existing *prejudices* about an *outgroup*, especially at times of economic hardship, and is expressed as aggression towards that group.

? What ethical questions are raised by Zillmann et al.'s study?

? Do you think that excitation transfer happens often in everyday life?

> **KEY TERM**
>
> **Deindividuation:** losing a sense of personal identity that may occur, e.g., when in a crowd or wearing a mask.

Individuals in a crowd experience a sense of deindividuation and this might explain why mobs act in an unruly way. However, this is not true of all "mobs", such as at a rock concert. Deindividuation is better described as increased conformity.

The Ku Klux Klan uniform provides both anonymity and a shared identity for its wearers.

individuals' adherence to group norms or standards—this often leads to desirable behaviour rather than to aggressive behaviour. For example, the death of Princess Diana on 31 August 1997 led crowds of tearful people to show their sadness and sense of loss, but did not lead to any undesirable or aggressive behaviour. Thus, there can be conformity to group norms without any aggression.

Evaluation

The major difficulty with using deindividuation as an explanation for aggression is the fact that it doesn't always lead to aggression. In fact, deindividuation can lead to higher levels of pro-social behaviour. For example, wearing a nurse's uniform leads to a loss of personal identity and adopting the norms for that uniform. Whereas wearing the uniform of a soldier might lead one to adopt more aggressive behaviours.

What happens is that deindividuation actually leads to increased conformity to the norm of the crowd. This can lead to desirable or undesirable behaviour depending on the specific situation and the particular group norms in operation. Deindividuation means one tends to relinquish personal control.

Social constructionism

Most of the theories of aggression are based on the assumption that it is fairly easy to decide whether someone is behaving aggressively. However, social constructionists such as Gergen (1997) argue that we impose subjective interpretations or constructions on the world around us. For example, tackles that seem like cynical fouls deserving a sending-off to the supporters of one team are regarded as perfectly fair by the supporters of the other team.

The social constructionist approach as applied to aggression is based on a number of assumptions:

To one team this looks like a foul; to the other, a justifiable defensive manoeuvre.

1. Aggressive behaviour is a form of social behaviour, and it is not simply an expression of anger.
2. Our interpretation or construction of someone else's behaviour as aggressive or non-aggressive depends on our beliefs and knowledge.
3. Our decision whether to behave aggressively or non-aggressively depends on how we interpret the other person's behaviour towards us.

Research evidence

The first assumption is supported by numerous cases in which an individual behaves aggressively towards someone else some time after being angered by that person. For example, in the days (thankfully past!) when teachers used to cane their students, the caning would often take place days after the student had behaved badly.

The second assumption is supported by the work of Blumenthal et al. (1972). They studied the attitudes of American men towards police and student behaviour during student demonstrations. Students with negative attitudes towards the police judged the behaviour of the police to be violent, whereas the sit-ins and other actions of the students were regarded as nonviolent. In contrast, men with positive attitudes to the police didn't regard their assaults on students or their use of firearms as violent. However, they condemned student sit-ins as violent acts deserving arrest. These findings suggest that our judgement that someone is behaving aggressively depends on the constructions we place on their behaviour.

How do we decide whether someone is behaving aggressively? According to the **norm of reciprocity**, if someone has done something to you, you are justified in behaving in the same way to that person. Evidence that the norm of reciprocity applies to aggressive behaviour was reported by Brown and Tedeschi (1976). Someone who *initiated* a hostile act against another person was seen as aggressive and unfair. In contrast, someone who attacked another person after having been provoked was regarded as behaving non-aggressively.

The third assumption of the constructionist approach was supported by Marsh, Rosser, and Harré (1978). They studied violent attacks by students in schools, and found that these attacks were neither random nor spontaneous. The attacks generally occurred in classes with less effective teachers, because the students interpreted this as a sign that the school authorities had written them off. This interpretation (although mistaken) produced anger and aggression.

Evaluation

The constructionist notion that our interpretation or construction of situations and people's behaviour determines our responses is valuable. Such interpretations or constructions depend on our attitudes and beliefs. Thus, we must distinguish between what *actually* happens in social situations and our interpretations.

On the negative side, social constructionists exaggerate the differences between different individuals' constructions of what has happened. There are many cases in which nearly everyone would agree that someone is behaving aggressively, for example if a defenceless old woman is suddenly attacked by a mugger and her handbag is stolen.

Effects of environmental stressors on aggressive behaviour

A number of environmental factors have been identified as triggers for aggression. We saw earlier that a gun might be a cue to aggression and Zillmann suggested that temperature might lead to excitation-transfer. Other environmental factors that may lead to aggression include intense noise and overcrowding. What these factors seem to have in common is that they all involve uncomfortable levels of internal arousal, which can in turn lead to aggressive behaviour.

Temperature

Baron and Bell (1976) studied the effects of heat on aggression by seeing how willing participants were to give electric shocks to another person. Temperatures within the range 92–95°F (33–35°C) generally increased the level of aggression. However, extreme heat led to a reduced level of aggression towards

? Can you think of any recent news items that could be interpreted in different ways according to which side a person supported?

? Are there situations where the norm of reciprocity does not apply?

KEY TERM

Norm of reciprocity: the cultural expectation that it is justified to treat others in the way they treat you.

EXAM HINT

In a question that specifies that you describe research studies as AO1, you might find it helpful to link the research to particular theories as AO2 (e.g., linking crowding to deindividuation), but do not describe the theories. Instead, discuss in an evaluative way how the research and theories support or contradict each other, and whether they have the same or different strengths and weaknesses.

Episodes of road rage may result when one driver makes the assumption that another has been deliberately aggressive. In fact, the apparently aggressive driver could be lost, in the wrong lane, driving an unfamiliar car, or in the middle of a row with a passenger, and the offensive behaviour could be completely unintentional.

another person who had provided a negative evaluation of the participant. In those conditions, the participants were very stressed. If they had given shocks to the other person, they would have had to deal with that person's angry reactions, and they felt unable to deal with the added stress.

In a naturalistic study, Baron and Ransberger (1978) showed that incidences of violence could be related to high air temperatures. They used collected data on incidents of group violence in the US as well as the corresponding weather reports. They found that when the temperature was moderately hot, around 84°F, violence was highest; when temperatures got any hotter, aggression declined. This confirms the finding that temperature can act as a stressor leading to the response of aggression.

However, other evidence doesn't support the notion that aggressive behaviour declines when the heat becomes extreme. Anderson (1989) considered the effects of temperature on various forms of aggressive behaviour, such as assault, rape, and murder. There was a steady increase in all of these aggressive acts as the temperature rose, with no indication of any reduction in extreme heat.

Cohn and Rotton (1997) carried out a thorough study on temperature and aggression in which they recorded the temperature every day for 2 years in Minneapolis. They confirmed Baron and Ransberger's (1978) finding that aggression is greatest when the weather is moderately hot. In addition, they found that the effects of temperature on aggression were greatest in the evening. They argued that this occurred in part because alcohol (which is known to increase aggression) is mostly consumed in the evening and more alcohol is drunk in hot weather than in cool weather. However, this doesn't explain why there is less aggression on extremely hot days than on moderately hot ones.

Most of the findings indicate that heat leads to increased aggression. This is not surprising—we say that someone who is angry is "hot under the collar", and we tell them to "cool down" or "chill out". Strong emotions are generally linked to high levels of physiological arousal, and anger is no exception to the rule.

Noise

Noise levels also act as a stressor and may lead to arousal and frustration as anyone living near Heathrow airport will tell you. Glass, Singer, and Friedman (1969) arranged for 60 undergraduates to complete a number of cognitive tasks, such as word searches, under one of four conditions: loud or soft noise which was played at random (unpredictable) or fixed (predictable intervals). There was also a no-noise condition. During the task physiological arousal was measured using the galvanic skin response (GSR, a measure of autonomic arousal or stress). After the task participants were asked to complete four puzzles. Two of them were insoluble. Frustration (stress) was measured in terms of the length of time that participants persisted at these tasks.

Participants did adapt to the noise. In the predictable noise condition, participants made fewer errors, and had lower GSR and higher task persistence than those in the random noise condition. Those in the no-noise condition made even fewer errors. This suggests that random noise has the greatest effect; but even predictable noise creates some stress. Glass et al. suggested that this is because we can "tune out" constant stimuli while still attending at a preconscious level, but unpredictable stimuli require continued attention, and this reduces our ability to cope with stress. Therefore noise is, in itself, a stressor. And such stressors may lead to aggression as described by the frustration–aggression hypothesis.

? Do you feel that the study by Glass et al. raises any clinical concerns?

You might think that it is only the intensity of noise that determines how stressful it is and how likely it is to produce an aggressive reaction. In fact, Borsky (1969) identified five factors other than intensity that cause noise to be regarded as stressful in real-life situations:

1. It is perceived as unnecessary.
2. Those responsible for the noise are thought to be unconcerned about its effects on others.
3. The individual dislikes other features of the environment (e.g., overcrowding).
4. The individual believes that noise is harmful to health.
5. The noise is associated with fear.

Donnerstein and Wilson (1976) carried out an important study. Initially, half the participants had their written work evaluated negatively or positively, it being assumed that negative evaluation would lead to anger. After that, all the participants had the chance to deliver electric shocks to the person who had evaluated their work—the strength of shock was taken as a measure of aggression. During this period of time, the participants were exposed to low or high intensity noise. The key finding was that intense noise only increased aggression in those participants who had been angered previously. Thus, noise is most likely to make people aggressive when they are already prepared to behave in an aggressive way (e.g., by being angered at their previous treatment).

Noise can cause aggression. However, it is important to note that the effects of noise depend on various factors including how it is interpreted and whether it is regarded as deliberate (e.g., noisy neighbours) or necessary. In addition, it is mostly people already feeling angry or upset who are most likely to react to intense noise with aggression.

Crowding and overcrowding

It is often argued that people will tend to behave in an aggressive way when there is severe *overcrowding* that leads to the psychological experience of *crowding*. Note that the experience of being surrounded by lots of other people depends very much on the precise situation. You probably dislike having many people very close to you on a crowded train but you may find it exciting when something similar happens when you're out clubbing!

Evidence indicating negative effects of crowding was reported by Loo (1979), who studied the behaviour of young children in a day nursery. The overall level of aggressive behaviour went up as the number of children in the nursery increased. In similar fashion, there are more acts of aggression and riots in prisons with a high density of prisoners than in those with a low density (McCain et al., 1980).

Studies of other species confirm the link between crowding and aggression. Calhoun (1962) carried out a study involving a steady increase in the number of rats living in a large enclosure. Even though the rats were well cared for, they grew

Do crowds always lead to negative behaviour? The feeling of crowding is likely to heighten the mood people are in rather than always making people feel aggressive.

increasingly aggressive as the enclosure became crowded. The level of aggression finally became so high that some of the young rats were killed.

Freedman (1973) suggests that the physiological arousal of a crowd heightens the mood you are in. In some situations, a crowd may often be associated with enjoyment, as in a rock concert, or pro-social behaviour, as at a peace gathering. However, if you are not enjoying yourself at such an event, you might feel stressed, or behave anti-socially.

The effects of crowding on behaviour depend very much on whether you have a sense of control. For example, Rodin, Solomon, and Metcalf (1978) packed lots of people into a lift. The person standing closest to the control panel (who therefore had the greatest control) was generally the least stressed person in the lift. In similar fashion, Indians living in very crowded housing were less unhappy and less inclined to behave aggressively when they perceived themselves to have control over their environment (Ruback & Pandey, 1991).

Crowding sometimes (but by no means always) leads to aggression and other undesirable forms of behaviour. The effects of crowding depend on the nature of the situation and the amount of control we have. We can cope better with crowding when the situation is one that we enjoy (e.g., clubbing) than when it is one we don't enjoy (e.g., a crowded train). It is much easier to remain calm in a crowded situation if we perceive we have at least some control over it.

Negative affect escape model

Baron (1977) has outlined a general theory to incorporate these findings—the negative affect escape model. According to this model unpleasant stimuli (e.g., noise, heat) usually increase aggressive behaviour, because this provides a way of reducing the negative affect. However, if the unpleasant stimuli become very intense, then there is often less aggressive behaviour as people try to escape or simply become passive.

Evaluation

It is not known why laboratory tests of this model tend to support it, whereas data from real-life situations do not (as described earlier). One possibility is that it may be easier to escape from unpleasant stimuli in the laboratory than in real life. Another possibility is that provoking stimuli in real life can be much more intense than in the laboratory. As a result, the high levels of negative affect generated by heat or noise are more likely to trigger aggressive behaviour in real life.

Biological Theories of Aggression

So far in this Section, we have focused on social psychological explanations of aggression. But we should not ignore the fact that there are other,

EXAM HINT

Include a discussion of the social versus the biological explanations of aggression to take advantage of the synoptic opportunity. Make a conclusion about the relative impact of nature–nurture. Draw from the physiological, genetic, and evolutionary approaches to support nature but consider how the great variety in expression of aggression across cultures suggests that social factors override biological ones.

contrasting explanations—namely, the purely biological explanations of aggression. Therefore we will deal with them only very briefly.

The physiological approach

One way to explain why men are more aggressive, in general, than women is in terms of the male hormone **testosterone**. Kalat (1998) reports that men aged 15–25, who have the highest levels of testosterone, also show the highest levels of violence as measured by crime statistics. Further evidence can be gleaned from the fact that in non-human animals, those males who have been castrated (and thus produce no male hormones) fight least. Female aggression has also been linked to hormones. For example, Floody (1968) reviewed research on pre-menstrual syndrome and found evidence to support the view that during this time of hormonal fluctuation women increase in irritability and hostility, and also are more likely to commit a crime.

The neurotransmitter **serotonin** has also been linked with increased aggression. For example, people with a history of criminal behaviour have been found to have low levels of serotonin (Virkkunen et al., 1987).

A third way of explaining aggression in physiological terms is with reference to brain anatomy. Raine, Buchsbaum, and LaCasse (1997) found significant differences in the brain structure of murderers and normal individuals, such as reduced activity in both sides of the prefrontal cortex and in the amygdala.

One major difficulty with physiological explanations of aggression is that it is difficult to know whether physiological correlates are causes or effects of aggressiveness.

The genetic approach

One classic study in the 1960s (Jacobs, Brunton, & Melville, 1965) found that a surprising number of men in prison had XYY sex chromosomes instead of the normal XY. The researchers supposed that the extra Y chromosome might make the men more aggressive. Later studies have found that such genetic abnormalities are in fact widespread throughout the general population and therefore can't explain aggression.

More recently, studies have identified genetic trends in twins and families. For example, Brunner et al. (1993) identified a common gene in male members of a Danish family who all exhibited abnormal aggressive behaviour. This potential "gene for aggression" was used as a defence argument in the 1995 trial of Stephen Mobley, who was eventually found guilty of murder despite testimony from his aunt that various members of his family over the last four generations had been inexplicably very violent, aggressive, and criminal.

The evolutionary or ethological perspective

Ethologists and evolutionary psychologists argue that aggression must be understood in terms of its natural function. Animals, especially males, are biologically programmed to fight over resources. One of the classic ethological accounts was from Lorenz (1966). His conclusions were based on observations of non-human animals in their natural environment. He felt that his view was equally applicable to humans because they are governed by the same laws of natural selection. He argued that aggression is a highly adaptive response because

KEY TERMS

Testosterone: a male hormone.
Serotonin: a neurotransmitter that is associated with lower arousal, sleepiness, and reduced anxiety.

an individual who is aggressive controls food, territory, and mating, and thus is the one most likely to survive to reproduce.

In non-human animals aggression does not generally result in harm to the animal towards which the aggression is directed. Any species where aggression leads to death or serious injury will eventually become extinct unless it evolves a form of natural regulation. However, the belief that animals have effective signals to turn off aggression has been challenged by a number of studies. For example, Goodall (1978) noted that appeasement gestures did not stop fighting among a troop of chimpanzees. Parallels between humans and animals may be oversimplified.

Psychoanalytic explanation

Freud proposed that aggression was related to innate instincts, i.e., biological drives. Each individual has a life wish (Eros) and a death wish (Thanatos). The death wish drives us towards self-destruction and, according to Freud, the not always unpleasant wish to return to lifelessness and the mother's womb. The life instinct tries to prevent the death instinct taking over, which results in a redirection of the desire for self-destruction. What would be self-aggression becomes aggression towards others. It is possible for the individual to channel this outward aggression into harmless activity such as sport. This is called catharsis, the release of pent-up energy. Freud felt that it was necessary to release our hostile and destructive impulses regularly otherwise they would result in undesirable behaviour.

Evaluation

Biological explanations of aggression have some practical usefulness in suggesting ways to reduce aggression, though not all of them are desirable (e.g., drugs to counter hormones) or successful (it is not clear whether sport increases or decreases aggression). The biological approach is highly deterministic, as we saw in the suggestion that some criminals might argue that their behaviour was not their fault. Biological explanations also cannot explain cultural variation in aggression.

SECTION SUMMARY
Nature and Causes of Aggression

What is aggression?

❖ Aggression involves intentional hurt.
❖ We can distinguish between:

— Person-oriented aggression (designed to hurt someone else and cause harm) and instrumental aggression (designed to obtain a desired award).
— Proactive aggression (aggressive behaviour initiated by the individual) and reactive aggression (an individual's reaction to aggression).

Theories of aggression: Social learning theory

❖ Bandura's social learning approach suggests that aggression is learned through:

— Direct reinforcement: traditional learning theory based on classical and operant conditioning.

— Indirect (vicarious) reinforcement: where observational learning takes place and then behaviour is imitated or modelled. The observer learns to imitate specific acts towards a specific model and also learns generally increased levels of aggression.

❖ What factors influence the imitation of aggression?

— Imitation is more likely if the model is similar and/or possesses desirable characteristics, and if the individuals have low self-esteem.
— Imitation is more likely if reinforcement is direct. Films provide less direct reinforcement than live models.
— Vicarious punishment leads to a reduced response, making imitation of aggression less likely (if you see someone being told off for something, you are less likely to do it yourself).
— Some behaviours may be disinhibited: individuals can unlearn pro-social behaviour when they witness anti-social behaviour, and become more aggressive.
— Research has also shown how children may learn aggression through modelling parents' aggressive coping tactics.
— Video games increase aggressiveness, especially in younger children. However, it is possible that aggression is a cause rather than an effect of video game playing. Many of the studies have involved only short-term effects.

❖ Cross-cultural evidence also supports social learning theory, such as Mead's classic studies of three New Guinea tribes.

❖ Social learning is an important explanation of aggression, and can be used to account for media influence and cultural differences, as well as the context-specific nature of aggressive behaviour.

❖ The essence is that aggression is learned through direct and indirect reinforcement, and also influenced by punishment and disinhibition.

❖ Some models are more effective than others. Social learning is not the only explanation; for example, biological factors are important in aggression too, as indicated by twin studies.

How social learning theory explains aggression

❖ The frustration–aggression hypothesis suggests that frustration always produces aggression, and aggression always depends on frustration.

❖ Criticisms of the hypothesis:

— Research evidence indicates that frustration leads to anger, though this may not turn into aggression.
— This hypothesis is oversimplified, for example justified frustration leads to less anger than unjustified frustration.
— The situation can be more important than frustration.
— Environmental cues may trigger aggression, as demonstrated by the weapons effect.

❖ Revising the hypothesis:

— The original hypothesis was modified by Berkowitz, in a cognitive-neoassociationistic approach.

Theories of aggression: The frustration–aggression hypothesis

— He argued that an aversive or unpleasant event causes negative feelings that activate tendencies towards aggression and flight. How we then behave depends on our interpretation of the situation.

Theories of aggression: Excitation-transfer theory

❖ This theory suggests that aggression is a consequence of a generally increased level of arousal; again arousal is interpreted using situational cues.

❖ This is similar to the cognitive labelling theory of emotion.

❖ There is research support for this theory but in real life we generally know *why* we are aroused and don't use situational cues.

Theories of aggression: Deindividuation

❖ When people experience deindividuation they may behave more aggressively, however they may also behave more pro-socially.

❖ Deindividuation leads to higher levels of conformity with group norms or standards and loss of personal control.

Theories of aggression: The social constructionist approach

❖ The social constructionist approach considers the question of how we interpret an aggressive behaviour—aggression is an evaluative rather than a descriptive concept.

❖ This approach enables us to distinguish between what actually happens and the interpretation different people place on it.

Theories of aggression: Environmental factors

❖ Environmental factors can act as a cue to aggression, as suggested by both frustration–aggression and excitation-transfer theories.

— High temperatures: have been shown to lead to increased aggression but very high temperatures may not have this effect, possibly because individuals don't feel they can deal with an aggressive response.

— Unpredictable noise: Research has shown that unpredictable noise may lead to arousal and frustration, which could be translated into aggression. However, the social context is important.

— Overcrowding is also associated with increased aggression, especially in situations in which the individual has little or no control.

❖ The negative affect escape model can be used to explain the effect of environmental factors. According to this model unpleasant stimuli usually increase aggressive behaviour, because this provides a way of reducing the negative affect. However, if the negative stimuli become very intense, there is often less aggressive behaviour as people try to escape or simply become passive. But real-life studies don't support this—which may be because in real life passivity is not an option.

Biological explanations of aggression

❖ As a counterpoint to these explanations we can consider biological explanations:

— Physiological explanations include the effects of hormones and neurotransmitters, and differences in brain anatomy.

— Individual differences in aggression may be genetic.

— Ethologists argue that aggression is adaptive behaviour.

— Freud suggested aggression was an innate instinct, a redirection of our desire for self-destruction which could be rendered harmless through catharsis and sport.

See also pages 44–50 of the revision guide.

❖ Biological explanations are deterministic and cannot account for cultural variation.

ALTRUISM AND BYSTANDER BEHAVIOUR

You must have met some people who were very helpful and co-operative, and others who were aggressive and unpleasant. Psychologists use the terms pro-social behaviour and anti-social behaviour to describe these very different ways of treating other people. **Pro-social behaviour** is behaviour that is of benefit to someone else. It includes actions that are co-operative, affectionate, and helpful to others. In contrast, **anti-social behaviour** is behaviour that harms or injures someone else. In the last Section we considered aggression. For the most part this is seen as an anti-social behaviour, though this is not always true. There are instances where an aggressive act may serve a pro-social purpose, i.e., acting in a manner that is helpful to others, such as when you push someone away because they were attacking another person. Helping behaviour, such as altruism, would appear to be pro-social but, as we will see, this isn't always true either.

Altruism

The clearest examples of pro-social behaviour involve what is generally called altruism. **Altruism** is voluntary helping behaviour that is costly to the person who is altruistic. It is based on a desire to help someone else rather than on any possible rewards. It has often been assumed that altruism depends on empathy. **Empathy** is the ability to share the emotions of another person, and to understand that person's point of view.

The empathy–altruism hypothesis

Eisenberg, Lennon, and Roth (1983) put forward a theory on moral development in children (see Chapter 5, Cognitive Development). This theory suggested that moral development was linked to the growth of empathy. Batson (e.g., 1987) argued that the same is true of adults. According to his **empathy–altruism hypothesis**, altruistic or unselfish behaviour is motivated mainly by empathy. He claimed that there are two main emotional reactions that occur when we observe someone in distress (adjectives describing each reaction are in brackets):

- *Empathic concern*: a sympathetic focus on the other person's distress, plus the motivation to reduce it (compassionate, soft-hearted, tender).
- *Personal distress*: concern with one's own discomfort, plus the motivation to reduce it (worried, disturbed, alarmed).

Evaluation

The basic assumption of the empathy–altruism hypothesis that altruistic behaviour depends on empathy is supported by most of the evidence obtained by Batson and his colleagues (see the Key Study on the next page). It is also supported by the developmental evidence discussed in Chapter 5, Cognitive Development. That evidence suggests that children's thinking and behaviour become more altruistic as their ability to empathise with others increases.

One limitation of the empathy–altruism hypothesis is that it is hard to be sure that people are offering help for altruistic reasons rather than simply to avoid the

KEY STUDY
Research evidence supporting the empathy–altruism hypothesis

Batson et al. (1981) devised a situation to test the empathy–altruism hypothesis. Female students observed a student called Elaine receiving a number of mild electric shocks. The students were then asked whether they would take the remaining shocks instead of Elaine. Some of the students were told that they were free to leave the experiment if they wanted. The other students were told that they would have to stay and watch Elaine being shocked if they refused to take the shocks themselves. All the students received a placebo drug that actually had no effects and were given misleading information about the drug, so that they would interpret their reactions to Elaine as either empathic concern or personal distress. It must be open to doubt whether all the participants believed this somewhat unlikely story!

Participants who could leave (interpreted reaction)		Participants who had to stay (interpreted reaction)	
Empathic concern	Personal distress	Empathic concern	Personal distress
Most offered to take shocks	Few offered to take shocks	Most offered to take shocks	Most offered to take shocks, motivated by social disapproval rather than desire to help

Most of the students in the two groups who felt empathic concern offered to take the remaining shocks regardless of whether they could easily escape from the situation. In contrast, most of those who felt personal distress offered to take the shocks when escape was difficult, but far fewer did so when escape was easy. Thus, those feeling personal distress were motivated to help by fear of social disapproval if they did not help, rather than by any real desire to help Elaine.

Batson et al. argued that the students feeling empathic concern helped Elaine for unselfish reasons. However, there are other possibilities. For example, they might have wanted to avoid self-criticism or social disapproval. In order to test this possibility, Batson et al. (1988) carried out a modified version of the 1981 study. Some of the female participants were told that they would only be allowed to help Elaine by taking some of her electric shocks if they did well in a difficult mathematical task. Someone who was motivated to help Elaine only to avoid social disapproval and self-criticism might well offer to help, but then deliberately perform poorly on the mathematical task.

This could be regarded as taking the easy way out. Many of those feeling personal distress did just that, and performed at a low level on the mathematical task. However, most of the students feeling empathic concern volunteered to help Elaine and did very well on the mathematical task. Their refusal to take the easy way out suggests that their desire to help was genuine, i.e., they were motivated by empathy–altruism.

Key study evaluation

Batson et al.'s study was intended to test the empathy–altruism hypothesis. However, mechanisms other than empathy may have played a part, including fear of social disapproval, or even the demand characteristics of the experimental situation. The students might easily have guessed that the experimenter was interested in their level of care for another person and behaved in what they thought was the expected or socially acceptable way.

It might also be interesting to speculate on the reasons why psychologists so often use the inflicting of electric shocks in their experiments, even if the shocks are only simulated. Mild shocks are often used in animal experiments, but their use in human experiments often seems contrived and artificial. How often do people find themselves in such a situation in real life?

Discussion points
1. Does this study seem to provide a good test of the empathy–altruism hypothesis?
2. Do you think that someone needs to experience empathy in order to behave altruistically?

In real life as opposed to experimental situations, altruistic behaviour may involve many years of commitment rather than a brief impulse.

disapproval of others, to avoid the feelings of guilt associated with failing to help, or to experience pleasure when the other person has received help. However, Batson and Oleson (1991, p.80) argued that the emerging pattern of findings means that "we must radically revise our views about human nature and the human capacity for caring". That may be overstating matters. As Batson et al. (1983) pointed out, genuine concern for others is often "a fragile flower, easily crushed by egotistic [self-centred] concerns". They provided some evidence for this assertion. Of participants feeling empathic concern, 86% were willing to take Elaine's place when she received mild shocks. However, this figure was reduced dramatically to only 14% when Elaine received painful shocks.

The experimental evidence relating to the empathy–altruism hypothesis is rather limited in some ways. The focus has been on short-term altruistic behaviour having only a modest effect on the participants' lives. In real life, however, altruistic behaviour can involve providing almost non-stop care for an ageing relative for several or many years. More generally, most of the research seems to lack external or ecological validity, meaning that it is doubtful whether the laboratory findings can be generalised to altruism in everyday life. In addition, the research tends to lack mundane realism, in that the situations used don't resemble natural ones.

Empathic joy hypothesis

Smith, Keating, and Stotland (1989) argued that the empathy–altruism hypothesis was inadequate. They put forward an **empathic joy hypothesis**, according to which empathic concern leads people to help a needy person, because this allows them to share in that person's joy at receiving successful help. It is predicted by this hypothesis that those high in empathic concern should be motivated to learn about their successful acts of helping more than about their unsuccessful ones. However, Batson et al. (1991) found that this was not the case. Indeed, those *low* in empathic concern were most interested in hearing about their successful altruistic behaviour. This and other evidence indicates that the empathy–altruism hypothesis is more accurate than the empathic joy hypothesis.

Evolutionary explanation

Evolutionary psychology is an approach to explaining social behaviour in terms of evolutionary processes. As we will see, the evolutionary approach provides an explanation of altruism that is radically different from the one offered by the empathy–altruism hypothesis. However, bear in mind that it is entirely

 Why might the behaviour of carers not be altruistic?

KEY TERMS

Empathic joy hypothesis: the notion that when people help a needy person they share that person's joy at being helped.

Evolutionary psychology: an approach that explains behaviour in terms of its function and adaptiveness (i.e., the extent to which a behaviour enhances survival and reproduction of the individual's genes).

Charities, aid agencies, and televised appeals rely on empathic concern from the public in order to raise funds.

possible that there is some validity to both theoretical approaches.

The theory of evolution proposes that any behaviour promoting the survival of an individual will be retained in future generations because it is naturally selected (the principle of **natural selection**). Individuals who don't possess such adaptive behaviours are likely to die and/or be unsuccessful at reproduction. However, this principle alone cannot explain altruism because an individual who behaves altruistically may die (for example, if they risk their life to help another), thus restricting the individual's reproductive success. Yet there are many examples of altruism in the animal world, such as the partridge that draws a predator away from its nest by pretending it has a broken wing and walking off in another direction. Batson (1983) tells the story of a red setter and young girl sitting in the back seat of a car when the car burst into flames. The dog jumped out of the car but jumped back in to save the child when he realised she was still in there. This is called the **paradox of altruism**. How can we account for this social behaviour when the theory of evolution would suggest that it would not be naturally selected?

Kin selection

It is possible to explain this paradox if one uses the **gene** rather than the individual as the basic unit of evolution, which is what is done by sociobiologists. Sociobiologists such as Maynard Smith (1964) used the concept of **kin selection** to describe the idea that a behaviour is adaptive if it promotes the survival of the **gene pool** to which the individual belongs rather than the individual alone. So, if an act of altruism assists the survival and reproduction of kin, then this behaviour is naturally selected.

The closer the kin, the more likely one should be to help. It should also be the case that one would choose to behave in an altruistic way to an individual who has greater reproductive potential. Burnstein, Crandall, and Kitayama (1994) tested these expectations by asking people to say how they would behave in

? Could socio-biological explanations account for cultural differences in helping behaviour?

KEY TERMS

Natural selection: the process by which certain traits (and the associated genes) are perpetuated because of the advantage they confer in terms of survival and increased reproduction.

Paradox of altruism: the paradox that altruistic behaviour has been naturally selected (as evidenced by the fact that it exists) despite the fact that such behaviour would appear to reduce the altruist's own survival and reproduction.

Gene: a unit of inheritance that forms part of a chromosome. Some characteristics are determined by one gene, whereas for others many genes are involved.

Kin selection: the view that the process of natural selection functions at the level of an individual's genes and thus any behaviour that promotes the survival and reproduction of all "kin" (genetic relatives) will also be selected.

Gene pool: the whole stock of different genes in a breeding population of any species.

hypothetical life-or-death situations (e.g., saving someone from a house on fire). People reported that they would be much more likely to help relatives than non-relatives, and to aid close kin over distant kin, the young over the old, the healthy over the sick, the wealthy over the poor, and the pre-menopausal woman over the post-menopausal woman. However, when it was a matter of an everyday favour, they gave less weight to kinship and opted to help either the very young or the very old over those of intermediate age, the sick over the healthy, and the poor over the wealthy. This suggests that altruism is driven by different principles from ordinary helpfulness.

Reciprocal altruism

It is also possible to explain altruism in evolutionary terms using the concept of "payback". One animal performs a favour for another with the presumption that, at a later date, this favour will be returned. Trivers (1971) used the term **delayed reciprocal altruism** to refer to this state of affairs. The most obvious problem with delayed reciprocal altruism (or reciprocity as it is also known) is the possibility of cheating. If someone behaves altruistically towards you, but you then refuse to help that person, then you have gained overall but they have lost.

Biological versus psychological altruism

It is possible that biological explanations can account for some aspects of human behaviour with regard to altruism, and this is referred to as biological altruism. However, in humans, altruistic behaviour may be more than this. People *think* about their actions. Their behaviour is influenced by personal choice, empathy, morals, and social norms. The behaviour of the bystander who drowned while saving passengers from an aircrash in the Potomac River illustrates all of these characteristics (see the box to the right).

In non-human animals, it is likely that altruistic behaviour is explained in terms of sociobiology, though this doesn't entirely explain the case of the red setter mentioned earlier. This could be an example of reciprocal altruism or mistaken kin identity (the red setter regards the child as kin because of being reared together). It is also possible that non-human animals are capable of empathy.

> **Rescue in the Potomac River**
>
> Washington, January 14, 1982. There was a hero, name unknown, in today's plane crash into the iced-over waters of the Potomac River just after the jet took off from Washington airport.
>
> To the rescuers in the helicopter, he was only a head in the water, a balding man, perhaps in his mid-50s, with a heavy moustache. He was clinging with five others to the tail section of the Air Florida 737, the only part of the plane still afloat. The helicopter crew threw down a yellow ring life preserver attached to a rope. "He could have gone on the first trip", said the helicopter pilot. "We threw the ring to him first, but he passed it to somebody else", a man who was bleeding badly from a head injury. "We went back five times, and each time he kept passing the ring to somebody else, including three ladies who were hanging onto the tail section."
>
> Finally, after making several trips and plucking everyone else from the water, the helicopter returned to pick up the man who had put the others first. "We flew back out to get him but he was gone."
>
> Adapted from *New York Times*, 14 January 1982, p.6.

Bystander Behaviour

One of the haunting images of our time is that of someone being attacked violently in the middle of a city, with no one being willing to help them. This apparent apathy or reluctance to help was shown very clearly in the case of Kitty Genovese. She was stabbed to death in New York as she returned home from work at 3 o'clock one morning in March 1964. Thirty-nine witnesses watched her murder from their apartments, but none of them intervened. Indeed, only one person called the police. Even that action was only taken after he had asked

> **KEY TERM**
>
> **Delayed reciprocal altruism:** one individual performs a favour for another on the assumption that the favour will be returned later on (also known as reciprocity).

CASE STUDY: THE KITTY GENOVESE MURDER
(As reported in somewhat exaggerated terms by the *New York Times*)

At approximately 3.20 in the morning on 13 March 1964, 28-year-old Kitty Genovese was returning to her home in a middle-class area of Queens, New York, from her job as a bar manager. She parked her car and started to walk to her second-floor apartment some 30 metres away. She got as far as a streetlight, when a man who was later identified as Winston Mosely grabbed her. She screamed. Lights went on in the nearby apartment building. Kitty yelled, "Oh my God, he stabbed me! Please help me!" A window opened in the apartment building and a man's voice shouted, "Let that girl alone!" Mosely looked up, shrugged, and walked off down the street. As Kitty Genovese struggled to get to her feet, the lights went off in the apartments. The attacker came back some minutes later and renewed the assault by stabbing her again. She again cried out, "I'm dying! I'm dying!" Once again the lights came on and windows opened in many of the nearby apartments. The assailant again left, got into his car and drove away. Kitty staggered to her feet as a city bus drove by. It was now 3.35 am. Mosely returned and found his victim in a doorway at the foot of the stairs. He then raped her and stabbed her for a third time—this time fatally. It was 3.50 when the police received the first call. They responded quickly and were at the scene within two minutes, but Kitty Genovese was already dead.

The only person to call the police, a neighbour of Ms Genovese, revealed that he had phoned only after much thought and after making a call to a friend to ask advice. He said, "I didn't want to get involved." Later it emerged that there were 38 other witnesses to the events over the half-hour period. Many of Kitty's neighbours heard her screams and watched from the windows, but no one came to her aid. The story shocked America and made front-page news across the country. The question people asked was why no one had offered any help, or even called the police earlier when it might have helped. Urban and moral decay, apathy, and indifference were some of the many explanations offered. Two social psychologists, Bibb Latané and John Darley, were unsatisfied with these explanations and began a series of research studies to identify the situational factors that influence whether or not people come to the aid of others. They concluded that an individual is less likely to provide assistance the greater the number of other bystanders present.

? Have you ever been in the situation where someone was in trouble and you did nothing? How did you feel? Can you explain why you did not help?

? How would you explain why none of the bystanders helped Kitty Genovese?

advice from a friend in another part of the city. This case is described in greater detail above.

The police asked the witnesses why they had done nothing to help Kitty Genovese. According to a report in the *New York Times*:

The police said most persons had told them they had been afraid to call, but had given meaningless answers when asked what they had feared. "We can understand the reticence of people to become involved in an area of violence", Lieutenant Jacobs said, "but when they are in their homes, near phones, why should they be afraid to call the police"?

Diffusion of responsibility

John Darley and Bibb Latané (1968) were interested in the Kitty Genovese case, and in the whole issue of bystander intervention. They tried to work out why Kitty Genovese was not helped by any of the numerous witnesses who saw her being attacked. According to them, a victim may be in a more fortunate position when there is just one bystander rather than several. In such a situation, responsibility for helping the victim falls firmly on to one person rather than being spread among many. In other words, the witness or bystander has a sense of personal responsibility. If there are many observers of a crime or other incident, there is a **diffusion of responsibility**, in which each person bears only a small portion of the blame for not helping. As a result, there is less feeling of personal responsibility. Darley and Latané demonstrated this in a series of studies that are described in the Key Study on the next page.

A related way of considering what is involved here is to think in terms of social norms or culturally determined expectations of behaviour. One of the key norms in many societies is the **norm of social responsibility**: we should help those who need help. Darley and Latané argued that the norm of social responsibility is strongly activated when only one person observes the fate of

KEY TERMS

Diffusion of responsibility: if there are many observers of an incident, each person feels they bear only a small portion of the blame for not helping.
Norm of social responsibility: the cultural expectation that help should be given to those in need of help.

KEY STUDY
Demonstrating the diffusion of responsibility

Darley and Latané (1968) tested their ideas in various studies. The participants were placed in separate rooms, and told to put on headphones. They were asked to discuss their personal problems, speaking into a microphone and hearing the contributions of others to the discussion over their headphones. They were led to think that there were one, two, three, or six people involved in the discussion. In fact, however, all of the apparent contributions by other participants were tape recordings.

Each participant heard that one of the other people in the discussion was prone to seizures, especially when studying hard or taking examinations. Later on, they heard him say, "I-er-I— uh-I've got one of these-er-seizure-er-er-things coming on and-and-and I could really-er-use some help so if somebody would-er-er-help-er-er-help-er-uh-uh-uh [choking sounds] . . . I'm gonna die-er-er-I'm . . . gonna die-er-help-er-er-seizure-er . . . [choking sounds, silence]."

Of those who thought they were the only person to know that someone was having an epileptic fit, 100% left the room and reported the emergency. However, only 62% of participants responded if they thought that there were five other bystanders who knew about it. Furthermore, those participants who thought they were the only bystander responded much more quickly than did those who thought there were five bystanders: 50% of them responded within 45 seconds of the onset of the fit, whereas none of those who believed there were five other bystanders did so.

Two other interesting findings emerged from the research of Darley and Latané. First, the participants who believed that there were five other bystanders denied that this had had any effect on their behaviour. This suggests that people are not fully aware of the factors determining whether or not they behave in a pro-social or helpful way. Second, those participants who failed to report the emergency were not apathetic or uncaring. Most of them had trembling hands and sweating palms. Indeed, they seemed more emotionally aroused than the participants who did report the emergency.

Discussion points
1. Why do you think the findings of Darley and Latané have had so much influence on subsequent research?
2. Should we be concerned about the artificiality of the situation used by Darley and Latané?

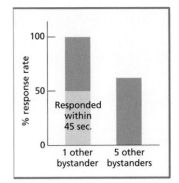

a victim. However, it is much less likely to influence behaviour when there are several bystanders.

In the years since the publication of Darley and Latané's (1968) groundbreaking research, several researchers have identified factors other than diffusion of responsibility which determine whether or not a victim will be helped. We will consider some of these factors, and then proceed to discuss some theories of bystander intervention.

Interpreting the situation
Ambiguous situations

In real life, many emergencies have an ambiguous quality about them. For example, someone who collapses in the street may have had a heart attack, or they may simply have had too much to drink. Not surprisingly, the chances of a bystander lending assistance to a victim are much greater if the situation is interpreted as a genuine emergency. Brickman et al. (1982) carried out a study in which the participants heard a bookcase falling on another participant, followed by a scream. When someone else interpreted the situation as an emergency, the participant offered help more quickly than when the other person said there was nothing to worry about.

Perceived relationships

In many incidents, the perceived relationship between those directly involved can have a major influence on the bystanders' behaviour. Shotland and Straw (1976) arranged for a man and a woman to stage a fight close to onlookers. In one condition, the woman screamed, "I don't know you". In a second condition, she screamed, "I don't know why I ever married you". When the onlookers thought the fight involved strangers, 65% of them intervened, against only 19% when they thought it involved a married couple. This suggests that bystanders are reluctant to become involved in the personal lives of strangers.

It is likely that one of the reasons why none of the bystanders went to the assistance of Kitty Genovese was because they assumed that there was a close relationship between her and her male attacker. Indeed, a housewife who was among the bystanders said, "We thought it was a lovers' quarrel".

Victim characteristics

Most bystanders are influenced by the victim's characteristics. This was shown by Piliavin, Rodin, and Piliavin (1969). They staged incidents in the New York subway, with a male victim staggering forwards and collapsing on the floor. He either carried a black cane and seemed sober, or he smelled of alcohol and carried a bottle of alcohol. Bystanders were much less likely to help when the victim was "drunk" than when he was "ill". Drunks are regarded as responsible for their own plight, and it could be unpleasant to help a smelly drunk who might vomit or become abusive.

Bystander characteristics: Individual differences

What characteristics of bystanders determine the likelihood that they will help a victim?

Bystanders who have some relevant skill to offer are more likely to get involved than those who don't know what to do.

Skills and expertise

Huston et al. (1981) argued that bystanders who have relevant skills or expertise are most likely to offer help to a victim. For example, suppose that a passenger on a plane collapses suddenly, and one of the stewardesses asks for help. It is reasonable to assume that a doctor is more likely to offer his or her assistance than someone lacking any medical skills. Huston et al. studied the characteristics of bystanders who helped out in dangerous emergencies. There was a strong tendency for helpers to have training in relevant skills such as life-saving, first aid, or self-defence.

Gender differences

Eagly and Crowley (1986) reviewed the literature on gender differences in helping behaviour. They found that men are more likely than women to help when the situation involves some danger, or when there is an audience. Men are more likely to help women than other men, especially when the women are attractive. In contrast, women are equally likely to help men and women.

Personality factors

It might be expected that bystanders with certain personality characteristics (e.g., sociable, warm-hearted, conscientious) would be more likely to help a victim than those with other personality characteristics (e.g., unsociable, reserved, expedient). There is evidence indicating that those who offer help tend to be other-oriented rather than self-oriented (Dovidio, Piliavin, & Clark, 1991). However, the effects of personality are typically rather small, especially when there is obviously an emergency.

Perceived similarity

Bystanders are usually most likely to help a victim if he or she is perceived as similar to themselves. However, there are some exceptions. Gaertner and Dovidio (1977) used a situation in which white participants heard a victim in the next room apparently being struck by a stack of falling chairs. When it was not clear whether or not there was an emergency (there were no screams from the victim), the white participants helped a white victim faster than a black one. The findings were different when the victim screamed, and so there was clearly an emergency. In that case, a black victim was helped as rapidly as a white victim.

What do these findings mean? They suggest that perceived similarity between the bystander and the victim often influences helping behaviour. However, the effects of perceived similarity can be wiped out by the demands of the situation if it is clear that there really is an emergency.

> **?** There is also evidence that people who have heard of research such as Gaertner and Davidio's study are more likely to intervene and help.

Town vs. country

It is often claimed that people living in large cities are less friendly and helpful than those living in small towns in rural areas. Evidence supporting this was reported by Amato (1983) in a study based on 55 Australian cities and towns. He found that almost 60% of individuals living in villages of under 1000 people were willing to help someone who had hurt a leg and collapsed onto the footpath compared to only about 10% of individuals living in large cities of over one million people.

Other activities

Bystanders don't only take account of the emergency itself. They also take into account the activity they were involved in when they came upon the emergency. Batson et al. (1978) sent their participants from one building to another to perform a task. On the way, they went past a male student who was slumped on the stairs coughing and groaning. Some of the participants had been told that it was important for them to help the experimenter by performing the task, and that they were to hurry. Only 10% of these participants stopped to help the student. However, if the participants were told that helping the experimenter was not very important, and that there was no hurry, then 80% of them helped the student.

> **?** Do you consider there are any ethical problems with studies like that of Batson et al.? Did the participants give their informed consent to take part?

Models of bystander behaviour

How can we make theoretical sense of the various findings on bystander intervention?

The decision model

? At any stage in Latané and Darley's model, why might a person answer "no"?

Latané and Darley (1970) put forward a **decision model**. According to this model, bystanders who lend assistance to a victim do so after working their way through a five-step sequence of decisions, producing a "yes" answer at each step. The complete decision-making sequence is as follows:

- Step 1: Is something the matter?
- Step 2: Is the event or incident interpreted as one in which assistance is needed?
- Step 3: Should the bystander accept personal responsibility?
- Step 4: What kind of help should be provided by the bystander?
- Step 5: Should the help worked out at step 4 be carried out?

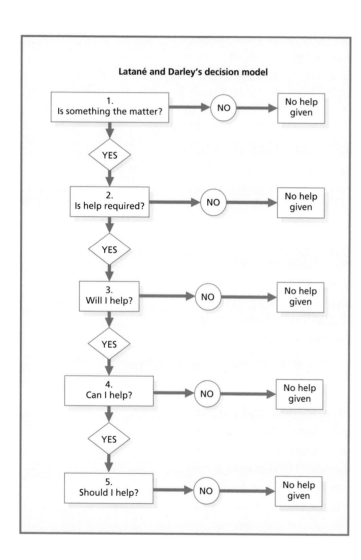

Latané and Darley's decision model

Evaluation

The decision model has two strengths. First, it assumes that there are several different reasons why bystanders do not lend assistance. The experimental evidence that we have discussed provides substantial support for that assumption. Second, the decision model gives a plausible explanation of why it is that bystanders so often fail to help a victim. If bystanders produce a "no" answer at any point in the decision sequence, then help will not be forthcoming.

On the negative side, the model doesn't provide a detailed account of the processes involved in decision making. For example, it seems reasonable to assume that bystanders who interpret the situation as an emergency and who also accept personal responsibility would nearly always lend assistance to the unfortunate victim. We need to know more about the processes involved when "yes" decisions at steps 1, 2, and 3 are followed by a "no" decision at steps 4 or 5.

KEY TERM

Decision model: Latané and Darley's model for predicting when an individual will help in an emergency situation, based on a series of decisions to be taken.

Another limitation of the model is that it de-emphasises the influence of emotional factors on the bystanders' behaviour. Bystanders who are anxious or terrified are unlikely to work carefully through the five decision-making stages contained in the decision model. The model assumes a rather logical sequence of thought. For example, consider the terrorist attacks on London on 7 July 2005. Many bystanders offered almost instant help to those wounded in the attacks, which suggests they didn't work through a series of questions before doing anything.

Arousal/cost–reward model

Piliavin et al. (1981) put forward an **arousal/cost–reward model**. According to this model, there are five steps that bystanders go through before deciding whether or not to assist a victim:

1. Becoming aware of someone's need for help; this depends on attention.
2. Experience of arousal.
3. Interpreting cues and labelling their state of arousal.
4. Working out the rewards and costs associated with different actions.
5. Making a decision and acting on it.

Would you stop to find out what the problem is?

The fourth step is perhaps the most important, and deserves more detailed consideration. Some of the major rewards and costs involved in helping and not helping are as follows:

- Costs of helping: physical harm; delay in carrying out other activities.
- Costs of not helping: ignoring personal responsibility; guilt; criticism from others; ignoring perceived similarity.
- Rewards of helping: praise from victim; satisfaction from having been useful if relevant skills are possessed.
- Rewards of not helping: able to continue with other activities as normal.

Evaluation

The arousal/cost–reward model provides a more complete account than the decision model of the processes involved in determining whether to provide help. As we saw in our review of the literature, bystanders often seem to take account of the potential rewards and costs associated with helping and not helping. It is also probably true that bystanders are generally more likely to think about the possibility of helping when they experience a state of arousal than when they do not.

On the negative side, it is implied by the arousal/cost–reward model that bystanders spend some time considering all of the elements in the situation and the other demands on their time before deciding what to do. In fact, people faced by a sudden emergency often respond impulsively and with very little thought. For example, this would appear to be the case with most of the bystanders who rapidly came to the assistance of those wounded in the London terrorist attacks on 7 July 2005. More generally, it is surely the case that bystanders often help those in need of assistance without engaging in a rational process of decision making.

Even if bystanders do consider the relevant rewards and costs, it is perhaps unlikely that they consider *all* of them. Another problem with the model is that it is not always the case that a bystander needs to experience arousal before helping in an emergency. Someone with much experience of similar emergencies (such as a doctor responding to someone having a heart attack) may respond efficiently without becoming aroused.

> **KEY TERM**
>
> **Arousal/cost–reward model:** Piliavin et al.'s view that whether a bystander helps a victim depends on his or her level of arousal, and on the rewards and costs of different possible actions.

Encouraging altruism
Observational learning

How can people be made more altruistic? According to social learning theory, observational learning from models could be an effective technique. Midlarsky and Bryan (1972) tested this notion in a study involving children observing a model giving valuable tokens to a charity. Ten days later, these children were more likely than other children to donate sweets to the same charity.

The importance of observational learning or modelling in everyday life was shown by Rosenhan (1970). He studied White Americans who had worked wholeheartedly in an altruistic way for the civil rights movement during the 1960s. Most of their parents had set them a good example by behaving in a consistently altruistic way, thus providing altruistic models for their children. Rosenhan also studied White Americans who had been less involved in the civil rights movement. Most of their parents had argued in favour of altruism, but were less likely to have *behaved* in an altruistic way. Thus, most of these parents failed to provide good models of altruistic behaviour. This may explain why their children had only been partly involved in the civil rights movement.

> **?** What other factors, apart from modelling, may be the cause of these children's low involvement in the civil rights movement?

Rewards

Another way of trying to increase altruism is by offering rewards for helping. This may be effective with young children who have not yet developed much empathic concern for others. However, rewards or reinforcement can have the opposite effect to that intended with older children. Fabes et al. (1989) promised toys to some children if they sorted coloured paper squares for children who were sick in hospital. Other children were not offered any reward for carrying out the same task. After a while, all of the children were told that they could continue to sort the coloured squares, but that they would not receive any reward for doing so. The children who had been rewarded were less likely to continue to be helpful than those who had not been rewarded. The findings were strongest among those children whose mothers believed in using rewards to make their children behave well.

Why are rewards so ineffective in producing altruistic behaviour? The main reason is that those who are rewarded for behaving helpfully are motivated by the thought of the reward rather than by the desire to help other people. As a result, removal of the rewards often causes the helpful behaviour to stop.

> **?** At what age, according to Eisenberg et al. (1983), would rewards be most effective? See page 232.

Social norms

The ways in which individuals behave are influenced greatly by social norms, which are the expected forms of behaviour within any given society. In order to encourage people to behave more altruistically, it may be necessary to alter some of the social norms within Western cultures. Piliavin et al. (1981, p. 254) argued that helping behaviour could be increased by means of re-training:

> *In our society, we are trained from an early age to see the problems of others as "none of our business" ... This tendency saves all of us a great deal of emotional distress, but it contributes ... to the increasing alienation and self-absorption of which we all are currently being accused. We may need more training as busybodies; respect for privacy prevents*

empathic arousal, and directs one's attention to the costs of intervention, specifically the cost of being thought intrusive.

One way to alter social norms is through media intervention, the topic of the next Section.

	Situation Rating	Costs	Rewards
■ **Activity:** Complete a table such as this one and rate each situation in order of likelihood of helping. Devise your own table or use this one to assess the public's views on helping. Compare their responses with Piliavin et al.'s reasons for helping or not helping. Do your results show any sex or age-group differences?	A pregnant woman drops her shopping bag		
	A blind person requests help to cross the road		
	There is a car crash on the motorway		
	A hitch-hiker is thumbing a lift on a lonely road		

Cultural differences in pro-social behaviour

Most of the research we have discussed was carried out in the United States. It is dangerous to assume that what is true in one culture is true in other cultures, and this danger is perhaps especially great with respect to altruism. For example, the reluctance of bystanders to help victims may be much greater in the United States and western Europe (in which most of the studies were conducted) than in other parts of the world. The dominant approach to life in the United States is based on self-interest rather than on any great altruistic concern for others. Darley (1991) described this approach as follows:

> *In the United States and perhaps in all advanced capitalistic societies, it is generally accepted that the true and basic motive for human action is self-interest. It is the primary motivation.*

Evidence that this selfish approach is not dominant in all cultures was reported by Whiting and Whiting (1975). They considered the behaviour of young children between the ages of 3 and 10 in six cultures (United States; India; Okinawa, an island in southwest Japan; Philippines; Mexico; and Kenya). At one extreme, Whiting and Whiting found that 100% of young children in Kenya were high in altruism. At the other extreme, only 8% of young children in the United States were altruistic. The other cultures were in between the two extremes.

EXAM HINT

Students often struggle with the AO2 in this area so consider these sources of evaluation: Assess the extent of cultural differences; how do the differences limit the generalisability of the research? Use the weaknesses of cross-cultural research (restricted samples, ethnocentrism, and so imposed etics) to evaluate the validity of research. Culture is a naturally occurring independent variable, which limits conclusions about cause and effect, and also other variables may be involved; so what other factors could explain differences in pro-social behaviour besides culture?

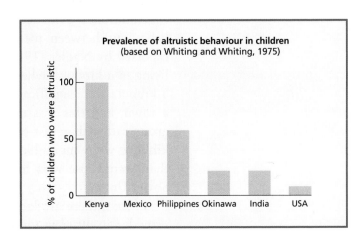

Prevalence of altruistic behaviour in children (based on Whiting and Whiting, 1975)

Eisenberg and Mussen (1989) reviewed several studies on cross-cultural differences in altruism. They concluded that there are large differences from one culture to another. In their own words:

Most children reared in Mexican villages, Hopi children on reservations in the Southwest [of America], and youngsters on Israeli kibbutzim are more considerate, kind, and cooperative than their "typical" middle-class American counterparts.

Individualism and collectivism

What do these findings mean? Several factors are involved. First, industrialised societies such as those in most parts of the United States and Okinawa place much emphasis on competition and personal success. This emphasis is likely to reduce co-operation and altruism. Second, the family structure in non-industrialised cultures such as those of Kenya, Mexico, and the Hopi is quite different from that in industrialised cultures. Children in non-industrialised societies are often given major family responsibilities (e.g., caring for young children), and these responsibilities help to develop altruistic behaviour. Third, it is possible that members of non-industrialised and collectivistic societies expect to receive more co-operation and help from others, in which case their behaviour may be less altruistic than it looks (Fijneman, Willemsen, & Poortinga, 1996).

Miller (1994) and Miller and Bersoff (1994) had made important contributions to our understanding of cultural differences in pro-social behaviour. Miller (1994) distinguished between individually oriented and duty-based interpersonal moral codes. According to the individually oriented moral code found in individualistic cultures (e.g., America, western Europe), help is provided to those whom we like and have a personal involvement with. In contrast, according to the duty-based moral code found in collectivistic cultures (e.g., many countries in the Far East), help is provided on the basis of fulfilling one's duty and obligations rather than on the basis of personal liking.

Miller and Bersoff (1998) reported evidence supporting the above distinction. They found that European Americans tended to regard their interpersonal responsibilities to family and friends as depending largely on their personal feelings. In contrast, Hindu Indians tended to regard their interpersonal responsibilities as depending on duty and thus uninfluenced by considerations of liking or personal involvement.

Additional evidence that there are important differences in pro-social behaviour between members of individualistic and collectivistic cultures was reported by Nadler (1986). Israelis living in towns were compared with Israelis living in a kibbutz (where the emphasis is on communal living). Those living on a kibbutz were significantly more liking to help others than were those living in a town, and this was especially true when the help provided would benefit a group rather than just one individual. Nadler (1993) found that those living in a kibbutz were more likely to seek help (presumably expecting to receive it) than were those who had recently arrived in Israel from America or from the Soviet Union.

In sum, there are large differences in the extent to which help is sought and provided in different cultures, with these differences depending in large measure

? Why might the behaviour of people in collectivist cultures be less altruistic than it first appears?

on whether any given culture is individualistic or collectivistic. It is important to note that the cross-cultural studies have generally focused on helping behaviour in social situations (e.g., within the family or other group). In contrast, most laboratory studies have much less of a social context, and participants in such studies may show little helping behaviour because they are typically interacting with strangers. These differences make it hard to compare findings in the laboratory and in the real world.

Individual variation

Apart from cultural differences, there are also important individual differences in altruistic behaviour *within* any given culture. Davis (1983) developed an Interpersonal Reactivity Index. This was designed to measure tendencies towards empathic concern (e.g., warmth, compassion) and towards personal distress (e.g., anxiety, uneasiness). He identified the characteristics of those who watched the annual Jerry Lewis muscular dystrophy telethon in the United States, and then gave their time, effort, and money to helping. As would be expected on Batson's empathy–altruism hypothesis, those who scored high on empathic concern were most likely to watch the programme and to help.

It is often assumed that women are more generally caring than men, and so we might expect that women would exhibit more helping behaviour. There is some evidence supporting this expectation (see Hogg & Vaughan, 2002), but the findings depend very much on the precise situation. For example, Przybyla (1985) considered the willingness of male and female students to help a member of the opposite sex who had knocked over a pile of papers. When the participants had just seen a sexually explicit videotape, far more males than females provided help (90% vs. 40%, respectively). However, there was no difference in helping behaviour between male and female students when no videotape had been seen previously.

SECTION SUMMARY
Altruism and Bystander Behaviour

❖ Altruism is an example of a pro-social behaviour. The altruist helps another at some cost to themselves and for no apparent reward.

What is altruism?

❖ According to the empathy–altruism hypothesis, altruistic or unselfish behaviour in adults is motivated mainly by empathy. When we observe someone in distress, we feel empathic concern and personal distress, and feel motivated to reduce it.

The empathy–altruism hypothesis

❖ In terms of the empathy–altruism hypothesis, it is hard to know whether people help others for altruistic reasons rather than to avoid feelings of guilt or the disapproval of others. In some situations egotistic concerns clearly govern behaviour. This model may apply to short-term altruistic acts, as in laboratory studies, but not be relevant to long-term altruism.

❖ The empathic joy model has been proposed as an alternative to the empathy–altruism hypothesis.

The empathic joy model

❖ However, it would predict that those high in empathic concern should be motivated to learn more about their successful acts of helping than about their unsuccessful ones. This is not supported by research.

Evolutionary explanation

❖ Evolutionary psychologists explain altruism as an adaptive behaviour. (If individuals are not altruistic, they are more likely to die, and/or be unsuccessful at reproduction.)

❖ According to Darwin's theory, altruism is a paradox but it can be explained by kin selection where the gene is seen as the unit of natural selection. Altruistic behaviour towards relatives promotes the survival of the gene pool and is naturally selected.

❖ People do say that they would be more likely to help relatives in emergency situations but would help non-relatives and people past their reproductive years when performing everyday favours. This suggests that altruism is driven by different principles from ordinary helpfulness.

❖ Reciprocal altruism can also be explained in evolutionary terms as long as no one cheats.

❖ Human behaviour may be understood in terms of psychological rather than biological altruism.

Bystander behaviour

❖ Bystander behaviour describes situations where an individual observes an emergency and does or doesn't offer to help.

❖ The classic real-life example was the case of Kitty Genovese.

❖ Factors that affect bystander behaviour:

— Diffusion of responsibility: Bystanders are often less likely to help a victim if there are many other bystanders, because there is a diffusion of responsibility. A lone person is more likely to respond to the norm of social responsibility.

— Ambiguous situations: It may be that individuals find it difficult to interpret the situation because it is ambiguous, or because it is not clear what relationship exists between the two people fighting, so may be less likely to help.

— Victim characteristics: Help may not be forthcoming if the victim appears to be responsible for their own plight (e.g., is drunk).

— Bystander characteristics: Help may also be less likely because of characteristics of the potential helper: some individuals have more skills and expertise, and people who offer help tend to be other-oriented rather than self-oriented. People prefer to help others who are similar, though this appears to be less true when there is a clear emergency. Help may be less forthcoming if you have another task on your mind.

The decision model

❖ The decision model can be used to co-ordinate all these factors:

— Is something the matter?
— Is assistance needed?
— Should I accept personal responsibility?
— What kind of help is needed?
— Should I do it?

❖ This model has the advantage of explaining the variety of different decisions that have to be made and why help is not always forthcoming.

❖ On the negative side not all the outcomes are clear and the model doesn't refer to the effects of emotion on decision making.

❖ The arousal/cost–reward model proposes a different five steps to helping behaviour:

The arousal/ cost–reward model

1. Becoming aware of the need for help
2. Arousal
3. Interpreting cues
4. Working out the rewards and costs associated with different actions
5. Making a decision and acting on it.

❖ Rewards and costs of helping and not helping are determined by various factors such as praise, physical harm, and public censure.

❖ This model has the advantage of including the importance of arousal in the decision to help, but it still suggests that people don't act impulsively. There are important cross-cultural and individual differences in helping behaviour.

❖ Observational learning: According to social learning theory, observational learning from models can encourage altruism. This can be seen in research by Rosenhan (1970).

Encouraging altruism

❖ Rewards: This may be effective with young children who have not yet developed much empathetic concern. However, it may have the opposite effect with older children as removal of the reward often causes the helpful behaviour to stop.

❖ Social norms: It may be necessary to alter some of the social norms, possibly through media intervention, to encourage altruism.

❖ In the United States, where much of the research was carried out, behaviour tends to be based on self-interest. Research shows that other cultures, such as in Kenya, are much more altruistic.

Cultural differences in pro-social behaviour

❖ Individualism: Industrialised societies place much emphasis on competition which can reduce altruism. Help is generally offered to those whom one likes in individualistic cultures.

❖ Collectivism: The family structure in non-industrialised cultures helps to develop altruistic behaviour, though in such societies mutual help means that behaviour may be less altruistic than it looks. More generally, helping is regarded as a duty within collectivistic cultures.

See also pages 51–60 of the revision guide.

❖ There are also individual differences within any culture, and people living in villages are more likely to help than those living in large cities.

Individual differences in altruistic behaviour

❖ It is often assumed that women are generally more caring than men.

MEDIA INFLUENCES ON PRO- AND ANTI-SOCIAL BEHAVIOUR

Explanations of Media Influence

When we use the term the "media" we are referring to any medium of communication: books, newspapers, magazines, music (pop songs) CDs, films,

DVDs or videotapes, and television. Most of the research in this area is focused on the last two kinds of media but we should remember that all other forms of media have strong influences. There was a fear, in Victorian times, that penny "novellas" would damage vulnerable minds. The medium has changed but the fear hasn't.

It is highly probable that massive exposure to television programmes (and especially violent ones) affects the beliefs of viewers in various ways, and may also affect their behaviour. In this Section we will consider the effects of the media on pro-social and anti-social behaviour, but first we might consider general explanations as to how the media exert an influence. It is very important to note that there are some similarities and overlaps among these explanations. In addition, most studies have not been designed in such a way that we can be confident that only one of the possible explanations is the most appropriate way of interpreting the findings.

Social learning theory

According to Bandura's social learning theory, one of the factors in media influence will be observational learning or modelling. We learn ways of behaving aggressively or altruistically from observing people on television behaving in this manner, and this behaviour may be imitated subsequently. This is especially likely if the behaviours are reinforced and/or the observer identifies with the characters on television, either because they are similar in terms of gender or age, or because they are admired. This might lead us to question the extent to which we may imitate cartoon characters as we are unlikely to identify with them.

The main prediction from social learning theory is that the behaviour produced by viewers of television will be rather similar to the behaviour they have observed. For example, if a character in a television programme stares angrily when frustrated, we would expect viewers to copy this angry stare rather than exhibiting other kinds of aggressive behaviour.

Disinhibition effect

The effect of cartoons may be explained in terms of disinhibition. Much of the time we exert conscious control over our behaviour, and feel we should inhibit behaviours that are seen to be anti-social. High levels of violence in the media promote the view that such behaviour is common and acceptable, and this reduces our normal inhibitions about behaving in this way. For example, you watch a scene that shows a son hitting his father when the father says the son must stay home, and this decreases your normal inhibitions about behaving in such a way.

This applies generally to anti-social rather than pro-social behaviour, but we might imagine that where people normally feel inhibited about helping in an emergency situation, portrayal of such behaviour in a television programme might disinhibit us in future. For example, normally we would feel inhibited about stepping in between two lovers having a quarrel, but a programme on television that showed how this may have been helpful might reduce our normal inhibitions, i.e., it would disinhibit us.

On the basis of this approach, we would expect disinhibition to increase as children watch an increasing number of violent programmes and this should lead to increased aggression. The more such programmes are watched, the more the violent behaviour shown in them is likely to seem appropriate.

EXAM HINT
The debate about anti-social behaviour is often misperceived as more important but make sure you are equally ready for either a pro-social or an anti-social question, as you could be asked to consider either.

Desensitisation

Desensitisation is a different concept from disinhibition. Here it is suggested that violent acts reduce our responsiveness. As Franzoi (1996) pointed out we gradually become less responsive to, and emotionally concerned by, acts of violence, because we have seen so many on television. In a study by Thomas et al. (1977), two groups of children watched a videotape of young children behaving aggressively. Their physiological reactions to this videotape were recorded. Those children who had seen a television programme containing much violence just before watching the videotape became less aroused physiologically than did those who had just watched a programme containing no violence. Such reduced responsiveness may be associated with an increased acceptance of violent behaviour.

On the basis of this approach (as with the disinhibition effect), we would expect that increased viewing of violent programmes should increase viewers' tendency to behave aggressively. However, what causes this to happen is different, in that it is assumed here that viewers become less sensitive to (and so less concerned about) violence when we watch it repeatedly.

> **?** How might you use the concept of desensitisation to explain an increase or decrease in pro-social behaviour?

Cognitive priming

Another reason why media violence may play a part in producing aggressive behaviour is because of **cognitive priming**. The basic idea is that the aggressive cues presented in violent television programmes lead to aggressive thoughts and feelings. When college students were asked to write down their thoughts while watching violent films (e.g., *The French Connection*), they reported numerous aggressive thoughts, increased anger, and a high level of physiological arousal.

Some of the most convincing evidence for the importance of cognitive priming was reported by Josephson (1987). Some Canadian boys were shown a television programme involving violence in the form of a gun battle, in which the snipers communicated with each other by means of walkie-talkies. The other boys watched a nonviolent programme about a motocross team. After they had watched the television programme, all of the boys played floor hockey. Before the game started, the referee gave the boys instructions either by walkie-talkie or in a tape recording. The boys who watched the violent programme and received instructions by walkie-talkie were more aggressive during the hockey game than were the boys who had watched the same programme but received instructions by tape recording. Thus, the walkie-talkie acted as a cognitive prime or cue to aggression.

The same principle could be applied to pro-social behaviour. However, relatively little research on the effects of television on either pro-social or anti-social behaviour has focused specifically on cognitive priming.

Stereotypes

Another means by which the media influence our behaviour is through the use of **stereotypes**. All media need to communicate a great deal of information in a relatively short time, so they use standard cultural and sub-cultural stereotypes such as foreigners given roles of the "enemy" (using foreign sounding names and/or accents). Men are also more often portrayed as criminals or aggressors. There are positive stereotypes as well, such as overweight people depicted as "jolly", and women portrayed as caring. Mulac, Bradac, and Mann (1985)

> **KEY TERMS**
>
> **Desensitisation:** the process of becoming less sensitive to stimuli the more they are encountered.
> **Cognitive priming:** the idea that cues, e.g., violent TV programmes, lead to thoughts and feelings that produce aggression.
> **Stereotypes:** social perception of an individual in terms of readily available features, such as skin colour or gender, rather than their actual personal attributes.

analysed the content of a number of children's programmes, and found strong gender stereotyping: males were more dynamic and female characters had greater socio-intellectual status and aesthetic quality.

These stereotypes can be anti-social in so far as they perpetuate prejudices. They may also be pro-social if they try to break down existing stereotypes.

Counter-stereotypes

One way to deal with the problem of stereotypes is to replace them with **counter-stereotypes**. Thus we see a successful lawyer in a wheelchair (for those who remember *Ironside*), women judges, and single fathers. It does appear that changing stereotypes has had positive consequences. For example, Greenfield (1984) found that *Sesame Street*'s use of ethnic and disabled minorities helped children from minority groups have a greater sense of cultural pride.

The influence of stereotypes on pro-social and anti-social behaviour can be assessed by comparing programmes using stereotypes with those using counter-stereotypes. As yet, there is relatively little such research.

Displacement effect

One of the more worrying aspects of television watching is that it replaces an individual's experience of the real world and creates norms that may be unrealistic. The **deviance amplification effect** is an example of this. Programmes that concentrate on disasters or extreme situations are much more popular than those dealing with rather humdrum aspects of life. News programmes, in particular, focus on unusual and often negative events. Gerbner and Gross (1976) found that people who watch a lot of television rate the outside world as being more dangerous and threatening than it actually is. It follows that violent programmes implying that violence is all around us should lead to more aggressive behaviour in viewers than programmes implying that violence is a rare event committed by a few dangerous individuals. Relatively little research has focused on this prediction.

Stimulation hypothesis

Finally we must remember that the media have enormous potential for education. This may be in terms of providing suitable models for children to imitate but may be most effective when individuals are placed in commonplace situations and methods of resolution are provided. So, for example, an individual is shown behaving anti-socially and the television character deals with the situation in a pro-social manner. One programme on American television, *Freestyle*, aimed to reduce sex-role stereotypes in children by presenting characters who try to engage in behaviours that are nonstereotypical, but the character finds this difficult. Eventually the difficulties are overcome and the character is rewarded for this (Johnston & Ettema, 1986).

However, there is a danger that children will imitate the anti-social behaviour and disregard the resolution! Lovelace and Huston (1982) claim that the most effective way of communicating a pro-social message may be to present the pro-social behaviour without any contrasting conflict or anti-social behaviour. However, the conflict resolution strategy can effectively convey pro-social behaviour if there are a variety of models showing pro-social actions, if the pro-social resolution is given sufficient time and attention, and if viewing conditions are

From the approximate total of 12,000 children under the age of 19 who died in Britain in 1996, only 2 were killed deliberately by strangers. Does this surprise you? How can the deviance amplification effect explain this?

KEY TERMS

Counterstereotypes: positive stereotypes, such as a lawyer in a wheelchair, used to counter the negative effects of stereotyping.

Deviance amplification effect: the creation of unrealistic norms, for example that the world is more dangerous than it really is.

adequate. A third technique, the presentation of unresolved conflict, can be useful in classroom or therapeutic situations where an adult can guide post-viewing discussion and activity, but it has unknown effects in unsupervised circumstances.

Media Influences on Pro-social Behaviour

The effects of television can be positive, and can lead to pro-social behaviour. In the same way that seeing people behaving violently on television can produce violent behaviour in viewers, so seeing people behaving in a caring way can increase caring behaviour.

Research evidence

Increased pro-social or helping behaviour as a result of watching television programmes has been found in children of various ages. Friedrich and Stein (1973) studied American preschool children, who watched episodes of a pro-social television programme called *Mister Rogers' Neighborhood*. These children remembered much of the pro-social information contained in the programmes, and they behaved in a more helpful and cooperative way than did children who watched other television programmes with neutral or aggressive content. They became even more helpful if they role-played pro-social events from the programmes.

> **?** Which past or present television programmes do you consider to be pro-social?

Sprafkin, Liebert, and Poulos (1975) studied 6-year-olds. Some of these children watched an episode of *Lassie*, in which a boy was seen to risk his life in order to rescue a puppy from a mine shaft. Other groups of children saw a different episode of *Lassie*, in which no helping was involved, or they saw an episode of a situation comedy called *The Brady Bunch*. After watching the programme, all of the children had the chance to help some distressed puppies. However, to do so they had to stop playing a game in which they might have won a big prize. The children who had watched the rescue from the mine shaft spent an average of over 90 seconds helping the puppies, compared with under 50 seconds by the children who had watched the other programmes. This shows that they imitated specific acts they had seen as is predicted by social learning theory.

Baran, Chase, and Courtright (1979) studied older children between the ages of 8 and 10. These children watched an episode of *The Waltons*, in which there was much emphasis on helping behaviour. These children were then found to behave in a more helpful or pro-social way than other children who had not seen the programme.

Rosenkoetter (1999) argued that pro-social television will only influence children's pro-social behaviour when they understand the moral message being communicated. Children who watched the most pro-social television programmes exhibited the most pro-social behaviour, and this was especially the case among children who had a good understanding of the moral lessons in those programmes.

Limitations
Duration of effect
Hearold (1986) reviewed more than 100 studies on the effects of pro-social television programmes on children's behaviour. She concluded that such programmes do generally make children behave in more helpful ways. Indeed, the beneficial effects of pro-social programmes on pro-social behaviour were on average

almost twice as great as the adverse effects of television violence on aggressive behaviour, perhaps because pro-social programmes are more likely to be specifically designed to produce certain effects on viewers. However, helping behaviour was usually assessed shortly after watching a pro-social television programme.

It is not altogether clear whether pro-social television programmes can have long-term effects on children's pro-social behaviour. In a study by Sagotsky, Wood-Schneider, and Konop (1981), children of 6 and 8 saw co-operative behaviour being modelled. Children of both ages showed an immediate increase in co-operative behaviour. However, only the 8-year-olds continued to show increased co-operation 7 weeks later. Wiegman, Kuttschreuter, and Baarda (1992) carried out a longitudinal study in Holland. They found that the viewing of pro-social behaviour on television didn't have any effect on subsequent pro-social behaviour.

Evidence that observational learning from a film can produce beneficial longer term changes in behaviour was reported by O'Connor (1980). Children who avoided playing with other children were shown a film of children playing happily together. Every child who saw the film played more with other children afterwards, and this effect seemed to last for a long time. Perhaps the effects were long-lasting because the children's initial experiences of playing with other children were so positive.

Situation-specificity

Lovelace and Huston (1982) suggested that learning from pro-social programmes is often situation-specific. In order to make the effects more generalised it is necessary to show ordinary people in a variety of everyday situations working together, helping each other, and being sensitive to each other. Dramatic story formats appear better suited than brief didactic scenes for influencing children's behaviour. Discussion with children after viewing and related play can enhance the effects of the TV programme.

Media Influences on Anti-social Behaviour

It has been calculated that the average 16-year-old in Western society has seen about 13,000 violent murders on television, and it seems reasonable to assume

INDEPENDENT STUDY IDEA: MEDIA INFLUENCES ON PRO-SOCIAL OR ON ANTI-SOCIAL BEHAVIOUR 1

One way of looking at media influences on the young is to do a content analysis of the amount of pro-social behaviour and the amount of anti-social behaviour on children's TV. You could do these separately or make a comparison between the two.

This needs some careful planning (but would be interesting and fun). Select what programmes you intend to use; do not bias the investigation by deliberating choosing one type of children's programme but it is unlikely you can use them all, so use a method that provides a representative sample aimed at a fairly wide age range.

You then need a fairly precise coding system. You must decide exactly what constitutes anti-social behaviour and then break these into categories (for example, one person hitting another, one cartoon character being hit by another, etc.). Do the same for pro-social behaviour. The easiest way to do this is carefully to watch some programmes before making any decisions.

You can then use the data in a variety of ways. Just a few suggestions are: a comparison of the content of different programmes, of groups of programmes aimed at different age groups, of the types of anti-social behaviour shown, of the types of pro-social behaviour, and of the amount of time spend in pro-social as compared to anti-social behaviour.

that this must have some effect on their behaviour. There is, indeed, a positive relationship between the amount of television violence children have seen and the aggressiveness of their behaviour. However, it is hard to interpret such correlational evidence. It may be that watching violent programmes causes aggressive behaviour. On the other hand, it may be that naturally aggressive children choose to watch more violent programmes than non-aggressive children.

Physical and verbal aggression

One of the more thorough studies of physical and verbal aggression was reported by Leyens et al. (1975). The participants were juvenile delinquents at a school in Belgium. They lived in four dormitories, two of which had high levels of aggressive behaviour and two of which had low levels. During a special Movie Week, boys in two of the dormitories (one high in aggression and the other low) watched only violent films, whereas boys in the other two dormitories watched only nonviolent films.

There was an increased level of physical aggression among the boys who saw the violent films, but not among those who saw the nonviolent films. The findings were more complex for verbal aggression. This increased among boys in the aggressive dormitory who saw violent films, but it actually decreased among boys from the non-aggressive dormitory who saw violent films. A final finding was that the effects of the violent films on aggression were much stronger shortly after watching them than they were later on. A limitation of this study is that the experimenters did not distinguish clearly between real and pretend aggression.

? Can you see any ethical issues in the Leyens et al. study?

CASE STUDY: MOVIE VIOLENCE

Since its release in 1994, the film *Natural Born Killers* has been surrounded by controversy and has sparked a long-standing debate about the effect of viewing intense violence on the human mind. The film follows the story of Mickey and Mallory Knox, a young couple who go on a killing spree across America, claiming 52 lives at random. Their flippant attitude towards the crimes they commit is portrayed as exciting and thrilling by the media and as a result their murderous behaviour catches the imagination of a generation of young impressionable people who idolise them. The notion of admiring cold-blooded killers may seem to be far-fetched, but alarming similarities have emerged between the reaction to the fictional Mickey and Mallory and other real-life killers. *Natural Born Killers* has been linked to at least a dozen murders, including two cases in France where the defence has blamed the film as providing inspiration for the crime.

In October 1998 the French courts sentenced Florence Rey to 20 years in prison for her part in a shoot-out that left five people dead. She was committing the crime with her boyfriend, Audry Maupin, who was killed in the shoot-out. Publicity material from the film was found in the flat that Rey shared with her boyfriend at the time of the shootings. The press latched on to this and called the pair "France's Natural Born Killers", and as in the film the vulgarity of the multiple murder was lost and replaced by a glamorous image of rebellion that was both enticing and thrilling. Before long, young Parisians were wearing a picture of the convicted woman on their T-shirts. This was the first time a real-life murderer had been idolised in public.

Stronger links between the film and a murder were discovered in the case of Véronique Herbert and her boyfriend Sébastian Paindavoine who lured their victim into a trap and then stabbed him to death. There was no motive for the attack and Herbert placed the blame on *Natural Born Killers*. She said, "The film coincided with my state of mind. Maybe I muddled up dream and reality. I wanted to eliminate someone, as if by magic . . . The idea of killing invaded me." In the light of such a testimony, can anyone deny the link between the sort of violence depicted in *Natural Born Killers* and Herbert and Paindavoine's gruesome act?

The pro-censorship lobby says the film and subsequent murders provide conclusive evidence that screen violence is rapidly translated into street violence. The image of killing, especially in a fictional world where the characters do not have to live with the consequences of their actions, can become a reality. Such allegations against a film cannot be dismissed and the controversy surrounding the subject matter has been fuelled by the similarities between Mickey and Mallory and the real-life murderers. However, there is an argument against censorship which states that *Natural Born Killers* was intended as a satire on the bloodlust of the media and American society and that it is society that should be held responsible for any acts of violence rather than the film itself.

The question of whether or not violence depicted in films and on TV leads to violent behaviour is often discussed and was hotly debated in relation to the Oliver Stone film *Natural Born Killers*. The film itself looks at media focus on violence and how it can be glamorised.

Direct vs. indirect aggression

Coyne, Archer, and Eslea (2004) argued that there is an important distinction between direct aggression (i.e., violent behaviour) and indirect aggression (e.g., spreading rumours). Indirect aggression is present in more programmes on British television than is direct aggression, but there has been remarkably little research on the effects of indirect aggression. Coyne et al. presented children aged between 11 and 14 with videos showing direct or indirect aggression. Both forms of aggression triggered aggressive behaviour in the children. However, viewing direct aggression led to more directly aggressive responses whereas viewing indirect aggression produce more indirectly aggressive responses. These associations between the type of aggression viewed and children's subsequent aggressive behaviour is as expected on social learning theory. These findings show very clearly the importance of considering the effects of viewing indirect aggression in future research.

Longitudinal research

Eron (1982) and Huesmann, Lagerspetz, and Eron (1984) reported on a major longitudinal study. First of all, the amount of television watched and levels of aggressiveness were assessed in some young children. Then aggressiveness and the amount of television watched were reassessed in the same participants several years later. One of the key findings was that the amount of television violence watched at a young age predicted the level of later aggressiveness (measured by the number of criminal convictions by the age of 30). This suggests that watching television violence may be one of the causes of aggressive behaviour. This is consistent with expectations from the desensitisation and disinhibition hypotheses discussed earlier. In addition, there was evidence that children who were aggressive when young tended to watch more violent television programmes several years later. This suggests that more aggressive individuals choose to watch more violent television programmes.

Absence of television

So far we have considered only studies in which television violence led to increased aggression. However, several studies have found no effect of television on aggression. Of particular interest is evidence obtained in the United States during the early 1950s. The Federal Communications Commission refused to issue any new television licences between the end of 1949 and the middle of 1952. As a result, television arrived in some parts of the United States several years before others. According to FBI crime statistics, the level of violent crime was no greater in those areas that had television than in those that did not which seems inconsistent with the desensitisation and disinhibition hypotheses discussed earlier. Furthermore, the introduction of television into an area did not lead to an increase in violent crime. However, the introduction of television was followed by an increase in the number of thefts (Hennigan et al., 1982). This may have occurred because the advertisements on television made many people more determined to acquire material possessions.

A similar study has recently been carried out on St. Helena in the south Atlantic, which is best known for the fact that Napoleon spent the last few years of his life there. Its inhabitants received television for the first time in 1995, but there is no evidence of any adverse effects on the children. According to Charlton (1998):

> *The argument that watching violent television turns youngsters to violence is not borne out, and this study on St. Helena is the clearest proof yet. The children have watched the same amounts of violence, and in many cases the same programmes, as British children. But they have not gone out and copied what they have seen on TV.*

Some of the evidence consisted of secret videoing of the children playing at school. Charlton reported that "Bad behaviour is virtually unheard of in the playground, and our footage shows that what is viewed is not repeated." What are the factors preventing television violence from influencing the children of St. Helena? According to Charlton: "The main ones are that children are in stable home, school, and community situations. This is why the children on St. Helena appear to be immune to what they are watching."

? Do you think that children from St. Helena would identify with characters in American television programmes? How does this affect the impact of the findings?

Evaluation

It is hard to evaluate the effects of television violence on aggressive behaviour. Many of the studies are limited in scope, focusing only on the short-term effects on behaviour of exposure to a single violent programme. Such studies can tell us little or nothing about the long-term effects of prolonged exposure to violent programmes. The somewhat inconclusive nature of the evidence was summarised as follows by Gunter and McAleer (1990):

> *the measurement of television's effects . . . is highly complex . . . we are still a long way from knowing fully the extent and character of television's influence on children's aggressive behaviour.*

? What characters in television programmes do children imitate today? Does such imitation have negative effects?

Wood, Wong, and Chachere (1991) reviewed 28 laboratory and field studies concerned with the effects of media violence on aggression in children and adolescents. It was found in both laboratory and field studies that exposure to media violence led to more aggressive behaviour towards strangers, classmates, and friends. In general, the effects were stronger under laboratory conditions.

Comstock and Paik (1991) reviewed more than 1000 findings on the effects of media violence. There are generally strong short-term effects, especially with respect to minor acts of aggression. In addition, there seem to be rather weaker long-term effects. They concluded that there are five factors that tend to increase the effects of media violence on aggression:

? Bearing in mind Comstock and Paik's five factors, what advice would you give film makers who do not wish to provoke aggression in their audiences?

1. Violent behaviour is presented as being an efficient way to get what one wants.
2. The person who is behaving violently is portrayed as similar to the viewer.

Children are exposed to violent images at an early age and often incorporate them into their play. How well do they distinguish between a play scenario and how they behave in real life?

3. Violent behaviour is presented in a realistic way rather than, for example, in cartoon form.
4. The suffering of the victims of violence is not shown.
5. The viewer is emotionally excited while watching the violent behaviour.

There are three final points that need to be made. First, much of the laboratory research in this area is very artificial. For example, the participants are instructed to view a programme from start to finish rather than suiting themselves as in real life. Second, there are likely to be important differences in the effects of real and mock aggression, but most research has not focused on this issue. Third, there has been an almost exclusive emphasis in research on the viewing of direct aggression (i.e., violence), but it is also important to consider what happens when people view indirect aggression.

Individual differences

A key issue is the extent to which all people are affected by violence on television. It may be that people with aggressive personalities are more drawn to such programmes and therefore the observed effects of television violence are an effect rather than a cause of aggressive tendencies. A second explanation is that only certain vulnerable individuals are affected by such violence. Most people can watch violence without significantly increased aggressiveness. However, theories of aggression tell us that some people become predisposed to aggression because of frustration, personality characteristics, or perhaps other environmental factors such as heat. In such circumstances violence on television might lead to increased interpersonal aggression. One particular group of vulnerable individuals are children, who may have as yet unformed personalities and are especially susceptible to the effects of disinhibition, desensitisation, and socially mediated models. This is why, of course, we prefer young people not to watch violence in the media.

Cross-cultural differences

Nearly all research on the effects of media violence has been carried out in the United States or the United Kingdom. As a result, we do not really know whether the findings would be the same in other cultures. One of the few cross-cultural studies was carried out by Huesmann and Eron (1986). They tested children and parents over a period of 3 years in Finland, Israel, Poland, and Australia. In the first three countries, the amount of television violence that young children had seen predicted their subsequent level of aggression, even when their initial level of aggressiveness was controlled for statistically. However, these findings were not obtained with Australian children. The overall findings suggest that media violence increases aggressive behaviour in most countries.

Other anti-social behaviours

Violence and aggression are not the only anti-social behaviours associated with the media. Prejudice can be inflamed by newspaper and other media reports.

Televised role portrayals and inter-racial interactions are sources of vicarious experience and contribute to the development and maintenance of stereotypes, prejudice, and discrimination among children. Limited portrayals of ethnic groups and of inter-ethnic interaction mean that children develop stereotypical views of our society.

Fairchild (1988) suggested a concept for an educational TV programme that would address the concerns emerging from research on the effects of media violence, the portrayal of minorities and women in the media, and the pro-social potential of TV. The pilot TV programme involved an inter-racial and cross-gender team of skilled young adults, cast in counterstereotypical roles, who travelled to other planets to solve problems of intergroup conflict. To reduce prejudice, the team of protagonists shared equal status and common goals, they co-operated in a fairly intimate context, and they enjoyed successful outcomes. Such programmes might help to encourage a sense of world community, promoting intercultural understanding, and impede the formation of the enemy image! Lofty and pro-social aims indeed.

 INDEPENDENT STUDY IDEA: MEDIA INFLUENCES ON PRO-SOCIAL OR ON ANTI-SOCIAL BEHAVIOUR 2
Do a similar study to the one on page 114 but this time use news broadcasts and compare the number of aggressive acts shown with the number of pro-social acts. There will almost certainly be more aggression shown than pro-social behaviour. Is this a true reflection of social behaviour or simply the (probably inevitable) consequence of the type of items reported on the news? Does this lead to a distorted view of how dangerous our lives are and does this, in turn, affect the way we behave?

SECTION SUMMARY
Media Influences on Pro- and Anti-social Behaviour

❖ The media is any means of communication: books, magazines, films, and television.

❖ The media may have effects on pro-social and anti-social behaviour.

What is the media?

❖ Social learning theory: The most obvious way to explain the potential influence of the media is social learning theory. Individuals model behaviours that they see or read about in the media, especially those that appear to be reinforced, and those of characters with whom they identify.

❖ The disinhibition effect: suggests that exposure to certain behaviours in the media reduces our normal inhibitions. This is likely to result in anti-social behaviour but could lead to pro-social behaviour as in reducing our reluctance to intervene in a lovers' quarrel.

❖ Desensitisation occurs when our normal sensitivities are dulled by overexposure.

❖ Cognitive priming acts like the weapons effect—cues in the media may trigger aggressive thoughts, thus increasing arousal and possibly aggressive behaviour.

❖ Stereotypes are inevitable in the media as a means of communicating lots of information very quickly. However they are anti-social because they perpetuate prejudices, though they can also be used pro-socially in the form of counterstereotypes. Counterstereotypes can be used to deal with the problem of stereotypes.

Explanations of media influence

❖ Displacement effect: Television may exert an anti-social effect by displacing real-life experiences (a displacement effect). The result may be that people who watch a lot of television see the world as much more deviant than it actually is (the deviance amplification effect).

❖ Simulation hypothesis: The media can stimulate thought and pro-social behaviour, especially when demonstrating ways of dealing with anti-social situations (conflict resolution). The danger is that the resolution is overlooked and the anti-social behaviour is imitated. Conflict resolution needs to be given adequate programme time and it is necessary to ensure that observers attend to the resolution.

Media influences on pro-social behaviour

❖ The pro-social effects of television have been shown in many research studies.
❖ There are limitations to this evidence:

— The demonstrated effects are fairly short term though there is some evidence of long-term effects.
— The pro-social behaviours that are learned may also be quite situation specific.

Media influences on anti-social behaviour

❖ Any correlation between amount of violent television watched and aggressive behaviour raises the issue of cause and effect:

— In one study, physical aggression increased following watching a violent film but verbal aggression only increased in boys who were previously classed as aggressive.
— In another study the amount of television violence watched at a young age predicted levels of later aggressiveness, a result that may be due to a cause or effect of aggressiveness.

❖ Nearly all the research focuses on the effects of direct aggression (i.e., violence) but viewing indirect aggression (e.g., spreading rumours) also increases aggressive responses.
❖ Absence of television:

— In the United States, areas without television broadcasts in the 1950s did not have lower rates of crime, although theft did increase after television reception was available.
— Observations in St. Helena, where television is relatively new, bear this out. However this is a stable society where children appear to be immune to what they are watching.

Evaluation of media influences on anti-social behaviour

❖ Most studies tell us little about the potential long-term effects.
❖ Overall the effects of media violence on aggression may be due to:

— Showing it as being an efficient way to get what one wants
— Portraying the violent individual as similar to the viewer
— Showing violent behaviour in a realistic way
— Not showing the suffering of the victims of violence
— Creating emotional excitement in the viewer.

See also pages 61–65 of the revision guide.

❖ Individuals with aggressive personalities will be more drawn to watching violent programmes and probably more affected.

❖ Children may be especially vulnerable to influence.

❖ Television violence appears to have similar effects in most countries.

❖ Pro- and anti-social behaviour goes beyond helpfulness and aggression; it can include attempts to reduce prejudice and promote world peace.

Other pro- and anti-social behaviours

FURTHER READING

The topics in this chapter are covered in greater depth by D. Clarke (2001) *Pro- and antisocial behaviour* (Routledge Modular Series) (London: Routledge), written specifically for the AQA A specification. Other useful sources are F.M. Moghaddam (1998) *Social psychology: Exploring universals across cultures* (New York: W.H. Freeman), and B. Gunter and J. McAleer (1997) *Children and television (2nd Edn)* (London: Routledge). Various chapters in M. Hewstone and W. Stroebe (2001) *Introduction to social psychology (3rd Edn)* (Oxford: Blackwell) provide coverage of most of the topics discussed in this chapter. Another useful reference is N. Hayes (1993) *Principles of social psychology* (Hove, UK: Psychology Press).

EXAMPLE EXAMINATION QUESTIONS

You should spend 30 minutes on each of the questions below, which aim to test the material in this chapter.

1. Describe and evaluate **one** social psychological theory of aggression. (24 marks)
2. Critically consider research into the effects of **two** environmental stressors on aggressive behaviour. (24 marks)
3. (a) Outline **two or more** explanations for human altruism and/or bystander behaviour. (12 marks)
   (b) Evaluate these and/or other explanations with reference to research studies. (12 marks)
4. (a) Outline research evidence relating to human altruism and/or bystander behaviour. (12 marks)
   (b) Assess the effects of cultural differences on pro-social behaviour. (12 marks)
5. Critically consider **two** research studies relating to media influences on *anti-social* behaviour. (24 marks)
6. "There is much public interest in the debate about the effects of violence in the media on the behaviour of young children; but why don't people focus more on the potentially pro-social influences?"
   Discuss the above quotation in relation to the pro- and anti-social effects of the media. (24 marks)

Examination Tips

Question 1. You must restrict yourself to describing one theory of aggression but may introduce other theories as a means of evaluation as long as this is explicit. It is desirable to do more than just say "I will evaluate my first theory by describing a second theory". True evaluation is achieved through genuinely comparing the theories and highlighting some features of your first theory through contrasts. Further evaluation may be achieved with reference to research studies and consideration of individual and cultural differences. The practical implications of the theory in, for example, reducing aggression are also a form of evaluation.

Question 2. The injunction "critically consider" requires that you describe (AO1) and then criticise this consideration—involving reference to both strengths and limitations. The term "research" refers to either theory or studies. The essay itself focuses on two environmental stressors. Therefore you should identify two stressors such as noise and temperature, and critically consider the research related to each.

Question 3. In part (a) the injunction "outline" requires that you offer no more than a summary description. You will not receive credit for detail in this answer but for breadth. Thus it may be better to offer as many explanations as possible. Note that the essay refers only to altruism and not to bystander behaviour. Any explanations of the latter would only receive credit if they account for altruism (or the lack of it). This must be explicit. Any research studies should be saved for part (b), where the focus should be on using the studies to evaluate the explanations rather than simply describing them. Use of phrases like "This shows that . . ." and "I would argue that . . ." should help you be evaluative rather than just descriptive.

Question 4. The emphasis is slightly different in this question, compared to question 3. Again the injunction for part (a) is "outline" but this time it is research evidence you are asked for (which was in part (b) last time), and also it is bystander behaviour that is the focus. Part (b) requires an assessment of cultural differences. There is a danger again that you will just describe such differences and/or the research studies that have demonstrated such differences. However, credit will be given for the extent to which you use such evidence effectively, in essence answering the question "Are relationships the same the world over?"

Question 5. Again, the injunction "critically consider" requires a description plus an evaluation including reference to strengths and weaknesses. You should identify two research studies only and describe each in terms of aims, procedures, findings, and conclusions. Evaluation can refer to any aspect of the study and may also refer to theories arising from the study (a possible strength). You must restrict yourself to anti-social behaviour, although evaluation might consider the reverse side of the coin—pro-social behaviour.

Question 6. This question requires that you make reference to the quotation in your answer. To maximise your marks you should fully engage with the quotation by making reference to the issues that it raises throughout your answer rather than just reiterating the quotation at the beginning and end. You are asked to discuss both pro- and anti-social effects and therefore need to be selective about the material you use, otherwise you will end up sacrificing depth (detail) for breadth.

WEBSITES

http://psychclassics.yorku.ca/Bandura/bobo.htm
  The classic study by Bandura et al. (1961) using the Bobo doll.

http://salmon.psy.plym.ac.uk/year2/aggression/aggression.html#overview
  Website examining the sociological and biological causes of aggression.

http://www.socialpsychology.org/social.htm#prosocial
  Links about pro-social behaviour.

http://faculty.babson.edu/krollag/org_site/soc_psych/latane_bystand.html
  An essay on bystander apathy, as epitomised by the Kitty Genovese murder incident of 1964.

http://observer.guardian.co.uk/comment/story/0,6903,389527,00.html
  Article from the Observer about the effects of the arrival of television on the remote island of St. Helena.

http://www.media-awareness.ca/english/issues/violence/index.cfm
  An abundance of links and articles regarding the sociological effects of violence in the media.

PHYSIOLOGICAL PSYCHOLOGY

Biological Rhythms p.125
- What are circadian, infradian, and ultradian rhythms?
- Why do we need biological rhythms?
- What happens when biological rhythms are disrupted, as in jet lag and shiftwork?

Sleep p.138
- What happens when people are deprived of sleep for long periods?
- Can people learn to sleep less?
- Is sleep just a waste of time?

Dreaming p.152
- Is REM (rapid eye movement) sleep the same as dreaming?
- Did Freud believe in dream dictionaries?
- Can dreams help you solve problems?

Biological Rhythms, Sleep, and Dreaming

There is a wide variety of biological rhythms—periodically recurring features of biological organisms, which are classified by the period of the cycle. In this chapter we explore biological clocks, and the external and internal cues that act as pacemakers for different cycles. Sleep is the most well-known cycle, and we look at some studies of sleep deprivation that attempt to tell us more about the function of sleep; we also discuss the theories explaining the purpose of sleep. Finally, we investigate the theories of dreaming, a behaviour that is little understood: when, what, and why do we dream?

BIOLOGICAL RHYTHMS

A rhythm is something that is regularly repeated. In living organisms there is a vast array of rhythms: plants open and close daily, people eat several times a day, birds migrate annually, and so on. These rhythms are repeated over different intervals and they are governed by both internal (**endogenous**) and external (**exogenous**) factors. In this Section we will critically consider research relating to different kinds of rhythm and how these rhythms are determined. We will also consider the consequences of disrupting these rhythms.

Different Kinds of Biological Rhythm

The three main categories are:

- **Circadian rhythm** (from two Latin words meaning "about" and "day"). Most of the biological rhythms possessed by human beings repeat themselves every 24 hours. According to Green (1994), mammals possess about 100 different biological circadian rhythms. For example, temperature in humans varies over the course of the 24-hour day, reaching a peak in the late afternoon and a low point in the early hours of the morning. Other examples of human circadian rhythms are the sleep–waking cycle and the release of hormones from the pituitary gland.

> **KEY TERMS**
> **Endogenous:** internally caused, as distinct from external causes (exogenous).
> **Exogenous:** based on factors external to the organism.
> **Circadian rhythm:** a biological rhythm that recurs approximately every 24 hours; "circa" and "dies" mean "around the day". The most obvious example is the sleep–wake cycle.

As many hormones have circadian rhythms, it is important to note the time a blood sample is taken, as this could affect interpretation of results.

- **Ultradian rhythm**, meaning rhythms of less than 1 day. A good example of an ultradian rhythm is to be found in sleep. While you are asleep you pass through cycles of lighter and deeper sleep, each cycle lasting about 90 minutes.
- **Infradian rhythm**, meaning greater than 1 day, for example those rhythms repeating once a month. Perhaps the best known example of an infradian rhythm in humans is the menstrual cycle, which typically lasts about 28 days. Those rhythms that repeat once a year are called **circannual rhythms**.

We will consider some circadian and infradian rhythms. An example of an ultradian rhythm, the stages of sleep, is discussed in the next Section.

The Sleep–Waking Cycle: A Circadian Rhythm

The 24-hour sleep–waking cycle is of particular importance, and is associated with other circadian rhythms. For example, bodily temperature is at its highest about halfway through the waking day (early to late afternoon) and at its lowest halfway through the sleeping part of the day (about 3am). Why is the sleep–waking cycle 24 hours long? One possibility is that it is strongly influenced by *external* events such as the light–dark cycle, and the fact that each dawn follows almost exactly 24 hours after the preceding one. Another possibility is that the sleep–waking cycle is *endogenous*, meaning that it is based on internal biological mechanisms or pacemakers that have a 24-hour periodicity. We will first consider endogenous factors and then move on to external (exogenous) ones.

Endogenous factors: The biological clock

How can we decide whether the sleep–waking cycle depends mainly on external or on internal factors? One approach is to study individuals who are removed from the normal light–dark cycle, e.g., by being kept away from daylight (but not from artificial light). Michel Siffre spent 2 months in a dark cave. At first, there was no very clear pattern in his sleep–waking cycle. Later on, however, he developed a sleep–waking cycle of about 25 hours rather than the standard one of 24 hours (Siffre, 1975). This suggests the influence of some internal, **biological clock**.

Other studies have supported this. Wever (1979) discussed studies on participants who spent several

Did you know?

The fact that there are circadian rhythms for many hormones has important applications in medicine. When a doctor takes a sample of blood or urine it is important to record the time of day at which the sample was taken in order to properly assess it. For example, the stress hormone cortisol is at its highest level in the morning. If an early morning sample of urine was tested for cortisol but was thought to have been taken later in the day, it might be assumed that the person was highly stressed.

Recent research has also suggested that biorhythms should be considered when prescribing medicines. It seems that the standard practice of taking a drug at regular intervals throughout the day may not only be ineffective, but can also be counterproductive or even harmful. Evidence shows that certain medical illnesses whose symptoms show a circadian rhythm respond better when drugs are co-ordinated with that rhythm (Moore-Ede et al., 1982).

KEY TERMS

Ultradian rhythm: a biological rhythm that recurs in a cycle of less than a day ("ultra" and "dies" = above or higher frequency than a day); e.g., the sleep stages.

Infradian rhythm: a biological rhythm that recurs in a cycle of more than 24 hours ("infra" and "dies" = below or lower frequency than a day); for example, the menstrual cycle.

Circannual rhythm: a biological rhythm that recurs approximately once a year, such as annual migration.

Biological clock: a biological pacemaker that governs rhythms such as the sleep–wake cycle. In humans, this function is located in the suprachiasmatic nucleus.

weeks or months in a bunker or isolation suite. Most of them settled down to a sleep–waking cycle of about 25 hours, though this is not a universal finding. Folkard (1996) studied one individual who had a 30-hour cycle.

Why would we have an endogenous rhythm lasting for 25 hours given that we normally experience a 24-hour day? In fact, there is a significant limitation with the above studies, because the participants could control their own lighting conditions (known as the free-running paradigm). Czeisler et al. (1999) compared the free-running paradigm with the forced desynchrony paradigm in which artificial 20- or 28-hour days were imposed on the participants. There was evidence for a 25-hour circadian rhythm in temperature with the free-running paradigm, but the temperature circadian rhythm averaged 24 hours and 10 minutes with the forced desynchrony paradigm. The message is that the endogenous circadian rhythm has a period of 24 hours, but this can be lengthened when people in artificial environments can turn the lights on whenever they want.

The main pacemaker for endogenous rhythms is the **suprachiasmatic nucleus** (SCN). This is a small group of cells in the **hypothalamus**. It is called "suprachiasmatic" because it lies just above the **optic chiasm**. This location is not surprising because it can then receive input fairly directly from the eye, and therefore the rhythm can be reset by the amount of light entering the eye. The SCN also generates its own rhythms, probably as a result of protein synthesis. It is likely that what happens is that the cells in the SCN produce a protein for a period of hours until the level inhibits further production, again for hours; next, when the protein level drops below another threshold, the SCN starts producing the protein again (Kalat, 1998). This generates the biological rhythm.

This rhythm then affects the sleep–wake cycle via the **pineal gland**. Electrical stimulation of the pineal gland produces the hormone **melatonin**, which makes a person feel sleepy (see the Key Study on the next page); when light levels are low more melatonin is released. Incidentally, in birds and reptiles, as opposed to mammals, light falls directly on the pineal gland, which is located just under the skull.

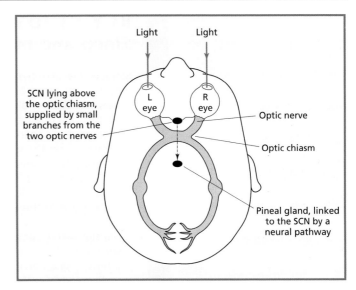

The visual pathway in the brain showing the connection to the suprachiasmatic nucleus (SCN) and onwards to the pineal gland.

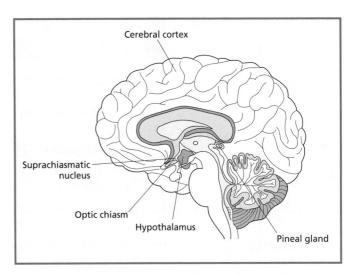

The endogenous mechanisms involved in regulating bodily rhythms.

KEY TERMS

Suprachiasmatic nucleus: a small group of neurones in the hypothalamus that act as a biological clock and help regulate the circadian rhythm.

Hypothalamus: the part of the brain that integrates the activity of the autonomic nervous system. Involved with emotion, stress, motivation, and hunger.

Optic chiasm: the point at which the optic nerves from each eye cross over to the opposite side of the brain.

Pineal gland: a very small endocrine gland located in the brain that produces melatonin, and is involved in the circadian rhythm.

Melatonin: a hormone produced by the pineal gland that increases sleepiness.

KEY STUDY
Sleep and melatonin

Some of the strongest evidence of the involvement of melatonin in the sleep–waking cycle was reported by Schochat, Luboshitzky, and Lavie (1997). They made use of the ultra-short sleep–wake paradigm, in which their six male participants spent 29 hours between 7am one day to noon the following day in the sleep laboratory. Throughout that time they spent 7 minutes in every 20 lying down in bed in a completely darkened room trying to sleep. This method allowed Schochat et al. to measure sleep propensity or the tendency to sleep at different times of day. The period of greatest sleep propensity is known as the "sleep gate", and starts in the late evening. Surprisingly, the period of lowest sleep propensity (known as the "wake maintenance zone") occurs in the early evening shortly before the sleep gate.

Schochat et al. measured the levels of melatonin by taking blood samples up to three times an hour during the 29-hour session. The key finding was as follows: "We demonstrated a close and precise temporal relationship between the circadian rhythms of sleep propensity and melatonin; the nocturnal [night] onset of melatonin secretion consistently precedes the nocturnal sleep gate by 100–120 min" (p.367). This close relationship between increased melatonin levels and increased sleep propensity does not prove that they are causally related. However, Schochat et al. discussed other studies that strengthen the argument that melatonin is important in determining sleep propensity. For example, individuals who suffer from insomnia find it much easier to get to sleep when they are given melatonin about 2 hours before bedtime.

Discussion points
1. What are some of the good features of the study carried out by Schochat et al.?
2. What are the limitations of their approach?

Evidence to support the functioning of the SCN comes from various studies. Morgan (1995) removed the SCN from hamsters and found that their circadian rhythms disappeared. The rhythms could be re-established by transplanted SCN cells from foetal hamsters. Morgan also transplanted the SCN cells from mutant hamsters (those bred to have shorter cycles than normal) and found that the transplanted hamsters took on the mutant rhythms. Silver et al. (1996) also showed that transplanted SCNs can restore circadian rhythm to an animal whose own SCN has been ablated.

There is also evidence of a second biological clock, again in the SCN. Nearly all participants in the long-term bunker studies showed evidence of two different patterns: one for their sleep–waking cycle and one for their temperature cycle (Wever, 1979). Folkard's (1996) study of Kate Aldcroft found that she developed a 30-hour sleep–wake cycle but a 24-hour temperature cycle. These findings indicate strongly that there are separate internal clocks controlling the sleep–waking cycle and temperature.

Exogenous factors
As we have seen, the SCN also receives direct information from the eye about the level of light. This means the SCN can be controlled internally but also can be reset by external cues. In fact recent evidence shows that humans may receive information about light from elsewhere in the body. Campbell and Murphy (1998) demonstrated that participants given regular light exposure on the backs of their knees had changes in their circadian rhythms in line with the light/dark they were exposed to. However, it is not clear how this information would get to the SCN.

? In this area of research, unlike other areas of psychology, single case studies are referred to by their full names rather than initials. Can you explain why that is?

Light is considered to be the dominant **zeitgeber**, the technical term for an external event that partially controls biological rhythms and literally means "time giver". An interesting study by Miles et al. (1977) documented the problems of a young man who was blind from birth. He had a strong 24.9-hour circadian rhythm despite the fact that he was exposed to a variety of zeitgebers such as clocks and radios. His problems in resetting his biological clock were so great that he had to use stimulants and sedatives to co-ordinate his sleep–wake cycle with the rest of the world. This demonstrates that light really is the dominant time-giver.

However, there is also evidence that shows that, where appropriate, light cues are disregarded. Luce and Segal (1966) pointed out that people living within the Arctic Circle still sleep for about 7 hours despite the fact that during the summer months the sun never sets. In certain circumstances other external cues take over, such as social customs that dictate when it is time to get up and go to bed. The sleep–wake cycle is more strongly controlled by endogenous factors, but these cues can be overridden. For example, if you were trapped in a dark cave, your need to stay awake to be able to respond to rescuers would overturn the messages to the SCN that it was dark and therefore time to go to sleep.

Can you think of anyone whose melatonin cycle differs from the norm?

Evidence that it can be difficult to override endogenous circadian rhythms was found in a study of American submariners (Kelly et al., 1999). Their work schedule consisted of 6 hours on duty followed by 12 hours off duty, thus producing an 18-hour day. In spite of this schedule and their ability to control their own lighting conditions, the submariners had an average circadian rhythm for melatonin lasting just over 24 hours. Why was this? The submariners in question had social contacts with people living on a 24-hour schedule and they were aware of clock time.

Conclusions

The findings discussed above suggest that there is, indeed, an endogenous sleep–waking cycle. However, the fact that there is sometimes a discrepancy between the endogenous sleep–waking cycle and the normal sleep–waking cycle indicates that external cues such as changes in light and dark also play a role in **entraining** our biological clock.

Both endogenous and exogenous signals are important and both cause us difficulties. Think of the difficulties people experience when working shifts. Darkness tells them they should be asleep. Think also of the difficulties related to jet lag—the light tells us we should be awake but our internal clock says it's time for sleep. We will consider the effects of these disruptions later.

There are good reasons why our biorhythms should be sensitive to *both* internal and external control. Without external control, animals wouldn't be sensitive to seasonal variations. They wouldn't shed hair in summer or grow extra

EXAM HINT

If you are asked to outline one or two biological rhythms or to discuss research into biological rhythms, a useful way to organise your answer is to consider the evidence for the role of endogenous and exogenous factors.

KEY TERMS

Zeitgeber: external events that partially determine biological rhythms.
Entraining: synchronising two or more things.

hair in winter. Some animals sleep at night, possibly because it is safer; other animals hunt at night because they are adapted for this. In either case the animal needs to respond to light cues. Light cues are not likely to be the only cues as far as seasonal variation is concerned. Air temperature would also be important as it would alter the nutritional needs in order to maintain core body temperature. Therefore we can see that responsiveness to external cues enables animals to adapt to environmental conditions, which is vital for survival.

However, if animals were solely at the mercy of environmental cues we would have very irregular biological patterns and this might be life threatening.

Indirect effects of circadian rhythms

So far we have focused mainly on a circadian rhythm directly related to underlying biological processes. There are other, more psychological rhythms that depend indirectly on basic circadian rhythms. For example, there are fairly consistent patterns of performance on many tasks throughout the day. People tend to peak at certain times of the day.

The classic work in this area was carried out by Blake (1967). He asked naval ratings to perform several tasks at five different times of day (08.00, 10.30, 13.00, 15.30, and 21.00). For most of the tasks, the best performance was obtained at 21.00, with the second-best level of performance occurring at 10.30. However, later studies found that peak performance on most tasks is reached at around midday rather than during the evening (M.W. Eysenck, 1982).

Why might people perform at their best at midday rather than earlier or later in the day? Relevant evidence was obtained by Akerstedt (1977). Self-reported alertness (assessed by questionnaire) was greatest at about noon, as was the level of adrenaline. Adrenaline is a hormone associated with states of high physiological arousal within the **autonomic nervous system** (ANS). However, it should be noted that the notion of physiological arousal is rather vague and imprecise. Furthermore, these are correlational data, and it is hard to be sure that the high level of midday performance *depends* on arousal.

After the midday peak there may be a trough. Blake (1967) found that most of his participants showed a clear reduction in performance at 13.00 compared to their performance at 10.30. This reduction in performance occurred shortly after lunch, and is commonly known as the "post-lunch dip". The explanation for this is that the physiological processes involved in digestion make us feel sluggish and reduce our ability to work efficiently. It is also noteworthy that the act of digestion is governed by the **parasympathetic branch** of the ANS, which leads to general relaxation, whereas physiological arousal is an effect of the antagonistic ANS branch, the **sympathetic branch**.

The Menstrual Cycle: An Infradian Rhythm

Infradian rhythms are bodily rhythms for which the cycle time is greater than one day. One of the clearest

---

? Are you a "morning" or an "evening" person, or neither?

■ **Activity:** Design a questionnaire to measure alertness and distribute it to volunteer participants. Ask them to complete it at regular intervals over several days. Analyse the data to see if there are "morning" and "evening" people, in terms of levels of alertness. What are the methodological problems you may encounter?

KEY TERMS

Autonomic nervous system: that part of the nervous system that controls vital body functions, which is self-regulating and needs no conscious control (automatic).
Parasympathetic branch: the part of the autonomic nervous system that monitors the relaxed state, conserving resources, and promoting digestion and metabolism.
Sympathetic branch: the part of the autonomic nervous system that activates internal organs.

examples of an infradian rhythm is the menstrual cycle in women. (In other mammals the cycle is longer or shorter than the human 28 days, but is still infradian.) This cycle is governed by hormones, an endogenous mechanism. **Hormones** are biochemical substances that are produced by endocrine glands and released into the bloodstream. Small amounts of such hormones have a large effect on target organs such as, in the case of the menstrual cycle, the ovaries and womb. The menstrual cycle is governed by the female hormones oestrogen and progesterone. These hormones cause the lining of the womb to become engorged with blood and one egg to ripen and be released. If the egg is not fertilised, then the lining of the womb is shed. On average this cycle takes 28 days. Here are the detailed phases of the menstrual cycle:

- *Follicular phase*: Follicle-stimulating hormone causes ovarian follicles (small sac-like structures) to grow around egg cells or ova, following by the ovarian follicles releasing oestrogens (sex hormones).
- *Ovulation phase*: Oestrogens lead to increased release of luteinising hormone and follicle-stimulating hormone from the anterior pituitary, causing a ruptured follicle to release its ovum or egg.
- *Luteal phase*: The ruptured follicle releases progesterone (sex hormone), so preparing the lining of the uterus for the implantation of a fertilised ovum or egg.
- *Pre-menstrual and menstrual phases*: The ovum or egg moves into the fallopian tube; if unfertilised, progesterone and oestrogen levels decrease.

The endogenous rhythm of the menstrual cycle can be affected by many external cues. Reinberg (1967) documented the duration of a woman's menstrual cycle during and after she spent 3 months in a cave, with only dim lighting. Her sleep–wake cycle lengthened slightly and her menstrual cycle became shorter during her stay in the cave. It took a further year for her cycle to return to normal. This suggests that light can influence the menstrual cycle, probably by generally affecting the action of the SCN and the circadian cycle, which then has implications for the infradian rhythm.

Even more interestingly there is evidence that a woman's menstrual cycle can be entrained by the menstrual cycle of other women; an example of exogenous control, albeit biological. Women who spend time together, such as girls living in boarding schools and nuns, appear to have synchronised menstrual cycles (McClintock, 1971). It is likely that this happens because of **pheromones**, biochemical substances that act like hormones but are released into the air rather than the bloodstream. These pheromones have no smell and aren't consciously detectable but they carry messages from one individual to another of the same species. Support for this comes from a study by Russell, Switz, and Thompson (1980; see the Key Study on the next page). But why would this happen? One possibility is that there might be an evolutionary advantage for a social group to have synchronised pregnancies so that all the women in the group were breastfeeding at the same time. This would mean that child care could be shared, which would be especially helpful if one mother died (Bentley, 2000). Members of other animal species certainly share feeding though; in fact, wet nursing in humans shows that you can continue to breastfeed even if your child was born much earlier.

KEY TERMS

Hormones: chemical substances produced by endocrine glands, and circulated in the blood. They only affect target organs and are produced in large quantities but disappear very quickly.

Pheromones: chemical substances produced by the body and secreted into the air. They act on conspecifics by being absorbed into their bloodstream. The pheromones then work like hormones.

? Can you think of any evolutionary advantages for synchronised menstrual cycles?

? Why was it necessary to use sexually inactive women in this study?

KEY STUDY
The effects of pheromones

Hormones are produced by the endocrine system and distributed in the blood so that their influence can be felt by target organs. Pheromones are biochemical substances, like hormones, but pheromones are released into the air and affect other individuals. Ants produce pheromones as a means of "telling" other ants where to find food. Most mammals use pheromones in sexual attraction, signalling when a female is in her fertile phase. In fact the pheromones of some animals are used to produce perfume. It has also been noted that pheromones may explain why women who live together, such as in boarding schools, have synchronised menstrual cycles.

To test this, Russell et al. (1980) arranged to apply the pheromones of one woman to a group of sexually inactive women. The donor's odour was collected from pads placed under her arms. Once every 24 hours the pads were replaced. The old pad was then dissolved in alcohol to remove any bacteria. Finally, the pad was rubbed on the upper lip of each participant. This was repeated daily for 5 months. Some of the women were in a control group where they received the same treatment but did not receive the odour. Participants did not know which group they were in. A record was kept of the participants' menstrual cycles.

At the end of the experiment four out of the five women in the odour group had menstrual cycles that synchronised to within a day of the odour donor.

Discussion points
1. Can you suggest any other explanations for the findings of this study?
2. What ethical issues might a researcher have to consider when conducting a study such as this?

Another example of the effect of external cues has been found in women working with men. It has been found that they have much shorter menstrual cycles. McClintock (1971) has suggested that male pheromones may reset a woman's biological clock. One possible explanation is that this would have adaptive value. Women who ovulate more often when men are present are likely to have more offspring and this would increase the genetic strain that has this characteristic response to male presence. At other times a short menstrual cycle would be disadvantageous because of the drain on resources.

Circannual Rhythms

Circannual rhythms are biological rhythms that last for about 1 year before repeating. They are more common in some animal species than in humans, and this is especially true of species that hibernate during the winter. Convincing evidence of a circannual rhythm in the gold-mantled ground squirrel was reported by Pengelley and Fisher (1957). They put a squirrel in a highly controlled environment with artificial light on for 12 hours every day, and a constant temperature of 0°C. Despite the fact that the external cues were unchanging, the squirrel hibernated from October through to the following April, with its body temperature dropping dramatically from 37°C before hibernation to 1°C during hibernation. The circannual rhythm for this squirrel was somewhat less than a year, having about 300 days' duration. It would appear that this circannual rhythm was endogenously controlled.

Migration is another circannual rhythm. In general it is thought that migration is controlled by alterations in day length and/or food supplies, both of which are external cues. However, this can't explain why birds living in the equator travel north because changes at that latitude in daylight and temperature over the year are minimal. It is possible that migration is also endogenously controlled. Gwinner (1986) kept wild birds in a controlled environment for 3 years, maintaining 12 hours of light each day. Nevertheless they showed signs of migratory restlessness, which does support the existence of an endogenous mechanism.

There is some evidence for circannual rhythms in humans. For example, Palinkas et al. (2001) studied men and women who spent the winter at McMurdo Station in Antarctica. There were circannual rhythms in thryotropin-stimulating hormone and mood, with both peaking in November and July and having their lowest levels during March and April. These findings suggested that "winter-over syndrome" (involving negative moods, anxiety, and confusion) is due in part to a low level of thyroid function.

A young seasonal affective disorder sufferer receiving phototherapy from a light box.

Seasonal affective disorder

Some people suffer from **seasonal affective disorder** (SAD), which resembles a circannual rhythm. The great majority of sufferers from seasonal affective disorder experience severe depression during the winter months, but a few seem to experience depression in the summer instead. The evidence suggests that seasonal affective disorder is related to seasonal variations in the production of melatonin, which is a hormone secreted by the pineal gland (Barlow & Durand, 1995). Melatonin affects production of serotonin, which is implicated in depression (see Chapter 8, Psychopathology). Melatonin is produced primarily at night, i.e., in darkness, and so more is produced during the dark winter months. As would be expected, seasonal affective disorder is more common in northern latitudes where the winter days are very short. Terman (1988) found that nearly 10% of those living in New Hampshire (a northern part of the United States) suffered from seasonal affective disorder, compared with only 2% in the southern state of Florida.

Phototherapy is recommended for the treatment of seasonal affective disorder (Barlow & Durand, 1995). This involves exposing sufferers to about 2 hours of intense light shortly after they wake up in the morning. It is assumed that this treatment reduces the production of melatonin. Lam et al. (2000) found that light treatment reduced or even eliminated depression. Natural light can also be effective. Wirz-Justice et al. (1996) found that patients with seasonal affective disorder were helped by taking morning walks.

The Consequences of Disrupting Biological Rhythms

In our everyday lives, there is usually no conflict between our endogenously controlled rhythms and external events or zeitgebers. However, there are situations in which there is a real conflict. Probably the two most important examples of such conflict are jet lag and shiftwork.

> **KEY TERM**
>
> **Seasonal affective disorder:** a disorder that nearly always involves the sufferer experiencing severe depression during winter months.

Jet lag can be a problem for airline staff who frequently cross time zones in the course of their work.

[?] Is it easier to override endogenous cues for sleep or for waking?

Jet lag

It is sometimes thought that jet lag occurs because travelling by plane can be time-consuming and tiring. In fact, jet lag occurs only when flying from east to west or from west to east, not from north to south. In other words it is related to changing time zones and depends on a discrepancy between internal and external time. For example, suppose you fly from Scotland to the east coast of the United States. You leave at eleven in the morning British time, and arrive in Boston at five in the afternoon British time. However, the time in Boston is probably midday. As a result of the 5-hour difference, you are likely to feel very tired by about 8 o'clock in the evening Boston time (which is 1am on your internal "clock").

Klein, Wegman, and Hunt (1972) found that adjustment of the sleep–waking cycle was much faster for westbound flights (going to the States) than for eastbound ones, regardless of whether you were travelling home or going away from home. For eastbound flights, re-adjustment of the sleep–waking cycle took about 1 day per time zone crossed. Thus, for example, it would take about 5 days to recover completely from a flight to Britain from Boston.

Why is it easier to adapt to jet lag when flying in a westerly direction? An important reason is that the day of travel is effectively lengthened when travelling west, whereas it is shortened when travelling east. It seems that phase delay (putting one's internal clock on hold) is easier to adapt to than phase advance.

People also generally cope better with staying up later than with getting up earlier, again because phase delay is easier. In other words, we don't like to be woken up when our body clock tells us we should be sleeping, but we can cope with being awake when our body clock says we should be asleep. A study by

CASE STUDY: MELATONIN AND AIRCREW

Melatonin is now available in US chemists and some claim it is the cure for jet lag. Jet lag can lead to fatigue, headache, sleep disturbances, irritability, and gastrointestinal disturbances—all with a potentially negative impact on flight safety. Interestingly, reported side-effects of melatonin use include many similar symptoms. Although some researchers claim melatonin is among the safest known substances, no large clinical evaluations have been performed to evaluate long-term effects.

Scientists believe melatonin is crucial for the functioning of our body clock. Studies suggest that treating jet lag with melatonin can not only resolve sleeping problems but also increase the body clock's ability to adjust to a new time zone. However, those in the medical community advise caution. Melatonin is not a universal remedy for everyone who must travel over many time zones. It is thought by some that it should not be used unless the user intends to spend more than 3 days in the new time zone. International aircrews will often cover several time zones, typically flying overnight west to east, spending 24 hours on the ground, then returning during the day

(east to west). This cycle is likely to be repeated several times before an extended period of sleep is possible. Melatonin usage to adjust the body clock in these circumstances is viewed by many scientists as inappropriate.

Timing the dose of melatonin is very important. Studies show that resynchronisation of the sleep–waking cycle only occurred if the subjects were allowed to sleep after taking the medication. In those participants unable to sleep after taking melatonin, the circadian rhythm was actually prolonged. More worryingly, melatonin's effect on fine motor and cognitive tasks is unknown and the nature of melatonin's sedative effects are uncertain.

Unfortunately, there are no published clinical studies evaluating flying performance while taking melatonin. The US Armed Forces are actively evaluating melatonin's aeromedical usefulness. Despite ongoing research, no US military service permits the routine use of melatonin by aviators. Significantly, aircrew participating in experimental study groups are not allowed to perform flying duties within 36 hours of using melatonin.

Schwartz, Recht, and Lew (1995) supported this. They analysed the results of American baseball games where teams had to travel across time zones to play opposing teams on the east or west coast (the time difference is 3 hours). West coast teams who travelled east (phase advance) had significantly fewer wins than east coast teams travelling west—which gives the east coast teams a distinct advantage. (Though, of course, it might simply be that the east coast teams were better!)

One suggestion to combat jet lag is to use melatonin to reset the body clock (see the Case Study on the previous page). An alternative is to adopt local eating times and bedtimes as soon as possible, so that these social cues help reset your biological clock.

? What are the dangers with taking melatonin?

Shiftwork

What about shiftwork? As they say, there are only two problems with shiftwork: you have to work when you want to be asleep, and you have to sleep when you want to be awake. The effects of shiftwork require serious consideration because it is a feature of our industrialised society. We need people in industry, transportation, and health care to work around the clock to maintain the systems underpinning our society. It is estimated that approximately 20% of people employed in the United States work in shifts (US Congress, 1991). Another reason to be concerned about shiftwork is that records show that more accidents occur at night—when people are working when they should be asleep. The industrial accidents at Chernobyl, Bhopal, and Three-Mile Island all occurred between 1am and 4am; and most lorry accidents occur between 4am and 7am. Moore-Ede (1993) estimated the cost of shiftworker fatigue in the US to be $77 billion annually as a result of both major accidents and also ongoing medical expenses due to shiftwork-related illnesses.

? Would you expect to find that industrial accidents are more likely to occur at certain times of day?

There are ways to lessen the effects of shiftwork by using different work patterns. Monk and Folkard (1983) identified two major types of shiftwork: (1) rapidly rotating shifts, in which the worker only does one or two shifts at a given time before moving to a different work time: (2) slowly rotating shifts, in which the worker changes shifts much less often (e.g., every week or month). There are problems with both shift systems. However, rapidly rotating shifts may be preferable. They allow workers to maintain fairly constant circadian rhythms, whereas slowly rotating shifts can cause harmful effects by causing major changes to individuals' circadian rhythms. On the other hand, research has found that it takes most people about a week before their circadian rhythms have adjusted to a new sleep–wake cycle, so one might expect slowly rotating shifts to be better. Rapid rotation means your rhythms are always disrupted (Hawkins & Armstrong-Esther, 1978). It might help if shiftworkers reset their biological clocks as quickly as possible. Research has shown that it is possible to reset biological clocks using bright lights as a substitute for sunlight to reset the SCN. Dawson and Campbell (1991) exposed workers to a 4-hour pulse of very bright light, which appeared to help them work better.

Another way to lessen the effects of shiftwork is by using phase delay rather than phase advance, as we noted in relation to jet lag. It would be better to rotate shifts with the clock rather than against it so one is doing early shifts and then later shifts, then night shifts and then back to early shifts. Czeisler, Moore-Ede, and Coleman (1982) tested this in a chemical plant in Utah, finding that the workers reported feeling better and much less tired on the job. The management also reported increased productivity and fewer errors. Another feature of what

EXAM HINT
You may be asked to discuss the consequences of disrupting biological rhythms. Again AO2 can seem daunting with this question so use the following:

- Draw conclusions from the research evidence about the optimal direction and length of shift patterns, and direction of flight.
- Consider the positive applications of this research in terms of real-world usefulness and validity.
- Consider applications of the findings on light and medication times.
- Consider methodological weaknesses such as some of the research studies are natural experiments and so we cannot conclude cause and effect.
- There is a lack of control in such research and so other factors may influence the effects, such as individual differences, i.e., "lark or owl".
- Social factors rather than just biological ones need to be considered—a shift worker may spend little time with the family, which could lead to conflict that might exacerbate the negative effects.
- Disruption of biological rhythms other than the sleep–wake cycle could contribute to the effects, e.g., the temperature cycle.

INDEPENDENT STUDY IDEA: THE EFFECTS OF SHIFTWORK
Interview some shiftworkers, using a questionnaire which could comprise both fixed response and open-ended questions. The aim is to find out what effects shift work has on them. Start by establishing what their shift pattern is: is it clockwise rotating shifts (e.g. 6pm–2am; 2–10pm; 10pm–6am); 12 hour shifts day and night; shifts that are mainly daytime ones, etc. Ask about sleep patterns (including how much they vary from one shift to another), mood, relationships, etc. (but be careful not to be too intrusive). Emphasise to them that you are mainly interested in whether their mood and general sense of well-being changes according to the shift they are doing. It would also be interesting to see if they would recommend any changes in their shift work patterns and compare this to Czeisler's recommendations.

Czeisler et al. did was to have slower shift changes. More specifically, there was a shift rotation every 21 days rather than every 7 days—this proved beneficial because the workers had more time to adjust to any given work pattern before it was changed again.

Evaluation

There is clear evidence from studies of jet lag and shiftwork that people's circadian rhythms are easily disrupted. However, the good news is that we are reasonably good at adapting to such disruptions even though it sometimes takes a few days for adaptation to be complete. It is important to distinguish between effects of jet lag and shiftwork on biological rhythms and on self-report measures. Self-report measures undoubtedly reflect the influence of several factors not directly related to underlying bodily changes. For example, we may almost be inclined to boast of suffering from jet lag, and some of the adverse effects of shiftwork on mood may be due to missed opportunities for spending time with friends.

It is important not to lose sight of individual differences—we don't all respond in the same way to jet lag or shiftwork. We can distinguish between people who are at their most alert early in the day (larks) and those who are most alert in the evening (owls). The circadian rhythms of owls adjust more rapidly than those of larks to shiftwork (Akerstedt & Froberg, 1976). Part of this may be because shiftworkers often sleep late in the morning, and it seems plausible that owls would find this easier than larks.

SECTION SUMMARY
Biological Rhythms

What are biological rhythms?

❖ Biological rhythms are regularly repeated features of biological organisms. They can be categorised into:

— Circadian rhythms: rhythms that repeat themselves once a day (such as the sleep–waking cycle)
— Ultradian rhythms: rhythms of less than one day
— Infradian rhythms: rhythms of greater than one day, (such as the menstrual cycle) including circannual rhythms, which repeat once a year.

❖ Research into the effects of light deprivation (e.g., in a cave) show that circadian rhythms can persist in the absence of daylight and other cues. This indicates the existence of an internal (endogenous) biological clock.

❖ The suprachiasmatic nucleus (SCN) in the hypothalamus acts as an endogenous pacemaker, generating its own rhythms:

— The SCN receives input directly from the eye so it can also be reset by light cues.
— The SCN sends output to the pineal gland, regulating the production of melatonin.
— High levels of melatonin are associated with sleepiness.

The sleep–waking cycle: Internal factors

❖ Light: the dominant external cue or zeitgeber (can partially control biological rhythms).

❖ Social routines: are important as shown by the circadian rhythms of people living within the Arctic Circle.

The sleep–waking cycle: External factors

❖ Both internal biological processes and external cues are important. We have an internal body clock, but it can be entrained by external cues.

Conclusions

❖ There are also circadian rhythms based on psychological processes such as task performance. There is evidence for a peak at midday followed by a possible trough after lunch. The peak might be due to high levels of adrenaline, and the trough due to eating lunch.

Psychological circadian rhythms

❖ This is an example of an infradian rhythm. It is governed by:

— Endogenous (internal) factors: the release of hormones from the pituitary gland
— Exogenous (external) factors: there is some evidence to show that light or pheromones produced by other women or by men affect the menstrual cycle.

The menstrual cycle

❖ In animals, circannual rhythms include hibernation and migration. They are governed by:

— Endogenous (internal) factors: shown by research evidence in squirrels and wild birds
— Exogenous (external) factors such as day length and temperature.

Circannual rhythms

❖ In humans, circannual rhythms include seasonal affective disorder:

— Depression can be caused by seasonal variation, possibly as a result of melatonin level alterations changing daylight hours
— Phototherapy is used as a treatment.

❖ When body rhythms are disrupted, as a result of discrepancies between internal and external time cues, there may be serious consequences.

❖ Jet lag is more pronounced when travelling in an easterly direction (phase advance) than westerly (phase delay).

Disrupting body rhythms

See also pages 70–78 of the revision guide.

❖ Shiftwork is an important example as the costs in terms of accidents and health are high. Solutions include:

— Rapidly rotating shifts to reduce the internal/external discrepancy
— Slowly rotating shifts to allow the body's natural rhythms to catch up
— Bright lights to reset the biological clock
— Phase delay changes in shift patterns.

SLEEP

Sleep is an important part of all our lives, generally occupying almost one-third of our time. There are various ways of trying to understand sleep. First of all we can describe it. The most obvious way to do this is in terms of an ultradian rhythm with a number of stages, each of which lasts about 90 minutes, repeated five or six times a night. Second, we can consider the question of what function is served by sleep. What happens when individuals are deprived of sleep? Why do all animals sleep? Why do different animals have different patterns of sleep?

Stages of Sleep: An Ultradian Rhythm

Early investigations discovered two surprising features of sleep. First of all it is not as passive as one might be led to think when watching someone asleep. Individuals are often quite active during sleep. Second, there are different kinds of sleep. Being asleep is not a total loss of consciousness but a descent into reduced consciousness passing through different levels of awareness and different kinds of brain activity.

The notion of different kinds of sleep is described using the concept of "stages". One implication of a "stage theory" is that the stages follow a regular sequence, which is the case with sleep stages. A second implication is that there are qualitative differences between stages. In the case of sleep, each stage is defined by a distinctive pattern of brain activity, i.e., a qualitative and not just a quantitative difference.

The development of the electroencephalograph (or EEG) was crucial in the investigation of sleep because, without it, we had no way of measuring what is going on when someone is asleep. In essence, scalp electrodes are used to obtain a continuous measure of the electrical or brain-wave activity, which is recorded as a trace. Without this method of objective recording, researchers relied on self-reporting, which tells us nothing about the physiology of sleep. Other useful physiological measures include eye-movement data from an electro-oculogram or EOG, and muscle movements from an electromyogram or EMG.

There are two main aspects to EEG activity: frequency and amplitude. Frequency is defined as the number of oscillations of EEG activity per second, whereas amplitude is defined as half the distance between the high and low points of an oscillation. In practice, frequency is used more often than amplitude to describe the essence of EEG activity.

• *Stage 1*: A person becomes relaxed and drowsy and brain waves are synchronised (i.e., peaks and troughs in the wave pattern across the brain occur at the same time). There are characteristic alpha waves (waves having a frequency of between 8 and 12 cycles per second) in the EEG. The transition from awake beta waves to the alpha waves of stage 1 is often accompanied by a **hypnogogic state**, in which we may experience hallucinatory images.

? What happens to you physiologically and psychologically when you are asleep?

EXAM HINT

Sleep, as an ultradian rhythm, is also relevant to questions on biological rhythms. Sleep deprivation studies can therefore also be used as studies to illustrate disrupting biological rhythms.

KEY TERM

Hypnogogic state: a state sometimes experienced during the first stage of sleep, accompanied by hallucinatory images.

- *Stage 2*: The EEG waves become slower and larger (theta waves of frequency 4–8Hz). There is little activity in the EOG. K-complexes are also characteristic of stage 2. This stage lasts about 20 minutes. It is still quite easy to be awakened at this stage.
- *Stage 3*: Sleep deepens as the brain waves slow down and the person is described as "descending the sleep staircase". The EEG consists mainly of long, slow delta waves (1–5Hz) with some sleep spindles.
- *Stage 4*: There is a majority of the long, slow delta waves present in smaller amounts in the previous stage, and very little activity in the EOG or the EMG. This is a deeper stage of sleep than any of the first three stages, and it is often known as slow-wave sleep (SWS). Body temperature drops (which is why you need bed covers). Growth hormones are secreted at this time. It is the time when sleepwalking occurs and also sleeptalking and "night terrors" (a particular kind of nightmare where the dreamer may appear to be awake but terrified).
- *Stage 5*: Rapid eye movement or REM sleep, in which there are rapid eye movements and a very low level of EMG activity. REM sleep has been called **paradoxical sleep**, because it is harder to awaken someone from REM sleep than from any of the other stages, even though the EEG indicates that the brain is very active. The body is also paralysed during REM sleep, which may serve the useful function of preventing us from acting out our dreams.

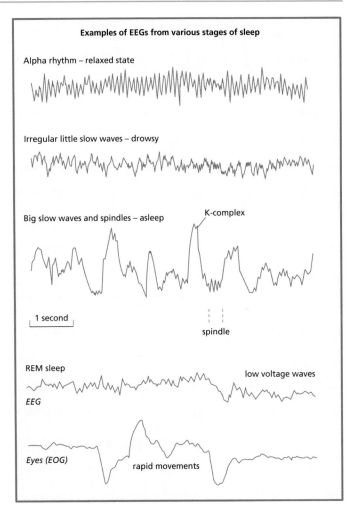

After the sleeper has worked through the first four stages of progressively deeper sleep, he/she reverses the process. Stage 4 sleep is followed by stage 3, and then by stage 2. However, stage 2 is followed by REM sleep (stage 5). After REM sleep, the sleeper starts another cycle, working his/her way through stages 2, 3, and 4, followed by stage 3, then stage 2, and then REM sleep again. A complete sleep cycle or ultradian cycle lasts about 90 minutes. Most sleepers complete about five ultradian cycles during a normal night's sleep, with progressively less SWS and more REM activity as morning approaches.

The proportion of the cycle devoted to REM sleep tends to increase from one cycle to the next.

Evaluation

The data on sleep stages are collected in highly artificial conditions. Participants have to spend the night in a sleep laboratory where they are wired up to various machines and may be woken during the night to report their dreams. As Hobson, Pace-Schott, and Stickgold (2000, p.803) pointed out, "Anyone who has ever slept in a sleep laboratory . . . knows that it is an inhospitable and unnatural

> **KEY TERM**
>
> **Paradoxical sleep:** a term used to describe REM sleep because of the behavioural contradictions (paradoxes): eye movement, heart rate, breathing, etc. are increased but the body is in a state of near paralysis and it is difficult to wake a person up.

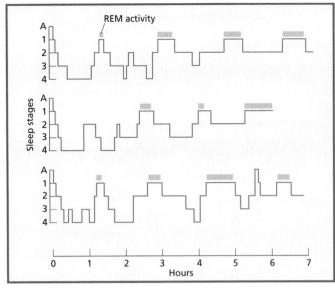

Cyclic variations in EEG during three typical nights' sleep. Note the increased REM activity as the night progresses, and reduced stage 4 sleep.

? Why do you think there are several stages of sleep?

EXAM HINT

The specification requires that you can relate the implications of sleep deprivation research to the theories of sleep. Note that restoration theories predict negative effects of sleep deprivation and that any lost sleep will need to be regained, whereas ecological theories do not. Use this to assess their validity.

setting that makes sleep more difficult and less deep than is possible in more naturalistic settings."

REM sleep and dreaming

REM sleep is the most interesting stage of sleep. Many people associate REM sleep with dreaming. Aserinsky and Kleitman (1955) first discovered this association, which was further investigated by Dement and Kleitman (1957; see the Key Study on page 153). Dement and Kleitman woke up their participants when they were in REM sleep, and most of them reported that they had just been dreaming. This link offered researchers an objective way to study dreams, or at least it would if REM sleep was the only time when dreams occurred. However, later research has shown that about 30% of sleepers in slow-wave sleep report having been dreaming when woken up (Green, 1994). This is a fairly high percentage, even though it is lower than the 70–75% for those awoken from REM sleep. But it does mean that REM sleep and dreaming are NOT equivalent. One reason that people think they don't dream in slow-wave sleep is because they are deeply asleep and, by the time they are awake, they have forgotten their dream. On the other hand, of course, it may be the case that 70% of people genuinely don't dream outside of REM sleep.

The dreams reported from REM sleep differ from those from other stages of sleep. Dreams during REM sleep tend to be vivid and detailed, whereas non-REM (NREM) dreams contain much less detail and are less coherent, with vague plots and concerning more commonplace things (McIlveen & Gross, 2000).

Theories of Sleep

Several theories of sleep function have been proposed over the years. However, most of them belong to two broad classes of theory:

1. Recovery or restoration theories.
2. Adaptive or ecological theories.

It may help to bear a few facts in mind as you are considering these theories. First, all animals sleep, which suggests that sleep serves some important function. The fact that the part of the brain that governs sleep is the oldest (in an evolutionary sense) also marks sleep out as a fundamental requirement of all animals.

Second, different species have quite different sleep requirements: they either sleep little and often, or for long periods at one time; or they sleep during the day or during the night, or they sleep one hemisphere at a time (as in the case of some dolphins). This suggests that sleep is an evolutionary adaptation to environmental conditions.

Finally, sleep deprivation studies show that there are some physical affects of both NREM and REM deprivation but these may be related to motivation as much as some kind of reduced capacity.

Recovery or restoration theories

An important function of sleep is probably to save energy and to permit the restoration of tissue. This notion is central to various recovery or restoration theories, such as those of Oswald (1980) and Horne (1988). These theories focus on the benefits of sleep for the physiological system. It is also possible that sleep conveys advantages to the psychological system. Thus, sleep may also serve to restore psychological functions.

According to Oswald's (1980) recovery theory, slow-wave sleep is useful for recovery processes in the body. There is a substantial release of growth hormone from the pituitary gland during slow-wave sleep, and this seems to provide strong support for the theory. This may stimulate protein synthesis and so contribute to the repair of tissues within the body. Oswald also argued that important recovery processes occur in the brain during REM sleep. In essence, Oswald claimed that NREM sleep is good for the body and REM sleep is good for the brain.

Horne (1988) put forward a recovery theory resembling that of Oswald (1980). However, he emphasised the fact that humans have periods of relaxed wakefulness during which there are rather low levels of energy expenditure. Repair of bodily tissues occurs during periods of relaxed wakefulness rather than during sleep itself. However, what is common to all recovery theories is the crucial assumption that sleep is essential for well-being and ultimately for survival. The disagreements concern the precise mechanisms involved in recovery and/or restoration.

Horne (2001) argued that sleep is important for the recovery of cerebral function especially that of the pre-frontal cortex. The pre-frontal cortex plays an important role in decision making and dealing with unexpected events, and sleep deprivation has strongly negative effects on those abilities (Harrison & Horne, 2000). As Horne pointed out, the notion that sleep permits recovery of cerebral function is most applicable to advanced mammalian species.

Physiological restoration

If physiological restoration is the function of sleep then we would expect that:

- Sleep deprivation would have serious effects because physiological restoration was prevented.
- Animals who use more energy would be likely to need to sleep more.
- More sleep would be likely to be required after periods of physical exertion.

The evidence from sleep deprivation studies suggests some negative effects, especially if an animal is deprived of SWS and/or REM sleep (evidence discussed shortly). Oswald (1980) identified SWS as being important in the recovery process, especially as it has been linked with the release of growth hormone and protein synthesis. There is also evidence of essential physiological processing during REM sleep. Stern and Morgane (1974) argue that the normal function of REM sleep is to restore levels of **neurotransmitters** after a day's activities. This is supported by evidence that some people on antidepressants show decreased REM, possibly because the drugs are increasing their neurotransmitter levels. The negative effects of REM rebound (see page 148) also support the view that REM sleep provides a restorative function.

However, as Horne (1988) argued, restoration may occur during waking hours even if it is less efficient or more resource intensive. Then loss of sleep would have an effect but not necessarily a serious one. So sleep deprivation effects alone are not sufficient evidence.

KEY TERM

Neurotransmitters: chemical substances that are released at the junction between neurons (a synapse) and that affect the transmission of messages in the nervous system.

The physiology of sleep

This is an alternative theoretical account of sleep, focusing on the physiological events of sleep rather than the psychological need for sleep.

The typical processes in human sleep are as follows. Darkness causes the *suprachiasmatic nucleus* (the SCN, our "biological clock") to produce *melatonin*, which in turn enhances the production of *serotonin*. This accumulates in the *pons*, a region of the hindbrain. In particular it accumulates in the *raphe nucleus*. When levels of serotonin have risen to an appropriate level this causes the *reticular activating system* (RAS) to shut down. The RAS is involved with levels of arousal or alertness (Moruzzi & Magoun, 1949).

Once a person is asleep, there are further physiological mechanisms that govern the sleep cycle:

1. The *raphe nucleus* (in the RAS) initiates NREM sleep. We know this from various studies. For example, Jouvet (1967) lesioned the raphe system in cats and found this resulted in sleeplessness, concluding that serotonin and the raphe nucleus initiate sleep (called the monoamine hypothesis because serotonin is a monoamine).
2. The *locus coeruleus* (shu-rule-us) produces *noradrenaline*, which leads to onset of REM sleep. The locus coeruleus is inactive during REM sleep and also much of our waking time. It appears to be involved in the special kind of arousal that helps form memories, which may explain why we do not always remember dreams.
3. The *pons* produces *acetylcholine*, which leads to REM sleep. We know this because drugs that stimulate the production of acetylcholine quickly change NREM to REM sleep (Baghdoyan, Spotts, & Snyder, 1993). The pons also transmits PGO (ponsgeniculate-occipital) waves, which lead to REM sleep. As a REM period continues, these PGO waves spread to more of the cerebral cortex. During prolonged periods of REM deprivation, the PGO waves emerge during other stages of sleep besides REM sleep. They may even occur when awake and are associated with strange behaviours such as hallucinations.

The three systems are:

- The serotonergic system of the raphe nuclei. Drugs that block serotonin prevent the onset of REM (Kalat, 1998).
- The noradrenergic system of the locus coeruleus. When noradrenaline levels fall REM sleep is impaired (Jouvet, 1967).
- The acetylcholinergic system of the pons. Drugs that block acetylcholine interfere with the continuation of REM sleep (Kalat, 1998).

? Why do you think small animals need relatively more slow-wave sleep than larger ones?

In terms of animals that use more energy, we should look at the evidence related to small mammals having comparatively high metabolic rates. Allison and Cicchetti (1976) surveyed 39 mammalian species to work out the amount of time spent in slow-wave sleep (SWS) and in REM sleep. Body weight and metabolic rate were found to be related to amounts of SWS, with smaller mammals having more SWS. In terms of REM sleep, vulnerability to danger (e.g., danger of being preyed upon) was found to be important, with those most vulnerable having less REM sleep than those least vulnerable. This makes sense given that REM sleep is a state from which it is very hard to awaken an animal.

Evidence of the effects of physical exertion can be found both in natural and laboratory experiments. Shapiro et al. (1981) studied runners who had taken part in an ultra marathon covering 57 miles. These runners slept about an hour and a half longer than normal on the 2 nights after the ultra marathon, and there was an especially large increase in the amount of time devoted to SWS. Researchers also cite the evidence that newborn infants (who experience enormous brain growth) have a very high percentage of their time asleep devoted to REM sleep (Green, 1994). On the other hand, Horne and Minard (1985) tried to exhaust their participants with numerous activities and found that they went to sleep faster but not for longer. It might be imagined that people who take very little exercise would sleep for less time than those who take an average amount of exercise, but there is little or no evidence to support this.

Psychological functions

As was mentioned earlier, one of the possible functions of sleep is to permit restoration of psychological functions. There are various studies in which associations were found between quality of sleep and mood. Naitoh (1975) discussed various studies concerned with the effects of 1 night's sleep deprivation on mood. The effects were consistently negative. Sleep-deprived individuals described themselves as less friendly, relaxed, good-natured, and cheerful than those who had not been sleep deprived.

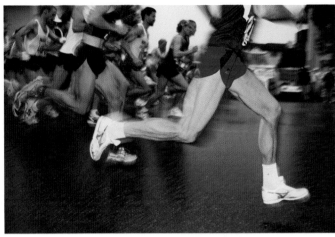

Although studies show that people need extra sleep following extreme exertion, there is no evidence that people who take little or no exercise reduce their sleeping time.

Insomniacs (who have persistent problems with sleeping) tend to be more worried and anxious than people who sleep normally. However, it is not clear whether their anxiety is a cause or an effect of sleep deprivation. It is usually assumed that it is more a question of people's worries and concerns disrupting sleep than of disrupted sleep causing worries. This is supported by Berry and Webb (1983), in a study in which they assessed self-reported anxiety. When people slept well during a given night, their level of anxiety on the following day was lower than when they had slept poorly.

So the evidence supports the view that lack of sleep causes depressed mood and increased anxiety, therefore suggesting that sleep has a role in the recovery of some psychological functions.

Evaluation of recovery theories

There is considerable support for the theory but there are also problems or inconsistencies. The notion that SWS may be related to protein synthesis doesn't make sense when one considers that amino acids, which are the ingredients of proteins, can't be stored in the body and only last for about 4 hours after a meal. This would mean that protein synthesis could only take place in the initial 4 hours of sleep and can't explain why we appear to need more than 4 hours' sleep (Bentley, 2000). Though we might mention the study by Webb and Bonnet (1978; see page 149) that did indeed find that people could be trained to reduce their sleep requirements to 4 hours nightly without apparent ill effects.

Another question is why we need to reduce consciousness during sleep. There is evidence that relaxed wakefulness during which there are rather low levels of energy expenditure could and does provide an opportunity for bodily repair. As was mentioned earlier, Horne (1988) emphasised the importance of periods of relaxed wakefulness (termed micro-sleep) for restoration. What evidence supports this position? Horne pointed out that most of Randy Gardner's problems during sleep deprivation (he remained awake for 264 hours; Horne, 1988—see below) were connected with brain processes rather than with other physiological processes in the body. The implication is that sleep is not essential for the repair of bodily tissues, which can happen at other times. The concept of micro-sleep can also explain why people don't always experience symptoms of sleep deprivation when they have had no sleep—they may have had periods of micro-sleep when apparently awake. However, considering that these periods are so brief it is difficult to see how much could be restored.

Types of sleep

We have seen that REM is one type of sleep, and the term NREM is used to describe the other stages of sleep. REM sleep has also been called paradoxical sleep because of the apparent paradox between being physically paralysed yet mentally active. Meddis (1979) used the terms **active** and **quiet sleep** for REM and NREM sleep respectively, and Horne (1988) referred to **core sleep** to describe those aspects of sleep that are more essential to survival, i.e., if we are deprived of core sleep this does seem to matter whereas other kinds of sleep appear to be less important. Finally there is **micro-sleep**, brief periods of relaxed wakefulness during the day when a person stares blankly into space and temporarily loses awareness. Such periods may permit some restorative functions to take place.

? Do you find that some worries and problems recede after a good night's sleep? Is this valid evidence for the function of sleep?

KEY TERMS

Active sleep: a term used to refer to REM sleep.
Quiet sleep: a term used to refer to NREM (non-rapid eye movement) sleep.
Core sleep: those aspects of sleep that are more essential to survival.
Micro-sleep: brief periods of relaxed wakefulness during the day when a person stares blankly into space and temporarily loses awareness. Such periods may permit some restorative functions to take place.

If restoration was the only function of sleep then we would expect to find consistent effects from sleep deprivation. The apparently inconsistent effects may be due to the fact that only some aspects of sleep provide a physiological and/or psychological restoration function, i.e., core sleep that includes SWS and also REM sleep. The importance of these stages of sleep is supported by the previously mentioned sleep-deprivation study on Randy Gardner. After his long period of sleep deprivation (11 days), there was much greater recovery of REM sleep and stage 4 slow-wave sleep than of the other stages of sleep. But then why do we have other sleep stages?

We can also argue that if sleep has a restorative function we would expect people who are more active to require more sleep. But we have seen that the evidence doesn't wholly support this view.

Finally, we can ask why, if sleep is restorative in all animals, there are so many different variations in the way that animals sleep. It may be that sleep serves an adaptive rather than a restorative function.

Adaptive or ecological theories

According to various theorists sleep can be regarded as an adaptive behaviour to fit in with one's habitat. In contrast with the theoretical views we have been discussing, such theorists doubt whether sleep is important for purposes of restoration or recovery.

Sleep as protection against predation

Meddis (1975a) proposed that the sleep behaviour shown by any species depends on the need to adapt to environmental threats and dangers. Thus, for example, sleep serves the function of keeping animals fairly immobile and safe from predators during periods of time when they cannot engage in feeding and other kinds of behaviour. In the case of those species that depend on vision, it is adaptive for them to sleep during the hours of darkness.

It follows that those species in danger from predators should sleep more of the time than those species that are predators. In fact, however, predators tend to sleep more than those preyed upon (Allison & Cicchetti, 1976). This might seem inconsistent with adaptive theories of sleep. However, species in danger from predators might benefit from remaining vigilant most of the time and sleeping relatively little. This seems like an example of having your cake and eating it, in the sense that any pattern of findings can be explained by the adaptive or ecological approach! Thus, it is not possible to falsify Meddis' theory.

Interesting evidence that the pattern of sleep is often dictated by the environmental threats faced by animals was reported by Pilleri (1979). Dolphins living in the River Indus are in constant danger from debris floating down the river. As a consequence, these dolphins sleep for only a few seconds at a time to protect themselves from the debris. However, it is hard to explain why they sleep at all if sleep is not essential!

Modest support for adaptive or ecological theories comes from a few reports of individuals leading healthy lives in spite of regularly sleeping for very short periods of time each day (e.g., Meddis, Pearson, & Langford, 1973). For example, Miss M., a cheerful 70-year-old retired nurse typically slept for only 1 hour per day. She generally sat on her bed reading or writing until about 2 in the morning, after which she would sleep for about 1 hour. When she was studied under laboratory conditions, she slept an average of 67 minutes per night.

Hibernation theory

Webb (1982) suggested a different adaptive account, called the hibernation theory. In this version of an ecological theory, sleep is seen as adaptive because it conserves energy in the same way that hibernation enhances survival by reducing physiological demands at a time of year when they would be hard to fulfil. The same principles could be applied to staying awake at night. Any animal that is not nocturnal will be twiddling its thumbs, so to speak, and might as well relax and save energy. The same could be said of nocturnal animals during the day. Animals that don't rest when not engaged in finding food use more energy and need more food, which may decrease their survival potential.

Evaluation of adaptation theories

We have already seen that there are problems with the predation theory, in terms of it being non-falsifiable. There are also problems with applying this theory to human sleep. It is possible that when our ancestors were evolving, sleep did provide an adaptive advantage for either or both safety and energy conservation. (This is called the environment of evolutionary adaptation—EEA—the period in human evolution during which time our genes were shaped and selected by natural selection to solve survival problems operating then, roughly between 35,000 and 3 million years ago.) However, one wonders why there hasn't been some move in the direction of less sleep when today there would be enormous advantages for an individual who needed very little sleep—think what you could do if you didn't have to sleep!

So far as humans are concerned, sleep is of little value in energy conservation. As Horne (2001, p.302) pointed out, "The energy saved by being asleep throughout the night rather than sitting relaxed but awake is trivial—the energy equivalent to a slice of bread."

The finding that vulnerable species tend to sleep less of the time than non-vulnerable or predator species seems to be the opposite of the "natural" prediction from adaptation theories. Even if the theory is modified to allow for predator species sleeping more of the time than vulnerable species, it is important to note that this is only correlational evidence—it would be dangerous to infer that belonging to a predator species causes animals to sleep longer.

Empson (1989) regards these adaptation theories as a "waste of time" because they propose that sleep itself is just wasting time so that the individual is safer and/or using less energy. Empson's criticism seems reasonable. But deprivation studies do suggest that lack of sleep has distinct consequences so it can't just be a waste of time, as suggested by ecological theories.

Bearing in mind the two theoretical approaches to sleep, explain why human babies sleep a lot.

Recovery or adaptation?

How can we decide between recovery and adaptive theories of sleep function? According to most recovery theories, sleep is absolutely essential to well-being. In contrast, sleep is generally rather less crucial according to adaptive theories. There are no reports of human beings who have managed without sleep and members of all species sleep at least some of the time. However, there are a few reports of individuals who led normal healthy lives in spite of regularly sleeping for very short periods of time each day (e.g., Meddis et al., 1973). The finding that severe sleep deprivation produces a range of adverse effects (see below) fits restoration/recovery theories better than adaptive or ecological ones. However, adaptive theorists would point out that the effects of sleep deprivation are rarely long-lasting.

Evidence against adaptive theories has been obtained from individuals with **fatal familial insomnia**. They sleep normally for many years, but then stop sleeping when about 35 or 40 years old. Individuals with fatal familial insomnia typically die within 2 years of the onset of the insomnia (Medori et al., 1992). Why do they die if sleep is not essential?

On balance, the recovery approach seems to provide a more thorough and well-developed account of sleep. However, it could be argued that these two approaches address somewhat different issues. The recovery approach provides some views on *why* sleep is important, whereas the adaptive approach also focuses on *when* different species sleep. More generally, Horne (1988) made the important point that sleep probably serves somewhat different purposes in different species. Thus, no single theory of the functions of sleep is likely to be adequate.

? When two different approaches address different issues within an area of psychology, is it possible to make a true comparison between them?

Research Studies of Sleep Deprivation

Considering that we spend almost 200,000 hours asleep in the course of a lifetime, it seems reasonable to assume that sleep must serve one or more key functions. However, it has proved hard to discover these functions. One way of trying to work out *why* we sleep is to deprive people of sleep and see what happens. It could be argued that the kinds of problems and impairments experienced by sleep-deprived individuals are those that sleep is designed to prevent.

People often cope surprisingly well when deprived of sleep. Consider, for example, the case of Peter Tripp. He was a New York disc jockey who took part in a "wakeathon" for charity. He managed to stay awake for 8 days or about 200 hours. He suffered from delusions and hallucinations (e.g., that his desk drawer was on fire). These delusions were so severe that it was hard to test his precise level of psychological functioning. However, it is unclear whether he showed any long-term effects from his wakeathon. One report suggests that he suffered psychological consequences months and even years later, but we don't know to what extent such behaviour was the result of his one bout of sleep deprivation. It should be noted that the whole study lacked adequate control and may relate only to the characteristics of this unique individual.

Horne (1988) discussed the case of Randy Gardner, a 17-year-old student who remained awake for 264 hours or 11 days in 1964. Towards the end of the 11-day period, he suffered from disorganised speech, blurred vision, and a small degree

KEY TERM

Fatal familial insomnia: an inherited disorder in which the ability to sleep disappears in middle age and is typically followed by death several months later.

of paranoia (e.g., thinking that other people regarded him as stupid because of his impaired functioning). In view of the fact that Randy Gardner missed out on about 80–90 hours of sleep, he had remarkably few problems. He was clearly less affected than Tripp by sleep deprivation, even though he remained awake for 3 extra days.

After his ordeal was over, Randy Gardner slept for 15 hours. He slept longer than usual for a few nights thereafter, before reverting to his normal sleep pattern. However, he did not recover more than 25% (about 20 hours) of the 80–90 hours of sleep he had missed. If sleep were essential we might expect that he would need to recover it all. He did, however, recover almost 70% of stage 4 deep sleep and 50% of REM sleep, with very small recovery percentages for the other stages of sleep. This suggests that stage 4 and REM sleep are of special importance.

You will note that these are studies of single individuals, because it is difficult to arrange large-scale deprivation experiments over a prolonged period of time—not many people are willing (or have the time) to go without sleep for 11 days! Hüber-Weidman (1976) documented the effects of sleep deprivation over time (see the Key Study on page 149). However, Horne (1988) reviewed numerous studies in which humans were sleep deprived, typically for periods of between 1 and 3 days. There were no reports of physical illness, but there was a very small drop in body temperature of about 0.5°C. According to Horne, these findings suggest that restorative processes occur effectively during the wakefulness of sleep deprivation.

Finally, it is also possible to conduct experimental studies with non-human animals. Rechtschaffen et al. (1983) placed two rats at a time on a disc above a water container. The EEG activity of both rats was monitored. One rat was not allowed to sleep, because the disc started to rotate and caused it to fall in the water whenever its EEG activity indicated that it was starting to sleep. In contrast, the other rat was allowed to sleep, because the disc stopped rotating when its EEG indicated sleep. All of the sleep-deprived rats died within 33 days, whereas the rats that were not sleep-deprived seemed in good health.

It is hard to be sure whether findings on rats also apply to humans. However, Lugaressi et al. (1986) studied a 52-year-old man who could hardly sleep at all because of damage to parts of his brain involved in sleep regulation. Not surprisingly, he became absolutely exhausted, and was unable to function normally. Eventually he died, possibly as a result of the sleeplessness, though the anxiety created by his condition may have contributed (as may also have been the case with the rats). The post-mortem examination revealed that he had lesions in those areas of his brain linked with control of sleep.

REM sleep deprivation

We saw in the case of Randy Gardner that he recovered more of his lost REM sleep than most other stages of sleep. Dement (1960) carried out a systematic study of REM and NREM sleep. Some of his participants were deprived of REM sleep over a period of several days, whereas others were deprived of NREM sleep. In general, the effects of REM sleep deprivation were more severe, including increased aggression and poor concentration. Those deprived of REM sleep tried to catch up on the REM sleep they had missed. They started to enter REM sleep 12 times on average during the first night in the laboratory, but this rose to 26

? What are the drawbacks of using case studies to collect evidence?

? How do you deprive someone of NREM sleep? If the answer is that you cannot, what does this say about the validity of Dement's research?

? Is it possible to study sleep deprivation in humans without encountering ethical difficulties?

times on the seventh night. When they were free to sleep undisturbed, most of them spent much longer than usual in REM sleep; this is known as a REM rebound effect.

Again research with non-human animals may be an important source of information. Jouvet (1967) used the "flower-pot technique" to test the consequences of REM deprivation in cats and other animals. He placed an upturned flower-pot in a large tank of water. The cats had to sit on the pots and eventually fell asleep. In NREM sleep they were able to remain sitting up, but with loss of muscle tone in REM sleep they slipped into the water and were abruptly awoken. Very soon they woke up as soon as their heads began to nod. In the end the cats died, leading to the conclusion that the lack of REM sleep had been fatal. It is possible, however, that again the stress of the whole experience may have also affected their health.

Task performance

There have been more controlled laboratory studies of sleep deprivation in humans than just the case studies described earlier (see M.W. Eysenck, 1982, for a review). Sleep deprivation over the first 3 days or so has few adverse effects on tasks that are complex and interesting. However, sleep-deprived individuals tend to perform poorly on tasks that are monotonous and uninteresting. This is especially the case when these tasks are performed in the early hours of the morning and need to be performed over a longish period of time. A good example is the vigilance task, in which the participants have to detect signals (e.g., faint lights) that are only presented occasionally.

? Many people feel that when they are tired they can't work at their best. What do psychologists suggest to be the reason for this depressed performance?

What do these findings mean? According to Wilkinson (1969, p.39), it is "difficult for us to assess the 'real' effect of lost sleep upon subjects' *capacity* as opposed to their *willingness* to perform". Wilkinson and others found that most of the adverse effects of sleep loss on performance could be eliminated if attempts were made to motivate the participants (e.g., by providing knowledge of results). It thus appears that poor performance by sleep-deprived individuals is usually due to low motivation rather than to reduced capacity.

Effects over time

It appears that impaired performance on boring tasks is one of the main problems caused by sleep deprivation over the first 3 nights of sleep loss. During the fourth night of sleep deprivation, there tend to be very short (2–3 second) periods of micro-sleep during which the individual is unresponsive (Hüber-Weidman, 1976; see the Key Study on the next page). In addition, this length of sleep deprivation sometimes produces the so-called "hat phenomenon". In this phenomenon, it feels to the sleep-deprived person as if he/she were wearing a rather small hat that fits very tightly. From the fifth night on, there may be delusions as reported by Peter Tripp, though Randy Gardner did not suffer from these so early on. From the sixth night on, there are more severe

Air traffic controllers have to be alert to tiny changes in flashing lights on their screens at all hours of the day or night; as the lights represent aircraft, motivation to be vigilant remains high.

problems such as partial loss of a sense of identity and increased difficulty in dealing with other people and the environment. Some of these symptoms were experienced by Randy Gardner. The term sleep-deprivation psychosis has been used to refer to these symptoms (Hüber-Weidman, 1976). However, this is probably an exaggerated description of the actual symptoms.

KEY STUDY
The effects of sleep deprivation

Hüber-Weidman (1976) reviewed a large number of sleep deprivation studies, and produced a summary of the findings:

- After one night of sleep deprivation people report not feeling very comfortable, but it is tolerable.
- Two nights: People feel a much greater urge to sleep, especially when the body temperature rhythm is lowest at 3–5am.
- Three nights: Tasks that involve sustained attention or complex processing become much more difficult, especially when they are boring. If the experimenter offers encouragement or the tasks are made more interesting, then performance is improved. This is again worst in the very early hours.
- Four nights: Micro-sleep periods start to occur while the sleep-deprived person is awake. These last about 3 seconds during which the person stares blankly into space and temporarily loses awareness. They also generally become irritable and confused.
- Five nights: The above effects continue and the person may start to experience delusions. It appears that cognitive abilities, such as problem solving, remain fairly unimpaired.
- Six nights: The person starts to show signs of "sleep deprivation psychosis", which involves a loss of a sense of personal identity, a sense of depersonalisation, and increased difficulty in coping with other people and the environment.

Discussion points

1. What conclusions can you draw from this review of studies about sleep deprivation?
2. What might be the purpose of micro-sleep?

Partial deprivation

Some research studies have looked at the effects of reduced sleep, rather than total deprivation as in the previous studies. Webb and Bonnet (1978) deprived their participants of 2 hours of sleep a night. The participants reported feeling fine. They did, however, go to sleep more quickly the next night and also slept for longer. A further study looked at the possibility of reducing sleep needs. Participants spent 2 months making themselves have gradually less and less sleep. Eventually they were able to have just 4 hours' sleep a night without apparent ill effects.

Health consequences

So far we have focused on the short-term effects of sleep deprivation. However, as you will probably

 INDEPENDENT STUDY IDEA: IS THERE A SLEEP DEBT?
Do people make up for lack of sleep during the week by sleeping longer at the weekend? Ask people to make a note of what time they go to sleep and wake up every night for at least a week. See if those who sleep comparatively little during the week make up for it at the weekends. Results can be analysed by first of all splitting the groups in two: low levels of sleep in the week and high levels of sleep in the week (you may need to discard some data if participants fall in between); then compare the total amount of sleep at weekends. You need a test of difference for independent groups. It's possible that results could go either way: the idea of a sleep debt would suggest that sleep at the weekends will be greater in the "low weekday sleep" group but if sleep is determined by individual differences and/or habit, then the "low weekday sleep" group will sleep less at weekends.

? What do partial deprivation studies tell us about the purpose of sleep?

agree, millions of people are actually chronically sleep deprived, meaning that they generally don't have as much sleep as they need. The National Sleep Foundation (2001) carried out a study in the United States on people who are chronically sleep deprived. It was found that several serious conditions including depression, nighttime heartburn, hypertension, and heart disease were associated with chronic sleep deprivation. In addition, sleep deprivation was associated with obesity and acceleration of the ageing process.

There is increasing evidence that other serious health problems are associated with chronic sleep deprivation. For example, the American Diabetes Association argued in 2001 that sleep deprivation increases the risk of developing diabetes. Chronic sleep deprivation impairs the ability of insulin to work effectively, and this in turn increases an individual's chances of becoming diabetic. Even more worryingly, it has been found that women having one or more almost sleepless nights per week have a greater risk of developing breast cancer (Hall, 2001). Note that this is correlational evidence, and it is possible that women who have potentially serious health problems may find it harder to sleep as a consequence.

Evaluation

Most of the research on sleep deprivation is concerned with the effects of being deprived of sleep for upwards of 24 hours. As we have seen, the effects are generally surprisingly small and tend not to be long-lasting. However, it is the potential adverse effects of chronic sleep deprivation in our 24/7 society that are of real concern. There is more and more evidence suggesting that chronic sleep deprivation is associated with a wide range of diseases, some of which are potentially fatal. However, it is generally unclear whether the sleep deprivation actually helps to trigger the disease or whether the early stages of the disease make it harder to achieve a full night's sleep. However, what is indisputable is that sleep deprivation is partly responsible for numerous car accidents and deaths. According to the National Highway Traffic Safety Administration in the United States, about 100,000 car crashes a year occur due to drivers falling asleep. These crashes led to 76,000 injuries and about 1500 deaths.

SECTION SUMMARY
Sleep

Stages of sleep

❖ As a person falls asleep their brain waves have progressively reduced frequency and amplitude, and bodily activity also slows down.
❖ Sleep consists of five separate stages.

— Of particular importance is stage 4 sleep: slow-wave (SWS) and deep.
— After this stage, the sleeper ascends the "sleep staircase" and enters a more active phase: stage 5 (REM sleep) during which most dreaming occurs.
— The sequence of five stages is repeated during the night with progressively less SWS sleep and more REM activity.

❖ Physiological measures such as the EEG, EOG, and EMG are used to measure physiological activity during sleep.

❖ Recovery theories of sleep propose that sleep has benefits for the physiological system and the psychological system.

❖ Physiological recovery:

— According to Oswald and Horne the physiological restoration of proteins and neurotransmitters takes place during sleep.

— SWS and REM sleep are likely to be most important in recovery.

— Support for this view comes from studies of sleep and REM deprivation, from evidence that smaller animals with higher metabolic rates sleep more, and evidence from studies of physical exertion.

❖ Psychological recovery:

— Various studies show that mood and anxiety may be negatively affected by lack of sleep.

❖ Problems with the restorative account:

— Can proteins be stored in the body?

— Why do we have to reduce consciousness when asleep rather than just relaxing?

— Why do we have other stages of sleep apart from core sleep?

❖ Adaptive theories suggest that sleep promotes survival so is naturally selected.

❖ Meddis suggested that sleep keeps animals safe at times of danger, such as during the night.

❖ Webb suggested that sleep, like hibernation, prevents an animal expending energy unnecessarily.

❖ Problems with adaptive theories:

— Criticisms focus on the non-falsifiability of the theory and the question of how much it can explain human sleep.

— Sleep deprivation can have harmful consequences, so sleep doesn't just "waste time".

❖ It may be that recovery theory explains *why* we sleep, whereas adaptation theory focuses on *when*.

❖ In general, however, the recovery/restoration approach accounts for more of the evidence.

❖ Case studies of prolonged sleep deprivation on a single occasion show few ill effects, but it is inappropriate to overgeneralise from these studies.

❖ Studies of non-human animals have found that sleep deprivation results in death, and this is supported by the case of a man who was unable to sleep and also died.

❖ REM sleep deprivation:

— Randy Gardner showed a greater need to recover REM sleep.

— Studies of REM deprivation in both humans and animals have shown greater effects from REM deprivation than sleep deprivation in general.

— This confirms the REM rebound effect.

Recovery/restoration theories of sleep

Adaptive theories of sleep

Recovery or adaptation?

Research studies of sleep deprivation

The effects of sleep deprivation

❖ According to controlled laboratory studies, deprivation may affect motivation rather than actual task performance.

❖ After more than 3 days there are increased periods of micro-sleep and, eventually, sleep deprivation psychosis.

❖ Studies of partial sleep deprivation indicate that people can cope with less sleep.

❖ Chronic sleep deprivation over a long period of time is associated with several serious diseases. However, since the evidence is only correlational, it is not altogether clear whether chronic sleep deprivation is one of the factors involved in *causing* these diseases.

See also pages 79–86 of the revision guide.

DREAMING

A photo montage illustrating eye movement during REM sleep.

Research Relating to the Nature of Dreams

Most (but by no means all) dreaming takes place during REM (rapid eye movement) sleep. We can thus use the duration of REM sleep during the night as one approximate measure of how long any given individual spends dreaming. It also means we can consider what other physiological activities are taking place simultaneously to try to find out why people (and other animals) dream. The fact that we devote so much time to dreaming (about 700 hours a year) suggests that dreams are likely to fulfil some important function or functions. As we will see, various theorists have tried to identify these functions.

We know that non-human animals have REM sleep—any cat or dog owner will describe episodes of twitching in their pet's sleep as if it were chasing rabbits. However, we have no way of finding what their subjective experiences actually are. In humans we can ask people to tell us about their dreams, though again we do not know how many of their dreams are forgotten, or to what extent their recall is distorted by the fact that they were asleep. A classic study by Dement and Kleitman (1957; see the Key Study opposite) aimed to provide researchers with a way of conducting objective research into dreams.

In fact, not all animals have REM sleep. It has not been observed in dolphins nor in the spiny anteater but otherwise appears to be common to all mammals. It is not found in fish, reptiles, and amphibians and only occasionally in some birds of prey. This suggests some link with higher order brain functioning.

EXAM HINT
You may be asked a question on the nature of dreams, which may seem a bit limiting. However, it is not if you use this content to assess the theories of dreaming:
• AO1 will be an outline of research into the content, duration, and type of dreaming.
• AO2 will involve assessing whether the research supports or contradicts the theories.
Avoid describing the theories as the question has not asked for this. Consider that different dreams may support different explanations; perhaps we have different dreams for different reasons.

KEY STUDY
An objective method for the study of dreaming

Dement and Kleitman (1957) sought to demonstrate a link between REM activity and dreaming, to facilitate research into dreaming. If one could demonstrate that REM activity was dreaming, then you could investigate the possible functions of dreaming by finding out what else was related to REM activity rather than having to rely on the subjective and unreliable reports of dreamers once they woke up.

If REM sleep is dreaming then we might expect:

- Dreams to be specific to REM sleep.
- The duration of REM activity and the subjective report of dreaming to be similar.
- The movement of the eyes to be related to the visual imagery of the dream. For example, if someone dreamt of playing basketball their eyes would move up and down.

Nine adults took part in the study. Typically a participant reported to the sleep laboratory just before their usual bedtime and went to bed in a darkened room. Electrodes were attached around the participant's eyes to measure eye movement (EOG), and to the participant's scalp to record brain activity as a measure of depth of sleep (EEG). At various times during the night a bell rang and woke the participants up. They were woken either randomly or during alternations of REM and NREM activity. The participant then spoke into a recording machine by their bed, saying (a) whether they had been dreaming and (b) describing the content of the dream. An experimenter was listening outside the room and, if he had further questions, he would come in and ask the participant about other details. On average participants were awoken six times a night.

Dement and Kleitman found that all participants had REM activity every night. REM periods lasted between 3 and 50 minutes. During that time the eyes were not constantly in motion but there were bursts of activity. Interestingly REM activity occurred at regular intervals for each individual. For one participant they were every 70 minutes, for another every 104 minutes. The average was an REM episode every 92 minutes.

Most dreams were recalled during REM sleep but some dreams were reported when patients were woken from NREM sleep. When participants were awoken during deep sleep they sometimes were rather bewildered and reported that they must have been dreaming, though they couldn't remember the dream. They recalled a mood, such as anxiety or pleasantness, but no specific content.

One way to estimate the length of the dream was in terms of the number of words the participant used to describe the dream. Another way was to ask the participant to estimate the length. Both were positively correlated with the length of REM activity.

There did appear to be some support for a relationship between eye movement and dream activity, for example, when one participant displayed horizontal eye movements (which were quite rare) they dreamt they were watching two people throwing tomatoes at each other.

Key study evaluation
A key criticism of this research is its artificiality. It is quite possible that sleeping in a laboratory would not be entirely representative of normal sleeping, and dreaming, patterns. Furthermore the fact that participants were awoken during the night might affect their behaviour, especially when one considers the effects of REM deprivation (see pages 147–148). Nevertheless this research did provide some useful data about dreaming—although it did not find an exclusive link between REM activity and dreaming.

Discussion points
1. What are the main findings of this study?
2. How could these findings be used to investigate the function of dreams?

In what way are REM sleep and dreams the same—and how are they different?

Remembering your dreams

Newborn babies spend about 9 hours a day in REM sleep, and adults 2 hours. You may not feel that you spend this amount of time dreaming. One reason is that maybe not all of REM sleep involves dreaming. Another reason is that we forget more than 95% of our dreams. What are these forgotten dreams about? Researchers have obtained some idea by using sleep laboratories, in which sleepers are woken up when the EEG and EOG records indicate that a dream is taking place. This allows the researcher to assess the content of dreams that probably would normally be forgotten, and these tend to be much more ordinary and less strange than the dreams we normally remember (Empson, 1989). This is important, because it shows that the dreams we normally remember aren't *representative* or typical of dreams in general. It would thus not be appropriate to produce a general theory of dreaming purely on the basis of the 5% of dreams we normally remember, aside from the problem of subjective recall.

One reason why dreams are forgotten may be that during REM sleep a part of the hindbrain—the locus coeruleus—is inactive. This structure may be important for the special kind of arousal that helps us form memories and may explain why we often have only partial recall for our dreams (Chiara, Pompeiano, & Tononi, 1996).

What do we dream about? Germain et al. (2000) found that the most typical theme in dreams involved the threatening situation of being chased or pursued. Other common themes were dreams of sexual experiences and of falling. More generally, Hall and van de Castle (1966) found that there were seven times as many dreams involving misfortune (e.g., mishaps, dangers) as good fortune (411 dreams vs. 58, respectively).

As you would probably guess, there are important sex differences in the content of their dreams (Tonay, 2003). Men's dreams tend to be set outdoors and often involve unfamiliar men. In contrast, women's dreams are more likely to be set inside their home or workplace and to involve familiar people. These differences are also found in sex dreams. Men typically dream about having sex with someone they don't know, whereas women dream about sex with their current partner or a previous partner.

It is important to note that we can't access other people's dreams directly. As Coenen (2000, p.923) pointed out, "A dream is what someone describes upon awakening and researchers infer a one-to-one relationship between the dream and the way it is reported. It is therefore impossible to exclude such confounding factors as poor memory, overestimation, suppression or the effects of psycho-emotional factors on recall."

Dreaming and consciousness

Are we conscious when we are dreaming? Empson (1989) identified various differences between dreaming and waking consciousness. First, dreamers typically feel that they have little or no control over their dreams, whereas we nearly always have a sense of conscious control in our waking lives. However, some people have **lucid dreams**, in which they know they are dreaming and can sometimes control the dream content. For example, LaBerge, Greenleaf, and Kedzierski (1983) studied a woman who was able to create lucid sex dreams that produced orgasms.

KEY TERM

Lucid dreams: dreams where the individual is aware that they are dreaming and can sometimes control the dream content.

Second, dreams often contain elements that would seem illogical or nonsensical in our waking consciousness. For example, dreams sometimes include impossible events or actions (e.g., someone floating above the ground), and they can also include various hallucinations and delusions.

Third, we tend to be totally absorbed by our dream imagery, reflecting what Empson (1989) described as the "singlemindedness of dreams". However, when we are awake, we can usually stand back from our conscious thoughts and avoid becoming dominated by them.

? Is it possible that there are different kinds of dreams and different functions?

Theories of the Functions of Dreaming

In what follows, we will be discussing five of the main theories of dreaming. These theories can be divided into two groups: neurobiological theories, which focus on the benefits of dreaming for the brain and nervous system, and psychological theories, which focus on what dreams can do for our psyche.

In considering these theories it is crucial to remember that REM sleep is not the same as dreaming. People don't always report dreams in REM sleep and they dream in NREM sleep. Some theories try to explain the function of REM sleep (and we presume this may explain dreaming) and other theories offer explanations of dreaming in general, in or outside of REM sleep. These are psychological theories.

Neurobiological theories of the functions of dreaming
Hobson and McCarley's activation-synthesis theory

Hobson and McCarley (1977) were impressed by the fact that the brain is as physiologically active during REM (rapid eye movement) sleep as it is during normal waking life. This led them to put forward the activation-synthesis theory

? Have you ever had a dream that incorporated external stimuli? When and why might this phenomenon be useful?

of dreaming. According to this theory, during dreaming there are high levels of activation in several parts of the brain (especially the pontine brain stem), including areas involved in perception, action, and emotional reactions. This activation is essentially *random* and is not related to any actual body activity since bodily movements are inhibited during REM sleep. The reason for this is both an output blockade at the top of the spinal column, which prevents commands for action being acted upon, and an input blockade, which inhibits processing of environmental stimuli. However, signals resembling those that normally come from the eyes and ears (but not the nose and mouth) are spontaneously generated within the hindbrain and midbrain structures of the brain. Dreamers generally interpret these internal signals as if they were produced by external stimuli, and this is the experience of dreaming.

A 1935 demonstration of an experiment developed at Harvard University, in which an electroencephalograph is used to detect the electrical changes in the brain that take place during periods of rest and activity.

How do dreamers react to the high level of random brain activation that occurs during REM sleep? According to Hobson (1988), dreamers try to make sense of it by synthesising or combining the information contained in the bursts of neural activity. As this activity is essentially random, it is often very difficult for dreamers to produce coherent dreams. Indeed, one might wonder how it is possible at all. According to Hobson (1988), "The brain is so inexorably bent upon the quest for meaning that it attributes and even creates meaning when there is little or none in the data it is asked to process."

Research evidence. There is physiological evidence to support the activation-synthesis theory. Research on cats indicated that there is apparently random firing of cells in cats' brains during REM sleep (Hobson, 1988). This then produces activation in the parts of the brain that are used in visual perception and the control of motor movements, and may be synthesised into a dream.

Hobson (1994) has also provided evidence of how internally generated signals are misinterpreted as external signals. He noted that cortical levels of the neurotransmitters noradrenaline and serotonin are lower during REM sleep than during NREM sleep or waking life. (It is worth noting here that this is contradictory evidence in relation to the restoration theory of sleep—where it is suggested that REM sleep is a time when neurotransmitter levels are replenished.) According to Hobson, these reduced levels of noradrenaline and serotonin prevent the effective use of attentional processes and of the capacity to organise information in a coherent way. This makes it easier for the brain to misinterpret internally generated signals as if they came from external stimuli or from responses. Hobson went on to argue that the problems of attention caused by low levels of noradrenaline and serotonin may also explain why we fail to remember the great majority of our dreams.

According to the theory, activation of the pontine brain stem and the presence of REM sleep ensure that dreaming will occur. Solms (2000) addressed this prediction by considering 111 cases of brain-damaged patients who dream either rarely or not at all. In direct contradiction of the theory, the pontine brain stem was completely preserved in nearly all of the patients and they had normal levels of REM sleep.

Evaluation. The greatest strength of the activation-synthesis theory is that it is based on detailed information on the physiological activity of the brain during dreaming. The theory can explain why smells and tastes rarely or never appear in our dreams—because only those parts of the brain involved with vision and hearing are activated. The activation-synthesis theory also accounts for the incoherent nature of many dreams. If dreams occur as a result of random activity in the brain, and attentional processes are not functioning effectively, then it is entirely understandable that we often find our dreams hard to understand.

An important limitation of the theory is that it doesn't provide a convincing account of the fact that some dreams (especially those we don't remember spontaneously) possess clear meaning and coherence. It may be true that the brain has a "quest for meaning", but this is hardly a detailed explanation of dream coherence. The theory is also of little value in explaining why it is that so many people have dreams relating to their present concerns or why many dreams are repetitive. This is puzzling if dreams are based on *random* brain activity. Though it might be that any synthesis that takes place draws on past experiences and therefore becomes meaningful to the dreamer.

We should also remember that activation-synthesis is related to REM activity, but dreaming also takes place at other times though in a different way. It is

? This contradictory evidence leads us to question the tendency of researchers to focus on evidence that supports their theory and reject other evidence. Is this in keeping with the aims of scientific research?

possible that NREM dreams may be the synthesis of different kinds of brain activity. Finally, the fact that many brain-damaged patients who rarely if ever dream have an intact pontine brain stem and intact REM sleep is inconsistent with the theory.

Crick and Mitchison's reverse-learning theory

Crick and Mitchison (1983) put forward a challenging approach to dreaming known as reverse-learning or unlearning theory. According to this theory, the main function of dreaming is to get rid of useless information stored in the brain. This information (which they called "parasitic information") uses up valuable space in the cortex, and so dreaming helps to free up some of this space for the storage of more useful information. More specifically, there are neuronal networks in the cortex. According to Crick and Mitchison, these networks are strongly interconnected, and this can lead to overloading. The elimination of unimportant information during dreaming allows the neuronal networks to function more efficiently.

What are the physiological processes involved in dreaming and the elimination of unwanted information? According to Blakemore (1988):

> *Dreams are, quite literally, a kind of shock therapy, in which the cortex is bombarded by barrages of impulses from the brainstem below, while a different mode of synaptic modification ensures that the unwanted elements of each circuit are unlearned.*

The subjective experience of dreaming is a kind of "read out" of the search and destroy activity. As with activation-synthesis theory, dreams are seen as an accidental by-product of a neurobiologically inevitable or necessary process.

Research evidence. It is hard to test reverse-learning theory. However, Crick and Mitchison (1983) claimed that the size of the cortex in different species of mammals provides support for their theory. The only mammals not having the REM sleep associated with dreaming are dolphins and spiny anteaters. With no REM sleep one might presume that these species are unable to get rid of useless information. According to Crick and Mitchison, these species only manage to function effectively because they have an unusually large cortex for mammals of their size and therefore have no need to jettison unwanted material.

On the other hand, it has been argued that the human cortex is much more highly folded than that of a dolphin or spiny anteater so that it may have just as much capacity. Yet another alternative explanation, put forward by Winson (1997), is that the dolphin and spiny anteater have to perform the clearing up operations while awake, which is why they need a larger cortex to cope with doing this at the same time as the daily processing tasks. Other animals have evolved an alternative strategy (i.e., REM sleep).

Evaluation. Reverse-learning theory represents an interesting approach to dream function. If dreaming is simply designed to allow us to erase valueless information, then it makes sense that we rarely remember the content of our dreams. As we have seen, we forget about 95% of our dreams, which is entirely consistent with the reverse-learning theory.

However, there are some major problems with the theory. First, dreams are often meaningful or significant (see the evidence related to problem-solving theory), whereas it would be predicted by the theory that they should be relatively meaningless. Second, there is evidence that foetuses engage in something resembling REM sleep. It is hard to believe that they are trying to forget meaningless information before they are even born! Though this is not inconceivable; for example, we know that there are large numbers of neuronal connections being organised during development. If a foetus is, say, trying out new motor programmes, some will be efficacious and some will be erroneous. Dreaming might, therefore, serve the same purpose.

Third, modern connectionist ideas about the brain suggest that we have a vast potential for information storage and there is no need to save space.

Comment on neurobiological theories

We have already noted that both theories see dreams as an accidental by-product of neurobiological processes. The theories have no explanation for why dreams should have meaning beyond the possibility that our cognitive processes have a tendency to impose meaning on any set of data.

One further issue is the question of REM and NREM dreaming. Both theories describe one basic explanation or function for dreams. But why would this apply to several different physiological states (REM and NREM activity)? It might be that other kinds of activity in NREM are also synthesised. We can probably at best conclude that these accounts of dreaming are partial explanations, and may only be related to REM activity.

Psychological theories of the functions of dreaming

Psychological theories start from the notion that dreams are psychological rather than physiological experiences, and therefore we would expect them to serve a psychological function. It may be coincidental that many dreams are in REM sleep.

Freud's wish-fulfilment theory

Probably the best-known theory of dreaming was put forward by Sigmund Freud (1900). He claimed that all dreams represent *wish fulfilment*, mainly of repressed desires (e.g., sexual desires). The source of this theory was his own dreams and the descriptions of dreams provided by his patients. In one of his dreams, Freud found himself with a patient, Irma, who was not recovering as well as Freud hoped and he blamed himself for this. In his dream Freud met Irma at a party and examined her. In the dream he saw a chemical formula for a drug prescribed by another doctor and realised that this other doctor had used a dirty syringe, and this was the source of Irma's problem. This meant that Freud was no longer to blame for Irma's illness. Freud interpreted this dream as wish fulfilment.

Such wish fulfilments are often unacceptable to the dreamer, leading Freud to describe dreams as "the insanity of the night". This unacceptability leads the dreamer to produce separate manifest and latent content. The **manifest content** of a dream is what the dreamer actually dreams, whereas the **latent content** is the true meaning of the dream. "Dream-work" transforms a forbidden wish into a

[?] Is it possible that REM "dreams" are a different process to more coherent "psychological" dreams?

[?] How easy is it to test Freud's wish-fulfilment theory? Is this a strength or weakness of the theory?

KEY TERMS

Manifest content: in Freud's theory, the actual or obvious content of a dream.
Latent content: in Freud's theory, the underlying meaning of a dream.

non-threatening form, thus reducing anxiety and allowing the dreamer to continue sleeping.

Psychoanalysis can be used to uncover the latent content. Indeed, according to Freud, dream analysis provides a *via regia* or royal road to an understanding of the unconscious mind. An important feature of such dream analysis involves working out the meaning of various dream symbols. Such symbols may be universal, such as poles, guns, and swords representing the penis, and horse-riding and dancing representing sexual intercourse. However, Freud suggested that many symbols were more likely to be personal and he didn't support the idea of "dream dictionaries" based on universal symbols. In one case, he was analysing a patient's dream about a wiggling fish. The patient suggested that this might represent a penis. However, Freud considered this and concluded that in fact the dream represented the patient's mother, who was a passionate astrologer and a Pisces (the astrological sign for a fish). Freud also famously said, with reference to a dream involving a cigar, yet another symbol for the penis, "Sometimes a cigar is only a cigar." In other words, not all dreams are symbolic and many dreams require careful individual rather than universal interpretation.

Research evidence. There is evidence that many dreams are relevant to current concerns. Hajek and Belcher (1991) studied the dreams of smokers who were involved in a programme designed to help them stop smoking. Most of the participants reported dreams about smoking during the course of treatment and for a year afterwards. Most of these dreams were what they called dreams of absent-minded transgressions or DAMITS. In these dreams, engaging in smoking was followed by feelings of panic or guilt.

Recent evidence provides some support for the general approach adopted by Freud. Solms (2000) found with brain-damaged patients that dreaming was eliminated when there was damage to a motivational system connected the midbrain to the limbic system and the frontal lobes. The relevance of this is that Freud's wish fulfilment theory focused very much on the importance of motivation in dreams. Solms also discussed brain-imaging evidence showing that the rational parts of the brain are relatively inactive during REM sleep (which explains why dreams are often incoherent) whereas the forebrain (a central part of the motivational system) is very active.

Hajek and Belcher (1991) found that dreaming about smoking seemed to help the ex-smokers. Those who had the most dreams about smoking (and about feeling bad about it) were less likely to start smoking again than those who had few such dreams. However, these are correlational findings, and don't show that the dreams were actually useful.

An obvious prediction from Freud's assumption that dreams represent wish fulfilment is that they should tend to be positive and enjoyable. In fact, however, as mentioned earlier, far more dreams involve negative than positive emotions (e.g., Hall & van de Castle, 1966).

Evaluation. Freud deserves credit for having put forward the first systematic theory of dream function. In view of the somewhat repressive nature of Austrian society at the end of the nineteenth century, the time of Freud's writing, it is likely

> **?** Is it strange that Freud's theory is associated with dream dictionaries, yet he didn't really subscribe to this view?

EXAM HINT

Avoid using anecdotal material in your answer, even if you have got lots of examples of wish-fulfilment. But do use your own dreams if it helps to understand the explanations. Whether the explanations account for recurring dreams is a useful way to assess explanatory power, i.e., do they explain dreaming fully?

KEY TERM

Psychoanalysis: Freud's set of theories about human behaviour; also the form of treatment for mental disorders he devised.

that some of the dreams of Freud's patients did represent wish fulfilment in a distorted form.

Freud argued that dreams can provide us with vital information about the unconscious thoughts and feelings of the dreamer. Most later theorists have been unwilling to go that far, but have accepted that dreams can tell us something about the thoughts and feelings of the dreamer. For example, it is claimed within activation-synthesis theory that dreamers have a "quest for meaning" that leads them to interpret the brain's activity in certain ways. Recent brain-imaging research and studies on brain-damaged patients indicate that motivational systems are very important in dreaming (as Freud claimed), and that the rational parts of the brain play only a modest role.

There are various problems with wish-fulfilment theory. First, it is improbable that there is much repression of unacceptable desires in today's liberal and permissive society. Hayes (1994) also pointed that, if dreams have a wish-fulfilment function, then we would expect in our society to find a stronger food and eating content.

Second, some dreams (nightmares) are very frightening, and it is hard to regard them as wish fulfilling even in a distorted way. Third, the latent content of a dream as identified through psychoanalysis generally seems open to question. In other words, dubious methods are used to identify the latent content of a dream. Although some dreams undoubtedly represent wish fulfilment (and not always in a distorted form!), it is unlikely that all dreams can reasonably be regarded as wish fulfilling.

■ Activity: Keep a "dream diary" for 2 weeks, noting down not only the content of your dreams but also any links you notice to events in your waking life. Which of the five theoretical approaches described here provides the best explanation for your dreams, or does each approach address a different aspect?

Webb and Cartright's problem-solving theory

If you have a problem on your mind, one piece of advice is to "sleep on it". This suggestion may not be as absurd as it seems as there are many reports of impressive problem solving during sleep. One of the most famous examples of a valuable dream was reported by the chemist Kekule. He had a dream about a ring of snakes, linked together with the tail of one in the mouth of another. This revealed to him the ring-like atomic structure of benzene molecules, a problem he was working on at the time.

Webb and Cartwright (1978) proposed that solving work, sex, health, and relationship problems was the purpose of dreaming. Like Freud's wish-fulfilment theory, problem-solving theory also suggests that dreams are a way of coping with problems. Dreams are a way of expressing current concerns. These concerns may relate to the wishes emphasised by Freud, but may also relate to fears (e.g., job insecurity, or health of a loved one). These concerns are often expressed in a symbolic way rather than directly. For example, students who are concerned they may fail a forthcoming examination may dream about falling over a cliff or tripping over something in the street.

However, in problem-solving theory, the manifest content of the dream is the true meaning of the dream rather than there being any latent content, though the dream may rely on metaphor, such as the ring of snakes as a representation of chemicals being linked together in a circular form.

Research evidence. Webb and Cartwright (1978) described a study where participants were given problems to solve and then allowed to go to sleep. Some were woken whenever they entered REM sleep. Those who had been allowed to sleep uninterrupted were able to provide more realistic solutions to the problems the next day, suggesting that their REM sleep had given them the opportunity to work through the problems.

In another study Cartwright (1984) interviewed women who were undergoing divorce and were either depressed or not depressed, and compared them with a non-depressed married group who had never considered divorce. All 29 participants were studied over a period of 6 nights in a sleep laboratory. The non-depressed divorcing women reported having longer dreams and ones that dealt with marital status issues. Such issues were absent from the dreams of the depressed group. Presumably the depression was associated with an inability to deal with problems and the ability to use dreams in this way helped the individuals to cope better. Hartmann (1973) also found that people who were experiencing various kinds of problems had more REM sleep than the less troubled individuals.

> **?** If we dream about personally relevant issues, why is it that we remember only a small fraction of our dreams?

Evaluation. This appears to be a reasonable account of dreaming and is supported by some research studies. For example, the theory explains why many of our dreams relate to current interests and concerns. However, there are things that the theory doesn't explain, perhaps most obviously why people and animals have dreams that are not related to the solution of problems! Many dreams are commentaries on life experiences and have no clear meaning. It would also seem to follow from problem-solving theory that it would be useful for us to remember our dreams. It seems puzzling that we remember fewer than 5% of our dreams. There is also the question of why sleep is necessary—we can also solve problems by engaging in another task for a while, as is indicated by the saying "a change is as good as a rest".

The most reasonable conclusion is that problem-solving theory helps to explain some dreams, but doesn't provide a comprehensive account of all types of dream. Finally, this approach, like all psychological approaches, is uninformative about the physiological processes involved in dreaming.

Survival strategy theory

Winson (1997) has recently put forward a theory of dreams that resembles problem-solving theory. According to Winson:

> *REM sleep is the information-processing period when memories and events of the day are juxtaposed [placed close together] with things that happened in the past to form a strategy for survival. What was this or that like? What better actions can I take in a similar situation in the future? All the indications are that REM sleep plays an important part in our survival.*

There is some support for this theory in the finding that people who are deprived of REM sleep find it hard to remember the key events of the previous day.

When awake, our thoughts are highly varied and serve different purposes. Why shouldn't the same be true when we are asleep?

Winson argued that the inhibition against movement found during dreaming is important: "If you didn't have this neural block on activity while you sleep, you would attempt to wake up and act out your dreams. Eye movements are not stopped because they don't interfere with sleeping."

Evaluation. It is hard to evaluate survival strategy theory, because relatively few studies have been designed specifically to test it. However, if dreams are designed to provide a survival strategy, it might be expected that most of them would be remembered. The fact that so few dreams are remembered suggests that many dreams do not provide useful guidance for future action.

SECTION SUMMARY
Dreaming

The nature of dreams

❖ During REM sleep: Dreams tend to be more vivid and detailed.

❖ Men's dreams generally involve people not known to them whereas women's dreams mostly involve familiar people.

❖ People forget more than 95% of their dreams and the dreams spontaneously remembered tend to be the more unusual ones.

❖ There are differences between the consciousness experienced during dreaming and that during waking.

Neurobiological theories of dreaming

❖ Neurobiological theories suggest that REM activity is the key to dreaming.

❖ Hobson and McCarley's activation-synthesis theory:

— Random electrical activity in the brain during REM sleep is interpreted by the brain as meaningful sensory data, resulting in the experience of a dream.

— Advantages of the theory: it is based on detailed information about brain processes.

— Disadvantages of the theory: it exaggerates the importance of the pontine brain stem and REM sleep in dreaming, and it doesn't explain adequately the existence of coherent dreams.

❖ Crick and Mitchison's reverse-learning theory:

— The main function of dreaming is to eliminate useless information stored in the brain, and so to free up space in the cortex.

— It is hard in this theory to account for meaningful dreams and to fit in with modern connectionist ideas related to the almost infinite capacity of neural networks.

Psychological theories of dreaming

❖ Psychological theories focus on the psychological benefits gained from dreams, whether they occur during REM sleep or not.

❖ Freud's wish-fulfilment theory:

— Dreams represent the fulfilment of mainly repressed desires. An individual copes with the repressed information by having dreams that express manifest content (the actual dream), rather than latent content (its true meaning) which can be discovered through dream analysis.

— Advantages of the theory: it may have been appropriate at the time it was written and can explain why dreams often represent our current concerns. Recent research indicates that parts of the brain involved in motivation are very active during dreaming whereas rational parts of the brain are not.

— Disadvantages of the theory: it is not clear why dreams aren't related to other concerns such as food, nor why we have nightmares.

❖ Webb and Cartwright's problem-solving theory:

— Dreams are a way of working through matters that are troubling us, often in a symbolic way.

— There is empirical support for this view, but it doesn't explain why not all dreams are related to problem solving.

❖ Winson's survival strategy theory:

— Dreams are related to problem solving as we combine past events to help form strategies for survival and remember those dreams that suggest adaptive strategies.

See also pages 87–93 of the revision guide.

FURTHER READING

The topics in this chapter are covered in greater depth by E. Bentley (2000) *Awareness: Biorhythms, sleep and dreaming* (London: Routledge), written specifically for the AQA A specification. The topics are also analysed in an accessible way in J.P.J. Pinel (2003) *Biopsychology (5th Edn.)* (Boston: Allyn & Bacon). V. Tonay (2003) *Every dream interpreted* (London: Collins & Brown Ltd.) provides interesting answers to crucial questions about dreams. S. Coren (1996) *Sleep thieves* (New York: The Free Press) offers readable coverage of biological rhythms and sleep.

EXAMPLE EXAMINATION QUESTIONS

You should spend 30 minutes on each of the questions below, which aim to test the material in this chapter.

1. (a) Describe **two** research studies into circadian biological rhythms. (12 marks)
   (b) Evaluate these studies. (12 marks)
2. Discuss the role of endogenous pacemakers in bodily rhythms. (24 marks)
3. "To sleep is to dream." Discuss explanations relating to functions of sleep. (24 marks)
4. Discuss the implications of findings from studies of sleep deprivation. (24 marks)
5. (a) Consider two or more neurobiological theories of the function of dreaming. (12 marks)
   (b) Evaluate these theories in terms of alternative theoretical accounts. (12 marks)
6. Discuss research findings relating to the nature of dreams (AQA, 2002). (24 marks)

Examination Tips

Question 1.   In part (a) you should present two research studies following the guidelines used at AS level, i.e., describe their aims, procedure, findings, and conclusions. Any evaluative comments are credited in part (b). Such evaluation may be positive (e.g., other research support, practical applications) or negative (e.g., poor methodology, lack of validity). Description of any other research studies would only receive credit where it offers some insight into (evaluation of) the initial two studies.

Question 2.   It is possible to use virtually everything you know in this essay because external factors can be used as a means of evaluation (as long as they are presented explicitly in this way). Therefore the likely problem in this essay will be lack of selectivity. In order to obtain high marks you need to supply depth and breadth, structure, and coherent elaboration. If you try to include everything you know it is likely to read like a list and lack sufficient detail (AO1 skill) and elaboration (AO2 skill).

Question 3.   You are not required to refer to the quotation in your answer but it is there to suggest a topic that you might consider when discussing the function of sleep. Your temptation might be to present a prepared essay on restoration and evolutionary theories, but you might also consider dreams. "Discuss" is an AO1 and AO2 term (describe and evaluate). Remember that both positive and negative evaluation is creditworthy.

Question 4.   This essay does not require you to describe studies of sleep deprivation but to discuss (describe + evaluate) the implications of these studies. This means that some description would be creditworthy but that AO1 credit will also come from a description of what the studies tell us. AO2 credit will come from the effective use of this material to present a critical argument (e.g., one that considers alternative viewpoints or the implications for theories). If you ignore the "partial sleep" research your final mark will be limited to a ceiling of 16 marks for partial performance.

Question 5.   "Consider" is an AO1 term and therefore in part (a) you are required to describe neurobiological theories. The "two or more" indicates that you could obtain full marks with reference to only two such theories. Part (b) is a straightforward evaluation with some hints about how you might do this.

Question 6.   The focus here is on the findings of research studies, i.e., what have researchers found about the nature of dreams from their studies? You might be tempted to write a list of different studies and their findings, which would be acceptable, but a better answer would use the findings themselves as the backbone of the essay. Evaluation could be in terms of methodological criticisms of the studies or the implications of the findings for theories of the function of dreaming. Remember that REM sleep is not the same as dreaming.

WEBSITES

http://www.websciences.org/sltbr/links.htm
   Useful links on the site of the Society for Light Treatment and Biological Rhythms.

http://www.circadian.com/
   This site includes a useful glossary of terms.

http://www.lboro.ac.uk/departments/hu/groups/sleep/
   A top UK sleep research centre at Loughborough University, UK.

http://www.crhsc.umontreal.ca/dreams/
   Dream and Nightmare Research Laboratory in Canada.

http://www.sleepnet.com/index.shtml
   Large site with lots of information and links about sleep-related issues (including dreams) and sleeping disorders.

http://sawka.com/spiritwatch/lucid.htm
   Papers on lucid dreaming.

http://www.sleephomepages.org/
   Collection of sleep-related portals.

http://www.asdreams.org/
   Association for the Study of Dreams.

DEVELOPMENTAL PSYCHOLOGY

Cognitive Development

Cognitive development concerns the mental changes that occur during an individual's lifetime. In this chapter our focus is on the changes in children's thinking as they get older.

DEVELOPMENT OF THINKING

Children change and develop in almost every way in the years between infancy and adolescence. However, some of the most dramatic changes take place in terms of cognitive development. The first systematic theory of cognitive development was proposed by a Swiss Psychologist, Jean Piaget (1896–1980). There are several other major theoretical approaches to cognitive development, including those of Vygotsky and the information-processing theorists.

Piaget's Theory

Jean Piaget put forward the most thorough account ever offered of cognitive development. Indeed, such is the richness of his contribution that only the bare outline of his account can be provided here.

Adaptation to the environment

Piaget was interested in how children learn and adapt to the world. In order for adaptation or adjustment to occur, there must be constant interactions between the child and the outside world. According to Piaget, two processes are of key importance:

- **Accommodation**: the individual's cognitive organisation is altered by the need to deal with the environment; in other words, the individual adjusts to the outside world.
- **Assimilation**: the individual deals with new environmental situations on the basis of his or her existing cognitive organisation; in other words, the interpretation of the outside world is adjusted to fit the individual.

Consider the example of an infant playing with different objects. The infant has acquired the concept of a rattle—if you shake a certain object it makes a particular noise. When the infant picks up a new object and this makes the same

---

KEY TERMS

Accommodation: in Piaget's theory, the process of changing existing schemas or creating new schemas because new information cannot be assimilated.

Assimilation: in Piaget's theory, dealing with new environmental situations by using existing cognitive organisation.

Jean Piaget, 1896–1980.

noise, the infant can *assimilate* this into his or her existing cognitive organisation. The new object fits in with previous knowledge. However, if the infant picks up another rattle-like object and discovers that makes a mewing sound, the infant must *accommodate* to this new class of objects and form a new concept.

The clearest example of the dominance of assimilation over accommodation is play, in which reality is interpreted according to the individual's whim (e.g., a stick becomes a gun). In contrast, dominance of accommodation over assimilation is seen in imitation, in which the actions of someone else are simply copied.

Schemas and equilibration

There are two other key Piagetian concepts: schemas and equilibration. **Schema** refers to organised knowledge used to guide action. It is a term that is now used throughout psychology but Piaget was one of the first psychologists to use it. Infants are born with innate schemas, such as a sucking schema. Through assimilation and accommodation these innate schemas develop into progressively more complex packets of knowledge about the world. The first schema infants develop is the body schema, when they realise there is an important distinction between "me" and "not me". This body schema helps the infant in its attempts to explore and make sense of the world.

Equilibration is based on the notion that the individual needs to keep a stable internal state (equilibrium) in a changing environment. The child tries to understand its experiences in terms of existing cognitive structures (i.e., schemas). If there is a new experience or a mismatch between the new experience and existing schemas this creates an unpleasant state of *disequilibrium* or lack of balance. The child then uses assimilation and accommodation to restore a state of equilibrium or balance. Thus, disequilibrium motivates the child to learn new skills and knowledge to return to the desired state of equilibrium.

An example of the dominance of assimilation over accommodation—pretending that hairbrushes are microphones.

Quantitative versus qualitative change

We can distinguish between two kinds of theorists in the area of child development. One group (e.g., behaviourists) argues that cognitive development only involves changes in the amount of knowledge available to the child, and the efficiency with which that knowledge is used in thinking. According to such theorists, there are no fundamental differences in cognition during development. As a child gets older it is a question of acquiring more knowledge. This is a

KEY TERMS

Schema: an organised packet of information stored in long-term memory.
Equilibration: using the processes of accommodation and of assimilation to produce a state of equilibrium or balance.

EXAM HINT

Questions on the development of thinking may be sub-parted so be ready to outline theory and applications as AO1 and also to use the applications and evaluation of the theory as AO2, depending on the question. Note if the question is on applications then the evaluation of the theory must be related consistently to the applications, i.e., how does each criticism affect the application of the theory?

quantitative change, a change in the amount of knowledge rather than the *kind* of knowledge or thinking (a qualitative difference).

The second group of theorists (e.g., Piaget) claim that the ways of thinking found in adolescence are very different from those of early childhood. There is a **qualitative change** in the kind of logic that the child uses. Most importantly, these qualitative changes are the result of innate maturational processes. One can use the analogy of a child learning to walk. No amount of practice will enable a child to walk before he or she is ready. This occurs when the child has matured sufficiently to have the requisite physical skills and co-ordination to do it. Piaget argued that the same was true of cognitive development and, just as learning to walk is a stage in a child's physical development, there are recognisable stages in a child's cognitive development.

Just as children must learn the alphabet before they can read, Piaget defined a set of stages that all children must pass through as they develop.

Stage theory

Piaget argued that all children pass through various stages. The main assumptions of a stage theory are as follows. First, the stages are determined by innate, maturational changes. Second, although the ages at which different children attain any given stage can vary, the *sequence* of stages should remain the same for all. Third, the cognitive operations and structures defining a stage should form an integrated whole. Despite the notion of a coherence to each stage, Piaget accepted that children in a given stage do not always adopt the mode of thought typical of that stage, and he coined the term **horizontal décalage** to refer to this. The word "décalage" means to move forwards or backwards in French, or simply "a difference". So the concept is Piaget's way of expressing the fact that development is not an even process, some changes progress more rapidly than other changes.

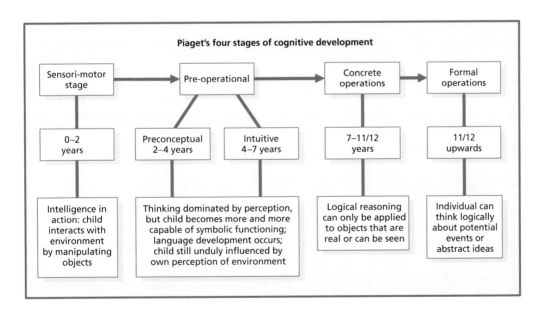

KEY TERMS
Quantitative change: change in how much there is of something; i.e., the quantity.
Qualitative change: change in how things are expressed, what it feels like, meanings or explanations; i.e., the quality.
Horizontal décalage: Piaget's concept that, at any stage of cognitive development, not all aspects of the stage will appear at the same time.

Piaget identified four major stages of cognitive development. The first is the **sensori-motor stage**, which lasts from birth to about 2 years of age. The second is the **pre-operational stage**, spanning the years between 2 and 7. The third is the **concrete operations stage**, which usually occurs between the ages of 7 and 11 or 12. The fourth stage is the **formal operations stage**, which follows on from the stage of concrete operations.

According to Piaget, at each stage there are changes in the way children think. These are qualitative changes. It might help to have an overview of these changes before looking at the specific features of each stage. In the first stage of cognitive development very young children deal with the environment by manipulating objects. This means that sensori-motor development (learning to co-ordinate one's senses with one's motor responses) is basically *intelligence through action*.

In the next stage, which is the stage of pre-operational thought, thinking becomes dominated by *perception*. This contrasts with the third stage, from 7 years onwards, where thinking is more and more influenced by logical considerations, in other words by the ability to engage in logical thinking that is internally consistent. In the pre-operational stage, a child might call all red cars "Daddy's car" because Daddy has a red car. There is a certain logic but it is flawed and not internally consistent—it would not hold up under questioning.

In the third stage of concrete operations, the child's thinking becomes truly logical reasoning; however it can only be applied to objects that are real or can be seen. During the final stage of formal operations, the older child or adult can think logically about potential events or abstract ideas. Examples of such abstract logical thinking include mathematics and thinking about hypothetical ethical issues.

The term "operations" is used to describe the internally consistent mental rules that are used in thinking. Thus "pre-operational" refers to the inability to use logical rules; "concrete operations" is the stage when operations depend on concrete examples; and "formal operations" is the ability to conduct abstract logical reasoning.

As you read through the descriptions of all four stages, remember the essence of these stages: knowledge through action, knowledge dominated by perception (what can be seen rather than logical deduction), knowledge through concrete logic, and finally knowledge through abstract reasoning.

> **?** You have become very adept at sensori-motor co-ordination. Can you think of some examples?

KEY TERMS

Sensori-motor stage: the first stage in Piaget's theory, at which children learn to co-ordinate their sensory and motor abilities.

Pre-operational stage: the second stage in Piaget's theory of cognitive development, from 2 to 7 years. The child can cope with symbols (such as using language) but cannot cope with adult internally consistent logic (operations).

Concrete operations stage: the third stage in Piaget's theory of cognitive development, from 7 to 11 years. The child can now use adult internally consistent logic but only when the problem is presented in a concrete way.

Formal operations stage: the final stage in Piaget's theory of cognitive development, from 11 onwards. Thinking now involves formal internally consistent adult logic and abstract thinking.

Reflexes: innate and automatic responses to stimuli.

Object permanence: an awareness that objects continue to exist when they can no longer be seen.

Sensori-motor stage (0–2 years)

This stage of cognitive development lasts from birth to about 2 years of age, with the infant learning a great deal by moving around. Initially, the baby's schemas consist largely of inborn **reflexes** such as sucking. However, these reflexes change somewhat with experience. For example, babies learn at a very early age to alter the shape of their lips so that they can suck more efficiently.

The key achievement of this stage is **object permanence**. This involves being aware that objects continue to exist when they are no longer in view. In the early part of the sensori-motor stage, the infant has no awareness at all of object permanence: it is literally a case of "out of sight, out of mind". Object permanence develops as the child actively explores his or her environment. Towards the end of its first year, the infant starts to display what is known as **perseverative search**. This involves the infant searching for a concealed object in the place in which it was found some time earlier, rather than in the place in which it was last seen. According to Piaget, this happens because the infant does not regard the object as existing independently of the infant's own behaviour. Perseverative search shows some features of object permanence. However, full object permanence is only achieved towards the end of the sensori-motor stage.

The development of imitation is a major achievement of the sensori-motor stage. Imitation allows the infant to add considerably to the range of actions of which it is capable. It develops slowly, becoming more precise over time. Towards the end of the sensori-motor stage, the infant shows evidence of **deferred imitation**, which is the ability to imitate behaviour that was seen before.

Evaluation of the sensori-motor stage. Piaget identified many of the main kinds of learning shown by infants during the first 2 years. However, he underestimated the abilities of infants in a number of ways. For example, Bower (1982) hid a toy behind a screen. When the screen was lifted a few seconds later, the toy was no longer there. Infants who were 3 or 4 months old showed surprise. This suggests that some aspects of object permanence are present much earlier than was claimed by Piaget. This was also found by Bower and Wishart (1972). They made an object disappear from sight by removing all light from it. However, infra-red television cameras revealed that very young children reached out for the object in the correct direction, suggesting that they had at least some aspects of object permanence.

According to Piaget, deferred imitation only develops towards the end of the second year of life. However, Meltzoff (1988) found that it could occur several months earlier than Piaget believed. Many 9-month-old infants were able to imitate simple actions 24 hours after they had observed them.

Some of Piaget's explanations have not been supported. Piaget assumed that infants showing perseverative search did not remember where the toy had been hidden. However, Baillargeon and Graber (1988) carried out a study in which 8-month-old infants saw a toy being hidden behind one of two screens. Fifteen seconds later they saw a hand lift the toy out, either from the place in which it had been hidden or from behind the other screen. The infants were only surprised

In the left-hand picture, the baby is reaching for a toy he can see. In the right-hand one, he searches in the same place for it, although in fact it is hidden under the cloth on his right.

? What reflexes are babies born with, and how might these develop into conscious activity?

? How could the development of a baby's first words be explained in terms of imitation?

KEY TERMS

Perseverative search: mistakenly searching for an object in the place in which it was previously found, rather than the place in which it is currently hidden.

Deferred imitation: in Piaget's theory, the ability to imitate behaviour that was observed at an earlier time.

Baillargeon and Graber found that 8-month-old infants were surprised when a cup they had seen being put behind the left-hand screen was then retrieved from behind the right-hand screen.

when the toy was lifted from behind the "wrong" screen, indicating that they did remember where it had been put. Thus, perseverative search does *not* occur simply because of faulty memory.

There is another problem with Piaget's explanation of perseverative search. He argued that perseverative search occurs because young children believe that an object's existence depends on their own actions. It follows from this explanation that children who only passively observed the object in its first location should *not* show perseverative search. In fact, infants show as much perseverative search under those conditions as when they have been allowed to find the object in its first location.

Pre-operational stage (2–7 years)

The child who completes the sensori-motor stage of cognitive development is still not capable of "true" thought. This child operates largely at the level of direct action, whereas the pre-operational child becomes more and more capable of symbolic functioning. The development of language is associated with the cognitive advances of pre-operational children. However, Piaget regarded language development as largely a consequence of more fundamental cognitive changes, rather than as itself a cause of cognitive advance. This is a fundamental feature of Piaget's theory.

Children show considerable cognitive development during the 5 years covered by the pre-operational stage. Accordingly, Piaget divided the pre-operational stage into two sub-stages: the preconceptual (2–4 years) and the intuitive (4–7 years). Two of the cognitive differences between children at the *preconceptual* and *intuitive* stages involve **seriation** and **syncretic thought**.

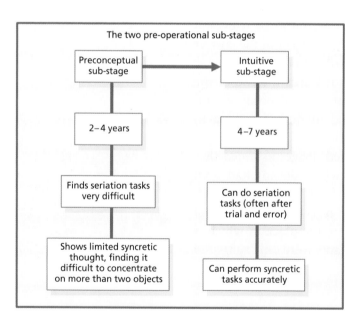

The two pre-operational sub-stages

Preconceptual sub-stage → Intuitive sub-stage

2–4 years | 4–7 years

Finds seriation tasks very difficult | Can do seriation tasks (often after trial and error)

Shows limited syncretic thought, finding it difficult to concentrate on more than two objects | Can perform syncretic tasks accurately

Seriation. Seriation tasks require children to arrange objects in order on the basis of a single feature (e.g., height). Piaget and Szeminska (1952) demonstrated that preconceptual children found this very hard to do, and even intuitive children often used a trial-and-error approach.

Syncretic thought. Syncretic thought can be revealed on tasks where children are asked to select various objects that are all alike. Intuitive children tend to perform this task accurately, for example selecting several yellow objects or square objects. Preconceptual children show limited syncretic thought. The second object they select is the same as the first on one dimension (e.g., size), but then the

> **KEY TERMS**
> **Seriation:** a child's ability to arrange objects in order on the basis of a single feature (e.g., height).
> **Syncretic thought:** a kind of thinking where new experiences are assimilated into rather vague and global schema. Syncretic thought occurs because young children focus on two objects at a time, and find it hard to consider the characteristics of several objects at the same time. It is characteristic of the preoperational stage.

Seriation tasks require children to arrange objects in order on the basis of a single feature, such as height.

third object is the same as the second on another dimension (e.g., colour). Thus, syncretic thought occurs because young children focus on two objects at a time, and find it hard to consider the characteristics of several objects at the same time. The most common example of this is lack of the ability to **conserve**, i.e., to recognise that quantity stays the same (is conserved) even when objective appearance changes. Piaget's conservation experiments are described in the Key Study below.

KEY STUDY
Conservation tasks

Pre-operational children are unduly influenced by their own perception of the environment. They tend to pay attention to only one aspect of the total situation (this is called **centration** by Piaget). The way in which centration produces errors is shown in studies of conservation. Conservation refers to understanding that certain aspects of a visual display do not vary in spite of changes in perceptual aspects. In his classic studies on conservation of quantity, Piaget presented children with two glasses of the same size and shape containing the same quantity of liquid. Once the child has agreed that there is the same quantity of liquid in both glasses, the liquid from one of the glasses is poured into a different glass that is taller and thinner. The child is then asked if the two glasses (the original one and the new one) contain the same amount to drink, or if one contains more. Pre-operational children fail to show conservation. They argue either that there is more liquid in the new container ("because it's higher") or that there is more liquid in the original glass ("because it's wider"). In either case, the child centres or focuses on only one dimension (height or width).

The pre-operational child fails on conservation tasks partly because of centration. However, the child also lacks crucial internalised cognitive operations, according to Piaget. Two cognitive operations are of special relevance to conservation tasks: reversibility and syncretic thought. Reversibility involves the ability to undo, or reverse mentally, some operation that has been carried out. Reversibility allows the realisation that the effect of pouring liquid from one container into another could be negated by simply pouring the liquid back into its original container. Syncretic thought involves the ability to take account of two or more aspects of a situation at the same time. In the case of conservation of quantity, it involves considering height and width together.

Key study evaluation
Piaget used the conservation of liquid task to show that pre-operational children lack the internalised cognitive operations of reversibility and syncretic thought. However, it might be interesting to try the same experiment with children from a non-Western environment, such as the bush people of the African Kalahari desert, who are not likely to be familiar with glass beakers filled with water. Would they show conservation or not? Would a lack of conservation necessarily mean that these children could not decentre?

Discussion points
1. In what real-life situations might the ability to conserve be important?
2. What are the limitations of Piaget's research (see the General Evaluation on pages 180–182)?

Egocentrism. Piaget argued that the thinking of pre-operational children is characterised by egocentrism. **Egocentrism** is the tendency to assume that one's way of thinking about things is the only possible way. Piaget studied egocentric thinking in pre-operational children by using the three mountains task. Children looked at a model of mountains, and then decided which picture showed the view that would be seen by someone looking at the display from a different angle. Children younger than 8 nearly always selected the photograph of the scene as they themselves saw it. According to Piaget, this error occurred because of their inability to escape from an egocentric perspective.

Egocentrism also involves a lack of differentiation between the self and the world, which makes the child unable to distinguish clearly between psychological and physical events. This produces:

A drawing of the model used in Piaget's three mountains task. Children were shown the model from one angle, then shown photographs of the model from other viewpoints, and asked to choose which view someone standing at one of the other labelled points would see. Pre-operational children usually selected the view from the point at which they themselves had seen the model.

- *Realism*: the tendency to regard psychological events as having a physical existence. Piaget (1967, p.95) provided the following example of realism in a conversation with a child called Engl: "Where is the dream whilst you are dreaming?" "Beside me." "Are your eyes shut when you dream? Where is the dream?" "Over there."

- *Animism*: the tendency to endow physical objects and events with psychological qualities. Young children often attribute consciousness to all things. For example saying "Don't do that or the book will cry."

- *Artificialism*: the tendency to consider that physical objects and events were created by people. For example, I (Michael Eysenck) was walking across Wimbledon Common with my daughter Fleur, aged 3, and told her the sun would come out when I had counted to 10. When it did so, she was very confident that Daddy could control the sun, and often begged me to make the sun appear on gloomy days!

Evaluation of Piaget's theory of the pre-operational stage. Piaget identified several limitations in the thinking of pre-operational children. He also provided a theoretical account, arguing that children at this stage lack important cognitive operations (e.g., reversibility). However, Piaget may have underestimated the cognitive abilities of pre-operational children. For example, Wheldall and Poborca (1980) claimed that children often fail on conservation tasks because they don't understand the question due to their limited understanding of language. Accordingly, they devised a version of the liquid conservation task that didn't involve the use of language (a nonverbal version). Only 28% of their 6- and 7-year-old participants showed conservation with the standard verbal version, but 50% did so when tested on the nonverbal version. These findings suggest that misunderstanding of language is one factor involved in non-conservation. However, the fact that half the participants were non-conservers with the nonverbal version indicates that other factors are also involved.

Other researchers have focused on the issue of whether posing two questions in the conservation task confuses younger children. They might think that, if there are two questions, then there must be two different answers. This research is discussed in the Key Study below.

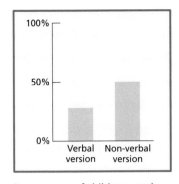

Percentages of children aged 6–7 years who showed conservation on the two versions of Piaget's conservation task (Wheldall & Poborca, 1980).

? Give a definition of operant discrimination learning and how it might be demonstrated in Wheldall and Poborca's study.

KEY STUDY
Asking one question in the conservation experiment

Piaget suggested that younger children cannot cope with conservation tasks because their thinking is not sufficiently mature. Rose and Blank (1974) and Samuel and Bryant (1984) proposed that younger children fail because they find being asked two questions confusing. The child may well think that the reason the experimenter asks the same question again is because he wants a different answer. This would be especially true because younger children are most susceptible to demand characteristics.

In Samuel and Bryant's study over 200 children aged between 5 and $8\frac{1}{2}$ years were given standard conservation tasks. Some children were given this in the "traditional form" where they were asked two questions: The child is shown the original display with two beakers of liquid or two rows of counters, and asked if the displays are the same. This is followed by the transformation where the water is poured into a taller, thinner glass or one row of counters is spread out. The child is then asked the question a second time.

Another group of children were only asked the question on the second occasion. This is the "one judgement condition". The children were tested on mass (two plasticine cylinders) as well as volume and number.

Younger children did cope better with the task in the one judgement condition than the standard condition; however, there continued to be age differences. In other words the older children always did better. It is, of course, possible that the younger children may still have felt intimidated by the experimental situation and been less able to cope.

Discussion points
1. What conclusions can be drawn from this study in terms of Piaget's theory?
2. What kinds of difficulty are encountered in research with children?

? Piaget's three mountains task required children to reverse a complicated image in their heads. Do you think a failure to do this necessarily shows egocentricity, or is there another explanation?

Bruner, Olver, and Greenfield (1966) argued that pre-operational children may fail to show conservation because they are influenced too much by the altered appearance of the visual display. First, they used the standard version of the liquid conservation task. Then they placed two beakers of different shapes behind a screen with only the tops of the beakers visible. Next water was poured from one beaker into the other behind the screen. When asked whether there was the same amount of water in the second beaker as there had been in the first, children of all ages between 4 and 7 showed much more evidence of conservation than they had in the standard version of the task. Finally, the children were given the standard conservation task for the second time. The percentage of 5-year-olds showing conservation more than trebled from 20% on the first test under standard conditions to about 70% on the second test. This shows that the pre-operational children were much more able to conserve when they recognised that appearances were misleading and that their learning could not be explained just by their readiness.

In addition, if Bruner asked the question "Is it still the same water?" this led to a marked increase in the number of children showing conservation. It was argued that such visual manipulation and questions increased the children's *sense of identity*. Identity involves realising that an object remains the same after it has been transformed.

Hughes (1975) argued that poor performance on the three mountains task occurred because the task did not relate to children's experience. He tested this argument by using a piece of apparatus in which two walls intersected at right angles to form what looked like a plus sign. A boy doll and a policeman doll were put into the apparatus, and the child was asked whether the policeman doll could see the boy doll. After that, the child was told to hide the boy so that the policeman could not see him. Nearly all the children could do this. Finally, a second policeman was used, and the children were told to hide the boy doll so that neither of the policemen could see him. According to Piaget, the children should have hidden the boy doll so that they themselves could not see him, and so should have failed the task. In fact, Hughes found that 90% of children between the ages of $3\frac{1}{2}$ and 5 performed the task successfully. Hughes concluded that the main reason why performance was much higher on his task than on the three mountains task used by Piaget was because his task was much more meaningful and interesting for young children.

A drawing of the two policemen version of Hughes' (1975) experimental set-up, in which the child is asked to hide a boy doll where neither of the policemen can see him. According to Piaget's egocentrism theory, children should hide the doll in sections A or B, where they themselves can't see him, but in fact Hughes found that 90% of children put the doll in section C—the only one the policemen cannot see.

It is worth re-emphasising the fact that, in all these studies, research showed that more children were capable of the tasks than Piaget had suggested but that differences between the age groups remained.

Concrete operations stage (7–11 years)

Piaget argued that the shift from pre-operational to concrete operational thinking involves an increasing independence of thought from perception (the evidence of your senses). Underlying this shift is the development of various cognitive operations of a logical or mathematical nature, including the actions implied by mathematical symbols (e.g., $+, -, \div, \times, >, <, =$). The most important cognitive operation is reversibility, which involves the ability to cancel out the effects of a perceptual change by imagining the opposite change. During the concrete operations stage, children can use the various cognitive operations only with respect to specific concrete situations. In the subsequent stage of formal operations, thinking is freed from the immediate situation.

Piaget argued that cognitive operations are usually combined or organised into a system or structure. For example, the operation "greater than" cannot really be considered independently of the operation "less than". Someone will fail to grasp the full meaning of "A is greater than B" unless he or she realises that this statement means that "B is less than A". Piaget coined the term *grouping* to refer to such sets of logically related operations. For example, consider the following problem: Tom is taller than Harry; Harry is taller than Dick. Is Dick shorter than Tom? Children who understand that the question is the same as "Is Tom taller than Dick?" are more likely to produce the correct answer.

The problem discussed in the previous paragraph is an example of the kind of task children can perform in the concrete operations stage that they couldn't perform previously. It is based on the notion of **transitivity**, which allows three elements to be placed in the correct order. Here is another example of a transitivity problem: if Mark is taller than Peter, and Peter is taller than Robert, then it follows from the notion of transitivity that Mark is taller than Robert. Concrete operational children can solve problems such as this one, but they can't apply the notion of transitivity to abstract problems, such as "if A > B > C, then is A greater than or smaller than C?"

Piaget argued that children should find it easier to achieve conservation on some tasks than on others. Conservation of number (e.g., realising that two rows of objects contain the same number of objects even when they are closer together in one row than in the other) involves fairly simple operations. All the child has to do is to pair each object in one row with an object in the other row. In contrast, consider conservation of volume. This can be tested by placing two identical balls of clay into two identical transparent containers filled to the same level with water. One ball of clay is then moulded into a new shape, and conservation is shown if the child realises that this will not change the amount of water it displaces. Conservation of volume is said to be harder to achieve than conservation of number because it involves taking account of the operations involved in the conservation of liquids and of mass. As predicted, conservation of volume is generally attained some years after conservation of number (e.g., Tomlinson-Keasey et al., 1979).

KEY TERM

Transitivity: understanding the relation between elements, for example, if *x* is greater than *y* and *y* is greater than *z*, then *x* is greater than *z*.

One of the tasks used to test conservation of number. Children are asked if there are the same number of beads in the two rows before and after they are rearranged.

This apparatus tests conservation of volume. Children are asked if the liquids will be at the same level again when the new shape of clay is put back into the glass. Conservation of volume is not usually attained until about the age of 11 or 12.

According to Piaget, most children acquire the various forms of conservation in the same order. First comes conservation of number and liquid at the age of about 6 or 7. Then comes conservation of substance or quantity and of length at about 7 or 8, followed by conservation of weight between the ages of 8 and 10. Finally, there is conservation of volume at about the age of 11 or 12.

Evaluation of Piaget's theory of the concrete operations stage. Children between the ages of 7 and 11 typically learn a range of cognitive operations related to mathematics and to logic. However, Piaget's approach is limited. Children during the concrete operations stage acquire an enormous amount of new knowledge, which contributes to their cognitive development. Much of this knowledge owes little to either mathematics or logic. Thus Piaget overlooked vast areas of cognitive development.

Piaget underestimated the importance of specific experiences in determining performance on conservation tasks. For example, children often show conservation of volume for substances with which they are familiar some time before they show conservation of volume for less familiar ones. For example, the children of Mexican potters showed slow development of conservation of volume using beakers, but fast development when a ball of clay was stretched into an oblong shape (Price-Williams, Gordon, & Ramirez, 1969). This is inconsistent with Piaget's stage-based account of cognitive development.

Formal operations stage (11 upwards)

Formal operational thought involves the ability to think in terms of many possible states of the world. This means one's thinking can go beyond the limitations of immediate reality, so one is not tied to perceptions and/or concrete reality. Thus adolescents and adults in the formal operations stage can think in an abstract way, as well as in the concrete way found in the previous stage of cognitive development.

Inhelder and Piaget (1958) suggested the following as a way to decide whether someone is using formal operations when solving a logical problem (such as the pendulum problem described below). If you ask a person to explain *how* they arrived at an answer to a logical problem, the formal operational thinker will report that they thought of a range of possibilities to account for the problem and used this range to generate hypotheses which could then be tested. The concrete thinker will have thought of a few alternatives and tried each one out in no particular order; when one possibility doesn't work another one is tried with no attempt to logically exclude certain possibilities.

The mathematical game *Mastermind*™ involves abstract logical thinking that occurs at the formal operations stage.

The pendulum problem. What kinds of problem have been used to study formal operational thought? One task used by Piaget involved presenting the participants with a set of weights and a string that could be lengthened or shortened. The goal was to work out what determines the frequency of the swings of a pendulum formed by suspending a weight on a string from a pole. The factors likely to be considered include the length of the string, the weight of the suspended object, the force of the participant's push, and the position from which the

? What can you do now, in terms of mental activities, that you were not able to do before you were 11?

pendulum is pushed. In fact, only the length of the string is relevant.

When pre-operational children are presented with this problem, they typically argue mistakenly that the strength of the push they give to the pendulum is the main factor. Concrete operational children often argue that the frequency of swinging of the pendulum is affected by the length of the string, but they aren't able to show that the other factors are irrelevant. In contrast, many formal operational children manage to carry out the necessary tests to show that *only* the length of the string influences the frequency of the swings of a pendulum. According to Piaget, the ability to solve the pendulum problem requires an understanding of a complicated combinatorial system.

Children were asked to work out what would affect the frequency of the swings of the pendulum (how many times it would go back and forth in a given period). They were asked to consider changing the weights on the pendulum, the length of the string, how hard they pushed it, and which direction it was pushed in.

Evaluation of Piaget's theory of the formal operations stage.   Piaget greatly exaggerated the role played by logical reasoning in adolescent and adult thought. Adults in their everyday lives typically deal with problems that have no single perfect solution, and that cannot be solved simply by the rigorous use of logic. Thus, a detailed understanding of mathematics and of logic is of limited value in most adult thinking. Bradmetz (1999) assessed formal operational thinking in 62 15-year-olds using various Piagetian tasks. His key finding was that only 1 out of the 62 participants showed substantial evidence of formal operational thought, although many other participants occasionally showed signs of such thought.

It is not clear to what extent even intelligent adults (e.g., university students) actually ever do reach the stage of formal operational thinking. For example, Wason and Shapiro (1971) devised a card selection task that requires abstract logical reasoning (see the Key Study below). If this task is given in a concrete form more individuals can solve it, suggesting that not all adults can cope with abstract reasoning.

KEY STUDY
Wason and Shapiro

Peter Wason devised the Wason selection task to study deductive reasoning. In the original version, there are four cards lying on a table. Each card has a letter on one side, and a number on the other side. Each participant is told that there is a rule that applies to the four cards. The participant's task is to select only those cards that need to be turned over in order to decide whether or not the rule is correct.

In one of the most used versions of this selection task, the four cards have the following symbols visible: R, G, 2, and 7, and the rule is as follows: "If there is an R on one side of the card, then there is a 2 on the other side of the card". What answer would you give? Most people select either the R card or the R and 2 cards. If you did the same, then you got the answer wrong. The

Rule: If there is an R on one side of the card, then there is a 2 on the other.

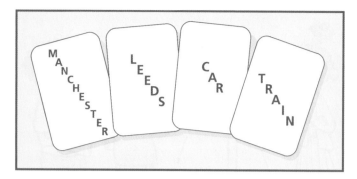

A more concrete version of the Wason selection task.

INDEPENDENT STUDY IDEA: VARIATIONS ON THE WASON TASK

It is possible to devise your own abstract and concrete versions of the Wason and Shapiro study. The advantage of this is that it's possible to do a cognitive developmental task on an older group of students. You could compare the same people on the concrete and abstract task—this would be nominal data (the number of people to do the task successfully) with a repeated measures design. You could also compare two age groups on their ability to do one or other of the tasks (the concrete and abstract). This would yield two separate sets of results, both of which could be analysed using a 2 × 1 chi-squared test (don't put them together in a 2 × 2 as some of them are related and chi-squared test can only be used on independent data). You may find bigger differences in the abstract than in the concrete task depending, of course, on which age groups you use.

starting point for solving the problem is to recognise that what needs to be done is to see whether any of the cards *fail* to obey the rule. From this point of view, the 2 card is irrelevant. If there is an R on the other side of it, then all that this tells us is that the rule *might* be true. If there is any other letter, then we have found out nothing about the validity of the rule.

The correct answer is to select the cards with R and 7 on them. This answer is produced by only about 5–10% of university students. The reason why the 7 card is necessary is that it would definitely disprove the rule if it had an R on the other side.

Wason and Shapiro (1971) argued that the abstract nature of the Wason task makes it hard to solve. They used four cards (Manchester, Leeds, car, and train), and the rule was, "Every time I go to Manchester I travel by car". The task was to select only those cards that needed to be turned over to prove or disprove the rule. The correct answer that the Manchester and train cards need to be turned over was given by 62% of the student participants, against only 12% when the task was presented in its abstract form. These finding suggest that most young adults have difficulties with formal operational thinking—like younger people, they can reason much better when dealing with concrete versions of tasks than with abstract ones.

Discussion points
1. Why do you think most people find the original version of the Wason selection task so difficult?
2. How can the Wason selection task be made easier?

General evaluation of Piaget's theory

Piaget's theory was an ambitious attempt to explain how children move from being irrational and illogical to being rational and logical. The notion that children learn certain basic operations (e.g., reversibility), and that these operations then allow them to solve a wide range of problems, is a valuable one. No one before Piaget had provided a detailed account of the ways in which children's thinking changes.

Much of the evidence Piaget obtained about children's cognitive development is flawed. He used the **clinical method**, which involves the experimenter discussing the task with the child in an unstandardised and rather unscientific way. A major problem with the clinical method is that it makes considerable demands on the language ability of the child. As a result, Piaget often underestimated the cognitive abilities of children.

Some of the major assumptions on which Piaget's theory is based are inadequate:

1. Stage development

Piaget assumed that all children go through the same sequence of four major cognitive stages. One of the great dangers with stage theories is that the differences between stages will be *overestimated*, whereas those within stages will be *underestimated*. For example, Piaget assumed that children who show conservation of quantity for one material possess the operation of reversibility. Thus, they should show conservation

KEY TERM

Clinical method: a form of unstructured interview where the interviewer starts with some predetermined set of questions, but as the interview proceeds these questions are adapted in line with the responses given. This kind of interview is used by clinicians when assessing mentally-ill patients.

with other materials. In fact, children generally show conservation of quantity for familiar materials some time before they show it for unfamiliar materials. Thus, successful performance depends on *specific* learning experiences as well as on the *general* cognitive operations emphasised by Piaget. In essence, cognitive development proceeds much more unsystematically than Piaget assumed.

 What problems does the clinical method pose for anyone attempting to carry out a longitudinal study of a child's development?

2. Performance and competence

Piaget argued that children who fail to solve a problem lack the necessary cognitive structures or competencies. There is an important distinction between performance (which is what the individual actually does) and competence (which is the underlying knowledge). As Shaffer (1993, p.268) pointed out, Piaget had a tendency "to equate *performance* with *competence* (and to ignore other factors that influence children's responses)." Donaldson (1978) drew a distinction between embedded and disembedded language. Embedded language is very much bound up in ongoing events, whereas disembedded language is not. Donaldson argued that children find it much harder to show the abilities they possess when problems are presented in disembedded language. In other words, the gap between competence and performance is greater when disembedded language is used. In similar fashion, students often find mathematics and statistics difficult, because they tend to be disembedded from the immediate experience of students. Donaldson's argument is illustrated by a study with McGarrigle (1974), which is described in the Key Study below.

KEY STUDY
McGarrigle and Donaldson

McGarrigle and Donaldson (1974) showed that there can be a large discrepancy between competence and performance. They presented 6-year-old children with two rows of counters, following a similar procedure to Piaget's classic conservation experiments. All the children agreed that there were equal numbers of counters in each row. In one condition, the experimenter deliberately messed up one of the rows. Only 16% of the children showed number conservation (i.e., argued that there were the same number of counters in each row). This finding suggests that very few of the children had the underlying competence necessary to show number conservation. However, the findings were very different in a second condition, in which a "naughty teddy bear" messed up one of the rows in what looked like an accidental way. In this condition, 62% of the children showed conservation, saying that there was no change in the number of counters.

Why did McGarrigle and Donaldson find such a large difference between the two conditions? The high level of performance in the "naughty teddy" condition must have occurred because most of the children in fact had a general understanding of number conservation. In the other condition, the fact that the experimenter deliberately altered the situation may have led the children to assume that the experimenter *intended* to change the number of counters in one of the rows. Whether or not that is correct, the fact remains that performance in the "Piaget" condition failed to reflect the underlying level of competence.

McGarrigle and Donaldson found that when an experimenter rearranged one of a pair of rows of counters, relatively few 6-year-old children thought that the two rows still contained the same number of counters. However, when a teddy bear appeared to mess up the counters accidentally, most children said that the numbers in the rows were still the same.

Key study evaluation

Recent research suggests that McGarrigle and Donaldson may also have been mistaken. It is possible that the children were so absorbed in the "naughty teddy" routine that they didn't actually notice the transformation and that is why, with naughty teddy, they said the display hadn't changed. To test this possibility, Moore and Frye (1986) arranged for naughty teddy to actually add a counter (or take one away). Children said no change had taken place, which suggests that they were simply not attending to the display at all.

However, the notion that children may fail to show number conservation because they think the experimenter intended to change the number was further supported by Light, Buckingham, and Robbins (1979). They tested 5- and 6-year-olds in pairs, with both members of each pair being given glass beakers of the same size and containing the same number of pasta shells. They were told the shells would be used to play a competitive game, and so it was essential they had the same number. Then the experimenter pretended to notice that one of the beakers had a badly chipped rim and so might be dangerous to handle. The shells were then transferred to another beaker of a different shape, and the children were asked whether the number of shells in each beaker was the same. Conservation was shown by 70% of the children in this incidental transformation condition, against only 5% in a standard intentional transformation condition. Presumably the change seemed less important when it was seen as merely incidental.

Discussion points

1. Why do you think that McGarrigle and Donaldson found such a large difference between their two conditions?
2. What problems for Piaget's theory arose from his failure to distinguish carefully between performance and competence?

3. Maturational processes

Piaget (1970) assumed that maturation of the brain and of the nervous system plays an important role in allowing children to move through the successive stages of cognitive development. He also assumed that new cognitive structures can develop when there is a *conflict* between what the child expects to happen and what actually happens. These assumptions are too vague to be of much value in understanding the forces producing cognitive development. Piaget provided a detailed *description* of the major changes in cognitive development, but he didn't offer an adequate explanation. He told us *what* cognitive development involves, but not *why* or *how* this development occurs. However, Piaget's approach has given rise to much research, and he remains the most significant theorist on cognitive development.

Vygotsky's Theory

Lev Vygotsky (1896–1934) was a Russian psychologist who emphasised the notion that cognitive development depends very largely on social factors. According to Vygotsky (1981, p.163):

Any function in the child's cultural development appears twice, or on two planes. First, it appears on the social plane, and then on the psychological plane.

As Durkin (1995) pointed out, the child can be thought of as an apprentice who learns directly from social interaction and communication with older children and

Lev Semeonovich Vygotsky, 1896–1934.

adults who have the knowledge and skills that the child lacks. This approach is very different from Piaget's, where the emphasis is on the *individual* acquiring knowledge through a process of self-discovery. However, there are some similarities between the two approaches. Vygotsky and Piaget agreed that activity forms the basis for learning and for the development of thinking. In addition, they both agreed that learning is most effective when the information presented to children is closely related to their current knowledge and abilities.

The role of culture

Social factors, or more generally "**culture**", play a key role in cognitive development because, according to Vygotsky, they enable **elementary mental functions** to be transformed into **higher mental functions**. Elementary functions are innate capacities such as attention and sensation. Such functions are possessed by all animals and these will develop to a limited extent through experience. However cultural influences are required to transform them into higher mental functions, such as problem solving and thinking. When Vygotsky used the concept of "culture" he was referring to the body of knowledge that is held by, for example, books and "**experts**" (persons with greater knowledge), and that is largely transmitted through language. Therefore cultural knowledge and language are the means by which cognitive development takes place.

If higher mental functions depend on cultural influences then we would expect to find different higher mental functions in different cultures. Gredler (1992) recorded an example of this. Children in Papua New Guinea are taught a counting system that begins on the thumb of one hand and proceeds up the arm and down to the other fingers, ending at 29. This means that it is very difficult to add and subtract large numbers and this limits mathematical calculations in that culture. We can see another example in the advent of the internet in our cultures. This has the potential of vastly changing the speed of cognitive development in children who can now access huge stores of knowledge.

> [?] Has use of the internet affected your own cognitive development?

Vygotsky's four stages

Vygotsky argued that there are four stages in the formation of concepts. He identified these four stages on the basis of a study in which children were presented with wooden blocks provided with labels consisting of nonsense symbols. Each nonsense syllable was used in a consistent way to refer to blocks having certain characteristics, such as circular and thin. The children were given the concept-formation task of deciding on the meaning of each nonsense syllable. Vygotsky's four stages were as follows:

Vague syncretic stage: the children failed to use systematic strategies and showed little or no understanding of the concepts. The approach adopted by children in this stage is not far removed from a random one.

Complex stage: non-random strategies were used, but these strategies were not successful in finding the main features of each concept.

Potential concept stage: systematic strategies were used, but they were limited to focusing on one feature

> **KEY TERMS**
> **Culture:** the rules, morals, and methods of interactions specific to a group of people.
> **Elementary mental functions:** innate capacities, such as attention and sensation. Such functions are possessed by all animals and these will develop to a limited extent through experience.
> **Higher mental functions:** according to Vygotsky those mental abilities, such as problem solving, that develop from elementary mental functions largely as a consequence of cultural influences.
> **Experts:** people with greater knowledge. This can include peers.

at a time (e.g., shape). This is very similar to Piaget's notion that pre-operational children fail on conservation tasks because they focus on only one feature at a time (e.g., shape).

Mature concept stage: systematic strategies relating to more than one feature at a time were used, and led to successful concept formation. Thus, children in this stage have attained a good understanding of concepts.

What happens as children proceed through these four stages? In essence, children's behaviour is initially controlled by the environment but there is a gradual emergence of voluntary regulation of behaviour and a great increase in understanding. For example, a young child perceives paper money as simply a patterned and coloured piece of paper, whereas an older child perceives it as money that can be used to buy things.

Zone of proximal development

What factors determine how well children are able to learn and to benefit from their interactions with other people? According to Vygotsky, the zone of proximal development is of fundamental importance to an understanding of cognitive development. The **zone of proximal development** was defined by Vygotsky (1978, p.86) as:

> *the distance between the actual developmental level as determined by independent problem solving and the level of potential development as determined through problem solving under adult guidance or in collaboration with more capable peers.*

The lower limit of the zone is the child's level of ability as it is displayed when he/she works on his/her own, and the upper limit is the child's potential level of ability when assisted by someone who has more knowledge than the child. Children are most likely to acquire new knowledge rapidly and without a sense of failure when they are moderately challenged by someone else.

Scaffolding

Wood, Bruner, and Ross (1976) developed Vygotsky's notion of a zone of proximal development. They introduced the concept of **scaffolding**, which refers

? Can you relate any, or all, of these stages to some of the Piagetian concepts you read about earlier?

KEY TERMS

Zone of proximal development: in Vygotsky's theory, capacities that are being developed but are not as yet functioning fully.
Scaffolding: the context provided by an adult or other knowledgeable person which helps the child to develop his or her cognitive skills.

Left to his own devices, could this boy make his sister a birthday cake? His mother uses scaffolding to create a situation in which he can begin to move to the top of a zone of proximal development.

to the context provided by knowledgeable people such as adults to help children to develop their cognitive skills. An important aspect of scaffolding is that there is a gradual withdrawal of support on any one task as the child's knowledge and confidence increase. Of course, many parents use scaffolding when interacting with their children even though they have never heard of scaffolding or of Vygotsky!

Moss (1992) reviewed a number of studies concerned with the scaffolding provided by mothers during the preschool period. There were three main aspects to the mothers' scaffolding strategies. First, the mother instructed her child in new skills that the child couldn't use on its own. Second, the mother encouraged her child to maintain useful problem solving tactics it had shown spontaneously. Third, the mother tried to persuade the child to discard immature and inappropriate forms of behaviour.

Language development

Vygotsky attached great importance to the development of language. He argued that language and thought are essentially unrelated during the first stage of development. As a result, young children have "pre-intellectual speech" and "pre-verbal thought". During the second stage, language and thought develop in parallel, and continue to have very little impact on each other. During the third stage, children begin to make use of the speech of others and talking to themselves (private speech) to assist in their thinking and problem solving. An important notion here is that of **intersubjectivity**. This refers to the process by which two individuals whose initial views about a task are different move towards an agreed understanding of what is involved.

Language development in Vygotsky's four stages

Vague syncretic stage	Complex stage	Potential concept stage	Mature concept stage
Pre-verbal thought and pre-intellectual language	Language and thought are developing in parallel, but have little impact on each other	Children make use of the speech of others, and talking to themselves, in thinking and problem solving	Talking to oneself becomes increasingly private

Finally, private speech is used routinely in problem solving, and language plays a part in the development of thinking. Thus, language becomes more and more central to cognitive development over the years. Private speech is initially spoken out loud, but then becomes increasingly internal. Language generally plays a crucial role when children learn from social interactions with others. Some of the processes involved were described by Berk (1994, p.62):

> *When a child discusses a challenging task with a mentor [someone providing guidance], that individual offers spoken directions and strategies. The child incorporates the language of those dialogues into his or her private speech and then uses it to guide independent efforts.*

Research evidence for Vygotsky's approach
Scaffolding

There is considerable experimental evidence that approaches to teaching based on the zone of proximal development and on scaffolding can be very effective. For example, Conner, Knight, and Cross (1997) studied the effects of scaffolding on 2-year-olds, who were asked to perform various problem-solving and literary tasks. Most previous studies had focused only on mothers' scaffolding, but Conner et al. also considered fathers' scaffolding. Mothers and fathers were

KEY TERM

Intersubjectivity: a process by which two individuals with different views about a task adjust those views so they become more similar.

Children who make use of inner speech tend to perform better on difficult or novel tasks than children who do not use much inner speech.

equally good at scaffolding, and the quality of scaffolding predicted the children's performance on the various tasks during the teaching session.

If scaffolding is to be of real value in education, its beneficial effects need to last well beyond the original teaching session. Accordingly, Conner et al. conducted a follow-up session. They found that the children who had originally received better scaffolding continued to perform better than those who had received poor scaffolding.

Social context

Wertsch et al. (1980) obtained evidence supporting Vygotsky's view that learning initially emerges in a social context. Mothers and their children between the ages of 2 and 4 were given the task of building a truck so that it looked like a model they could refer to. When the mothers of the younger children looked at the model, this was followed by their children looking at the model on about 90% of occasions. However, the older children's looking behaviour was much less influenced by what their mothers were doing. Thus, social factors in the form of the mother's looking behaviour had much more impact on younger than on older children, as expected by Vygotsky.

Inner speech

Vygotsky's notion that inner speech can be of value in thinking has received support, for example the study by Berk (1994), which is described in the Key Study below. In another study (Hardyck & Petrinovich, 1970), participants read an easy or difficult text. Half were told not to use inner speech, whereas the remainder were free to do so. Comprehension of the difficult text was significantly higher when the participants were allowed to use inner speech, but the use of inner speech did not affect comprehension of the easy text. This is consistent with other evidence indicating that inner speech is of most value when tasks are difficult (Eysenck & Keane, 1995). Behrend, Harris, and Cartwright (1992) used whispering and observable lip movements as measures of inner speech. Children who used the most inner speech tended to perform difficult tasks better than children who made little use of inner speech.

KEY STUDY
Berk

Convincing evidence of the important role played by inner speech was reported by Berk (1994). She found that 6-year-olds spent an average of 60% of the time talking to themselves while solving problems in mathematics. Those whose speech contained numerous comments about what needed to be done on the current problem did better at mathematics over the following year. This confirmed Vygotsky's view that self-guiding speech can make it easier for children to direct their actions. Presumably this self-guiding speech made it easier for the children to focus their attention on the task in hand.

Vygotsky argued that private speech diminishes and becomes more internal as children's level of performance improves. Berk (1994) discussed a study in which 4- and 5-year-old children made Lego™ models in each of three sessions. As predicted by Vygotsky, the children's speech became increasingly internalised from session to session as their model-making performance improved. Thus, as Vygotsky assumed, private speech is of most value to children when they are confronted by novel tasks that they do not fully understand.

Parents can provide their children with an excellent start in acquiring skills if they support and encourage attempts to learn through play.

Key Study evaluation
The usefulness of Vygotsky's theory of diminishing speech depends on what is meant by "speech". For example, some children with learning difficulties are unable to speak but can perform quite well on many types of tasks. Children who are born profoundly deaf and whose families are hearing often find speech difficult or impossible to acquire, but their intelligence is sometimes unimpaired. It is interesting to speculate whether deaf children of deaf parents who grow up using sign language can use signs as their own private "speech" in the way described by Vygotsky.

Discussion points
1. How important do you think that private speech is in children's thinking?
2. Why does private speech become less frequent when children begin to master a task?

Evaluation of Vygotsky's approach

There are several significant strengths of Vygotsky's theoretical approach. As he argued, children's cognitive development does depend importantly on the social context and on guidance provided by adults and other children. Piaget underestimated the importance of the social environment, and Vygotsky deserves credit for acknowledging the key role it plays in cognitive development. It follows from Vygotsky's approach that there should be major differences in cognitive development from culture to culture, whereas Piaget argued that children everywhere go through the same sequence of cognitive stages in the same order. The universal stages emphasised by Piaget have been found in numerous cultures. However, there are also important cultural differences in cognitive development, especially with respect to the *speed* of that development.

There are several limitations with Vygotsky's theoretical approach. First, he has been criticised for exaggerating the importance of the social environment. Children's rate of cognitive development is determined by their level of motivation and interest in learning, as well as by the social support they receive.

Second, the account he offered is rather sketchy. He didn't make it clear precisely what kinds of social interaction were most beneficial for learning (e.g., general encouragement versus specific instructions). According to Durkin (1995, p.380), the followers of Vygotsky "offer only superficial accounts of how language is actually used in the course of social interactions".

Third, social interactions between, for example, parent and child don't always have beneficial effects. Indeed, social interactions can make matters worse rather than better. As Durkin (1995, p.375) pointed out, "People confronted with an opposing point of view . . . dig their heels in, get hot under the collar, refuse to budge, exploit their knowledge as a source of power and control, and so on."

Fourth, Vygotsky assumed that social interactions enhanced cognitive development because of the instruction provided. However, there are other reasons why children benefit from social interactions. Light et al. (1994) found on a computer-based task that children learned better in pairs than on their own, even when the other child was merely present and did not say anything. This is known as **social facilitation**, and occurs because the presence of others can have a motivational effect.

Fifth, it would seem from Vygotsky's account that nearly all learning should be fairly easy if children receive the appropriate help from adults and other

? Does social facilitation only apply to young children? Are there times when it might apply to older individuals?

KEY TERM

Social facilitation: the enhancement of an individual's performance when working in the presence of other people.

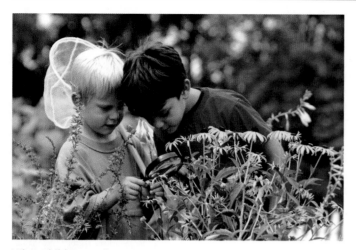

When children are in company they tend to be more motivated to learn and investigate.

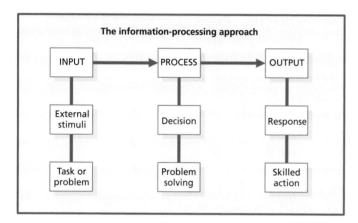

children. In fact, young children often take months or years to master complex skills even when well supported in their schools and homes. This suggests that Vygotsky ignored genuine constraints on children's learning.

Vygotsky developed his theory during the last 10 years of his life, before he died of tuberculosis at the tragically early age of 38. At least some of the weaknesses of his approach might have been resolved had he lived longer.

Information-processing Approach

Most cognitive psychologists have used the information-processing approach in their attempts to understand adult cognition. According to this approach, the human mind is like an information-processing system consisting of a small number of *processes* (e.g., attention) and *structures* (e.g., long-term memory). This system is used in flexible ways to handle all kinds of cognitive tasks ranging from simple mathematics to reading a novel, and from studying French to playing chess.

There have been several attempts to apply the information-processing approach to the topic of cognitive development. In what follows, we focus on two theories using this approach within the general context of Piagetian theory.

Approach of Case and Pascual-Leone: Neo-Piagetian approach

Case (1974) and Pascual-Leone (1984) were both strongly influenced by Piaget's theoretical approach, although they didn't accept all his views. They agreed with Piaget that children actively structure their understanding, and that children move from pre-concrete to concrete thinking, and then on to abstract thinking. More specifically, Case and Pascual-Leone made use of various assumptions. First, they argued that it was desirable to consider cognitive development within an **information-processing framework**. Second, they claimed that it was preferable to focus on *specific* components of cognitive processing rather than the more *general* schemas emphasised by Piaget. Third, they argued that much of cognitive development depends on an increase in mental capacity or mental power. These areas of agreement and disagreement with Piaget led them to develop a neo-Piagetian theory of cognitive development.

According to Pascual-Leone (1984), a key aspect of mental capacity is "M". This refers to the number of schemes or units of cognition a child can work with at any given time. M increases as children grow up, and this is one of the main reasons for cognitive development. Pascual-Leone assumed that increased M or processing capacity resulted from neurological development.

? Can you recall trying to master a skill, such as multiplication or telling the time, which seemed impossible to grasp but is now automatic?

KEY TERM

Information-processing framework: an approach to understanding cognitive processes by making analogies with computing and information technology.

The information-processing approaches of Pascual-Leone and Case revolve around the notion of schemes or basic units of cognition, which resemble Piaget's schemas. Case (1974) identified three kinds of schemes:

Figurative schemes	Operative schemes	Executive schemes
Internal representations of items of information with which a subject is familiar or of perceptual configurations he or she can recognise	Internal representations of function (rules), which can be applied to one set of figurative schemes in order to generate a new set	Internal representations of procedures, which can be applied in the face of particular problem situations, in an attempt to reach particular objectives
For example: recognising one's own school from a photograph	For example: deciding that two photographs depict the same school	For example: looking at a work colleague and deciding whether to work goals or an operative scheme related to social goals

According to this theory, a child's ability to solve a problem depends on four basic factors. First, there is the range of schemes the child has available. Second, there is the child's M-power or mental capacity, which increases with age. Third, there is the extent to which the child uses its available M-power. Fourth, there is the relative importance the child gives to perceptual and non-perceptual cues.

How do children acquire new schemes? Case (1974) suggested they can be formed by modifying existing schemes. Alternatively, new schemes can be acquired by the combination or consolidation of several existing schemes.

Research evidence

This theory can be applied to many of Piaget's findings. For example, Piaget found that children below the age of 7 generally didn't realise that the amount of water remains the same when poured from one container into another that is taller and thinner. Piaget argued that this is because these children don't understand the logic of conservation. According to Pascual-Leone (1984), it is often because the children don't have enough mental capacity to hold all the relevant schemes in mind. Suppose the conservation task were made easier by filling the containers with beads and allowing children to count the number of beads. Piaget would still expect the children to fail, because they haven't learned the underlying logic. In contrast, Case and Pascual-Leone would predict more success, because the demands on mental capacity have been reduced. The evidence supports the neo-Piagetians rather than Piaget (e.g., Bower, 1979).

The value of the neo-Piagetian approach can also be seen in a study discussed by Case (1992). Children and adolescents aged between 10 and 18 drew a picture of a mother looking out of the window of her home who could see her son playing peekaboo with her in the park on the other side of the road. The younger participants found it very hard to do this. They could draw the mother in the house and the boy in the park, but they didn't have enough mental capacity to

Despite possessing generally inferior cognitive-processing capabilities, a child with more experience of playing chess, will be able to recall chess positions better than their less practised opponent.

If schemas or schemes are hypothetical structures, why might this be a limitation of theories that include them?

integrate the two parts of the drawing. In contrast, the older participants produced an integrated drawing, because they had greater M-power.

Evaluation

There are some clear advantages to the neo-Piagetian approach compared with Piaget's. First, the general approach has been applied with great success to the study of adult cognition, and it is reasonable to extend that approach to children's cognition. Second, Piaget argued that children fail to solve problems because they lack the necessary logical or other structures, rather than because of processing limitations. However, many problem-solving failures in children depend on processing limitations or insufficient M-power. Third, the concepts (e.g., different types of schemes) used by theorists such as Case and Pascual-Leone are easier to measure than Piaget's schemas.

On the negative side, there are problems in testing the theory. First, it is often hard to work out how many schemes are required to solve a task, or to decide how many schemes are used by a given child.

Second, it is hard to calculate someone's mental capacity. There is a danger of assuming that success results from sufficient mental capacity and failure results from insufficient mental capacity, without actually measuring mental capacity at all. When that happens, the findings are simply re-described.

Third, it is very difficult to distinguish between changes in strategies and changes in M-space or mental capacity. In fact, Case (1985) admitted that children's cognitive development may depend more on changing strategies than on basic mental capacity.

COMPARISON OF THE THREE MAIN APPROACHES		
Information-processing	**Vygotsky**	**Piaget**
Children's intellectual development is explained in terms of automatic processes	Children are participating in an interactive process whereby knowledge becomes individualised through socially and culturally determined knowledge	Children's intellectual development can be seen in terms of the individual's adaptation to the environment

Practical Applications to Education

The theories of cognitive development put forward by Piaget, by Vygotsky, and by information-processing theorists have been very influential in the field of education. Here, we will focus on the ways in which their ideas have had an impact on education in schools. However, note that many of the educational methods discussed are also used very successfully by parents and others outside the school context.

Piaget's approach

Piaget himself didn't focus very much on the usefulness of his theory for educational practice. However, many people working in education have done precisely that. The Plowden Report in 1967 suggested that some of Piaget's ideas should be used in schools. Years later, the Nuffield Science approach to education was based on the Piagetian notions that children should be actively involved in learning, and that concrete practical work should precede the more abstract

Do you think that children receive more "education" in school or at home?

aspects of science. Next we consider three ways in which Piagetian theory has been applied in education.

What can children learn?

According to Piaget, what children can learn is determined by their current stage of cognitive development. Thus, it is very much limited to what they are "ready" to learn. More specifically, children can only deal successfully with tasks making use of the various cognitive structures and operations they have already mastered.

This prediction has received little support. Several attempts have been made to teach concrete operations to preschool children. The ability to perform concrete operational tasks is normally learned at about the age of 7. Thus, it shouldn't be possible on Piagetian theory for much younger children to perform them successfully. However, provision of suitable training to 4-year-olds usually leads to reasonably good performance on such tasks (Brainerd, 1983). In other words, Piaget underestimated the ability of children to cope with new kinds of intellectual challenge.

Piaget recommended that disequilibrium be created by asking children difficult questions.

How should children be taught?

According to Piaget, children learn best when they engage in a process of active **self-discovery**. Children apply the processes of assimilation and accommodation to their active involvement with the world around them. Teachers can encourage this by creating a state of disequilibrium, in which the child's existing schemas or cognitive structures are shown to be inadequate. Disequilibrium can be created by asking children difficult questions, and by encouraging them to ask questions.

Some of these ideas can be applied to playgroup practices and to children playing with toys. According to Piaget, children will obtain the most benefit from playgroups and from toys when actively involved in a process of self-discovery. In what Piaget called mastery play, the child uses new motor schemas in several different situations. This helps to strengthen the child's learning.

Piaget's preferred educational approach can be contrasted with the more traditional approach, in which the teacher provides relatively passive children with knowledge. Piaget argued that this approach (sometimes called **tutorial training**) is much less effective than self-discovery. In his own words, "Every time we teach a child something, we prevent him from discovering it on his own."

Brainerd (1983) reviewed the relevant studies. He concluded that, "although self-discovery training can produce learning, it is generally less effective than tutorial learning". Meadows (1994) arrived at a similar, but broader conclusion: "Piagetian theory emphasises the individual child as the virtually independent constructor of his own development, an emphasis that under-values the contribution of other people to cognitive development and excludes teaching and cultural influences." Note, however, that it is difficult to compare the effectiveness of different teaching methods. We really need large-scale studies involving teachers with a very clear grasp of the methods they have been told to use teaching children of equivalent ability over a fairly lengthy period of time. As you can imagine, few studies match up to these requirements.

Socio-cognitive conflict. The notion of disequilibrium was developed by neo-Piagetians such as Doise and Mugny (1984). They argued that cognitive

> **?** Most children in Western societies spend many years in school. What implications might this have for trying to apply Piaget's universal theory to all children?

KEY TERMS

Self-discovery: an active approach to learning in which the child is encouraged to use his or her initiative in learning.

Tutorial training: a traditional approach in which the teacher imparts knowledge to fairly passive students.

development involves the resolution of **socio-cognitive conflict,** which is produced by exposure to the differing views of others. Thus, they emphasised social factors in learning more than Piaget did.

Evidence indicating the importance of socio-cognitive conflict was reported by Ames and Murray (1982), in a study on children aged 6 and 7 who had failed on conservation tasks. Some children were given corrective feedback, and others were exposed to children who already knew about conservation. Still others were paired with children who had also failed to conserve, but who had provided a *different* wrong answer from theirs. Children in the last condition showed the greatest improvement in ability to conserve. Presumably this happened because socio-cognitive conflict and the need to consider the task in detail were greatest in this condition.

The neo-Piagetians also emphasised the importance of **social marking,** which involves conflict between an individual's cognitive understanding and some social rule. Doise et al. (1981) studied conservation of liquid in children between the ages of 4 and 6 who didn't initially show conservation. Social marking was induced in some pairs of children by reminding them of the social rule that both children deserved the same reward. Other pairs of children were not reminded of this rule. The children in the social marking condition saw a conflict between the social rule and the apparently different amounts of liquid in the two containers, and this helped them to show conservation. This approach offers useful guidance to educators in suggesting what particular interventions are helpful.

What should children be taught?

Piaget claimed that cognitive development depends very much on children learning a range of schemas or cognitive structures (e.g., operations). Many of these schemas are based on mathematical or logical principles. It follows that it should be useful for children to study mathematics and logic, as well as science subjects that provide illustrations of these principles at work. Of crucial importance is the notion that the learning material mustn't be too complex and far removed from the child's existing schemas. According to Piaget, children can only learn effectively when they possess the relevant underlying schemas that can be accommodated to new experiences.

The major weakness of Piaget's position is that the cognitive structures he emphasised are of rather limited value for many kinds of learning. It is not clear that concrete and formal operations are of much relevance to the learning of foreign languages or of history. Thus his approach applies only to a small number of subjects taught at school.

Evaluation

Piaget's ideas have influenced educational practice in several countries. Self-discovery and the creation of disequilibrium can be very useful in learning, especially with intelligent students who are able to engage in independent thinking. In addition, as Piaget argued, it is often preferable for students to deal with concrete problems before proceeding to abstract ones. However, Piaget's influence has been of limited value. In some cases (e.g., tutorial training), the more traditional approach seems to be superior to Piaget's alternative approach.

? Which group would be predicted to do best according to Vygotsky's theory?

? What school subjects are difficult to link with Piaget's theory? Which subjects fit well with the theory?

KEY TERMS

Socio-cognitive conflict: intellectual conflict produced by exposure to the differing views of others.
Social marking: conflict between an individual's cognitive understanding and a social rule.

Vygotsky's approach

Vygotsky's key contribution to educational practice was the notion that children typically learn best in a social context in which someone who is more knowledgeable carefully guides and encourages their learning efforts. Thus, children can be regarded as apprentices who are taught the necessary skills by those already possessing them by means of scaffolding. Effective teachers or tutors will generally reduce their control over the learning process when children are performing successfully, but will increase their control when children start making errors.

Vygotsky's ideas are relevant at home as well as in the school environment. Some parents don't make use of scaffolding, and do not discuss issues with their children in a way appropriate to their level of understanding. As a result, the children tend to have poor concentration, and find it hard to develop activities (Meadows, 1994).

To be an effective tutor, this father needs to avoid interfering while his son is managing alone, but be prepared to help when the boy gets stuck.

Peer tutoring

According to Vygotsky, it is important for those involved in educating children to focus on the children's zone of proximal development. It could be argued that the ideal tutors are children who are slightly older and more advanced than the children being taught. Such tutors have useful knowledge to communicate to the children being taught. They should also remember the limitations in their own knowledge and understanding when they were 1 or 2 years younger. The approach we have just described is known as **peer tutoring**, and it has become increasingly popular in schools.

Peer tutoring is generally effective. Barnier (1989) looked at the performance of 6- and 7-year-olds on various spatial and perspective-taking tasks. Those who were exposed to brief sessions of peer tutoring with 7- and 8-year-old tutors performed better than those who were not. The benefits of peer tutoring have been found in various cultures. Ellis and Gauvain (1992) compared 7-year-old Navaho children and Euro-American children who performed a maze game. They were tutored by either one or two 9-year-old tutors working together. The children from both cultures benefited more from the paired tutors than from the individual ones, and the benefit was the same in both cultures. There were some cultural differences in the teaching style of the tutors: the Euro-American tutors gave many more verbal instructions, and were generally less patient.

Learning through play

Vygotsky also argued that children can learn much through play. According to Vygotsky (1976, p.552):

> *In play, the child functions above his average age, above his usual everyday behaviour, in play he is head high above himself.*

Why is this? A key reason is because children at play generally make use of some aspects of their own culture. For example, they may pretend to be a fire-fighter or a doctor, or they may play with toys that are specific to their culture. This relationship to their own culture enhances learning.

Evaluation

The scaffolding provided by peers or by teachers can be very effective in promoting effective learning at school. However, the Vygotskyan approach has various

> **KEY TERM**
>
> **Peer tutoring:** teaching of one child by another, with the child doing the teaching generally being slightly older than the child being taught.

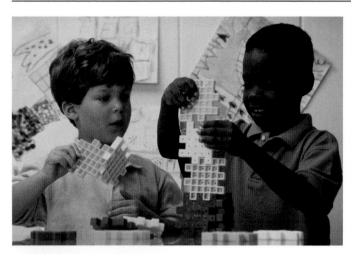

Peer tutoring: a boy shows his school friend how the puzzle fits together.

? Does thinking about the ideas underlying a task link more closely with the Piagetian or the information-processing approach?

? Think back to your own experiences at school: which method helped you to learn most successfully?

limitations. First, as Durkin (1995, p.375) pointed out, the whole approach is based on the dubious assumption that, "helpful tutors team up with eager tutees to yield maximum learning outcomes". In fact, as Salomon and Globerson (1989) pointed out, there are several reasons why this assumption is often incorrect. For example, if there is too much status difference between the tutor and the learner, the learner may become uninvolved in the learning process. Another possibility is what Salomon and Globerson called "ganging up on the task", in which the tutor and learner agree that the task is not worth doing properly.

Second, Durkin (1995) argued that the Vygotskyan approach may be better suited to some kinds of tasks than to others. Many of the successful uses of scaffolding have been on construction tasks of various kinds. In contrast, Howe, Tolmie, and Rodgers (1992) studied peer tutoring on a task concerned with understanding motion down an incline. Peer tutoring was of very little benefit, whereas thinking about the underlying ideas proved useful.

Third, the main focus of the Vygotskyan approach to education is on the contribution made by the tutor or expert to the understanding of the child or apprentice. In fact, it is probable that the success or otherwise of scaffolding depends crucially on the responsiveness of the tutor to the thoughts and actions of the child. In other words, those who favour Vygotsky's approach sometimes emphasise *external* factors in learning (e.g., the instructions given by the tutor) while minimising *internal factors* (e.g., the child's natural curiosity and motivation in the learning process). For example, Vygotsky (1930/1981, p.169) argued as follows: "We never find a child who would naturally develop arithmetic functions in nature . . . These are external changes coming from the environment and are not in any way a process of internal development". However, Vygotsky did emphasise the importance of the knowledge that the child brings to any given learning situation.

Piaget vs. Vygotsky

Forman and Cazden (1985) found that collaboration as recommended by Vygotsky and conflict as recommended by the neo-Piagetians both have a role to play. They studied 9-year-olds who had to carry out an experiment on chemical reactions. Collaboration among the children was very useful early on when the apparatus had to be set up. Later on, however, when they had to make decisions about how to carry out the experiment (e.g., which combinations of elements would produce which effects), conflict seemed to be more useful than collaboration. An important implication of this study is that any given teaching method is likely to work better in some situations than in others.

At a superficial level, it may appear that the approach to education following from Vygotsky's ideas is radically different from that of Piaget. As DeVries (2000) pointed out, Vygotsky seemed to emphasise factors external to the child (e.g., tutors, teachers) in promoting learning, whereas Piaget emphasised internal factors (e.g., adaptation), with the child in charge of the learning process. In fact, however, Vygotsky and Piaget were both fully aware of the importance of external and internal factors, and it is possible to develop educational practices that reconcile their views (see below).

The approach known as Cognitive Acceleration through Science Education (CASE) started about 20 years ago for use in secondary schools in the UK. It was designed explicitly to combine the insights of Piaget and Vygotsky to enhance students' learning and understanding. CASE has five main features with a typical lesson based on working them in the order listed:

1. *Concrete preparation*: This involves the teacher setting the scene for what is to come, ensuring that the students understand the scientific terms that will be used, and know how to use any equipment.
2. *Cognitive conflict*: This is created by exposing students to unexpected ideas or findings that don't fit their preconceptions and that can't easily be understood on the basis of their current ways of thinking.
3. *Construction*: This involves resolving the cognitive conflicts that have been created by means of discussions either involving small groups or the entire class.
4. *Metacognition*: This involves asking students open-ended questions that require students to explain their thinking and really focus on tricky issues.
5. *Bridging*: This involves relating students' new understanding to other aspects of science and their everyday experience. For this to be successful, teachers need to have identified good examples to produce the required bridging.

As mentioned earlier, these five features of CASE are based at least in part on the ideas of Piaget and Vygotsky. For example, the teacher uses his/her greater knowledge than the students to provide information during the concrete preparation and bridging phases as would be recommended by Vygotsky. The cognitive conflict phase resembles Piaget's emphasis on the importance of disequilibrium, and the phase of metacognition requires students to engage in a process resembling self-discovery. Finally, the construction phase resembles in some ways the peer tutoring approach based on Vygotsky's approach. The CASE approach has been so successful that it has led to the development of similar teaching methods for subjects other than science ones. These teaching methods include Cognitive Acceleration through Mathematics Education (CAME) and Cognitive Acceleration through Technology Education (CATE).

Information-processing approach
Task analysis and error analysis
There are several implications of the information-processing approach for education. Of greatest importance, teachers should engage in a careful task analysis of the information they want to communicate to the children in their class. A task analysis involves breaking down the target activity (the information) into constituent elements. This is necessary to ensure that the material is presented in the most effective way so that the child understands the task. It is also of value in identifying the reasons why some children perform a task inaccurately. If teachers have a clear idea of the information and processes needed to perform the task, they can analyse children's errors to see which rules or processes are being used wrongly. We will consider a concrete example of these implications.

Brown and Burton (1978) used errors to identify children's problems in mathematics. They used the term "bug" to refer to the systematic errors in the

How was reading taught in your school? What rules of spelling do you remember?

arithmetic rules used by children. For example, a child might claim that $736 - 464 = 372$ and that $871 - 663 = 218$ because he or she is using the mistaken rule that subtractions in the hundreds, tens, and units columns are never affected by what has happened in the column to the right. Brown and Burton devised computerised games that provided teachers with training in identifying bugs. As a result, teachers detected bugs more quickly than before, and they appreciated that some errors in mathematics are due to faulty rules rather than simply to lack of attention.

Other implications

Two other implications are as follows:

Implication 1. Parts of the information-processing system (e.g., attention, short-term memory) have very limited capacity, and so teachers should present tasks so these limited capacities are not overloaded. For example, Beck and Carpenter (1986) argued that children often find it hard to understand what they read because their processing capacity is focused on identifying individual words and parts of words. Accordingly, they gave children huge amounts of practice in identifying and making use of sub-word units (e.g., syllables). This led to substantial increases in the speed and accuracy of word recognition plus enhanced comprehension of the reading material.

Implication 2. Children benefit from gaining **metacognitive knowledge** about cognitive processes; such knowledge involves understanding the value of various cognitive processes (e.g., knowing that processing of meaning will enhance long-term memory). Children often lack important metacognitive knowledge. For example, to understand a text fully, readers need to focus on the structure of the text (e.g., its main theme). However, children typically lack this metacognitive knowledge, and focus on individual words and sentences. Palincsar and Brown (1984) gave children specific training in thinking about the structure of the texts they were reading. This led to a significant increase in their comprehension ability.

Evaluation

The information-processing approach has proved of use in education, because it provides techniques for identifying the processes and strategies required to complete tasks successfully. However, the approach is limited in several ways. First, we often cannot identify the underlying processes. Second, it is often hard to assess accurately a given child's capacity limitations, and so the point at which overload will occur is not easy to predict. Third, the information-processing approach often indicates *what* task processes are involved without specifying *how* those processes are acquired.

> **?** What metacognitive knowledge do you have in relation to taking exams?

> **KEY TERM**
>
> **Metacognitive knowledge:** knowledge about the usefulness of various cognitive processes relevant to learning.

SUMMARY OF THE DIFFERENT APPROACHES TO EDUCATION		
Piaget	**Vygotsky**	**Information-processing**
Child-centred discovery ("discovery learning")	Teacher–child interaction ("social learning")	Development of skills, strategies, and rules

SECTION SUMMARY
Development of Thinking

❖ Theories of cognitive development aim to describe and explain the way that children's thinking changes as they get older.

Theories of cognitive development

❖ According to Piaget, the child acquires knowledge and can adapts to his/her environment by:

Piaget's theory

— Accommodation (adjustment)
— Assimilation (taking in).

❖ The infant is born with innate knowledge (schemas) that change through interactions with the environment and the driving force is equilibration (internal balance).

❖ There are recognisable stages in a child's cognitive development as a result of qualitative changes. All children pass through the same sequence but not necessarily at the same age.

❖ There are four stages of cognitive development:

Piaget's stages of cognitive development

— Sensori-motor: intelligence develops through action
— Pre-operational: thinking dominated by perception and lacking internally consistent logic
— Concrete operations: logical thinking applied to concrete objects
— Formal operations: logical thinking can be applied to potential events or abstract ideas.

❖ This stage is characterised by innate schemas (reflexes), object permanence, perseverative search, imitation, and deferred imitation.

The sensori-motor stage

❖ Evaluation:

— Piaget underestimated the abilities of infants at this stage.
— The perseverative search does not involve the child's active participation.

❖ This stage is subdivided into preconceptual and intuitive stages.

The pre-operational stage

❖ It is characterised by an inability to demonstrate seriation, syncretic thought (e.g., conservation), centration, egocentric thought (e.g., three mountains experiment), realism, animism, and artificialism.

❖ Evaluation:

— Piaget underestimated the cognitive abilities of children at this stage but age differences remain.
— Children may fail the conservation task because they don't understand the question, or because they are confused by two questions.
— Certain visual tasks or questions can increase sense of identity and conservation ability.
— Making the task more meaningful reduces egocentric reasoning.

❖ Children's thinking is no longer dominated by perception.

The concrete operations stage

❖ Logical reasoning develops, though it is restricted to concrete situations only.

❖ Children learn mathematical operations, reversibility, and transitivity. Conservation of volume is harder to achieve than conservation of number; children can conserve in familiar situations.

❖ Evaluation:

— This account may focus too exclusively on logical thinking.

Formal operations stage

❖ This stage is illustrated by the pendulum problem, solving problems through hypothesis testing.

❖ Evaluation:

— Piaget exaggerated the role of logical reasoning in adult thought which can involve problem solving in situations where there aren't logical solutions.
— Not all adults may reach this stage.

Evaluating Piaget's theory

❖ In general, Piaget's underestimation of children's abilities may be due to his use of the clinical method.

❖ Other general criticisms are related to:

— The notion of stages: cognitive development may not be as systematic as the concept of stages suggests
— The distinction between performance and competence
— The vagueness of maturation and conflict as concepts to explain why development takes place
— Piaget's account may be descriptive rather than explanatory.

Vygotsky's theory

❖ Cognitive development depends largely on social factors. Children can achieve more with the assistance of others than they can achieve on their own.

❖ Culture and "experts" transform elementary functions into higher mental functions, moving through the zone of proximal development.

❖ Movement through the zone of proximal development is assisted by scaffolding and language (including intersubjectivity).

❖ Research supports the value of scaffolding, the social context, and inner speech in cognitive development.

Evaluating Vygotsky's theory

❖ Vygotsky's approach can explain cultural differences because it is based on the social context.

❖ However, criticisms include:

— The importance of social factors may have been overestimated.
— Social interactions may result in opposing reactions rather than learning or may simply motivate behaviour (e.g., social facilitation).
— One might expect learning to be much faster than it is if all that was required was the guidance of experts.

Information-processing approach

❖ According to Case (1974) and Pascual-Leone (1984) Piaget's theory can be adapted to focus on:

— Cognitive development within an information-processing framework
— Specific components of cognitive processing rather than general schemas
— How cognitive development depends on increases in mental capacity
— M (processing capacity) increases with neurological development.

❖ There are three basic units of cognition (schemes): figurative, operative, and executive. Over time children increase their range of schemes by modifying or combining existing schemes.

❖ Cognitive development is the result of increased M-power (mental capacity), and the ability to use it.

❖ Evaluation:

— Information processing can explain Piagetian research findings by arguing that young children have insufficient mental capacity to hold all the relevant schemes in mind.

— This approach fits well with cognitive research generally.

— However, it is hard to assess which schemes are being used and to measure M-power.

❖ According to Piaget what children can learn is determined by their current stage of cognitive development. Research has not supported this.

Practical applications to education: Piaget

❖ How do children learn?

— Children learn best when engaged in a process of active self-discovery.

— However, research has shown that the tutorial method is more effective.

❖ The neo-Piagetians attach importance to socio-cognitive conflict (exposure to different views), and social marking as a way to promote effective learning at school.

❖ Piaget argued that the study of mathematics, logic, and science is valuable for the development of cognitive schemas.

❖ According to Vygotsky the social context enhances learning. Teachers scaffold the learner by increasing or decreasing support as required.

Practical applications to education: Vygotsky

❖ How do children learn?

— Peer tutoring

— Conflict can work well with some learning tasks, and collaboration with others

— Play is useful in learning because it is often involves cultural activities

— Tutors are not always helpful, especially when the tutor is insensitive to the pupil's needs.

❖ The Vygotskian approach isn't useful in all situations, such as conceptual understanding.

❖ Vygotsky's approach has been combined with Piaget's in various teaching methods including CASE.

❖ Teaching should be based on:

Practical applications to education: Information processing

— A sound understanding of the knowledge and processes required to perform different tasks (task analysis and error analysis).

— Preventing overload of short-term memory and on developing children's metacognitive knowledge.

❖ This is a useful approach that enables us to identify strategies required to complete tasks successfully. However, it is not possible to identify all underlying processes.

See also pages 100–113 of the revision guide.

DEVELOPMENT OF MEASURED INTELLIGENCE

What is Intelligence?

In this Section we are concerned with the factors involved in the development of children's intelligence test performance (measured intelligence). An obvious starting point is to consider the meaning of intelligence. According to Sternberg (1985, p.45), intelligence is:

mental activity directed towards purposive adaptation to, and selection and shaping of, real-world environments relevant to one's life.

Intelligence tests

In 1905, Binet and his associate Simon produced a wide range of tests measuring comprehension, memory, and other cognitive processes. This led to numerous later tests. Among the best known of such tests are the Stanford–Binet test produced at Stanford University in 1916, the Wechsler Intelligence Scale for Children, and, in the 1970s, the British Ability Scales.

These and other tests measure several aspects of intelligence. Many contain vocabulary tests in which individuals are asked to define the meanings of words. Tests often also include problems based on analogies (e.g., "Hat is to head as shoe is to ___"), and tests of spatial ability (e.g., "If I start walking northwards, then turn left, and then turn left again, what direction will I be facing?"). They also include vocabulary tests to assess an individual's level of verbal ability.

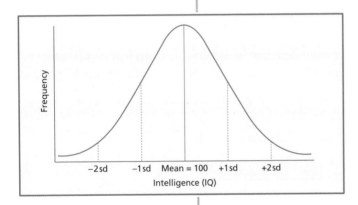

All the major intelligence tests share key similarities. They have manuals that spell out how the test should be administered. This is important, because the wording of the instructions often affects the tested person's score. The major tests are also alike in that they are **standardised tests**. Standardisation of a test involves giving it to large, representative samples of the age groups for which the test is intended. The meaning of an individual's score can then be evaluated by comparing it against the scores of other people.

It is possible with most standardised tests to obtain several measures of an individual's performance. These measures are mostly of a fairly specific nature (e.g., arithmetic ability or spatial ability). However, the best-known measure is the very general IQ or **intelligence quotient**. This reflects performance on all of the sub-tests contained in an intelligence test, and is thus regarded as an overall measure of intellectual ability.

How is the IQ calculated? An individual's test performance is compared against the scores obtained by other children of his or her age or by other adults in the standardisation sample. Most intelligence tests are devised so that the overall scores are normally distributed: we do not know what the "real" distribution of intelligence looks like. The normal distribution is a bell-shaped curve in which there are as many scores above the mean as below it. Most scores cluster fairly close to the mean (see the graph), and there are fewer and fewer scores as you move away from it. The spread of scores in a normal distribution is usually indicated by a statistic known as the standard deviation. In a normal distribution, 68% of the scores fall within one standard deviation of the mean or average, and 95% fall within two standard deviations.

Intelligence tests have a mean of 100 and a standard deviation of about 15. Thus, an IQ of 116 is one standard deviation above the mean, and indicates that the individual is more intelligent than 84% of the population. That is because 50% fall below the mean, and a further 34% between the mean and one standard deviation above it.

Limitations: Those with high IQs do not usually perform well on all of the tests within an intelligence test battery, nor do those with low IQs perform poorly on every test. As a result, tests are usually constructed to obtain measures of various abilities (e.g., numerical, spatial, reasoning, perceptual speed). We can obtain a more accurate assessment of an individual's intelligence by considering the profile of his/her performance across these abilities than by focusing only on IQ.

KEY TERMS

Standardised tests: psychological tests that have been used with large groups of individuals in order to establish a set of "standards" or norms.

Intelligence quotient: a measure of general intellectual ability that can be calculated by dividing mental age by chronical age; abbreviated as IQ.

There tends to be a gap between such definitions of intelligence and the type of intelligence assessed by intelligence tests. Sternberg offered a broad definition of intelligence, which includes the ability to cope successfully with life. In contrast, most intelligence tests measure basic cognitive abilities such as thinking, problem solving, and reasoning. These cognitive abilities are of value when coping with life, but successful individuals tend also to possess various "streetwise" skills not assessed by most intelligence tests. (There is a further discussion of intelligence, and the evolution of this ability, in Chapter 7, Evolutionary Explanations of Human Behaviour.)

Measured intelligence

The most common measure of intelligence is the intelligence quotient or IQ, obtained from intelligence tests (see the box to the left). This is a measure of general intelligence that does not take account of the fact that some people are much more intelligent in some ways than others. For example, consider the case of a boy called Christopher. His tested IQ was 75 or less, which is substantially below the population average of 100. In spite of that, he could speak 17 languages, and many of them fluently (Smith & Tsimpli, 1991).

Environmental factors (e.g., cultural differences)

There are various environmental factors that may influence the validity of measures of intelligence. A few of the relevant factors are discussed below.

Socio-economic culture. Children may not be well motivated to do their best. Zigler, Abelson, and Seitz (1973) studied the intelligence test performance of preschool children from poor and middle-class backgrounds. Those from poor backgrounds showed gains of almost 10 points of IQ after a play session or when tested a second time, indicating that their IQ assessed in the normal way was an underestimate. In contrast, middle-class children showed a much smaller increase of about 3 IQ points when given a play session or tested a second time.

> **Reliability and validity**
>
> Good intelligence tests have high reliability and validity. **Reliability** refers to the extent to which a test provides consistent findings, and **validity** refers to the extent to which a test measures what it is supposed to be measuring. The question of validity is important when considering the use of IQ tests in different cultural settings. In such situations we might ask whether it is valid to test one cultural group using a test derived from another cultural definition of intelligence.

Cultural differences. It is difficult to assess intelligence properly across different cultures. As Triandis (1994, p.58) pointed out:

> *When we measure something in another culture, we are most likely to get answer to the question, Do they do our tricks as well as we do our tricks? rather than Do they do their tricks well ... Different ecologies [environments] reward different tricks.*

We can see the force of what Triandis (1994) was saying when we consider that most intelligence tests are devised by white, middle-class psychologists from Western societies. As a result, the tests they produce may underestimate the intelligence of those from other cultures or social backgrounds. Some support for this point of view was reported by Williams (1972), who devised the Black Intelligence Test of Cultural Homogeneity (BITCH; see also later). This test was aimed at black American children, and white American children did less well on this test than most standard ones.

> **KEY TERMS**
>
> **Reliability:** the extent to which a method of measurement or a research study produces consistent findings across situation or overtime.
>
> **Validity:** the extent to which something is true. This may be applied to a measurement tool, such as a psychological test, or to the "trueness" of an experimental procedure both in terms of what goes on within the experiment (internal validity) and its relevance to other situations (external validity).

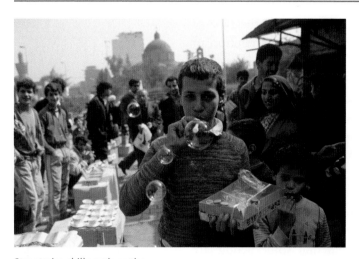

Streetwise skills such as the commercial, bargaining, and economic abilities these children possess are not measured by conventional intelligence tests.

? Why do you think drawing might be less valued than a practical skill like wire-shaping in some cultures?

Intelligence tests don't take account of the fact that cultures vary in the skills that are valued. For example, Serpell (1979) compared the performance of English and Zambian children on two tasks. The English children did better at a drawing task, whereas the Zambian children did better on a wire-shaping task. This illustrates the fact that differences between cultures are qualitative rather than quantitative, i.e., no one culture is better than any other culture (a quantitative difference), there simply are variations (a qualitative difference).

Sternberg (reported in Sternberg & Ben Zeev, 2001) studied Kenyan children who had considerable knowledge about natural herbal medicines that can be used to fight infection in that country. Those Kenyan children having most knowledge tended to perform *worse* than the other children on conventional verbal tests of intelligence. The implication is that the skills that are important in the Kenyan culture differ considerably from those regarded as important in Western cultures.

Sternberg et al. (2002) argued that children in many cultures may perform poorly on conventional intelligence tests mainly because they have received very little teaching in the skills needed on those tests. One way of comparing intelligence across cultures in a fairer way might be to use dynamic testing in which individuals are tested on two separate occasions with training in the skills assessed by the tests being provided between testings. Sternberg et al. used dynamic testing with children in Tanzania. There were substantial improvements in the children's performance on an intelligence test on the second testing occasion, suggesting that they had abilities not revealed on the first testing occasion.

Heredity and environment

Why are some children more intelligent than others? At the most general level, there are only two factors that could be responsible: heredity and environment. Heredity consists of each person's genetic endowment, the instructions that tell your body to produce hair of a particular colour, or blood of a particular blood group, or an easy or difficult temperament. Environment consists of the situations and experiences encountered by people in the course of their lives. It is generally assumed that individual differences in intelligence depend on both heredity and environment. As we will see, many psychologists have tried to determine the relative importance of heredity and environment in determining intelligence. However, the Canadian psychologist Donald Hebb (1958) argued that this is an essentially meaningless issue. He claimed that it is like asking whether a field's area is determined more by its length or by its width. Of course, its area depends equally on both length and width. In similar fashion, Hebb argued, intelligence depends equally on both heredity and environment.

Hebb's argument is not as convincing as it sounds. Even though it is clear that the area of a field depends equally on its length and width, we can still reasonably ask whether the areas of different fields vary more because of differences in their lengths or in terms of their widths. In the same way, we can ask whether individual differences in intelligence depend more on differences in genetic endowment or on environmental differences.

Those who believe in the importance of heredity draw a distinction between the **genotype** and the **phenotype**. The genotype is the genetic instructions that each individual is given at conception. These instructions offer a blueprint for characteristics and behaviour but are meaningless until they can be expressed through the environment. The phenotype consists of an individual's observable characteristics. So far as intelligence is concerned, we cannot access the genotype. All that can be done is to assess the phenotype by means of administering an intelligence test.

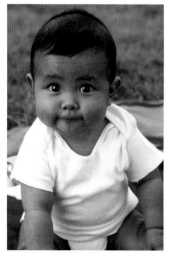

We can see a person's phenotype, but their genotype lies hidden.

The Role of Genetics

Twin studies

The most popular method of assessing the relative importance of heredity and environment in determining individual differences in intelligence is to conduct a twin study. There are two kinds of twins: **monozygotic twins** and **dizygotic twins**. Monozygotic (MZ) twins derive from the same fertilised ovum, and have essentially identical genotypes. It is for this reason that they are often called identical twins. Dizygotic (DZ) twins derive from two different fertilised ova. As a result, their genotypes are no more similar than those of ordinary siblings. Dizygotic twins are sometimes called fraternal twins.

What would we expect to find in a twin study? If heredity is very important, then monozygotic twins should be considerably more similar in intelligence than dizygotic twins. On the other hand, if environmental factors are all-important, then monozygotic twins should be no more alike than dizygotic twins.

What does the evidence suggest? A review based on 111 studies was published by Bouchard and McGue (1981; see the Key Study below). They left out the findings from Burt's (1955) study, because there is clear evidence that he made up some or all of his data. The mean correlation coefficient for monozygotic or identical twins was +0.86, indicating that monozygotic twins are generally very similar to each other in intelligence. The mean correlation coefficient for dizygotic or fraternal twins was +0.60, indicating only a moderate degree of similarity in intelligence. Similar findings were reported in another large-scale review of numerous studies by McCartney, Harris, and Bernieri (1981). The mean correlation for identical twins was +0.81 compared to +0.59 for fraternal twins.

KEY STUDY
Bouchard and McGue

In spite of the problems, much useful information has been obtained from studying twins. Identical or monozygotic twins derive from the same fertilised ovum, and so have essentially identical genotypes. In contrast, fraternal or dizygotic twins derive from two different fertilised ova, and so their genotypes are no more similar than those of two ordinary siblings. If heredity influences intelligence, then we would expect to find that identical twins are more alike in intelligence than are fraternal twins.

In their review of 111 studies, Bouchard and McGue (1981) reported that the mean correlation for identical twins was +0.86, and +0.60 for fraternal

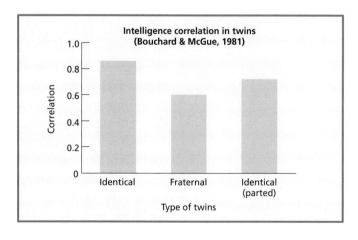

twins. Thus identical twins are more similar in intelligence than are fraternal twins, and this suggests that heredity plays a part in determining individual differences in intelligence. However, the environment is generally more similar for identical twins than for fraternal twins (Loehlin & Nichols, 1976).

Below are the correlations indicating the similarity of IQ between different groups of relatives. In general terms, relatives who have greater genetic similarity tend to be more similar in IQ. However, relatives having greater genetic similarity tend to live in more similar environments than those with less genetic similarity, which makes it hard to interpret the findings. As Bouchard and McGue (1981) concluded, "Most of the results of studies of family resemblance...can be interpreted as either supporting the genetic or the environmentalist theory."

Relationship	Mean correlation
Siblings reared apart	+0.24
Siblings reared together	+0.47
Single parent—offspring reared apart	+0.22
Single parent—offspring reared together	+0.42
Half-siblings	+0.31
Cousins	+0.15
Adopted parent and adopted child	+0.19

Discussion points
1. How convincing is the evidence reviewed by Bouchard and McGue for the notion that heredity plays an important role in determining individual differences in intelligence?
2. Most of the correlations reported by Bouchard and McGue were based on studies in a small number of Western cultures. Would the same findings be obtained in other cultures?

The fact that monozygotic twins were much more similar in intelligence than dizygotic twins suggests that heredity is of major significance in determining intelligence. However, that is on the assumption that the degree of environmental similarity experienced by monozygotic twins is the same as that experienced by dizygotic twins. However, monozygotic twins are treated in a more similar fashion than dizygotic twins in the following ways: parental treatment; playing together; spending time together; dressing in a similar style; and being taught by the same teachers (Loehlin & Nichols, 1976). When these data were considered in detail by Kamin (1981), it emerged that there was an effect of similarity of treatment on similarity of intelligence in the form of IQ.

Twins who live apart
In a few twin studies, use has been made of identical twins brought up apart in different families. Such twin pairs would seem to be of particular value in deciding on the relative importance of genetic factors and of environment in determining intelligence. Those arguing that genetic factors are of most importance would expect such twins to resemble each other closely in intelligence. In contrast, those favouring an environmentalist position would argue that placing twins in different environments should ensure that they are not similar in intelligence. According to Bouchard and McGue's (1981) review, the mean correlation coefficient for monozygotic twins brought up apart is +0.72.

The findings from identical twins brought up apart seem to provide convincing evidence for the importance of genetic factors. However, there are problems with the evidence. Many of the identical twins brought up apart grew up in different branches of the same family. Other identical twins were actually brought up together for several years before being separated. Thus, many pairs of identical twins actually experience rather similar environments. As a result, at least some of the similarity in IQ of identical twins brought up apart is due to environmental rather than genetic factors. However, the identical twins in the Minnesota Study of Twins Reared Apart were separated in infancy and reared in different environments. In spite of this, their IQs correlated about +0.75 (Bouchard et al., 1990). Note that the fact that the correlation for identical twins brought up apart is always lower than that for identical twins brought up together is strong evidence that environmental factors are important in determining individual differences in intelligence.

Monozygotic twins tend to experience a greater degree of environmental similarity than dizygotic twins.

Evaluation

The evidence from twin studies suggests that individual differences in intelligence are about 50% due to genetic factors and 50% due to environmental factors. You might have expected this figure to be 75% for genetic factors because of the correlations reported above, but when this correlation is translated into a **heritability estimate** then account is taken of total variability in the population. The details need not concern you but this is an important feature of understanding the relationship between heredity and environment.

In any group of individuals, the more similar the environmental factors shared by the group, the greater will be the effect of genetic factors in determining individual differences in intelligence. Consider the example of a set of seeds. If these seeds are planted in the same pot (identical environment) then any differences must be due to genetic variation, whereas if the seeds are planted in different soils then the environmental factors become part of the equation. In terms of humans, this means that if everyone in a society were exposed to precisely the same environmental conditions, then *all* individual differences in intelligence would be due to genetic factors! On the other hand, in societies in which there are enormous environmental differences between various sections of the community, the role of genetic factors in producing individual differences in intelligence would be rather small.

When considering children raised in the *same* environment, a different argument needs to be considered. The general concept of a shared environment assumes that all children (or seeds) will have the same experiences in that environment. When we consider different environments it is obvious that individuals will have different experiences, but recently researchers have recognised that the same environment does not mean the same *experiences*. Dunn and Plomin (1990) found that children reared in the same environment actually had very different experiences. Differences in their abilities and behaviours couldn't be due to the shared environment. They were due (a) to genetic differences and (b) to differences in experience. The latter is referred to as the *non-shared environment*.

> **KEY TERM**
>
> **Heritability estimate:** an estimate of the importance of genetic factors which takes account of total variability in the population. It is calculated by working out the ratio between the genetic variability of the particular trait and total variability in the whole population.

? Can you give examples of large differences in environment between communities living in the same society?

In terms of our twin studies, the figure of 50% of individual differences in intelligence being due to heredity applies only to the small number of cultures that have been studied so far. In some cultures this figure may be smaller or larger depending on how similar the environment is.

There are other reasons to be cautious about accepting the apparently obvious conclusion from twin studies that intelligence is 50% genetic. First, there are problems with many of the studies, and it is often unclear whether environmental similarity has been properly controlled.

Second, intelligence is assessed by means of IQ obtained from standard intelligence tests. It is debatable whether IQ is an adequate measure of intelligence.

Third, the role of heredity in determining individual differences in intelligence tends to increase with age. According to Plomin (1990), about 30% of individual differences in intelligence among children are due to heredity, and this figure increases to 50% in adolescence, and to more than 50% in adult life. This puzzling change may occur because environmental differences are *smaller* among adults than among children and this is what makes heredity *appear* to contribute more as children grow into adults.

Fourth, Turkheimer et al. (2003) compared the heritability of IQ in children from poor and wealthy families. Heritability was about 70% among the wealthy children compared to only 10% among the poor children. The implication of this finding is that there is much more variation in the environments of poor children than of wealthy ones.

Adoption studies

Another method of assessing the role of genetic and environmental factors in intelligence is by adoption studies. The measured intelligence of adopted children might depend more on genetic factors (the intelligence inherited from the biological parents) or it might depend more on environmental factors (related to the intelligence of the adoptive parents).

Horn (1983) discussed the findings from the Texas Adoption Project, which involved almost 500 adopted children. The correlation between the adopted children and their biological mothers for intelligence was +0.28, indicating that there was only a moderate degree of similarity in intelligence. The correlation between the adopted children and their adoptive mothers was even lower at +0.15. Both of these correlations are so low that it is hard to make any definite statements about the roles played by heredity and environment, though it does suggest a greater role for heredity.

Change over time

Loehlin, Horn, and Willerman (1989) found that there were some differences in the findings when the adopted children were tested again 10 years later. Now the children had an increased correlation with their biological mothers but less with their adoptive mothers. Shared family environment between the adopted children and their adoptive mothers was reduced in importance, whereas genetic factors had a greater influence on the adopted children's intelligence than had been the case 10 years earlier.

The notion that shared family environment has less influence on intelligence as children become older received additional support in a review by Plomin

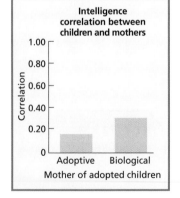

The correlations between adopted children and their adoptive mothers, and between adopted children and their biological mothers, are so low that they do not allow us to make any definite statements about the roles played by heredity and environment in intelligence.

(1988). He reported that the correlation between genetically unrelated children growing up together in adoptive families was about +0.30 for intelligence when they were still children. However, the correlation dropped to zero in adolescence and adulthood. The major reason for this change is presumably because environmental factors outside the home become increasingly important from adolescence onwards. The zero correlation indicates that the influence of any environmental factors within the home doesn't seem to be long-lasting.

? What environmental factors might be expected to influence the development of IQ?

Evaluation of adoption studies

The findings of the study by Capron and Duyne (1989, see the Key Study below) are consistent with those from twin studies in suggesting that about 50% of the variance in intelligence scores is due to genetic factors. However, less clear findings have emerged from other adoption studies (e.g., Horn, 1983), in part because of the problems of interpretation posed by selective placement (children placed in homes similar to those of their biological parents). In many studies, some of the correlation between adopted children and their biological parents is due to selective placement rather than to genetic factors.

KEY STUDY
Capron and Duyne

Capron and Duyne (1989) reported a very impressive adoption study. They made use of four very different groups of adopted children. These groups involved all four possible combinations of biological parents of high or low socio-economic status and adoptive parents of high or low socio-economic status. The predictions are fairly straightforward. The measured intelligence of the adopted children should be related mainly to the socio-economic status of the biological parents if genetic factors are of more importance

| High SES biological parent + High SES adoptive parent | Low SES biological parent + High SES adoptive parent |
| High SES biological parent + Low SES adoptive parent | Low SES biological parent + Low SES adoptive parent |

(because high SES parents are more intelligent and have high IQ children), but should be related mostly to the socio-economic status of the adoptive parents if environmental factors are more important. In fact, the effects of the socio-economic status of the biological and of the adoptive parents were much the same. These findings suggest that genetic and environmental factors were of about equal importance in determining the intelligence of the adopted children.

This study is important for various reasons. First, it is hard to interpret the findings from most adoption studies because of selective placement, which involves adoption agencies placing adopted children into families resembling those of their biological parents in terms of educational and social backgrounds. When there is selective placement, it is hard to disentangle the effects of heredity and environment. The design of the study by Capron and Duyne largely eliminated the issue of selective placement. Second, the use of groups in which there was a large difference between the socio-economic status of the biological parents and that of the adoptive parents is unusual, but has the advantage of making it easier to assess the relative impacts of heredity and environment.

Discussion points
1. Why is the study by Capron and Duyne of importance?
2. Are adoption studies more or less useful than twin studies in trying to decide on the relative importance of heredity and environment in determining individual differences in intelligence?

GENERAL CRITICISMS OF IQ TESTS, ADOPTION STUDIES, AND TWIN STUDIES

IQ tests	Adoption studies	Twin studies
Debatable whether IQ is an adequate measurement of intelligence	Selective placement makes it hard to determine the effects of heredity and environment	Environmental similarity often occurs
Cultural differences not always considered	Heredity is less well controlled than in twin studies	Twins raised separately were actually raised by different branches of the same family
		Twins had spent some years together before being separated

Social and Cultural Influences: Environmental Factors

We have seen from the findings of twin and adoption studies that environmental factors are of major importance in producing individual differences in measured intelligence. Somewhat more direct evidence for the role of the environment comes from studies in which entire communities have gone through large-scale environmental changes. Wheeler (1932, 1942) studied the members of an isolated community in Tennessee in the United States. This community gradually became more integrated into society as schools and roads were built, and communications with the outside world developed. The children in this community originally had a mean IQ of 82. Ten years later, the children's mean IQ was 93. It seems likely that the environmental changes, in some way, boosted the children's IQ.

How else might one explain this increase in IQ?

The limitation of Wheeler's study is that we don't know which of the many environmental changes within the Tennessee community studied were of most importance in affecting intelligence. As might be expected, there is good evidence that the amount of schooling is important. For example, Ceci (1991) reviewed studies showing that children who start school after the age of 6 have lower IQs than other children. In addition, children's IQs are lower if they miss long periods of schooling through illness or some other reason, and there is a small decline in IQs over the summer holiday.

Evidence that environmental influences can have a dramatic effect on intelligence was reported by Skeels and Dye (1939). They studied children who were initially raised in an orphanage in the United States. Some of the children remained in the orphanage whereas others went to a school for the mentally retarded and then were adopted. At the age of 7, the adopted children had average IQs 36 points higher than they had had at the age of 2. In contrast, the children who remained in the orphanage showed an average drop in IQ of 21 points.

The HOME inventory

In order to understand in more detail how the environment affects intelligence, what we need to do is to compare the effects of several different aspects of the environment. One suitable measure is the Home Observation for Measurement of the Environment (or HOME) inventory (Caldwell & Bradley, 1984). This inventory provides measures in the following six environmental categories:

- Emotional and verbal responsivity of parent
- Avoidance of restriction and punishment
- Organisation of physical and temporal environment

- Provision of appropriate play materials
- Parental involvement with child
- Opportunities for variety in daily stimulation.

Gottfried (1984) has addressed the issue of which of these aspects of the home environment have the greatest impact on children's IQs. The evidence from a number of studies indicated that provision of appropriate play materials, parental involvement with the child, and opportunities for variety in daily stimulation predicted children's subsequent IQs better than did any of the other three aspects.

A stimulating environment has been said to encourage a child's development. What might this environment include?

There is a potential problem with this approach. The findings discussed by Gottfried (1984) are correlational in nature, and so they can't be used to show that a stimulating home environment actually increases children's IQs. It is possible that more intelligent parents are more likely than less intelligent ones to provide a stimulating home environment for their children, and that it is the parental intelligence rather than the home environment they provide that is of importance.

Yeates et al. (1983) addressed the causality issue in a longitudinal study of young children. The mother's IQ predicted children's IQs at the age of 2 better than did scores on the HOME inventory. However, the HOME inventory predicted the IQs of the same children at the age of 4 better than did the mother's IQ. These findings suggest that a stimulating home environment is beneficial for children's intellectual development, and that this beneficial effect becomes stronger as children develop.

The Rochester study

Sameroff et al. (1993) reported the findings of the Rochester Longitudinal Study, in which hundreds of children were followed from birth to adolescence. The researchers identified 10 environmental factors that jointly accounted for 49% of individual differences in IQ. This study is reported in detail in the Key Study on the next page.

Operation Headstart

Another way to study the effects of environmental factors on the development of (measured) intelligence is to consider enrichment programmes such as Operation Headstart. In the 1960s there was a political move in the United States to set up an intervention programme that would help disadvantaged children. It was argued that such children lacked some of the early benefits enjoyed by more middle-class children in terms of, for example, health and intellectual stimulation, and that therefore they were disadvantaged even before they started school. Such disadvantages inevitably only got worse and perpetuated a cycle of failure.

In 1965 the first Headstart programmes were run involving half a million children. When the children were compared with a control group after the first year there were small IQ gains; however, these were short lived and the financial

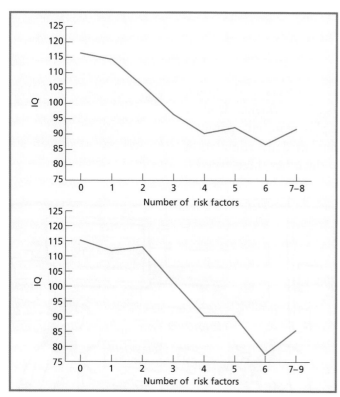

These graphs show the negative association between IQ and number of environmental risk factors. The top graph presents data for mean 4-year-old IQ scores, and the bottom graph presents data for mean 13-year-old IQ scores.

KEY STUDY
The Rochester Longitudinal Study

Sameroff et al. (1987, 1993) conducted a longitudinal study in New York State to investigate the factors that might be linked to intellectual delay in young children. They selected pregnant women to be part of their study and followed their 215 children, testing the children's IQs at age 4 and 13 (at this point 152 families remained in the sample). The families represented a range of socio-economic backgrounds, maternal age groups, and number of other siblings.

Sameroff et al. identified 10 family risk factors that were related to lower IQ:

- Mother has a history of mental illness.
- Mother did not go to high school.
- Mother has severe anxiety.
- Mother has rigid attitudes and values about her child's development.
- Few positive interactions between mother and child during infancy.
- Head of household has a semi-skilled job.
- Four or more children in the family.
- Father does not live with the family.
- Child belongs to a minority group.
- Family suffered 20 or more stressful events during the child's first 4 years of life.

There was a clear negative association between the number of risk factors associated with a child and the child's IQ, as illustrated in the graph above. At age 4 this correlation was −0.58. At age 13 it was −0.61. At the age of 4, high-risk children were 24 times as likely to have IQs below 85 than low-risk children. It was calculated that, on average, each risk factor reduced the child's IQ score by 4 points.

This study shows that environmental factors can be of great importance, and indicates what factors may be especially important. Sameroff et al. (1998) point out that the results have important implications for intervention, suggesting that changing environments should be more effective than relying on individual children's resilience under conditions of accumulated risk.

Key study evaluation

Where there are so many interrelated factors, it is not clear whether social class or specific parental behaviours are more important. It is also possible to explain the findings in terms of genetic factors. It is possible that low socio-economic level parents are biologically less intelligent, whereas those with more intelligence become better educated and are able to have higher living standards.

Discussion points

1. Select one of the risk factors and suggest how it might affect intellectual development.
2. What are the political implications of this study?

costs of the programme were over 150 million dollars (Zigler & Muenchow, 1992). Follow-up studies presented a more encouraging picture. Lazar and Darlington (1982) reported that the Headstart children were less likely to be placed in special classes, were more likely to go to college and, in terms of social benefits, were less likely to need welfare assistance or become delinquent. Seitz (1990) also found higher IQs in the Headstart children when they were tested in adolescence, suggesting a delayed effect. This indicates that IQ can be affected by environmental factors.

Evaluation

Other programmes have found evidence to support this. For example, the Carolina Abecedarian Project (Ramey, 1993) focused on low intelligence mothers and their infants, running a special day-care programme from infancy and giving extra medical attention. By school age the children had higher IQs than a control group but this declined soon thereafter.

Other studies have also tended to find rather minimal effects but this may be because other environmental factors overwhelm the comparatively small influence of the school.

One criticism that has been raised, in terms of methodology, is that the control groups used in the Operation Headstart evaluation may not have actually been comparable because allocation to such groups was not strictly random. However this was not true of the Abecedarian Project. Ramey, Campbell, and Ramey (1999) reviewed 10 studies that randomly allocated children to the two conditions and concluded that there was firm evidence that Headstart did boost IQ, and that the greater the deprivation suffered by the children the greater the gains achieved by Headstart.

Flynn effect

Surprising evidence that environmental factors can have a substantial effect on intelligence was reported by Flynn (1987, 1994). He obtained evidence from 20 Western countries, each of which showed the **Flynn effect**: a rapid rise in average IQ in most Western countries in recent decades. More specifically, Flynn (1987) reported that there had been an increase of 2.9 points per decade in nonverbal IQ and of 3.7 in verbal IQ. This rapid increase can't be due to genetic factors that would take thousands of years to have any effect.

What aspects of the environment account for the Flynn effect? Here are some likely factors:

- Increases in the number of years of education
- Greater access to information (e.g., television, internet)
- The increased cognitive complexity of the average person's job now compared to several decades ago
- More generally, a large increase in the number of middle-class families.

It is also possible that most people have become more familiar with intelligence tests over the years, and so the Flynn effect might be due to a practice effect. This could explain some of the increase in IQ but it is improbable that such large IQ increases could be due totally to practice at taking tests. A final possibility is that people's diets have improved over the years. As is discussed below, there is accumulating evidence that dietary supplements can enhance IQ, and so diet has been linked to intelligence.

KEY TERM

Flynn effect: steady rise in average IQ in several countries in recent decades.

Diet and intelligence

There has been increasing interest in recent years in the possibility that changes in diet by increased vitamin and mineral supplements could produce increases in IQ. Such beneficial effects on IQ have been reported in a number of studies. Benton (2001) reviewed the evidence from 13 studies. Dietary supplements increased nonverbal IQ more reliably than verbal IQ—this makes sense if nonverbal tests reflect biological functions that might be influenced by diet. Another general finding was that only a minority of children benefit from dietary supplements, primarily those whose normal diet only provides them with low levels of vitamins and/or minerals. It is noteworthy that nearly all the studies have been carried out in Western countries in which presumably most children have reasonably adequate diets. There might be more powerful effects of dietary supplements on IQ in poor countries in which many children have severely deficient diets.

Cultural background and intelligence

How might cultures differ in their perception of what makes someone intelligent?

It is difficult to compare intelligence in different cultures because the meaning of the word varies from one culture to another. We can distinguish between individualistic and collectivistic cultures. In individualistic cultures (e.g., the United States, northern Europe) there is a focus on individuals being independent and accepting responsibility for their own behaviour. In collectivistic cultures (e.g., many Asian and African cultures), the focus is on the group rather than the individual. As might be guessed, definitions of "intelligence" in collectivistic cultures tend to emphasise social considerations. For example, Chewa adults in Zambia focus on social responsibilities, obedience, and co-operativeness as key ingredients in intelligence (Serpell, 1982); in Zimbabwe, the word for intelligence is *ngware*, which means to be careful and prudent in social relationships. We will shortly be considering ways of trying to assess intelligence across different cultures.

Much research over the years has involved comparing different groups or cultures, with an emphasis on comparisons between white and black people in the United States. The mean difference in IQ between white people and black people in the United States is about 15 points (favouring white people), and this has caused much political controversy. The 15-point difference is only an average figure, and about 20% of black people have a higher IQ than that of the average white person (namely, 100). Most psychologists have assumed that the difference between white people and black people is due entirely to the environmental deprivation suffered by black people. However, Jensen (1969) and H.J. Eysenck (1981) argued that genetic differences might be involved. They claimed (in the absence of any convincing evidence whatsoever) that blacks are genetically inferior to whites in intelligence.

This debate has rumbled on. In 1988, Rushton published research that claimed to demonstrate significant differences in the IQs between white and black children. Quite incredibly the data were based on IQ tests that, although they purported to be "culture-free" (see later), actually rewarded those children who were taught basic arithmetic in school. The white children assessed were US schoolchildren. The black children were from Africa and didn't have the same access to school concepts. It is not surprising that they did less well.

More recently, Herrnstein and Murray (1994) published the controversial book *The Bell Curve*, in which they argued that there are genetic differences in IQ.

CHAPTER 5 Developmental Psychology: Cognitive Development **213**

According to their prejudiced views, since these differences are inevitable, there is little point in trying to educate individuals who will never progress beyond a fixed potential. This illustrates the extremely political nature of this debate.

What is "race"?

The first point to make about this controversial issue is that it is of very little scientific interest, in that it is unlikely to tell us anything about the processes involved in human intelligence. This makes it strange that so much time and money have been spent in studying this issue.

The second point is that the issue is based on the incorrect assumption that white people and black people form separate biological groups. There is more genetic variation *within* any so-called racial group than *between* racial groups. Indeed, the whole notion of "race" has been questioned, and seems to have no precise scientific definition. Altogether this suggests that there is little scientific validity in using the term "race".

The third point is that we cannot carry out definitive research on this issue. We cannot measure accurately the levels of deprivation experienced by black people, nor can we compare the genetic endowment of white people and black people. Even H.J. Eysenck (1981, p.79) admitted that the issue cannot be resolved by experimental evidence: "Can we . . . argue that genetic studies . . . give direct support to the hereditarian position? The answer must, I think, be in the negative. The two populations (black and white) are separate populations, and none of the studies carried out on white people alone, such as twin studies, are feasible."

In addition, such research poses major ethical issues. Extreme groups, such as the National Front, have used the findings to promote racial disharmony, which is totally unacceptable. Many working in this area have been insensitive to the dangerous political uses to which their research was likely to be put, and it is an issue that would have been better left unexplored.

Reasons for differences in black and white performance

A major reason why black people perform less well than white people on intelligence tests is because of environmental deprivation. Mackintosh (1986) compared white and West Indian children in England. Some of the children were matched for father's job, number of brothers and sisters, family income, and other measures relevant to deprivation, whereas the others were unmatched. In one study, there was a 9-point difference between unmatched groups, but only a 2.6-point difference in the matched groups. Thus, there were very small differences in intelligence between the two groups when they were equated for the level of deprivation.

Brooks-Gunn et al. (1996) found that the average IQ of white children was about 15 points higher than that of black children. However, they also found that the whole difference could be explained by the greater poverty and deprived home environments experienced by the black children.

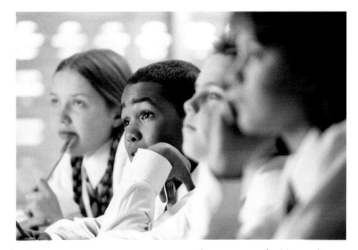

When groups of white and West Indian children were matched for levels of environmental deprivation, only very small differences in intelligence were found.

The fact that IQ tests generally do record differences between black and white individuals might be explained in terms of physical and/or social deprivation associated with lower incomes, poorer housing conditions, lower education, and so on. Alternatively these differences can be explained in terms of cultural variation. According to Vygotksy (earlier in this chapter), cognitive development is very much linked to cultural inputs and therefore we would expect to find differences between cultural groups. Such variations were mentioned earlier (see pages 201–202). In order to assess cognitive abilities such as intelligence more fairly one needs to develop culture-fair tests.

Culture-fair tests

Nearly all intelligence tests have been devised by white, middle-class psychologists. It is likely that Australian aboriginals or black people brought up in a very different culture would be disadvantaged by this cultural divide when taking an intelligence test. In similar fashion, members of minority groups might also be disadvantaged when confronted by standard intelligence tests. This issue is important. Legislation designed to ensure equal opportunities for everyone has been passed in Britain, the United States, and numerous other countries. If intelligence tests are biased against certain groups, then there is a real danger that people's rights to have equal opportunities are being infringed.

How should we proceed? According to Sternberg (1994, p.595):

We need to take into account culture in considering both the nature and the assessment of intelligence. Simply translating a test from one language to another scarcely constitutes doing so. Rather, we need to be sensitive to cultural differences that may artificially inflate the scores of one group over another due to the kinds of materials or tasks used to measure intelligence.

? Why do you think that some "culture-fair" tests produce larger differences in intelligence across cultural groups than standard intelligence tests?

One way to do this is to construct what are known as "culture-fair" tests, which consist mainly of abstract and nonverbal items that should not be more familiar to members of one group than another. However, strangely such culture-fair tests tend to produce larger differences in intelligence across cultural groups than are found when conventional verbal tests of intelligence are used (Sternberg, 1994)! In addition, attempts to "translate" American standard tests into Black dialect show no differences. For example when the Stanford–Binet intelligence test was translated into what is known as "Black English" (the English dialect spoken by many Black Americans) and given to black children by black testers, the black children's IQ scores were about the same as when the test was given in its standard form (Quay, 1971).

However, rather different findings were obtained with the Black Intelligence Test of Cultural Homogeneity (BITCH), which was designed for Black Americans. White American children did no better than black American children on this test, and sometimes performed worse (Williams, 1972). This suggests that there are cultural differences embedded in tests. The reason why the black children's performance didn't improve on the translated test may be because this is based on the assumption that cultural differences are purely linguistic. In reality it is unlikely to be simply a matter of translating a test.

Sternberg (2003) reported on progress with his Rainbow Project, which has involved designing and evaluating a new intelligence test that is broader than traditional IQ tests. The new test assesses creative and practical skills as well as analytical ones. Of particular interest, students who do very well on the creative and practical tests were more ethnically diverse than those who excelled in the visual memory and analytical tests. The message is that it is important to sample a wide range of abilities to provide an adequate assessment of any individual's or group's intelligence.

Evaluation of the Heredity/Environment Debate

The studies discussed in this Section indicate that major environmental changes can produce significant changes in IQ. Thus, they strengthen the notion that intelligence depends to a major extent on environmental factors. However, it hasn't proved possible to determine precisely *which* aspects of the environment are most effective in influencing intellectual development. For example, consider the findings of Sameroff et al. (1993; see the Key Study on page 210). They found that environmental factors such as the mother not going to high school and the head of household having a semi-skilled job were associated with low IQ in the children. This doesn't prove a causal relationship. It is possible that genetic factors play a part in producing these environmental factors *and* in producing low IQ in the children.

Twin studies and adoption studies show clearly that genetic factors play a part in explaining individual differences in intelligence. We should be very wary about assigning precise figures to the importance of genetic factors, but the notion that genetic factors account for somewhere between 40% and 60% of individual differences in intelligence in Western cultures is probably about right.

There is a final point that is very important. It is sometimes assumed that heredity and environment have *independent* effects on an individual's level of intelligence. However, this is generally incorrect. For example, the number of years of education is an important environmental factor influencing intelligence. However, it tends to be those with the genes for high intelligence who receive the most years of education. Thus, there are complex *interactions* between genes and environment, and so it is very difficult to disentangle the effects of heredity and environment.

> **EXAM HINT**
>
> The specification requires you to consider the role of genetic factors and environmental factors. Use issues such as culture bias and the nature–nurture debate to maximise synopticity. If the question specifies genetic factors do bring in environmental factors and vice versa, but make sure you do this effectively by highlighting how the factors contrast, rather than describing the opposing argument. Conclude that the factors are not separate influences and consider how genetics and environment interact.

SECTION SUMMARY
Development of Measured Intelligence

❖ Intelligence enables one to cope successfully with life.
❖ Most intelligence tests measure cognitive abilities, but not "streetwise" skills.

What is intelligence?

❖ IQ is the most common measure of intelligence.
❖ IQ is not always accurate because of social and cultural biases in tests.
❖ The key question is whether IQ is related more to:

Measured intelligence

— Heredity: genetic makeup
— Environment: situations and experiences.

Twin studies

❖ Twin studies can research the importance of heredity and environment on intelligence. Twins can be:

— MZ: same genetic makeup, i.e., identical
— DZ: different genetic makeup, i.e., non-identical.

❖ MZ twins reared together are much more similar than DZ twins in terms of IQ (but this may be partly because MZ twins are treated more similarly).
❖ Studies of twins reared apart also support the genetic position (though in some cases the twins were reared in very similar environments).
❖ Evaluation:

— Individual differences in intelligence are 50% due to genetic factors and 50% due to environment factors.
— This figure may be due to the small number of cultures in which the studies have taken place.
— IQ is an imperfect measure of intelligence.
— Heritability is lower in young children.
— Adoption studies generally confirm the findings of twin studies, but may be biased by selective placement.

Influence of environmental factors

❖ Twin and adoption studies show that environmental factors are influential.
❖ The HOME inventory suggests an increased IQ is due to the following environmental factors (though it is hard to prove a causal link):

— Provision of appropriate play materials
— Parental involvement with the child
— Variety in daily stimulation.

❖ The Rochester study identified environmental factors, such as the mother not going to high school or having severe anxiety, that were associated with lower IQ.
❖ Operation Headstart demonstrated some positive effects from environmental enrichment.
❖ The Flynn effect identified a rapid rise in IQ in Western countries in recent years, supporting environmental factors, and possibly diet.

Cultural background and intelligence

❖ Individualistic and collectivistic cultures differ in their definition of intelligence.
❖ There is an average difference in IQ found between American white and black people (about 15 IQ points). This could be explained by genetics but this is a highly political argument.
❖ Criticisms of investigations into race differences include:

— They tell us little about the nature of intelligence.
— They assume that we can identify distinct racial groups.
— They assume that controlled research is possible whereas we cannot truly isolate genetic and environmental factors.
— There are important ethical issues.

See also pages 114–120 of the revision guide.

Reasons for differences in black and white performance

❖ Environmental deprivation is probably responsible for most supposed racial differences.
❖ IQ tests are potentially socially and culturally biased. Some research suggests that the effects are not as great as has been claimed. Truly culture-fair tests do show differences.

DEVELOPMENT OF MORAL UNDERSTANDING

What are Morals?

What is meant by the term "morality"? According to Shaffer (1993), morality implies "a set of principles or ideals that help the individual to distinguish right from wrong and to act on this distinction".

Why is morality important? Society cannot function effectively unless there is some agreement on what is right and wrong. Of course, there are moral and ethical issues (e.g., animal experiments) on which individual members of a given society have very different views. However, if there were controversy on all major moral issues, society would become chaotic.

Shaffer argued that human morality has three components. First, there is the *emotional component*. This is concerned with the feelings (e.g., guilt) associated with moral thoughts and behaviour. Second, there is the *cognitive component*. This is concerned with how we think about moral issues, and make decisions about what is right and wrong. Third, there is the *behavioural component*, which is concerned with how we behave. It includes the extent to which we lie, steal, cheat, or behave honourably.

SHAFFER'S COMPONENTS OF HUMAN MORALITY

Emotional	Cognitive	Behavioural (not covered here)
Feelings associated with moral behaviour	How we think about moral issues, and decide between right and wrong	How we behave
Theorists: • Freud • Eisenberg	Theorists: • Piaget • Kohlberg • Gilligan	Theorists: • Bandura • Mischel
Approach: • Psychodynamic/social cognition	Approach: • Cognitive-developmental	Approach: • Social learning

---

Why should we distinguish among these components? There is often a significant difference between the components. We may know at the cognitive level that it is wrong to cheat, but we may still cheat at the behavioural level. Some people lead blameless lives (behavioural component), but still feel guilty (emotional component). The title of this Section is the "development of moral *understanding*". Emotional and cognitive components are part of moral understanding. The behavioural component is a means of assessing the value of theories of moral understanding and seeing how moral understanding relates to behaviour.

The distinction among different moral components is also useful in comparing theories of moral development. Freud and Eisenberg emphasised the emotional component; Piaget, Kohlberg, and Gilligan focused on the cognitive component; and social learning theorists concentrated on the behavioural component.

? How is moral understanding different from moral behaviour?

EXAM HINT

Questions in the exam will be on moral reasoning and/or pro-social reasoning, so you can choose whether to focus on one of these, or both.

Freud's model of the mind

Theories of the Development of Moral Thinking

Psychodynamic theory

Sigmund Freud (1856–1939) argued that the human mind consists of three parts: the **id, ego,** and **superego.** The id deals with motivational forces (e.g., the sexual instinct); the ego is concerned with conscious thinking; and the superego is concerned with moral issues. The superego is divided into the conscience and the ego-ideal. Our conscience makes us feel guilty or ashamed when we have behaved badly, whereas our ego-ideal makes us feel proud of ourselves when we have behaved well in the face of temptation. (See pages 240–245 for a more detailed description of Freud's theory of personality.)

Freud suggested that the superego develops at the age of 5 or 6. Boys develop sexual desires for their mother, leading to an intense rivalry with their father and a desire to get rid of this rival. This state of affairs is known as the **Oedipus complex.** It makes boys feel very fearful, because they are afraid that their father will discover their true feelings. Boys also suffer from a **castration complex**—the discovery that girls lack a penis leads them to become very anxious about being castrated by their father.

The anxieties that boys have as a result or regarding their father as a rival and fearing castration are resolved through the process of **identification,** in which boys come to identify with their father (who is powerful and can protect them) and no longer see him as a rival. Identification leads them to imitate or copy the beliefs and behaviour of their father and to repress (i.e., banish from consciousness) their sexual feelings for their mother. As part of the identification process, boys adopt their father's moral standards, and this leads to the formation of the superego. According to Freud, the superego is "the heir of the Oedipus complex".

According to Freud, similar processes occur in girls. Freud (1933) argued that girls are "mortified by the comparison with boys' far superior equipment" (known as penis envy) for which they blame their mother. Girls also suffer from castration complex, believing that they have lost their penis. This causes girls to desire the father's penis. Thus, their father becomes their love-object and they substitute their "penis envy" with a wish to have a child. These desires are so threatening that they are rapidly repressed. There is a resolution similar to the Oedipus conflict in which girls identify with their mother because they are very frightened of losing her love. However, Freud concluded that girls have weaker superegos (and so inferior moral development) than boys because of their weaker identification with the same-sex parent. This is an example of gender bias, an issue that is discussed in more detail in the Section "Gender Development" in Chapter 6, Social and Personality Development. However, Freud admitted

? Freud developed his ideas about the Oedipus complex at a time when lone-parent families were very rare. What bearing do you think this may have had on his theorising?

KEY TERMS

Id: in Freudian theory, that part of the mind containing the sexual instinct.
Ego: the conscious, rational mind; one of the three main parts of the mind in Freud's theory.
Superego: in Freudian theory, the part of the mind concerned with moral issues.
Oedipus complex: in Freudian theory, the notion that young boys desire their mother sexually and so experience rivalry with their father.
Castration complex: in Freudian theory, the young boy's fear that he will be castrated by his father for desiring his mother.
Identification: to become associated with a person or a thing; this increases the likelihood of imitation.

that, "the majority of men are far behind the masculine ideal [in terms of superego strength]".

Research evidence

The main evidence available to Freud consisted of the accounts of his patients as they tried to remember their childhood. Most of these patients were middle-class Austrian women suffering from various forms of neurosis or anxiety disorders. Strangely, in spite of the fact that Freud treated hundreds of patients, he only included detailed accounts of about 12 cases in his published work! One celebrated case concerns Little Hans' (see page 376) experiences of desire for his mother and guilt about his father. Such evidence is weak because it is based on Freud's possibly biased interpretations of what Little Hans had to say, and, in the case of older patients' recollections, a reliance on their fallible memories. Another problem was identified by Meadows (1986, p.162):

> there could be no refuting evidence since a demonstration that a person did not experience an Oedipus complex, feel penis-envy, etc., might be taken as evidence for the perfect repression [motivated forgetting] of the person's Oedipus complex, penis-envy, etc.

Freud argued that fear of the same-sex parent was of crucial importance in the development of the superego. Thus parents who are aggressive and administer a lot of punishment might be expected to have children with strong superegos. In fact, the opposite seems to be the case. Parents who make the most use of spanking and other forms of punishment tend to have children who behave badly and who experience little guilt or shame (Hoffman, 1988; see also the Key Study below).

Freud's theory suggests that punishment should develop a strong superego in the child. However, children who receive a lot of physical punishment tend to behave badly and experience little guilt or shame.

KEY STUDY
Parental role in moral development

The child's early stages of moral development depend very much on its parents. Hoffman (1970) identified three major styles used by parents in the moral development of their children:

1. *Induction*: explaining why a given action is wrong, with special emphasis on its effects on other people.
2. *Power assertion*: using spankings, removal of privileges, and harsh words to exert power over a child.
3. *Love withdrawal*: withholding attention or love when a child behaves badly.

Brody and Shaffer (1982) reviewed studies in which parental style influenced moral development. Induction improved moral development in 86% of

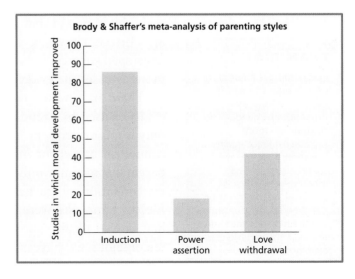

those studies. In contrast, power assertion improved moral development in only 18%, and love withdrawal in 42%. As power assertion had a negative effect on moral development in 82% of the studies, it is a very ineffective parenting style. Power assertion produces children who are aggressive and who do not care about others (Zahn-Waxler, Radke-Yarrow, & King, 1979).

Induction is effective because it provides the child with useful information that helps the development of moral reasoning. Another reason is that induction encourages children to think about other people. Considering the needs and emotions of others is of vital importance if moral development is to occur.

The findings tell us there is an association between parental use of induction and good moral development. The main reason for this association is probably that inductive parenting benefits children's moral development, but that may not be the whole story. Children who are well behaved are more likely to be treated in a reasonable, inductive way by their parents.

In contrast, children who are badly behaved and aggressive may cause their parents to use power assertion. Thus, parenting style affects children's behaviour, but children's behaviour may also affect parenting style.

Discussion points
1. Explain how each style might be related to moral behaviour.
2. What components of morality are left out of this account?

Freud's hypothesis that girls have weaker superegos than boys has been disproved. Hoffman (1975) discussed a number of studies in which the behaviour of children on their own was assessed in order to see whether they did the things they had been told not to do. There was no difference between boys and girls in most of the studies. When there was a sex difference, it was the girls (rather than the boys) who were better at resisting temptation. However, it could be argued that ability to resist temptation is not a good measure of superego strength.

Cross-cultural studies have confirmed the findings of Hoffman (1975). Snarey (1985) reviewed 17 studies from 15 different countries around the world. Sex differences in moral development were found in only three of those studies. However, as we shall see, Kohlberg concluded that men *were* more advanced in their moral development—although this evidence has also been criticised by Gilligan, who like Freud suggested that girls were at least different in their moral orientation.

Evaluation

Freud put forward the first detailed theory of moral development. His basic assumptions that parents have a major influence on the moral development of their children, and that many moral values are acquired in the early years of life, are correct. However, most of his specific hypotheses (e.g., that girls have less developed superegos than boys), are not supported by research evidence. Indeed, in many cases the evidence actually contradicts Freud's hypotheses.

There are several general criticisms of Freud's approach. The main source of evidence used by Freud was adults' memories of their childhood. However, not only is this evidence prone to distortion by the person who is remembering, it also cannot be proved or disproved. Freud didn't see child patients, but dealt with parents, sometimes only through letters, which has led to speculation about his interpretation of particular behaviours. Freud claimed that the Oedipus and Electra complexes were unconscious phases that a child passed through on his or her way to identifying with the same-sex parent. However, if these phases are unconscious we have no way of proving that they did in fact happen, except indirectly through interpretations of children's behaviour.

? If the ability to resist temptation is not a good measure of superego strength, how else might you assess it?

EXAM HINT

You might get a question on the extent to which moral understanding is influenced by gender and cultural variations. Provide evidence against variations first, i.e., the theories suggest that moral development is universal. Do not describe the theories, as you must use them as evidence and then use the variations as evidence for.

Another general criticism of the psychodynamic approach stems from the way in which the theories are formulated. Freud's theory tends to "work backwards", for example, the result leads to the formation of a hypothesis. Freud did not so much predict behaviour as analyse it once it had happened. Finally, the period in which Freud was working must be considered. His patients mostly came from middle-class families, which at the time were ruled by strict disciplinarian regimes. At this point in history, the family would have had the most influence on the developing child. However, today, outside pressures such as peer groups, school, and even television and the internet may prove as influential as the family in a child's development.

In modern society, television could be considered to be one of the major influences on a child's moral development.

There are several specific inadequacies with Freud's theory. First, he exaggerated the role of the same-sex parent in the development of children's morality. The evidence indicates that the opposite-sex parent and other children also generally play an important role (Shaffer, 1993).

Freud attached too much weight to emotional factors in morality and not enough to the cognitive processes partly determining moral behaviour. Theorists such as Piaget and Kohlberg argued that such cognitive processes are the key to moral development. It could also be argued that Freud neglected the behavioural component of morality, which was studied in depth by the social learning theorists.

Freud claimed that children make more dramatic progress in moral development at about the age of 5 or 6 than they do in later childhood or adolescence. In fact, there are large changes in moral reasoning between the ages of 10 and 16 (e.g., Colby et al., 1983; see also Kohlberg's theory on page 255).

Cognitive-developmental theory: Piaget
According to Jean Piaget (e.g., 1932), children's thinking goes through a series of stages (see the first Section of this chapter). He argued that children's moral reasoning also proceeds through a number of different stages.

Stages in moral development
Piaget developed his ideas about moral reasoning by playing marbles with children. He was interested in seeing how well they understood the rules of the game, how important they thought it was to obey those rules, and so on. His observations led him to propose the following stages of moral development:

? In what way is moral reasoning related to moral understanding?

1. *Premoral period* (0–5 years): children in this stage have very little understanding of rules or other aspects of morality.
2. *Stage of moral realism* or **heteronomous morality** (heteronomous means "subject to externally imposed rules") (5–10 years): children at this stage are rather rigid in their thinking—they believe that rules must be obeyed no matter what the circumstances. Children at this stage think that rules are made by important other people (e.g., parents), and that how bad an action is stems from its consequences. There are two other key features of the moral

> **KEY TERM**
>
> **Heteronomous morality:** younger children base their judgements of right and wrong on the severity of outcome and/or externally imposed rules.

Piaget (1932) found that moral reasoning in children between the ages of 5 and 10 is partially influenced by the notion of immanent justice. If the adult has set a rule that the toy is not to be played with, the child is likely to obey, for fear of punishment.

reasoning of children at this stage. First, they believe in **expiatory punishment**: the naughtier the behaviour, the greater should be the punishment; however, there is no idea that the punishment should fit the crime. For example, a child who drops a freshly baked cake on the floor should be spanked. Second, children between the ages of 5 and 10 strongly favour the notion of fairness. This leads them to believe in **immanent justice**, which is the idea that naughty behaviour will always be punished in some way.

3. *Stage of moral relativism* or **autonomous morality** (10 years upwards): children at this stage think more flexibly about moral issues. They understand that moral rules evolve from human relationships, and that people differ in their standards of morality. They also understand, reasonably, that most rules of morality can be broken sometimes. If a violent man with a gun demands to be told where your mother is, it is perfectly acceptable to tell a lie and say that you do not know. Children now think that the wrongness of an action depends far more on the individual's intentions than on the consequences of his/her behaviour. Second, children in this stage believe in **reciprocal punishment** rather than expiatory punishment. Thus, the punishment should fit the crime. Third, children in this stage have learned that wrong-doers often avoid punishment. Thus, they no longer believe in immanent justice.

What causes development?

According to Piaget, two main factors cause changes in moral reasoning. First, young children are egocentric in their thinking, seeing the world only from their own point of view. At about the age of 7, they become less egocentric. Their growing awareness that other people have different views allows them to develop more mature moral reasoning. Moral development lags behind cognitive development because it depends on the cognitive changes occurring first.

Second, older children develop flexible ideas of morality because they are exposed to the different views of other children of the same age. This leads them to question their own values.

Evidence

Children in most Western societies go through Piaget's stages of moral development in the order specified by Piaget (Shaffer, 1993). There is also evidence to support many of the details of the theory. For example, Piaget (1932) argued that children in the stage of moral realism judge actions by their consequences rather than by the actor's intentions, and he obtained evidence for this. Children in this stage were told about a boy called John who opened a door, and by so doing broke 15 cups on the other side of the door. They were also told about Henry, who broke one cup while trying to reach some jam he had been told not to get. Even though John had no idea there were any cups there, he was still regarded as being naughtier than Henry because he broke more cups (see the box on the next page).

PIAGET'S STAGES OF MORAL DEVELOPMENT

Premoral	Moral realism (heteronomous morality)	Moral relativism (autonomous morality)
0–5 years old	5–10 years old	10 years upwards
Little understanding of rules and other aspects	Rigid thinking: rules must be obeyed	Development of flexibility in moral issues
	Actions are judged by their consequences	Understanding that people differ in moral standards. Rules can be broken and wrong behaviour is not always punished
	Belief in: • Expiatory punishment • Immanent justice	Belief in: • Reciprocal punishment

Piaget's moral stories

Piaget used moral stories to investigate what moral decisions children reached. An example is given below with a sample interview with a child.

STORY 1: A little boy who is called John is in his room. He is called to dinner. He goes into the dining room. But behind the door there was a chair, and on the chair there was a tray with 15 cups on it. John couldn't have known that there was all this behind the door. He goes in, the door knocks against the tray, "bang" to the 15 cups and they all get broken!

STORY 2: Once there was a little boy whose name was Henry. One day when his mother was out he tried to get some jam out of the cupboard. He climbed up on a chair and stretched out his arm. But the jam was too high up and he couldn't reach it and have any. But while he was trying to get it, he knocked over a cup. The cup fell down and broke.

Below is a characteristic response for a child in the stage of moral realism:

Questioner:	"What did the first boy do?"
Child:	"He broke 15 cups."
Questioner:	"And the second one?"
Child:	"He broke a cup by moving roughly."
Questioner:	"Is one of the boys naughtier than the other?"
Child:	"The first one is because he knocked over 15 cups."
Questioner:	"If you were the daddy, which one would you punish most?"
Child:	"The one who broke 15 cups."
Questioner:	"Why did he break them?"
Child:	"The door shut too hard and knocked them over. He didn't do it on purpose."
Questioner:	"And why did the other boy break a cup?"
Child:	"Because he was clumsy. When he was getting the jam the cup fell down."
Questioner:	"Why did he want to get the jam?"
Child:	"Because he was alone. Because the mother wasn't there."

Piaget (1932), pp.122 and 129.

Evaluation

Piaget was right that there are close links between cognitive development in general and moral development in particular. Another strength of his theoretical approach is that most children in Western societies show the shift from moral realism to moral relativism predicted by Piaget.

On the negative side, young children have more complex ideas about morality than was assumed by Piaget, and some of their moral thinking is more advanced than he claimed. Piaget's assumption that 10- and 11-year-old children have reached an adult level of moral reasoning is incorrect. This was shown in a study by Colby et al. (1983) (described later), who found large changes in moral thinking between the ages of 10 and 16.

Piaget argued that children at the stage of moral realism follow the rules of parents and other authority figures in an uncritical way. However, this only applies to certain parental rules (e.g., those about honesty and stealing). They are much less willing to allow their parents to make and enforce rules about who they may have as their friends or what they should do in their free time (Shaffer, 1993). This problem may arise because Piaget used the game of marbles and rather simplistic stories as a means of investigating moral behaviour.

Finally, Piaget focused on children's views concerning moral issues, and so dealt with their knowledge of how they ought to behave. However, their thinking may be rather different from their actual behaviour when faced with a moral dilemma. More generally, Piaget tended to neglect the behavioural component of morality. He also paid little attention to the emotional component of morality (which was emphasised by Freud).

Cognitive-developmental theory: Kohlberg

Lawrence Kohlberg (1927–1987) agreed with Piaget that we need to focus on children's cognitive structures to understand how they think about moral issues. However, Kohlberg's theory differs in several ways from that of Piaget. For example, Kohlberg believed that moral reasoning often continues to develop through adolescence and early adulthood.

Moral dilemmas

The main experimental approach used by Kohlberg involved presenting his participants with a series of moral dilemmas, and then asking them a series of predetermined questions of what they would have done and why. These questions are of key importance because Kohlberg was endeavouring to investigate moral reasoning—how individuals think about moral decisions, rather than moral behaviour.

Each dilemma required them to decide whether it is preferable to uphold some law or other moral principle, or to reject the moral principle in favour of some basic human need. To make clear what Kohlberg (e.g., 1963) did, we will consider one of the moral dilemmas he used.

Do you think that you sometimes behave differently from your moral principles?

In Europe, a woman was dying from cancer. One drug might save her, a form of radium that a druggist in the same town had recently discovered. The druggist was charging 2000 dollars, ten times what the drug cost him to make. The sick woman's husband, Heinz, went to everyone he knew to borrow the money, but he could only get together about half of what the drug cost. He told the druggist that his wife was dying and asked him to sell it cheaper or let him pay later. But the druggist said "No". The husband got desperate and broke into the man's store to steal the drug for his wife.

The moral principle in this dilemma is that stealing is wrong. However, it was the good motive of wanting to help his sick wife that led Heinz to steal the drug. It is precisely because there are powerful arguments for and against stealing the drug that there is a moral dilemma. (See the Key Study on the next page for another example of Kohlberg's dilemmas.)

? In what way are Kohlberg's moral dilemmas different from Piaget's moral stories?

Kohlberg's theory

Kohlberg (1976) developed his stage theory of moral development on the basis of a cross-sectional study, where 72 boys aged between 10 and 16 were interviewed about moral dilemmas, such as the "Heinz dilemma", above. Further details of this research are given in the Key Study on the next page. By analysing the answers participants gave in the interviews, Kohlberg identified different stages and levels of moral reasoning.

Kohlberg followed Piaget in assuming that all children follow the same sequence of stages in their moral development. However, Kohlberg's three levels of moral development (with two stages at each level) do not correspond closely to Piaget's:

Level 1: Pre-conventional morality. At this level, what is regarded as right and wrong is determined by the rewards or punishments that are likely to follow, rather than by thinking about moral issues. Stage 1 of this level is based on a *punishment-and-obedience orientation*. Stealing is wrong because it involves disobeying authority, and leads to punishment. Stage 2 of this level is based on the notion that the right way to behave is the way that is rewarded. There is more attention to the needs of other people than in stage 1, but mainly on the basis that if you help other people, then they will help you.

? Think of an example to illustrate each of Kohlberg's six stages.

Level 2: Conventional morality. The greatest difference between level 1 and level 2 is that the views and needs of other people are much more important at

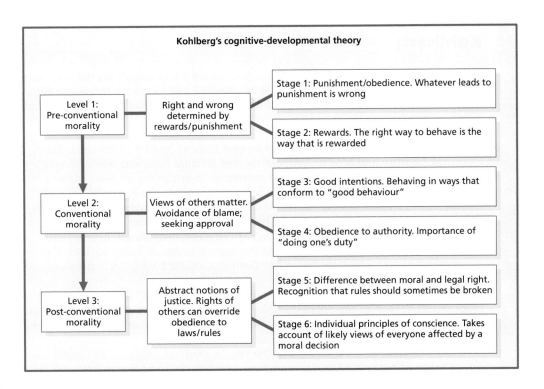

Kohlberg's cognitive-developmental theory

Level 1: Pre-conventional morality → Right and wrong determined by rewards/punishment → Stage 1: Punishment/obedience. Whatever leads to punishment is wrong

Stage 2: Rewards. The right way to behave is the way that is rewarded

Level 2: Conventional morality → Views of others matter. Avoidance of blame; seeking approval → Stage 3: Good intentions. Behaving in ways that conform to "good behaviour"

Stage 4: Obedience to authority. Importance of "doing one's duty"

Level 3: Post-conventional morality → Abstract notions of justice. Rights of others can override obedience to laws/rules → Stage 5: Difference between moral and legal right. Recognition that rules should sometimes be broken

Stage 6: Individual principles of conscience. Takes account of likely views of everyone affected by a moral decision level 2 than at level 1. At this level, people are very concerned to have the approval of others for their actions, and to avoid being blamed by them for behaving wrongly. At stage 3, the emphasis is on having good intentions, and on behaving in ways that conform to most people's views of good behaviour. At stage 4, children believe that it is important to do one's duty, and to obey the laws or rules of those in authority.

Level 3: Post-conventional or principled morality. Those at the highest level of post-conventional or principled morality recognise that the laws or rules of authority figures should sometimes be broken. Abstract notions about justice and the need to treat other people with respect can override the need to obey laws and rules. At stage 5, there is a growing recognition that what is morally right may differ from what is legally right. Finally, at stage 6, the individual has developed his or her own principles of conscience. The individual takes into account the likely views of everyone who will be affected by a moral decision. Kohlberg (1981) described this as a kind of "moral musical chairs". In practice, it is very rare for anyone to operate most of the time at stage 6.

Research evidence
Kohlberg assumed that all children follow the same sequence of moral stages. The best way of testing this assumption is to carry out a longitudinal (long-term) study to see how children's moral reasoning changes over time. Colby et al. (1983) conducted a 20-year study of 58 American males (see the graph on the next page). There was a substantial drop in stage 1 and stage 2 moral reasoning between the ages of 10 and 16, with a compensatory increase in stage 3 and stage 4 moral reasoning occurring during the same time period. Most impressively for Kohlberg's theory, all of the participants progressed through the moral stages in exactly the predicted sequence.

KEY STUDY
Kohlberg

Kohlberg (1976) developed his stage theory of moral development on the basis of a cross-sectional study, where 72 boys aged between 10 and 16 were interviewed about moral dilemmas, such as the "Heinz dilemma" on page 224 or the one described below.

In a country in Europe, a poor man named Valjean could find no work, nor could his sister and brother. Without money, he stole food and medicine that they needed. He was captured and sentenced to prison for six years. After a couple of years, he escaped from the prison and went to live in another part of the country under a new name. He saved money and slowly built up a big factory. He gave his workers the highest wages and used most of his profits to build a hospital for people who couldn't afford good medical care. Twenty years had passed when a tailor recognised the factory owner as being Valjean, the escaped convict whom the police had been looking for back in his hometown.

The interviews consisted of a predetermined set of questions, such as "Should the tailor report Valjean to the police?", "Why or why not?", "Does a citizen have a duty or an obligation to report an escaped convict?", "Suppose Valjean were a close friend of the tailor. Should he then report Valjean?"

Each interview lasted 2 hours and the results enabled Kohlberg to classify each boy in terms of his level of moral reasoning. The original sample was followed for a further 20 years (Colby et al., 1983). The boys and men were tested six times in all, at 3-yearly intervals. The graph on the right shows how moral reasoning developed. At age 10 the children displayed mainly stage 2 reasoning but there were examples of stages 1 and 3. By the age of 22 no one used stage 1 reasoning, and stages 3 and 4 were predominant. By the age of 36, and the end of the study, there was still very little evidence of stage 5 reasoning (about 5%).

Kohlberg's findings were confirmed in a study by Walker, de Vries, and Trevethan (1987) who developed a modified set of nine stages to allow for the fact that reasoning often falls between two of Kohlberg's stages. They still found general agreement with Kohlberg, for example that the equivalent of stage 2 type reasoning dominates at age 10 and stage 3 at age 16.

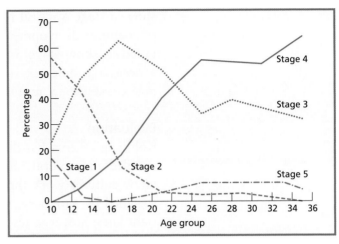

Kohlberg's moral stages studied longitudinally over a 20-year period encompassing ages 10 to 36.

Key study evaluation
Kohlberg's theory addresses some of the problems of Piaget's approach, in that it is more flexible and less tied to specific age-based stages of development. Meta-analyses have shown that the six stages of Kohlberg's theoretical framework apply across most cultures, and it is almost universally the case that individuals work through the various stages in the same order. However, individual differences in experience or cultural differences may affect the speed with which a person moves through the stages. For example, in some cultures children can work, be married, or be regarded as full members of adult society at much younger ages than Western children. It is possible that these individuals move through Kohlberg's stages much earlier than Western children do. In addition, some children's lives do not conform to the stereotypical well-balanced family background with a strong moral sense of right and wrong that seems to lie behind some of Kohlberg's stages. This may also have a profound effect on a child's moral development.

Discussion points
1. How adequate do you find Kohlberg's use of moral dilemmas to study moral development?
2. What do you think of Kohlberg's stage-based approach to moral development?

In order to demonstrate that his moral stages were universal, Kohlberg (1969) studied the moral reasoning of children in other countries: Britain, Mexico, Taiwan, Turkey, USA, and Yucatan, finding the same pattern of development. He did find that development tended to be slower in non-industrialised countries. Colby and Kohlberg (1987) reported longitudinal studies in Turkey and Israel that produced similar results. Snarey (1985) reviewed 44 studies from 26 cultures. People in nearly all cultures went through the stages of moral development identified by Kohlberg in the same order. There was little evidence for any stage-skipping or for people returning to an earlier stage of moral development.

However, Kohlberg's claim that the moral thinking of any given individual will be consistently at the same stage has not been supported. Rubin and Trotter (1977) gave their participants several moral dilemmas, and found that many of them responded very differently from one dilemma to the next.

Kohlberg assumed that certain kinds of general cognitive development must occur before an individual can advance a stage in his or her moral reasoning. For example, those whose moral reasoning is at stage 5 make use of abstract principles (e.g., of justice), which presumably requires them to be good at abstract thinking. Tomlinson-Keasey and Keasey (1974) found that those girls of 11 and 12 who showed stage 5 moral reasoning were good at abstract thinking on general tests of cognitive development. However, some of the girls could think abstractly, but failed to show stage 5 moral reasoning. Thus the ability to think abstractly is a necessary (but not sufficient) requirement for someone to attain stage 5 or post-conventional morality.

Evaluation

Kohlberg's theory has the advantage over Piaget's theory in that it provides a more detailed and accurate account of moral development. It appears that children in many cultures work through the various stages of moral reasoning in the order specified by Kohlberg, which would suggest that the theory seems to be on the right lines; however, research in the last decade has questioned this. For example, Miller, Bershoff, and Harwood (1990), in research in India, found that the moral code used tended to give priority to social duties as contrasting with Americans' priority for individual rights. Though later studies have found that, where serious moral issues are concerned, Indian and American views in relation to social responsibilities were more similar (Berry et al., 1992). Ma (1988) conducted work in China and produced an adaptation of Kohlberg's original theory that included Chinese perspectives such as the "Golden Mean" (behaving as most people in society behave) and "Good Will" (acting in a way that complies with nature). It may be that there are significant cultural differences, especially at the highest level of post-conventional morality, but also some similarities.

Shweder, Mahapatra, and Miller (1990) proposed an alternative post-conventional morality that functions in India. This is based on conceptions of natural law and justice, rather than individualism and social equality.

A further critical issue is the question of whether most people develop beyond stage 4 at all (Shaver & Strong, 1976). In addition, it has proved difficult to make a clear distinction between stage 5 and stage 6 moral reasoning (Colby et al., 1983).

Kohlberg focused on the verbal responses when his participants were given artificial moral dilemmas, rather than on actual moral behaviour. People's responses to those dilemmas may not predict how they would behave in real-life situations. The evidence is somewhat inconsistent. Santrock (1975) found that children's level of moral reasoning did not predict whether they would cheat when given the chance. However, there is more evidence among adults that the stage of moral reasoning can predict behaviour. Kohlberg (1975) compared cheating behaviour among students at different levels of moral reasoning. About 70% of the students at the pre-conventional level were found to cheat, compared with only 15% of those at the post-conventional level. Students at the conventional level were intermediate (55%). This does appear to support a link between reasoning and behaviour.

Finally, Kohlberg did not consider the emotional component of morality in any detail. For example, the development of emotions such as shame and guilt is important within moral development. This is addressed by theories of pro-social development.

> ? Can you think of an example of how Kohlberg's levels of moral development emphasise individual rights?

> ? Why might there be more cross-cultural similarities over serious moral issues?

> ? Which is of greater usefulness: a theory of moral reasoning or moral behaviour?

Kohlberg's study of cheating behaviour

Gilligan's theory

Gilligan (1977) argued that a major problem with Kohlberg's theory was its focus on male morality, an **androcentric bias**. The participants in the baseline study were all males and Gilligan claimed that essentially Kohlberg had produced a theory that was centred on the way that men approach moral decisions—making decisions in terms of justice rather than in terms of care, whereas women emphasise the morality of care over that of justice. According to Gilligan and Wiggins (1987), these gender differences have their origins in early childhood. Women are the main caregivers in most societies, and girls learn the morality of care through their strong attachment to their mother. In contrast, boys are less attached to their mother. They tend to identify with their father, who is often perceived as an authority figure. This identification process leads boys to develop the morality of justice.

Gilligan carried out numerous interviews with women, as a result of which she proposed a stage theory of moral development differing in various ways from the one proposed by Kohlberg. According to Gilligan's theory, there are three stages. During the first stage, the emphasis is on self-interest, which resembles the pre-conventional stage identified by Kohlberg. During the second stage, there is self-sacrifice (resembling Kohlberg's conventional stage) with children focusing more on the importance of being considerate towards the needs of others. During the third stage (resembling Kohlberg's post-conventional stage), there is integration, with the emphasis being on the importance of doing one's best not to hurt anyone else by one's actions.

Gilligan supported her views with research (see the Key Study below). Kohlberg's male focus may explain why he found that men were more morally developed than women; he reported that most women were at stage 3 of moral development, whereas men were at stage 4.

KEY STUDY
Gilligan and Attanucci

Carol Gilligan (1977, 1982) proposed a theory in response to what she regarded as Kohlberg's androcentric bias. Kohlberg initially based his theory on interviews with male participants, which suggests that bias may have been introduced. Gilligan argued that a less biased theory should take female views into account and should also consider moral decisions in real life rather than simply asking participants about hypothetical decisions.

Gilligan (1982) conducted her own research, interviewing women who were facing a real-life dilemma. She interviewed 29 women who were deciding whether or not to have an abortion. She analysed the interviews and concluded that people rely on two different moral injunctions: not to treat others unfairly and not to turn away from someone in need (a "justice" or a "care" orientation). Gilligan suggested that Kohlberg's research was constrained by the assumption that there is only one moral perspective, that of justice. The alternative, care, is observed mainly by women, who tend to be concerned more about people's feelings than about what is "fair". According to Gilligan, Kohlberg showed sexist bias by regarding the morality of justice as superior to the morality of care.

Gilligan developed her own stage theory from her interview analyses and Gilligan and Attanucci (1988) used this for a further analysis of male and female behaviour.

Gilligan and Attanucci expected that female participants would favour a care orientation and males would favour a justice orientation. A key feature of this study was that moral reasoning was to be tested in the context of real-life dilemmas,

> **KEY TERM**
>
> **Androcentric bias:** a bias in favour of males. An androcentric theory is based on research data on males and then applied to all human behaviour.

Stage	Justice	Care
1	1J Uphold moral standards and withstand pressure to deviate	1C Concern with what others say and how choices might affect relationships
2	2J Justice should be tempered with mercy. One should consider the feelings of others, but principles are most important	2C Sacrificing one's own concerns to the welfare of others. Relationships are more important than conventional rules
3	3J Although there are "exceptions to the rule", everyone is best served by obedience to universal laws	3C Attempting to apply moral rules while valuing the individual and trying not to hurt anyone

providing greater ecological validity. Eighty men and women aged between 14 and 77 from various walks of life were asked a set of questions about moral conflict and choice, such as "Have you ever been in a situation of moral conflict where you had to make a decision but weren't sure what was the right thing to do?", "Could you describe the situation?", "What were the conflicts for you in that situation?", "What did you do?", "Do you think it was the right thing to do?", "How do you know?". Each participant was interviewed individually for approximately 2 hours, and their answers analysed and classified as care only, care focus (more than 75% care considerations), care justice (less than 75% of either), justice focus, or justice only.

	Care focus and care only	Care justice	Justice focus and justice only
Women	12	12	10
Men	1	15	30

THEORIES OF MORAL DEVELOPMENT

Theory	Methods	Criticisms
Psychodynamic	Personal accounts from adults about their childhood experiences	Relies on accuracy of person's memory. Many of Freud's hypotheses have been proved wrong
Piaget's cognitive-developmental theory	Telling short stories to illustrate moral points revealed a shift from moral realism to moral relativism	Piaget may have underestimated the young child's ability to take account of people's intentions. Piaget ignored the behavioural and emotional components of morality
Kohlberg's cognitive-developmental theory	Through the use of artificial dilemmas, Kohlberg described six stages of moral development that seem to be stable across most cultures	Most people do not seem to develop beyond stage 4. The distinction between stages 5 and 6 is not clear. Kohlberg also placed little emphasis on the behavioural and emotional components of morality

Key study evaluation

It might be worth noting that the findings of Gilligan's original research study involved a relatively small number of women, and a rather unsystematic and potentially biased method of interviewing.

Convincing evidence that men and women are actually very similar in their moral reasoning has been found in studies in which people discuss moral dilemmas they have experienced. In contrast to what would be predicted by Gilligan's (1982) theory, men as well as women focus on interpersonal responsibility and the well-being of others at least as much as they consider laws and justice (Walker et al., 1987). Jaffee and Hyde (2000) carried out an analysis of over 100 studies of moral reasoning. Overall, there was a very small tendency for males to show more justice reasoning than females, and a slightly larger (but still small) tendency for females to show more care reasoning than males.

Discussion points
1. Do you think that other ethnic groups (non-American) would respond in the same way?
2. What ethical concerns are raised by Gilligan's research?

Theories of Pro-social Reasoning

Nancy Eisenberg felt that Kohlberg's emphasis on justice and fairness overlooked a key aspect of morality, that of "pro-social" moral reasoning. In Chapter 3, Pro- and Anti-social Behaviour, we discussed pro-social behaviour in adults, behaviours that aim to benefit others. One particular kind of pro-social behaviour—altruism—aims to help others at a possible cost or risk to the altruist. Why do people behave altruistically? The "empathy–altruism model" (Batson, 1987) suggested that when we see someone else in distress we feel empathy for their distress and are motivated to reduce their and our distress. Empathy describes the ability to comprehend what someone else is feeling.

Eisenberg argued that empathy was a fundamental part of moral development. In order to behave in a just or caring way towards others, one must feel empathy.

Eisenberg's theory

Eisenberg believed, like Piaget and Kohlberg, that changes take place in moral reasoning in parallel with the maturation of general cognitive abilities. Eisenberg particularly emphasised the growth of role-taking skills—the ability to assume the perspective and take the part of another person. These skills in turn assist in the growth of empathy and thus pro-social moral reasoning.

According to Eisenberg, Lennon, and Roth (1983) there are five levels or stages in the development of pro-social reasoning, as shown in the box on the next page.

Research evidence

This theory has been tested by asking children of different ages to decide what they would do if faced by various dilemmas. One of the dilemmas was as follows:

One day a girl named Mary was going to a friend's birthday party. On her way she saw a girl who had fallen down and hurt her leg. The girl asked Mary to go to her house and get her parents so that they could come and take her to a doctor. But if Mary did . . . she would be late for the party and miss the ice cream, cake, and all the games. What should Mary do?

Eisenberg-Berg and Hand (1979) found that young children tended to be self-centred. Most of them decided that Mary should go to the party and leave the injured girl on her own. In contrast, older children generally decided that it was

> **EXAM HINT**
>
> You may be asked for one, two, or two or more theories of moral understanding/pro-social reasoning. Kohlberg and Eisenberg provide very detailed theories, so do remember you don't need to cover them both in equal depth, and any further theories should be dealt with in less detail.

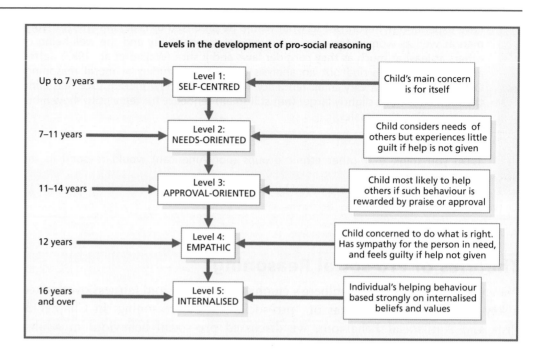

Levels in the development of pro-social reasoning

Up to 7 years →	Level 1: SELF-CENTRED	Child's main concern is for itself
7–11 years →	Level 2: NEEDS-ORIENTED	Child considers needs of others but experiences little guilt if help is not given
11–14 years →	Level 3: APPROVAL-ORIENTED	Child most likely to help others if such behaviour is rewarded by praise or approval
12 years →	Level 4: EMPATHIC	Child concerned to do what is right. Has sympathy for the person in need, and feels guilty if help not given
16 years and over →	Level 5: INTERNALISED	Individual's helping behaviour based strongly on internalised beliefs and values

more important to help the injured girl than to go to the party. Of course, the opinions expressed by children when given such dilemmas may not correspond to their behaviour in everyday life. However, Eisenberg-Berg and Hand obtained some evidence that the level of pro-social reasoning revealed by the dilemmas *does* predict actual behaviour. Sharing behaviour was more common among children at level 2 of pro-social reasoning than among those at level 1.

Eisenberg et al. (1991) found that empathy (which develops during level 4) plays an important role in producing pro-social thinking. Adolescents given the dilemma about Mary and the injured girl were more likely to decide that Mary should help if they thought about the injured girl's feelings of pain and anxiety.

According to the theory of Eisenberg et al. (1983), empathy only develops from about the age of 12. However, evidence that empathy may influence pro-social behaviour several years earlier was reported by Zahn-Waxler et al. (1979). Many children between the ages of 18 and 30 months showed obvious concern when they saw other children in distress. The infants may have experienced empathy because their mothers had a particular way of dealing with them when they harmed another child. Their mothers emphasised the distress that their behaviour had caused to the other child. The mothers said things such as, "Don't hit Mary—you've made her cry" or "Put that bat down—you've hurt John".

If the mother of an aggressive child emphasises how much the other child is being hurt, the aggressive child is more likely to feel empathy and stop the undesirable behaviour.

Evaluation

Eisenberg's theory provides a perspective on the development of moral understanding that is different from that of Kohlberg. It emphasises the importance of emotional factors and focuses on pro-social reasoning rather than issues of wrong-doing. Nevertheless there are strong parallels between this theory and Kohlberg's stage account. As a result, it can be regarded as a broadening of Kohlberg's original approach (Bee, 1995) with an increased emphasis on emotional factors.

Eisenberg's approach is potentially of value to parents and others involved with children in that it shows how to raise helpful and altruistic children. For example, emphasising that the consequences of an action matter, and acting as pro-social models for children's behaviour are both useful approaches for parents to take.

Sociobiological theory

A different approach to understanding the development of pro-social behaviour can be found in sociobiological theory, based on evolutionary principles. According to the theory of evolution, any behaviour that promotes survival and reproduction will be naturally selected and remain in a species' repertoire. Individuals who possess **adaptive** characteristics have a competitive advantage over individuals without such characteristics. This theory can explain many animal behaviours, but it cannot explain altruism because an individual who dies or is injured saving another has reduced their chances of reproduction. Therefore we should not observe altruistic behaviour in the animal world—yet we do.

Sociobiologists offered an explanation for this. It is not the survival of the individual that matters but the survival of the genes. Thus, if an individual dies in order to ensure the survival of other genetically related individuals then this altruistic behaviour is adaptive. This is called **kin selection**.

Sociobiologists further suggest that, if an individual behaves in a pro-social manner towards another, this behaviour may be returned at a later date, thus enhancing the survival of both individuals. This is called **reciprocal altruism** (Trivers, 1971).

Sociobiological theory suggests that we behave pro-socially because we inherit this characteristic. We inherit it because it is adaptive. This is a biological account of the development of pro-social behaviour and is further discussed in Chapter 3, Pro- and Anti-social Behaviour.

> **KEY TERMS**
>
> **Adaptive:** the extent to which a behaviour increases the reproductive potential of an individual and survival of its genes.
> **Kin selection:** the view that the process of natural selection functions at the level of an individual's genes and thus any behaviour that promotes the survival and reproduction of all "kin" (genetic relatives) will also be selected.
> **Reciprocal altruism:** a form of mutual benefit where a selfless act is performed with the expectation that the favour will be returned at a later date. Such behaviour is adaptive as long as cheating doesn't occur.

SECTION SUMMARY
Development of Moral Understanding

❖ Morals are concerned with right and wrong and are vital for society to function.
❖ There are emotional, cognitive, and behavioural components associated with morality.

❖ According to Freud, moral development depends on children's identification with the same-sex parent at about the age of 5 or 6.
❖ This process is called the Oedipus complex in boys and penis-envy (or according to Jung, the Electra complex) in girls.
❖ Moral strength is predicted to be weaker in girls because the resolution is less complete.
❖ Evaluation:
  — Research evidence doesn't support a link between harsher parents and greater morality, though it may be important to consider the parents' intentions rather than their behaviour.

What are morals?

Psychodynamic theory: Freud

— Research also shows that women do not have weaker moralities.

— Freud's basic assumptions about age and parental influence are correct.

— However, he exaggerated the role of the same-sex parent, ignored cognitive and behavioural elements, and suggested that moral development ceased after the age of 6.

Cognitive-developmental theory: Piaget

❖ Piaget's stage theory can be applied to moral reasoning.

❖ Piaget observed children's behaviour in games with marbles and identified three major stages:

1. The premoral period
2. Stage of moral realism: associated with consequences rather than intentions (heteronomous morality, expiatory punishment, immanent justice)
3. Stage of moral relativism: associated with intentions rather than consequences (autonomous morality and reciprocal punishment).

❖ Development occurs because of decreasing egocentricity and increasing negotiations with others that lead children to question their own values.

❖ Evaluation:

— Young children have more complex ideas about morality than Piaget assumed.

— Piaget oversimplifies moral thinking and overestimates moral reasoning.

— Piaget assumed that heteronomous children follow their parents in all things, but they may treat some decisions differently.

— Piaget focused on moral reasoning rather than on either moral behaviour or emotional factors.

Cognitive-development theory: Kohlberg

❖ Kohlberg researched moral dilemmas to expand Piaget's theory, producing a 6-stage theory of moral reasoning (two stages per level).

❖ The three levels are:

1. Pre-conventional morality
2. Conventional morality
3. Post-conventional or principled morality.

❖ Evaluation:

— Kohlberg's original cross-sectional study, his longitudinal study, and cross-cultural research has supported this stage theory.

— But individuals can operate at several levels at one time.

— Being able to think abstractly does not guarantee level 3 of moral reasoning.

— There is some doubt if people generally develop beyond stage 4, and whether the stages can predict moral behaviour.

— Kohlberg overlooked the emotional component of morality.

Gilligan's theory

❖ Gilligan proposed a distinction between a male morality of justice and a female morality of care.

❖ She argued that there are three stages of moral development: self-interest, self-sacrifice, and integration.

❖ Evaluation:

— The evidence provides only very modest support for the proposed gender difference in moral development.

❖ Eisenberg's five-stage theory suggests that empathy is a key element of moral and pro-social behaviour and emphasises the growth of role-taking skills.

Theories of pro-social reasoning

❖ Evaluation:

— Research used dilemmas and found support for the theory, although empathy may appear earlier than was predicted.
— The theory emphasises emotional factors and focuses on pro-social reasoning rather than on issues of wrong-doing.
— It can be seen as a broadening of Kohlberg's original approach.

See also pages 121–128 of the revision guide.

❖ Sociobiological theory suggests pro-social behaviour is inherited to ensure the survival of kin.

FURTHER READING

The topics in this chapter are covered in greater depth by J. Henderson (2001) *Development of thinking* (London: Routledge), written specifically for the AQA A specification. There is good coverage of most aspects of cognitive development in K. Durkin (1995) *Developmental social psychology: From infancy to old age* (Oxford: Blackwell). A very readable account of Piaget's work can be found in the chapter on "Jean Piaget" by Peter Bryant in *Seven pioneers of psychology* (1995) edited by R. Fuller (London: Routledge). Factors associated with the development of intelligence test performance are discussed by M.W. Eysenck (2004) *Psychology: An international perspective* (Hove, UK: Psychology Press). A book written for A level students is by M. Jarvis (2001) *Angles on child psychology* (Cheltenham, UK: Stanley Thornes).

EXAMPLE EXAMINATION QUESTIONS

You should spend 30 minutes on each of the questions below, which aim to test the material in this chapter.

1. Discuss the applications of **one or more** theories of cognitive development. (24 marks)
2. (a) Describe Vygotsky's theory of cognitive development. (12 marks)
   (b) Evaluate this theory with reference to research evidence and/or other theories of cognitive development. (12 marks)
3. (a) Describe **two** studies that illustrate the role of genetic factors in the development of measured intelligence. (12 marks)
   (b) Evaluate the extent to which these, and/or other studies, provide insight into the role of genetics in the development of intelligence. (12 marks)
4. Discuss the role of genetics **and** cultural differences in the development of measured intelligence. (24 marks)
5. Discuss **one or more** theories of the development of moral understanding. (24 marks)
6. Critically consider the influence of gender and cultural variation on moral development. (24 marks)

Examination Tips

Question 1. "Discuss" is an AO1 and AO2 term. The words "applications" and "theories" are both plural and therefore you must cover more than one application (although the applications may just concern education) and more than one theory. Evaluation may be achieved through reference to research studies but may also involve comparisons between the differing theoretical perspectives.

Question 2. Vygotsky's theory of cognitive development is explicitly named in the specification (as is Piaget's theory and the information-processing approach), thus it is legitimate to specifically ask for a description of one of these theories/approaches. In part (a) you should aim for a balance between depth and breadth (i.e., cover a number of aspects of the theory, but not as a "shopping list"; detail is required). In part (b) you are given some guidance about evaluation but can include other considerations, such as practical applications and methodological/logical flaws.

Question 3. When describing studies you can use the same guidelines as for AS level: write something about the aims, procedures, findings, and conclusions. Criticisms of such studies will not be creditworthy here as part (a) is AO1 marks only. The studies selected must illustrate the role of genetic factors but you do not need to explain this link as that is the topic for part (b). Since the second part is AO2 you must ensure that you are presenting an argument about the role of genetic factors and using research studies to support this argument. You should not offer any further *descriptions* of research studies.

Question 4. This essay requires consideration of both nature and nurture. It is not explicitly required that you use research studies and, given the potential breadth of the material, you may do better to limit your descriptions of such studies and emphasise the arguments for each position. The essay asks about the role of genetics/cultural differences not the evidence to support this, though such evidence may form part of your *critical* consideration. You will need to be selective in order to compose a well-structured and well-detailed response in 30 minutes. Marks will be lost if you try to cover too much evidence and end up with an essay lacking in detail.

Question 5. In the specification there are no named theories for moral understanding, unlike the theories of cognitive development; Piaget and Kohlberg are given as "e.g."s. Therefore no question can be asked about a named theory. This essay offers you the opportunity to take the depth or breadth route—either lots of theories in minimal detail or few theories in more detail. For top marks you need to achieve a balance between depth and breadth. Evaluation can be achieved through contrasting different theories, a consideration of whether moral understanding is related to moral behaviour, reference to research studies and their methodological problems, gender bias in theories of moral understanding, and so on.

Question 6. "Critically consider" is an AO1 and AO2 term. You should consider/describe gender *and* cultural variation, and then evaluate the extent that such variations affect moral development. Support for your argument can be achieved through the use of research (theories and/or studies). It is possible to conclude that such variation actually has no effect (i.e., morals are universal), and this position should be explored as part of a balanced answer (the injunction "critically" requires a consideration of both the strengths and limitations of the argument).

WEBSITES

http://www.piaget.org
   The Jean Piaget Society.
http://www.funderstanding.com/vygotsky.cfm
   Information on the life and works of Lev Vygotsky.
http://www.indiana.edu/~intell/sternberg.shtml
   Website on Robert J. Sternberg, including video interviews with the cognitive psychologist himself on his theories on human intelligence and IQ testing.
http://www.allthetests.com/intelligence.php3
   Selection of intelligence tests.
http://www.vtaide.com/png/Kohlberg.htm
   Notes on Kohlberg's six stages of moral judgement.

DEVELOPMENTAL PSYCHOLOGY

Personality Development p.239

- What is personality?
- How sexual was Freud's psychosexual theory of personality development?
- Why do social learning theories suggest that people have no consistent personality?

Gender Development p.257

- How do we acquire a gender identity as we are learning gender role behaviours?
- Can a biological male be successfully reared as a female?
- What is a gender schema?

Adolescence p.275

- What is the main "task" for the adolescent?
- Are relationships with parents or peers more important in adolescence?
- How different would it be to be a teenager in Samoa?

Social and Personality Development

In this chapter we continue to look at the development of behaviours through childhood and into adolescence. A "big" question in psychology is how personality develops.

PERSONALITY DEVELOPMENT

What is Personality?

A definition that captures much of what psychologists mean by **personality** was provided by Child (1968, p.83). He described it as "more or less stable, internal factors that make one person's behaviour consistent from one time to another, and different from the behaviour other people would manifest in comparable situations".

As Hampson (1988) pointed out, the four key words in Child's definition are "stable", "internal", "consistent", and "different". According to Child's perspective, personality is relatively stable or unchanging over time; moods or emotional states may change dramatically over shortish periods of time, but personality does not; personality is internal, and must not be equated with external behaviour; behaviour (e.g., restlessness, lack of eye contact) is relevant, but only because it allows us to draw inferences about someone's underlying personality. If personality is moderately stable over time, and if personality determines behaviour, then it should follow that individuals will behave in a reasonably consistent fashion on different occasions. Finally, there are individual differences in personality, and these differences are revealed by different ways of behaving in a given situation. For example, extraverted people will talk more than introverted ones in a social group.

Freud's account of personality development remains highly influential, so we will start by examining this.

The Psychodynamic Approach

"Psychodynamic" refers to any approach that emphasises the processes of change and development, and moreover any theory that deals with the dynamics of behaviour (the things that drive us to behave in particular ways). Glassman

---

KEY TERM

Personality: semi-permanent internal predispositions that make people behave consistently, but in ways that differ from those of other people.

Sigmund Freud, 1856–1939.

(1995) points out that the psychodynamic approach is distinguished from the cognitive approach chiefly because of this element of motivation. The psychodynamic approach focuses on the role of internal processes (such as motivation) and of past experience shaping personality.

We owe the origins of the psychodynamic approach to Freud, who put forward what is often referred as psychoanalytic theory. However, since Freud's psychoanalytic theory is the best-known psychodynamic theory, we will use the term "psychodynamic" to refer to Freud's ideas as well as those who followed in his footsteps. We will also consider Erikson's psychosocial theory.

Freud's psychodynamic theory

Freud made many theoretical contributions to psychology including a theory of personality and a method of treatment for mental disorder (discussed in Chapter 9, Treating Mental Disorders). Sigmund Freud treated patients with mental disorders (especially neurotic illnesses) in Vienna in the late nineteenth century and first half of the twentieth century. Freud realised that the causes of most neurotic illnesses are psychological (e.g., anxiety created by worrying about future threats). His understanding of these psychological causes is revealed in his case studies, such as that of Anna O (see the Case Study below). Freud had the

---

CASE STUDY: ANNA O

Freud's theory was largely based on the observations he made during consultations with patients. He suggested that his work was similar to that of an archaeologist, who dug away layers of earth before uncovering what he was seeking. In a similar way, the psychiatrist seeks to dig down to the unconscious and discover the key to the individual's personality dynamic.

One of his patients was Anna O, a girl of 21 who had a high degree of intelligence. Her illness first appeared while she was caring for her father, whom she tenderly loved, during a severe illness that led to his death. Anna O developed a severe paralysis of both right extremities, disturbance of eye movements, an intense nausea when she attempted to take nourishment, and at one time for several weeks a loss of the power to drink, in spite of tormenting thirst. Freud's report explains how she occasionally became confused or delirious and mumbled several words to herself. If these same words were later repeated to her when she was in a hypnotic state, she would engage in deeply sad, often poetically beautiful, day dreams. These day dreams commonly took the situation of a girl beside the sick-bed of her father as their starting point. Anna O jokingly called this treatment "chimney sweeping". Freud's colleague Dr Breuer soon hit upon the fact that through such cleansing of the soul more could be accomplished than a temporary removal of the constantly recurring mental "clouds".

During one session, the patient recalled an occasion when she was with her governess, and how that lady's dog, that she abhorred, had drunk out of a glass. Out of respect for the conventions the patient had remained silent at the time of the incident, but now under hypnosis she gave energetic expression to her restrained anger, and then drank a large quantity of water without trouble, and woke from hypnosis with the glass at her lips. The symptom of being unable to drink thereupon vanished permanently.

Freud comments, "Permit me to dwell for a moment on this experience. No one had ever cured an hysterical symptom by such means before, or had come so near to understanding its cause. This would be a pregnant discovery if the expectation could be confirmed that still other, perhaps the majority of symptoms, originated in this way and could be removed by the same method.

"Such was indeed the case, almost all the symptoms originated in exactly this way, as we were to discover. The patient's illness originated at the time when she was caring for her sick father, and her symptoms could only be regarded as memory symbols of his sickness and death. While she was seated by her father's sick-bed, she was careful to betray nothing of her anxiety and her painful depression to the patient. When, later, she reproduced the same scene before the physician, the emotion that she had suppressed on the occurrence of the scene burst out with especial strength, as though it had been pent up all along.

"In her normal state she was entirely ignorant of the pathogenic scenes and of their connection with her symptoms. She had forgotten those scenes. When the patient was hypnotised, it was possible, after considerable difficulty, to recall those scenes to her memory, and by this means of recall the symptoms were removed."

Postscript: Anna O was actually Bertha Pappenheim. Jones (1953) claims that her recovery was not as successful as Breuer suggested. She had many relapses and was institutionalised for a while. In later life Bertha remained cool about psychoanalysis, refusing to allow the orphans she cared for to be treated by this method.

Adapted from Sigmund Freud (1910)
The origin and development of psychoanalysis.
American Journal of Psychology, 21, 181–218.

profound insight that neuroses could be treated effectively by psychological means, and he developed psychoanalysis as the first systematic psychological treatment for mental disorders.

Freud's case studies of pathological (diseased) behaviour led him to propose a theory of normal personality development. In particular, he suggested that adult personality is the result of an interaction between innate drives (such as the desire for pleasure) and early experience (the extent to which early desires were gratified). Freud proposed that individual differences in personality can be traced back to the way the early conflicts between desire and experience were handled (in the case of Anna O her conflicts arose when caring for her dying father). These conflicts remain with the adult and exert pressure through unconsciously motivated behaviour. In order to understand how these conflicts arise we first have to look at the structure of the personality.

The structure of the personality

Freud assumed that the mind is metaphorically divided into three parts. First, there is the **id**. This contains innate sexual and aggressive instincts, and is located in the unconscious mind. The sexual instinct is known as libido. The id works in accord with the **pleasure principle**, with the emphasis being on immediate satisfaction. Second, there is the **ego**. This is the conscious, rational mind, and it develops during the first 2 years of life. It works on the **reality principle**, taking

? To what extent do you think it is useful to create metaphorical concepts such as these? Are there associated dangers?

account of what is going on in the environment, i.e., in reality. Third, there is the **superego**. This develops at about the age of 5 and embodies the child's conscience and sense of right and wrong. It is formed when the child adopts many of the values of the same-sex parent (the process of identification discussed in Chapter 5, Cognitive Development).

Freud also assumed that there were three levels of the mind: the conscious, the preconscious, and the unconscious. The conscious consists of those thoughts currently the focus of attention. The preconscious consists of information and ideas that could be retrieved easily from memory and brought into consciousness. The unconscious consists of information that is either very hard or almost impossible to bring into conscious awareness.

Defence mechanisms

An important part of Freud's theory was the notion that there are frequent *conflicts* among the id, ego, and superego. Conflicts cause the individual to experience anxiety, and this leads the ego to devote much time to trying to resolve these conflicts. The ego protects itself by using a number of **defence mechanisms** (strategies designed to reduce anxiety) that contribute to the formation of adult personality.

KEY TERMS

Id: in Freudian theory that part of the mind containing the sexual instinct.

Pleasure principle: the drive to do things that produce pleasure or gratification.

Ego: the conscious, rational mind; one of the three main parts of the mind in Freud's theory.

Reality principle: Freud's explanation for the motivating force of the ego; it is a drive to accommodate the demands of the environment in a realistic way.

Superego: in Freudian theory, the part of the mind concerned with moral issues.

Defence mechanisms: strategies used by the ego to defend itself against anxiety.

What kinds of experience might be so upsetting that they are kept out of conscious awareness?

Some of the defences that contribute to the formation of adult personality include:

1. *Repression*. Keeping threatening thoughts out of consciousness. For example, a person may not remember a dental appointment because it is going to be painful.
2. *Displacement*. Unconsciously moving impulses away from a threatening object and towards a less threatening object. For example, someone who has been made angry by their boss may go home and kick the cat.
3. *Projection*. An individual may attribute their undesirable characteristics to others. For example, someone who is very unfriendly may accuse other people of being unfriendly.
4. *Denial*. Refusing to accept the existence or reality of a threatening event. For example, patients suffering from life-threatening diseases often deny that these diseases are affecting their lives.
5. *Intellectualisation*. Thinking about threatening events in ways that remove the emotion from them. An example would be responding to the sinking of a car ferry with considerable loss of life by thinking about ways of improving ferry design.

Anna Freud (1946) used the concept of ego defences to explain the development of personality. For example, "defences against instincts" are the result of developmental conflicts where a child learns defensive behaviours in order to control undesirable instinctive behaviours.

Psychosexual development

Freud described early personality development as a series of stages, where in each stage the child's energy or **libido** is focused on a body region. The term "libido" was Freud's word for the psychological and sexual energy produced by the id. When Freud used the word "sexual" he was *not* referring to sexuality as in sexual intercourse but rather to a more general physical and sensual arousal. According to Freud (1921), libido is "the energy . . . of those instincts which have to do with all that may be comprised under the word 'love' ".

These five stages are psychosexual because of this psychological and sexual energy.

1. *Oral stage*: this occurs during the first 18 months of life. During this stage, the infant obtains satisfaction from eating, sucking, and other activities using the mouth.
2. *Anal stage*: this occurs between about 18 and 36 months of age. Toilet training occurs during this stage, which may cause conflict.
3. *Phallic stage*: this occurs between 3 and 6 years of age. The genitals become a key source of satisfaction during this stage. At about the age of 5, boys acquire the **Oedipus complex**, in which they have sexual desires for their mother and therefore want to get rid of their father who is a rival (see Chapter 5, Cognitive Development). They then also fear their father who might realise what they are thinking. This complex is resolved by identification with their father, involving adopting many of their father's attitudes and developing a superego. Freud argued that girls come to recognise that they don't have a

KEY TERMS

Libido: Freud's term for the psychological energy that is associated with sexual drives. At each stage of psychosexual development, the libido becomes focused on a part of the body.

Oedipus complex: in Freudian theory, the notion that young boys desire their mother sexually and so experience rivalry with their father.

penis and blame their mother for this. The girl's father now becomes her love-object and she substitutes her "penis-envy" with a wish to have a child. These desires threaten the girl's relationship with her mother, and so she identifies with the mother.

4. *Latency stage*: this lasts from 6 years of age until the onset of puberty. During this stage, boys and girls spend very little time together.

5. *Genital stage*: this starts from the onset of puberty and continues throughout adult life. During this stage, the main source of sexual pleasure is in the genitals.

> Note that the term "sexual" is roughly equivalent to "physical pleasure".

FREUD'S STAGES OF PSYCHOSEXUAL DEVELOPMENT

Stage	Approximate age	Summary
Oral	0–18 months	Satisfaction from eating, sucking, etc.
Anal	18–36 months	Interest in and satisfaction from anal region
Phallic	3–6 years	Genitals become source of satisfaction
Latency	6 years old to puberty	Boys and girls spend little time together
Genital	From onset of puberty	Genitals are main source of sexual pleasure

---

Personality development

In a sense there are three strands to Freud's theory of personality development: the structure of the personality (id, ego, and superego), defence mechanisms, and stages of psychosexual development. Personality itself develops as an outcome of these three strands. If a child experiences severe problems or excessive pleasure at any stage of development, this leads to **fixation**, in which basic energy or libido becomes attached to that stage for many years. Later in life, adults who experience very stressful conditions are likely to show **regression**, in which their behaviour becomes less mature and like that displayed during a psychosexual stage at which they fixated as children. According to Freud, these processes of fixation and regression play important roles in determining adult personality.

Some personality types are shown in the diagram below, along with descriptions and a link to the stage of psychosexual development at which

> **Useful mnemonic**
>
> To help you remember Freud's stages of psychosexual development, the following mnemonic is made from the initial letter of each stage: Old Age Pensioners Love Greens!

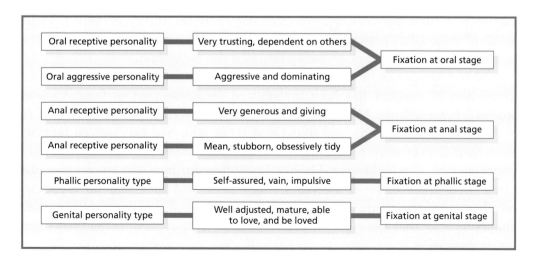

Freud's personality types.

> **KEY TERMS**
>
> **Fixation:** in Freud's theory, spending a long time at a given stage of development because of problems or excessive gratification.
> **Regression:** returning to earlier stages of development when severely stressed.

fixation may have occurred. As you can see, each stage (with the exception of the latency stage) is associated with one or two personality types. There are links between the main activities at any given stage and the personality type or types associated with it. For example, toilet training occurs during the anal stage. Some children in this stage will be difficult and try to retain their faeces, whereas others will do their best to defecate as quickly as possible to please their parents. The former are likely to develop an anal retentive personality whereas the latter will tend to develop an anal receptive personality.

Case studies

Freud's theory was based on the data he collected in his interactions with patients. He never made any notes during a therapeutic session, feeling that any lack of attention during therapy would interfere with its progress and believing that he would be able to record all the important details afterwards. It is likely that these notes were biased by his own expectations and selective recall. In fact, Freud recorded only a very few case histories such as those of Anna O, described earlier, and Little Hans (see page 376).

What problems might arise in using retrospective data?

Little Hans was an unusual case study because it was the only one involving a child, which highlights the fact that Freud's account of child development was almost entirely based on retrospective accounts. It was also, as we have noted, a theory of normal development based on observations of pathological behaviour.

Other research evidence

Much evidence supports Freud's general point that childhood experiences influence the development of human adult personality. For example, Franz et al. (1996) found that adult levels of depression at the age of 41 were predicted well by parental coldness when they were only 5 years old. In addition, an overall measure of difficult childhood experiences (e.g., divorce, frequent moves, death of a parent) predicted depression in middle age. Of course, this doesn't prove that the details of Freud's theory of psychosexual development are correct.

There is support for some of the personality types identified by Freud. For example, Kline and Storey (1977) found the three main characteristics of the anal retentive character (stubbornness, meanness, orderliness) were often found together in the same person. There is also evidence that some people possess all the characteristics of the oral aggressive character (Kline, 1981). Evidence for the existence of these personality types does *not* show the theory is correct. Freud assumed these adult personality types depend on specific childhood experiences, but there is practically no convincing evidence this is the case.

Other evidence can be used to support Freud's theory. The topic of repression in relation to memory has been investigated (and was part of your AS level studies). For example, Myers and Brewin (1994) asked female participants to recall childhood memories and found that those who had experienced hostility from their fathers were most likely to repress such memories. In another study, young women who had received hospital treatment for incidents involving sexual abuse were tracked down 17 years later—38% said they had no conscious recollection of the events for which they were treated (Williams, 1994). Both studies indicate that some people deal with anxiety by repressing the events that create anxiety.

Freud's work was largely with middle-class women in Vienna in the 1890s and 1900s. How relevant do you think his ideas are to other cultures, particularly given the social changes since then?

Evaluation of psychodynamic theory

Freud was absolutely correct in arguing that adult personality depends in part on the experiences of early childhood. He also has the distinction of having put forward probably the first systematic theory of personality. Another plus point is that there is evidence for the id and ego. For example, Freud argued that dreams often involve sexual encounters because the libido is freed from the constraints of the ego. Solms (2000) found with brain-damaged patients that dreaming was eliminated when there was damage to a motivational system resembling the libido. Solms also discussed brain-imaging evidence showing that the rational parts of the brain (resembling the ego) are relatively inactive during dreaming, whereas the forebrain (a central part of the motivational system) is very active. Finally, at least some of the personality types identified by Freud (e.g., anal retentive character) seem to exist.

There are several points on the negative side. First, it is hard to establish accurately what childhood experiences any given adult has had, but this needs to be done to test the theory. Second, it is even harder to prove that early childhood experiences have actually influenced the development of adult personality many years later. Third, as Westen and Gabbard (1999) pointed out, "Psychoanalysts seriously shoot themselves in the foot by never evolving from case study methods [based on individual patients] as their primary mode of knowledge generation and hypothesis testing". Fourth, Freud exaggerated the importance of sex as *the* major motivational force, perhaps because he developed his theory at a time of great sexual repression. Understandably this may have caused sex to be something that was repressed in many minds (Banyard & Hayes, 1994). A number of neo-Freudians (e.g., Erik Erikson) have emphasised social rather than sexual influences.

? Considering that Freud was working in a strict Victorian society, why was sexual behaviour so strongly emphasised in his theory of development?

Erikson's psychosocial theory

Erikson's (1959) starting point was the notion that conflicts between the natural processes of maturation and the expectations of society create various crises that the child must try to resolve. Erikson's theory of psychosocial development resembled Freud's theory of psychosexual development in some ways (e.g., stage-based

PSYCHOSOCIAL DEVELOPMENT—ERIKSON'S STAGES 1–8						
Stage	Age	Name	Life crisis	Positive characteristics	Negative characteristics	Social focus
1	0–1	Infancy	Trust vs. mistrust	Trust in self and others	Mistrust in self and others	Mother
2	2–3	Toddler	Autonomy vs. shame	Becoming independent	Sense of shame and doubt	Parents
3	4–5	Preschool	Initiative vs. guilt	Shows initiative	Experiences guilt	Family
4	6–12	Childhood	Industry vs. inferiority	Shows industry	Sense of inferiority	School, friends, home
5	13–19	Adolescence	Identity vs. role confusion	Identity	Role confusion	Peer group
6	20–30	Early adulthood	Intimacy vs. isolation	Intimacy	Isolation	Friends
7	30–60	Middle adulthood	Generativity vs. stagnation	Generativity	Stagnation	Household
8	60+	Old age	Integrity vs. despair	Wisdom	Despair	Humankind

approach; notion that we have an ego, id, and superego), but its emphasis was much more on the role of social factors and on the development of the ego. There are eight stages of psychosocial development. Everyone goes through these stages in the same order, but people vary enormously in terms of how successfully they cope with each stage. Each stage has possible positive and negative outcomes associated with it; children who have negative outcomes have to deal with their unresolved crises later in life.

The eight stages are outlined in the box above, and the first four are described in detail.

- *Stage 1.* Infancy (0–1 year): the infant develops either trust *or* mistrust in itself and others; the mother or mother figure is the central person in the child's life.
- *Stage 2.* Toddler (2–3 years): the child either becomes more independent *or* has a sense of shame and doubt. Erikson (1959, p.102) described "the sinister forces which are leashed and unleashed, especially in the guerrilla warfare of unequal wills; for the child is often unequal to his own violent drives, and parent and child unequal to each other". The parents are the central figures.
- *Stage 3.* Preschool (4–5 years): the child shows initiative *or* experiences guilt. According to Erikson (1959, p.74), "Being firmly convinced that he *is* a person, the child must now find out *what kind* of a person he is going to be . . . he wants to be like his parents, who to him appear very powerful and beautiful, although quite unreasonably dangerous". The family is of central importance.
- *Stage 4.* Childhood (6–12 years): the child shows industry and works hard *or* develops a sense of inferiority. According to Erikson (1959, p.82), the child's approach during this stage is, "I am what I learn". This learning takes place

at school and in friends' houses as well as at home, because the child's social world is expanding.

Children generally show a mixture of the positive and negative outcomes identified here. For example, most infants in stage 1 develop some trust as well as some mistrust. Children for whom the outcomes of each stage are mainly positive develop a stronger and more positive sense of self than children for whom most of the outcomes are negative.

Research evidence

Erikson relied heavily on clinical evidence to provide support for his theory, gathered in his work as a practising therapist. Although such evidence can indicate that a theory is on the right lines, it is generally too anecdotal and imprecise to confirm the theory's details. However, there is some experimental evidence providing indirect support for aspects of Erikson's theory. For example, Erikson argued that trust was a positive outcome of stage 1, whereas mistrust was a negative outcome. The work of Ainsworth on attachment behaviour is relevant (examined in your AS level studies). Ainsworth and Bell (1970) identified three forms of attachment of an infant to its mother. Secure attachment, which is most useful for the infant's psychological development, involves a high level of trust. In contrast, the less desirable resistant attachment and avoidant attachment both involve mistrust and anxiety.

Erikson's general notion that the development of the self during stage 4 (ages 6–12) is increasingly influenced by friends and by schoolmates has received support in the work of Damon and Hart (1988). They asked children of different ages to describe themselves and found that children between the ages of 8 and 11 are much more likely than those between 4 and 7 to describe themselves in comparison with other children. The older children also tended to use more internal, psychological terms to describe themselves, whereas younger children focused on visible and tangible properties and possessions to define themselves, such as "I've got black hair" rather than "I'm a kind person".

> **?** What are the major drawbacks of using mainly clinical evidence to formulate a theory, as Erikson did?

Evaluation

Erikson's psychosocial theory possesses various significant strengths. First, its focus on social processes and the development of the ego greatly enlarged the scope of psychodynamic theory. Second, the notion that children face a series of conflicts or crises, with the consequences for their sense of self depending on how well these conflicts are resolved, is a valuable one. Third, Erikson would seem to be correct in arguing that most of the conflicts experienced by infants lie within the family, whereas later conflicts (e.g., in stage 4) spread out to include school and peers.

There are several limitations of the theory. As Miller (1993, p.172) pointed out:

> *Erikson's theory does not explain in any detail how a child moves from stage to stage or even how he resolves the crisis within a stage. It states what influences the movement (for example, physical maturation, parents, cultural beliefs, to what extent earlier crises were resolved), but not specifically how the movement comes about.*

Second, there is little convincing evidence for Erikson's theory. As Dworetzky (1996, p.369) pointed out:

> *hard scientific proof for Erikson's theory is not easy to come by because of the difficulty of examining each of Erikson's stages under controlled laboratory conditions or by other scientific methods.*

The point is that some theories simply do not lend themselves to the kind of research where cause and effect relationships can be indicated. Erikson's emphasis on individual experience rather than observable behaviour means that it has proved quite difficult to test in a scientific manner.

Third, one reason why it is hard to test Erikson's theory is because most of the evidence is correlational. For example, suppose we find that children who show signs of independence at stage 2 develop a stronger sense of self in later childhood than those who do not. This does not prove that independence at stage 2 *caused* a strong sense of self.

Fourth, there is a danger with any stage theory that it presents far too tidy an account of what happens. For example, a conflict between trust and mistrust is said to be central only to the first stage of development, but it could well be argued that this conflict keeps recurring through most people's lives. This may be especially true nowadays when millions of people change jobs and partners far more often than used to be the case.

Social Learning Approaches

A contrasting approach to the explanation of personality is to consider development purely from the point of view of social interactions. Both Freud and Erikson involved social factors in their account; however, the key to the psychodynamic approach was the explanation of how these external factors interact with internal development. The social learning approach is almost entirely lodged in external social experiences.

Social learning theory

Social learning theory proposes that all behaviour is the consequence of conditioning: direct or indirect. Classical and operant conditioning theories explain learning as the consequence of association or reinforcement respectively. Social learning theory extended this to include indirect, or vicarious reinforcement. Personality is learned in the same way as everything else is learned.

Consider the following example. One aspect of personality is humour. A child may tell a joke to a circle of friends and find that they all laugh along with him. This is rewarding and thus increases the likelihood that the child will tell the joke again. If, however, the joke raises no laughter but instead the other children tease him for being little use at telling jokes, then the child is less likely to repeat this behaviour. Thus we have the elements of direct reinforcement (reward) and punishment (decreases the likelihood of a behaviour being repeated).

To continue the example, the same child may watch someone else telling a joke—successfully getting laughs from everyone. This may lead the child to imitate the behaviour of the successful joke teller. This is called vicarious reinforcement. The child observed someone else's behaviour being rewarded and this encouraged him to model his own behaviour on the successful behaviour.

? According to Erikson, what is the main "cause" of personality development?

EXAM HINT
There is a lot of theoretical content on Freud so make sure you are selective. Also, if you are asked for two or more theories use social learning theory rather than the neo-Freudian theory or Erikson's theory, to bring more breadth to your answer.

If their father responds with humour to their practical joke, these children will experience direct reinforcement, and are likely to repeat this behaviour in the future!

The key elements of social learning are observation, vicarious reinforcement, and modelling or imitation. The essential difference between social learning and learning theory is that the former includes *indirect* learning, which means that cognitive factors must be involved. In order to recall a behaviour to be modelled there must be some internal representation of this model. Traditional learning theory specifically rejected the use of cognitive factors in explanations of behaviour. The essence of social learning theory was expressed as follows by Albert Bandura (1977, p.12):

> *Virtually all learning phenomena resulting from experience occur on a vicarious [second-hand] basis by observing other people's behaviour and its consequences for them. The capacity to learn by observation enables people to acquire large, integrated patterns of behaviour without having to form them gradually by tedious trial and error.*

The origins of social learning theory lie in the work of Bandura (b.1925). In the 1950s, he was conducting research into adolescent aggression and felt that learning theory was too simplistic as an explanation for the phenomena that he was observing. Consider the description of his early experiments on aggression that is given in the box below.

Observational learning

Of the hundreds of studies Bandura was responsible for, one group stands out above the others—the Bobo doll studies. He made a film of one of his students, a young woman, essentially beating up a Bobo doll. In case you don't know, a Bobo doll is an inflatable, egg-shaped balloon creature with a weight in the bottom that makes it bob back up when you knock it down. Nowadays, it might have Darth Vader painted on it, but back then it was simply "Bobo" the clown.

The woman punched the clown, shouting "sockeroo!" She kicked it, sat on it, hit it with a little hammer, and so on, shouting various aggressive phrases. Bandura showed his film to groups of kindergartners who, as you might predict, liked it a lot. They then were let out to play. In the playroom, of course, were several observers with pens and clipboards in hand, a brand new Bobo doll, and a few little hammers.

And you might predict as well what the observers recorded: a lot of little kids beating the daylights out of the Bobo doll. They punched it and shouted "sockeroo", kicked it, sat on it, hit it with the little hammers, and so on. In other words, they imitated the young lady in the film, and quite precisely at that.

This might seem like a real nothing of an experiment at first, but consider: these children changed their behaviour without first being rewarded for approximations to that behaviour! And while that may not seem extraordinary to the average parent, teacher, or casual observer of children, it didn't fit so well with standard behaviouristic learning theory. Bandura called the phenomenon observational learning or modelling, and his theory is usually called social learning theory.

From http://www.ship.edu/~cgboeree/bandura.html

Bandura's Bobo doll study emphasised the importance of observation and imitation as part of the learning process.

Steps in the modelling process

Bandura suggested that there are four steps in the modelling process:

1. *Attention.* If you are going to learn anything, you have to be paying attention. Certain characteristics of the model influence attention. If the model is attractive, or prestigious, or appears to be particularly competent, you will pay more attention. And if the model seems more like yourself, you pay more

attention. Parents, peers, and the media are obvious models that command attention.

2. *Retention*. It is obvious that the model must be remembered and recalled. This stage requires reference to cognitive processes.

3. *Reproduction*. You may observe someone telling a joke well but that doesn't mean you can imitate it. Imitation requires personal skills. An interesting feature of imitation is that just imagining oneself doing the activity can improve performance. Athletes, for example, improve their own performance through imagination as well as direct practice.

4. *Motivation*. Finally you need to be motivated to perform the action, which depends on direct and indirect reinforcements and punishments. The first part of the equation is that you observe a behaviour (observational learning) but, after that the likelihood you will repeat it is related to vicarious reinforcement or punishment.

Two specific aspects of social learning theory as developed by Bandura (1977, 1986) help to explain personality development. These are the concepts of reciprocal determination and self-efficacy. Learning is influenced by self-regulation (reciprocal determinism)—we use our cognitive processes to regulate and control our own behaviour, often giving ourselves self-rewards if we achieve a good level of performance. Learning is also affected by self-efficacy—our beliefs about how well we will cope with various situations or tasks.

Reciprocal determinism

According to learning theory and conditioning theories generally, we are shaped by external factors (e.g., external rewards and punishments), and these lead us to behave in predictable ways. However, Bandura stressed that social learning theory does *not* represent the individual as a helpless victim of circumstance. Nor did Bandura subscribe to the idea that one can somehow add up internal and external factors and thus explain personality. Bandura felt this was an oversimplification and that it was the *interaction* that was all important (1973, p.43):

> The environment is only a potentiality, not a fixed property that inevitably impinges on individuals and to which their behaviour eventually adapts. Behaviour partly creates the environment and the resultant environment, in turn influences the behaviour.

KEY TERM

Reciprocal determinism: Bandura's concept that what one learns is affected by one's characteristics (personality, beliefs, and cognitive abilities). Personality isn't simply determined by the environment, but the individual also shapes the environment.

Bandura (1977, 1986) called this interaction **reciprocal determinism**. The personal characteristics of an individual influence what they select to do in the social environment. These characteristics include personality, beliefs, and cognitive abilities, and these will then determine who a person chooses to spend time with, what kind of activities they take part in, and what they avoid. These selections then, in turn, affect what skills and behaviours are reinforced and what ultimately is learned. An aggressive child, for example, may find that this behaviour is rewarding because the child gets to play with a certain toy. Increased aggressiveness will further shape the child's environment because it may discourage certain other children from playing with the aggressive child. It may just be other aggressive children who maintain the friendship and this will shape the original child's continuing behaviour. People are both products of and producers of their environment.

Self-efficacy

Bandura also stressed the effect of an individual's perceived abilities on his or her learning. This sense of perceived effectiveness is called **self-efficacy**. It is the individual's perception or assessment of his/her ability to cope satisfactorily with given situations. According to Bandura (1977, p.391), self-efficacy judgements are concerned "not with the skills one has but with judgements of what one can do with the skills one possesses".

An individual's sense of self-efficacy in any given situation depends on four factors:

1. That individual's previous experiences of success and/or failure in that situation.
2. Relevant vicarious experiences, based on observing someone else cope successfully or unsuccessfully with the situation; this is observational learning.
3. Verbal (or social) persuasion: your feelings of self-efficacy may increase if someone argues persuasively that you have the skills needed to succeed in that situation.
4. Emotional arousal: high levels of arousal are often associated with anxiety and failure, and can serve to reduce feelings of self-efficacy.

? What other effects might high levels of emotional arousal have, for example, in a competitive sports situation?

Research evidence

There is much evidence from studies of children to show the importance of observational learning. Children who see someone else (the model) behave aggressively and being rewarded for this show observational learning, in that they then behave aggressively themselves (Rosekrans & Hartup, 1967). Those children who see the aggressive model punished do not behave aggressively because of the potential threat of punishment.

A child who has previously been successful in a situation is more likely to expect to succeed again, whereas one who has previously done poorly may be reluctant to put in much effort or show much interest.

> **KEY TERM**
>
> **Self-efficacy:** an individual's assessment of his or her ability to cope with given situations.

? What might result is some people underestimating their abilities?

In a general sense, Bandura's approach leads to the prediction that children should develop more "selves" as they develop friendships with more people. Relevant evidence was reported by Harter and Monsour (1992). They asked children of 12, 14, and 16 to describe themselves with their parents, with their friends, and at school. Among the 12-year-olds, about one-third of the attributes they used to describe themselves in their relationship with their parents were also used to describe themselves with friends and at school. In contrast, 16-year-olds tended to describe themselves very differently in the three situations, suggesting that they had developed a number of selves.

The importance of self-efficacy has been shown numerous times. Stajkovic and Luthans (1998) combined the findings from 114 studies concerned with the relationship between self-efficacy and work-related performance. The average correlation between self-efficacy and performance was +0.38, meaning that those high in self-efficacy had significantly better performance than those low in self-efficacy.

Kitsantas (2000) studied the effects of self-efficacy and of self-regulation in overweight students who had failed to lose weight and previously overweight students who had managed to lose weight. Those students who had lost weight had greater self-efficacy than those who had not. In addition, those who had lost weight used more self-regulation strategies (e.g., planning how much weight to lose; monitoring their weight; seeking help from others) than those who remained overweight.

Evaluation

An important difference between Bandura's social learning theory and other theories is the notion that people possess more and more different "selves" as they experience an increasing number of situations and activities. There is no strong evidence, but Bandura (1986) may well be right that our sense of a single, integrated self is an illusion. Bandura emphasises the importance of observational learning, self-efficacy, and self-regulation as factors influencing behaviour, and there is convincing evidence that all of these factors are of real importance.

There are various limitations with the social learning theory approach. First, it isn't specifically a *developmental* theory—Bandura doesn't spell out in detail how children's personality changes in the course of development. Second, the emphasis is too much on cognitive factors and not enough on emotional ones— much human motivation and behaviour is influenced by our emotions rather than by cool calculation. Third, As Hergenhahn and Olson (1999, p.12) pointed out, "Little is said in social learning theory about the biological, hormonal, or maturational influences on personality development". Fourth, Bandura has focused mainly on predicting and understanding people's behaviour in *specific* situations rather than in broad areas of life. As a result, it is not clear that his theory provides much understanding of individual differences in personality. Indeed, Bandura is sceptical of the notion of personality (see below).

Situationalism and Mischel

Bandura suggested that personality isn't a stable trait of an individual. This was apparently supported by Mischel (1968). He found that personality measures rarely correlated more than about +0.30 with behaviour in any given situation. Mischel concluded that personality predicts behaviour poorly, and that behaviour is overwhelmingly determined by the situation in which the individual finds himself/herself. Strangely, however, Mischel didn't actually assess how important the situation is in determining behaviour! When this was done by Sarason, Smith, and Diener (1975) in an analysis of numerous studies, it turned out that individual differences in behaviour were determined only slightly more by the situation than by personality. In a sense, the real problem is that psychologists don't fully understand which factors cause individuals to behave differently from each other in different situations!

Mischel and Peake's (1982) theory referred to the "consistency paradox", the intuitive belief that people are consistent across situations; a belief that stems from our tendency to categorise everything. However, research has failed to show this consistency. Mischel and Peake confirmed this inconsistency in a study where different individuals were asked to rate the behaviour of 63 students in various situations. The observers were asked to focus on their conscientiousness, and included family and friends of the students plus unknown observers. Mischel and Peake found almost zero correlation in behaviour ratings (i.e., personality) between the different situations.

Mischel (1968) argued instead that individuals exhibit *behavioural specificity*, that is their behaviour is specific to certain situations. In fact their behaviour is determined by the situation because it is reinforced for that situation. An individual will behave aggressively in one situation and meekly in another depending on the reinforcements received. This is *selective reinforcement*.

Mischel (1968) pointed out that the reason we may think that personality is consistent is because we tend to see people in similar situations and therefore they appear to be consistent. People offer excuses for why they are sometimes inconsistent, such as saying, "I'm usually very punctual but when it's raining it throws me off". One advantage of Mischel's theory, therefore, is that he can explain personality inconsistency.

> **?** Mischel suggested that our different selves are related to different situations. Bandura also suggested that each individual has different selves, but suggested an alternative source. What is it?

Person variables

Mischel (1993) suggests that there are important individual differences in the way we think and therefore learn, and this inevitably leads to differences in personality development. For example, if you put two people in the same situation they actually behave differently. It is not simply the situation that affects behaviour but the individual's prior learning experience. Mischel calls these differences **person variables**, the product of the individual's total history that in turn mediates the manner in which new experiences affect him/her.

1. *Cognitive and behavioural construction competencies.* What can you do? This refers to an individual's ability to construct particular cognitions and behaviour. These competencies are related to an individual's past experiences (e.g., the way an individual resolves conflicts will be based on what they have used and found effective in the past).
2. *Encoding strategies and personal constructs.* How do you see it? The selective attention, interpretation, and categorisation of events substantially alter the impact of any stimulus on behaviour. This helps to explain why two people having the same experience see it differently. For example, a middle-aged person may find it offensive when a famous actor swears on television, whereas a teenager may find it amusing.

> **KEY TERM**
>
> **Person variables:** the ways that people differ, such as beliefs and cognitive abilities.

3. *Expectancies.* What will happen? Specific expectancies about the consequences of different behaviours in a specific situation are developed on the basis of direct experience, instructions, and observational learning. For example, we are much more confident of succeeding in situations in which we have succeeded in the past than in situations in which we have failed.

4. *Subjective stimulus values.* What is it worth? What are your goals? Individuals decide whether to perform a specific behaviour based on the given value of the outcome. This value system develops on the basis of direct experience, instructions, and observational learning. For example, a person who values peace and solitude will be more attracted by someone who likes walks in the country than someone who likes shopping.

5. *Self-regulatory systems and plans.* How can you achieve it? A person regulates his/her own behaviour by self-imposed goals or standards and self-produced consequences. For example, a girl working in a shop who hopes to become a manageress might report that other employees are pilfering, whereas another shop girl who hates the store and intends to quit soon might keep quiet.

Evaluation

The notion that the situation has a large effect on behaviour gains support from studies of context-dependent learning as examined in your AS level studies (e.g., Abernethy, 1940). There is no doubt that people do learn things in relation to contexts, and that we cannot predict very accurately how an individual with a given personality will behave in a given situation (e.g., Mischel, 1968; Mischel & Peake, 1982).

However, people do generalise learning from one situation to another, which suggests that not all aspects of our personality are situation-specific. If this were the case we would have a sense of fragmentation, whereas most individuals feel a unity about themselves. It appears that a sense of unified self is important to mental health.

It should be noted that people's behaviour appears inconsistent when we consider small and unreliable pieces of behaviour, but can become much more consistent when extended samples of behaviour are used. For example, Epstein (1977) correlated ratings of sociability based on two samples of behaviour. When each sample was only 1 day in duration, the correlation was only +0.37, but this increased to +0.81 when each sample was 14 days in duration.

An important reason for believing that there are genuine differences in personality comes from studies in which an individual's self-assessment of his/her personality is compared with the ratings provided by others who know that individual well. When this is done, there is reasonable agreement on that individual's personality between the individual himself/herself and the raters (e.g., McCrae & Costa, 1990).

SECTION SUMMARY
Personality Development

What is personality?

❖ Personality consists of stable, internal, and consistent characteristics that make each of us different.

❖ According to the psychodynamic approach, personality can be shaped by:

— Internal processes such as motivation
— Past experience.

❖ Freud developed a theory of personality (psychoanalytic theory) as a way to explain pathological (unhealthy) behaviour.

❖ The personality consists of the id, ego, and superego:

— The id and ego are often in conflict because they are driven by the opposing pleasure and reality principles.
— Conflicts cause the individual to experience anxiety.
— The ego protects itself against anxiety using defence mechanisms such as repression, displacement, projection, denial, and intellectualisation.

❖ So Freud concluded: innate drives interact with early experiences and may produce conflicts that lead to unhealthy behaviours.

Freud's psychodynamic approach

❖ Psychosexual development is the attachment of the libido (child's energy) to various body regions at different stages of development:

— Oral stage
— Anal stage
— Phallic stage: important in moral development and includes the Oedipus (Electra) complex, which leads to identification
— Latency stage
— Genital stage.

Psychosexual development

❖ Personality development is the consequence of over- or undergratification at any stage, leading to a fixation (libido attached to that stage).

❖ Anxiety later in life leads to regression to a previously fixated stage.

❖ Freud based his theory on the following research:

— Case studies of adults, women, and disturbed individuals
— Extensive self-analysis
— Studies of repression (motivated forgetting)
— Perceptual defence.

Research evidence for the psychodynamic approach

❖ Evaluation:

— Rather weak research support based on a unique group of individuals.
— Case histories produce rich data but can be biased.
— But Freud's emphasis on childhood and on the unconscious has endured.
— His overemphasis on sexual forces may be a reflection of his historical period.

❖ Erikson focused on the role of social factors in development.

❖ He outlined eight stages of development, where there are conflicts to be resolved at each stage for healthy development:

— Trust vs. mistrust
— Autonomy vs. shame

Erikson's psychosocial theory

— Initiative vs. guilt
— Industry vs. inferiority
— Identity vs. role confusion
— Intimacy vs. isolation
— Generativity vs. stagnation
— Integrity vs. despair.

❖ Resolution does not mean that one or the other extreme is developed; individuals generally experience a mixture of each outcome.

Research evidence for the psychosocial theory

❖ Research support comes from:

— Erikson's clinical studies
— Attachment research that indicates the importance of trust
— Studies that show how peers influence self-development.

❖ Evaluation:

— The focus on social processes enlarged the scope of psychodynamic theory, and the notion of crises has been useful.
— However, the theory does not explain how crises are resolved nor is the research evidence very convincing. It is rather too tidy an account to be realistic.

The social learning approach

❖ This focuses on external social influences on the development of personality.
❖ Social learning theory explains learning in terms of direct and indirect reinforcement. Personality is learned like everything else.
❖ Social learning incorporated cognitive explanations by suggesting that we model our behaviour on others and therefore need an internal representation of that behaviour.
❖ Bandura suggested:

— There are four steps in the modelling process: attention, retention, reproduction, and motivation.
— Personality develops as an interaction: people are both products of and producers of their environment (reciprocal determination).
— An individual's sense of perceived effectiveness (self-efficacy) also influences personality development: previous experiences, relevant vicarious experiences, persuasion, and emotional arousal all create self-efficacy.

❖ Evaluation:

— Well supported by research evidence
— But the theory would predict that individuals should develop multiple selves—which is not congruent with personal experience. (However, it may be that our sense of a single, integrated self is an illusion.)
— Social learning theory is not truly a developmental theory.

Situationalism and Mischel

❖ This theory expands on the notion that there is no consistency in self or personality: personality is not stable.
❖ Mischel proposed:

— We think people are consistent because we often see them in similar situations (the "consistency paradox").

— Individuals exhibit behaviour specific to certain situations (behavioural specificity).

— We learn to behave differently in different situations because of selective reinforcement.

— There are five person variables that are influenced by experience and influence learning: construction competencies, encoding strategies, expectancies, subjective stimulus values, and self-regulatory systems and plans. These jointly explain how personality develops.

❖ Evaluation:

— This theory is supported by research into context-dependent learning.

— However, the notion of a fragmented self is allied to mental disorder; we need to have a sense of unity in our personality to function effectively.

See also pages 133–142 of the revision guide.

GENDER DEVELOPMENT

What is Gender?

When a baby is born, the key question everyone asks is, "Is it a boy or a girl?" As the baby develops, the ways in which it is treated by its parents and other people are influenced by its **sex**. In the fullness of time, the growing child's thoughts about itself and its place in the world are likely to depend in part on whether it is male or female. Here we are concerned with some of these issues.

It is important to note that some of these terms used in this section are fairly closely related to each other. For example, most children develop a gender identity during the early years of childhood in which they have an increasing awareness of being male or female. In order to have a full sense of being male or female, it is necessary to be aware of the kinds of expectations that others have about the ways in which males and females should think and behave (this is gender role). Thus, in practice gender identity and gender role tend to be found together in most children.

Observed Gender Differences

Fixed **gender stereotypes** are in decline. Few people accept any more that men should go out to work and have little to do with looking after the home and the children, whereas women should stay at home and concern themselves only with the cleaning and children. However (regrettably) many stereotypes still exist. It is important to consider the actual behaviour of boys and girls. Do the sexes really differ in their behaviour?

One of the most comprehensive studies of sex differences (and quite an old one) was conducted by Eleanor Maccoby and Carol Jacklin (1974). They reviewed over 1500 studies of sex differences and concluded that there were only four significant differences between boys and girls for which there was convincing evidence:

- Girls have greater verbal ability than boys; this difference has been found at most ages during childhood.
- Boys have greater visual and spatial abilities than girls.
- Boys have greater arithmetical ability than girls, but this difference only appears during adolescence.
- Boys are more aggressive than girls physically and verbally. This may have been true in 1974, but more recent research indicates that girls are often more aggressive verbally than boys.

KEY TERMS

Sex: the biological fact of being male or female as determined by a pair of chromosomes.
Gender stereotypes: the social perception of a man or a woman based on beliefs about gender roles.

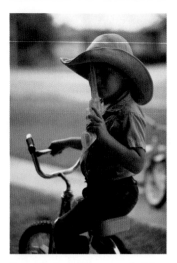

Boys playing with guns—is this nature or nurture?

Golombok and Hines (2002) reviewed sex differences in the first 2 years of life. Girl infants tend to stay closer to adults than do boy infants, but boys are more upset by situations outside their control than are girls. In addition, girls on average learn to talk at an earlier age than boys. Shaffer (1993) pointed out some other **gender** differences in behaviour later in childhood. Girls show more emotional sensitivity than boys. For example, girls from the age of about 5 are more interested than boys in babies, and respond more attentively to them. Girls have less developmental vulnerability than boys, with more boys showing mental retardation, language disorders, and hyperactivity.

Most observed differences between boys and girls are modest. However, there are large sex differences in A-level performance. In a report published in 2005, it was shown that girls achieved better A-level performance than boys in 74% of the state schools surveyed. In 43% of the schools, girls achieved over 10% better results than boys. A similar picture was found in independent schools. Girls outperformed boys in 71% of those schools, and obtained over 10% better results in 20% of them. The precise reasons are not known, but it is likely that girls are more likely than boys to be motivated to work hard for their exams.

In general, there are fewer and smaller differences between the genders than is generally assumed. Why is there this gap between appearance and reality? We tend to misinterpret the evidence of our senses to fit our stereotypes. Condry and Condry (1976) asked college students to watch a videotape of an infant. The ways in which the infant's behaviour was interpreted depended on whether it was referred to as David or Dana. The infant was said to be "angry" in its reaction to a jack-in-the-box if it had been called David, but "anxious" if it had been called Dana.

■ Activity: Gender stereotypes

Make a list of stereotypes that are often used to describe males and females. Now categorise them in terms of gender or biology. Are there any that could be supported by evidence, and what evidence could be considered valid?

Psychological Theories of Gender Development

In the following accounts our interest is, in particular, on the development of **gender identity** (your own sense of your gender) and on **gender roles** (what you learn about appropriate behaviour for males and females).

Psychodynamic theory

Part of Freud's psychodynamic theory was designed to account for gender development (see pages 242–243 for a fuller account). Most theories of gender development are based on the assumption that environmental and cultural influences are of crucial importance. In contrast, Freud de-emphasised such influences, arguing that "anatomy is destiny".

As we saw earlier, Freud argued that boys develop an Oedipus complex, in which they have sexual desires for their mother combined with intense fear of their father. Part of this fear arises because boys think that their fathers may castrate them. The Oedipus complex is resolved by a process of identification with the father. Girls resolve a different crisis at the same age, bemoaning the fact

KEY TERMS

Gender: the psychological characteristics associated with being male or female, i.e., masculinity and femininity.
Gender identity: one's concept of being male or female, a fundamental part of the self concept.
Gender roles: those behaviours, attitudes, and interests that are considered appropriate for one gender and not the other.

that they lack a penis, which they believe has been lost. They have sexual desires for their father. However, fearing the anger of their mother, they identify (somewhat less strongly than boys) with their mother. According to Freud, identification (imitating the beliefs and behaviour of the same-sex parent) plays a major role in the development of gender stereotypes.

Chodorow (1978) developed an alternative psychoanalytic theory, according to which most young children develop a close relationship with their mother. This relationship then sets the pattern for future relationships. Girls can develop a sense of gender identity based on their close relationship with another female (their mother). By so doing, they associate femininity with feelings of closeness. In contrast, boys have to move away from their close relationship with their mother in order to develop gender identity, and this can make them regard masculinity and closeness as not being associated.

Fathers may play a major role in the development of sex-typed behaviour in their sons.

Research evidence

There is some evidence that the father plays a major role in the development of gender stereotypes in boys. Boys whose fathers are missing during the time at which the Oedipus complex develops (around the age of 5) showed fewer gender stereotypes than boys whose fathers were present throughout (Stevenson & Black, 1988). There is also evidence (discussed later) that there are major changes in gender development at around the age of 5.

> **?** What does psychoanalytic theory tell us about the development of gender identity?

Evaluation

Freud's theory of the development of gender identity is incorrect in nearly every respect. His account tells us more about his powers of imagination than about what actually happens. There is no real evidence that boys fear castration or that girls regret not having a penis. Freud argued that the identification process depends on fear, so it might be expected that a boy's identification with his father would be greatest if his father was a threatening figure. In fact, however, boys tend to identify much more with a warm and supportive father than with an overbearing and threatening one (Mussen & Rutherford, 1963).

Freud's theory of gender development should be regarded largely as a historical curiosity rather than a useful theoretical contribution. However, it was the first systematic attempt to identify a series of developmental stages within which gender development can be understood. Freud focused on the influence of the same-sex parent in influencing gender development in children. By so doing, he ignored the impact of the opposite-sex parent, other members of the family, and other children.

Freud's general approach was limited in various ways, as can be seen if we relate it to other theoretical approaches. The emphasis in Kohlberg's cognitive-developmental theory and in gender-schema theory (both discussed later) is more on the cognitive factors involved in gender development. The emphasis in social learning theory (discussed next) is more on the behavioural aspects of gender development.

> **?** How might Freud have used his focus on the influence of the same-sex parent to explain homosexuality?

Social learning theory

According to social learning theory (e.g., Bandura, 1977, 1986), the development of gender occurs as a result of the child's social experiences. Generally, children learn to behave in ways rewarded by others and to avoid behaving in ways punished by others. This is known as direct tuition. As society has expectations about the ways in which boys and girls should behave, the operation of socially delivered rewards and punishments will tend to produce gender stereotypes and gender-appropriate behaviours.

Bandura also argued that children can learn gender stereotypes by observing the actions of various models of the same gender, including other children, parents, and teachers. This is known as observational learning, and was discussed earlier in the chapter. It has often been argued that much observational learning of gender stereotypes in children depends on the media, and especially television.

According to social learning theory, boys and girls learn gender stereotypes and gender roles from observing others in their society and from exposure to that society's media. As a result, gender stereotypes and gender roles would be predicted to vary from culture to culture depending on the particular emphases within each one.

Note that the social learning theory approach has been broadened into a social cognitive theory by Bussey and Bandura (1999). According to this new theory, observational learning and direct tuition are important as was assumed within social learning theory. In addition, however, it is assumed that children use self-regulatory mechanisms to compare their own behaviour against their own standards of how they should behave. Furthermore, when children decide which aspects of others' behaviour to imitate, they typically choose forms of behaviour they think will increase their feelings of self-efficacy or mastery.

Parents may try to discourage what they see as sex-inappropriate behaviour in a variety of ways. This little girl is helped out of the tree, while her brother is permitted to continue climbing.

Research evidence

Gender stereotypes are learned in part through direct tuition. Fagot and Leinbach (1989) carried out a long-term study on children. Parents encouraged gender-appropriate behaviour and discouraged gender-inappropriate behaviour in their children even before the age of 2. For example, girls were rewarded for playing with dolls, and discouraged from climbing trees. Those parents who made the most use of direct tuition tended to have children who behaved in the most gender-stereotyped way. However, these findings are not altogether typical. Golombok and Hines (2002) reviewed numerous studies on the parental treatment of boys and girls. There was a modest tendency for parents to encourage gender-stereotyped activities, but boys and girls received equal parental warmth, encouragement of achievement, discipline, and amount of interaction. The tendency for parents to parents to encourage gender-stereotyped activities is hard to interpret. It may reflect the parents' wishes or it may occur more because their sons have pre-existing tendencies to behave differently from their daughters.

Direct tuition is also used by other children. Fagot (1985) studied the behaviour of children aged between 21 and 25 months. Boys made fun of other boys who played with dolls or with a girl, and girls did not like it when one of them started playing with a boy. There are similar pressures from their peers among older children in the years before adolescence. Those who fail to behave in a gender-stereotyped way are the least popular (Sroufe et al., 1993).

Observational learning was studied by Perry and Bussey (1979). Children aged 8 or 9 watched male and female adult models choose between gender-neutral activities (e.g., selecting an apple or a pear). Afterwards, they tended to make the same choices as the same-sex models. These findings suggest that observational learning plays an important role in gender development. However, Barkley et al. (1977) reviewed the literature, and found that children showed a bias in favour of the same-sex model in only 18 out of 81 studies.

Children between the ages of 4 and 11 watch about 3 hours of television a day, which adds up to 1000 hours a year. It would be surprising if this exposure had no impact on children's views of themselves and on gender stereotypes via observational learning. Most of the research indicates there is a modest link between television watching and gender stereotypes. Frueh and McGhee (1975) studied the television viewing habits of children aged between 4 and 12. Those children who watched the most television tended to show more gender-stereotyped behaviour in terms of preferring gender-stereotyped toys. However, this is only correlational evidence, and so we don't know that watching television led to gender-stereotyped behaviour.

INDEPENDENT STUDY IDEA: CONTENT ANALYSIS

A content analysis is a useful way of investigating whether sex role stereotypes are used in children's television programmes. In small groups choose several children's programmes from a variety of TV channels. Carefully choose a coding system, consisting of about 46 categories, to use for the investigation. For example, you could look at the role of every adult character in the programme—does it conform to a sex role stereotype or not? You will analyse this with a chi-squared test and you must be careful to use all data and for that data to be independent. In the category cited above you would need to note every role played by an adult and decide "yes" or "no" to whether it is sex stereotyped. Within this category you could also look at whether the male roles are more or less likely to be sex-role stereotyped than the females. Your table would look like this:

	Sex-role stereotyped	Non sex-role stereotyped	Total
Male character			
Female character			
Total			

Repeat this for your other categories.

If possible, carry out the same study on children's television programmes from the past, many of which are available on videotape or DVD. Use the same categories and do a chi-squared to see if there's a difference between these and the more recent programmes. It would make the analysis easier if, in this case, you combined the male/female characters, so the table then looks like this:

	Sex-role stereotyped	Non sex-role stereotyped	Total
Present day programmes			
Older programmes			
Total			

? Do you think the Canadian study by Williams (1986) would be able to demonstrate a causal relationship between television and gender-role stereotyping? What other factors in children's lives might have played a part?

Williams (1986) examined gender-role stereotypes in three towns in Canada nicknamed: "Notel" (no television channels), "Unitel" (one channel), and "Multitel" (four channels). Gender-role stereotyping was much greater in the towns with television than in the one without. During the course of the study, Notel gained access to one television channel. This led to increased gender-role stereotyping among children.

Some of the strongest evidence that television can influence gender development was reported by Johnston and Ettema (1982). In the *Freestyle* project, there was a series of television programmes in which non-traditional opportunities and activities were modelled. These programmes produced significant attitude changes away from gender-role stereotypes, and these changes were still present 9 months later. However, the effects on behaviour were rather small.

Evidence for self-regulation (emphasised within social cognitive theory) was reported by Bussey and Bandura (1992). Children at the age of 4 were asked how they would feel if they played with various same-gender or opposite-gender toys. Unsurprisingly, the boys felt very positive about playing with toys such as robots but negative about playing with baby dolls or kitchen sets, whereas girls showed the opposite pattern. These internal feelings form part of self-regulation and probably influence children's choice of toys.

Evaluation

One of the strengths of the social learning approach is that it takes full account of the social context in which the development of gender occurs. As social learning theorists have claimed, some gender-stereotyped behaviour occurs because it has been rewarded, and gender-inappropriate behaviour is avoided because it has been discouraged or punished. There is also evidence that observational learning is important, but perhaps more with older than with young children. The prediction that there should be important differences in the roles of males and females across cultures has received much support, and is discussed later on. Finally, there is support for the importance of self-regulation as emphasised in social cognitive theory.

There are several limitations of social learning theory. First, as Durkin (1995, p.179) pointed out:

Research into the effects of the principal mechanisms emphasised by the theory (parental reinforcement, modelling) has not led consistently to the conclusion that they have a major influence.

Second, some aspects of social learning theory suggest that gender is *passively* acquired through reward and punishment. In reality, children make an active contribution to their own development and this factor is recognised in later versions of social learning theory, such as Bandura's (1986) social cognitive theory, in which the emphasis is on the self and the role it plays in influencing behaviour (see page 250 for a description of reciprocal determinism).

Television programmes that show men and women taking part in non-traditional sex-typed activities have been found to produce some attitude changes among viewers, but the effects on behaviour were small.

Third, social learning theorists mistakenly assume that learning processes are very similar at any age. For example, consider young children and adolescents watching a film in which a man and a woman are eating a meal together. The observational learning of the young children might focus on the eating behaviour of the same-sex person, whereas the adolescents might focus on his or her social behaviour. Approaches such as Kohlberg's cognitive-developmental theory and gender-schema theory (discussed shortly) are better equipped to explain developmental changes in learning and cognition.

Fourth, social learning theory focuses on the learning of *specific* ways of behaving. This ignores the fact that there is also a considerable amount of general learning. For example, children seem to acquire gender schemas (organised beliefs about the sexes; Martin & Halverson, 1987), and it is hard to explain how this happens in terms of social learning theory.

Cognitive-developmental theory: Kohlberg

Lawrence Kohlberg (1966) put forward a cognitive-developmental theory of gender role development. The essence of his approach can be seen by contrasting it with social learning theory. According to Kohlberg (1966, p.85), "the child's sex-role concepts are the result of the child's active structuring of his own experience; they are not passive products of social training". Social learning theory contrasts with cognitive-developmental theory in arguing that rewarding behaviour is behaviour that *others* regard as appropriate. Cognitive-developmental theorists suggest that rewards are gained from doing things that fit one's own concept of gender identity, i.e., gender-appropriate behaviour is self-rewarding.

> **?** What is meant by a "cognitive-developmental theory", as distinct from a cognitive theory?

There are other important differences between social learning theory and Kohlberg's theory. According to social learning theory, children develop a gender identity as a result of attending to same-sex models. According to Kohlberg, the causality goes in the other direction: children attend to same-sex models because they have already developed a consistent gender identity. It follows from this theory that children find it rewarding to behave in line with their consistent gender identity. In the words of Kohlberg (1966, p.89), "I am a boy; therefore I want to do boy things; therefore the opportunity to do boy things . . . is rewarding."

The notion of gender identity is of great importance within Kohlberg's cognitive-developmental theory. Children go through three stages in the development of gender identity:

1. *Basic gender identity* (age 2 to $3\frac{1}{2}$ years): boys know they are boys, and girls know they are girls. However, they believe it would be possible to change sex.
2. *Gender stability* ($3\frac{1}{2}$ to $4\frac{1}{2}$ years): there is an awareness that sex is stable over time (e.g., boys will become men), but less awareness that sex remains stable across different situations, such as wearing clothes normally worn by

KOHLBERG'S STAGES IN THE DEVELOPMENT OF GENDER IDENTITY		
Basic gender identity	**Gender stability**	**Gender consistency**
2–$3\frac{1}{2}$ years	$3\frac{1}{2}$–$4\frac{1}{2}$ years	$4\frac{1}{2}$–7 upwards
Aware of sex, but believes it can change	Aware that sex is stable over time, but not over situations	Realises sex remains the same, regardless of time or situation

? Do behaviours that are considered "boy things" and "girl things" remain constant over time? Are there illustrative examples from your childhood that are different from your parents' childhood?

members of the opposite sex. When a doll was dressed in transparent clothes so there was a discrepancy between its clothing and its genitals, children in this stage decided on its sex on the basis of clothing (McConaghy, 1979).

3. *Gender consistency* (4½ to 7 years upwards): children at this stage realise that sex remains the same over time and over situations. This is like Piaget's notion of conservation (see Chapter 5, Cognitive Development).

Research evidence

There is evidence that children do, indeed, progress through the three stages proposed by Kohlberg. In a cross-cultural study, Munroe, Shimmin, and Munroe (1984) found that children in several cultures had the same sequences of stages on the way to full gender identity.

One of the predictions of Kohlberg's theory is that children who have reached the stage of gender consistency will pay more attention to the behaviour of same-sex models than children at earlier stages of gender development. Slaby and Frey (1975) tested this prediction. Children between the ages of 2 and 5 were assessed for gender consistency, assigned to a high or a low gender consistency group, and shown a film of a male and a female performing various activities. Those who were high in gender consistency showed a greater tendency to attend to the same-sex model than those low in gender consistency.

According to Kohlberg (1966), children find it rewarding to behave in line with their consistent gender identity.

More evidence of the importance of gender consistency was reported by Ruble, Balaban, and Cooper (1981). Preschoolers high and low in gender consistency watched television commercials in which toys were represented as being suitable for boys or for girls. These advertisements had more effect on the attitudes and behaviour of boys and girls high in gender consistency. This offers a more complex perspective on the role of the media in gender behaviours than social learning theory because it suggests that it is not simply a case of exposure to stereotypes in the media but what children bring with them to their media use.

Evaluation

Gender identity does seem to develop through the three stages proposed by Kohlberg. As predicted by the theory, the achievement of full gender identity increases gender role behaviour. In more general terms, the notion that gender development involves children actively interacting with the world around them is valuable, as is the notion that how they interact with the world depends on the extent to which they have developed a consistent gender identity.

There are various problems with Kohlberg's theory. First, gender-role behaviour is shown by most boys and girls by the time of their second birthday. This is several years before they have reached gender consistency, and so it cannot be argued that *all* gender role behaviour depends on gender consistency.

Second, Kohlberg (1966, p.98) argued that, "the process of forming a constant [gender] identity is . . . a part of the general process of conceptual growth". In other words, the formation of gender identity depends mainly on *internal* processes relating to developmental changes in thinking. This approach tends to ignore the *external* factors (e.g., reward and punishment from parents) that determine much early gender role behaviour. More generally, Kohlberg's focus was too much on the individual child, and not enough on the social context that largely determines gender development.

Third, Kohlberg exaggerated the importance of cognitive factors in producing gender role behaviour. Huston (1985) pointed out that Kohlberg's theory leads to the prediction that there should be a close relationship between cognitions about gender and gender-typed attitudes and behaviour. In fact, the relationship is not very strong, and is weaker in girls than in boys. It is not clear how these findings can be explained by Kohlberg's theory.

EXAM HINT

You will not be directly examined on gender-schema theory as it is not on the specification, but we have included coverage of it here for background.

Cognitive-developmental theory: Gender-schema theory

Martin and Halverson (1987) put forward a rather different cognitive-developmental theory known as gender-schema theory based on the assumption that children want to learn about their gender much earlier than was suggested by Kohlberg. They argued that children as young as 2 or 3 years who have acquired basic gender identity start to form **gender schemas**, which consist of organised sets of beliefs about the sexes. The first schema formed is an ingroup/outgroup schema, consisting of organised information about which toys and activities are suitable for boys and which are suitable for girls. Another early schema is an own-gender schema containing information about how to behave in gender-stereotyped ways (e.g., how to dress dolls for a girl). Some of the processes involved in the initial development of gender schemas may include those emphasised by social learning theorists.

Schema-consistent activities

A key aspect of gender-schema theory is the notion that children don't simply respond passively to the world. What happens instead is that the gender schemas possessed by children help to determine what they attend to, how they interpret the world, and what they remember of their experiences. Thus, as Shaffer (1993, p.513) argued, "Gender schemas 'structure' experience by providing an organisation for processing social information."

Schema-inconsistent activities

Research evidence

According to the theory, gender schemas are used by children to organise and make sense of their experiences. If they are exposed to information that doesn't fit one of their schemas (e.g., a boy combing the hair of his doll), then the information should be distorted to make it fit the schema. Martin and Halverson (1983) tested this prediction. They showed 5- and 6-year-old children pictures of schema-consistent activities (e.g., a girl playing with a doll) and schema-inconsistent activities (e.g., a girl playing with a toy gun). Schema-inconsistent activities were often misremembered 1 week later as schema-consistent (e.g., it had been a boy playing with a toy gun).

KEY TERM

Gender schemas: organised sets of beliefs about gender behaviour.

[?] In what other contexts
have you come across
"schema"? How should you
define it?

Another study that supports gender-schema theory was reported by Bradbard et al. (1986). Boys and girls between the ages of 4 and 9 were presented with gender-neutral objects such as burglar alarms and pizza cutters. They were told that some of the objects were "boy" objects, whereas others were described as "girl" objects. There were two key findings. First, children spent much more time playing with objects that they had been told were appropriate to their gender. Second, even a week later the children remembered whether any given object was a "boy" or a "girl" object.

A study by Masters et al. (1979) also supports gender-schema theory. Young children of 4 and 5 were influenced in their choice of toy more by the gender label attached to the toy (e.g., "It's a girl's toy") than by the gender of the model seen playing with the toy. As Durkin (1995) pointed out, children's behaviour seems to be influenced more by the schema, "This is a boy's toy" or "This is a girl's toy" than by a desire to imitate a same-sex model.

Serbin et al. (1993) found that boys and girls in middle childhood possessed comparable amounts of gender stereotypic knowledge in their gender schemas. The natural prediction from gender-schema theory is that there would be no difference between boys and girls in gender-typed behaviour. In fact, boys showed more gender-typed behaviour than girls, which is hard to explain on gender-schema theory.

Is it possible to reconcile the differences between gender-schema theory and Kohlberg's theory? According to Stangor and Ruble (1989), what happens is that gender schemas *and* gender consistency both develop during the early years of childhood. Gender schemas contain information about various kinds of gender-appropriate activities and behaviour; they also contain knowledge about the extent to which the child is motivated to perform certain gender-appropriate forms of behaviour.

Evaluation

One of the main strengths of gender-schema theory is that it helps to explain why children's gender-role beliefs and attitudes often change rather little after middle childhood. The gender schemas that have been established tend to be maintained because schema-consistent information is attended to and remembered. Another strength of the theory is its focus on the child as being actively involved in making sense of the world in the light of its present knowledge.

The limitations of gender-schema theory resemble those of Kohlberg's theory. The theory emphasises too much the role of the individual child in gender development, and de-emphasises the importance of social factors. In addition, it is likely that the importance of schemas and other cognitive factors in determining behaviour is exaggerated within the theory. Another problem is that the theory doesn't really explain *why* gender schemas develop and take the form they do. In addition, the theory doesn't explain why boys exhibit more gender-typed behaviour than girls (Serbin et al., 1993).

[?] Think about your own
family. Are there specific
domestic chores that are
done by particular
members of the family?
Can they be categorised by
gender?

Finally, it is assumed within the theory that it should be possible to change children's behaviour by changing their schemas or stereotypes. In fact, as Durkin (1995, p.185) pointed out, "greater success has been reported in attempts to change concepts than attempts to change behaviour or behavioural intentions". In a similar way, many married couples have *schemas* relating to equality of the sexes and equal division of household chores, but this rarely has much effect on their *behaviour*!

Biological Theories of Gender Development

Biological theories differ, and contrast with, psychological theories because they are largely focused on the influence of our biological sex on gender behaviour.

Biosocial theory

There are various obvious biological differences between boys and girls. These biological differences produce hormonal differences between the sexes at a very early stage of development. For example, the male sex hormone testosterone is present in greater amounts in male than female foetuses from about the age of 6 weeks, whereas the opposite is the case for the female sex hormone oestrogen (see Durkin, 1995). It has been argued that basic biological and hormonal factors are important in gender identity, and in the development of greater aggressiveness in boys than in girls. However, as Willerman (1979) pointed out:

> One should not expect too much of the genetic differences between males and females. The two sexes have forty-five/forty-six of their chromosomes in common, and the one that differs (the Y) contains the smallest proportion of genetic material.

The "Y" chromosome is denoted in this way because it is missing some of the information that is on the "X" chromosome, which is why males are more susceptible to recessive disorders—they only need one gene on that pair because there is no partner on the Y chromosome.

There are other biological differences between human males and females. For example, Taylor et al. (2000) discussed sex differences in the role of **oxytocin**, which is a hormone produced as part of the response to stress and which makes people less anxious and more sociable. Its effects are reduced by male sex hormones but increased by the female hormone oestrogen. Another difference involves the hypothalamus, a structure in at the base of the brain that regulates male and female reproductive behaviour. Parts of the hypothalamus are larger in men than in women, and are larger in men than in male-to-female transsexuals (Kimura, 2002). Thus, gender identity and sexual orientation may depend in part on the hypothalamus.

The ideal way of testing biological theories of gender development would be to study individuals in which there is a clear distinction between **sexual identity** (based on biological factors) and the way in which they are treated socially. Thus, for example, if an individual was born a boy but was treated as a girl, would biological or social factors be more important in their gender development? The ideal study has not been carried out, but approximations to it are discussed next.

Research evidence

Suggestive evidence in support of the biological approach to gender development has been obtained in animal studies. For example, Young, Goy, and Phoenix (1964) gave doses of testosterone to pregnant monkeys. This male sex hormone produced greater aggressiveness and higher frequency of rough-and-tumble play in the mothers' female offspring.

However, gender is not necessarily a matter of biological sex. Early research evidence appeared to suggest that individuals would accept their sex of rearing

---

KEY TERMS

Oxytocin: a hormone produced as part of the response to stress that reduces anxiety and increases sociability.

Sexual identity: maleness or femaleness based on biological factors.

and learn appropriate gender role behaviours in association with the gender assigned at birth. For example, about 500 people in Britain have what is known as testicular feminising syndrome. They are male in the sense that they have male chromosomes and testicles. However, their bodies do not respond to the male sex hormone testosterone. As a result, they develop a female body shape and their breasts develop. Mrs Daphne Went has testicular feminising syndrome. She had always thought of herself as a woman, but when she found it impossible to become pregnant she consulted a doctor and found that she was biologically male and had no internal female organs. Nevertheless, she felt that she was a woman and elected to stay in that role, adopting two children (Goldwyn, 1979). This, of course, is a case study of one, which makes it hard to draw firm conclusions. It also isn't entirely clear whether we can say that Mrs Went was influenced by social factors (reared as a girl) or biological ones (exposure to male hormones).

Other case studies recorded by Money and Ehrhardt (see the Key Study below) at first appeared to support Goldwyn's conclusion. However, the evidence now

? In the case of Mrs Went, what factor or factors do you think were responsible for her gender identity?

KEY STUDY
Money and Ehrhardt

Money and Ehrhardt (1972) discussed cases of females who were exposed to male sex hormones prior to birth. The reason for this was as a treatment to prevent miscarriage in mothers who had a previous history of such difficulties. The effect of the hormones on the foetus was not considered.

Even though their parents treated them as girls, they tended to be tomboys. They played and fought with boys, and avoided more traditional female activities. In addition, they preferred to play with blocks and cars rather than with dolls. However, many of these girls were given the hormone cortisone to prevent them from becoming too masculine anatomically. One of the effects of cortisone is to increased activity level, and this may have made their behaviour more like that expected of boys.

A further consideration is that male hormones during prenatal development have the effect of masculinising the brain (Geschwind & Galaburda, 1985). This is what makes men behave in a male fashion, such as having a more dominant right hemisphere of the brain, and thus would have the same effect on biological females. Therefore, in such cases the individual is, at least in some sense, biologically male.

However, evidence that social factors can override biology was also reported by Money and Ehrhardt. They studied male identical twins, one of whom had had his penis very severely damaged during a circumcision operation. Money advised the parents that the best solution would be to reassign the boy's gender and rear him as a girl, giving him female hormones at puberty. The parents endeavoured to raise the boy as a girl, calling her Brenda and rewarding gender-appropriate behaviour. Money reported that Brenda played with girls' toys such as dolls and a doll's house, whereas his brother asked for a garage. He was neater and more delicate in his behaviour than his identical twin.

A book by Colapinto (2000) describes quite a different reality, of a child who was totally confused and more boyish than his/her brother. Eventually, in adolescence, Brenda chose to return to being a man and later married.

Money had used the case to argue that social factors can overrule biology and many feminists embraced this view because it suggested that many gender prejudices and gender differences are social creations. The reality of this one natural experiment suggests that biology may be more important than some people wish to recognise.

Discussion points
1. How much can studies of such unusual cases tell us about ordinary gender development?
2. Do these cases persuade you that biological factors play a part in gender development?

appears to suggest that biological sex may have a greater influence than was once thought.

Further support for this latter view comes from a study by Imperato-McGinley et al. (1974) of a family in the Dominican Republic. Four of the sons in the family appeared biologically to be female at birth, and were reared as girls. However, at the age of about 12, they developed male genitals and started to look like ordinary adolescent males. In spite of the fact that all four of them had been reared as girls, and had thought of themselves as females, they seemed to adjust well to the male role. According to Gross' account (1996, p.584), "They have all taken on male roles, do men's jobs, have married women and are accepted as men." These findings suggest that biological factors can be more important than social ones in the formation of gender identity.

Collaer and Hines (1995) reviewed the sometimes confusing and inconsistent findings from numerous studies. They argued that there is good evidence for at least three effects. First, male sex hormones increase the likelihood that the child will enjoy rough-and-tumble play and physical activity generally. Second, exposure to high levels of male sex hormones at an early age affects sexual orientation in adolescence. Third, male sex hormones lead to an increase in aggressive behaviour.

Evaluation

Most of the evidence suggests that biological factors play *some* role in gender development. Of particular interest are those studies in which there is a fairly direct conflict between biological and social factors, as was the case with the four children in the family from the Dominican Republic. It seemed as if biological factors outweighed social factors. However, it needs to be remembered that the relevant evidence has been obtained from very unusual cases, and it is hard to know whether the findings obtained can be generalised to the ordinary population.

It is important to note that biological theories cannot provide more than a partial explanation. Such theories do not explain the impact of social factors on gender development, and they don't account for the substantial changes in gender roles that have occurred in Western societies in recent decades. As Durkin (1995, p.173) pointed out:

> *Biological theories stress the demands of parenting and the possible implications of possible differences in abilities, but have little to say about the other distinguishing characteristic that has evolved in this [human] species: its ability to articulate, share, reflect upon, and change its social practices. Biosocial theory, on the other hand, is an attempt to combine elements of both approaches [i.e., biological and social approaches].*

Finally, biological theories predict that the roles and status of men and women should be fairly constant across cultures. In fact, however, there are actually substantial cross-cultural differences (discussed shortly).

? What might be some of the ethical problems encountered by researchers conducting studies into the links between sexual identity and biology?

Evidence suggests that the formation of a child's gender identity is subject to both biological and social influences.

Evolutionary theory and cultural differences

Many aspects of gender behaviour have been explained through evolutionary theory and this is discussed at length in Chapter 7, Evolutionary Explanations of Human Behaviour.

Briefly, the argument is that males and females look and behave differently because such behaviours are adaptive. All animals strive to maximise reproduction because this ensures the survival of the individual's **genes**. Thus, adaptive behaviours remain in the gene pool and other behaviours disappear. One of the main implications of this approach is that there should be similarity in the gender roles of males across cultures and the same should be true of females. If there are major differences in gender roles across cultures, this would suggest that environmental factors associated with particular cultures are important.

Males produce millions of sperm at almost no physical cost. Females produce eggs in limited quantities and at a greater physical cost. Therefore females must ensure that each reproduction is as successful as possible. Thus, women seek men with good genes who can provide resources to help look after a growing child (see the Key Study by Buss, 1989, on page 301). "Good genes" may be in terms of physical strength or intelligence or any characteristic that might be passed on to sons in the next generation because this would ensure that these sons are selected by other females, and the original mother's genes are thus further perpetuated. This is called the **sexy sons hypothesis** (see page 303). Alternatively, "good genes" may be in terms of robustness, as proposed by the **handicapping theory**: robust genes are indicated by the male's ability to sustain characteristics incurring a cost (e.g., a peacock's elaborate tail).

Females also look for resources, which may be in terms of money, land, or power. Davis (1990) found that when men advertised for a mate they tended to emphasise their wealth or other resources, and women indicated that they were looking for a high-status, wealthy man, and mentioned their own physical attractiveness.

? What does this sociobiological view tell us about gender identity and gender roles?

Research evidence

Cross-cultural studies have supplied evidence that there are some universal similarities in gender behaviour, which supports sociobiological theory. For instance, Mead's (1935) classic studies of three cultural groups in New Guinea indicated some gender differences but also gender similarities. In the Mundugumor, both men and women adopted the aggressive, instrumental style of behaviour that is supposed to be more characteristic of males. In the Arapesh, both sexes adopted the caring, expressive style commonly associated with females. Most dramatically, the females in the Tchambuli behaved in an assertive and independent fashion, whereas the males were nurturant and dependent.

At first sight this evidence would seem to suggest that there *are* gender differences and this could be explained in term of social rather than biological, inherited factors. However, within each cultural group the males were *more* aggressive than the

> **KEY TERMS**
>
> **Genes:** units of inheritance that form part of a chromosome. Some characteristics are determined by one gene, whereas for others many genes are involved.
>
> **Sexy sons hypothesis:** the notion that females mate with the most attractive males so that their own sons will inherit these characteristics and thus be attractive to other females. Related to the runaway process.
>
> **Handicapping theory:** according to this theory, females select males who have a handicap because this suggests the male must be genetically robust. Symmetry may be a handicap because of its physiological cost.

women. Even in the Tchambuli it was the men who did most of the fighting in time of war. This supports the idea of inherited gender role behaviours.

Other research has supported these findings. Williams and Best (1982) explored gender stereotypes in 30 different national cultures. In each country 100 male and female students were asked to look at a list of adjectives and state whether they were associated with men or women, or both, in their culture. Williams and Best found that there were many similarities across the various cultures. Men were seen as more dominant, aggressive, autonomous, and taking a more *instrumental role*, whereas women were more nurturant, deferent, and interested in affiliation, being encouraged to develop an *expressive role*. This finding was also supported by Barry, Bacon, and Child (1957) (see the Key Study below).

KEY STUDY
Barry, Bacon, and Child

Socialisation pressures in 110 non-industrialised countries were explored by Barry, Bacon, and Child (1957). They considered five characteristics:

- Nurturance (being supportive)
- Responsibility
- Obedience
- Achievement
- Self-reliance.

There was more pressure on girls than on boys to be nurturant in 75% of the non-industrialised societies, with none showing the opposite pattern. Responsibility was regarded as more important in girls than in boys in 55% of the societies, with 10% showing the opposite. Obedience was stressed for girls more than for boys in 32% of societies, with 3% showing the opposite. There was more pressure on boys than on girls to acquire the other two characteristics. Achievement was emphasised more for boys in 79% of societies (3% showed the opposite), and self-reliance was regarded as more important in boys in 77% of societies, with no societies regarding it as more important in girls.

These findings indicate that the gender-role stereotypes of females being expressive and males being instrumental are very widespread. Related findings were obtained by Williams and Best (1990). Similar gender stereotypes to those found in the United States were present in 24 other countries in Asia, Europe, Oceania, Africa, and the Americas.

Discussion points
1. Are you surprised at the cross-cultural similarities in expectations of males and females?
2. Why do you think there are such consistent gender-specific expectations?

INDEPENDENT STUDY IDEA: GENDER DIFFERENCES—SOCIOBIOLOGICAL
You could use a questionnaire to explore some of the areas covered by Barry, Bacon, and Child (1957). It would be too difficult to look at different cultures, but within British society you could compare attitudes to boys and to girls. Devise a questionnaire that puts various scenarios to people and ask them to judge how concerned they might be if their son/daughter behaved in this way, how important it is that they achieve certain goals, etc. Because the purpose of the study would be very obvious if you used a repeated measures design, it's almost certainly better to use an independent groups design, i.e., ask two separate groups of people (one referring throughout to a son, the other to a daughter) who are carefully matched on all important variables (age, sex, whether they have children, etc.). If you use fixed responses, you have quantitative data to analyse. It may be useful to add a couple of open ended questions so as to increase the material for discussion.

In most Western societies, there are now more female than male university students.

Wood and Eagly (2002) discussed cross-cultural findings relating to gender roles obtained from a very large number (181) of non-industrialised cultures. Men were dominant in 67% of those cultures, especially those in which there was much warfare and men's economic contribution was much greater than that of women. However, neither sex was dominant in 30% of cultures, and women were dominant in 3%. There were also large cultural differences in responsibility for obtaining food. Men had the primary role in obtaining food in cultures dependent on hunting or fishing, but women had the main role when food gathering was involved. Thus, there were important differences in the roles of men and women across cultures.

Cultural change also applies to historical differences. There have been great changes in most Western societies in recent years. In the mid-twentieth century, many fewer women than men went to university. Nowadays the number of female university students exceeds that of male students in several countries. There is a similar pattern in employment. In spite of these changes, many of the old stereotypes have changed very little. Bergen and Williams (1991) found in the United States that stereotypical views of the sexes in 1988 were remarkably similar to those expressed in 1972. This might be taken as an indication that gender roles are biologically driven.

Evaluation

Some cross-cultural studies have indicated that the cultural expectations and stereotypes for boys and girls are surprisingly similar in otherwise very different cultures. However, Williams and Best (1992) found that such consensus was strongest in collectivist societies and weaker in individualist societies where gender equality is more influential. This again suggests a cultural difference—the

EXAM HINT

There is a lot of theoretical content on gender development so select two explanations for AO1, e.g., social learning theory and Kohlberg's gender constancy, and then use Freud's "anatomy is destiny" evolutionary explanations to provide counterperspectives.

GENDER IDENTITY AND GENDER ROLES

	Gender identity	Gender roles
Psychodynamic theory	Learned through identification with same-sex parent during the phallic stage (aged 3–6 years)	Learned after identification
Cognitive-developmental theory	Consistent gender identity appears around age 4	Gender identity leads child to acquire gender stereotypes
Gender-schema theory	Basic gender identity appears around $2\frac{1}{2}$ and child begins to develop gender schemas	Gender schemas organise knowledge about gender stereotypes and role
Social learning	Learned by attending to same-sex models	Learned through vicarious reinforcement and modelling
Biosocial	Determined largely by biological sex	A combination of biological and social influences
Evolutionary	Biological	Adaptive and biological

effect of different socialisation practices. Some large differences in gender roles have been obtained in non-industrialised cultures (Wood & Eagly, 2002). Overall, it is clear that the evolutionary approach provides no more than a very partial explanation of gender roles.

SECTION SUMMARY
Gender Development

❖ Gender is a fundamental part of our self-concept.

❖ Some gender stereotypes are outdated but others are real, such as differences in verbal ability, interest in babies, and performance at school. The differences are exaggerated by our expectations.

What is gender?

❖ Gender development is largely determined by biological factors (anatomy is destiny). Theories were developed by Freud and Chodorow:

Psychodynamic theory

❖ Freud:

— Identification with the same-sex parent plays a major role in the development of sex-typed behaviour.

— Freud's theory is very limited.

❖ Chodorow:

— Both sexes identify with their mother; boys ultimately have to move away from this close relationship in order to establish their gender identity.

— There is some evidence to support this view: boys without fathers when under the age of 5 show fewer gender stereotypes but in general the support is thin. Boys should identify more with a threatening father but they don't.

❖ Gender development occurs through social experiences and observation.

Social learning theory

❖ Social cognitive theory develops this to suggest that children use self-regulatory mechanisms to decide what behaviour to imitate.

❖ According to research, gender stereotypes are learned by:

— Direct tuition: parents encourage gender appropriate behaviour and discourage gender inappropriate behaviour.

— Other children also use direct tuition through peer pressure.

— Observational learning, involving either live models or the media.

❖ Evaluation:

— Social learning theory takes full account of the social context in which the development of gender occurs.

— However, social learning theorists focus on learning specific forms of behaviour rather than on general types of learning; they tend to regard children as passive rather than active; and they ignore age differences in receptiveness.

❖ According to this theory:

Cognitive-developmental theory: Kohlberg

— Gender identity is a prerequisite to acquiring gender roles (opposite way round to social learning theory).

— Children develop gender identity in three stages: basic gender identity, gender stability, and gender consistency.

❖ Evaluation:

— Research supports the existence of these three stages, as well as the fact that achievement of gender consistency leads to the predicted increase in sex-typed behaviour.
— However, it appears that children begin to acquire gender concepts before gender consistency. The theory also exaggerates internal and cognitive factors and lacks emphasis on social context.

Cognitive-developmental theory: Gender-schema theory

❖ According to this theory:

— Young children who have acquired basic gender identity start to form gender schemas to organise new experiences.
— Information that is inconsistent with gender schemas tends to be misremembered.

❖ Evaluation:

— This theory can explain why gender-role beliefs often change rather little after middle childhood.
— Many of the same criticisms apply as for cognitive-developmental theory. There is also evidence that gender schemas are not always in accord with gender behaviours.

Biological theories of gender development

❖ Biological theories of gender development contrast with the social approach.
❖ The effects of biological factors can be studied by looking at cases of individuals reared in opposition to their biological sex.
❖ Evaluation:

— Social factors are influential but, in some cases at least, biological factors are ultimately important (however, these are very unusual cases).
— Biosocial theory is an amalgam of biological and social factors.

Evolutionary theories of gender development

❖ Evolutionary theories explain gender development in terms of evolutionary processes:

— Women select males in terms of good genes to enhance the perpetuation of their own genetic line.
— They also select men with resources to help look after their offspring.
— These are examples of gender role behaviour.

❖ Evaluation:

— Cross-cultural studies show universal male and female behaviours, strongest in collectivist cultures, suggesting some biological basis.
— However, the evolutionary approach is only a partial explanation of gender roles.

See also pages 143–149 of the revision guide.

ADOLESCENCE

It is often assumed that adolescence is a very "difficult" period of life, with adolescents being highly stressed and moody. It is further assumed that adolescents are stressed because they have to cope with enormous changes in their lives. Some of these changes are in sexual behaviour following puberty. There are also large social changes, with adolescents spending much more time with others of the same age and much less time with their parents than they did when they were younger. Adolescence is also a time at which decisions need to be made about the future. Adolescents need to decide which examinations to take, whether or not to apply to university, what to study at university, and so on.

Adolescence is certainly a period of change, and adolescents do have various pressures on them. However, as we will see, it is *not* true that all adolescents become stressed at this time, and some research suggests that adolescents are at no greater risk of being in crisis than adults of all ages. However, rates of mental disorder do peak in adolescence, and moods become more extreme and unstable (Rutter et al., 1976; see the Key Study below).

? Is it possible that adolescence is less stressful today than it was 30 years ago?

KEY STUDY
The Isle of Wight Study

Rutter et al. (1976) conducted a very large-scale study of adolescents living on the Isle of Wight. The aim of the investigation was to find out more about adolescent turmoil and to further explore Bowlby's hypothesis that early separation was associated with later maladjustment and delinquency. Rutter et al. interviewed 2300 9- to 12-year-olds and their families. The sample was divided into good, fair, and poor families. A good family was defined as one with warm, loving, and secure relationships.

In terms of psychiatric disturbance, Rutter et al. found a small peak in adolescence. Even though there was more psychiatric illness in adolescence than childhood, such disturbance was rare but a reasonable number reported feelings of inner turmoil. Where there were psychiatric problems these had mostly been ongoing since childhood, but in cases where problems did first appear in adolescence there were often family problems, which may have acted as a stressor.

In terms of early separation, the study found that, in good and fair homes, separation did not lead to delinquency. When early separation had been due to illness, it was not related to delinquency, but when separations were due to stress in the home the children were four times more likely to become delinquent. This led Rutter et al. to conclude that it is not separation *per se* that causes delinquency, but the stress that often surrounds separation.

Discussion points
1. What conclusions can be reached about the factors that may cause disturbance in adolescence?
2. Data about early childhood was collected retrospectively. How may this have affected the reliability of the data?

When does adolescence begin and end? It is convenient to assume that it covers the teenage years from 13 to 19. However, some girls enter puberty at the age of 10 or 11, and so become adolescent before they become teenagers. There are also numerous 20- and 21-year-olds who continue to exhibit many of the signs of adolescence. Adolescence cannot only be defined in terms of age, because some people enter and leave adolescence years earlier than others. In spite of these

EXAM HINT

A key issue to consider is whether adolescence is a time of crisis or not, as this is a good source of AO2 marks.

considerations, we will assume that the stage of development known as adolescence largely centres on the teenage years.

Theories of Social Development in Adolescence: The Psychodynamic Approach

At the beginning of this chapter, we considered psychodynamic theories of personality. Such theories, derived from Freud's approach, are characterised by the view that the child goes through innate stages during development and each stage is associated with a focus on some aspect of development. Life experiences interact with innate urges to produce adult personality. Freud proposed that, during adolescence, the focus is on adult sexuality (the genital stage) and on independence. These ideas were further developed in Erikson's more psychosocial theory. Of central importance, the changes and upheaval in the lives of adolescents lead in early adult life to the formation of an identity or sense of who they are.

Erikson's theory

Erik Erikson (1902–1994), like Freud, used the idea of crises during stages of an individual's life that needed to be resolved before moving on to the next stage. If these crises were not resolved development could not proceed normally. There are two key differences between Erikson and Freud. First, Erikson's crises were not psychosexual but were psychosocial, resolving social rather than physical conflicts. Second, Erikson mapped eight different stages (and crises) across the entire lifespan in contrast with Freud's stages that stop after adolescence. These stages are outlined on pages 246 and 247. In adolescence, the crisis is one of identity.

Erikson's ideas about adolescence stemmed from his observations of emotionally disturbed adolescents during therapy. His views have been influential, and have helped to create the general impression that most adolescents are stressed and uncertain about themselves and about the future. Erikson (1950, 1968, 1969) also argued that adolescents typically experience **identity diffusion**, which involves a strong sense of uncertainty. They need to achieve a sense of identity, which can be defined as "a feeling of being at home in one's body, a sense of 'knowing where one is going', and an inner assuredness of anticipated recognition from those who count" (Erikson, 1950, p.165). Adolescents find it hard to do this, because they are undergoing rapid biological and social changes, and they need to take major decisions in almost all areas of life (e.g., future career). In other words, adolescents typically face an **identity crisis**, because they don't know who they are, or where they are going. Erikson (1950, p.139) argued that the typical adolescent thinks about himself or herself in the following way: "I ain't what I ought to be, I ain't what I'm gonna be, but I ain't what I was."

? What do psychologists mean by identity? What is an "identity crisis"? Is an identity crisis healthy or maladaptive?

KEY TERMS

Identity diffusion: an identity status in which the individual has not focused on identity issues and has made no definite future commitments.

Identity crisis: the state of lacking a clear sense of what one is; it is most common in adolescence and early adulthood.

Erikson (1969, p.22) spelled out in more detail what is involved in this identity crisis:

> *Adolescence is not an affliction but a normative crisis, i.e., a normal phase of increased conflict . . . What under prejudiced scrutiny may appear to be the onset of a neurosis is often but an aggravated crisis which might prove to be self-liquidating and, in fact, contributive to the process of identity formation.*

Thus, Erikson seemed to think that it was almost essential for adolescents to go through an identity crisis in order to resolve the identity issue and move on to the formation of a stable adult identity. As we will see, this is an exaggeration of what normally happens.

According to Erikson (1968), adolescents experienced uncertainty about their identity—called identity diffusion. This uncertainty has four major components:

1. *Intimacy*: adolescents fear commitment to others because it may involve a loss of identity.
2. *Diffusion of time*: this "consists of a decided disbelief in the possibility that time may bring change and yet also of a violent fear that it might" (Erikson, 1968, p.169).
3. *Diffusion of industry*: this involves either an inability to concentrate or enormous efforts directed towards a single activity.
4. *Negative identity*: this involves "a scornful and snobbish hostility towards the role offered as proper and desirable in one's family or immediate community" (Erikson, 1968, p.173).

A scornful and snobbish hostility towards the role offered in one's family.

Erikson (1969) assumed that there are some important differences between males and females in identity development: females develop a sense of identity later than males, allegedly because they realise that their identity and social status will depend very much on the type of man they choose to marry. It is unlikely that a theorist would make such assumptions in the greatly changed society in which we now live!

One final point needs to be made about Erikson's theoretical approach. Adolescence typically lasts for several years, and an identity crisis could possibly develop at any point within the teenage years. According to Erikson (1968), however, an identity crisis is more likely to occur in late adolescence than at any earlier time.

> ■ **Activity: Erikson's theory**
> Consider Erikson's theory in the context of other variables in an adolescent's life:
> 1. Ingroups: what major stresses, influences, and decisions are part of an adolescent's life?
> 2. Do you think that most adolescents accomplish identity formation adequately? If not, why not?
> 3. Erikson's theory is a stage theory. Can one scheme fit all individuals?

Research evidence

Some of the evidence is consistent with the notion that adolescents experience high levels of stress. Smith and Crawford (1986) found that more than 60% of students in secondary school reported at least one instance of suicidal thinking, and 10% had attempted suicide. In fact, suicide is the third-highest cause of death

---

Suicide is a major cause of death in teenagers

The stress experienced by adolescents may be reflected in the statistics for attempted and completed suicides. Young men seem particularly at risk: the suicide rate in young men aged 15–19 has doubled since 1985 and suicide is the commonest cause of death in men under 35 (Men's Heath Forum, 2002). Although the rates are highest among 20- to 24-year-olds, the Health Development Agency warns that suicidal behaviour is probably established in the earlier, teenage, years.

There appears to be something about young men that gives them problems in coping with emotional situations and sharing their feelings together with a reluctance to acknowledge suicidal thoughts. Support for this contention comes from studies carried out in the UK, which indicate that the majority of young male suicide victims have made no contact with support services in the year before their death. A survey in Northern Ireland indicated that talking to an advice service ranked lowest amongst 16- to 24-year-olds when asked to identify how they coped with depression. Even when young men have rung a helpline especially set up to provide help for them, the large majority remain silent: of almost 209,000 calls made to a young men's helpline operated by the Campaign Against Living Miserably (CALM) between July 1997 and July 2004, nearly 186,000 were silent.

Academic pressure, family break up, and relationship problems are all causes of mounting stress and anxiety for young people. A study in Avon (Vassilas & Morgan, 1997) found that although 80% of young male suicides had had no contact with their GP, psychiatrist, or other support agency in the month prior to their suicide, many had experienced interpersonal stresses in the 72 hours prior to death, giving the impression that many of theses suicides were impulsive.

Health authorities and many voluntary organisations are sufficiently concerned about these very high suicide rates that there are now many programmes aimed at providing support, information, and advice to help prevent young suicide. If you suspect that any of your friends are at risk, or if you yourself are feeling suicidal, there is help available.

---

among Americans aged between 15 and 24. In Britain, suicide is the highest cause of death in males in that age range.

One of the implications of Erikson's theory is that adolescents should have low self-esteem because of the uncertainties they face. However, the evidence doesn't support this. If there are changes in self-image during adolescence, those changes are more likely to be positive than negative (Marsh, 1989). Of course, some adolescents do show reduced self-esteem, but this is only common among those who experience several life changes (e.g., change of school, divorcing parents) in a fairly short period of time (Simmons et al., 1987).

Why should a number of critical life changes reduce an adolescent's self-esteem?

Brown and Lohr (1987) found that self-esteem was low in adolescents who didn't belong to any cliques (small groups of friends who meet together very frequently). This makes sense if we assume that membership of a clique gives adolescents a kind of "social identity" (Coleman, 1974). However, it is not clear from Brown and Lohr's findings whether not belonging to a clique reduced their self-esteem or whether it was their low self-esteem that stopped them from belonging to a clique in the first place.

Adolescents in different cultures have quite different educational experiences, and life experiences generally. How might these experiences affect adolescent development?

There is also some evidence that adolescents are not always highly emotional. For example, Larson and Lampman-Petraitis (1989) assessed the emotional states of American children between the ages of 9 and 15 on an hour-by-hour basis, finding that the onset of adolescence was *not* associated with increased emotionality. On the other hand, a study by Csikszentmihalyi and Larson (1984) found that adolescent Americans displayed extreme mood swings in the space of 1 hour whereas adults typically take several hours to change from one mood to another.

The evidence generally indicates that problems are more likely to occur early rather than late in adolescence. For example, Larson et al. (1996) found that boys experienced less positive emotion in their family interactions at the ages of 12 and 13, and girls did the same at the ages of 14 and 15. After that, however, the level of positive emotion increased in late adolescence, returning to the level of childhood.

Some studies have addressed the issue of sex differences in identity formation. Douvan and Adelson (1966) obtained support for Erikson's position. Adolescent girls had greater problems than adolescent boys with identity development, and this seemed to be because they focused on the changes in their lives that would result from marriage. In contrast, Waterman (1985) reviewed several studies, and concluded that there was only "weak and inconsistent evidence" that boys and girls follow different routes to identity achievement.

Evaluation

Erikson was correct in his argument that adolescents and young adults typically experience major changes in identity, and that these changes can cause uncertainty and doubt. However, Erikson overstated the case when he focused on the notion of an identity crisis that all adolescents go through. Offer et al. (1988, pp.83–84) reviewed the literature, and came to the following measured conclusion:

> *The most dramatic . . . findings are those that permit us to characterise the model American teenager as feeling confident, happy, and self-satisfied—a portrait of the American adolescent that contrasts sharply with that drawn by many theorists of adolescent development, who contend that adolescence is pervaded with turmoil, dramatic mood swings, and rebellion.*

Another criticism is that most of Erikson's theorising was about male adolescents, and he had relatively little to say about female adolescents. This led Archer (1992, p.29) to argue as follows:

> *A major feminist criticism of Erikson's work is that it portrays a primarily Eurocentric male model of normality.*

In other words, Erikson's theoretical views are limited because they show signs of both gender and culture bias.

Erikson initially argued that identity in males and females differed for biological and anatomical reasons, for example, he referred to the "inner space" or womb as the basis for female identity. However, he changed his mind somewhat thereafter. Erikson (1968, p.273) argued that:

> *nothing in our interpretation . . . is meant to claim that either sex is doomed to one . . . mode or another; rather . . . these modes "come more naturally".*

Erikson didn't carry out any experimental studies to test his theoretical ideas. The ideal approach would have been to conduct a longitudinal or long-term study in which individuals were observed over a period of years starting before adolescence and continuing until after adolescence. In fact, as was mentioned earlier, Erikson relied mainly on his observations of adolescents undergoing therapy. He obtained evidence of an identity crisis in this biased sample, but this doesn't mean that all adolescents are the same and in fact they aren't.

Finally, Erikson's views merely *describe* what he regarded as typical of adolescent thinking and behaviour. He didn't provide a detailed *explanation* of the processes responsible for creating an identity crisis, nor did he indicate in detail the processes responsible for resolving it.

While searching for an identity, adolescents are already having to cope with physiological changes, changing roles, relationships, the prospect of future work and/or education, and other pressures. All this as they try to discover who they really are, and how they are seen by others.

Erikson uses all these areas of uncertainty, and more, to suggest an identity crisis that adolescents are bound to go through. He has been criticised for his concept of a *single* identity, and for his research sampling, which has been seen as too small in number and too male-biased. Erikson's ideas about identity are oversimplified, and more elaborate accounts have been given by Marcia and others. Marcia recognised that multiple identities are possible. Others have criticised Erikson's view that *all* adolescents suffer from an identity crisis.

Erikson was one of the first to develop a stage account of human development, but his stage theories fail to take individual differences fully into account. One stage or plan cannot apply to all people, and much evidence suggests that no two people with basically the same environment will behave in the same way.

CASE STUDY: ANNE FRANK

Anne Frank was a Jewish teenager in the Netherlands during the Second World War. She and members of her family spent 2 years hiding from the occupying Nazis in a secret annexe at the back of a warehouse in Amsterdam, during which time Anne kept a diary of day-to-day events and her thoughts and feelings. Anne was 13 years old when the family went into hiding, and she experienced the difficulties faced by all adolescents as well as the almost unbearable situation of being confined with seven other people, facing hunger, boredom, and the constant fear of discovery. After a year and a half in the secret annexe, Anne wrote:

Everyone thinks I'm showing off when I talk, ridiculous when I'm silent, insolent when I answer, cunning when I have a good idea, lazy when I'm tired, selfish when I eat one bite more than I should, stupid, cowardly, calculating, etc., etc. *All day long I hear nothing but what an exasperating child I am, and although I laugh it off and pretend not to mind, I wish I could ask God to give me another personality, one that doesn't antagonize everyone.*

After the war, only one member of Anne Frank's family had survived; her father Otto, who edited and published his daughter's diaries. Because of the social climate of the time (1947) Otto Frank edited out many references Anne had made to her sexual feelings and some passages in which she wrote with anger and sometimes hatred about her mother and other family members. A new edition of the diaries, published in 1997, gives a fuller picture of Anne Frank as a normal adolescent, struggling to come to terms with all the changes in her extraordinary and tragically short life.

Marcia's theory

James Marcia focused on the ways in which adolescents form an identity, which he regarded as a structure of beliefs and ideas regarding the self. According to Marcia (1980, p.159), "The better developed this structure is, the more individuals appear to be of their own . . . strengths and weaknesses . . . The less developed this structure is, the more confused individuals seem to be about their own distinctiveness from others and the more they have to rely on external sources to evaluate themselves." One of the challenges of adolescence is to develop a sense of identity by developing a structure of beliefs about themselves.

Marcia (1966, 1980) was much influenced by Erikson's (1963) notion that adolescents are likely to experience an identity crisis. However, he argued that better methods of assessing adolescents' state of identity diffusion or identity formation were needed. He also argued that Erikson's ideas were oversimplified, and that there are actually various different ways in which adolescents can fail to achieve a stable sense of identity.

Marcia's first assumption was that, at any point in time, each adolescent has an identity status. Marcia investigated the possible different kinds of identity status by using a semi-structured interview technique to explore what adolescents thought about occupational choice, religion, and political ideology. In each of these three areas an individual was classified on two dimensions: (1) Have various alternatives been considered seriously in each of the three areas? (crisis); and (2) Have firm commitments been made in those areas? (commitment). Marcia (1967, p.119) defined the key terms here as follows:

> *Crisis refers to times during adolescence when the individual seems to be actively involved in choosing among alternative occupations and beliefs. Commitment refers to the degree of personal investment the individual expresses in an occupation or belief.*

Marcia concluded from these interviews that there are four possible identity statuses that may be experienced during adolescence:

1. **Identity diffusion**: identity issues have not been considered in detail and no firm commitments have been made for the future.
2. **Foreclosure**: identity issues have not been considered seriously, but future commitments have been made in spite of this.
3. **Moratorium**: there has been an active exploration and consideration of alternatives, but no definite future commitments have been made; this corresponds to Erikson's identity crisis.
4. **Identity achievement**: various alternatives have been carefully considered, and firm future commitments have been made.

Marcia (1966) assumed that adolescents would tend to move from one of the low-identity statuses (foreclosure and diffusion) to one of the high-identity statuses (moratorium and achievement). Adolescents would change their identity status because of the growing external and internal pressures on them to enter the adult world. Not all adolescents would pass through each stage.

Research evidence

Marcia's development of Erikson's ideas was largely intended to facilitate empirical research. The stages identified on the previous page are the outcome of Marcia's own research and have received general support from other studies, such as Meilman's (1979) research, described in the Key Study on the next page. Meilman did find evidence of all four identity

? In order to assess the degree of crisis an adolescent was in, what question(s) did Marcia ask?

KEY TERMS

Identity diffusion: an identity status in which the individual has not focused on identity issues and has made no definite future commitments.

Foreclosure: an identity status during adolescence in which the individual has not focused on identity issues, but has nevertheless made definite future commitments.

Moratorium: an identity status in adolescence in which the individual has focused on identity issues, but has made no definite future commitments.

Identity achievement: in adolescence an identity status in which the individual has focused on identity issues, and has made definite future commitments.

statuses but also discovered that many of the characteristics typically associated with adolescence were in fact not typical at all. Some individuals *never* experienced an identity crisis and many individuals had still failed to achieve a stable identity by their mid-20s.

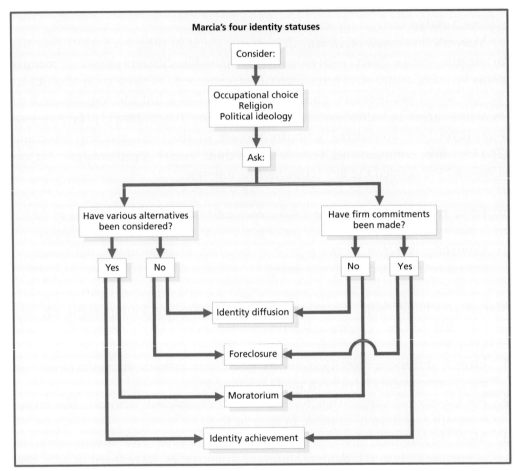

KEY STUDY
Meilman

Some support for Marcia's general approach was reported by Meilman (1979). He assessed the identity statuses of young males ranging in age between 12 and 24 using Marcia's semi-structured interview technique. All of the 12-year-olds and nearly all of the 15-year-olds had one of the low-identity statuses. Among the 15-year-olds, 64% had identity diffusion and 32% had foreclosure. Among the 18-year-olds, 48% had identity diffusion and 24% had foreclosure, with 20% having identity achievement. The proportion of identity achievers increased to 40% among the 21-year-olds, and to 56% among the 24-year-olds.

There are two surprising features of Meilman's findings. First, large numbers of people in their early 20s had still failed to achieve a stable identity, indicating that problems over identity are often by no means confined to the years of adolescence. Second, it appears that only a small minority of individuals at any age are in the moratorium period, suggesting that an identity crisis is fairly infrequent during or after adolescence.

Discussion points

1. Does it make sense to put adolescents and young adults into one of only four categories?
2. What confidence can we have in the opinions expressed by the participants in semi-structured interviews?

Marcia (1966) assumed, as did Erikson, that any given adolescent either has or hasn't forged an identity for himself/herself. In other words, identity formation is all or none. That assumption is an oversimplification, as was shown by Archer (1982). The identity statuses of adolescents varying in age between 12 and 18 were assessed in the areas of occupational choice, gender roles, religious values, and political ideologies. Only 5% of these adolescents had the same identity status in all four areas, indicating that the great majority of adolescents are at different stages of development towards identity formation in different areas of life.

Erikson (1968) and Marcia (1966) both seem to have assumed that adolescents who have achieved a stable sense of identity are unlikely to go back to an earlier, pre-identity stage. However, Marcia (1976) carried out a follow-up after his initial study, and found that some adolescents who had achieved a sense of identity had returned to the foreclosure or diffusion identity status 6 years later.

Identity status depends more on social and cultural factors than Marcia (1966) assumed. For example, Munro and Adams (1977) found that college students were more likely than those of the same age in full-time work to be in the moratorium period with respect to religious and political identity. Perhaps time spent at university provides more opportunity for exploration and questioning than is available in the workplace.

One of the key differences between Marcia's theory and that of Erikson is that Marcia argued that there are different ways in which an adolescent can fail to have achieved a sense of identity. Evidence that it is important to distinguish among the moratorium, foreclosure, and diffusion categories was reported by Marcia (1980). Those in the moratorium status felt much more positive about themselves and about the future than did those in the diffusion and foreclosure statuses. These findings are hard to explain from Erikson's theory, because the moratorium status comes closest to his notion of identity crisis.

> ? What experiences might cause an adolescent to go back to an earlier identity status?

Evaluation

Marcia's theory is more realistic than that of Erikson, in that it recognises that there are several possible identity statuses. However, it is open to most of the same criticisms. Semi-structured interviews conducted at one point in time cannot provide much evidence about the ways in which adolescents change and develop during the teenage years. It is also not clear whether the answers given by adolescents in these interviews are accurate, or whether they are simply telling the interviewer what they think he/she expects to hear. Furthermore, there is a large difference between describing four identity statuses found among adolescents and explaining in detail how these statuses arise and are replaced by other statuses.

Marcia's whole approach is rather limited. This was shown by Archer (1992, p.33), who asked the following awkward question:

> ? Marcia used semi-structured interviews to assess adolescents' identity status. What might be a better method to choose?

> *Why do we expend all this energy conducting these interviews, listen to these people share life stories, and then walk away with only these four little letters—"A" for identity achievement, "M" for moratorium, "F" for foreclosure, and "D" for identity diffusion?*

Some studies have focused on the factors within the family that may lead adolescents to have different identity statuses. Adolescents in either the identity

? From your own experience, do you think Erikson was right, or do you prefer Marcia's more elaborate ideas?

achievement or moratorium statuses tend to have affectionate parents and the freedom to be individuals in their own right (Waterman, 1982). Adolescents in the identity foreclosure status tend to have close relationships with domineering parents, and those in the identity diffusion status tend to have distant relationships with aloof or uninvolved parents (Waterman, 1982). This suggests that crises are not resolved by individuals.

Finally, there may be important differences in identity formation between generations not taken into account by Marcia. Waterman and Waterman (1975) compared fathers and sons, and found that fathers tended to have identity foreclosure whereas sons had identity diffusion or moratorium. Thus, it is possible that Marcia's theory is only really applicable to a particular point in historical time.

Theories of Social Development in Adolescence: The Sociological Approach

Erikson and Marcia focused on crises in adolescence, and how healthy psychological development was related to the resolution of crises. The sociological approach takes the view that adolescence is indeed a transitional process. However, the reason for this is not because there are personal crises to be overcome but rather that *external* factors steer the adolescent in the direction of transition. These external factors include culturally determined pressures from the family, from peers, the school, and other social influences such as the mass media. The net result is that the adolescent is placed under pressure at a time when he/she may be feeling most vulnerable. Vulnerability is due to those physical and psychological changes associated with puberty.

Coleman's focal theory

G. Stanley Hall (1904) suggested that adolescence is a time of "storm and stress" during which the child must experience the turbulent history of the human race in order to reach maturity, referred to as "recapitulation theory".

This view of crisis in adolescence was disputed by Coleman (1974) who argued that, in reality, most adolescents do not experience severe difficulties because they are usually able to "focus on" (thus focal theory) individual problems as they occur. Coleman agreed with the psychoanalytic view that adolescence was a time of role change and thus a time when social adjustments need to be made, but he didn't agree that crisis was inevitable or healthy. Instead, those adolescents who experience crisis may well have other ongoing, externally caused problems that make the adjustment more difficult.

Research evidence

Evidence to support Coleman's views comes from a large-scale study, involving 800 boys and girls aged from 11 to 17. Coleman and Hendry (1990) interviewed the young people asking them to discuss topics that were anxiety-provoking, such as self-image, being alone, occupational choice, and peer, sexual, and parental relationships. Each issue had a different distribution curve, peaking in importance over a particular age. Concerns about peer relations, for example, peaked earlier than occupational choice. In addition, some adolescents came to these issues earlier than normal, and others experienced them later. Adolescent life, therefore, can be seen as a mixture of stability and adjustment in different areas of life at different times. The coincidence of a number of important issues all peaking at once could cause problems, but, generally, adolescents navigate carefully through this stage of life, choosing whether to engage with particular issues immediately or later. In this way, they manage their own life stage and are generally successful in coming through unscathed.

Evaluation

There appears to be no reason to suppose that adolescence is necessarily a time of storm and stress, or that such crises need to be weathered for healthy personality development. At the same time it is clear that adolescents do have adjustments to make to their physical and psychological identities.

It may be that Erikson and Marcia, on the one hand, and Coleman on the other, were using the word "crisis" in a rather different sense. Erikson's understanding of a crisis was that it was a fairly normal developmental event, whereas Coleman may well be referring to a more serious disturbance caused by a number of conflicts all occurring at the same time.

Eccles et al. (1993) put forward a somewhat different explanation of the stress experienced by many adolescents. They pointed out that most Western cultures have many laws and rules limiting the behaviour of adolescents—these include minimum ages for drinking alcohol in pubs, minimum voting ages, and so on. As a result, adolescents in Western cultures are often deprived of the opportunities they want to express their needs.

Adolescence is traditionally considered an emotionally turbulent time, marked by an increase in distance (both emotionally and physically) from parental control, as the child strives for independence.

Relationships in adolescence

A key part of the sociological approach is to emphasise the role of socialisation in adolescent development, especially the role of family and peers in socialising the adolescent. "Sociological" means that it is concerned with the effects that social groups have on the individual. A classic picture is of the adolescent breaking his or her ties with the family and substituting the influence of the family with peer group culture.

The theoretical approaches of Erickson and of Marcia are of relevance to the issue of relationships in adolescence. Interactions with peers and opposite-sex relationships can play an important role in adolescents' development of a sense of identity. Conversely, as Erickson pointed out, adolescents in a state of identity confusion may fail to establish strong friendships or relationships because they fear commitment to others.

Relationships with parents

Adolescence is traditionally seen as a time of conflict between parents and their children. There are various ways of explaining why this may be. The cognitive-developmental view (e.g., Piaget) might suggest that the young people's newly achieved abilities of hypothetical and abstract thought might lead them to start considering their own opinions, leading them into philosophical arguments with parents. Peterson and Zill (1986) found that children in the stage of formal operations (aged 11 upwards) were more likely to have heated arguments with their parents, though we cannot be certain whether this is *because* of the stage of formal operations.

Older children can be surprisingly confident about debating.

A second explanation, from the sociobiological perspective, is that adolescent strivings for independence are adaptive because this enables the adolescent to become directed towards the peer group and ready for entry into adulthood. The psychoanalytic view was also one that regarded independence as a crucial aim of this stage and a necessity for future healthy psychological development.

Some studies have found conflict but many have found that most adolescents are actually quite happy with the situation at home. For example, Offer et al. (1988) surveyed adolescents in various countries (Australia, Bangladesh, Hungary, Israel, Italy, Taiwan, Turkey, United States, and West Germany) and found that 91% denied holding a grudge against their parents and a similar number said their parents were not ashamed of them. More strikingly, Apter (1990) studied adolescent girls in the UK and in the USA. The key finding was that most adolescent girls identified their mother as the person to whom they felt closest.

Smetana (1988) identified two different kinds of dispute. One concerns domains under the control of the adolescent, such as sleeping late at the weekend, and the other concerns parental domains, such as not cleaning up after a party, or thieving. The latter were regarded as legitimate areas for parents to continue to exert control whereas the former could lead to parent–child disputes.

Baumrind (e.g., 1991) has made an important contribution to our understanding of the relationship between parents and children/adolescents, arguing that there are two basic dimensions of parenting style:

1. Parental responsiveness: this dimension is concerned with the extent to which parents are supportive and cater for their children's special demands.
2. Parental demandingness: this dimension is concerned with the extent to which parents discipline their children and are willing to confront them when they are disobedient.

Low and high levels on these two dimensions give four types of parenting: uninvolved (low on both dimensions), authoritative (high on both dimensions), authoritarian (low on responsiveness but high on demandingness), and indulgent (high on responsiveness but low on demandingness). Children and adolescents whose parents are authoritative are more competent socially and in general than those whose parents are non-authoritative (Baumrind, 1991). Baumrind (1991) reported that children and adolescents whose parents are uninvolved performed the worst overall. Adolescents with authoritarian parents generally perform well at school but suffer from fairly poor social skills and elevated levels of depression. Finally, adolescents from indulgent homes have good social skills and high self-esteem, but tend to perform poorly at school.

In relation to the issue of independence, one might think that adolescents who become emotionally dependent on their peers are compensating for lack of support from home. However, Ryan and Lynch (1989) make an important point that, just in the same way as a securely attached infant is better equipped to form relationships away from primary caregivers, the same is true of adolescents. Therefore, adolescent independence is likely to be the result of good family relationships rather than the outcome of conflict.

Allen and Land (1999) argue along similar lines. According to them, adolescents need to feel securely attached to one or both parents at least as much

? Are independent adolescents more or less likely to have good relations with their parents?

as when they were children. A key role of the parents is to support their adolescent children as they seek independence or autonomy. More generally, the relationships between adolescents and their parents become more *flexible* than when they were younger. An important factor in maintaining strong relationships between adolescents and their parents is that many adolescents are better able than children to take account of their parents' wishes as well as their own.

Evaluation. The notion that adolescents are constantly at war with their parents is a serious distortion of the typical situation. It is undeniable that adolescents sometimes have arguments with their parents, but most adolescents still feel a strong sense of attachment to one or both parents. When considering conflicts within the family, it is important to note that the parents are not always blameless. As we have seen, parenting style has a substantial effect on children (e.g., Baumrind, 1991), and some parenting styles leave much to be desired (e.g., uninvolved). Additional evidence that parents are sometimes responsible for parent–child conflicts was reported by Montemayor et al. (1993). Interactions between fathers and their adolescent children were more negative and full of conflict when the fathers in question were suffering from mid-life stress.

Relationships with peers

There is no doubt that peers do become increasingly important during adolescence. Palmonari, Pombeni, and Kirchler (1989) surveyed Italian 16- to 18-year-olds and found that 90% identified themselves as belonging to a peer group. We can see the importance of peer relationships by considering what happens when adolescents don't belong to a peer group. Buhrmester (1992) found that adolescents who had close peer group relationships were also less prone to anxiety and depression, suggesting that belonging to a peer group provides emotional support. However, it could be argued that what is actually happening is that depressed adolescents find it difficult to form close relationships.

One feature of adolescent behaviour is the image of being different while at the same time adolescents are actually highly conformist within their own social group.

Kirchler et al. (1991) argued that adolescents who fail to establish peer relationships and spend most of their time at home are likely to find it difficult to establish their independence and to engage in adult relationships later on.

An important role of the peer group is social conformity. Costanzo and Shaw (1966) conducted conformity experiments along the lines of those of Asch, using participants aged between 7 and 21. They found that conformity peaked at around 11–13 years. Berndt (1979) investigated conformity using hypothetical situations where the participant was encouraged by another (a peer or an adult) to behave in an anti-social or pro-social way (e.g., stealing a sweet or helping someone with homework). Berndt found that conformity to adults' suggestions decreased with age, whereas the reverse was true of peer conformity. Pro-social conformity peaked around the age of 11–12 whereas anti-social conformity occurred slightly later, at 14–15 years.

Harris (1997) argues that this tendency towards conformity is vital in adolescent development. According to **group socialisation theory**, children and adolescents are shaped far more by their peers than they are by their parents. Only this can explain why siblings are often so very different from each other. Siblings have genetic similarities and they share the same home influences yet they are so different. This must be because they are largely socialised by peers. This makes sense when you consider that, ultimately, we all have to function in the world outside our own home and thus it is important to orient ourselves towards peers rather than families as we get older.

There are important differences between males and females in friendships. In general, female adolescents attach more emotional importance to their same-sex and their opposite-sex friendships than do adolescent males (Lempers & Clark-Lempers, 1993). Strong evidence for gender differences in same-sex friendships was reported by Johnson and Aries (1983) in analyses of conversational patterns. Female friends focused on personal problems, family problems, and intimate relationships, whereas male friends discussed sports, shared activities, and hobbies.

There are some individual differences in peer relationships that depend on differences in parenting styles. For example, Fuligni and Eccles (1993) questioned nearly 2000 11-year-olds, and found that peer orientation was higher in adolescents who rated their parents as more authoritarian and where adolescents felt they had few opportunities to be involved in decision making. Adolescents who experience a democratic parenting style may rely less on their peers.

Evaluation. There are several advantages associated with adolescents having a wide range of same-sex and opposite-sex friendships. The other side of the coin is that adolescents who don't form peer relationships may suffer from anxiety and depression, and may also find it harder to become independent in adulthood. It is important to note that the nature of peer relationships among adolescents depends on various factors including the parental style to which they have been exposed. In addition, same-sex friendships tend to be more intimate and more focused on emotional issues in girls than in boys.

We have discussed peer relationships in a separate section from relationships with parents. However, as we have seen, there are important links between them. In one study, Gauze (1994) found that adolescents often discussed peer relationships with their mothers (but tended not to do so with their fathers).

EXAM HINT

AO2 can be a challenge in a question on relationships with parents and peers, so think about how the research challenges the stereotypes that parents and adolescents are in conflict, and that peer conformity is all pervasive. You can use the research as evidence for and against the theories of social development, and use the next section on cultural variations to discuss the ethnocentrism of research.

KEY TERM

Group socialisation theory: the view that children are socialised by groups outside the home, especially their peer groups, rather than the family.

There is a general limitation of most research on peer relationships, namely, that it is difficult to know *why* the findings are as they are. This occurs in part because we can't exercise experimental control over the number and nature of peer relationships of any given adolescent. As a result, we can describe what happens but we typically can't establish clearly the causal factors responsible.

Cultural differences

The account of adolescence that has been presented so far is largely related to European or so-called "Western" culture. In fact, however, there are enormous individual and cultural differences in the adolescent experience (Durkin, 1995).

For example, it is generally accepted within Western culture that adolescence is a period of life that extends for several years and only gradually comes to an end in the late teens or early 20s. In contrast, teenagers in many non-industrialised cultures go through "rites of passage" in which they move very rapidly from being regarded as children to becoming perceived as adults. These rites of passage are very diverse, but often involve some large religious or other ceremony.

The individualist and collectivist dimension

Adolescents in the United States and other Western societies generally take several years to achieve a clear sense of adult identity. However, that doesn't necessarily mean that similar processes are at work in other cultures. Markus and Kitayama (1991) drew a distinction between societies in which the self is perceived as *independent* and those in which the self is perceived as interdependent. Societies (e.g., the United States or Western Europe) in which the self is independent tend to be described as individualistic, egocentric, and self-contained. Societies (e.g., those in the Far East) in which the self is interdependent are described as **collectivist**, connected, or relational. In the latter societies, many of the key decisions of early adulthood aren't taken directly by the individual concerned. For example, there may be an arranged marriage, and the individual may be expected to do the same job as his/her father or mother. In such societies, the whole nature of adolescence is different from that in **individualist** societies.

No adolescence

Historically, the concept of adolescence is also not universal. Shaffer (1993) claimed that adolescence is an "invention" of the twentieth century. He argued that, when it became illegal to employ children, this created a new section of the population, an "adolescent peer culture", which was isolated from those who were younger and older. They weren't able to identify with younger children and were now kept separate from the adult working population. Up until this time there was no "adolescent" phase. It was G. Stanley Hall, writing at the beginning of the nineteenth century, who first identified this period of development. According to Gross (1996), the concept of a "teenager" is even more recent, being coined in the 1950s. Adolescence is therefore historically a new concept and is also culturally specific.

Evidence that adolescence in the Western sense is not universal was discussed by Condon (1987) in his analysis of the Inuit of the Canadian arctic at the start of the twentieth century. In that society, young women were regarded as adult at puberty. By the time of puberty, they were usually married, and soon thereafter started to have children. Young men were treated as adult when they could build

? What are the distinctive features of a collectivist society?

EXAM HINT

You could be set a question on cultural differences so consider some of the following as ideas for discussion: Does adolescence exist across cultures? Is it a period of conflict and even delinquency across cultures? What evidence is there for differences within cultures? What conclusions can be drawn from these variations?

KEY TERMS

Collectivist: a culture where individuals share tasks, belongings, and income. The people may live in large family groups and value interdependence.

Individualist: a culture that emphasises individuality, individual needs, and independence.

Difficult living conditions may force adolescents to move straight from childhood to adulthood in order to survive.

an igloo, hunt large animals on their own, and support themselves and their families. The difficult living conditions in the arctic meant there was no time for teenagers to spend several years thinking about what they were going to do with their lives.

Sub-cultural differences

Within Britain there are many cultural groups, and for adolescent members of minority groups there may be particular problems related to identity formation in adolescence because their path to adulthood is not clear-cut. Weinreich (1979) reported findings on different groups of adolescent girls in the United Kingdom. Immigrant girls (especially those from Pakistani families) had higher levels of identity diffusion than did girls from the dominant culture. It is fairly common to find that adolescents from ethnic minorities take longer to achieve identity status, perhaps because their lives are more complex and confusing than those of the majority group (Durkin, 1995).

Delinquency

A different kind of sub-culture from ethnic minorities is the delinquent sub-culture. Much of this Section has presented the view that young people generally negotiate adolescence with relatively little stress and conflict. But there is a minority for whom this is not true. Hargreaves (1967) studied the different sub-cultures within a school population of 14- to 15-year-old boys in the north of England. The study identified two opposed sub-cultures: a group of academically successful boys, who were also the ones most liked by the teachers and were often prefects, and the "delinquescent" low achievers. Popularity in this group was related to anti-social behaviour. These data suggest that children not achieving at school turn to other sources to define success or acceptance, thus forming delinquent sub-cultures.

It is difficult to assess the intellectual ability of such delinquents because they also usually lack the motivation to do well on IQ tests, therefore their poor performance may be due to low motivation rather than low IQ.

One of the possible explanations for delinquency is reputation management theory (Emler, 1984). This follows on from the research of Hargreaves and proposes that for all adolescents the main task is identity formation. For those who can define their reputation in terms of academic success, identity is not a problem. But other adolescents reject socially sanctioned values either because they are academically unsuccessful or because they may distrust the rewards offered by conventional social systems. This view is supported by the social nature of delinquency. Emler, Reicher, and Ross (1987) found that most adolescent crime was committed in the company of others. Reicher and Emler (1986) argue that the peer context is critical in constructing social and personal identity and, for some adolescents, delinquency is their main route to doing this. In addition, this can explain why boys are more likely to be delinquent than girls—because there is greater pressure on them to do well at school and therefore failure is more deeply felt (Emler & Reicher, 1995).

A final factor associated with delinquency in adolescents is socio-economic status. Pettit et al. (1999) studied 12- and 13-year-olds rated by teachers as having (or not having) behaviour problems (e.g., behaving aggressively). The adolescents with behaviour problems generally came from unsafe, working-class neighbourhoods.

Evaluation

The nature of adolescence and the kinds of identity emerging from that period of life vary considerably from one culture to another and can also be found at the sub-cultural level. This should come as no surprise—in order for someone to function effectively as an adult in a given culture they have to think and behave in ways that are acceptable within that culture. At one time, most cross-cultural research was carried out by Western psychologists who in many cases were not very sensitive to the realities of the cultures they were studying. In addition, they would use tests and other measures devised in Western cultures and often inappropriate for use in other cultures. Thankfully, the situation is slowing changing as more cross-cultural research is carried out by psychologists who grew up in the culture they find themselves studying.

SECTION SUMMARY
Adolescence

❖ Adolescence roughly covers the teenage years, but is better defined in psychological terms rather than by age.

❖ It is a time of many changes but it is not necessarily experienced as stressful.

What is adolescence?

❖ This approach emphasises biologically driven stages in development.

❖ According to Erikson:

Erikson's theory

— Adolescents experience an identity crisis, which is necessary in order to resolve the identity issue and to move on to the formation of a stable adult identity.

— Adolescents experience uncertainty (identity diffusion) revolving around intimacy, diffusion of time, diffusion of industry, and negative identity.

— Females have greater problems than males with identity development.

— An identity crisis is more likely towards the end of adolescence.

❖ Evaluation:

— There is some evidence of stress during adolescence but low self-esteem may be explained by other changes not associated with adolescence *per se*.

— There appears to be little support for sex differences in identity development or for identity crisis later in adolescence.

— Erikson may have relied too much on limited observations of a biased sample of emotionally disturbed adolescents.

— The account is more descriptive than explanatory.

Marcia's theory

❖ This approach aims to find more exact ways of assessing identity crisis and a more complex formulation of how adolescents achieve a stable sense of identity.

❖ According to Marcia:

— There are four identity statuses that may be experienced during adolescence: identity diffusion, foreclosure, moratorium, and identity achievement.
— Crisis and commitment determine the passage through these statuses.

❖ Evaluation:

— A number of Marcia's (and Erikson's) assumptions have not been supported by research:
— Not all individuals ever reach identity achievement.
— The identity statuses are less all-or-none than Marcia suggested.
— There may be a return to earlier stages.
— Social and cultural factors have been shown to be important.
— The interview method may produce inaccurate data, and the classification scheme is ultimately reductionist.
— However, Marcia showed that the identity crisis takes various different forms (diffusion, foreclosure, and moratorium).

The sociological approach

❖ This suggests that transition is forced on the adolescent because of external factors (e.g., pressures from the media) rather than internal identity crises.

❖ The "storm and stress view":

— According to Coleman's focal theory this view is generally wrong because most adolescents are able to focus on areas of development one at a time, and thus remain fairly unstressed.
— Research evidence supports this.

Relationships with parents

❖ The role of parents in development is emphasised by the sociological approach. Parent–adolescent conflict may be related to:

— An increased ability to think abstractly (cognitive-developmental view).
— An adaptive behaviour to promote independence (sociobiological and psychoanalytic view).

❖ Evaluation:

— Many adolescents do not experience conflict with their parents over fundamental issues such as moral principles.
— Discord may be related to social living and not to the relationship itself.
— Adolescent independence is likely to be the result of good family relationships rather than the outcome of conflict.

Relationships with peers

❖ Peers become increasingly important during adolescence as they offer emotional support and are a source of social conformity (and security).

❖ Adolescents are more conformist than younger children, especially with respect to their peers.

❖ Group socialisation theory suggests that peer influence is important because it prepares adolescents to cope with the wider adult world.

❖ Individual and cultural differences are both related to social processes:

    Cultural differences

— In collectivist cultures the society rather than the individual constructs identity.

— In some non-Western cultures there is no adolescent period. This may also apply to our own culture in the past.

❖ Sub-cultural variation also exists, including delinquent sub-culture. For some adolescents delinquency may be the only route to social identity, which leads to the assumption that delinquency is sometimes a necessary part of adolescence.

See also pages 150–159 of the revision guide.

FURTHER READING

The topics in this chapter are covered in greater depth by T. Abbott (2001) *Social and personality development* (London: Routledge), written specifically for the AQA A specification. A useful reference for theories of personality can be found in C.S. Hall, G. Lindzey, and J.B. Campbell (1997) *Theories of personality* (New York: John Wiley). There are chapters on gender and adolescence in K. Durkin (1995) *Developmental social psychology: From infancy to old age* (Oxford: Blackwell). J. Kroger (1996) *Identity in adolescence* (London: Routledge) is part of a Routledge series on "adolescence and society" edited by John Coleman.

EXAMPLE EXAMINATION QUESTIONS

You should spend 30 minutes on each of the questions below, which aim to test the material in this chapter.

1. Discuss one explanation of personality development. (24 marks)
2. Distinguish between psychodynamic and social learning approaches to the explanation of personality development. (24 marks)
3. (a) Outline **two** explanations of the development of gender identity and/or gender roles. (12 marks)
   (b) Evaluate these explanations. (12 marks)
4. "Narrow gender concepts inevitably limit a person's behavioural repertoire and mean that an individual has to behave in a rigid fashion. People who are less gender-stereotyped are freer to behave in ways that are appropriate to the situation and this is psychologically healthier."
   Discuss the effects of gender roles and/or gender identity on behaviour. (24 marks)
5. Critically consider research into social development in adolescence. (24 marks)
6. Discuss the findings of research into cultural differences in adolescent behaviour. (24 marks)

Examination Tips

Question 1. "Discuss" is an AO1 and AO2 term, therefore you should describe your chosen theory of personality and then evaluate it. For good marks the description needs to be well-detailed. Evaluation/commentary (AO2) is best if it is embedded in the essay rather than "tacked on" at the end. You might make reference to research studies, methodological flaws in such evidence, and/or make comparisons with other theories. Practical applications are a means of positive evaluation.

Question 2. "Distinguish between" is an AO1 and AO2 term, therefore you should describe both theories but also aim to draw out the similarities and differences in doing so. It is this compare/contrast that will earn you the AO2 marks. There are numerous ways of contrasting theories such as in terms of their potential for research and their actual research support; in terms of their cultural or gender bias, with respect to the extent the theory covers the life span, and so on. You can use lots of different theories as the question requires that you contrast the two approaches not two theories.

Question 3. In part (a) the injunction "outline" is used to signal that breadth rather than depth is required here. "Outline" requires a summary description only. You need to cover two explanations of how gender identity and/or gender roles develop and should provide a summary description of each explanation. In part (b) you are required to offer any kind of evaluation, which might be achieved through reference to research evidence, a consideration of the conclusions of such studies and their methodology, comparisons with other explanations of gender identity, and any practical applications. Make sure you give a full 15 minutes to the second part or you will lose valuable marks.

Question 4. In this question you are not required to specifically address the quotation, though it may help in directing your response. The essay requires consideration of the relationship between gender identity/roles and actual behaviour. How does our identity influence the way we behave? You should describe the relationship between roles/identity and behaviour, and at the same time assess the value of such understanding. Upon what sort of evidence is this knowledge based? Is this evidence sound?

Question 5. "Research" can be either theories or studies. If you describe studies then you may evaluate them with reference to theories and vice versa. When describing studies you can use the same guidelines as for AS level: write something about the aims, procedures, findings, and conclusions. The essay is quite open-ended so it will probably be necessary to be selective in the way you structure your response, otherwise you risk providing too much breadth and not enough detail to communicate good understanding.

Question 6. The essay requires a focus on the findings only of research (theories and/or studies) and therefore no credit will be given for information about procedures or conclusions except where these are relevant to our knowledge of findings and/or used as an evaluation of the findings. For example, it is likely that you will criticise such findings in terms of the validity of the research procedures. Such criticism may be positive or negative. Note that the essay is limited to cultural differences in adolescent behaviour but such differences arguably include many things, for example, historical and gender differences (it may be desirable to be explicit about why these count as "cultural").

WEBSITES

http://www.ship.edu/~cgboeree/perscontents.html
   Large site covering personality theories.
http://www.personalityresearch.org
   Great ideas in personality, lots of material and links on personality theories and research.
http://www.personalityresearch.org/glossary.html
   Glossary of personality terms, with links to related glossaries.
http://www.spsp.org
   Society for Personality and Social Psychology homepage.
http://www.freud.org.uk/
   The homepage of the Freud Museum, London, which includes links to many Freud-related sites on the internet.
http://www.freudfile.org/
   Provides information about the life and work of Sigmund Freud, including online resources.
http://www.psy.pdx.edu/PsiCafe/KeyTheorists/Erikson.htm
   A site about Erik Erikson, including critiques and links.
http://www.gwu.edu/~tip/bandura.html
   Overview of Bandura's Social Learning Theory.
http://www.ship.edu/~cgboeree/bandura.html
   Introduction to Bandura's theories.
http://www.nd.edu/~rbarger/kohlberg.html
   Summary of Kohlberg's stages of moral development.
http://www.aber.ac.uk/media/Students/hzi9402.html
   Essay on the effect of television on the development of gender roles in children.
http://www.stanford.edu/group/adolescent.ctr/
   Stanford Center on Adolescence.

COMPARATIVE PSYCHOLOGY

Human Reproductive Behaviour p.298

- Why does a peahen find a peacock's tail attractive?
- What traits do women find attractive in men?
- Why do females usually end up being the ones to care for offspring?

Evolutionary Explanations of Mental Disorders p.315

- If mental disorders are inherited, how can we explain why such genes persist? One would think they would *not* be naturally selected.
- Is it because some aspects of mental disorders are actually adaptive?
- Or is it because of "genome lag"?

Evolution of Intelligence p.327

- Why might an intelligent individual be more likely to survive and reproduce?
- Is intelligence a sexy trait?
- Are people with larger brains more intelligent?

Evolutionary Explanations of Human Behaviour

Charles Darwin was struck by the fact that most species seem well designed for the environment in which they find themselves. He referred to "the innumerable cases in which organisms of every kind are beautifully adapted to their habits of life—for instance, a woodpecker or tree-frog to climb trees, or a seed for dispersal by hooks and plumes" (from Darwin's autobiography; see Ridley, 1996, p.9).

According to Darwin's (1859) theory of evolution, the reasons why so many species are well adapted to their environment are as follows:

1. *Variation*: Individuals within a species differ from each other in their physical characteristics (e.g., height) and in their behaviour.
2. *Inheritance*: At least some of the variation among members of a species is inherited. As a result, offspring tend to resemble their parents more than other members of the species.
3. *Competition*: The members of most species produce far more offspring than can survive. Darwin (1859) worked out that a pair of elephants could have about 19 million descendants alive 750 years after their birth if there were no problems of survival, given the expected reproductive productivity of any pair of mating elephants. In fact, however, there is competition for mates, food, and places to live.
4. *Natural selection*: Those members of a species surviving the process of competition who go on to breed will tend to have characteristics better suited to the environment than those who don't. Thus, there is **natural selection** or survival of the fittest (in the sense of survival or reproductive success rather than physical fitness!).
5. *Adaptation*: As a result of natural selection, successive generations will tend to be better adapted to their environment. They will possess characteristics allowing them to obtain food and to reproduce.

In sum, the key to evolution by natural selection is differential reproductive success. Thus, those members of a species well adapted to their environment are more likely to reproduce than those poorly adapted. Over hundreds or thousands

---

KEY TERM

Natural selection: the process by which certain traits (and the associated genes) are perpetuated because of the advantage they confer in terms of survival and increased reproduction.

Evolutionary explanations—key summary points

- According to the theory of evolution, most species are well adapted to their environment because of variation, inheritance, competition, natural selection, and adaptation.
- The key to evolution by natural selection is differential reproductive success.
- Evolutionary psychologists seek to apply insights from the theory of evolution to explain human behaviour.

of generations, this gradual process of natural selection can produce substantial changes within any given species. However, changes occasionally occur rapidly when there are **mutations** or changes in single **genes** during reproduction.

A crucial question is whether this evolutionary account is as appropriate for explaining human behaviour as non-human behaviour, given that we are influenced by language and consciousness. According to those working within the field of **evolutionary psychology**, it does make sense to explain much human behaviour in evolutionary terms. However, even evolutionary psychologists generally admit that there are also very important cultural factors to take into account when accounting for human behaviour. For example, as we will see, evolutionary psychologists have much to say about human sexual behaviour. However, there are large differences in the frequency of sexual activity, the number of partners, and so on between cultures. These cultural differences are difficult to explain in evolutionary terms.

On the face of it, it seems as if many humans are *not* very well adapted to their environment. For example, what is the advantage associated with suffering from a serious mental disorder? According to the evolutionary perspective, we should look for an answer by considering what may have happened hundreds of thousands of years ago. It is possible that what we now call mental disorders were useful or adaptive in the far distant past.

The above point is really important. It is often assumed that evolutionary psychologists believe that humans are well-adapted in most respects to their environment. This assumption is false, because it can take thousands of generations for natural selection to produce substantial genetic changes. As Buss (1999, p.20) pointed out, "We carry around a Stone-Aged brain in a modern environment. A strong desire for fat, adaptive in a past environment of scarce food resources, now leads to clogged arteries and heart attacks."

HUMAN REPRODUCTIVE BEHAVIOUR

Natural Selection and Sexual Selection

Sexual reproduction involves two parents creating a new individual by combining their genes. If an individual doesn't reproduce, then that's the end of his/her genes (unless an individual helps a close relative to reproduce). Therefore, any characteristic that maximises an individual's ability to reproduce successfully is highly adaptive and likely to be naturally selected. Individuals with these genes go on to form successive generations.

Charles Darwin formulated this theory of evolution by natural selection but there are inconsistencies with this theory. When we look at other species, there are some characteristics that seem positively detrimental to the survival of individual animals. For example, stags have huge antlers that must be a disadvantage when trying to escape from a predator. You would think that stags with small antlers would be naturally selected and therefore we wouldn't see any stages with larger antler. To solve this problem, Darwin (1871) outlined the principle of **sexual selection**. He argued that if a characteristic such as the stag's antlers

KEY TERMS

Mutations: genetic changes that can then be inherited by any offspring.

Genes: units of inheritance that form part of a chromosome. Some characteristics are determined by one gene, whereas for others many genes are involved.

Evolutionary psychology: an approach that explains behaviour in terms of its function and adaptiveness (i.e., the extent to which a behaviour enhances survival and reproduction of the individual's genes).

increases the individual's changes of reproduction, then this characteristic will be adaptive because that stag will have more offspring. The antlers serve to increase the stag's reproductive fitness. The next question is, "Why would stags with larger antlers have increased chances of reproduction?" The answer is because stags fight for the right to be the dominant male and to have the right to access the harem of females.

We will start this Section with a general consideration of sexual selection in non-human animals before considering the human species.

Anisogamy and parental investment

Males produce sperm and females produce eggs. Sperm and eggs are both gametes, meaning reproductive cells.

- Males produce sperm in thousands at relatively little physiological cost. Therefore, their best strategy is to mate with many females, because this should result in the maximum number of offspring to perpetuate their genetic line.
- Females produce eggs, each of which contains a store of food for the growing embryo. This incurs some cost to the female and so eggs aren't generally produced in thousands.

Fertilisation of a human egg by a sperm, an example of anisogamy, where the gametes of the two sexes are dissimilar.

The difference between egg and sperm is called **anisogamy**, a type of sexual reproduction in which the games or reproductive cells of the two sexes are dissimilar. It is rare to find animals in which the two gametes are the same size (isogamy), but it does occur in, for example, paramecium, a tiny freshwater organism.

Of key importance is the notion of **parental investment**, which Trivers (1972) defined as, "any investment by the parent in an individual offspring that increases the offspring's chance of surviving (and hence reproductive success) at the cost of the parent's ability to invest in other offspring". In mammals, female investment in her offspring is greater than male investment, in part because of the female's efforts during pregnancy. For example, female elephant seals are pregnant for several months before giving birth to a pup that may weigh as much as 50kg or 8 stone. After the pup is born, the mother loses up to 200kg or 31 stone in weight during the first weeks of feeding.

It is important to note that Trivers (1972) didn't argue that females in every species would have greater parental investment than males. His key notion was that the sex having more parental investment would tend to be more selective when mating than would the other sex.

Human species

Female parental investment is typically much greater than male parental investment in the human species. As Buss (1999, p.102) pointed out:

A man in human evolutionary history could walk away from a casual coupling having lost only a few hours or even a few minutes. A woman in

As the female will invest considerably more in her offspring than her male counterpart, she must select a mate carefully. The male must therefore compete with his rivals to ensure that he wins this mating opportunity.

evolutionary history risked getting pregnant as a result, and therefore could have incurred the cost of that decision for years.

What are the implications of the female's greater parental investment in her offspring? According to Trivers (1972), "Where one sex invests considerably more than the other, members of the latter will compete among themselves to mate with members of the former." Thus, women will typically be more discriminating than men in their choice of sex partners, because the consequences of mating with an unsuitable partner are potentially much greater for women than for men. If males have to fight for the right to have sex with females, then natural selection would have favoured those characteristics making it easier to compete. For example, it might have led to men being larger than women, and also more aggressive physically. Similar processes based on natural selection have operated in virtually all other species of mammal.

As we have seen, human males can maximise their reproductive potential by having sex with numerous females. This should lead them to seek women who are fertile. One way to do this is to seek younger women. In contrast, females can only bear a limited number of children, and they invest heavily in each one during the 9 months of pregnancy and for several years thereafter. It follows that they should prefer men who have good resources and who are willing to be committed to them over long periods of time.

Several studies have produced support for this view. Buss (1989; see the Key Study on the next page) conducted a cross-cultural study to show that men and women in many different cultures follow the patterns of behaviour predicted by evolutionary theory for the factors most valued in a mate. His findings are consistent with those of Davis (1990), who considered the content of personal advertisements in newspapers. Women advertising for a mate emphasised their physical beauty and indicated they were looking for a high-status, wealthy man. In contrast, men emphasised their wealth of other resources, and made it clear they were looking for a physically attractive younger woman. In other words, women regard men as "success objects", whereas men regard women as "sex objects". These findings fit with the much greater parental investment of women than of men. Evidence that doesn't fit evolutionary theory is discussed shortly.

More evidence supporting the prediction from evolutionary theory that females should be more selective than males in their choice of sexual partners was reported by Clark and Hatfield (1989). Attractive male and female students approached students of the opposite sex, and said, "Hi, I've been noticing you around town lately, and I find you very attractive. Would you have sex with me?" As you have probably guessed, this offer was received much more eagerly by male students than by female ones. None of the

■ **Activity:** Westen (1996, p.706) commented on the behaviour of men and women: "Consider the Casanova who professes commitment and then turns out a few months later not to be ready for it; the man who gladly sleeps with a woman on a first date but then does not want to see her again, certainly not for a long-term relationship; or the women who only date men of high status and earning potential."

Westen suggested that all of these behaviours can be explained in evolutionary terms. Try to do this for yourself, by making a list of the different behaviours along with the evolutionary explanations for them. You also might consider why some people might find Westen's comments sexist and offensive.

KEY STUDY
Cross-cultural support for the evolutionary account of mate choice

One way of testing the evolutionary theory of human sexual selection is by carrying out a cross-cultural study of preferred characteristics in mates. If the theory is correct, there should be clear differences in those characteristics preferred by men and by women, and these differences should be consistent across cultures. Some support for these predictions was reported by Buss (1989), who obtained data from 37 cultures in 33 countries. He found that males in virtually every culture preferred females who were younger than them, and so likely to have good reproductive potential. In contrast, females in all cultures preferred males who were older, and thus more likely to have good resources. As predicted, females rated good financial prospects in a potential mate as more important than did males. It could be argued that males should value physical attractiveness in their mates more highly than females, because of its association with reproductive potential. In 36 out of 37 cultures, males valued physical attractiveness in mates more than did females. Finally, males tended to value chastity in a potential mate more than did females, but the difference between the sexes was not significant in 38% of the cultures sampled.

Key study evaluation
The findings of Buss (1989) are of key importance, but they are less clear-cut than they seem for three main reasons. First, they don't actually show that sex differences in mate preference are consistent across cultures. In fact, there were much smaller sex differences in more developed cultures than in less developed ones on most measures, including preferred age differences, importance of financial prospects, and the value of chastity in a mate. Second, the evolutionary approach is more concerned with behaviour than with the preferences assessed by Buss. In fact, the actual average age difference between husband and wife across cultures was 2.99 years, which is similar to the preferred age differences for males (2.66 years) and for females (3.42 years). However, it is by no means clear that there would be this level of agreement between preferences and behaviour for the other measures obtained by Buss. Third, cultural differences were about six times greater than sex differences overall. Since evolutionary psychologists largely discount cultural differences, this shows a real limitation in the evolutionary approach.

Discussion points
1. Does this research provide strong support for the evolutionary approach?
2. Why do you think that sex differences in mate preference vary between Western and non-Western cultures?

? Using words like "selection" and "choice" suggests that these behaviours are intentional—but they aren't. How could this difficulty with description be overcome?

female students accepted the invitation, whereas 75% of the male students did. Some of the male students who declined the invitation apologised that they couldn't because they were seeing their girl-friend that night! These findings support the view that men are easily persuaded to have sex, whereas women are more choosy. However, it should be noted that we don't know whether the students' actual behaviour would have been consistent with what they said.

Parental investment
In humans, joint parental investment is important because of the long time it takes for offspring to pass through childhood. There are many customs we observe that help females ensure that male parental investment will be forthcoming. For example, traditionally when a man asks a woman for her hand in marriage, he would have been expected to show that he would be able to provide for a family. Women might also provide material goods in the form of what was called their "bottom drawer" or their dowry. In order to be ready to set up a family, it was

Joint parental investment ensures the optimal chance of survival for the offspring.

important to ensure that the necessary resources were there. Marriage itself is a way of trying to ensure that the female has some rights over her husband and that (even if he should depart) she will continue to gain support from him.

In Western society today, we are observing some reversal of sex roles. A number of men stay at home to care for their children while their partners go out to work. In general, men are far more willing to take on traditionally female tasks such as nappy changing and child-minding duties than used to be the case. This reflects the fact that humans are not necessarily subject only to biological forces and can adapt through conscious choice. However, we shouldn't get carried away—it is only about 1% of men who actually stay at home and look after the children!

We need to introduce two terms at this point. The competition between males for the right to fertilise females is called **intrasexual selection** ("intra" means "within"). In contrast, the tendency of females to exercise choice and select the best male available is called **intersexual selection** ("inter" means "between").

Intrasexual selection

Dimorphism, the difference between males and females, arises because of intrasexual competition. If males have to compete, they need to be able to fight and this tends to result in larger males who have antlers for fighting or colourful tail feathers to attract females. Typically, females don't have to compete with other females in order to mate.

There are generally fewer sexually receptive females than males in any population, and as a result there is competition between males for the scarce resource. This means that dominant males carefully control their hard-won access to impregnate the females. However, non-dominant males have developed other strategies. **Sneak copulation** is an example of this—a non-dominant male discreetly copulates when the first male isn't looking. Some male elephant seals pretend to be females, and are then able to join a harem and sneak copulate when the bull is occupied elsewhere. In order to counteract this, males must be very possessive of their females and/or have sex in private. In the Coho salmon, there are two male forms. One is much smaller than the other and lurks behind rocks (being small helps with this) to fertilise female eggs surreptitiously. The longer-maturing and larger hooknose male fights for the opportunity to fertilise eggs with other males. The fact that both forms persist shows that both strategies pay off.

Another strategy is called sperm competition. Males may compete at the level of their sperm for the right to fertilise an egg. Once a male has inseminated a female, another male's sperm may arrive and there

Soay sheep

Research by Brian Preston at the University of Stirling (Motluk, 1999) parallels findings on stages. The 3-year study of 100 wild soay sheep on St. Kilda's Isle, Scotland, showed that the larger rams were most successful in mating, seeing off the smaller rams so that they could mate 10 times or more a day. Blood tests on the lambs showed that the majority born from matings that took place early in the 5-week reproductive season in November and December were fathered by the larger rams. However, lambs born from matings in the last 2 weeks of the season had an equal chance of being fathered by larger or smaller rams. This shows that at the start of the mating season the larger rams were more successful, and selection was for heaviness. The later fall in success rates could be explained by the larger rams actually running out of sperm: too much success leads to failure!

KEY TERMS

Intrasexual selection: sexual selection based on competition for mates among the same-sexed (generally male) members of a species.

Intersexual selection: sexual selection based on the members of one sex (usually female) selecting or choosing opposite-sexed mates.

Dimorphism: the existence of two forms, such as male and female forms of the same species.

Sneak copulation: mating by a non-dominant male when the dominant male is not looking.

is evidence that the most recently arrived sperm have the advantage.

Intrasexual selection in a few species takes very unusual forms. Abele and Gilchrist (1977) observed the mating habits of *Monoliformes dubius*, which is a worm that lives in rats' intestines. Males of this species apply cement to the female's genital opening after they have mated with her! This is done to prevent other male worms from fertilising her. They also have the charming habit of applying cement to the genital areas of other males so that they can't mate.

Intersexual selection

In this section, we consider some of the key factors involved in intersexual selection (choosing a mate of the opposite sex). We start with two theories that have been applied mainly to other species but that may be relevant to the human species. After that, we focus more directly on the human species. In human sexual relations, it tends to be the female who does the choosing, and so we focus on the factors that make some men more attractive than others to women. We also consider some of the physical characteristics men find attractive in women.

Fisher's hypothesis: The runaway process

Fisher (1930) proposed that females are initially attracted to those features of males having survival value. For example, a bird with a fairly long tail may be better at flying and so at finding food than one with a short tail. A female will prefer a male with a long tail because her offspring are likely to inherit this characteristic (assuming that the long tail was an inherited characteristic). With successive generations, males with a more exaggerated form of the long tail are the ones selected by females, so the characteristic becomes more and more exaggerated. Fisher called this the **runaway process.**

This hypothesis has also been described as the **sexy sons hypothesis** because females will benefit from mating with a male with desirable characteristics as these will be passed to hers sons. As a result, their reproductive chances will be enhanced because they are "sexy". Thus, the mother's genes will be perpetuated.

As long as the advantages outweigh the disadvantages, the exaggerated characteristic will be perpetuated. It is thought that one reason why the giant deer

> **Mating by proxy**
>
> Researcher Matt Gage of Liverpool University was studying an insect pest, the flour beetle, which destroys stored grain (Walker, 1999). He hoped to find clues to methods of control from the reproductive cycle of the beetles, and he stumbled on a strange strategy of "mating by proxy". This appears to stem from the crowded populations of flour beetles, which are highly promiscuous. The males mate with many females in just a few minutes, and so the females have a succession of matings. Each male uses his spiny genitals to scrape out the previous male's sperm before replacing it with his own. The ousted sperm stick to the outside of the male's genitals and survive the journey to the next female, in whom they are deposited. According to Gage, one in eight females was fertilised by a male with whom they hadn't mated. So far, it seems that this strategy is unique in the animal world.

It is a good intersexual strategy, in evolutionary terms, for females to be coy because it permits time to assess a male's fitness (likelihood of reproductive success). Marilyn Monroe knew how to act coyly, as can be seen in this still from the comedy *The Seven Year Itch*.

 According to Fisher, why will successive generations of birds have longer and longer tails?

KEY TERMS

Runaway process: Fisher's theory that some inherited characteristics become more and more exaggerated because females actively select mates with this feature. Also called "sexy sons hypothesis".

Sexy sons hypothesis: the notion that females mate with the most attractive males so that their own sons will inherit these characteristics and thus be attractive to other females. Related to the runaway process.

The principle of natural selection might seem to predict that large antlers would reduce a stag's chances of survival. However, this prediction is not supported by our observations—stags do have large antlers. The antlers increase reproductive success and thus are adaptive.

became extinct was because its antlers had simply become too large through the runaway process. Fossil records show antlers spanning as much as 3 metres. Andersson (1982) supplied experimental evidence to support this hypothesis (see the Key Study below).

The handicap process

The main alternative to Fisher's hypothesis is Zahavi's (1977) handicap hypothesis. According to this hypothesis, a male adornment such as a long tail is a handicap. The argument is that a male bird that is able to survive in spite of having a significant handicap is likely to be genetically superior to other birds. Thus, females who prefer handicapped males may be selecting those who tend to possess good genes for survival. Therefore, this theory is also called the "good genes" theory, but in this case the good genes are in terms of survival and reproduction. This contrasts with Fisher's view that the good genes would be good in the sense that they would lead to attractive offspring.

The basic notion behind the handicap hypothesis can be seen if we consider a concrete example. Suppose two men are running around a track at the same speed, but one of them is carrying a heavy load. We would assume that the man handicapped by the load is stronger and fitter than the other man. Certain behaviours imply or *indicate* robust genes.

Hamilton and Zuk (1982) put forward a specific version of the handicap hypothesis. They argued that males are only likely to have a long tail or other sexual adornment if they are in good health. An individual who isn't in good health couldn't manage to survive with such an extra drain on energy. Thus, male animals with these adornments are attractive to females because they are likely to be free of diseases.

[?] The terms "good taste" and "good sense" have sometimes been used to describe these theories. Considering Fisher's and Zahavi's hypotheses, which one do you think is the "good taste" hypothesis and which is the "good sense" one?

KEY STUDY
Long tails in widow birds

Perhaps the most interesting form of intrasexual selection occurs when some characteristic (e.g., a long tail) evolves over the generations because it is attractive to members of the opposite sex. For example, the males of several species (e.g., peacocks, birds of paradise) are elaborately adorned, and their adornment seems to make them more attractive to females for mating purposes. This form of intrasexual selection may seem straightforward, but it is not really so. For example, the peacock's very long and large tail reduces its chances of escaping from a predator. In addition, it has to eat more because of the weight of its tail.

It seems reasonable to assume that such adornments have developed because females find them attractive. However, it is always useful to have good evidence for any assumption. Andersson (1982) studied long-tailed widow birds in Kenya. The male of the species is fairly small (about the size of a sparrow) but its tail is about 40 centimetres (16 inches) in length. Andersson cut the tails off some males to reduce their length to about 14 centimetres or 6 inches. He lengthened the tails of other males by sticking the detached pieces of tail on to them with superglue, making their tails about 65 centimetres or 26 inches long. Andersson found that the males with the artificially lengthened tails had the greatest mating success, indicating that female widow birds are attracted to long tails in male birds.

Discussion points
1. Why is the research by Andersson of particular value?
2. Do you think this research provides a good explanation of long tails in male widow birds?

[?] Can you explain why Andersson's approach is more convincing than one based on correlational evidence?

Møller (1990) tested Hamilton and Zuk's version of the handicap hypothesis with barn swallows in Denmark. First, Møller showed that female swallows preferred males with long tails: males with artificially lengthened tails paired up more rapidly with female swallows than did normal males. Then he found that baby swallows reared in nests containing numerous blood-sucking mites were more likely to have reduced growth or to die than were those raised in nests with relatively few mites. Finally, he found that male swallows with long tails had offspring with fewer mites on them than did males with short tails. Thus, as predicted by the handicap hypothesis, male barn swallows with longer tails are healthier than those with shorter tails, because they have greater resistance to parasites such as blood-sucking mites.

Intersexual selection in humans

When we see someone for the first time, we generally pay a lot of attention to their face. What facial characteristics are regarded as attractive? Langlois et al. (1994) found that male and female computer-generated composites or "averaged" faces were regarded as more attractive than the individual faces from which the averaged faces were formed. One reason for this is that averaged faces are more symmetrical than individual faces, and symmetry is associated with attractiveness (Grammer & Thornhill, 1994). Of particular importance from the perspective of evolutionary psychology, individuals having average faces are thought at less risk of carrying potentially harmful genetic mutations.

Women whose faces resemble those of young children are often perceived as attractive. For example, photographs of females with relatively large and widely separated eyes, a small nose, and a small chin are regarded as more attractive. These findings are consistent with the notion in evolutionary psychology that men seek young women who are most likely to be fertile. However, wide cheekbones and narrow cheeks in women are also seen as attractive (Cunningham, 1986), and these features are not usually found in young children.

Cunningham (1986) also studied physical attractiveness in males. Men having features such as a large, square jaw, small eyes, prominent cheekbones, and thin lips were regarded as attractive by women. These features can be regarded as indicating maturity, as they are rarely found in children. Some of these features (e.g., large jaw, prominent cheekbones) depend in part on male sex hormones (e.g., testosterone). Since testosterone is thought to have adverse effects on the immune system, it could be argued that these facial features indicate men who are generally healthy and whose immune system is strong enough to cope with high levels of testosterone (Thornhill & Gangestad, 1999).

Earlier we discussed a study by Davis (1990), who found that women advertising for a mate tended to emphasise their physical beauty as would be predicted by evolutionary theory. However, that study begged the question of whether that kind of advertisement is actually effective in attracting replies from men. Evidence that matters are more complex

Concar (1995) proposed that the reason we find a symmetrical face attractive is because symmetry implies physical fitness, and denotes a genetic predisposition for reproductive success.

> **INDEPENDENT STUDY IDEA: MATE CHOICE 1**
> You can do a replication of Davis (1990) using "personal" ads from a local or national newspaper. Analyse 30–50 "male seeks female" ads and a similar number of "female seeks male" ones. Choose various categories that can be analysed on all the ads, such as "mentions height" (Tall man seeks . . .; petite woman seeks . . .); other physical features (hair colour, size, etc.), profession. You need to differentiate between what people seek and what they say about themselves. Analyse the differences by using a series of chi-squared tests (male/female X does mention characteristic/does not mention characteristic). Do not try to combine the data into one large table as it is not all independent. Your alternative hypothesis is that men and women will both seek and mention different characteristics. You need a specific hypothesis for each characteristic, such as: women will mention features associated with attractiveness more than will men, men are more likely than women to mention profession, men are more likely to seek a younger female, and so on. There's plenty to discuss: the bias of the sample of ads, the bias of the sample of "participants" (the people writing the ads), and so on.

than might have been imagined was reported by Strassberg and Holtz (2003). Fictitious advertisements were used in which a hypothetical woman was described as "very attractive", "passionate and sensitive", or "financially successful and ambitious". Evolutionary psychologists would predict that the first advertisement would produce the most interest from men, but it was actually the last advertisement that attracted the most replies.

What physical features in women signal high fertility? Zaadstra et al. (1993) found two such features: (1) body mass index (BMI), which is based upon the relationship between height and weight; and (2) waist-to-hip ratio. More specifically, they found that women having BMIs between 20 and 30 and waist-to-hip ratios under 0.70 were the most fertile on average. Of the two measures, waist-to-hip ratio was the better predictor of female fertility. According to evolutionary psychologists, features predicting fertility should be important in mate selection. Consistent with that prediction, Singh (2002) found that women with a waist-to-hip ratio of 0.70 were judged to be the most attractive. Another finding was that models and winners of pageants over a 60-year period had remarkably stable waist-to-hip ratios.

The evidence concerning BMI is less supportive of evolutionary psychology. Rubinstein and Caballero (2000) found that there had been a steady decrease in BMI for the winners of the Miss America Pageant between 1923 and 1999. Anderson et al.'s (1992) findings across 54 cultures are more striking. In essence, women with a slender body were preferred in cultures in which the food supply was very reliable (e.g., most Western cultures), whereas women with a heavy body were preferred in cultures in which the food supply was very unreliable. On the face of it, these large cultural differences seem inconsistent with the evolutionary approach. However, it could be argued that heavy women in cultures with very unreliable food supplies are better equipped than slender women to survive food shortages and to provide nourishment for their children.

In sum, the evidence discussed here is mostly reasonably in line with expectations from evolutionary psychology. In addition, there is the cross-cultural research of Buss (1989) discussed earlier showing that women prefer older men and men prefer younger women. However, cross-cultural studies (e.g., Anderson et al., 1992; Buss, 1989) have generally reported substantial differences across cultures, and such differences are not readily explained by evolutionary accounts. We also need to bear in mind that there may be important differences between expressed preferences when participants look at photographs and actual behaviour. Thankfully, most people whose physical features are far removed from the evolutionary ideal nevertheless manage to have sexual relationships and children.

INDEPENDENT STUDY IDEA: MATE CHOICE 2

Do all men seek the same physical characteristics in the women with whom they desire to have a sexual relationship, as implied by evolutionary theory of mate choice and supported by the research of Buss (1989)? Or are there, contrary to evolutionary theory, differences based on the "fashion" of the time? One way of investigating this within one sample of men is to gather together, from magazines or the internet, a series of full-length photos of women of child-bearing age, all fairly attractive but different shapes and possibly from different cultures and different generations (a picture of Marilyn Monroe and Greta Garbo at a fairly young age, for example). Avoid personal photos. Ask a selection of men from two different age groups to rate them on attractiveness by ranking them in order of attractiveness. If the theory's correct, you would expect no great difference in the ratings between the men, regardless of the age of the men. You could analyse it by comparing men from two different generations and using a test of difference for independent groups. Use the mean score of attractiveness for each female given by each age group of men. It's the null hypothesis that you are expecting to support if evolutionary theory is correct and this has implications for the level of significance you may choose to use.

EXAM HINT

Parental investment could come up as a question and is often seen as a bit limiting, so think about how to structure the content to ensure you achieve depth and breadth. For example, consider the factors in parental investment and how the costs of parenting influence mating strategies, such as sexual selection and jealousy. Ensure that you use post-modernism, and social constructionism as a counterperspective.

Mating systems

There are a number of different social systems for mating: one male and one female, or one male and several females, and so on.

Monogamy

Monogamy refers to one male pairing with one female ("mono" means "on"). In some animals, monogamy is for life (e.g., in swans). This is called perennial monogamy. In other animals such as songbirds, monogamy may be for one breeding season only (annual monogamy).

Seals commonly practise polygyny, in which several females are defended and mated by one male.

Polygamy

Polygamy is one individual of one sex mating with many individuals of the other sex ("poly" means "many"). **Polygyny** refers to one male and many women ("gyny" means "female"). A common example of this is the harem where one man has many wives. There is also serial polygyny, in which a male bonds with a female for a while and then moves on to another.

Polygyny has obvious advantages for males as they gain by maximising their reproduction. One might think from an evolutionary point of view that females would prefer monogamy because then have a mate to provide resources solely for them. However, polygyny can also provide a high level of resources and has proved a successful way to rear children—this is the case, for example, with lions. Females in a harem have a dominant male with presumably "good" genes because that male fought successfully with others for the right to mate. The group will share parental care and resources. Songbirds were thought to be monogamous, but it has been found that, when resources are plentiful, a male will do better to engage a second or even third mate (Lack, 1968). In this situation, the female continues to get the same level of support from the male.

Polyandry describes a mating system in which one female has many males ("andry" means "male"). This is rare in humans but has been documented in Tibet, where a woman may marry two or more brothers. This is necessitated by the harsh living conditions where it takes at least two men to manage a farm. With two brothers, all parents share a genetic interest in all of the children (Dickemann, 1979).

Polygynandry

Polygynandry, or promiscuity, is where many males mate with many females. Such promiscuity is rare in the animal kingdom but has been observed in chimpanzees and songbirds such as the dunnock. Halliday and Arnold (1987) identified several advantages for promiscuity, including the following:

1. It may produce greater genetic diversity in the offspring.
2. It may persuade a number of males to guard the brood.
3. It may reduce the negative effects of males engaging in sexual competition.

> **KEY TERMS**
>
> **Monogamy:** a mating system in which a male and a female remain together over a long period, with both of them generally contributing to parental care.
> **Polygyny:** a mating system in which a male mates with several females, but females usually mate with only one male; parental care is usually provided by the female.
> **Polyandry:** a mating system in which one female mates with many males.
> **Polygynandry:** a mating system in which many males mate with many females (also known as promiscuity).

Women are promiscuous, naturally

"So many men, so little time!" The actress Mae West jested about it, but scientists—male ones anyway—are convinced they have proved it. Women—far from being naturally monogamous—are, like men, naturally promiscuous. Biologists believe that women are genetically programmed to have sex with several different men in order to increase their chances of healthy children.

This theory helps to explain the high incidence of mistaken paternity. One study suggested that as many as one in seven people may not be the biological child of the man he or she thinks is the father.

Two recent reports have added to a growing body of evidence that females from across the animal kingdom—including birds, bees, fish, scorpions, crabs, reptiles, and mammals—are promiscuous. Promiscuity is suggested by the "good gene" theory, as shown in the great weed warbler. The female warbler may nest with a male with a small song repertoire but she will seek "extra-pair copulation" with males with big song repertoires, which tend to live longer. This way she gets the best offspring (from mate 2) and they are looked after (by mate 1).

"We don't all get the exact partner we want, we make some kind of compromise. That's true of humans as well. A woman might find a man who is good at providing food and looking after children, but she doesn't necessarily want him to be the father of her kids," says Tim Birkhead, professor of evolutionary psychology.

The only comfort that men can take from the animal world is that females have an incentive not to have all the offspring from adulterous liaisons.

"If they are totally unfaithful to their social partner, they might just be abandoned," said Birkhead.

Adapted from A. Brown (2000) "Women are promiscuous, naturally." *The Observer*, 3 September.

Mating systems, parental investment, and parental care

The choice of mating system for any species is related to parental investment (see the box on the left). In the stickleback, it is the male who has made the large investment in terms of energy and polygyny is the rule—one male mates with many females. In species in which both partners share care, monogamy is likely because both partners benefit from protecting their investment.

Which comes first, mating system or parental investment? It is parental investment that dictates how much investment is made from the start. However, it appears in non-human animals that if a partner can desert and his/her reproductive success is enhanced by this, then he/she will desert thus affecting the mating system. For example, in the case of animals where eggs are fertilised externally (as in the stickleback), the female can leave first because the male fertilises the eggs after she has laid them. In most cases, this results in male care and polyandry. It may also result in no care. If there are sufficient eggs, then both parents have protected their investment through sheer numbers.

In the case of internal fertilisation, the male can desert and often does. The female, who had made a major investment in pregnancy, is likely to stay and care. This will result in polygyny or monogamy. The partner left "holding the baby" generally ends up caring for the offspring. A partner who leaves enhances his/her own reproductive success because he/she can go off and breed again, *unless* in leaving this reduces the chance of their current offspring surviving—then they stay! If the presence of both parents is important to ensure the survival of current offspring, then it pays for both parents to stay.

Mating systems and parental care

1. Monogamy: there is a pair bond between a male and a female, which may last for an entire breeding season or even a lifetime; often both parents protect the eggs or young, and co-operate in rearing the offspring.
2. Polygyny: a male mates with several females, whereas a female usually mates with only one male; females are more likely than males to provide the parental care.
3. Polyandry: a female mates with several males, whereas a male usually mates with only one female; in this mating system, males generally provide the parental care.
4. Polygynandry or promiscuity: males and females both mate with several members of the opposite sex; parental care may be provided by members of either sex.

Are humans monogamous by nature?

The answer is probably no. In spite of the fact that humans are basically regarded as a monogamous species (Grier & Burk, 1992), there is evidence from studies across different cultures that humans tend towards polygyny (see the pie chart on the right).

There is other evidence of our natural tendency to polygyny. The fact that humans exhibit dimorphism (males and females are very different in shape) is evidence of competition and polygyny. Males only have to compete when females are a scarce resource. Such conditions favour polygyny. Where competition between males is great, males have to develop means of winning any competition for females. One way of doing this is through fighting, so males tend to be bigger. Another way is through attracting females, so males develop special plumage or other attractive features. However, the dimorphism in humans is less pronounced than in some animals (e.g., peacocks), which suggests human have a low degree of polygyny.

Another means by which males compete is through sperm competition (see the box below). Males who have to compete need to produce more sperm and hence have larger testicles. Chimpanzees have huge testicles, relative to body weight, in comparison with gorillas (60g : 50kg compared with 10g : 250kg). Therefore, we would expect great competition among male chimpanzees but little in gorillas. This fits with the fact that chimpanzees have a mainly polygynandrous system whereas gorillas live in harems (polygyndy). Where does the human male fit in? The average male testicle size is 2.5in long by 1.25in wide. This compares unfavourably against the blue whale, each of whose testicles are 2.5ft long and

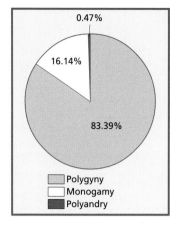

Human mating systems in traditional cultures prior to Western influence.

Mating systems and the size of testicles

Imagine a naked man standing next to a chimpanzee, a gorilla, and an orangutan. Which one has the biggest testes? Most people would say the gorilla, and most people would be wrong. The largest ape, at 350–450 pounds, has testicles that weigh, together, only a bit more than an ounce. Humans and orangutans, although lighter than gorillas, are slightly better endowed, with 1.5 ounces. Surprisingly, the smallest male in our line-up, the 100 pound chimpanzee, has over 4 ounces worth of testicles.

For decades scientists puzzled over this and then came up with the answer in what's called *sperm competition theory*. It goes like this:

Males of a species will have large testicles if they need to make lots of sperm: this occurs when other males are mating at the same time with the same females. On the other hand, it's quite sufficient to have small testicles when there is little competition. Let's take the gorilla and the chimpanzee as examples.

Gorillas live in small groups usually consisting of one fully adult male, two or three females, and their offspring. When a female gorilla is ready to mate, normally only one male adult is there as a partner. When there is more than one male around, the alpha male can usually monopolise the females. His success in parenting depends more on his brute force than the amount of sperm he produces. The 400 pound gorilla can therefore afford to have relatively tiny testicles because the only sperm racing for the female's ovum (egg) will be his own.

Compare this with chimpanzees. They live in large loose groups of both males and females. When a female chimpanzee is ready to mate there is a host of males ready to attend, most of whom will mate with her in a single day. That means lots of sperm from different individuals all competing to be the first one to reach the egg. The male with the biggest testicles will produce the most sperm, so he is the most likely to fertilise the female. Hence evolution for the chimpanzee moves in the direction of large testicles.

The theory that there is a relationship between testicular size and mating behaviour was supported by research that examined the mating system of a wide variety of primates, from lemurs to baboons to humans. In most species in which the female has more than one partner during any one period of fertility, males' testicles are larger than you would predict from body size. In contrast, in those species that are either monogamous or in which one male defends a harem of females, the testicles are either smaller than you would predict from body size or right on the line.

Now the question you're all asking. What of humans? They are right on the line, neither bigger nor smaller than would be predicted from body size and suggesting that sperm competition has played a role, but not a huge one, in the evolution of our sexual anatomy and behaviour.

Based on: K. Stewart (1998, February 15).
The Davis Enterprise.

weigh 100lb. Human male testicles are intermediate between chimpanzees and gorillas (10g : 70kg), which suggests a tendency towards polygyny or even polygynandry.

Human males have the largest penis of all primates: 5–6 inches compared to 3 inches for chimpanzees and only 1.5 inches for gorillas. Why is this? Speculations include the notion that a large penis attracts females, that it delivers sperm closer to the female's eggs and so maximises the chances of fertilisation, or that it frightens other males.

Evaluation of mating systems

Evolutionary psychologists have realised recently that the concept of mating systems doesn't quite work. An approach based on mating systems exaggerates the extent to which sexual behaviour is similar within any given species. More specifically, this approach ignores the considerable individual differences in sexual behaviour within a species.

An alternative approach is based on mating *strategies*. According to this approach, the sexual behaviour of individual males and females of a given species depends on the precise circumstances in which they find themselves. We have seen this is the case with birds, where there is a tendency to switch from one system to another in response to general environmental conditions. The same can be seen in human societies. Under some conditions, polygamy may be the best option for both males and females.

> **Mating systems and the environment**
>
> Crook (1964) studied many species of weaver bird and related mating strategies and social organisation to ecology:
>
> - In the forest, insect food is dispersed and relatively scarce. Therefore, parents form monogamous bonds and feed solitarily. They reduce predation risks through light colouration and camouflaged nests.
> - In the savannah, seed food is abundant in patches. Efficient foraging is achieved by groups rather than individuals, but there are few nesting sites, so what there is must be shared. This favours competition, intraspecies rivalry, and brighter plumage. Polygyny is likely because the males who gain the best nest sites can attract several females.

Therefore, the current view is that the most adaptive strategy is for a species to have a range of options and be flexible about changing to fit varying environmental conditions. This is preferable to conforming closely to the mating system that any given species is "supposed" to follow. In some bird species (e.g., dunnocks; Davies & Lundberg, 1984), all four mating strategies are exhibited at different times.

In human societies, the tendency is towards polygyny. Indeed, Smith (1984) estimated that this mating strategy was found in 83% of traditional cultures before they began to come under Western influence. However, monogamy will dominate when the benefits of polygyny for the male are outweighed by the benefits of monogamy, for example, when male help is essential to female success. Like all species, humans have a set of alternative strategies that are selected in relation to prevailing conditions.

Explaining other human reproductive behaviours
Adultery

In songbirds, it has been observed that under good environmental conditions males may manage several nest sites to maximise their reproduction. We could translate this into adultery in human terms. Males, given the chance, have nothing to lose and everything to gain by adultery unless they are found out.

Ridley (1993) reported that over 20% of children in the UK are the offspring of males other than their presumed father. This suggests that women may be as adulterous as men. Why are women adulterous? As we have seen, there are advantages for both sexes from promiscuity. Women may stand to gain by improving the quality of their offspring by selecting different mates, whereas males can increase the quantity. If a woman is found out and loses her partner, she risks losing protection and resources. Her protection may lie in making sure she has good emotional ties with her partner/husband.

Can we believe the astonishing figure provided by Ridley? In fact, there is reason to doubt that mistaken paternity is as high as 20%, because the data were obtained from a small and self-selected sample. A more recent study carried out in Switzerland (Sasse et al., 1994) was based on a more representative sample of 1600 children. Sasse et al. found that fewer than 1.4% of the children were raised by a presumed father who was actually not their biological one.

Chastity

Wilson (1975) claimed that women and men adopt different sexual strategies because women have to devote a considerable amount of time to their offspring during pregnancy and in the years afterwards. In contrast, men can maximise their reproductive potential by having sex with numerous women. Women can be certain that any child is really theirs, whereas men lack this certainty. As a result, men feel a need to control female sexuality so they can be as sure as possible that any child they protect and look after carries their genes. It follows from these considerations that men should attach more importance than women to chastity. This prediction was supported by Buss (1989). He found that males valued chastity more than females in 62% of the 37 cultures he considered, and there was no gender difference in the remaining 38% of cultures. Thus, there wasn't a single culture in which chastity was more highly valued by females.

Jealousy

Evolutionary psychologists argue that cuckoldry (discovering their partner has had sex with someone else) causes more jealousy in males than in females. The explanation is as follows. Men can only justify their parental investment in a child provided the child was actually fathered by them. If their partner is unfaithful, they cannot be sure that any child is theirs. In contrast, women always know for certain whether any child is theirs regardless of whether their partner is faithful or not.

Buunk et al. (1996) obtained support for the above prediction in a study involving participants from the United States, Germany, and The Netherlands. Participants were asked whether they would be more distressed if their partner enjoyed passionate sex with another person or if their partner formed a close emotional bond with someone of the opposite sex. In all three countries, men showed a greater tendency than women to be more distressed by the thought of their partner having sex with someone else, whereas women were more distressed by the thought of their partner having a close emotional bond. They also found that thoughts of their partner's sexual unfaithfulness caused greater physiological arousal in men than in women in all three countries.

There are two limitations with the study by Buunk et al. (1996). First, DeSteno et al. (2002) argued with supporting evidence that many people's decisions are influenced by the belief that one type of infidelity implies the existence of the

? Do males and females become jealous for the same reasons?

other. Many women believe that a man's emotional infidelity implies sexual infidelity as well, whereas a man can be sexually unfaithful without any real emotional involvement with the other woman. Thus, women may have decided that emotional infidelity was more distressing because of the high probability that sexual infidelity would also be involved ("double shot" of infidelity). Second, Buunk et al. studied involved in hypothetical situations. Harris (2002) studied actual infidelity, and found that males and females were equally distressed by it.

Evaluation

As we have seen, evolutionary psychology has been used to explain numerous forms of human behaviour in terms of their value for reproduction. The aim of any behaviour, or rather its adaptiveness, is directed at maximising the reproductive success for the individual. What is indisputable is that evolutionary psychology has provided several original theoretical insights into human sexual behaviour. More generally, the basic assumption that we can gain some understanding of current human behaviour by considering how it may have been influenced by natural selection is a valuable one.

What are the limitations of evolutionary psychology? First, it de-emphasises the importance of social and cultural influences. There have been enormous changes in human sexual behaviour and in sexual attitudes over the past 50 years, and these changes simply can't be explained in evolutionary terms. Another example comes from Buss's (1989) research on mate preferences in numerous cultures. In opposition to the evolutionary perspective, culture was substantially more important than gender in accounting for variation in the factors regarded as important in mate preference.

Second, evolutionary arguments are difficult to falsify. For example, it could be claimed that *monogamous* relationships are likely when resources are poor, because then a man would be unlikely to attract more than one female, let alone sustain more than one female and their offspring. On the other hand, it might be argued that *polygyny* is likely in times of scarce resources, because women would do better to group together and share the gathering of whatever is available. In lion prides, the females do the hunting as well as the child care, so it is not always necessary to have a male as provider.

Third, and related to the second point, the explanations offered by evolutionary psychologists can't be tested directly by carrying out controlled experiments. Evolutionary psychologists explain current human behaviour in terms of adaptive processes occurring hundreds of thousands of years ago, but most of these explanations are no more than speculative. Worryingly, any type of behaviour can be explained by claiming it is adaptive in an evolutionary sense if it is desirable (e.g., parenting) or maladaptive due to slow changes in our genetic make-up if it is undesirable (e.g., eating fatty foods). In this way, evolutionary psychologists can "explain" everything, but not in a convincing way.

Fourth, evolutionary psychology needs to, "put a little less evolution and a little more psychology into its explanations" (de Waal, 2002, p.189). In other words, the direct relevance of evolution to psychology is not always clear.

Nevertheless, evolutionary accounts of reproductive behaviour can't be said to be boring!

The ability to wrestle with a mammoth went down well with the ladies.

Evolutionary psychology: A comment

Evolutionary psychology—EP for short—is more than just a product of academia. It is a phenomenon of evolution all by itself. It has existed as a separate discipline for barely 20 years, yet it appears to be taking over the world. Evolutionary psychologists (EPs) conclude that human behaviour can best be understood, not with foreground reference to the contemporary social conditions, but by attributing it to processes that took place in the Stone Age. It is an EP axiom that the most basic human instinct is to reproduce and that men and women go about this in different ways. After all, our distant forebears had distinctly separate needs: women, being the carriers and bearers of children in perilous conditions, had an interest in choosing mates who were hearty, healthy, and liked to stick around to fight off marauding mammoths and maybe barbecue them too; men by contrast had more to gain from promiscuity, partly because they didn't pay for it with pregnancy, partly because for them it was the most effective way of fulfilling their prime directive of perpetuating their genes.

Steven Rose accuses EPs of having a "Flintstones view" of the human past based on "endless speculation". Rose sees EPs as gripped by chronic tunnel vision, "insisting on groping for some adaptionist explanation for everything when all sorts of local or social factors might easily account for the activity they're trying to study". Some EP findings are extrapolated from studies of other species. Rose has particular scorn for these "dubious animal behaviourists writing scientific pornography".

EP lends a momentum and veneer of intellectual validity to the media's obsession with sex. The press is cluttered with EP pronouncements. We've been informed, for example, that all over the world the key indicator to a man of a woman's fertility is the relationship of her hip measurement to that of her waist. A ratio of 0.7 is deemed ideal. How do we know? Because an EP from the University of Texas did a survey.

One of the most vaunted EPs is David Buss, who used evidence from 37 different cultures to make the case that men and women everywhere played the mating game in different ways, with men being interested in more casual sex and women being more concerned about commitment. And, of course, the explanation for these findings could only be evolutionary, disproving the theories of social scientists who have held that such differences have cultural—and therefore—alterable explanations. "What we have is in fact just the opposite," said Buss. Make way for the new cocks of the walk.

Adapted from an article by D. Hill in The Observer
Sunday 27 February 2000.

SECTION SUMMARY
Human Reproductive Behaviour

❖ Natural selection: behavioural characteristics are passed on to successive generations because of the advantages they confer in terms of survival.

❖ Sexual selection: Characteristics are selected because they increase the reproductive fitness of the individual in mating contests.

Natural selection and sexual selection

❖ Females in most species (including human) are much more discriminating than males in their choice of sexual partner because:

— Males produce sperm at little physiological cost whereas females produce eggs at large cost.
— Females usually have greater parental investment in their offspring.

Anisogamy and parental investment

❖ Men and women emphasise different features when selecting a mate as predicted by evolutionary theory.

❖ Male reproductive success is enhanced by fertilising as many eggs as possible, which costs relatively little.

❖ However, males have to compete with other males to mate with females. The fewer females available, the greater the competition between males.

❖ This is called intrasexual selection:

— Intrasexual selection results in dimorphism because competition between males leads to increased size and adornments to attract females.
— Non-dominant males have developed other adaptive strategies to promote their reproductive success, such as sneak copulation and sperm competition.

Intrasexual selection

Intersexual selection

❖ Female reproductive success is enhanced by having few offspring but ensuring that these offspring survive and are healthy, so they want to select the best mate.

❖ Choosing a mate of the opposite sex is called intersexual selection.

❖ There are two opposing theories for intersexual selection:

— Fisher's runaway hypothesis: females choose males with characteristics that promote survival. Over time, these characteristics become exaggerated. Females continue to choose males with these characteristics because they have "sexy" sons.

— Zahavi's handicap theory: females choose males with a handicap because this indicates genetic robustness, and sometimes health.

❖ Females also select males for non-genetic benefits, such as resources.

Human intersexual selection

❖ Factors that attract men to women:

— Average, symmetrical faces
— Faces that resemble those of young children
— In western cultures: women whose body mass index is between 20 and 30 and whose waist-to-hip ratio is under 0.70.

❖ Factors that attract women to men:

— Average, symmetrical faces
— Faces that suggest maturity.

Types of mating systems

❖ Each different mating system offers advantages for both sexes:

— Monogamy: Related to shared parental care and ensures help for females in terms of resources.
— Polygyny: Maximises reproductive success for males and may offer advantages for females in terms of shared care and good genes.
— Polyandry: Rare in humans but has benefits when males are related.
— Polygynandry: May offer advantages in terms of greater genetic variation for both males and females.

❖ The choice of mating strategy for any individual is related to parental investment:

— The parent left "holding the baby" is often the one who stays and does the caring.
— If both parents are needed to ensure offspring survival then it pays for them both to stay.

See also pages 166–173 of the revision guide.

❖ It is more appropriate to talk in terms of mating strategies rather than systems, as each species appears to practice different strategies in response to prevailing conditions, rather than having one system.

Mating systems in humans

❖ Evidence suggests that human males are polygynous by nature, based on observations of human societies.

❖ The testicular effect also suggests a tendency towards polygynandry, in that women too are seeking extra-pair copulations.

❖ Adultery: There is evidence that both men and women are adulterous. Men encourage chastity as a means of preventing this.

❖ Jealousy: may also have evolved as a strategy to prevent adultery, although men may be more concerned with sexual jealousy and women with emotional jealousy.

Other human
reproductive behaviours

❖ Evolutionary accounts of human reproductive behaviour de-emphasise the importance of social and cultural influences and are difficult to falsify.

Evaluation of
evolutionary psychology

EVOLUTIONARY EXPLANATIONS OF MENTAL DISORDERS

The mental disorders anorexia nervosa and bulimia nervosa were considered as part of your AS level studies, and mental disorders are further considered in your A2 studies, in Chapter 8, Psychopathology. In this Section we will focus on evolutionary explanations for mental disorders and direct you to read about the symptoms of particular disorders and alternative explanations in Chapter 8.

Evolutionary Explanations of Human Mental Disorders

In terms of mental disorders, the basic argument is that (1) mental disorders can be observed in humans and the historical record shows this is not a recent development, (2) some mental disorders are inherited, (3) the persistence of such disorders suggests that they may have some adaptive value. This seems hard to accept when one considers the disabling nature of mental disorders such as anorexia nervosa, depression, and schizophrenia. This would lead us to expect that a person with a mental disorder would have reduced reproductive success and, if such disorders are inherited, this would result in the disappearance of such disorders. Why, then, have these disorders *not* disappeared?

Genome lag

It is argued that most of our inherited behaviours stem from the time of the **environment of evolutionary adaptation (EEA)**, the period in human evolution during which our genes were shaped and naturally selected to solve survival problems operating then. This was roughly between 35,000 and 3 million years ago. Some of these behaviours are not especially adaptive today, but they have not been eliminated from our behavioural repertoire by natural selection. This is called "genome lag" because the evolution of the genome has lagged behind environmental changes. This makes sense given the fact that natural selection typically takes hundreds or thousands of generations to exert any large effects on the genes.

One example of this is our response to stressors. In your AS level studies, you learned about the way animals, including humans, respond to stressors. The initial rush of adrenaline, and the "fight or flight" response, is important for survival. In common with other animals, the stress response enabled our very distant ancestors to respond appropriately to environmental threats, such as stampeding buffalo, which really did threaten survival. Those individuals who had a rapid and effective stress response were more likely to survive. Now, we have a physiological stress mechanism that is not suited to our lifestyle.

> **KEY TERM**
>
> **Environment of evolutionary adaptation (EEA):** the period in human evolution during which our genes were shaped and naturally selected to solve survival problems that were operating at that time (between 35,000 and 3 million years ago).

Fight or flight is of little use in the modern world.

Modern stressors are things like noise, overcrowding, and pressure of too much work. They are often things over which we have no control. In such situations a stress response is not very adaptive. First of all running away is unlikely to be desirable—it would probably be more adaptive to respond to a stressor with parasympathetic arousal (relaxation). Second, modern stress situations are often ongoing and therefore we do end up in the state described by Selye's GAS model (described in your AS level course). This was not the original outcome of the stress response. In our evolutionary past we saw the threat (say a buffalo), became aroused (in terms of the **autonomic nervous system**), ran away, and the stressor was gone, so autonomic activity could return to normal. Today our stressors remain with us, and we end up ill. In relation to mental illness we can argue that humans are not adapted to urban life and the stressors of this environment may underlie mental disorder.

Evaluation

On the other hand, it could be argued that today's environment and that of the EEA are not that different. Many aspects of our day-to-day life are probably the same and we have the same concerns—finding resources, forming relationships, raising children, coping with death and injury, and so on. Cartwright (2001) wryly comments that "One of the ironies of the modern condition is that we launch high tech satellites into orbit around the planet to beam down soap operas and pornography."

It is also possible that the reason for this genome lag is that the genes continue to offer some benefits, and that is why they remain in our gene pool. Temple Grandin, a high-achieving autistic, has argued this point:

Aware adults with autism and their parents are often angry about autism. They may ask why nature or God created such horrible conditions as autism, manic depression, and schizophrenia. However, if the genes that caused these conditions were eliminated there might be a terrible price to pay. It is possible that persons with bits of these traits are more creative, or possibly even geniuses . . . If science eliminated these genes, maybe the whole world would be taken over by accountants. (Sacks, 1995, p.278)

Increased fitness

Temple Grandin's argument leads us to a second possibility—that the genes underlying certain mental disorders are also responsible for other, more desirable traits. Evolutionary theory has been used to explain certain disease symptoms and offer advice on suitable forms of treatment. Symptoms such as vomiting, coughing, running a temperature, and avoidance of certain foods may be a necessary part of the body's response to physical illness and thus are desirable and adaptive. For example, when lizards are ill they seek a warm place to lie in the sun. This is part of their normal temperature regulation as they are cold-blooded, but when they are ill they appear to tolerate even hotter conditions. Kluger (1991) found that if lizards who are ill are prevented from obtaining this extra warming, the result is that they die. This suggests that fever may be a way of killing off the pathogens associated with an illness.

It could be argued that similar principles apply to mental illness, and that some of the symptoms can be seen as adaptive behaviours. For example anxiety, and the

KEY TERM

Autonomic nervous system: that part of the nervous system that controls vital body functions, which is self-regulating and needs no conscious control (automatic).

Sickle cell anaemia

There are a number of well-established cases of maladaptive genes surviving against apparent odds in the human gene pool. A simple change to the base sequence on our DNA is known to cause the distressing condition of sickle cell anaemia. This condition occurs when an individual inherits a defective gene from both parents, and results in a proliferation of sickle-shaped cells in the blood. These cells are quickly broken down by the body, and the result is that the blood does not flow smoothly and parts of the body are deprived of oxygen. The physical symptoms range from anaemia, physical weakness, pain, damage to major organs, brain damage, and heart failure. There is no cure for the condition, which causes the deaths of about 100,000 people world-wide each year. Sickle cell anaemia is by far the most common inherited disorder among African-Americans and affects one in 500 of all African-American children born in the USA.

The reason that sickle cell anaemia has such high frequency among African-Americans, and the fact that natural selection has not eliminated it (many of those suffering die before they can reproduce), is probably due to the fact that in Africa possession of one copy of the sickle cell gene confers some resistance to malaria. People who inherit only one copy of the sickle cell gene are said to have the sickle cell trait and only some of their red blood cells are oddly shaped. The malarial parasite (*Plasmodium*) cannot complete its life cycle in the mutant cells and therefore those with the sickle cell trait are resistant to malaria. It is the prevalence of malaria in African countries that explains why this apparently maladaptive gene survived in the gene pool and is now found among African-Americans.

Adapted from Allison (1954).

associated responses to it, are adaptive behaviours that ensure we focus on genuine threats in the environment. Increased fitness also explains sickle cell anaemia (see the box above) and similarly it has been argued that aspects of mania (as part of manic depression) may be traits of the greatest world leaders.

Alternatively, the mental disorder gene or set of genes may be linked in some way to increased fertility, and this would explain why it is perpetuated. Either way the characteristic remains naturally selected.

Other possible explanations

Some mental disorders may persist not because they are associated with characteristics that have been naturally selected, but simply because they aren't weeded out, as they manifest themselves after breeding. This can be seen in the condition called Huntington's chorea, a genetic condition that only appears in middle life and is inevitably fatal. A child whose parent has developed Huntington's chorea has a 50 : 50 chance of developing it himself/herself.

Another possibility is that the gene for a disorder is recessive and therefore would only be expressed when passed to a child by *both* parents. For example, that is the case with haemophilia, a condition in which one's blood doesn't clot and may result in bleeding to death. Most people carrying this gene don't exhibit the disorder because they have only one of the gene pair. Thus, the gene continues to be passed on silently, only occasionally being expressed when both parents are carriers and they both pass the gene to their offspring. This means there is little opportunity for natural selection for (or against) this gene.

Applying Evolutionary Explanations to Mental Disorders

The three main disorders that will be examined in Chapter 8, Psychopathology, are schizophrenia, depression, and anxiety disorders. Here we will consider possible evolutionary explanations for each of them.

Schizophrenia

Schizophrenia is a complex and serious disorder with a range of subtypes (see page 344). Symptoms include delusions, hallucinations, and disorganised behaviour. The research evidence strongly suggests that there is a genetic basis for schizophrenia. This evidence comes from twin and adoption studies, as well as studies of biochemical abnormalities (see pages 347–348). At the same time there is also evidence of an important environmental component because when one identical twin develops schizophrenia the other one often does not. The **diathesis–stress model** expresses this relationship: individuals are born with a predisposition for the disorder but it is only expressed when environmental stressors act as a trigger. Of relevance for the discussion here, there is some evidence that schizophrenia existed tens of thousands of years ago. For example, some Australian Aborigines suffer from schizophrenia even though they were isolated from all other human groups for nearly all of the past 60,000 years (Torrey, 1987).

Group-splitting hypothesis

Stevens and Price (1996, 2000) have developed an evolutionary account of schizophrenia called the **group-splitting hypothesis**. The characteristics of the schizoid personality serve an adaptive function under certain conditions. These characteristics include mood changes, bizarre beliefs, hallucinations, delusions, and strange speech. A "crazy" individual may act as a leader and enable one subgroup to split off from a main group, a valuable function at times when the main group has become too large to be optimum. As group size increases so do risks from predation, difficulties in finding enough food, and intragroup rivalries. Dunbar (1996) estimated that between 100 and 150 was an optimum group size. Thus, it is argued that schizophrenia is an adaptation that served the useful function of making it easier for group splitting to occur.

There are many examples of schizoid personalities who have become leaders. A recent example was the cult leader David Koresh of the Branch Davidians who died with a group of followers at Waco, Texas in 1995. One member reported that "David was planning to lead the group to Israel to re-take Jerusalem. He taught that there would be a big battle between the forces of the world and his people." In this instance the plans may have been too crazy, but one might imagine that some leaders are possessed by extraordinary ideas that do mean a radical and healthy change for the group.

How plausible is the group-splitting hypothesis? In its favour, some schizophrenics have delusions of grandeur, hallucinations, and bizarre beliefs that might have been appealing to members of a group that had become too large. On the other hand, schizophrenics often have incoherent speech and a relative absence of emotion and motivation—not the most obvious characteristics of a charismatic leader! An alternative to the group-splitting hypothesis is the notion that schizophrenia is associated with shamanism (Polimeni & Reiss, 2002). The shaman is a medicine man or key religious figure, and shamans are often thought to be able to communicate with spirits. It is possible that some of the characteristics of schizophrenia (e.g., auditory hallucinations, delusions of grandeur) would have been useful qualities for shamans to have. As with the group-splitting hypothesis, this is a speculative viewpoint. Most schizophrenics don't seem to have the personal qualities needed in a charismatic shaman.

Origin of language theory

Crow (2000) has suggested that schizophrenia is the price that humans pay for language. This would explain the central paradox of schizophrenia—that despite the fact that the disorder should reduce reproductive capacity, the apparently genetic condition persists. In contrast, language has clear adaptive advantages in terms of enabling the users to engage in precise communication. It may also have advantages for reproductive success because it enables the user to be superior in intersexual selection.

According to Crow, there was a genetic mutation on the Y-chromosome more than 150,000 years ago that led to the development of both language and schizophrenia. Crow argues that a disorder like schizophrenia involves a breakdown in the brain's internal linguistic controls. Schizophrenics often believe they are hearing voices and/or they use atypical language. In some individuals, language may not be lateralised (located only in the left hemisphere, which is the normal state of affairs). This disrupts certain mechanisms of language, such as the ability of an individual to distinguish his/her thoughts from the speech output that he/she generates and the speech input that he/she receives and decodes from others. The result is schizophrenia.

Crow's theory is an interesting one. Humans differ from other primates in that the great majority of us are right-handed. This may be related to the fact that for most people language processing occurs mainly in the left hemisphere. The proposed linkage between schizophrenia and language is strengthened by the finding that adults with schizophrenia tend to be less strongly right-handed than most people (Francks et al., 2003). It is also true that schizophrenics have several problems with language, for example, suffering from auditory hallucinations and incoherent speech.

There are several limitations with Crow's theory. First, most of the symptoms of schizophrenia have very little to do with language—for example, lack of emotion and motivation; disorganised movements; and social impairments. Second, most genetic changes occur over very long periods of time lasting hundreds of thousands of years. This makes it unlikely that genetic changes leading to language and to schizophrenia occurred rapidly. Third, the theory emphasises the deficient language skills of schizophrenics. In fact, however, the hallucinations and delusions of schizophrenics are generally grammatically correct (Polimeni & Reiss, 2002).

> **?** The ability to use language is usually adaptive. When might this not be true?

Depression

There are two categories of depression: unipolar and bipolar disorder or depression. Unipolar disorder or major depression is a condition in which the individual suffers only from depression, whereas bipolar disorder involves mood swings between depression and mania (characterised by great excitement and activity). Most of the millions of people suffering from depression would find it hard to believe that their condition has adaptive value—indeed, they are desperate to be rid of the depression. However, as we will see, there *are* reasonable arguments that depression does serve one of more useful functions.

Unipolar disorder

When might it be useful to feel depressed?

Several theories have been put forward to explain why depression evolved. Here we will consider two of the main ones: the rank or social competition hypothesis and the social navigation hypothesis. According to the rank or social competition hypothesis (e.g., Price et al., 1994), it is important for survival that an individual who is the loser in a contest (i.e., loses rank) should accept the loss to prevent further injury from re-engaging with the person who has defeating him/her, an act of "damage limitation". This is often a realistic (if unpalatable) reaction. Thus, the adaptive significance of depression is that it discourages the individual from further efforts and allows him/her to adjust to the new situation. When people accept that they have lost rank or their position in the dominance hierarchy, it is natural for them to become depressed, to become lethargic or lacking in energy, and to engage in self-doubt. This theory can easily be extended to encompass other kinds of losses or defeats such as the death of a parent or being dumped by one's partner.

The rank or social competition hypothesis provides a fairly convincing account of many of the symptoms of depression. For example, the lack of motivation shown by depressed individuals is easily explained if depression is triggered by the need to adjust to be demoted in the social dominance hierarchy. As predicted by the theory, there is evidence that recovery from depression often occurs only when the individual suffering from depression finally abandons some desired goal that has become unobtainable (e.g., Nesse, 2000). However, it is not altogether clear on this hypothesis why depression can last for several years—how long would we expect such a process of adjust to last? It is also important to bear in mind that depression can undoubtedly be caused by many factors including genetic ones. The social competition hypothesis focuses on important environmental factors (i.e., major losses) triggering depression, but that is only part of the story.

Social navigation hypothesis

According to the social navigation hypothesis (Watson & Andrews, 2002), depression is adaptive because it leads to appropriate attempts decide what should be done after an important loss of some kind. According to Watson and Andrews, depression serves two valuable functions with respect to social problem solving. First, depression increases the focus on accurate analysis and solution of major problems facing the individual. Watson and Andrews described this as the social rumination function. Second, the obvious distress and unhappiness displayed by depressed individuals may help to persuade other people to help them or at the very least to make some concessions to them. This is the social motivation function of depression. In turn, this can lead to what Watson and Andrews called unintentional "fitness extortion". In effect, the depressed individual's message (even though he/she is not consciously aware of it) is that those close to them should provide help and assistance so they don't have to put up with the misery inflicted on them by the depressed individual.

It follows from the social navigation hypothesis that depressed individuals should recover as and when their social problems are resolved. As predicted, recovery from depression is speeded up when depressed individuals have strong social support (e.g., Brugha et al., 1997). There is some evidence that depressed individuals can be more realistic than non-depressed ones in their thinking (this is known as depressive realism). For example, it is well established that non-depressed individuals have a self-serving bias—they attribute success to their own ability but attribute failure to bad luck. In contrast, depressed individuals often seem more realistic, in that they are less inclined to take all the praise when things go well and accept no responsibility when things go badly (Ackermann & DeRubeis, 1991).

What are the limitations of the social navigation hypothesis? First, it is generally accepted that severe depression is associated with extremely low levels of motivation. This hardly sounds like the ideal state to be in to engage in complex social problem solving! Second, it could be argued that the hypothesis is far too optimistic about what happens to depressed individuals. Depressed people who make their partner's life a misery through their depression often find themselves losing their partner rather than receiving the help they seek. Third, the fact that approximately 5% of clinically depressed individuals commit suicide (Bostwick & Pankratz, 2000) is difficult to reconcile with the alleged adaptive functions of depression emphasised by the social navigation hypothesis. Fourth, other reasonable explanations are available (e.g., the "genome lag" account). Nesse and Williams (1995) suggest that rates of depression are increasing and it is possible that depression is a consequence of life in highly developed, urban societies that are very competitive. People, especially young people, are presented with many images of ideal lives and material possessions by the media. Such competition and longing leads individuals to feel dissatisfied, and depressed.

Bipolar disorder

There is stronger evidence for the inheritance of bipolar disorder than for unipolar disorder, again from twin studies and adoption studies. It has been suggested that the manic phase of bipolar disorder is related to creativity, lack of inhibition, and charismatic leadership, and thus would be an adaptive trait. Many species hibernate during the winter and are most active during the summer months. In that context, it is interesting that nearly all individuals with seasonal affective disorder suffer from severe depression during the winter months rather than the summer. It is also of interest that there is some evidence that patients with bipolar disorder are more likely to have manic phases in the warmer times of the year. For example, Carroll (1991) found that the peak time for manic episodes was early spring for one group of bipolar patients and late summer for another group. It could be argued that there is adaptive value in being most active during the time of the year when there are the most hours of daylight and food is in plentiful supply.

Winston Churchill, Abraham Lincoln, Vincent Van Gogh, Graham Greene, Ludwig van Beethoven . . . the list is endless. These have all been said to be sufferers of manic depression or bipolar disorder. The argument is that creativity

Winston Churchill was said to have suffered from bipolar disorder.

is linked in some way to the same genes that underlie bipolar disorder. Without one we would not have the other.

Evaluation

We have seen that various accounts have suggested that depression is adaptive in some way. However, we need to ask ourselves whether the severe disadvantages of such a debilitating disorder outweigh any possible adaptive value it might have. It is possible that some tendency towards mood swings may have adaptive value. Indeed, women who experience moderate mood swings are happier than those who don't (Diener et al., 1999).

Anxiety disorders

"Anxiety disorders" are a group of mental disorders characterised by levels of fear and apprehension disproportionate to any threat posed. Anxiety, like depression, is an emotion. Anxiety, like stress, is adaptive. Anxiety places an animal in a state of arousal (the "fight or flight" response), ready to deal with an environmental threat. Anxiety also ensures that situations of danger are approached cautiously. Such useful forms of anxiety can become crippling and disabling when the anxiety becomes disproportionate to the situation. For example, it is natural to experience slight fear and apprehension before an important social occasion, but the extreme anxiety that social phobics experience when faced by such an occasion is very disabling and often leads them to avoid many social events.

Phobias

A phobia is a strong and irrational fear of something, and the emotion of fear may have some adaptive value. One of the most intriguing facts about phobias is that people rarely develop phobias for potentially dangerous objects that were only invented fairly recently. For example, few people have car phobia, even though tens of thousands of people a year are killed by cars. However, millions of people in Western cultures have spider or snake phobias, even though they have very rarely seen spiders or snakes and most of the ones they have seen are harmless.

Seligman (1970) used the term **"preparedness"** to describe the tendency for members of a species to be biologically predisposed to acquire certain conditioned responses more easily than others. One of these responses would be a fear of things that were probably associated with danger to primitive humans, such as insects, heights, and small animals. Consider poisonous snakes for example—you may only have one chance to escape and so there would be survival value in having an innate predisposition to avoid them. The notion of preparedness may also be useful in explaining agoraphobia (a fear of public places). It may have been advantageous for our remote ancestors to spend most of their time in their own territory and avoid the dangers of straying too far from it. In similar fashion, our remote ancestors may have had much to fear from other people, and this could help to explain the origins of social phobia (extreme fear of social situations).

Tomarken, Mineka, and Cook (1989) presented their participants with a situation in which various stimuli were sometimes followed by electric shock.

EXAM HINT
The explanations of genome lag and increased fitness can be linked to depression and anxiety (phobias and obsessive-compulsive disorder), but do consider more specific explanations of phobias in-depth, such as "learned preparedness".

KEY TERM
Preparedness: the notion that each species finds some forms of learning more "natural" and easier than others.

The stimuli used included snakes, spiders, and a damaged electrical outlet. Participants exaggerated how often snakes and spiders had been followed by electric shock but didn't do so with the damaged electrical outlet. Thus, we are more likely to associate the fear of an electric shock with objects that were dangerous in our evolutionary past (e.g., snakes, spiders) than with potentially dangerous objects that have only recently come into existence (e.g., damaged electrical outlet).

Cook and Mineka (1989) reported good evidence for preparedness in a study on laboratory-bred monkeys who had never encountered a snake before. The monkeys watched a monkey reared in the wild reacting with strong fear to a snake. After that, they very quickly acquired a fear of snakes when shown a toy snake. However, no fear developed these monkeys when they saw a wild-reared monkey apparently reacting with strong fear to a rabbit. Presumably the monkeys responded so fearfully to the toy snake because of biological preparedness.

What are the limitations with the evolutionary approach based on the notion of preparedness? First, there is much stronger evidence for a fear of spiders in Western cultures such as those in Europe than in other cultures (e.g., those in Africa). This doesn't fit the theory because we would expect on the preparedness view that fear of spiders would be universal. Second, there are several relatively rare phobias that can't easily be explained in evolutionary terms. For example, consider arithmophobia (fear of numbers), triskaidekaphobia (fear of the number 13), and cherophobia (fear of gaiety). Third, we often need to engage in speculation when applying the notion of preparedness. For example, consider carnophobia (fear of meat) and myrmecophobia (fear of ants). Do these phobias occur because our remote ancestors had to deal with meat that could poison them and with dangerous ants? The only honest answer is that we don't know.

INDEPENDENT STUDY IDEA: FEAR READINESS

In a correlational study by Bennett-Levy and Marteau (1984) that supported the idea that we are born with a readiness to fear certain animals, with possibly adaptive advantages, participants rated 29 animals in terms of perceived ugliness, perceived harmfulness, and their own fear of the animal. Fear was strongly correlated with the animal's appearance; greater fear was associated with greater difference to the human form.

McIlveen, Higgins, and Wadeley (1992) highlighted a flaw in the original study in that perceived harmfulness was not controlled for, and this could explain the findings.

In your study you could compile a list of feared and not-feared animals and ask participants to rate them on perceived fear, harmfulness, and strangeness using a 3-point scale for each item. In other words, rate, for example, perceived harmfulness of a spider on a 1–3 scale, where 3 is very harmful. Then place all the participants' results together, so you have a total score for the fearfulness of spiders, their harmfulness, and their strangeness. Finally, correlate fear and harmfulness, fear and strangeness, and harmfulness and strangeness.

Obsessive-compulsive disorder

This disorder is characterised by a combination of obsessive thoughts and compulsive acts. The compulsive rituals are often concerned with hygiene, such as washing oneself or cleaning for several hours each day to eradicate any possible contamination. Another common form of compulsive behaviour is checking (e.g., returning home to make absolutely certain the front door is locked).

In principle, there is an infinite list of possible obsessions and compulsions that patients with obsessive-compulsive disorder might suffer from. In practice, however, most (but nothing like all) of their obsessions and compulsions revolve around washing and checking. Why is this the case? Throughout most of human history, many (or even most) people died prematurely because they were living in unhygienic conditions that led to disease. Accordingly, it was totally adaptive for individuals to be very concerned with hygiene issues and to wash themselves thoroughly several times a day. Historically, too, most human beings until fairly recently lived in potentially dangerous environments with little protection from wild animals or adverse climate. Accordingly, it was sensible for them to check carefully that everything in their environment was in order.

Perhaps the most adaptive function of symptoms such as washing and checking relates to the behaviour of mothers with a newborn child. In our ancestral past, it was probably essential for mothers to be very concerned that their newborn was in a hygienic environment in order to ensure its survival. Of relevance, Buttolph and Holland (1990) found that 69% of mothers with obsessive-compulsive disorder reported that the symptoms became worse either during pregnancy or very early in the child's life.

Abed and de Pauw (1999) have offered an evolutionary account of obsessive-compulsive disorder based on some of the ideas discussed above. According to them, obsessions are uncontrollable thoughts that produce strong aversive states (e.g., disgust, fear). These obsessional thoughts are the product of a brain system that Abed and de Pauw termed the "Involuntary Risk Scenario Generating System". This system allows individuals to work out ways and means of avoiding harm in safety without having to confront real-life dangers.

If the obsessions and compulsions of patients with obsessive-compulsive disorder fulfil an adaptive function, we might expect this disorder to be found in most or even all cultures. This is, indeed, the case. If these obsessional thoughts and compulsions are adaptive, we might also expect many normal individuals to report them. Rachman and de Silva (1978) found that 80% of normals reported obsessional thoughts and/or compulsions or impulses, with 54% reporting both.

On the negative side, the obsessional thoughts and compulsions of patients with obsessive-compulsive disorder are often very disturbing to them and severely disrupt their everyday functioning. Thus, we shouldn't exaggerate any adaptive value they may have. In addition, some of the thoughts and actions of obsessive-compulsive disorder patients seem to have no possible adaptive value. For example, some patients wish repeatedly that their spouse would die, and others have repeated urges to shout out obscenities at work.

Evaluation of Evolutionary Explanations of Human Mental Disorders

This is a fairly new field and therefore the explanations perhaps lack refinement and/or research evidence at present.

A prerequisite to the evolutionary argument is that the behaviour must be inherited, or at least there must be an inherited predisposition to the disorder. Evolutionary explanations can account for the fact that many mental disorders do run in families. It is important to remember that the mental disorders are not adaptive in themselves, but they are linked to behaviours that are adaptive. However, it doesn't make sense to argue that suicide resulting from depression is adaptive. (For a general evaluation of evolutionary psychology, refer back to the box on page 313.)

There is a potential benefit from the evolutionary approach in its application to the treatment of mental disorders—**evolutionary psychiatry**. Nesse and Williams (1995) argued the strengths of this approach by making an analogy with the way physical diseases are viewed. If a patient has a cough it is more useful to understand the function of the cough, which may then lead you to the root of the problem. Instead what psychiatry currently does, in terms of the cough analogy, is to understand the neural mechanisms underlying the cough and describe when coughing takes place, and perhaps catalogue different kinds of cough. Through this analogy we can see that mental illnesses might be more profitably treated—and/or accepted—if we understand the function of the behaviours. This permits us to understand the adaptive nature of apparently maladaptive behaviours.

Finally we should remember that there are a number of different approaches that can be used as a means of evaluation of evolutionary explanations. These alternatives are presented in Chapter 8, Psychopathology.

> **KEY TERM**
>
> **Evolutionary psychiatry:** an application of the evolutionary approach to treating mental disorders through understanding the function of the behaviours involved in the disorder.

SECTION SUMMARY
Evolutionary Explanations of Mental Disorders

❖ The persistence of inherited mental disorders suggests they probably have some adaptive value, or be related to behaviours that have some adaptive value.

❖ Possible explanations include:

— Genome lag
— Increased fitness
— Characteristics appear after breeding, so are not selected against
— Genes are recessive and thus rarely exposed to selective pressure.

Why seek evolutionary explanations for mental disorders?

❖ Suggests that modern behaviours evolved at a time when selective pressures were different (during the EEA):

— The pressures of modern life may turn once adaptive behaviours into maladaptive ones.
— Alternatively, as there are only small differences between the EEA and life today, the genes responsible for mental disorders may be linked to behaviours that continue to be desirable.

Genome lag

❖ Certain responses to physical illness are seen as adaptive and the same might be true for symptoms of mental disorders.

❖ The same gene for a mental disorder may increase creativity and/or reproductivity, and thus remains naturally selected.

Increased fitness

Evolutionary explanations for schizophrenia	❖ There is strong evidence that a predisposition for schizophrenia is inherited: — The group-splitting hypothesis claims that schizophrenia has the useful function of making it easier for group splitting to occur, and thus helps to ensure that human groups are the optimal size. — The origin of language theory suggests that schizophrenia is the price humans pay for language, because schizophrenia involves a breakdown in the brain's internal linguistic controls.
Evolutionary explanations for depression	❖ Unipolar disorder (major depression) is related to lowered mood (sadness), which may have adaptive significance because it prevents one being overactive in inappropriate situations: — The rank or social competition theory of depression proposes that depression is adaptive because it discourages an individual who has lost rank in a fight from further fighting (damage limitation). — The social navigation hypothesis proposes that depression is adaptive because it leads to a focus on solution of major problems and it can persuade others to provide help. This hypothesis is too optimistic about the likely consequences of being depressed. ❖ The manic phase of bipolar disorder may be related to creativity and other adaptive traits.
Evolutionary explanations for anxiety disorders	❖ Anxiety disorders are characterised by high levels of anxiety, which like stress, can be adaptive. But anxiety can become disabling under certain circumstances. ❖ Phobias: — May be based on innate predispositions to be afraid of potentially harmful animals (preparedness). — Operant conditioning then exaggerates natural fears. ❖ Obsessive-compulsive disorder: — Involves intense anxiety from the obsessive thoughts. — Rituals reduce anxiety and are thus rewarding. — Many of the symptoms of obsessive-compulsive disorder may be exaggerated forms of appropriate behaviour for mothers to display towards their offspring. — Both ritual behaviour and a predisposition to obsessive-compulsive disorder are possibly inherited.
See also pages 174–180 of the revision guide	
Evaluation of evolutionary explanations for mental disorders	❖ Evolutionary explanations depend on evidence for the inherited predisposition to mental disorders. ❖ More research is needed but this approach benefits from taking a functional approach rather than the more descriptive one of traditional psychiatry. ❖ Evolutionary explanations can be evaluated with reference to other explanations for mental disorders, discussed in Chapter 8, Psychopathology.

EVOLUTION OF INTELLIGENCE

What is Intelligence?

One general definition of intelligence is as follows: "the all-round mental ability (or thinking skills) either of humans or of lower animal species". According to that definition, intelligence can be regarded as equivalent to a set of mental abilities. These abilities would include problem solving, reasoning, memory, and language. Many non-human species possess at least some of these abilities, as we saw in the Section on memory in non-human animals.

The notion that intelligence consists of various mental abilities with some species having more of these abilities is a reasonable one. However, it is probably more appropriate to argue that intelligence should be regarded as the ability to deal effectively and adaptively with the environment. An animal that can respond more effectively to the environment will be more likely to survive and reproduce. Unfortunately, it is no easy matter to apply this approach when comparing several species. As Rifkin (1995) pointed out, "What is lacking is a good definition of intelligence that will tell us something about how an animal copes with its own ecology [natural environment] and not how closely it approximates human behaviour." In spite of its complexities, we will be focusing in this Section on the evolution of human intelligence relying in part on evidence from other species to help in the task of trying to work out how human intelligence developed over millions of years.

The human brain

If we want to understand the evolution of human intelligence, it is indisputable that we must consider above all else the human brain. The first point that needs to be emphasised about the human brain is that we mustn't regard all of its parts as being of comparable relevance to intelligence. We can see this by considering the work of MacLean (1970). He argued that the human brain can be thought of as a three-layered (or triune) system with each of the layers representing an important evolutionary development. The oldest of the three layers is deep down in the brain stem and is generally thought of as our reptilian brain. It is involved in basic functions such as breathing and eating. This layer is irrelevant to human intelligence.

Later on in evolutionary history, a second layer became wrapped around the first one. This layer is involved in preservation of the species, being concerned with functions such as pleasure seeking, emotions, feeding, fighting, and escape from pain. This layer is almost irrelevant to human intelligence. Finally, there is the third and most recent layer in evolutionary terms. This layer includes the neocortex or cerebral cortex and is overwhelmingly the most important for intelligence and for thinking. We can see how crucial the neocortex is to human intelligence by considering its size relative to the more primitive parts of the brain in humans and other primates. As Dunbar (1998) pointed out, the neocortex is no larger than the medulla (part of the reptilian brain involved in breathing and swallowing) in insectivores but is 20–50 times larger than the medulla in the anthropoids. In humans, the neocortex is an amazing 105 times larger than the medulla!

MacLean's (1982) notion of the triune brain provides a useful overview of the main divisions of the brain. His views are inevitably oversimplified given the overall complexity of the human brain. It is not really the case that the brain can

The cerebral cortex

The outer layer of the human brain is called the **cerebral cortex**. When you look at the brain, it is mostly cortex that you see but it is only 2 millimetres thick. The cerebral cortex has a bumpy, folded appearance and it is these bumps that greatly increase its volume. If you flattened the cortex out it would cover a square measuring 50 × 50cm. It is grey in colour because it largely contains cell bodies rather than the axons that link one area of the brain to another.

The cortex is what distinguishes the brain of mammals from the brain of lower animals. And the human brain has a far larger frontal cortex than other mammals (darker areas in diagram below). The cortex has great importance for our ability to perceive, think, and use language, and is highly related to intelligence.

Cerebral cortex

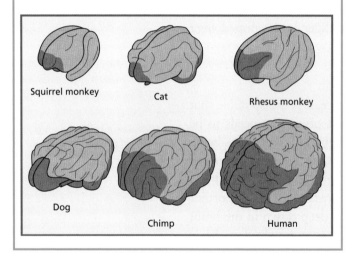

Squirrel monkey

Cat

Rhesus monkey

Dog

Chimp

Human

KEY TERM

Cerebral cortex: the surface layer of the forebrain or cerebrum.

be neatly subdivided into just three parts. In addition, there are important differences within different parts of each layer. For example, within the neocortex there are areas specialised for visual processing and other areas specialised for language processing.

Brain size and intelligence

The size of the human brain is not that impressive in some ways. For example, the elephant brain is about four times the size of the human brain. However, things look more promising if we consider the so-called "encephalisation quotient", which is the actual brain size of a species divided by its expected brain size on the basis of its body mass (Jerison, 1973). Humans score seven on this measure, which is more than any other species.

When we look back over the course of evolution, we discover that the human brain has increased dramatically in size. According to Stewart (1997), seven million years ago our ancestors had a brain that was only about 400 cubic centimetres (cc). Brain size didn't change much for millions of years after that, but by the time we get to the period 2.5 millions years ago with *Homo habilis* the brain size had almost doubled to about 700cc. *Homo habilis* then evolved into *Homo erectus*, who had a brain size of about 1000cc and had a socially complex life. Over the past 500,000 years, human brain size increased again and is now about 1350cc. You might imagine that it is a significant advantage to have a large brain, but real costs are involved. For example, our brains consume 20% of the total energy we produce.

Is intelligence related to brain size? There is evidence from various primate species to suggest that the answer is, "Yes". For example, Rumbaugh, Savage-Rumbaugh, and Washburn (1996) trained animals from 12 different primate species to perform a task (e.g., picking up a square instead of a triangle to find food). After that, the animals were trained to perform a second task (e.g., picking up a circle instead of a hexagon). Performance on the second task was facilitated by having previously done the first task among the larger-brained primates (e.g., gorillas, chimpanzees) but the first task interfered with performance on the second task among the smaller-brained primates (e.g., lemurs, talapoins).

When psychologists first studied the links between brain size and intelligence, it was found that there was practically no relationship. However, these early studies were very limited because the findings were based on inaccurate estimates of brain size. One technique was based on skull size, but that provides a very imprecise

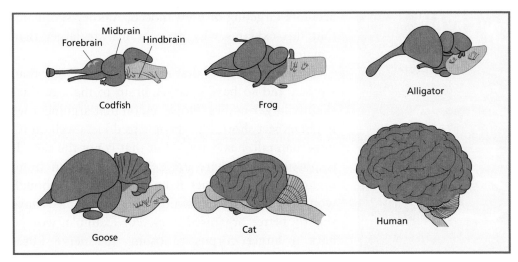

As you can see, higher animals have progressively more forebrain, the area of the brain involved in higher-order thinking. In mammals this forebrain has become highly folded. This development suggests a link between physical characteristics of the brain and intelligence.

estimate. Another technique was to measures the sizes of the shrunken brains of people who had recently died. Nowadays we can obtain good measures of brain size in living people by using brain-imaging techniques such as magnetic resonance imaging (MRI). Since male brains are larger than female ones, what is typically done is to use MRI to correlate brain size with intelligence in each sex separately. Alternatively, use is made of brain-to-body size to take account of the fact that females generally have smaller bodies than males.

The general finding is that there is a moderate association or correlation between brain size and intelligence. For example, Willerman et al. (1991) assessed brain size in male and female students. They reported that IQ correlated +0.51 with brain-to-body size and the correlation was slightly less when absolute brain volume was considered. Most other researchers have reported similar findings but the correlations have tended to be somewhat lower.

> **?** Why is it necessary to use brain : body ratio in this correlation?

What we have been discussing is correlational evidence, and we can't use correlations to prove causes. Of particular importance, brain development is related in part to the mother's health and nutrition during pregnancy, which is when most brain growth occurs. It is also the case that babies fed breast milk tend to have higher IQs later in life (Lucas et al., 1992), perhaps because breast milk contains fatty substances important to brain growth. We also know there is evidence relating nutritionally enhanced diets to increases in IQ (Benton, 2001; see Chapter 5). Thus, as Peters (1995) argued, the relationship between brain size and IQ may be influenced by nutritional factors—good nutrition benefits brain-size development and intelligence.

Gender differences

On average, men have larger brains than women, but there are generally no sex differences in average IQ. However, some sex differences have been reported for relatively specific abilities. For example, males have a slight advantage over females in visuospatial abilities and in aiming at targets (Kimura, 1992). According to Ankney (1995), this advantage may have occurred originally because men in hunter-gatherer societies needed hunting abilities such as navigational skills and

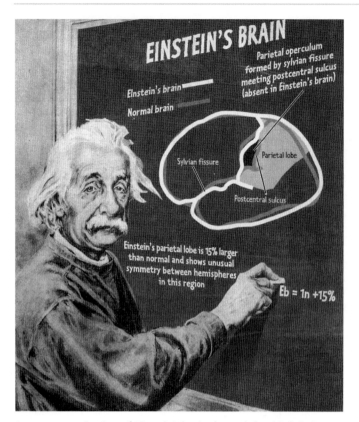

A recent examination of Einstein's brain showed that his inferior parietal region, which is linked to imagery and mathematics, was 15% wider than average. Furthermore, the groove that normally runs from the front of the brain to the back did not extend all the way, suggesting that Einstein's brain cells were packed close together, permitting more interconnections. © *The Times*.

accurate targeting of prey. Indeed, Ankney speculates that this explains why male brains are larger than female ones.

It could be argued that men tend to be larger than women and so have a larger brain to manage their slightly larger bodies. However, on that argument we might expect short, light people to do less well on IQ tests than tall, heavy ones, but that is not the case. It is possible that there are sex differences in brain organisation as distinct from overall size. Although women have smaller brains, they appear to have slightly better organised ones. For example, women have a larger corpus callosum (the nerve fibres connecting the two brain hemispheres) and this means slightly better communication within the brain (Johnson et al., 1996).

Brain organisation and intelligence

Perhaps brain organisation is more important than size, or at least equally important. For example, consider studies on the brain of the great scientist Albert Einstein who died on 18 April 1955. His brain was normal in size and structure—if anything it was a little *smaller* than the average brain since it weighed 1230 grams compared to the average adult male brain of 1400 grams. However, the neurons in Einstein's prefrontal cortex were more tightly packed than those of other adult males. This may be the cause or the effect of his intellectual powers, but the fact remains that it wasn't size but organisation that was related to intelligence.

Racial differences

It has sometimes been claimed that there are racial differences in brain size. For example, Rushton (1992) estimated cranial capacity of different groups within the US Army. He reported that the average was 1468 cm³ for Caucasoid soldiers, 1464 cm³ for Mongoloid soldiers, and 1449 cm³ for Negroid soldiers. Note that the difference between the highest and the lowest group is only a little over 1% and so probably has no real significance. In subsequent research, Rushton and Ankney (1995) produced more striking findings based using MRI. This time the cranial capacity estimates were 1416 cm³ for Mongoloid Americans, 1380 cm³ for Caucasoid Americans, and 1359 cm³ for Negroid Americans—the difference between the highest and lowest group is now about 4%. However, these figures were adjusted to take account of group differences in body weight, and some experts (e.g., Peters, 1995) argue that the adjustments were invalid.

How can we explain these racial differences in brain size? According to Rushton and Ankney (1995), we should focus on human evolutionary history. The ancestors of Negroid Americans lived in the warmest conditions, whereas the ancestors of Mongoloid Americans lived in the coldest conditions. If living in cold conditions requires more problem solving (e.g., finding shelter, gathering food), then we can provide an evolutionary account of racial differences in brain size. However, this account is very speculative.

There are several limitations with the data on racial differences in brain size. First, the cranial measures often used provide only an indirect (and probably inadequate) assessment of brain size, although this is not true of MRI data. Second, Rushton has consistently used an oversimplified grouping of races, and the whole concept of race is a complex and controversial one. Third, estimates of cranial capacity *within* any given group often vary considerably, thus shedding doubt on the value of these estimates. For example, Rushton (1991) discussed findings showing that Air Force personnel had estimated brain sizes that were 68 cm^3 greater in 1967 than in 1950. This difference is larger than any of the racial group differences reported by Rushton!

In sum, it is not clear that there are genuine racial differences in brain size. Even if it is established at some point in the future that such differences do exist, it would still be very difficult to know how to interpret them.

Evolutionary Factors in the Development of Human Intelligence

Intelligence must have evolved because it was an adaptive ability for any individual to possess. Could it be that an individual with more intelligence had greater reproductive success? Why might this be the case? Of particular importance, precisely why has the human brain grown so dramatically in size in the course of evolution? As we will, see there are several possible explanations of the large increases in intelligence and brain size that have occurred within the human species. Two types of explanations are of particular importance. First, our ancestors must have devoted much of their time and effort to ensuring that they had plentiful food supplies. According to ecological theories, brain size and the development of intelligence in any given species depended on how challenging it was for that species to have adequate access to food. Second, many primate species including the human species are essentially social and live in groups. According to social theories, the information-processing demands of operating effectively in social groups were important in the development of intelligence during the course of evolution.

Ecological theories of intelligence

Dunbar (1998) discussed three ecological hypotheses that emphasised different problems that primate species have to cope with when seeking food for survival. First, there is the dietary hypothesis. According to this hypothesis, primate species eating food that is distributed patchily need larger brains than primate species eating food that is more widely available. The reason why they need larger brains is because of the greater demands on their memory systems when trying to locate food. In general terms, fruits are more patchily distributed than leaves. Thus, it is predicted that frugivores (fruit-eating primates and other species) will have larger brains than folivores (leaf-eating primates and other species).

There is evidence that frugivorous primates have larger adult brains relative to body size than is the case with folivorous primates (Clutton-Brock & Harvey, 1980). However, the dietary hypothesis received much

> **EXAM HINT**
> There are three theories of factors in intelligence and you will only have approximately 600 words in timed conditions. So think about the structure of your essay. For example you could achieve depth by allocating 250 words to one factor, then 150 to each of the other two, leaving 50 for a conclusion.

A chimpanzee forages for insects with a stick; chimpanzees are skilled extractive foragers.

less support from a more detailed analysis carried out by Dunbar (1998). He considered the relationship between percentage of fruit in the diet and relative size of the neocortex (of key importance for intelligence) in 20 primate species. According to the dietary hypothesis, there should have been a strong correlation between these two measures. In fact, however, there was essentially no correlation at all. A criticism of Dunbar's findings is that he focused only on percentage of fruit in the diet. It is possible that more positive findings with respect to the dietary hypothesis might have been obtained if he had considered the *importance* of fruit in each species' diet—for example, a certain fruit may provide essential nutrients for a given species even though it doesn't account for a high percentage of the diet.

Second, there is the mental maps hypothesis. According to this hypothesis, species that cover a wide area in their search for food (large range size) and/or spend a large proportion of the day in foraging will have larger brains than those species that cover only a small area while foraging. The reason is that the former species need large-scale mental maps that impose additional memory loads on them. Frugivores tend to roam over larger areas than folivores in their foraging for food, and this provides a measure of support for the hypothesis. However, negative evidence was reported by Dunbar (1998). Across 20 primate species, there was essentially no correlation between range size and the size of the neocortex.

Third, there is the extractive foraging hypothesis. According to this hypothesis, primate species vary in terms of how easy or difficult it is to extract food. The key assumption is that species that have difficulty in extracting food (e.g., they need to use tools to gain access to it) will have larger brains than those having immediate access to food they have found. Dunbar (1998) divided primate species into four categories in terms of their use of extractive foraging: skilled, unskilled, specialised, and non-extractive foragers. Chimpanzees provide a good example of skilled extractive foragers: "Found stones are used to hammer open nuts on wood or stone anvils, sticks are used to pick up ants, stems and vines to 'fish' for termites in their mounds or ants" (Byrne, 2004, p.34). Dunbar reported across 20 primate species that there was no relationship between complexity of extractive foraging and relative neocortex size. A criticism of the extractive foraging hypothesis is that it is hard to provide a satisfactory definition of difficulty of extractive foraging.

Parker and Gibson (1979) reported that there was little relationship between complexity of extractive foraging (e.g., tool use) and intelligence across several species of mammal. According to them, tool use in intelligent primate species shouldn't be thought of as a cause of intelligence in those species, but rather as a consequence of their high level of intelligence. However, it is difficult to use correlational evidence to decide between these two possibilities.

Social theories of intelligence

Primates are predominantly social animals, and all monkeys and apes live in social groups. Group living confers many advantages on individuals, such as increasing survival and reproductive potential. A group can cope better with predators by having lookouts or using strategies to confuse predators. In addition, groups can often forage more effectively than individuals by using co-operative hunting, and group living facilitates mating.

A crucial feature of social or group living is that it presents situations that require problems to be solved to ensure that individuals survive long enough to reproduce. For example, an individual has to be aware of the inter-relationships within the group, needs to co-operate with other group members in foraging, and so on. An individual who can solve social problems is more likely to survive and to reproduce. Therefore, this ability is favoured by natural selection. As social groups increase in size, so does the complexity of information processing needed to keep track of interpersonal relationships within the group. As a consequence, we can see how the problems of being successful within social groups could have been of relevance in the increase in human brain size.

Machiavellian intelligence

In addition to the problems posed by group living, social life requires an ability to understand the intentions of others. This is called the **Theory of Mind**. If you possess a Theory of Mind, you have an understanding of others' thoughts and emotions, recognising that they are different from your own. This ability allows you to make predictions of how others will behave. Individuals without a Theory of Mind find social relationships more difficult. There is evidence that autistic individuals lack a Theory of Mind (Baron-Cohen, Leslie, & Frith, 1985) and they are also characterised by their social withdrawal. Theory of Mind is likely to be favoured by natural selection since it promotes social relationships.

The Theory of Mind is of relevance to Byrne and Whiten's (1988) notion of **Machiavellian intelligence**, which involves the ability to manipulate the social environment effectively by using other members of the social group as tools. Individuals who are high in Machiavellian intelligence need to understand other people's thoughts and to be able to predict their future behaviour, and possession of a Theory of Mind is necessary in order to do this. This requires complex information processing, and so only species with large brains and developed intelligence will exhibit Machiavellian intelligence.

Two ways in which Machiavellian intelligence manifests itself is through the formation of alliances and through deception. An individual can gain an important advantage by deceiving other group members about his/her real intentions, but must at the same time be sensitive to deception by others. In many primate species, mutual grooming is one way in which alliances are formed. Alliances are useful, because they increase the chances that individuals within an alliance will receive support from when they are threatened.

Some support for the notion of Machiavellian intelligence in higher primates was reported by Harcourt (1992). Alliances are found in nearly all primate species, but we can distinguish between alliances that apply only in the here and now versus those that also offer the prospect of assistance in the future. Future-oriented alliances (which are more complex than the here-and-now ones) are only in the more intelligent primate species such as humans and apes. Further support was obtained in research by Dunbar (1998). The size of the group involved in grooming is often used as a measure of alliance size in primate studies, and Dunbar reported that alliance size was greater in primate species having large relative neocortex size. Byrne (1995) considered the role of deception. Species with large relative neocortex size use tactical deception more often than species with small relative neocortex size.

The Machiavellian intelligence hypothesis has been broadened and extended and is often referred to nowadays as the social brain hypothesis. According to this hypothesis, intelligence and brain size will tend to be greater in those species having complex social structures. More specifically, "The social brain hypothesis implies that constraints on group size arise from the information-processing

? Dunbar's evidence is correlational. Are there any disadvantages of correlational studies?

capacity of the primate brain, and that the neocortex plays a major role in this" (Dunbar, 1998, p.184).

It is not easy to assess the complexity of social structures within a species, but Dunbar (1998) used social group size as an approximate measure. Dunbar reported a moderately strong correlation between relative neocortex size and social group size across 20 primate species, thus supporting the social brain hypothesis. He also noted that similar findings had been found by other researchers among bats, carnivores, and insectivores. Dunbar carried out additional analyses to decide which processes within the neocortex were of most importance to primates in maintaining complex social structures. He found that those parts of the neocortex concerned with visual perception or memory were not important—what really matters is the part of the neocortex concerned with manipulating information about social relationships.

Overall evaluation

We have now considered various ecological and social hypotheses or theories. In general, it has proved more difficult to find evidence supporting ecological hypotheses than social ones, but it is very likely that both types of hypotheses are of relevance in the evolution of intelligence. Most ecological and social hypotheses have had surprisingly little to say about language. Language is obviously hugely important in terms of communicating with other members of one's social group, and it makes it easier to understand others' motives and behaviour. In similar fashion, language can facilitate foraging behaviour—if someone else can give you precise instructions as to the location of food, that may save you much time. However, while the acquisition of language may well be one reason why relative neocortex size is larger in humans than in other primate species, it can't explain why there are large differences in relative neocortex size across primate species none of which possesses language.

We have discussed the two types of hypotheses separately for ease of communication, but it is likely that they have *interacted* with each other throughout the course of evolution. As Stewart (1997) pointed out, "It is unlikely that the evolution of primate intelligence can be definitively shunted into one category or another [ecological or social]. While ecology may have provided the initial conditions, cognitive evolution undoubtedly soon spiralled into a complex, interconnected web of adaptation, co-evolution [evolving together], and co-option of cerebral traits to cope with changing ecological and social conditions." Thus, we may need to combine elements of the ecological and social hypotheses to achieve full understanding.

There is a final issue to consider. Nearly all the evidence relating to the ecological and social hypotheses is correlational in nature—which means that it is very difficult to establish any *causal* links. For example, primate species with relatively large neocortices tend to live in larger social groups. Does having a relatively large neocortex lead primates to live in larger groups or does living in larger groups in some way trigger an increase in the size of the neocortex? The only honest answer is that we aren't really sure exactly *why* the correlation or association between size of neocortex and group size exists.

Meat-sharing hypothesis

During the course of evolution, meat became an important source of food for our ancestors. Meat contains saturated fat and helped to provide those ancestors with the energy they needed as their brains increased in size. Meat would often have been a relatively scarce resource because of the need to spend much time engaged in hunting wild animals. These considerations led Stanford (1999) to argue that the sharing of meat within the members of a group played an important role in the development of human intelligence. According to Stanford's meat-for-sex hypothesis, males who had access to meat would trade some of their meat with females in return for sex. Males who were at or near the top of the dominance hierarchy would have sexual access to females without such trading, and so it was mainly lower-ranking males would have engaged in exchanging meat for sex.

The meat-for-sex hypothesis may sound rather fanciful, but Stanford (1999) obtained evidence consistent with it. He studied chimpanzees in Tanzania who find it very difficult to obtain enough food for survival. When a group of chimpanzees manages to kill an animal for food (generally a colobus monkey), they share out the meat. As predicted by the meat-for-sex hypothesis, lower-ranking male chimpanzees often exchanged meat for sexual favours. Sexually receptive females were generally more successful than other females at obtaining meat.

It could be argued that findings from chimpanzees may have little or no evidence to humans. However, Hill and Kaplan (1988) studied various human hunter-gatherer cultures (e.g., the Ache culture in Paraguay). They reported that the Ache share meat within their group, and there is direct evidence of meat being exchanged for sex. The most skilful hunters are the ones who receive the most sexual favours from Ache women. If we assume that skilful hunters tend to be more intelligent than less skilful ones, the meat-for-sex hypothesis could help to explain how human intelligence has developed over thousands of generations.

Sexual selection theory

There is another possible explanation for why intelligence developed and the human brain increased in size. It could be that intelligence is a trait that was *sexually* selected (as distinct from naturally selected). Intelligence is seen as a sexy trait, in the same way that a peacock's tail feathers are sexy. Intelligence would include behaviours like the ability to be entertaining or to be successful at hunting. Females prefer men who are intelligent, and this means that the trait of intelligence becomes progressively stronger. This would be an example of the runaway hypothesis for intersexual selection (see page 303). Miller (1998) suggests that this sexual selection explains why men have been more creative in the arts than women—in this way they could demonstrate their intelligence and so win the sexual favours of a woman.

There was selective pressure on females as well because they needed larger brains to decode the male's new abilities—abilities to entertain, produce art and music, and also to use language. Thus, there is selective pressure on both males and females to be intelligent.

Some support for the sexiness of intelligence comes from surveys of what characteristics people seek in partners. Miller (1996) reports that intelligence consistently comes at the top of the list in spite of the fact that it is not *directly* related to such obvious indicators of reproductive success as health, fertility, and command of resources. However, in Western cultures there is a correlation of +0.3 between IQ and earnings, and there is a tendency for more intelligent people to live longer than less intelligent ones. According to evolutionary psychologists, there is probably some other way in which intelligence is related to sexual

Do you agree that women have been less creative in the arts than men? What reasons could you give for this belief?

Do you think that intelligent members of the opposite sex are more "sexy"?

selection (what people find attractive in a mate). The answer is that intelligence is a runaway trait. In order to evaluate this argument, you might consider research on interpersonal relationships (see Chapter 2, Relationships), which indicates that numerous factors in addition to intelligence are related to interpersonal attraction.

An argument favouring the view that sexual selection is responsible for intelligence is the fact that the human brain has increased in size tremendously (and the male brain is larger than the female brain even when different body weight is taken into account). Sexual selection exerts the kind of pressure that could explain the dramatic (and fairly rapid in evolutionary terms) increase in human brain size because it directly selects for reproductive success.

SECTION SUMMARY
Evolution of Intelligence

Is brain size related to intelligence?

❖ The human brain : body ratio is comparatively large, and the human brain has increased dramatically in size over several million years. There must be some advantage to a large brain, because such increased size incurs a cost.

❖ Comparative studies support the view that an animal with a larger brain is capable of more intelligent behaviour. However:

— There are three main layers in the brain, and the only one that is really crucial for intelligence is the neocortex.
— Comparative studies run the risk of underestimating abilities because animals are tested on unnatural tasks.

❖ A second approach is to look at the correlation between IQ and brain size:

— Recent studies using MRI have found a significant positive correlation.
— However, IQ tests have been questioned in terms of validity.

Accounting for the differences in human brain size

❖ Brain size is partly inherited, but it is also related to very early environment and diet.
❖ Sex: males have larger brains but they don't have higher IQs. This discrepancy may be due to the fact that women's brains are better organised, so compensating for the smaller size. Organisation may be more important than size.
❖ Race: it is claimed that there are racial differences in brain size, but it is difficult and controversial to interpret these differences.

Ecological theories of intelligence

❖ The development of intelligence depends on:

— Diet
— Mental maps needed for foraging
— Extractive foraging.

❖ Evaluation of ecological theories:

— None of these factors are reliably associated with relative neocortex size across primate species.

❖ Intelligence evolved as a result of various factors:

— The problems presented by group living and the demands of information processing within large groups.
— Social life requires a Theory of Mind and may involve the need for Machiavellian intelligence.

Social theories of intelligence

❖ Evaluation of social theories:

— Humans find it easier to solve social problems, supporting the link between social living and intelligence.
— Most social animals are intelligent, but there is some question about which comes first: intelligence or social life.
— Group size correlates highly with relative neocortex size across primate species, as is predicted by social theories. However, it is difficult to interpret what causes what on the basis of such correlational evidence.

❖ The meat-sharing hypothesis:

— Males who had access to meat would exchange it in return for the sexual favours of females.
— This hypothesis may help to explain the development of human intelligence but it is limited and omits many relevant social factors.

Other theories for the development of human intelligence

❖ Sexual selection:

— Intelligence is a sexy, "runaway" trait in males. Females also have to be intelligent to appreciate the male's abilities. Thus there is selective pressure on both males and females to be intelligent.
— Support for this comes from the fact that people consistently select intelligence as the trait they look for in a mate.
— In addition sexual selection for intelligence can also explain the rapid growth in the human brain because sexual selection selects directly for reproductive success.

See also pages 181–188 of the revision guide.

FURTHER READING

The topics in this chapter are covered in greater depth by J. Cartwright (2001) *Evolutionary explanations of human behaviour* (London: Routledge), written specifically for the AQA A specification. Reproductive strategies are intelligently discussed in a lavishly illustrated book by R. Short and M. Potts (1999) *Ever since Adam and Eve: The evolution of human sexuality* (Cambridge: Cambridge University Press). The evolution of mental illness is discussed by A. Stevens and J. Price (2000) *Evolutionary psychiatry (2nd Edn)* (London: Routledge).

EXAMPLE EXAMINATION QUESTIONS

You should spend 30 minutes on each of the questions below, which aim to test the material in this chapter.

1. (a) Outline evolutionary explanations for human reproductive behaviour. (12 marks)
   (b) Critically assess these explanations. (12 marks)
2. (a) Describe evolutionary explanations of parental investment. (12 marks)
   (b) Assess the implications of these evolutionary explanations
   of parental investment. (12 marks)
3. Discuss **two** evolutionary explanations of human mental disorders. (24 marks)
4. Critically consider evolutionary explanations of depression. (24 marks)
5. Discuss evolutionary factors in the development of human intelligence (AQA, 2004). (24 marks)
6. Discuss the relationship between brain size and intelligence (AQA, 2002). (24 marks)

Examination Tips

Question 1. The injunction "outline" requires a summary description rather than one given in detail. Therefore, in this question, your aim is to provide a number of different explanations rather than focusing on the detail. Your descriptions should nonetheless contain enough information to communicate understanding. In part (b) you are required to present evaluation of the explanations, including a consideration of both their strengths and weaknesses. Such critical assessment may involve reference to research support or to the relevance of such explanations for human behaviour. Note that, if research studies are used, then credit will not be given for a description of the studies but for the effective use of such material.

Question 2. Evolutionary explanations (AO1) of parental investment can include a range of material beginning with relative size and number of gametes. Darwinian and selfish gene approaches involve successful reproduction and rearing of the young (i.e., investment in parental care). Courtship and mating have elements related to parenting rather than "good" genes, e.g., resources. Whatever you use, remember the focus is on parental behaviour, not mating in general. Implications (AO2) include sex differences in parental investment and reproductive behaviour, species and cultural differences in patterns of parental behaviour, and changes over time in human parental patterns.

Question 3. "Discuss" is an AO1 and AO2 term. The question requires that you describe and evaluate two explanations. This can be achieved by explaining two different mental disorders (such as schizophrenia and depression) or by considering two general explanations (such as genome lag and increased fitness). When evaluating these explanations you might offer a contrast with other evolutionary or non-evolutionary explanations. It is important to use such contrasting evidence effectively to be awarded high marks. Research studies would also be useful for evaluation, as would practical applications.

Question 4. "Critically consider" is an AO1/AO2 term that further demands a consideration of both strengths and weaknesses. Thus you need to describe two or more evolutionary explanations of depression (because "explanations" is plural), and evaluate these as suggested in question 3. It is legitimate for the examiner to ask specifically about depression as it is given as an "including" in the specification.

Question 5.   The question requires you to consider how we can use the theory of evolution to explain why and how intelligence appeared in humans. You must include at least two factors and should aim to provide sufficient detail for each factor. Evaluation may be through the use of research studies (which may be criticised themselves) as well as an analysis of the logical nature of the arguments presented. The extent to which you use the material effectively rather than just, for example, describing research studies will determine the number of marks awarded.

Question 6.   The AO1 material here would include a description of relationships across different species between brain size and intelligence, perhaps including brain evolution and its possible role in human evolution and our ultimate success as a species. AO2 could be approached from many angles. Brain size does not correlate perfectly with intelligence, different brain structures may be more or less important in intelligence, small-brained animals can show learning and intelligent behaviour. There are problems in defining intelligence across species, e.g., do language and self-awareness count as "intelligence"? General but relevant commentary can provide very effective AO2.

WEBSITES

http://www.literature.org/authors/darwin-charles/the-origin-of-species/
   Text from Darwin's *The Origin of Species*.
http://www.ucmp.berkeley.edu/history/evotheory.html
   A fantastic website, hosting a timeline of evolutionary theories and more.
http://www.ocfoundation.org/
   Obsessive–Compulsive Foundation homepage.
http://www.thegreatdebate.org.uk/GDarticles.html
   A host of links and articles on topics such as sexual selection and Darwinism.

INDIVIDUAL DIFFERENCES

Schizophrenia p.341
- Are all schizophrenics a danger to society?
- What evidence is there to support the view that schizophrenia is inherited?
- In terms of causation, are psychological factors important as well?

Depression p.355
- How is clinical depression distinguished from the kind of depression we all experience occasionally?
- How do endogenous depression and reactive depression differ?
- Are some individuals more prone to becoming depressed than others?

Anxiety Disorders p.370
- Which phobia is the most disabling?
- Are some individuals genetically predisposed to becoming phobic?
- Has everyone with a phobia had a bad experience with their feared object?

Psychopathology

What is **psychopathology**? According to Davison and Neale (1996), it is "the field concerned with the nature and development of mental disorders" (p.G20). Psychopathology is the subject matter of this chapter.

SCHIZOPHRENIA

Causes of Mental Disorder

One of the key issues in abnormal psychology is to understand *why* some people suffer from psychological disorders such as depression or schizophrenia. When considering the causes of a mental disorder, it is helpful to start by distinguishing between two categories of factors:

Biological factors, as used by the **medical model**, for example:

- *Genetic factors*: twin studies, family studies, and adoption studies may indicate that some people are genetically more vulnerable than others to developing a disorder because of the genes they have inherited.
- *Biochemistry*: individuals with unusually high or low levels of certain brain chemicals may be vulnerable to psychological disorders.

Psychological factors, as used by **behavioural, cognitive, humanistic,** and **psychodynamic models**, for example:

- *Cultural factors*: cultural values and expectations may be important in causing some disorders; for example, most Western cultures emphasise the desirability of thinness in women, and this may help to trigger eating disorders.

KEY TERMS

Psychopathology: this is an area of psychology in which the focus is on the nature of mental disorders and the factors that cause them to exist.
Medical model: a model of abnormality based on the medical approach to treating physical illness; the model assumes that all illnesses (physical and psychological) have an underlying biochemical or physiological basis.
Behavioural model: a model of abnormality based on the behaviourist approach (behaviourism). Mental illness is explained in terms of classical and operant conditioning.
Cognitive model: a model of abnormality that emphasises the role of cognitive factors in mental disorders. The view is that thinking in a maladaptive way leads to disordered behaviour.
Humanistic model: a model of abnormality based on the humanistic approach that emphasises the uniqueness of each individual, a focus on the present rather than the past, the importance of subjective experience, and the drive of each individual to be self-righting and to self-actualise.
Psychodynamic model: a model of abnormality, based on the psychodynamic (psychoanalytic) approach, which emphasises the influence of early experiences and of repressed emotions that are expressed unconsciously.

- *Social factors*: individuals who experience severe life events (e.g., divorce, unemployment) may be at risk for various psychological disorders, as may those who lack social support or belong to poorly functioning families.
- *Experiential factors*: interactions with the environment result in learning or conditioning, which may explain some mental disorders such as phobias.

These factors *interact*. For example, someone may have a very high or a very low level of a given brain chemical because of genetic factors or because he/she has recently experienced a severe life event. Another example concerns the impact of cultural expectations on eating disorders. This is clearly not the *only* factor causing eating disorders, because the overwhelming majority of women in Western societies don't suffer from eating disorders. Eating disorders occur in individuals who are exposed to cultural expectations of thinness *and* who are vulnerable (e.g., because of genetic factors).

The multi-dimensional approach

The description of causal factors raises the questions of whether a disorder is caused by a *single* factor or many of them. According to one-dimensional models, the origins of a psychological disorder can be traced to a single underlying cause. For example, it might be argued that severe depression is caused by a major loss (e.g., death of a loved one), or that schizophrenia is caused by genetic factors. All one-dimensional models are now regarded as greatly oversimplified. They have been replaced by multi-dimensional models, in which it is recognised that abnormal behaviour is typically caused by several different factors.

The multi-dimensional approach to psychopathology is often expressed in the form of the **diathesis–stress model**. According to this model, the occurrence of psychological disorders depends on two factors:

1. *Diathesis*: a genetic vulnerability or predisposition to disease or disorder.
2. *Stress*: some severe or disturbing environmental event. Note that the term "stress" is used in a very broad sense and might include, for example, drug-taking or any event that places an extra burden on the individual psychologically and/or physically.

The key notion in the diathesis–stress model is that both diathesis or genetic vulnerability *and* stress are necessary for a psychological disorder to occur.

Clinical Characteristics of Schizophrenia

Schizophrenia is a very serious condition that is extremely difficult to treat effectively. On average, the rates of schizophrenia during the course of a person's life are about 1% of the population (see page 345). The symptoms exhibited vary somewhat, but typically include problems with attention, thinking, social relationships, motivation, and emotion. According to DSM-IV-TR (the *Diagnostic and Statistical Manual, Volume 4, 2000*), the criteria for schizophrenia include:

1. Two or more of the following symptoms, each of which must have been present for a significant period of time over a 1-month period: delusions, hallucinations, disorganised speech, grossly disorganised, or catatonic (rigid)

? Can you relate the diathesis–stress model to the dichotomy of nature and nurture?

KEY TERMS

Diathesis–stress model: the notion that psychological disorders occur when there is a genetically determined vulnerability (diathesis) and relevant stressful conditions.

Schizophrenia: a severe condition in which there is a loss of contact with reality, including distortions of thought, emotion, and behaviour.

behaviour; and negative symptoms (lack of emotion, lack of motivation, speaking very little or uninformatively); only one symptom is needed if the delusions are bizarre, or if the hallucinations consist of a voice commenting on the individual's behaviour.

2. Continuous signs of disturbance over a period of at least 6 months.

3. Social and/or occupational dysfunction or poor functioning.

Schizophrenics generally have confused thinking, and often suffer from delusions. Many of these delusions involve what are known as "ideas of reference", in which the schizophrenic patient attaches great personal significance to external objects or events. Thus, for example, a schizophrenic seeing his neighbours talking may be convinced that they are plotting to kill him.

Schizophrenics often suffer from hallucinations. Delusions arise from mistaken interpretations of actual objects and events, but hallucinations occur in the absence of any external stimulus. Most schizophrenic hallucinations consist of voices, usually saying something of personal relevance to the patient. McGuigan (1966) suggested that these auditory hallucinations occur because patients mistake their own inner speech for someone else's voice. He found that the patient's larynx was often active during the time that the auditory hallucination was being experienced. More recent studies have confirmed this explanation of hallucinations (Frith, 1992).

Language impairments characterise schizophrenia. Patients may repeat sounds (echolalia) or use invented words (neologisms). Their speech may seem illogical and involve abrupt shifts from one theme to another. This is described as "knight's move thinking" because, in chess, the knight is only permitted to move in an L-shape (e.g., two squares forward and one to the right). In some cases the patient's speech can be so jumbled that it is described as "word salad". The impairment of language has led some theorists to suggest that there is a link between the evolution of language in humans and schizophrenia—that schizophrenia is the price we pay for having language (see the box on page 347).

Finally, there are some schizophrenics whose behaviour is even more bizarre. One of the most common behavioural abnormalities is to remain almost motionless for hours at a time. Some patients make strange grimaces or repeat an odd gesture over and over again.

There are positive and negative symptoms. Positive symptoms include delusions, hallucinations, and bizarre forms of behaviour. Negative symptoms include an absence of emotion and motivation, language deficits, general apathy, and an avoidance of social activity. The positive symptoms are more important than the negative ones in terms of diagnosing a patient with schizophrenia—of the five categories of symptoms identified within DSM-IV, four are positive and only one is negative. However, patients with several negative symptoms often respond poorly to drugs and are generally hard to treat.

About one-third of patients have a single episode or a few brief episodes of schizophrenia and then recover fully. Another third have occasional episodes

Schizophrenics often suffer from delusions, misinterpreting ordinary events, such as conversations between other people, as being about themselves.

EXAM HINT

You need to know the clinical characteristics of each disorder but you should only ever use this material in the exam if it has been asked for in a sub-part (a) AO1 question.

of the disorder throughout their lives and, in between these, they function reasonably effectively. The remaining third deteriorate over a series of episodes, each of which becomes progressively more incapacitating. Those patients for whom schizophrenia comes on suddenly tend to have a better prognosis, and the same is true for patients where the positive symptoms predominate.

Types of schizophrenia

According to DSM-IV-TR (2000), there are five main types of schizophrenia:

1. *Disorganised schizophrenia*: this type involves great disorganisation, including delusions, hallucinations, incoherent speech, and large mood swings.
2. *Catatonic schizophrenia*: the main feature is almost total immobility for hours at a time, with the patient simply staring blankly.
3. *Paranoid schizophrenia*: this type involves delusions of various kinds.
4. *Undifferentiated schizophrenia*: this is a broad category that includes patients who don't clearly belong within any other category.
5. *Residual schizophrenia*: this type consists of patients who don't have any prominent positive symptoms (e.g., hallucinations, delusions) but who have various negative symptoms (e.g., lack of emotion).

CASE STUDY: **A SCHIZOPHRENIC**

A young man of 19 (WG) was admitted to the psychiatric services on the grounds of a dramatic change in character. His parents described him as always being extremely shy with no close friends, but in the last few months he had gone from being an average-performing student to failing his studies and leaving college. Having excelled in non-team sports such as swimming and athletics, he was now taking no exercise at all. WG had seldom mentioned health matters, but now complained of problems with his head and chest. After being admitted, WG spent most of his time staring out of the window, and uncharacteristically not taking care over his appearance. Staff found it difficult to converse with him and he offered no information about himself, making an ordinary diagnostic interview impossible. WG would usually answer direct questions, but in a flat emotionless tone. Sometimes his answers were not even connected to the question, and staff would find themselves wondering what the conversation had been about. There were also occasions when there was a complete mismatch between WG's emotional expression and the words he spoke. For example, he giggled continuously when speaking about a serious illness that had left his mother bedridden. On one occasion, WG became very agitated and spoke of "electrical sensations" in his brain. At other times he spoke of being influenced by a force outside himself, which took the form of a voice urging him to commit acts of violence against his parents. He claimed that the voice repeated the command "You'll have to do it".

Adapted from Hofling (1974).

What clinical characteristics of schizophrenia can be seen in this Case Study of WG?

Biological Explanation: Genetic Factors

There are various ways of trying to decide whether or not genetic factors are important in schizophrenia. Below we consider three approaches: twin studies, family studies, and adoption studies. After that, we evaluate the overall evidence to see what conclusions can reasonably be drawn.

Twin studies

Some of the most striking support for genetic factors was reported by Rosenthal (1963). He studied quadruplets, in which all four girls were identical to each other. Amazingly, all four of them developed schizophrenia, although they did differ somewhat in age of onset and the precise symptoms. They were known as the Genain (dreadful genes) quadruplets. It may be worth noting that they did also have a dreadful and aberrant childhood so, as with most evidence, the conclusion is not clear-cut.

Much of the evidence concerning the involvement of genetic factors in schizophrenia comes from the study of twins, one of whom is known to be schizophrenic. Researchers want to establish the probability that the other twin is also schizophrenic—a state of affairs known as **concordance**. Gottesman (1991) summarised about 40 studies. He reported that the concordance rate was about 48% if you have a monozygotic or identical twin with schizophrenia, but only 17% if you have a dizygotic or fraternal twin with schizophrenia. These findings strongly suggest that genetic factors are important—the reason why identical twins have much higher concordance than fraternal twins is because they are much more similar genetically (100% similarity vs. 50% similarity, respectively). Gottesman also reported that the concordance rate for identical twins brought up apart was very similar to that for identical twins brought up together—this suggests that the high concordance rate for identical twins is *not* due to them being treated in a very similar way within the family.

Torrey (1992) argued that many of the twin studies were inadequate. He reviewed eight studies in which representative samples were used and allocation of twin pairs to identical or fraternal was done with reasonable certainty. Overall, the concordance rate for identical or MZ twins was 28% compared to only 6% for fraternal or DZ twins. These figures are much lower than those reported by Gottesman (1991) but in line with figures reported by Joseph (2003). Joseph considered the nine most recent twin studies on schizophrenia, finding that the concordance rate was 22.4% for identical twins and 4.6% for fraternal twins. If you consider that the lifetime risk of schizophrenia in the general population is only 1%, then you have a substantially increased chance of schizophrenia if you have a twin (especially identical) with the condition.

Identical (monozygotic) twins are not only genetically identical; they are also more likely to be treated identically by their family.

Family studies

Gottesman (1991) reviewed concordance rates from family studies. If both your parents have schizophrenia, then you have a 46% chance of developing schizophrenia as well. The concordance rate is 16% if one of your parents has schizophrenia, and it is 8% if a sibling has schizophrenia. These concordance

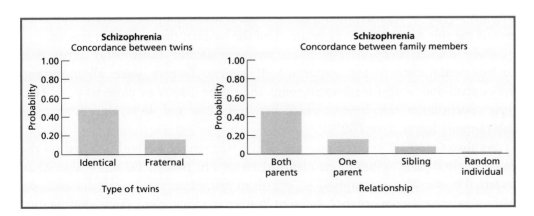

Research by Gottesman (1991) indicates that schizophrenia tends to run in families.

KEY TERM

Concordance: when a disorder or condition is found in both twins.

rates should be compared against the 1% probability of someone selected at random suffering from schizophrenia.

Gottesman and Bertelsen (1989) reported some convincing findings on the importance of genetic factors. One of their findings was that their participants had a 17% chance of being schizophrenic if they had a parent who was an identical twin and who had schizophrenia. This could be due to either heredity or environment. However, they also studied participants with a parent who was an identical twin and didn't have schizophrenia, but whose identical twin did. These participants also had a 17% chance of being schizophrenic. Thus, what is of most importance is the genes that are handed on by the parents.

Adoption studies

Schizophrenia
Concordance with adoption

The notion that genetic factors are important in producing schizophrenia is supported by adoption studies. One approach is to look at adopted children, one of whose parents has schizophrenia. Tienari (1991) did this in Finland. He managed to find 155 schizophrenic mothers who had given up their children for adoption, and they were compared against 155 adopted children not having a schizophrenic parent. There was a large difference in the incidence of schizophrenia in these two groups when they were adults: 10.3% of those with schizophrenic mothers had developed schizophrenia compared with only 1.1% of those without schizophrenic mothers.

Wahlberg et al. (1997) reported additional findings from the study started by Tienari suggesting that environmental factors are important as well as genetic ones. They studied the environment provided by the adopted families in terms of whether it was low or high in communication deviance—a tendency to communicate in unclear and confusing ways. Children at genetic risk because they had schizophrenic mothers had very good psychological health if they were raised by adopted families low in communication deviance; indeed, they were even healthier than children with no genetic risk! In contrast, children at genetic risk raised by adopted families high in communication deviance showed high levels of thought disorder.

Evaluation

What are the limitations of twin and family studies of schizophrenia?

We will start by evaluating the evidence from twin studies. In spite of large differences in the concordance rates reported across studies, two findings have been obtained repeatedly: (1) identical and fraternal twins with a co-twin having schizophrenia are much more likely than a random member of the population to suffer from schizophrenia; (2) among twins having a co-twin with schizophrenia, identical twins are at significantly greater risk than fraternal twins. These findings strongly suggest that genetic factors play a role in the development of schizophrenia, even if the role is less than was assumed on the basis of the early twin studies.

Twin studies also provide much ammunition for those who argue that environmental factors are important. If genetic factors were all-important, the concordance rate for identical twins should be 100% or close to it. In fact, their concordance rate is somewhere between 22% and 48%, figures that are substantially lower than 100%.

As Joseph (2003) pointed out, use of the twin-study method is based on the equal environment assumption: identical twins are treated no more alike than fraternal twins. This assumption is difficult to test. However, Joseph discusses six studies in which concordance rates of fraternal twins were compared against those of non-twin siblings. Since the genetic similarity is the same in both cases, we might imagine that the concordance rates would be the same. In fact, however, the concordance rates are consistently higher for fraternal twins than for non-twin siblings. This suggests that there may be something special about twins making it dangerous to draw general conclusions from them.

The evidence reported by Gottesman indicates clearly that schizophrenia runs in families. Furthermore, as predicted by the genetic hypothesis, the concordance rate is much higher between relatives having high genetic similarity. However, the fact that family members who are more similar genetically tend to spend more time together means that environmental factors are also indicated in this evidence.

The evidence from adoption studies also indicates that genetic factors are important in the development of schizophrenia. However, an important qualification on that was reported by Wahlberg et al. (1997): children at high genetic risk seemed to do very well if their adopted families provided a supportive environment. Thus, we need to consider genetic *and* environmental factors together in order to predict accurately how likely any given person is to develop schizophrenia.

In sum, the evidence from twin, family, and adoption studies indicates that genetic factors are of some importance in the development of schizophrenia. The consistency of the evidence is impressive. However, there are two other major conclusions. First, environmental factors are clearly important; indeed, they are probably more important than genetic ones. Second, if we are to understand fully what determines schizophrenia, it is essential to study genetic and environmental factors at the same time.

> **Biological explanation: The evolutionary approach**
>
> Several intriguing evolutionary explanations have been suggested for schizophrenia. These are discussed in greater detail in Chapter 7, Evolutionary Explanations of Human Behaviour.
>
> In essence the evolutionary view is that schizophrenia is at least in part genetic and the gene for schizophrenia must offer some advantage in order to explain why it has remained in the gene pool.
>
> One possibility is the **group-splitting hypothesis** (Stevens & Price, 1996). The personality characteristics of the schizophrenic include bizarre beliefs, hallucinations, delusions, and strange speech. A "crazy" individual may act as a leader and enable one subgroup to split off from a main group, a valuable function at times when the main group has become too large to be optimum.
>
> A second explanation has been advanced in relation to the origin of language. Crow (2000) has suggested that schizophrenia is the price that humans pay for language. He points out that schizophrenia involves a breakdown in the brain's internal linguistic controls. Schizophrenics often believe they are hearing voices and/or may use atypical language. Thus schizophrenia is an outcome of linguistic ability, when the processor goes wrong.

Biological Explanation: Biochemistry

Genetic factors may lead to differences in brain chemistry, so that it is the brain chemistry that is the immediate causal factor. Biochemical abnormalities may be important in the development and maintenance of schizophrenia. For example, schizophrenia may result in part from excess levels of the neurotransmitter dopamine (Seidman, 1983). A slightly different view is that neurons in the brains of schizophrenic patients are oversensitive to dopamine.

The dopamine hypothesis

Three kinds of evidence have been used to suggest that the neurotransmitter (chemical substance) dopamine plays a role in schizophrenia. First, the drug chlorpromazine has proved useful in the treatment of schizophrenia. The main reason for its effectiveness seems to be that it blocks dopamine receptors.

KEY TERM

Group-splitting hypothesis: an account of schizophrenia in which the schizophrenic individual acts as a leader to split a group that has become too large to function well.

Second, the drug L-dopa, which increases dopamine levels, can produce many of the symptoms of schizophrenia. L-dopa has been given to patients suffering from Parkinson's disease, which is caused by low levels of dopamine in parts of the brain. It is effective in treating some of the symptoms of the disease, but an unwanted side-effect is the presence of various schizophrenic symptoms.

Third, there is evidence on the effects of amphetamine. This is a drug that produces a functional excess of dopamine, meaning that the brain responds as if there were too much dopamine. High dosages of amphetamine can produce some of the symptoms of schizophrenia (e.g., paranoia, auditory hallucinations). In similar fashion, the symptoms of schizophrenic patients often become worse when they are given amphetamine, which activates dopamine (van Kammen, Docherty, & Bunney, 1982).

Problems with the dopamine hypothesis

It is difficult to assess brain levels of dopamine in schizophrenic patients. Indeed, this can only be done in a *direct* way by post-mortem (after death) assessment. It is also possible to assess dopamine levels in an *indirect* way. However, this involves a needle being inserted into the schizophrenic's spine, a technique that can be dangerous. The findings have generally been negative—schizophrenic patients don't seem to produce more dopamine than other people.

Supporters of the dopamine hypothesis have increasingly argued that the dopamine receptors of schizophrenics are more sensitive than those of normal controls. That could explain why schizophrenics seem to behave as if they had high levels of dopamine. Brain-imaging studies have produced rather variable results. It has sometimes been found that schizophrenics have more than twice as many dopamine receptors of a given type than controls (Gjedde & Wong, 1987), but no difference between schizophrenics and controls was found in another study (Farde et al., 1990).

In sum, it is likely that dopamine is of importance in understanding some of the symptoms of schizophrenia. However, it has proved difficult to identify precisely *how* dopamine exerts its effects.

[?] Does the evidence indicate whether schizophrenics might have excess dopamine (or serotonin), or are just more sensitive to it?

Biological Explanation: Brain Structure and Early Development

Several researchers have argued that brain abnormalities may be involved in schizophrenia. There are several sophisticated techniques for studying the brain, some of which have been used to study brain structure in schizophrenics. Pahl, Swayze, and Andreasen (1990) reviewed almost 50 studies, the great majority of which found abnormally large lateral ventricles (liquid-filled cavities) in the brains of schizophrenics. Further evidence of the involvement of the ventricles was reported by Suddath et al. (1990). They used magnetic resonance imaging (MRI) to obtain pictures of brain structure from monozygotic or identical twin pairs in which only one twin had schizophrenia. The schizophrenic twin generally had more enlarged ventricles and reduced anterior hypothalamus. Indeed, the differences were so large that the schizophrenic twin could be identified readily from the brain images in 12 out of 15 twin pairs.

[?] Could you use this knowledge to diagnose schizophrenia? How reliable would the diagnosis be?

Enlarged ventricles can occur because the brain areas surrounding them have decreased in volume. There is much evidence that the brain volume of schizophrenics is less than that of normals. There is also evidence that there are progressive decreases in schizophrenics' brain volume over time. For example, Mathalon et al. (2001) found that adult patients with schizophrenia had more rapid reductions in total brain volume than did healthy controls. With such evidence, however, it is difficult to know whether the reduced brain volume plays any role in the development and/or maintenance of schizophrenia or whether it is merely a consequence of having schizophrenia.

Neurodevelopmental hypothesis

Schizophrenia is generally diagnosed when someone is in their late teens or early twenties. As a result, it might seem odd to look at early childhood and even at the period before birth in order to obtain insights into the causes of schizophrenia. However, precisely that is what has been done by supporters of the neurodevelopmental hypothesis, according to which brain lesions occurring very early in development (possibly before birth) can make the individuals affected vulnerable to schizophrenia.

There is evidence supporting the neurodevelopmental hypothesis. For example, Wright et al. (1999) reported data from several countries on the incidence of schizophrenia in children born to mothers who had 'flu during pregnancy. There was an elevated risk of schizophrenia in these children, especially when the mother had 'flu between the fourth and seventh months of the pregnancy. The effect is not very large, but it is highly significant statistically.

Susser et al. (1996) considered the effects of a severe famine lasting several months in parts of Holland during the Second World War. Children who were conceived during the famine had twice the normal risk of developing schizophrenia subsequently. Presumably prenatal nutritional deficiency was responsible.

Walker et al. (1994) studied family home movies taken during the early childhoods of children who did or didn't develop schizophrenia subsequently. At a very early age (sometimes as early as 2), the children who would develop schizophrenia had more motor abnormalities, more negative emotional expressions, and more odd hand movements. This is intriguing evidence that there may be early signs that someone will develop schizophrenia many years later.

Evaluation

There is increasing evidence that a range of factors occurring either prior to birth or in the early years of childhood can significantly increase the risk of developing schizophrenia in late adolescence or early adulthood. According to the neurodevelopmental hypothesis, many of these factors cause brain lesions, and these brain lesions in turn play a role in the development of schizophrenia. At present, we don't have a detailed account of how these factors cause brain lesions, and we certainly don't even have clear evidence that they actually do cause brain lesions. However, the findings that schizophrenics have larger ventricles and smaller brain volume than normals suggest that it is fruitful to consider brain abnormalities when trying to explain schizophrenia.

Psychological Explanation: Social Factors

If schizophrenia was determined entirely by genetic factors, then the concordance rate for monozygotic or identical twins would be close to 100%. As it is actually

To what extent do you think that it is important to relate the different types of schizophrenia to the different explanations?

under 50% (perhaps well under 50%), several social or environmental factors must contribute to the development of schizophrenia.

Interpersonal communication

Some theorists have argued that there are abnormal and inadequate patterns of communication within the families of schizophrenic patients. Bateson et al. (1956) put forward a **double-bind theory**, according to which the members of families of schizophrenics communicate in a destructively ambiguous fashion. For example, the mother will tell her child that she loves him, but in a tone of voice that doesn't indicate love. The double-bind theory accounts in part for the confused thinking of schizophrenic patients. However, it suffers from the serious problem that there is very little evidence supporting it. The same lack of good evidence surrounds the similar theory of Lidz et al. (1965), who argued that schizophrenia occurs as a result of destructive parental interactions with their children.

However, there is some evidence that the families of schizophrenics tend to have inadequate interpersonal communication. Mischler and Waxler (1968) found that mothers talking to their schizophrenic daughters were rather aloof and unresponsive. However, the same mothers behaved in a much more normal and responsive way when talking to their normal daughters. Thus, the presence of a schizophrenic patient in the family may cause poor communication patterns rather than the other way around.

We can look at poor communication patterns in another way. There is evidence that the fragmented and incoherent communication patterns shown by some parents towards their schizophrenic child are due to the parents' genetic susceptibility to schizophrenia (Hooley & Hiller, 2000).

In sum, it is often the case that communication patterns within families having a schizophrenic child are poor and/or disturbed. However, as we have seen, there are various explanations of this observation, and it doesn't seem to be the case that poor communication patterns help to cause schizophrenia.

Expressed emotion

In spite of the lack of support for double-bind theory, there is evidence that the interactions within families can play a key role in maintaining the symptoms of individuals who are already suffering from schizophrenia. What seems to be important is the extent to which a family engages in **expressed emotion**, which involves criticism, hostility, and emotional overinvolvement. Individuals who have suffered from schizophrenia and who live in families with high expressed emotion are nearly four times as likely to relapse compared with those who live in families with low expressed emotion (Kavanagh, 1992).

The direction of causality is not clear in studies of expressed emotion. One possibility is that expressed emotion within the family causes relapse. Another possibility is that individuals who are in poor psychological shape are more likely to provoke expressed emotion from members of their family.

EXAM HINT

The question will usually stipulate whether biological or psychological explanations are to be considered. Do use the alternative explanations as counterperspectives, but be careful—one link sentence to introduce them is not enough. You must consistently contrast the counterperspective with the explanation(s) you've covered as AO1. Do not describe the counterperspective; instead explain what insights it provides that the AO1 explanations do not. Also consider whether the different explanations share any strengths or weaknesses, or whether the weakness of one can be used to highlight the strength of the other.

KEY TERMS

Double-bind theory: an explanation for schizophrenia that suggests that the disorder is a learned response to mutually exclusive demands being made on a child, which can be met or avoided.

Expressed emotion: a way of describing the behaviour of certain families. These behaviours include too much criticism, hostility, and emotional overprotectiveness.

Other social factors

Other social factors may be important. Mednick and Schulsinger (1968) studied individuals between the ages of 15 and 25 with a schizophrenic mother. Those individuals were more likely to develop the negative symptoms of schizophrenia if there had been pregnancy and birth complications, and they were more likely to develop the positive symptoms if there was instability within the family.

The social causation hypothesis

Social factors are emphasised by the **social causation hypothesis**. This hypothesis was designed to explain why it is that schizophrenics tend to belong to the lower social classes. According to this hypothesis, members of the lower social classes have more stressful lives than middle-class people, and this makes them more vulnerable to schizophrenia. The key issue here is whether belonging to the lower social classes makes individuals likely to develop schizophrenia, or whether developing schizophrenia leads to reduced social status, the **social drift hypothesis**. There is some evidence that being in the lower social classes can precede the onset of schizophrenia. Turner and Wagonfeld (1967) found that the fathers of schizophrenics tended to belong to the lower social classes.

Stress

Finally, stressful life events sometimes help to trigger the onset of schizophrenia. Day et al. (1987) carried out a study in several countries. They found that schizophrenics tended to have experienced a high number of stressful life events in the few weeks before the onset of schizophrenia. It is not easy to interpret this finding. It may have occurred because stress plays a role in triggering schizophrenia.

> [?] If one of your relatives has suffered from a mental disorder, what reasons are there for you not to worry that you may also develop the same disorder?

> **KEY TERMS**
>
> **Social causation hypothesis:** the view that schizophrenia may be related to the greater stress experienced by members of the lower class, whereas middle classes have less stressful lives.
>
> **Social drift hypothesis:** the view that more schizophrenics are members of the lower classes, not because of the social causation hypothesis, but because they drift into the lower classes due to their inability to cope.

What environmental factors may be of importance in triggering schizophrenia?

The fact that there is only a concordance rate of around 50% in identical twins reared together has raised interesting questions for psychologists. What environmental factors could possibly be so different that an identical genetic vulnerability could trigger this debilitating disease in one twin and not the other?

In a fascinating article, Ingram (2004) uses the case study of one pair of identical male twins, Corven and Michael, to speculate on the nature of these risk factors. He likens the genetic vulnerability to a speeding car and the risk factors to speed cameras. Activating a single speed camera causes a little upset in terms of points on the licence, but not a great deal and may be the equivalent of developing mildly eccentric behaviour, whereas triggering several cameras can lead to loss of a driving licence, the equivalent of full blown schizophrenia.

So what might these risk factors be? Ingram emphasises that the suggestions he makes are tentative but nevertheless gives a picture of "how the genetic car drives through the speed cameras of life".

The fertilised egg that developed into Michael (the non-schizophrenic twin) arrived in the womb 2 hours ahead of Corven. The two zygotes developed separate placentas: Michael's placenta was larger and more effective than Corven's which meant that he received more nutrients. The twins had identical genes but their pre-natal environments were already quite different.

Both twins have a gene that breaks down an essential component of nerve cells. The nutrients that counteract this effect are mainly found in fish and meat, neither of which their

mother ate as she is a vegetarian. Normally this would not be a problem since these nutrients are available in small amounts in vegetables and nuts. However, competing as the twins were for these nutrients, Michael, with the larger placenta, took the lion's share while Corven did not get an adequate amount. Michael's nerve cells grew satisfactorily while Corven's did not. For Corven, the first speed camera had been triggered.

The twins also have a gene that slows down the growth of glia cells, cells that maintain connections between nerve cells in the brain. Five weeks into her pregnancy their mother developed influenza and the virus from this together with antibodies used to fight it entered the bloodstream of the twins via the placenta. Again, for a single healthy developing embryo, this is not usually a problem. However, the virus further weakened the action of the glia cells—an effect that was more severe in Corven than in Michael because of Corven's existing deficiency in nutrients. This virus was the second speed camera.

Later speed cameras are even more speculative and may never be known, but pressures of work, stress of personal relationships, even cannabis, may all be risk factors.

The parents of schizophrenics often agonise over why this has happened and whose fault it is. But it may be no-one's fault—just too many speed cameras on the route to adulthood. But remember—risk factors can be biological and pre-natal—they are not necessarily life event or family induced stressors.

Ingram, N. (2004, April 26–28). Schizophrenia: Destiny in your genes? *Psychology Review, 10.*

However, it may have occurred because patients in the early stages of schizophrenia are more likely to behave in ways that will cause stressful life events to occur.

Cognitive Explanation: Self-monitoring

We have considered several biological, social, and environmental factors that may be involved in the development of schizophrenia. Frith (1992) has argued that there may also be important cognitive factors. More specifically, he claimed that positive symptoms of schizophrenia (e.g., delusions of control, auditory hallucinations) may occur because schizophrenics have problems with self-monitoring. What happens is that patients fail to keep track of their own intentions, as a consequence of which they mistakenly experience their own thoughts as alien. According to Frith, similar failures of self-monitoring can lead schizophrenics to attribute agency for some of their motor movements to other people.

Experimental support for this self-monitoring theory comes in a study by McGuire et al. (1996). They studied schizophrenics who suffered from hallucinations, and found that these patients had reduced activity in those parts of the brain involved in monitoring inner speech.

In sum, self-monitoring theory is a promising approach to understanding schizophrenia. It will be of interest to see whether failures of self-monitoring relate to any of the other factors we have been discussing.

Conclusion

The diathesis–stress model proposes that a complete explanation of any mental disorder is likely to involve both a predisposition to the disorder and a stressor that triggers the appearance of the symptoms. This can be seen to apply to schizophrenia where there is clear evidence of a genetic link, yet we have seen that not everyone who inherits the genetic component (as in identical twins) becomes schizophrenic. We can explain this in terms of the psychological factors that trigger the disorder, such as troubled families or stressful life events. There are also biological factors to take into account, such as the possible role of dopamine. In addition, as is emphasised in the neurodevelopmental hypothesis, brain lesions at an early age may make individuals more vulnerable to developing schizophrenia many years later. What is indisputable is that several factors play a part in causing schizophrenia, and so a multi-dimensional approach is required.

Another way of considering the factors associated with schizophrenia is in terms of whether they occur a long time before its onset (as with a diathesis) or occur only shortly beforehand (as with stress). Genetic factors and early brain lesions are examples of factors occurring a very long time prior to schizophrenia. In contrast, factors such as stressful life events or disrupted communication patterns may exert their influence immediately prior to the onset of schizophrenia.

The importance of understanding the causes of schizophrenia lies in the decision of what form of treatment is desirable. Biological explanations lead to biological methods of treatment and behavioural explanations to behavioural methods of treatment. The topic of treating mental disorders is examined in the next chapter. In terms of schizophrenia, the most successful therapy has been drug therapy, a biological approach. This doesn't offer a cure but provides relief for sufferers and, in the case of schizophrenics who may cause injury to others, protects the general public as long as such individuals continue to take their medication.

? What are the practical applications of theories of schizophrenia?

EXAM HINT
Use the fact that schizophrenia is not one illness to conclude that to understand the causes a multi-perspective is needed.

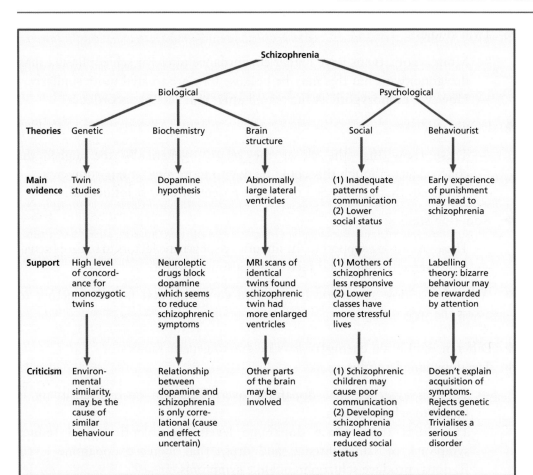

Theories of schizophrenia: strengths and weaknesses.

SECTION SUMMARY
Schizophrenia

❖ Causes of a mental disorder can be grouped into:

— Biological factors: genetics, brain biochemistry, brain structure
— Psychological factors: cultural, social, experiential.

❖ These factors can interact.

❖ The multi-dimensional approach recognises that abnormal behaviour is typically caused by several different factors. For example, the diathesis—stress model combines genetic vulnerability with stress as joint causes of mental disorder.

❖ Schizophrenia is diagnosed when there are continuous signs of disturbance for at least 6 months.

❖ Such signs would include two or more:

— Positive symptoms: delusions, hallucinations, bizarre forms of behaviour
  And/or
— Negative symptoms: lack of emotion, lack of motivation.

❖ Schizophrenia is classified into different types: disorganised, catatonic, paranoid, undifferentiated, and residual schizophrenia.

Causes of schizophrenia

Clinical characteristics of schizophrenia

Biological explanation: genetic factors

❖ Twin studies:

— Monozygotic twins have higher concordance rates for schizophrenia than dizygotic twins but this may be because they are treated more similarly.
— However monozygotic twins reared apart still show concordance.

❖ Family studies:

— These show that the closer the relative genetically the higher the concordance, though this could be due to more similar environments.
— The genes that are handed on by the parents are most influential.

❖ Adoption studies:

— These give strong support to the importance of genetic factors in schizophrenia.
— However, environmental factors are also important.

❖ We need to look at genetic factors and environmental factors together to assess the risk.

Biological explanations: biochemistry

❖ Differences in brain chemistry may be due to genetic factors.
❖ The dopamine hypothesis:

— There is evidence that dopamine overproduction or oversensitivity is linked to schizophrenia.
— The drugs that reduce dopamine levels (neuroleptics) also reduce symptoms of schizophrenia, and drugs that increase dopamine levels (L-dopa) produce schizophrenic-like symptoms.

❖ Evaluation of the dopamine hypothesis:

— Schizophrenics don't seem to produce more dopamine that other people, although it is difficult to assess the levels.
— Brain-imaging studies have produced variable results.
— It is difficult to identify how dopamine exerts its effects.

Biological explanations: brain structure and early development

❖ Brain abnormalities may be involved in schizophrenia.
❖ Schizophrenics have been found to have abnormally large lateral ventricles, shown by twin studies.
❖ This may be a cause or an effect; if it is a cause then it may be related to genetic factors.
❖ Neurodevelopmental hypothesis:

— Suggests that factors prior to birth and in early childhood can cause brain lesions, which can lead to schizophrenia.
— There is increasing evidence to support this hypothesis but as yet the findings are limited.

Psychological explanations: social factors

❖ Social or environmental factors must also contribute to the development of schizophrenia. These can include:

— Interpersonal communication: the double-bind theory proposes that schizophrenics' families communicate in a destructively ambiguous fashion, which could explain the confused thinking characteristic of schizophrenia.

— High levels of expressed emotion within families: this may help maintain schizophrenia, or may be a response to a schizophrenic family member.

— Positive and negative symptoms: may be related to certain family events such as birth complications.

— Social causation hypothesis: suggests that the stress of being in the impoverished lower classes leads to schizophrenia, which can explain the higher incidence of schizophrenia in such populations. Equally the social drift hypothesis can explain this link.

— Stress: other stressors may trigger schizophrenia, a view supported by the fact that individuals have often experienced a high number of stressful life events in the few weeks before the onset of schizophrenia.

See also pages 198–207 of the revision guide.

❖ Symptoms of schizophrenia may occur because of problems with self-monitoring.
❖ This is a promising approach to understanding schizophrenia.

Cognitive explanations: self-monitoring

DEPRESSION

Clinical Characteristics

The number of people in the Western world suffering from depression is about 15–20 times more than the number suffering from schizophrenia. There is a key distinction between *major depression* (sometimes called unipolar disorder) and *bipolar disorder* (also known as bipolar depression). According to DSM-IV-TR (2000), the diagnosis of a major depressive episode requires that five symptoms occur nearly every day for a minimum of 2 weeks. These symptoms are as follows:

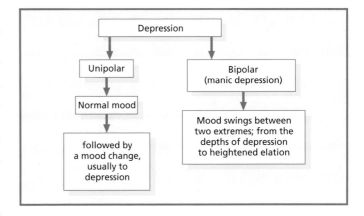

- *Emotional symptoms*: sad, depressed mood; loss of pleasure in usual activities.
- *Motivational symptoms*: changes in activity level; passivity; loss of interest and energy.
- *Somatic symptoms*: difficulties in sleeping (insomnia) or increased sleeping (hypersomnia); weight loss or gain; tiredness.
- *Cognitive symptoms*: negative self-concept, hopelessness, pessimism, lack of self-esteem, self-blame, and self-reproach; problems with concentration or the ability to think clearly; recurring thoughts of suicide or death.

Patients with bipolar depression (generally called bipolar disorder) experience both depression and mania (a mood state involving elation, talkativeness, and unjustified high self-esteem). About 10% of men and 20% of women become clinically depressed at some time in their lives. Over 90% of them suffer from unipolar rather than bipolar depression.

In addition to the distinction between unipolar and bipolar depression, there is also a distinction in unipolar depression between reactive and endogenous depression. **Reactive depression** is caused by some stressful event(s), such as the death of a close friend. The event triggers an episode of depression. **Endogenous depression** is caused from within the person, for instance it may be due to

CASE STUDY: MANIC BEHAVIOUR IN MANIC DEPRESSION

Robert B had been a successful dentist for 25 years, providing well for his wife and family. One morning he woke up with the idea that he was the best dental surgeon in the world, and that he should try to treat as many people as possible. As a result, he set about enlarging his practice from 2 chairs to 20, planning to treat patients simultaneously. He phoned builders and ordered the necessary equipment. After a day of feeling irritable that there had been delays, he decided to do the work himself and began to knock down the walls. When this proved difficult, he became frustrated and began to smash his X-ray equipment and washbasins. Robert B's family were unaware of his behaviour until patients began to phone his wife after being turned away from the dental surgery. When she mentioned the phone calls to him, Robert B "ranted and raved" at her for 15 minutes. She described her husband as looking "haggard, wild-eyed, and run down", and his speech was "over-excited". After several days of this behaviour, Mrs B phoned her daughters and asked them to come over with their husbands to help. On the evening of their visit Robert B began to "brag about his sexual prowess and make aggressive advances towards his daughters". When one of his sons-in-law tried to intervene he was attacked with a chair. Robert B was admitted to hospital, and subsequently it was found that he had had a history of such behaviour.

The AQA A specifications include unipolar (major) depression only. How might you use information about bipolar disorder?

Is the evidence of genetic factors in depression stronger or weaker than in schizophrenia?

hormonal imbalances. Neither of these categories is represented in the classification schemes DSM and ICD, but the distinction is important for understanding the causes of depression. Endogenous depression is linked to biological factors, whereas with reactive depression an individual may have a genetic predisposition to depression but it is psychological factors that are a primary cause.

Biological Explanation: Genetic Factors

As with schizophrenia, there are three main kinds of studies that can be carried out to try to establish whether genetic factors are important: twin studies; family studies; and adoption studies. We will first of all consider the evidence and then evaluate it.

Twin studies

The clearest evidence about the role of genetic factors in the development of major depression and bipolar depression or disorder comes from studies on monozygotic and dizygotic twins. Allen (1976) reviewed the relevant studies. For unipolar disorder, the mean concordance rate was 40% for monozygotic or identical twins, whereas it was only 11% for dizygotic or fraternal twins. For bipolar disorder, the mean concordance rate was 72% for monozygotic twins, compared with 14% for dizygotic twins. Similar findings were reported in a large study by Bertelsen, Harvald, and Hauge (1977). They found a concordance rate for major depression of 59% for identical twins and of 30% for fraternal twins. For bipolar disorder, the concordance rate was 80% for identical twins and 16% for fraternal twins.

More recent studies have produced similar findings. McGuffin et al. (1996) found the concordance rate for major depression was 46% compared to 20% for fraternal twins. Craddock and Jones (1999) found with bipolar disorder that the concordance rate was 40% for identical twins compared to between 5% and 10% for fraternal twins, siblings, and other close relatives. In the population at large, about 5% have been diagnosed with major depression and 1% with bipolar disorder, and all of the figures for identical and fraternal twins are much higher.

These findings suggest that genetic factors are involved in both types of depression, and that their involvement is probably greater for bipolar than for major depression. Berrettini (2000) linked bipolar disorder to genes on chromosomes 4, 6, 11, 12, 13, 15, 18, and 22. Problems of interpretation with these findings are discussed in the Evaluation section below.

Family studies

Family studies suggest the involvement of genetic factors. Gershon (1990) presented the findings from numerous family studies in which depression was assessed in the first-degree relatives of patients with depression. For both major depression and bipolar disorder, the rates of depression were about two to three times the rates in the general population. Sullivan et al. (2000) obtained similar findings for major or unipolar depression in a review of several family studies.

One particular study claimed to identify a gene that might be responsible. Egeland et al. (1987) studied the Amish, a small religious community living in Pennsylvania. The community has a relatively low incidence of major depressive illness, in comparison with the surrounding communities, but one family that was studied had an extremely high level of bipolar disorder. Eleven out of eighty-one members had bipolar disorder. On examination of their genes it was found that two marker genes on chromosome 11 appeared to be different. Importantly, these genes were "neighbours" of those genes that are involved in the production of monoamines, a biochemical implicated in depression (see later). Unfortunately, Hodgkinson (1987) studied extended families in Iceland and didn't find any evidence of the different genes in relation to bipolar disorder.

The Amish people of Pennsylvania have a relatively high incidence of bipolar disorder. One study found that this predisposition might be carried on chromosome 11, but the finding has not been replicated.

Adoption studies

Additional evidence supporting the notion that genetic factors are of importance comes from adoption studies. Wender et al. (1986) found that the biological relatives of adopted sufferers from major depression were about seven times more likely than adoptive relatives to have had major depression themselves. In similar fashion, it has been found with adopted children who later developed depression that their biological parents were eight times as likely as their adoptive parents to have suffered from clinical depression (Wender et al., 1986).

Sullivan et al. (2000) discussed two other adoption studies on major or unipolar depression. Neither of these studies produced strong evidence for a genetic influence on major depression. However, the studies were limited—one diagnosed major depression in a very indirect way and the other had very little information about the biological parents.

Evaluation

Twin studies can provide the most convincing evidence as to the extent of any genetic influences on unipolar and bipolar depression or disorder. As we have seen, the concordance rates for both types of depression are much higher for identical twins than for fraternal twins, suggesting that genetic factors are important. The concordance figures are more convincing for bipolar disorder than for unipolar disorder, suggesting that genetic influences are stronger for bipolar disorder. However, it isn't known whether the identical and fraternal twin pairs experienced equally similar environments. As a result, it is possible that some of the higher concordance rate for identical twins reflects environmental rather than genetic influences—perhaps they tend to grow up in stressful family environments.

The data from family studies are harder to interpret, because relatives who are the most similar genetically tend on average to spend the most time together. That means that it is difficult (or even impossible) to disentangle genetic and environmental effects. Thus, the findings from family studies can provide no more than weakfish evidence that genetic factors may be involved in producing unipolar and bipolar disorder. Finally, the findings from adoption studies are unclear—there are relatively few studies and important information was not collected.

Biological Explanation: Biochemistry

There has been much interest in the possibility that depressed patients might have either elevated or reduced levels of various neurotransmitters. Numerous theories have been put forward in this area, many of them based on the notion that low levels of the neurotransmitters noradrenaline and serotonin may play a role in the development of depression. It has also been suggested that there may be increased levels of these neurotransmitters when bipolar disorder patients are in their manic phase.

The permissive amine theory

Kety (1975) put forward a **permissive amine theory** of mood disorder. According to this theory, the level of noradrenaline is generally controlled by the level of serotonin. When the level of serotonin is low, however, noradrenaline levels are less controlled, and so they may fluctuate wildly. A third neurotransmitter, dopamine, is also involved.

Noradrenaline, serotonin, and dopamine are all neurotransmitters of the monoamine (catecholamine) group, which explains the name "permissive amine" theory. **Neurotransmitters** act at the synapses, or junctions, between neurons in the brain. They may either facilitate or block nervous transmission. Noradrenaline is associated with physiological arousal in general, a fact you may recall from your studies of stress at AS level. Serotonin is also related to arousal and sleep; increases in serotonin generally reduce arousal. Dopamine is normally inhibited by serotonin and has been linked with schizophrenia (see page 347). Under normal conditions all three neurotransmitters play a role in arousal and also are related to mood.

It is suggested that, in depression, serotonin levels are low as a consequence of individual differences that are inherited, and the abnormal serotonin level prevents adequate control of the other two neurotransmitters. Support for this hypothesis comes from studies that establish a link between mood and these monoamines, and from studies of the effects of anti-depressant drugs.

Mood and monoamine transmitters

Teuting, Rosen, and Hirschfeld (1981) compared the substances found in the urine of depressed patients and normals. Compounds that are produced as a by-product of the action of enzymes on noradrenaline and serotonin were present in smaller amounts in the urine of depressed patients. This finding suggests that depressed patients have lower levels of noradrenaline and serotonin.

Subsequent research has often produced findings that don't fit the theory. For example, Thase et al. (2002) found that depressed patients (especially those with severe depression) had increased levels of noradrenaline—this is the opposite of what is predicted.

What role was suggested for dopamine and serotonin in relation to schizophrenia?

KEY TERMS

Permissive amine theory: the view that mood disorders result from low levels of serotonin leading to reduced control of noradrenaline levels, both of which are neurotransmitters in the amine group.
Neurotransmitters: chemical substances that are released at the junction between neurons (a synapse) and that affect the transmission of messages in the nervous system.

Evaluation

It is very likely that depressed patients have disrupted functioning of various neurotransmitters. However, it is clear that no simple theory will fit the facts, and findings opposite to theoretical predictions greatly weaken the theory discussed here.

The complexity of what is involved was shown by Rampello et al. (2000), who reported that patients with major depressive disorder had an imbalance in several neurotransmitters including noradrenaline, serotonin, dopamine, and acetylcholine. Another issue is that there are generally problems of interpretation even when significant differences in the level of some neurotransmitter are found in depressed patients and controls—did the difference play a part in the development of depression or is the difference merely a consequence of patients having developed depression?

> ### Depression and diet
>
> Explanations of depression that are based on biological factors are generally related to endogenous depression, that is, depression that is caused by internal factors. There is some evidence that what you eat may affect your mood and may, in extreme cases, lead to depression.
>
> Tryptophan is a substance that is found in some foods, such as maize and other starchy foods. Delgado et al. (1990) found that acute tryptophan depletion (ATD) induces a temporary relapse in patients suffering from major depressive disorder. This is supported in a study by Smith et al. (1997) who found that women experienced depression when tryptophan was removed from their diets. In addition it has been suggested that serotonin may be involved in some cases of eating disorder, and that the reason why bulimics often eat a lot of starchy foods is in order to increase their levels of tryptophan and serotonin.

Anti-depressants

Anti-depressant drugs such as the monoamine oxidase inhibitors (MAOIs) increase the active levels of noradrenaline and serotonin in depressed patients, and typically reduce the symptoms of depression (see Chapter 9, Treating Mental Disorders). Lithium carbonate, which is very effective in reducing manic symptoms in bipolar disorder, is thought to decrease the availability of noradrenaline and serotonin. These drug effects suggest the potential importance of altered levels of serotonin and noradrenaline. The most prescribed anti-depressant drugs nowadays are known as selective serotonin re-uptake inhibitors (SSRIs), of which the most celebrated is Prozac. The SSRIs are chemically unrelated to the older MAOIs, but also tend to increase the availability of serotonin.

Evaluation

The major anti-depressant drugs rapidly affect neurotransmitter levels, but generally take much longer to reduce the symptoms of depression or mania. It is possible that the MAOIs reduce depression by increasing the sensitivity of receiving neurons, and it takes time for this increased sensitivity to occur.

It is important to note that these drug effects can't provide *direct* evidence of what causes depression in the first place. For example, aspirin can cure a headache, but that doesn't mean that it was an absence of aspirin that produced the headache! MacLeod (1998) called this the **treatment aetiology fallacy**—the mistaken notion that the success of a given form of treatment reveals the cause of the disorder.

Biological Explanation: Endocrine System

The **endocrine system** produces hormones having an influence over a huge range of behaviours: growth, menstruation, sleep, sexual activity, and so on. There are various conditions linked to hormone changes in which depression is a major symptom. Examples include premenstrual syndrome (PMS), postpartum

> **KEY TERMS**
>
> **Treatment aetiology fallacy:** the mistaken belief that the effectiveness of a form of treatment indicates the cause of a disorder.
>
> **Endocrine system:** a system of a number of ductless glands located throughout the body which produce the body's chemical messengers, called hormones.

depression (PPD), and seasonal affective disorder (SAD). The latter is discussed on page 133.

Premenstrual syndrome (PMS)

The female menstrual cycle involves changes in the levels of oestrogen and progesterone over the monthly cycle. In the week or two prior to menstruation, some women develop symptoms such as irritability, bloating, breast tenderness, mood swings, decreased ability to concentrate, depression, headache, acne, and constipation. These changes are related to the hormonal fluctuations.

Abramowitz, Baker, and Fleischer (1982) studied the female admissions to one psychiatric hospital and found that 41% entered on the day before (or the first day of) their menstrual period. Another study, this time looking at women in the normal population, found depressive symptoms during the premenstrual period in about 43% of the women interviewed (Halbreich et al., 1982).

The linkage between premenstrual syndrome and depression could explain part of the reason why more women than men suffer from depression. However, there are several other possible explanations. More women than men have suffered from child abuse, and such abuse predicts adult depression (Butcher et al., 2004).

Postpartum depression (PPD)

About 20% of women report moderate depression in the period after giving birth and a few of these women become chronically depressed. In extreme cases severe depression has led mothers to commit infanticide. Symptoms include sadness, anxiety, tearfulness, and trouble sleeping. These symptoms usually appear within several days of delivery and go away by 10–12 days after the birth.

Women who have recently given birth undergo massive hormonal changes and this is one possible explanation for postpartum depression. A further possibility is that levels of the stress hormone cortisol are very low after birth (see later) and this may make it difficult for women to cope with stress in the period after birth. The fact that some men suffer from postpartum depression suggests that psychological factors may also be involved. That is also suggested by the finding that mothers lacking social support are more likely to experience postpartum depression (Miller, 2002).

Evaluation

In many cases women who suffer postpartum depression have previously had episodes of clinical depression. This suggests that PPD is a combination of hormonal imbalances and a pre-existing predisposition to depression. Lack of emotional support, low self-esteem, and unrealistic ideas about motherhood are also found in cases of PPD, suggesting that psychological factors are important.

Research on life events indicates that major life changes are stressful even when the events themselves are basically positive because we have to adjust to the new situation. That is probably a relevant factor so far as PPD is concerned.

Cortisol

The role of cortisol (a human stress hormone) may be important in depression generally. Levels of cortisol tend to be elevated in depressed patients. For example, elevated levels of blood plasma levels of cortisol have been found in about 30% of

Is PPD likely to be due entirely to biological factors?

depressed outpatients and 70% of severely depressed hospitalised patients (Thase et al., 2002).

The notion that cortisol may be relevant to depression has been examined by using the dexamethasone suppression test. Dexamethasone suppresses cortisol secretion in normals, but about 50% of depressed patients show very little suppression (Howland & Thase, 1991). Presumably this happens because the levels of cortisol are so high in these patients that they cannot be easily suppressed. However, high levels of non-suppression are found in patients suffering from various other mental disorders, so non-suppression may reflect general mental distress rather than being specific to depression.

Evaluation

It is interesting and important that most severely depressed patients have elevated levels of cortisol. However, there are two limitations with the cortisol research. First, reduced suppression on the dexamethasone suppression test is also found in anxiety disorders and other mental disorders, and so high levels of cortisol are not specific to depression. Second, high cortisol levels may be a result of depression rather than forming part of the cause.

 High levels of cortisol are not specific to depression. Can the same be said for dopamine?

Biological explanation: The evolutionary approach

Several intriguing evolutionary explanations have been suggested for depression. These were discussed in detail in Chapter 7, Evolutionary Explanations of Human Behaviour.

In essence the evolutionary view is that depression is in part genetic and the gene for schizophrenia must offer some advantage in order to explain why it has remained in the gene pool.

Depression could be an adaptive response to certain situations. Nesse and Williams (1995) suggest that in certain situations it may be a better strategy to sit tight and do nothing. For example, our hunter-gatherer ancestors might have increased their survival if they were disinclined to venture out in bad weather but instead experienced low mood and stayed indoors. However, what was an adaptive response in the past may no longer be so. Nesse and Williams argue that in competitive urban societies depression is increasing because we are not psychologically equipped to deal with the pressures. We retreat to "sit and wait". This is referred to as "genome lag". Our genetic make-up fits us for the **environment of evolutionary adaptation**, not for now.

The *rank theory of depression* suggests that it is important for survival that an individual who is the loser in a contest (i.e., loses rank) should accept the loss to prevent further injury from re-engaging his (or her) defeater, an act of "damage limitation". The adaptive significance of depression is that it discourages the individual from further efforts.

Aspects of bipolar depression have also been explained in evolutionary terms. It has been suggested that the manic phase of bipolar disorder is related to creativity and charismatic leadership, and thus would be an adaptive trait.

Psychological Explanation: Psychodynamic Approach

Freud's psychoanalytic theory is an example of the psychodynamic approach. Freud argued that depression is like grief, in that it often occurs as a reaction to the loss of an important relationship. However, there is an important difference, because depressed people regard themselves as worthless. What happens is that the individual identifies with the lost person, so that repressed anger towards the lost person is directed inwards towards the self. This inner-directed anger reduces the individual's self-esteem, and makes him or her vulnerable to experiencing depression in the future.

Freud distinguished between actual losses (e.g., death of a loved one) and symbolic losses (e.g., loss of a job). Both kinds of losses can produce depression by causing the individual to re-experience childhood episodes when they experienced loss of affection from some significant person (e.g., a parent).

KEY TERM

Environment of evolutionary adaptation (EEA): the period in human evolution during which our genes were shaped and naturally selected to solve survival problems that were operating at that time (between 35,000 and 3 million years ago).

Job loss may cause depression affecting the person's belief in his or her abilities and future prospects.

What about bipolar disorder? According to Freud, the depressive phase occurs when the individual's superego or conscience is dominant. In contrast, the manic phase occurs when the individual's ego or rational mind asserts itself, and he/she feels in control.

In order to avoid loss turning into depression, the individual needs to engage in a period of mourning work, during which he/she recalls memories of the lost one. This allows the individual to separate himself/herself from the lost person, and so reduce the inner-directed anger. However, individuals very dependent on others for their sense of self-esteem may be unable to do this, and so remain extremely depressed.

Evaluation

There is evidence that depression is caused in part by loss events. For example, Finlay-Jones and Brown (1981) found that depressed patients experienced more stressful life events than normal controls in the year before onset of the depression, and most of them were loss events. However, the details of the psychodynamic approach are incorrect. Freud would predict that the repressed anger and hostility of depressed people would emerge at least partly in their dreams, but Beck and Ward (1961) found no evidence of this. Freud would also predict that depressed people should express anger and hostility mainly towards themselves. In fact, they express considerable anger and hostility towards those close to them (Weissman, Klerman, and Paykel, 1971).

Finally, it follows from Freud's theory that individuals who experienced some major loss early in their lives should be more vulnerable than others to developing clinical depression in adult life. The evidence is inconsistent, but often suggests that early loss doesn't predict adult depression (Crook & Eliot, 1980), though the opposite was found by Bifulco et al. (1992; see box on the left).

> ### Separation and loss
>
> You might also consider **anaclitic depression**, from your AS level studies, which is a state of resigned helplessness and loss of appetite in young children who have been separated from their mothers. Bowlby's (1969) theory of attachment proposed that there might be long-term emotional damage as a consequence of early loss. Bifulco, Harris, and Brown (1992) offered support for this in a study of about 250 women who had lost mothers, through separation or death, before they were 17. They found that loss of their mother through separation or death doubles the risk of depressive and anxiety disorders in adult women. The rate of depression was especially high among those whose mothers had died before the child reached the age of 6.

Psychological Explanation: Behavioural Approach

Reinforcement

Lewinsohn (1974) put forward a behavioural theory based on the notion that depression occurs as a result of a reduction in the level of **reinforcement** or reward. This relates to the psychodynamic view that depression is caused by the loss of an important relationship, because important relationships are a major source of positive reinforcement. There is also a reduction in reinforcement with other losses, such as being made redundant. People who become depressed because of a major loss may be reinforced in being depressed by the sympathy and understanding shown by other people.

Lewinsohn's behavioural theory clearly presents an oversimplified view of the causes of depression. For example, many people experience major losses without becoming depressed, and the theory doesn't explain how this happens. The theory also omits any consideration of other causes of depression such as genetic factors.

> **KEY TERMS**
>
> **Anaclitic depression:** a severe and progressive depression resulting from prolonged separation from a caregiver.
>
> **Reinforcement:** a behaviour is more likely to re-occur because the response was agreeable. Both positive and negative reinforcement have agreeable consequences.

Finally, evidence showing that depressed individuals have fewer positive reinforcements and experience more negative events doesn't prove that depression is caused by these factors. It is entirely possible that individuals who are already depressed have low activity levels and so are unlikely to receive much positive reinforcement in their lives.

Learned helplessness

Seligman's (1975) theory and research on learned helplessness have probably been more influential than any other behavioural approach to depression. **Learned helplessness** refers to the passive behaviour shown when animals or humans believe punishment is unavoidable. In his original studies, Seligman exposed dogs to electric shocks they could not avoid. After that, they were put in a box with a barrier in the middle. The dogs were given shocks after a warning signal, but they could escape by jumping over the barrier into the other part of the box. However, most of the dogs passively accepted the shocks, and didn't learn to escape. Seligman described this as learned helplessness, and argued that it was very similar to the behaviour shown by depressed people.

Evaluation of learned helplessness research

Seligman used dogs to illustrate how lack of control over one's experiences might contribute to feeling helpless. In his experiments each dog was "yoked" with another dog. The first dog learned to escape from electric shocks, whereas whether the second dog received a shock or not depended on the expertise of its partner. Later in the experiment the dogs were separated and put into a "shuttle box" where they could escape an electrified floor by jumping over a partition. The dogs that had previously learned to avoid shocks soon learned to jump the partition. However, the dogs that had been yoked behaved passively and gave up trying to escape soon after being put in the shuttle box.

From this research it appears that the most important factor in the animals' behaviour was not the electric shocks, but the failure to learn avoidance. The dogs had learned that they were helpless, so they displayed inappropriate behaviour in the shuttle box and didn't try to escape. Seligman went on to propose that depression in humans may be due to learned helplessness. For example, stressful situations may be experienced as unavoidable and not under the control of the individual.

Although symptoms of learned helplessness in Seligman's dogs and symptoms of depression in humans do appear to be similar, there are problems with these conclusions. The experiments were carried out on dogs in controlled conditions, but do the findings apply to humans in society? Later research indicated that what may be important is not so much the learned helplessness that a person feels, but the way in which the individual might perceive and react to the stressful situation.

Psychological Explanation: Cognitive Approach

Abramson et al. (1978) developed Seligman's learned helplessness theory by focusing on the thoughts of people experiencing learned helplessness. Abramson et al. started by arguing that people respond to failure in various ways:

- Individuals either attribute the failure to an *internal* cause (themselves) or to an *external* cause (other people, circumstances). For example, your boyfriend

---

? What is wrong with applying the results of a laboratory experiment on dogs to humans in society?

? Why might Seligman's experiments be considered unethical today?

? How might the idea of learned helplessness be applied to battered wife syndrome?

EXAM HINT

The behavioural and cognitive explanations of depression can be linked so use the fact that traditional behavioural explanations do not account for cognition as a criticism. Remember there are different types of depression so you should link this to the need for an idiographic (individual-based) approach rather than a nomothetic (looks for universal explanations) approach.

KEY TERM

Learned helplessness: passive behaviour produced by the perception that punishment is unavoidable.

Individuals suffering from depression see themselves as failures, and often attribute this to faults within themselves that cannot be changed.

KEY TERM

Cognitive triad: negative thoughts about the self, the world, and the future, found in depressed clients.

finishes your relationship and you are convinced it is because of your moodiness (internal cause) or the fact that you have little money for nice clothes (external cause).

- Individuals either attribute the failure to a *stable* cause (likely to continue in future) or to an *unstable* cause (might easily change in future). For example, the moodiness may be a permanent feature of your character (stable) or perhaps it is just because exams are looming ahead (unstable).
- Individuals either attribute the failure to a *global* cause (applying to a wide range of situations) or to a *specific* cause (applying to only one situation). For example, you may be moody with everyone (global) or just with your boyfriend because you didn't feel that he really loved you (specific cause).

People with learned helplessness attribute failure to internal, stable, and global causes. In other words, they feel personally responsible for failure, they think the factors causing that failure will persist, and they think that those factors will influence most situations in future. In view of these negative and pessimistic thoughts, it is no wonder that sufferers from learned helplessness are depressed.

The key issue is causality—do these negative attributions help to trigger depression or do they only occur as a consequence of being depressed? Lewinsohn et al. (2001) found evidence supporting the view that negative attributions *are* involved in producing depression. They studied adolescents who experienced many negative life events over a 12-month period. Those who had strongly negative attributions at the start of the study were much more likely to develop major depressive disorder than those who initially didn't have negative attributions.

Depressive schemas

Beck and Clark (1988) also argued that cognitive factors may play an important role in the development of depression. They referred to depressive schemas, which consist of organised information stored in long-term memory. Beck and Clark's (p.26) cognitive theory is as follows:

The schematic organisation of the clinically depressed individual is dominated by an overwhelming negativity. A negative cognitive trait is evident in the depressed person's view of the self, world, and future . . . As a result of these negative maladaptive schemas, the depressed person views himself as inadequate, deprived and worthless, the world as presenting insurmountable obstacles, and the future as utterly bleak and hopeless.

The term **cognitive triad** is used to refer to the three elements: the depressed person's negative views of himself or herself, the world, and the future.

The cognitive triad

"I am helpless and inadequate"

"The world is full of insuperable obstacles"

"I am worthless, so there's no chance of the future being better than the present"

Measuring depressive symptoms

Beck (1967) developed the most widely used inventory of depressive symptoms. Each question assesses one symptom of depression, and provides a score for severity of that symptom on a scale of 0 to 3. The symptoms are divided into mood, thought, motivation, and physical characteristics. The inventory is not intended to be used to diagnose depression, but just to assess the range of symptoms present and the severity.

Research has shown that a "normal" American college student would score above 3 or 4. Mildly depressed students score between 5 and 9, and a score above 10 suggests moderate to severe depression. If an individual scored more than 10 for a period of more than two weeks, he or she should seek help.

Adapted from D.L. Rosenhan and M.E.P. Seligman (1989) *Abnormal psychology* (2nd Edn). London: Norton.

Beck Depression Inventory (Beck, 1967)
An individual is asked to describe how they are feeling right now.

Mood A (sadness)
0   I do not feel sad.
1   feel blue or sad.
2a I am blue or sad all the time and I can't snap out of it.
2b I am so sad or unhappy that it is quite painful.
3   I am so sad or unhappy that I can't stand it.

Mood B (interest in others)
0   I have not lost interest in other people.
1   I am less interested in other people now than I used to be.
2   I have lost most of my interest in other people and have little feeling for them.
3   I have lost all of my interest in other people and don't care about them at all.

Thought C (pessimism)
0   I am not particularly pessimistic or discouraged about the future.
1   I feel discouraged about the future.
2a I feel I have nothing to look forward to.
2b I feel that I won't ever get over my troubles.
3   I feel that the future is hopeless and that things cannot improve.

Thought D (failure)
0   I do not feel like a failure.
1   I feel I have failed more than the average person.
2   I feel I have accomplished very little that is worthwhile or that means anything.
3   I feel I am a complete failure as a person (parent, husband, wife).

Motivation E (work initiation)
0   I can work about as well as before.
1a It takes extra effort to get started at doing something.
1b I don't work as well as I used to.
2   I have to push myself very hard to do anything.
3   I can't do any work at all.

Motivation F (suicide)
0   I don't have any thoughts of harming myself.
1   I have thoughts of harming myself but I would not carry them out.
2a I feel I would be better off dead.
2b I feel my family would be better off if I were dead.
3a I have definite plans about committing suicide.
3b I would kill myself if I could.

Physical G (appetite)
0   My appetite is no worse than usual.
1   My appetite is not as good as it used to be.
2   My appetite is much worse now.
3   I have no appetite at all any more.

Physical H (sleep loss)
0   I can sleep as well as usual.
1   I wake up more tired in the morning than I used to.
2   I wake up 1–2 hours earlier than usual and find it hard to get back to sleep.
3   I wake up early every day and can't get more than 5 hours of sleep.

Beck, A.T. (1967). *Depression: Clinical, experimental, and theoretical aspects*. New York: Hoeber.

Evaluation

Depressed people undoubtedly have the kinds of negative thoughts described by Abramson et al. (1978) and by Beck and Clark (1988). Do these negative thoughts help to cause depression, or do they merely occur as a result of being depressed? Lewinsohn et al. (1981, p.218) carried out a prospective study in which negative attitudes and thoughts were assessed *before* any of the participants became depressed. Here are their conclusions:

Future depressives did not subscribe to irrational beliefs, they did not have lower expectancies for positive outcomes or higher expectancies for negative outcomes, they did not attribute success experiences to external causes and failure experiences to internal causes ... People who are vulnerable to depression are not characterised by stable patterns of negative cognitions.

Most of the evidence suggests that negative thoughts and attitudes are caused by depression rather than the opposite direction of causality. However, Nolen-Hoeksma, Girgus, and Seligman (1992) found that a negative attributional style

? Identify some of the symptoms of depression that are given in this Case Study.

? Suggest two possible factors that may have caused Paul's depression.

CASE STUDY: MAJOR (UNIPOLAR) DEPRESSION

Paul was a twenty-year-old college senior majoring in chemistry. He first came to the student psychiatric clinic complaining of headaches and a vague assortment of somatic problems. Throughout the interview, Paul seemed severely depressed and unable to work up enough energy to talk with the therapist. Even though he had maintained a B+ average, he felt like a failure.

His parents had always had high expectations for Paul, their eldest son, and had transmitted these feelings to him from his earliest childhood. His father, a successful thoracic surgeon, had his heart set on Paul's becoming a doctor. The parents saw academic success as very important, and Paul did exceptionally well in school. Although his teachers praised him for being an outstanding student, his parents seemed to take his successes for granted. In fact they often made statements such as "You can do better". When he failed at something, his parents would make it obvious to him that they not only were disappointed but felt disgraced as well. This pattern of punishment for failures without recognition of successes, combined with his parents' high expectations, led to the development in Paul of an extremely negative self-concept.

From Sue et al. (1994) *Understanding abnormal behaviour* (p.373) (Boston: Houghton Mifflin).

in older children predicted the development of depressive symptoms in response to stressful life events. Therefore negative thoughts may make people vulnerable to depression.

Therapies based on this cognitive view of depression have proved very successful, as discussed in the next chapter of this book. However, we must be careful about suggesting that the success of a treatment reveals the cause of the disorder, a problem called the treatment aetiology fallacy, described earlier.

Psychological Explanation: Social Factors

Patients suffering from major depression typically experience an above average number of stressful **life events** in the period before the onset of depression. For example, Brown and Harris (1978) carried out an interview study on women in London. They found that 61% of the depressed women had experienced at least one very stressful life event in the 8 months before interview, compared with 19% of non-depressed women. However, many women manage to cope with major life events without becoming clinically depressed. Of those women who experienced a serious life event, 37% of those without an intimate friend became depressed, compared with only 10% of those who had a very close friend. This suggests that social support (another social factor) may moderate the effects of life events on depression.

The findings of Brown and Harris (1978) have been replicated several times. Brown (1989) reviewed the various studies. On average, about 55% of depressed

KEY TERM

Life events: experiences that are common to most people and involve change from a steady state; they are a means of explaining why some people become ill.

LIFE EVENTS

Rank	Life event	Stress value
1	Death of a spouse	100
2	Divorce	73
3	Marital separation	65
13	Sex difficulties	39
23	Son or daughter leaving	29
38	Change in sleeping habits	16
41	Vacation	13

Adapted from T. Holmes and R. Rahe (1967), The social readjustment rating scale. *Journal of Psychosomatic Research, 11*, 213–218.

patients had at least one severe life event in the months before onset, compared with only about 17% of controls.

Evaluation

There are three main limitations of most life-event studies. First, the information is obtained retrospectively several months afterwards, and so there may be problems in remembering clearly what has happened. Second, it is often unclear whether life events have caused depression or depression caused the life events. For example, depression may play an important part in producing life events such as marital separation, or marital separation may cause depression. Third, the meaning of a life event depends on the context in which it happens. For example, losing your job is very serious if you have a large family to support, but may be much less serious if you are nearing the normal retirement age and have a large pension. This third limitation does not apply to the research of Brown and Harris (1978), because they took full account of the context in which the life events occurred.

■ **Activity:** Compile a set of everyday situations or problems (e.g., not doing well in a particular subject, being late for school, not handing in homework). Ask each other about these problems and decide from the participants' answers which factors are involved. Draw up a table of responses like the examples here.

Example:

Question 1 Are there any subjects that you are not doing well in, and if so, why do you think this is?

Participant A: I'm hopeless at maths, it's my own fault. (Internal factor)

	Internal	External	Stable	Unstable	Global	Specific
Q1	✓					
Q2						

Participant B: I'm doing badly in maths, because the teacher is awful. (External factor)

	Internal	External	Stable	Unstable	Global	Specific
Q1		✓				
Q2						

Explanations for Depression

By now you may be bewildered at the large number of factors that play a role in producing major depression and bipolar disorder. However, bear in mind that this is exactly in line with what would be predicted from the multi-dimensional approach to mental disorder. You should also bear in mind that some of the factors we have talked about are probably related to each other. For example, genetic factors in individuals who develop depression may be at least partially responsible for their abnormal patterns of neurotransmitter and hormone levels.

Most of the evidence can be fitted into the diathesis–stress model, in which the occurrence of a mental disorder is most likely when there is a diathesis (genetic vulnerability or predisposition) *and* stress in the broadest sense. We have seen that there is good evidence from twin and family studies that genetic factors are involved in depression. So far as stress is concerned, Freud argued that actual and symbolic losses in early childhood play a part in the development of depression.

? How might the diathesis–stress model be used to explain depression?

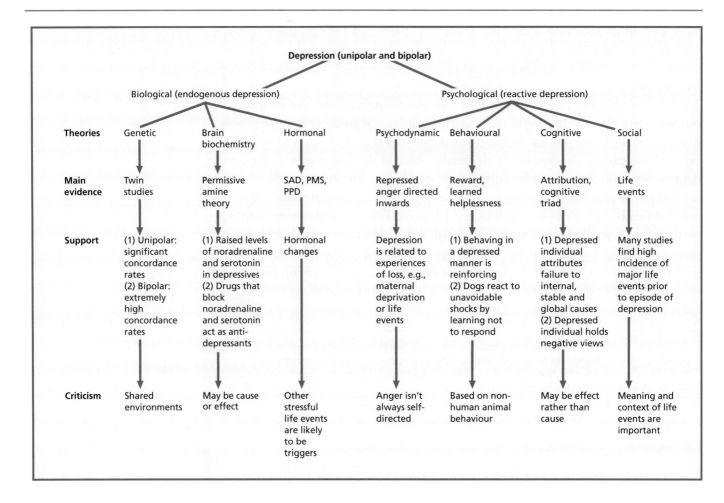

It has also been found that depressed individuals often have an excess of negative life events in the months prior to the onset of depression. Finally, there are cognitive factors such as negative attributions and depressive schemas. These cognitive factors influence the ways in which individuals respond to life events and can increase the impact of such events.

SECTION SUMMARY
Depression

Characteristics of depression

❖ Unipolar (major) depression is characterised by the following symptoms having been present daily for more than 2 weeks:

— Emotional symptoms such as lowered mood.
— Motivational symptoms such as loss of interest.
— Somatic symptoms such as insomnia or hypersomnia and tiredness.
— Cognitive symptoms such as negative self-concept and thoughts of suicide.

❖ Unipolar depression can be categorised into:

— Endogenous depression: mainly due to biological factors.
— Reactive depression: primarily psychological.

❖ Bipolar depression is much rarer and includes episodes of mania.

❖ Twin studies:

— Suggest that genetic factors are involved in both types of depression, but are stronger for bipolar disorder.
— Some of the higher concordance rates could reflect environmental rather than genetic influences.

❖ Family studies:

— Evidence for the role of genetic factors comes from family studies with higher than normal incidence among first-degree relatives.
— But it is difficult to disentangle genetic and environmental effects.

❖ Adoption studies:

— Studies of adopted children show much higher incidence of depression in their biological rather than adoptive parents.
— But there are relatively few studies and a lack of information.

❖ The permissive amine theory:

— This suggests low levels of serotonin lead to fluctuations in noradrenaline and dopamine. All three are neurotransmitters of the monoamine group.
— Support comes from studies of monoamine levels in the urine of depressed individuals (levels were low) and the fact that monoamine oxidase inhibitors (MAOIs) reduce depression.
— However, this evidence is indirect and it is not clear whether the neurotransmitters are a cause or an effect of depression. Evidence based on drug action is subject to the treatment aetiology fallacy.

❖ Changes in endocrine production are also linked to depression in:

— Premenstrual syndrome (PMS): occurs during a time of hormonal change just before menstruation.
— Postpartum depression (PPD): might be a combination of hormonal imbalances and a predisposition to depression; psychological factors such as poor emotional support are also implicated.
— Seasonal affective disorder (SAD).

❖ Levels of cortisol appear to be abnormally high in depressed individuals, though cortisol is also linked to anxiety and may be a cause or an effect of depression.

❖ Depression is a response to loss:

— Repressed anger towards the object of loss is directed inwards, reducing the individual's self-esteem.
— Losses in adulthood lead to re-experiencing the emotions felt in childhood relating to loss of affection from some significant person (e.g., a parent).
— Evidence shows that women who experienced early loss through death of their mother were more prone to depression later.
— Mourning one's losses helps to prevent depression.

❖ Some predictions from this theory are not borne out:

— Repressed anger and hostility do not appear in dreams.
— Depressed people do not just direct anger inwards.
— Vulnerability to depression following early loss is not always the case.

Biological explanations: genetic factors

Biological explanations: biochemistry

Biological explanations: endocrine system

Psychological explanations: psychodynamic approach

Psychological explanations: behavioural approach

❖ Losses may reduce positive reinforcement, which explains depression.
❖ Attention gained from being depressed may itself be rewarding and perpetuate the behaviour.
❖ Research has demonstrated that individuals may learn to behave in a helpless manner (learned helplessness), a response similar to depressed behaviour.

Psychological explanations: cognitive approach

❖ Depressed individuals attribute failure to internal, stable, and global causes.
❖ A different cognitive approach focuses on the role of depressive schemas. The individual has negative views of himself/herself, the world, and the future (the cognitive triad).
❖ Most of the evidence suggests that negative thoughts are caused by depression rather than vice versa, though one study found that children with a negative attributional style were later more prone to depression.

See also pages 208–216 of the revision guide

Psychological explanations: social factors

❖ An important social factor in depression is the effect of major life events. Depression often occurs when a person has to cope with a number of these.
❖ The impact of major life events may be lessened by another social factor—support from friends.
❖ A limitation to this approach: life events mean different things to different people.

Concluding the explanations for depression

❖ Many factors can be responsible for depression: this is the multi-dimensional approach.
❖ Most of the factors fit into the diathesis–stress model.
❖ Factors can relate to each other.

ANXIETY DISORDERS

A number of disorders are classified as "anxiety disorders" because they share one clinical characteristic: anxiety. Anxiety is an adaptive response that is important to ensure survival. In certain circumstances it is important for an animal to experience anxiety because it places it in a state of heightened arousal ready to respond to the danger. However, anxiety can become a chronic and disabling response. An individual with an anxiety disorder experiences anxiety that is quite disproportionate to any threat that is posed. Anxiety disorders are worryingly common. For example, more than 20 million Americans are affected by an anxiety disorder each year, with women being more likely to be affected than men.

ICD-10 and DSM-IV-TR include the following anxiety disorders: phobias (phobic anxiety disorders), panic disorder, generalised anxiety disorder, obsessive-compulsive disorder, and reaction to severe stress and adjustment disorder (e.g., post-traumatic stress disorder). In this Section we will consider one of these: phobias. However, there will also be coverage of some other anxiety disorders.

Phobias

Phobias involve a high level of fear of some object or situation, with the level of fear being so strong that the object or situation is avoided whenever possible. There are various different categories of phobia: specific phobia, social phobia, and agoraphobia. We will describe each type of phobia in turn.

Comparisons

About 6% or 7% of the population suffer from phobias. Some phobias are more disruptive of everyday life than others. Agoraphobia and social phobia are usually very disabling, whereas specific phobias such as snake or spider phobias generally have less impact on the phobic's enjoyment of life. About 50% of all phobics seen clinically suffer from agoraphobia with panic disorder.

Types of phobia

Specific phobia

Specific phobia involves strong and irrational fear of some specific object or situation. Specific phobias include fear of spiders and fear of snakes, but there are hundreds of different specific phobias. DSM-IV identified four major subtypes of specific phobia:

* Animal type.
* Natural environment type: this includes fear of heights, fear of water, and fear of storms.
* Blood-injection-injury type.
* Situational type: this includes fears about being in various situations, such as in a plane, a lift, or an enclosed space (claustrophobia).

In addition, there is a fifth category labelled "other type". This covers all specific phobias that don't fit any of the four major subtypes.

According to DSM-IV-TR, these are the major diagnostic criteria for specific phobia:

* Marked and persistent fear of a specific object or situation.
* Exposure to the phobic stimulus nearly always produces a rapid anxiety response.
* The individual recognises that his/her fear of the phobic object or situation is excessive.
* The phobic stimulus is either avoided or responded to with great anxiety.
* The phobic reactions interfere significantly with the individual's working or social life, or he/she is very distressed about the phobia.
* In individuals under the age of 18, the phobia has lasted for at least 6 months.

> Unusual phobias include *triskaidekaphobia*, the fear of the number 13; *batophobia*, fear of being close to high buildings; and *nephophobia*, a fear of clouds.

Social phobia

Social phobia involves extreme concern about one's own behaviour and the reactions of others. Social phobics have marked and persistent fear of social situations, and such situations are either avoided or responded to with great anxiety. Social phobia is a serious condition because the phobic reactions of social phobics generally interfere significantly with their working and/or social life. Social phobia is more common in females than in males, with about 70% of sufferers being female. According to Barlow and Durand (1995, p.186), social phobia "tends to be more prevalent in people who are younger (aged 18–29 years), less educated, single, and of lower socioeconomic class".

Agoraphobia

Agoraphobia involves great fear of open or public places. Agoraphobia on its own is rather rare, as was pointed out in DSM-IV-TR. In most cases, the panic disorder

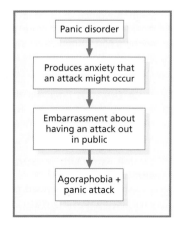

CASE STUDY: A PHOBIA

A young student in his first year at university was referred to a therapist after seeking help at the student health centre. During initial interviews he spoke of feeling frightened and often panicking when heading for his classes. He claimed he felt comfortable in his room, but was unable to concentrate on his work or to face other people. He admitted to fears of catching syphilis and of going bald. These fears were so intense that at times he would compulsively scrub his hands, head, and genitals so hard that they would bleed. He was reluctant to touch door handles and would never use public toilets. The student admitted that he knew his fears were irrational, but felt that he would be in even more "mental anguish" if he did not take these precautions.

In later sessions with the therapist, the student's history revealed previous concerns about his sexual identity. As a child he harboured feelings of inferiority because he had not been as fast or as strong as his peers. These feelings were reinforced by his mother who had not encouraged him to play rough games in case he got hurt. At puberty the student had also worried that he might be sexually deficient. At a summer camp he had discovered that he was underdeveloped sexually compared with the other boys. He had even wondered if he was developing into a girl. Although he did in fact mature into a young man, he constantly worried about his masculine identity, even fantasising that he was a girl. The student admitted that at times his anxiety was so great that he considered suicide.

Adapted from Kleinmuntz (1974).

starts before the agoraphobia. Individuals who are very frightened of having panic attacks feel less secure when away from familiar surroundings and people, and know that they would be very embarrassed if they had a panic attack in public. These concerns lead them to avoid open or public places, and so agoraphobia is added to the panic disorder (see the Case Study below).

Panic disorder with agoraphobia is defined by the following criteria in DSM-IV-TR:

- Recurrent unexpected panic attacks.
- At least one panic attack has been followed by at least 1 month of worry about the attack, concern about having more panic attacks, or changes in behaviour resulting from the attack.
- Agoraphobia, in which there is anxiety about being in situations from which escape might be hard or embarrassing in the event of a panic attack.
- The panic attacks are not due to use of some substance.

CASE STUDY: SARAH—A CASE OF AGORAPHOBIA

Sarah, a woman in her mid-30s, was shopping for bargains in a crowded department store during the January sales. Without warning and without knowing why, she suddenly felt anxious and dizzy. She worried that she was about to faint or have a heart attack. She dropped her shopping and rushed straight home. As she neared home, she noticed that her feelings of panic lessened.

A few days later she decided to go shopping again. On entering the store, she felt herself becoming increasingly anxious. After a few minutes, she had become so anxious that a shopkeeper asked her if she was OK and took her to a first-aid room. Once there her feelings of panic became worse and she became particularly embarrassed at all the attention she was attracting.

After this she avoided going to the large store again. She even started to worry when going into smaller shops because she thought she might have another panic attack, and this worry turned into intense anxiety. Eventually she stopped shopping altogether, asking her husband to do it for her.

Over the next few months, Sarah found that she had panic attacks in more and more places. The typical pattern was that she became progressively more anxious the further away from her house she got. She tried to avoid the places where she might have a panic attack, but as the months passed, she found that this restricted her activities. Some days she found it impossible to leave the house at all. She felt that her marriage was becoming strained and that her husband resented her dependence on him.

Adapted from J.D. Stirling and J.S.E. Hellewell (1999) *Psychopathology* (London: Routledge).

What is the definition of a panic attack?

According to DSM-IV-TR, a panic attack involves intense fear or discomfort, with four or more bodily symptoms suddenly appearing. These symptoms include palpitations, shortness of breath, accelerated heart rate, a feeling of choking, nausea, sweating, chest pain, feeling dizzy, and fear of dying. Panic attacks can be distinguished from other types of anxiety by the fact that they are typically short in duration and of great intensity.

People between the ages of about 25 and 29 are most likely to develop panic disorder. About 75% of those who suffer from agoraphobia are female. One reason why men show less agoraphobic avoidance than women is because they are more likely to drink heavily so that they can go out in public (Barlow & Durand, 1995).

Stage-fright: an example of fear when facing the scrutiny of others.

? Can you suggest other reasons why more women than men are agoraphobic?

Post-traumatic stress disorder (PTSD)

Post-traumatic stress disorder (PTSD) is triggered by a specific event such as war or a natural disaster (e.g., a hurricane). As would be expected, the chances of developing PTSD are generally much greater if the traumatic event is life threatening than when it is not. According to DSM-IV-TR, there are three main categories of symptoms associated with PTSD: (1) re-experiencing the traumatic event; (2) avoidance of stimuli associated with the event; and (3) increased arousal, producing problems with sleep and difficulties with concentration. Some individuals are more vulnerable than others to developing PTSD—when numerous people are exposed to the same traumatic event (e.g., a sinking ship), what typically happens is that develop PTSD whereas others do not.

Obsessive-compulsive disorder

Patients with obsessive-compulsive disorder (OCD) suffer from intrusive obsessive thoughts or images that are often accompanied by compulsive behaviours carried out in order to try to prevent some feared event. More specifically, according to DSM-IV-TR, obsessions consist of persistent and recurrent intrusive thoughts, images, or impulses that are regarded as disturbing. For example, a patient with obsessive-compulsive disorder may think about attacking or killing someone they dislike intensely. In contrast, compulsions consist of overt repetitive behaviours (e.g., hand washing or checking) or covert mental acts (e.g., counting). The great majority of OCD patients suffer from both obsessions and compulsions. Most patients with OCD realise that their obsessions and compulsions are excessive and senseless, but they find them very difficult to control.

Biological Explanation: Genetic Factors

The main evidence on genetic factors in the development of the phobias comes from twin studies, although some family studies have also been carried out. As we will see, genetic factors seem to play a role in the development of most phobias.

Torgersen (1983) and Noyes et al. (1986) studied twins and families of people suffering from panic disorder with agoraphobia.

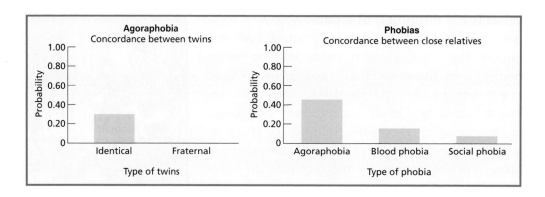

Twin and family studies

As far as panic disorder with agoraphobia is concerned, Torgersen (1983) considered pairs of monozygotic or identical twins and dizygotic or fraternal twins, at least one of whom had panic disorder. The concordance rate was 31% for identical twins against 0% for fraternal twins. Harris et al. (1983) found that the close relatives of agoraphobic patients were more likely to be suffering from agoraphobia than were the close relatives of non-anxious individuals. Noyes et al. (1986) found that 12% of the relatives of agoraphobics also had agoraphobia, and 17% suffered from panic disorder. Both of these percentage figures are greater than for controls.

As far as specific phobia is concerned, Fyer et al. (1990) found that 31% of close relatives of individuals with specific phobias also had a phobia. More striking findings were reported by Ost (1989) in a study on blood phobics. In 64% of the cases, these blood phobics had at least one close relative who also suffered from blood phobia. The findings from these two studies are consistent with the notion that genetic factors are involved. Stronger evidence based on twin studies involving 1708 female twins was reported by Kendler et al. (1999). They obtained estimates of heritability (a measure of the involvement of genetic factors in which the higher the figure the greater the role of genetic factors). Heritability was moderately high for blood-injury phobia, animal phobia, and situational phobia.

As far as social phobia is concerned, Fyer et al. (1993) discovered that 16% of the close relatives of social phobics developed the same disorder, against only 5% of the relatives of individuals without social phobia. However, Skre et al. (1993) found that the concordance rate for social phobia was similar in identical and fraternal twin pairs, leading them to conclude that social phobia is caused mainly by environmental influences. Kendler et al. (1999) argued that the involvement of genetic factors in various phobias had been under-estimated in the past because unreliability of diagnosis of phobias had been ignored. They took account of this unreliability when analysing the data from numerous female identical and fraternal twins. They concluded that genetic factors are moderately important in the development of social phobia.

More unusual phobias: *dextrophobia*, fear of objects at the right side of the body, and *xanthophobia*, fear of the colour yellow; and *genuphobia*, fear of knees.

Evaluation

The evidence from twin and family studies suggests that genetic factors are of moderate important in determining panic disorder with agoraphobia, specific phobias, and social phobia. In their large-scale twin study, Kendler et al. (1999) found that there was very little difference in the importance of genetic factors in determining social phobia and various specific phobias. However, there are various limitations with the evidence. First, as Kendler et al. pointed out, reliability of diagnosis of phobias has often been poor, and this would have the effect of reducing concordance rates in twin studies. Second, it may be misleading to assume that genetic factors are specific to a *single* form of phobia. There is evidence that genetic vulnerability is more general than that—for example, if you have a twin suffering from social phobia, you may be at risk of developing panic disorder with agoraphobia as well as social phobia (Kendler, 1995). Third, environmental factors may explain at least some of the effects reported. For example, a close relative of someone suffering from a phobia may develop the same phobia because he/she imitates the behaviour displayed by the patient or because they are both exposed to a stressful family environment. With twins, the higher concordance rates for identical than for fraternal twins may occur in part because identical twins are exposed to more similar environments than fraternal twins.

> **Biological explanation: The evolution of phobias**
>
> If phobias develop because of accidental pairings of a neutral and a fearful or aversive stimulus, then people could become phobic to almost anything. In fact, many more people have phobias about spiders and snakes than about cars, even though we see cars much more often and they are considerably more dangerous. Seligman (1971) argued that the objects and situations forming the basis of most phobias were real sources of danger hundreds or thousands of years ago, and only those individuals who were sensitive to such objects and situations were favoured by evolution. Thus, there is a "preparedness" or biological predisposition to be sensitive to, and to become phobic about, certain stimuli rather than others.
>
> (Phobias were discussed in Chapter 7, Evolutionary Explanations of Human Behaviour.)

Biological Explanation: Neurophysiology

It is possible that individuals who generally have a high level of physiological arousal are more vulnerable to the development of phobias. There is some evidence that patients suffering from panic disorder with agoraphobia or with social phobia have high levels of arousal (Lader & Mathews, 1968). However, it isn't clear from such evidence whether the high levels of arousal helped to cause the phobia, or whether the phobia led to the increased arousal.

Evaluation

Other evidence suggests that panic disorder with agoraphobia is often *not* associated with increased physiological activity. There have been several studies in which panic patients have been exposed to biological challenges such as inhalation of a mixture of carbon dioxide and oxygen. These biological challenges often produce panic attacks in patients suffering from panic disorder with agoraphobia, but rarely do so in normal controls. In terms of physiological responses, the effects of biological challenge on heart rate, respiratory rate, blood pressure, and so on are comparable in patients and in normal controls (see M.W. Eysenck, 1997, for a review). Thus, patients suffering from panic disorder with agoraphobia differ from normal controls in the way they *interpret* their bodily symptoms rather than in terms of their actual physiological responsiveness. Thus, these findings support a *cognitive* rather than a physiological account of panic disorder with agoraphobia.

? In what way do these data suggest a cognitive rather than a physiological interpretation of panic disorder?

Psychological Explanation: Psychodynamic Theory

According to Freud, phobias are a defence against the anxiety that is produced when the impulses of the id or sexual instinct are repressed or forced into the

CASE STUDY: LITTLE HANS

The case study of Little Hans (the 5-year-old phobic boy) is unusual for several reasons. It is Freud's only analysis of a child rather than an adult. This enabled Freud to test his hypotheses about child sexuality. The case study was also unusual in that Freud's analysis was indirect as almost all of the interviews and observations were made by the boy's father and passed on to Freud. Hans' father was Max Graf, a music critic and early supporter of Freud and member of the psychoanalytic society. Hans' father wrote to Freud when the boy was 5 years old, describing the main problem: "He is afraid a horse will bite him in the street, and this fear seems somehow connected with his having been frightened by a large penis." Freud only met Hans on two occasions. The recording of information and direct interviews were undertaken by Hans' father who then corresponded and discussed the case at length with Freud.

The chief features of the case history (chronologically) are outlined here:

- Hans was fascinated by his "widdler" (his penis). He observed that animals had big ones and it was likely that his parents had big ones too because they were grown up.
- Hans spent a lot of time alone with his mother over the summer holiday and realised he liked having her to himself. He wished his father would stay away. He also felt hostile towards his new baby sister who further separated Hans from his mother. He expressed this indirectly in his fear of baths because he thought his mother would drop him (in fact, he *wished* his mother would drop his little sister, a desire which was projected elsewhere because of the anxiety it aroused).
- There were two strands to his anxiety about horses. First, Hans once heard a man saying to a child "Don't put your finger to the white horse or it'll bite you." Second, Hans asked his mother if she would like to put her finger on his widdler. His mother told him this would not be proper. Therefore, it is suggested that Hans learned that touching a white horse or a widdler was undesirable. Hans' desire (libido) for his mother created a sense of anxiety and fear that she might leave him if

he persisted. Unconsciously this anxiety was projected elsewhere: he became afraid of being bitten by a white horse.
- More anxiety was created by the fact that Hans' mother told Hans that, if he played with his widdler it would be cut off. Hans' father told Hans that women have no widdler. Hans reasoned that his mother's must have been cut off—and she might do the same to him.
- There were two pieces of symbolism. First, Hans had a dream about two giraffes, he took away the crumpled one and this made the big one cry out. This might represent Hans' wish to take away his mother (crumpled one) causing his father to cry out (big giraffe—possible symbol of penis). Hans sat on the crumpled one (trying to claim his mother for himself). Second, Freud suggested to Hans that the black around the horses' mouths and the blinkers in front of their eyes were symbols for his father's moustache and glasses. Hans might envy these symbols of adulthood because they could give him the right to have a woman's love.
- Hans developed further anxieties about horses. Hans told his father that he was afraid of horses falling down, and if they were laden (e.g., with furniture) this might lead them to fall down. Hans also remembered seeing a horse fall down and thinking it was dead; since he secretly wished his father would fall down dead this made Hans feel more anxious.
- Hans now became preoccupied with bowel movements ("lumf"). His sister was lumf-like, as was a laden cart. So laden vehicles represented pregnancy and when they overturned it symbolised giving birth. Thus the falling horse was both his dying father and his mother giving birth.
- Finally, Hans became less afraid of horses. He developed two final fantasies which showed that his feelings about his father were resolved: (1) "The plumber came and first he took away my behind with a pair of pincers, and then he gave me another, and then the same with my widdler"; (2) Hans told his father that he was now the daddy and not the mummy of his imaginary children, thus showing that he had moved from wishing his father dead to identifying with him.

---

unconscious. This theory is illustrated in Freud's case study of Little Hans, who developed a phobia of horses, described in the Case Study above.

Little Hans

According to Freud, Little Hans was sexually attracted to his mother, but was very frightened that he would be punished for this by his father. Horses resembled his father in that their black muzzles and blinkers looked like his moustache and glasses, and so Little Hans transferred or displaced his fear of his father on to horses.

Separation anxiety

According to the psychodynamic approach (e.g., Bowlby, 1973), **separation anxiety** in children may make them more likely to develop panic disorder with agoraphobia as a result. Separation anxiety occurs when a child experiences the threat of separation from an important caregiver such as its mother or father. However, there is little evidence that patients suffering from panic disorder with agoraphobia experienced more childhood separation anxiety than other people.

KEY TERM

Separation anxiety: the sense of anxiety felt by a child when separated from their attachment figure.

Evaluation

It would be predicted from the account in the case Study on the left that Hans would have shown a phobic reaction every time he saw a horse. In fact, he *only* showed his phobia when he saw a horse pulling a cart at high speed, though this was further explained by the link between the laden cart and Hans' repressed feelings about his sister. However, the account of Little Hans is of historical importance because it was the first systematic description of specific phobia.

Little Hans only showed his fear of horses when he saw them pulling a cart at speed—he was not frightened of horses without carts, or of horses pulling carts at a walking pace.

A general criticism of Freudian explanations that applies here is that it is possible to produce an account for anything using these concepts. In addition we can explain Hans' phobia in other, simpler ways. The horse phobia originally developed after Hans had seen a serious accident involving a horse and cart moving at high speed, and this may have produced a conditioned fear response (see the Key Study on the next page).

In general the psychodynamic approach has not received much support, and it ignores many factors associated with phobias (e.g., genetic and social).

> **?** How would you suggest that a behaviourist might explain Hans' fear of horses (you might consider the accident that Hans witnessed)?

Psychological Explanation: Behavioural Approach

Classical and operant conditioning

According to the behaviourists, specific phobias develop through two kinds of conditioning. First, a neutral or conditioned stimulus can come to produce fear if, on several occasions, it is presented at the same time as an unpleasant or unconditioned stimulus. For example, Watson and Rayner (1920) studied an 11-month-old boy called Albert (see the Key Study on the next page). He was a calm child, but the loud noise produced by striking a steel bar made him cry. He became frightened of a rat when the sight of the rat was paired seven times with a loud noise. This involved classical conditioning.

What happened after that was that the fear produced by the previously neutral stimulus (i.e., the rat) was reduced by avoiding it thereafter. "Albert not only became greatly disturbed at the sight of a rat, but this fear had spread to include a white rabbit, cotton wool, a fur coat and the experimenter's (white) hair" (Jones, 1925). However, it has often proved hard to condition people to fear neutral stimuli by pairing them with unpleasant ones in the laboratory (Davison & Neale, 1996).

The development of phobias can be explained by Mowrer's (1947) two-process theory. The first stage involves classical conditioning (e.g., linking the white rat and the loud noise). Then the second stage involves operant conditioning, because avoidance of the phobic stimulus reduces fear and is thus reinforcing.

Some of the evidence supports the conditioning account. According to Barlow and Durand (1995), about 50% of those with specific phobia of driving remember a traumatic experience while driving (e.g., a car accident) as having caused the onset of the phobia. Barlow and Durand also noted that nearly everyone they have treated for choking phobia has had some very unpleasant choking experience in the past.

> **?** Can a conditioning account explain the relative frequency of different phobias?

Albert is shown the rat at the same time as he hears a loud noise.

KEY STUDY
The classical conditioning of the fear response

John B. Watson was taken with Pavlov's concept of **classical conditioning** and believed that it could make psychology a more objective science. With his assistant Rosalie Rayner (Watson & Rayner, 1920), Watson sought to demonstrate that one could explain complex human behaviours using the principles of classical conditioning. They did this by exposing the 11-month-old Albert first to a neutral stimulus (a white rat), and then pairing this with a loud noise. The loud noise was an unconditioned stimulus that produced an unconditioned fear response. Albert quickly learned to show the same fear response to the white rat, thus demonstrating how fear can be learned when a previously neutral stimulus is paired with something that naturally provokes fear.

Mowrer (1947) suggested that phobias are actually the result of a slightly more complex process, involving both classical and operant conditioning. This is called two-process theory. In the first stage, the fear response is learned through classical conditioning (e.g., linking the white rat and the loud noise). The second stage involves **operant conditioning**, where avoidance of the phobic stimulus serves to reduce fear and acts as a negative reinforcement (stamping the behaviour in).

There is evidence to support this theory. Barlow and Durand (1995) report that about 50% of those with a specific phobia of driving remember a traumatic experience while driving as having caused the onset of the phobia. On the other hand, Menzies and Clarke (1993) found that only 2% of individuals suffering from water phobia reported a direct fearful experience with water. DiNardo et al. (1988) found that many normal people had experienced fearful encounters with dogs but did not develop a phobia of dogs, though 50% of dog phobics had had a fearful encounter with a dog.

Key study evaluation

Not all research has found it possible to condition people to fear neutral stimuli by pairing them with unpleasant ones in the laboratory (Davison & Neale, 1996), and research into phobias has not found that all phobics have had prior traumatic experiences. For example, Menzies and Clarke (1993) carried out a study on child participants suffering from water phobia. Only 2% of them reported a direct conditioning experience involving water. DiNardo et al. (1988) found that about 50% of dog phobics had become very anxious during an encounter with a dog, which seems to support conditioning theory. However, they also found that about 50% of normal controls without dog phobia had also had an anxious encounter with a dog! Thus, these findings suggest that dog phobia does *not* depend on having had a frightening encounter with a dog.

Clearly there are ethical concerns in relation to this study, especially as Albert was never reconditioned. Watson and Rayner acknowledged these ethical issues from the outset. They said they conducted the research with hesitation but decided that it was justifiable because children do experience fearful situations in day-to-day life and therefore they were not exposing Albert to anything out of the usual. They also did intend that he should be reconditioned.

Discussion points

1. How might one explain why only some individuals go on to develop a phobia after a fearful experience?
2. How convincing is the behavioural or conditioning account of specific phobias in the light of the evidence?

Evaluation

According to the conditioning account, phobias develop as a result of accidental pairings of a neutral and an aversive stimulus. The obvious prediction from that account, namely, that we could become phobic to almost anything, doesn't fit the facts. As we saw earlier, we seem to be "prepared" to become phobic to stimuli that were dangerous in the long-distant past but not to other stimuli (e.g., cars).

In order to obtain support for the conditioning account of specific phobias, we need to show that phobic patients are much more likely than other people to have had a frightening experience with the phobic object. However, the crucial normal control group is often missing. Consider, for example, the study by DiNardo et al. (1988; see the Key Study on the left), in which both dog phobics and normal controls without dog phobia had had anxious encounters with dogs! Following from Seligman's (1971) ideas discussed earlier, it is possible that we are "prepared" to develop fear and phobia for large animals. More convincing evidence was reported by Hackmann et al. (2000). In their study, 96% of social phobics remembered some socially traumatic experience that had happened to them (often in adolescence). For example, they were harshly criticised in public or started blushing.

Keuthen (1980) reported that half of all phobics couldn't remember any highly unpleasant experiences relating to the phobic object. Those who favour a conditioning account have argued that phobics often forget conditioning experiences that happened many years previously. In order to reduce this problem, Menzies and Clarke (1993) carried out a study on child participants suffering from water phobia. Only 2% of them reported a direct conditioning experience involving water.

However, in defence of the behaviourist view it could be argued that children often have very poor recall for events in early childhood. They may also have repressed the memory of a traumatic event or may not have realised that the event involved water (for example the traumatic event may have taken place beside a stream and thus the sound of water created a phobia). Finally, the behaviourist concept of **stimulus generalisation** suggests that a fear response may be learned about one thing (Albert's fear of a white rat) but then generalised to other apparently quite different things (Albert also reportedly showed a fear reaction to Santa Claus).

Menzies and Clarke (1993) found that phobias do not necessarily develop as a result of a frightening encounter directly with the phobic object. Many people are phobic of snakes, despite having never encountered a real one.

? How might a fear response in a child be rewarded or reinforced?

Modelling and information transmission

Bandura (1986) developed conditioning theory by showing the importance of modelling or observational learning. Individuals learn to imitate the behaviour of others, especially those whose behaviour is seen to be rewarded or reinforced. Mineka et al. (1984) found that monkeys could develop snake phobia simply by watching another monkey experience fear in the presence of a snake. Another possible way in which phobias could be acquired is through information transmission. What happens is that fear-producing information about the phobic object leads to the development of a phobia. Öst (1985) described the case of a woman who was a severe snake phobic. She had been told repeatedly about the dangers of snakes, and had been strongly encouraged to wear rubber boots to protect herself against snakes. She finally reached the point where she wore rubber boots even when going to the local shops.

Some phobias can be acquired through modelling or information transmission. However, modelling or observational learning seems to be of less importance in producing specific phobias in humans than in other species (Menzies & Clarke, 1994), and there are only a few well-documented cases in which information transmission has led to phobias (see M.W. Eysenck, 1997). Merckelbach et al. (1996) argued on the basis of the evidence that claustrophobia or fear of enclosed spaces rarely occurs as a result of modelling or information transmission; in contrast, "In small-animal phobias, but also blood-injection-injury phobia, the predominant pathways to fear are modelling and negative information transmission" (p.354).

Phobia summary: overall prevalence of phobias in population studies: specific phobia 4–7%, agoraphobia 2–3%, social phobia 1–2%, other phobias 1–2%.

KEY TERM

Stimulus generalisation: the tendency for stimuli similar to the conditioned stimulus, to produce a weaker form of the conditioned response, with those stimuli most similar to the conditioned stimulus producing the greatest response.

Psychological Explanation: Cognitive Approach

According to cognitive therapists such as Beck and Emery (1985), anxious patients have various **cognitive biases**, which cause them to exaggerate the threats posed by external and internal stimuli. There is good evidence for cognitive biases in phobics. As far as specific phobics are concerned, Tomarken et al. (1989) presented individuals who were high and low in fears of snakes or spiders with a series of fear-relevant and fear-irrelevant slides. Each slide was followed by an electric shock, a tone, or nothing. The phobic participants greatly overestimated the number of times fear-relevant slides were followed by shock. This is known as covariation bias or **illusory correlation**, where individuals perceive relationships where none exist, thus demonstrating a bias. This could help to account for the high level of anxiety produced by phobic stimuli.

Further evidence for cognitive biases in specific phobics was reported by Arntz et al. (1993) in a study on spider phobics. When confronted by a spider, 91% of the spider phobics reported fear of becoming crazy and 64% said they might die because of fear.

Social phobia

Social phobics have two cognitive biases that may contribute to their condition. First, they attend excessively to their own behaviour in social situations, and so fail to notice the effect they are having on other people (Stopa & Clark, 1993). Second, they interpret their behaviour in social situations to be more negative than it appears to observers (Stopa & Clark, 1993). These cognitive biases lead social phobics to exaggerate how inadequate their social behaviour is, and so help to explain why they fear social situations.

Panic disorder

Clark et al. (1988) assessed the ways in which patients suffering from panic disorder or panic disorder with agoraphobia interpret a range of ambiguous events. These patients showed a cognitive bias for their own bodily sensations. For example, they tended to interpret an increase in heart rate as indicating that there was something wrong with their heart. These findings fit in well with Clark's (1986) cognitive theory of panic disorder, according to which panic disorder patients tend to interpret their bodily sensations in a catastrophic or life-threatening way. This makes them more anxious, and this in turn increases the tendency to have catastrophic thoughts about their bodily sensations.

Why do agoraphobics with panic disorder misinterpret their bodily sensations? One possibility is that some previous physical illness has made them more concerned than most people about their bodily well-being. Relevant evidence was reported by Verburg et al. (1995). Of their panic disorder patients, 43% had suffered from at least one respiratory disease, compared with only 16% of patients with other anxiety disorders.

Cause or result?

There is clear evidence that phobic patients have a range of cognitive biases, which lead them to misinterpret their phobic stimuli. However, it has proved very hard to show that these cognitive biases play a part in *causing* phobias rather than simply being a result of having a phobia. The strongest evidence that cognitive

Yet more unusual phobias: *captoptrophobia*, fear of mirrors; *lachanophobia*, fear of vegetables; *pogonophobia*, fear of beards.

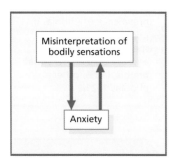

KEY TERMS

Cognitive biases: a predisposition to think in a certain way.
Illusory correlation: the perception of a relationship between things where none exists in reality.

Research at the US Air Force Academy showed that those recruits who were aware of, and anxious about, their own bodily sensations, such as increased sweating, raised heart rate, or shortness of breath, were more likely to suffer panic attacks as their training progressed.

biases may be causally involved in phobias was obtained in an unpublished study by Schmidt (discussed in M.W. Eysenck, 1997). He assessed the cognitive tendency to respond anxiously to one's own bodily sensations among recruits to the US Air Force Academy who went through stressful basic training. Those with the greatest sensitivity to their own bodily sensations at the start of training were most likely to experience panic attacks thereafter.

Evaluation

Individuals suffering from various phobias have cognitive biases that lead them to interpret phobic stimuli as being far more threatening and dangerous than is actually the case. It seems reasonable that such exaggerated cognitive interpretations could produce the high levels of anxiety found in phobics. However, the crucial issue is whether these cognitive biases occur *before* the onset of the phobia and so possibly influence its development or whether they occur only *afterwards* as a consequence of being phobic. A study by Mathews and Mackintosh (2000) is of some relevance here. They showed that manipulating a situation so that normal individuals learned to interpret ambiguous stimuli in a threatening way increased their anxiety levels. Thus, cognitive biases can produce effects on anxiety. However, we don't know whether cognitive biases cause heightened anxiety in phobics.

Psychological Explanation: Social Factors

Parental rearing styles

It is possible that parental rearing styles have an important impact on the development of phobias. This hypothesis was considered by Gerlsman, Emmelkamp, and Arrindell (1990). They reviewed the literature on parental rearing practices in anxious patients, focusing on the dimension of affection and control or overprotection. They found that phobics (especially social phobics and agoraphobics) were lower than normal controls on parental affection and higher on parental control or overprotection.

Parental practices may well play a part in the development of social phobia. Arrindell et al. (1989) found that social phobics claimed that their parents were rejecting, lacking in emotional warmth, or overprotective. However, it is difficult to interpret such findings. As Hudson and Rapee (2000, p.115) pointed out, "Children born with anxious temperaments may influence the way parents respond to them. This is likely to occur in a context in which a parent is anxious and therefore more likely to overprotect." There are other ways in which parents may influence the development of social phobia. Adult social phobics reported that their parents overemphasised the opinions of others, failed to stress the importance of family sociability, and tended to isolate their family from others (Bruch & Heimberg, 1994).

Evaluation

How might the diathesis–stress model be used to explain the development of phobias?

Studies on rearing practices have the limitation that they are based on information obtained years after the event. Another limitation is that all we have are correlations or associations between rearing practices and anxiety disorders. Correlations cannot prove causes—for example, it is possible that is the anxiety shown by their children that leads parents to be overprotective or rejecting. At best, therefore, the evidence from parenting styles can be no more than suggestive.

Life events

There is evidence that phobic patients tend to experience more serious life events than normal controls in the year or so before the onset of the phobia. In a study

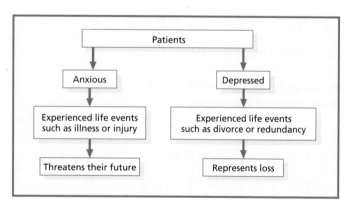

by Kleiner and Marshall (1987), 84% of agoraphobics reported having experienced family problems in the months before they had their first panic attack. In similar fashion, Barrett (1979) found that panic disorder patients reported significantly more undesirable life events in the 6 months prior to onset of their anxiety disorder than did controls over a 6-month period. Andrews (1988, p.171) considered studies on panic disorder with agoraphobia: "Four controlled studies supported the clinical wisdom that panic and agoraphobia tend to follow an especially severe period of stress, stress that was . . . much more pronounced than that reported by normal subjects over a comparable period."

Finlay-Jones and Brown (1981) found a difference between anxious and depressed patients in terms of the kinds of life events they had experienced in the 12 months prior to onset of their disorder. Both groups had experienced an above-average number of life events, but those of anxious patients tended to be danger events (involving future threats), whereas those of depressed patients tended to be loss events (involving past loss).

Evaluation

The main problem with most studies is that the information about life events is obtained some time after the events in question. As a result, some events may have

EXAM HINT

Questions will only be set on one anxiety disorder. If the anxiety disorder is phobias, make sure you include evolutionary explanations such as Seligman's "learned preparedness" theory, and consider the interaction of evolution and learning, to increase the synopticity of your answer.

been forgotten, or are remembered in a distorted form. Another is that of establishing whether the life events helped to cause the phobia or whether high levels of anxiety played a part in causing the life events. For example, someone in the early stages of developing social phobia might avoid social occasions and be so unapproachable that his/her behaviour triggers the severe life event of marital separation.

What other life events fit into Finlay-Jones and Brown's categories of "threatens the future" and "represents loss"?

SECTION SUMMARY
Anxiety Disorders

❖ Anxiety is important for survival. But when anxiety is quite disproportionate to any threat that is posed but it can become disabling. This is an anxiety disorder.

What are anxiety disorders?

❖ Examples of anxiety disorders include:

— Panic disorder
— Generalised anxiety disorder
— Obsessive-compulsive disorder
— Adjustment disorder (e.g., post-traumatic disorder)
— Phobias.

❖ Characteristics of specific phobias (e.g., claustrophobia, fear of flying, fear of spiders) include:

What are phobias?

— Persistent fear
— Excessive anxiety response to feared object leading to avoidance
— Awareness that anxiety is excessive
— Interference with working or social life.

❖ Social phobias (e.g., shyness, fear of public speaking) are distinguished by fear of exposure to unfamiliar people and certain social situations.

❖ Agoraphobia (panic disorder with agoraphobia) is usually preceded by panic attacks:

— A fear of having such an attack in public leads the sufferer to avoid going out.
— The agoraphobic worries about future panic attacks and is anxious in situations where escape would be difficult.
— Panic attacks are characterised by palpitations, shortness of breath, accelerated heart rate, a feeling of choking, nausea, sweating, chest pain, feeling dizzy, and fear of dying.
— Many of these disorders are more common in women, and in younger people.

❖ Post-traumatic stress disorder is triggered by a specific event. Some individuals are more vulnerable to PTSD than others.

❖ Obsessive-compulsive disorder includes obsessive intrusive thoughts and overtly repetitive behaviours which are difficult to control.

❖ The role of genetic factors in panic disorder with agoraphobia has been demonstrated in twin and family studies.

Biological explanations: genetic factors

❖ The picture is similar for specific phobias and social phobia.

❖ Social phobia is more likely to occur in individuals with a very introverted personality.

Biological explanations: neurophysiology	❖ Phobics may have higher levels of arousal, though this could be a cause or an effect of an anxiety disorder. ❖ Tests using biological challenges on patients suffering from panic disorder with agoraphobia show: — Patients differ in the way they interpret their bodily symptoms rather than in terms of their actual physiological responsiveness. — This supports support a cognitive model rather than a physiological model.
Psychological explanations: psychodynamic theory	❖ According to Freud, phobias are a means of coping with the anxiety produced from repression (e.g. of sexual desires). ❖ This is illustrated by the case of Little Hans: — The boy's fear of horses was explained as a means of dealing with the guilt he felt about having sexual desires for his mother. — However, one could explain this fear as a conditioned response. ❖ The psychodynamic approach also suggests that early separation anxiety may predispose individuals to develop panic disorder with agoraphobia.
Psychological explanations: behavioural approach	❖ Phobias develop as a result of two-process theory: — Classical conditioning: the neutral object is paired with something that creates anxiety. — Operant conditioning: avoidance of the feared stimulus reduces anxiety and is reinforcing. ❖ The experiment with Little Albert demonstrated classical conditioning of a fear response. ❖ However, research indicates that phobias do not depend on having previous frightening encounters, and people who do have frightening encounters don't always develop phobias. ❖ Modelling and information transmission are behavioural explanations that may apply to some specific phobias.
Psychological explanations: cognitive approach See also pages 217–225 of the revision guide.	❖ Phobics have cognitive biases which cause them to exaggerate the threat posed by certain stimuli. This is supported by the bias produced by illusory correlations. ❖ According to the cognitive theory of panic disorder, such patients interpret their bodily sensations in a catastrophic way. This may occur because of past serious illnesses that made them anxious about bodily sensations. ❖ There is some evidence that such biases are a cause rather than an effect.
Psychological explanations: social factors	❖ Phobics may have experienced low parental affection and high parental control or over-protection. ❖ Anxiety disorders may occur when a person experiences an above average number of life events. ❖ Anxious patients tend to experience danger events, whereas depressed patients experience loss events.

FURTHER READING

The topics in this chapter are covered in greater depth by J.D. Stirling and J. Hellewell (1999) *Psychopathology* (London: Routledge), written specifically for A level students. Most of the topics discussed in this chapter are dealt with by M.W. Eysenck (2004) *Psychology: An international perspective* (Hove: Psychology Press) in Chapter 22. J.N. Butcher, S. Mineka, and J.M. Hooley (2004) provide good coverage of psychopathology in their book, *Abnormal Psychology (12th Edn)* (London: Pearson).

Another good source is G.C. Davison and J.M. Neale (2004), *Abnormal psychology (7th Edn)* (Chichester: Wiley).

EXAMPLE EXAMINATION QUESTIONS

You should spend 40 minutes on each of the questions below, which aim to test the material in this chapter. Unlike questions from Unit 4 of the examination, covered in Chapters 1–6 of this book, the questions in the Individual Differences section of the Unit 5 examination, covered in this chapter and Chapter 9, are marked out of 30 and an additional criterion is used in assessment: synopticity. "Synopticity" is defined as your "understanding and critical appreciation of the breadth and range of different theoretical perspectives and/or methodological approaches relevant to any questions" (AQA specification).

1. Describe and evaluate the possible contributions of biological factors to schizophrenia. (30 marks)
2. (a) Outline the clinical characteristics of schizophrenia. (10 marks)
   (b) Outline **one** explanation of schizophrenia, and evaluate this explanation in terms of research studies **and/or** alternative explanations. (20 marks)
3. "There are many different kinds of depression, for example unipolar and bipolar, and endogenous and reactive."
   Discuss the possible explanations for depression, including the evidence on which these explanations are based. (30 marks)
4. (a) Outline the clinical characteristics of depression. (5 marks)
   (b) Discuss psychological explanations of depression. (25 marks)
5. Describe and evaluate possible contributions of biological factors to any **one** anxiety disorder. (30 marks)
6. Critically consider the research evidence for psychological explanations of any **one** anxiety disorder. (30 marks)

Examination Tips

Question 1. The descriptive part of this essay concerns biological explanations for schizophrenia, of which there are a large range. Candidates usually present the evidence for such explanations as part of the descriptive material and then evaluate the methodology of such studies or the logic of the explanations. Further evaluation can be given in terms of alternative explanations, such as social and family relationships. It is important to ensure that such alternatives are not just further descriptions but are used explicitly and exclusively as evaluations. Using alternative explanations contributes to the synoptic element of the essay as do any links you are able to make across the specification, such as reference to stress research or evolutionary, behaviourist, and psychodynamic explanations.

Question 2.   The division of marks in this question is unusual as some of the AO1 marks are in part (b). In part (a) you are asked for a straightforward list of characteristics. The injunction "outline" is used to indicate that breadth rather than detail is required, though some detail is necessary to demonstrate understanding. You should spend just over 10 minutes on this part of the answer. In part (b) there are 5 marks for another outline, this time of one explanation. If you choose the biological explanation you can include, under this umbrella, a number of different kinds of biological explanation, and leave the research studies to form part of your evaluation. As in question 1, ensure that any alternative explanations used are not just tacked on with a linking sentence "I can evaluate the biological explanations by looking at alternatives", but that you make a genuine effort to use alternative explanations as a point of contrast and evaluation.

Question 3.   You are not required to refer to the quotation in your answer but it is there to suggest ways of answering the question. "Discuss" is an AO1 and AO2 term. You are invited to describe any explanations of depression and the evidence on which they are based. The likely problem is that you will have too much to write and therefore, in order to produce a good answer, need to be selective in the way you approach this question, concentrating on the explanations you can give in the greatest detail. You might use other explanations as a form of evaluation, or simply mention them briefly at the end, saying that they have little support. You might also select explanations that are most likely to demonstrate most synopticity.

Question 4.   This question, like question 2, has an unusual mark division. Part (a) requires a summary description of the clinical characteristics of depression. You should spend about 5 minutes on this. In part (b) "discuss" is an AO1 and AO2 term. There are 10 marks for a description of psychological explanations and a further 15 marks for an evaluation of these explanations. Thus you should divide your time accordingly. It may be advisable to use evidence as a form of evaluation rather than description, and present a range of explanations in order to attract synoptic credit.

Question 5.   The specification requires knowledge of only one anxiety disorder. If you present more than one, they will all be marked but credit only given to the best one. This is not good practice in an examination and it would be better to use further knowledge of this kind as a form of evaluation (e.g., "other anxiety disorders are also explained like this"). The comments written for question 1 apply here.

Question 6.   In this essay you are required to focus on research evidence rather than explanations. A critical consideration of such evidence involves reference to both strengths and limitations of, for example, the methodology, practical application and/or ethics of such research. Further evaluation may be in terms of how the evidence may be used to construct explanations. As always bear the synopticity issue in mind.

WEBSITES

http://www.schizophrenia.com/
Schizophrenia information and links.

http://mentalhelp.net/
Huge site about mental disorders and treatment.

http://schizophrenia.mentalhelp.net/
Schizophrenia area of the Mentalhelp site.

http://www.mentalhealth.com/
Major site with lots of information about disorders, diagnosis, and treatments, as well as numerous links to other sites.

http://www.rcpsych.ac.uk/info/schiz.htm
Schizophrenia information on the website of the Royal College of Psychiatrists, UK.

http://www.depression.com/
Major "news" site about depression.

http://www.depressionalliance.org/
A comprehensive website with links to research articles and news on latest developments in the treatment of depression.

http://www.mentalhealthcare.org.uk/
Information and links regarding conditions affecting mental health, inlcuding research articles on Bipolar disorder and Schizophrenia.

http://www.blarg.net/~charlatn/Depression.html
A personal account of major depression by a sufferer; this site also includes many links.

http://www.beckinstitute.org/
Beck Institute for Cognitive Therapy and Research, under the leadership of its President, the founder of Cognitive Therapy, Aaron T. Beck.

http://phobialist.com/
Huge list of phobia, which professes to offer no explanations or cures!

http://www.socialphobia.org/
In-depth information and links about social phobia, the most common anxiety disorder.

http://www.nlm.nih.gov/medlineplus/phobias.html
Phobia links.

http://www.hydra.umn.edu/fobo/hans1.html
The case of Freud's Little Hans.

Biological (Somatic) Therapies p.389

• Is electroconvulsive therapy dangerous?

• When is it preferable to chemotherapy?

• Why is psychosurgery still used?

Behavioural Therapies p.405

• If some mental disorders are learned, can they be "unlearned"?

• Are behavioural therapists guilty of unethical manipulation of another person's behaviour?

• Is it acceptable to treat the symptoms and not the underlying causes of mental disorder?

Alternatives to Biological and Behavioural Therapies p.414

• Why are cognitive therapies increasingly popular?

• What is cognitive-behavioural therapy?

• Why is psychoanalysis only suitable for some people?

Treating Mental Disorders

This chapter is concerned with the main therapies used to treat mental disorders: biological (somatic), behavioural, cognitive-behavioural, and psychodynamic. There are important issues surrounding the use of these therapies, such as their effectiveness and the ethics of their use.

9

BIOLOGICAL (SOMATIC) THERAPIES

Medical doctors have claimed that mental illness resembles physical illness and the causes of mental illnesses resemble those of physical illnesses. According to this medical model, so-called mental illness depends on some underlying organic problem, and the best form of treatment involves *direct* manipulation of the physiological system within the body. **Somatic therapy** (a major part of which is drug therapy) is the term for this method of treatment.

The early history of somatic therapy was not very encouraging. As far back as the Middle Ages, those suffering from mental illness had holes cut in their skulls to allow the devils allegedly causing the illness to escape. This practice, which is known as **trepanning**, cannot be recommended. It did not produce any cures, and many of those subjected to trepanning didn't survive the operation.

Psychosurgery

Psychosurgery is the use of brain surgery to reduce psychological or behavioural disorders. Pioneering work was carried out by Antonio Egas Moniz in the 1930s. He used the surgical method of **prefrontal lobotomy**, in which fibres running from the frontal lobes to other parts of the brain were cut. In the film, *One Flew Over the Cuckoo's Nest*, a lobotomy operation ends Randle Patrick McMurphy's rebellion against the hospital authorities. Moniz and others claimed that this operation made schizophrenic and other patients less violent and agitated, and much easier to manage. This form of psychosurgery caught on to such an extent that about 70,000 lobotomies were carried out between 1935 and 1955.

> **KEY TERMS**
> **Somatic therapy:** a form of treatment for mental illness involving manipulations of the body (e.g., drug treatment).
> **Trepanning:** cutting holes in the skull so that the devils thought to cause mental illness can escape. It is still used to relieve pressure inside the cranial cavity.
> **Psychosurgery:** sections of the brain are removed or lesions are made to treat a psychological condition.
> **Prefrontal lobotomy:** a form of psychosurgery where the fibres running from the frontal lobes to other parts of the brain are cut. Lobotomies typically make patients calmer but there are side-effects include apathy, diminished intellectual powers, impaired judgements, and even coma and death.

The four major models of abnormality

There are four major models of abnormality, which were covered in your AS level studies. Each of these models provides explanations of the origins of mental disorders, and each is associated with certain forms of treatment.

The **medical model** proposes that the causes of mental disorders resemble those of physical illnesses. Clusters of symptoms can be identified and a diagnosis made, followed by suitable treatment. There is some evidence that infection, genetics, biochemistry, and/or neuroanatomy may account for mental disorders. If the causes are physical then the treatments should be physical as well, and the medical model recommends direct manipulation of the body processes, such as using drugs, ECT, and psychosurgery. This model is less appropriate for disorders with psychological symptoms, such as phobias.

The **behavioural model** suggests that mental disorders are caused by learning maladaptive behaviour via conditioning or observational learning. Logically, anything that is learned can be unlearned using the same techniques. The approach is best for explaining (and treating) those disorders that emphasise external behaviours, such as phobias. The behavioural model is oversimplified and more appropriate to non-human animal behaviour. Ethically, there are advantages such as the lack of blame attached to a person with a mental disorder, but the treatments can be psychologically painful and manipulative.

According to the **psychodynamic model**, the roots of mental disorder are to be found in unresolved conflicts and traumas from childhood. This model may focus too much on the past at the cost of understanding current problems, and too much on sexual problems rather than interpersonal and social issues. Ethical concerns include the problem of false memory syndrome and the sexist nature of the theory. The approach is best for conditions where patients have insight, such as some anxiety disorders, though it has not proved very effective with phobias.

The **cognitive model** takes the view that distorted and irrational beliefs are crucially involved in most mental disorders. Limitations of the cognitive model include the problem of whether distorted thinking is a cause or an effect, and the circularity of the explanations. The model suggests that individuals are in part to blame for their problems. The cognitive-behavioural model is a recent and popular development, combining both cognitive and behavioural approaches.

Lobotomies typically made patients calmer. However, the side-effects were so serious that they are very rarely performed any more. These side-effects include apathy, diminished intellectual powers, impaired judgements, and even coma and death. In view of all these serious side-effects, it is clear that performing lobotomies poses immense ethical issues.

More modern methods of psychosurgery

One of the criticisms of lobotomies was their very imprecise nature. Since lobotomies were first performed, various more refined techniques have been introduced. The **prefrontal leukotomy** involves drilling

Assumptions of the medical model

All mental disorders have a physical cause (micro-organisms, genetics, biochemistry, or neuroanatomy).

- Mental illnesses can be described in terms of clusters of symptoms.
- Symptoms can be identified, leading to the diagnosis of an illness.
- Diagnosis leads to appropriate physical treatments.

KEY TERMS

Medical model: a model of abnormality based on the medical approach to treating physical illness; the model assumes that all illnesses (physical and psychological) have an underlying biochemical or physiological basis.

Behavioural model: a model of abnormality based on the behaviourist approach (behaviourism). Mental illness is explained in terms of classical and operant conditioning.

Psychodynamic model: a model of abnormality, based on the psychodynamic (psychoanalytic) approach, which emphasises the influence of early experiences and of repressed emotions that are expressed unconsciously.

Cognitive model: a model of abnormality that emphasises the role of cognitive factors in mental disorders. The view is that thinking in a maladaptive way leads to disordered behaviour.

Prefrontal leukotomy: a more precise form of psychosurgery than the prefrontal lobotomy, which involves drilling two holes in either side of the skull and inserting needles to sever specific nerve fibres, thus effecting a functional removal of areas of the frontal lobes.

two holes in either side of the skull and inserting needles to sever specific nerve fibres, thus effecting a functional removal of areas of the brain.

Stereotactic neurosurgery is an even more refined method that requires only a small opening to be made in the patient's skull, under local anaesthesia. Then, a thin straight probe is introduced into the brain, and using a remarkably precise system of geometrical co-ordinates, it is targeted onto the internal structure of the brain that the neurosurgeon wants to remove. In this way, quantities of nervous tissue as small as a few cubic millimetres, totally inside the brain, can be lesioned without destroying other parts of the brain.

In the film *One Flew Over the Cuckoo's Nest*, Jack Nicholson played Randle Patrick McMurphy, who inspired and awakened his fellow patients, while falling out with the authorities. Eventually, the character is lobotomised, and becomes calmer and easier to handle, but loses all his intellectual spark and energy.

This method is used in surgeries that target specific regions of the brain; for example amygdalotomies and cingulotomies. In an **amygdalotomy**, the amygdala, which is the part of the brain involved in anger, is destroyed by directing fine wire electrodes at it through a small hole drilled in the skull. Strong currents are then passed through the electrode, destroying the tissue around its tip. Cosgrove and Ballantine (1996) described their recent work using **cingulotomy** to relieve emotional distress and reduce abnormal behaviour. The target of their operations, the cingulate gyrus, is a thin ribbon of grey matter believed to play a role in human emotional states.

Effectiveness

Amygdalotomies were carried out on violent criminals, especially in the United States during the 1950s and 1960s. The operations were usually a success, in that those operated on became less aggressive. However, there were very serious side-effects. Patients often became confused, lacking in motivation, and unable to work (Eysenck & Eysenck, 1989). For example, Thomas R. was a 34-year-old engineer who couldn't work after an amygdalotomy. He was found on one occasion walking about with his head covered by bags, rags, and newspapers. He justified his

Early somatic therapy

There have been many bizarre treatments for mental illness over the course of history, from blood-letting and purging (use of laxatives) to ice baths. In 1810, Dr Benjamin Rush invented the restraining chair illustrated here. Herman and Green (1991) quote his description of its effectiveness:

I have contrived a chair and introduced it to our Hospital to assist in curing madness. It binds and confines every part of the body. By keeping the trunk erect, it lessens the impetus of blood toward the brain . . . It acts as a sedative to the tongue and temper as well as to the blood vessels.

Rush coined the word *Tranquilliser* as a name for his apparatus and patients were confined in it for up to 24 hours at a time. No one today would be surprised that this would subdue anyone, regardless of their mental state.

KEY TERMS

Stereotactic neurosurgery: a refined method of psychosurgery that requires only a small opening to be made in the patient's skull, under local anaesthesia.

Amygdalotomy: a form of psychosurgery where the amygdala, which is the part of the brain involved in anger, is destroyed using strong electrical currents.

Cingulotomy: a form of psychosurgery where the cingulate gyrus is destroyed using strong electrical currents to reduce aggressive behaviour.

behaviour by saying he was frightened other bits of his brain might be destroyed. As a result of all the side-effects resulting from amygdalotomy, this form of psychosurgery is almost never carried out any more.

Between 1991 and 1995, Cosgrove et al. (1996) performed cingulotomies on 34 patients suffering from depressive or anxiety disorders. They claimed that there was improvement in about one-third of the patients, all of whom had severe illnesses that had proved resistant to all other available therapies. Psychosurgery is sometimes effective if it is performed precisely and on the right patients. However, there are ethical issues surrounding such permanent damage. In the UK, the Mental Health Act requires a patient's consent for psychosurgery, as well as an opinion from a second doctor.

Electroconvulsive Therapy

Electroconvulsive therapy (ECT) has its origins in the observation that epileptics rarely suffered from schizophrenia. It was thought that perhaps, in some way, the seizures associated with epilepsy would prevent schizophrenia. In the 1930s, a psychiatrist, Sakel, injected insulin into patients, which led to convulsions and coma. The behaviour of some schizophrenic patients did improve. In 1938, two Italian psychiatrists, Cerletti and Bini, first used electric shock to induce seizures.

What used to happen in ECT was that a strong electric current was passed for about half a second between two electrodes attached to each side of the depressed patient's forehead. This current caused almost immediate loss of consciousness and a convulsive seizure. Nowadays, an electric current of between 70 and 130 volts is generally passed through only the non-dominant brain hemisphere, and an anaesthetic and muscle relaxants are given before the treatment itself. As a result, the patient is unconscious during ECT and there are fewer muscular spasms than before. Additional precautions include giving the patient oxygen before and after treatment, and using a mouth gag to prevent the patient biting his or her lips and tongue.

In the past there were cases of broken bones and bruising as a consequence of the restraints that were used, but today the whole treatment is considerably more humane. The convulsion lasts for a maximum of 2 minutes and is only visible as a slight twitching of facial muscles and perhaps the person's toes. Typically a patient will receive between six and nine treatments over a period of a month.

A very early example of an induction coil device used in 18th-century electric-shock therapy. Today, aversion therapy utilises much more sophisticated methods and equipment.

Effectiveness

ECT is now rarely used for schizophrenia; however, it appears to be successful for cases of severe depression. Fink (1985) concluded, from a review of studies on

ECT using measures such as suicide rates, that it is effective in over 60% of psychotic-depressive patients. Rey and Walter (1997) found that about 65% of patients with major depression benefited from ECT. However, Sackheim, Nordlie, and Gur (1993) found that there was a high relapse rate within a year suggesting that relief was temporary and not a cure. ECT has also been used in cases of acute mania. The evidence suggests that ECT is effective in 80% of patients with acute mania who had previously failed to improve with medication (Mukherjee et al., 1994).

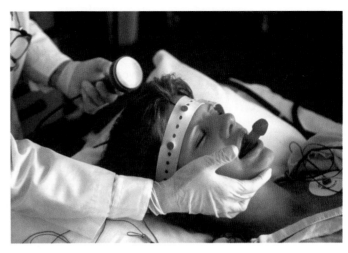

Electroconvulsive therapy has been found to be quite effective in cases of severe depression, though the reasons why it might be effective are uncertain.

Why is ECT sometimes used rather than drugs in the treatment of depression? The main reason is that some severely depressed patients fail to respond to drugs, but do respond to ECT. Janicak et al. (1985) found that 80% of all severely depressed patients respond well to ECT, compared with 64% given drug therapy. It might be suggested that the greater improvement rates for ECT are due to patients' expectations about the successfulness of the therapy rather than the shocks themselves. However, patients undergoing a "sham" ECT procedure in which no shocks are presented show much less improvement than those receiving ECT (Barlow & Durand, 1995). A useful feature of ECT is that it typically reduces depression more rapidly than do anti-depressant drugs. This is of special value when there are concerns that a depressed patient may commit suicide.

Appropriateness

On the negative side, we have little idea of precisely why ECT is so effective and therefore might question how appropriate it is to use as a therapy. One might justify its use by saying that it works, but this is no better than justifying kicking the television as a method of repair for the same reason (assuming that kicking the television does occasionally work—probably because of some third intervening variable).

Current understanding suggests three possible explanations for the effectiveness of ECT. First, ECT may act as a punishment. If maladaptive behaviours have been learned, then punishment will extinguish that S-R link. However, sub-convulsive shocks don't appear to change behaviour but are as unpleasant as those shocks that do cause convulsions. As ECT is now done under anaesthetic it also may be less of a punishment in any case.

Second, it has been suggested that the convulsions lead to memory loss and allow some restructuring of disordered thinking. However, unilateral ECT leads to minimal memory disruption yet is still effective.

The third explanation is linked to the permissive amine theory of mood disorders (see page 358). ECT appears to lower the level of noradrenaline and reduce serotonin re-uptake, which will reduce depression. However, for some patients ECT produces a permanent cure, and the alteration of neurotransmitter levels would be temporary.

It would clearly be desirable to develop safer options to ECT. One such approach is based on transcranial magnetic stimulation (TMS) in which magnetic pulses briefly disrupt the functioning of a given brain area. TMS has several

EXAM HINT

As there are a number of biological theories there is potentially a lot of AO1 material, so remember to be selective. For instance, focus on chemotherapy in depth and then cover ECT or psychosurgery in less depth.

advantages over ECT: it is painless; the parts of the brain affected can be targeted fairly precisely; and it has less serious side-effects. Klein et al. (1999) reported significant improvement in more than 50% of severely depressed patients who received TMS.

Ethical considerations

The link between ECT and abuse remains, and it is still seen by many as a form of punishment and a sign of the control wielded by psychiatrists. Any technique that involves direct intervention with brain states is viewed with suspicion. However, as we have seen, safer and less invasive techniques have been developed. Some depressed patients who don't respond to drugs are in danger of committing suicide, and it could be argued that it is ethical to give such patients ECT to minimise the chances that they will kill themselves. An important ethical safeguard is that patients are only given ECT after consent has been given by the patient or by a close relative.

Chemotherapy

Chemotherapy (also known as drug therapy) has been used in the treatment of several disorders. In this discussion, we will focus on chemotherapy or drug therapy as applied to depression, anxiety disorders, and schizophrenia.

Depression

Drug therapy has been used in the treatment of patients suffering from major depression and from bipolar disorder (see Chapter 8, Psychopathology). It has been argued that depression involves a shortage of **monoamines**, which are a type of neurotransmitter including dopamine, serotonin, and noradrenaline. It follows that an effective therapy for depression might involve using drugs that increase the supply of these neurotransmitters. Two groups of such drugs are the monoamine oxidase inhibitors (MAOIs) and the tricyclics. The MAOIs work by inhibiting monoamine oxidase, which leads to increased levels of neurotransmitters such as noradrenaline and serotonin. Tricyclics also enhance the action of monamines in a slightly different way (see the diagram below).

> Given that the full implications of ECT are poorly understood, do you think it is ever right to administer such treatments to vulnerable patients?

KEY TERM

Monoamines: a group of neurotransmitters that are chemically similar, such as serotonin, dopamine, and noradrenaline. They are also called catecholamines.

The action of anti-depressants on the synapse

Depressed individuals tend to have lower levels of monoamines, especially serotonin.

Tricyclics, e.g., imipramine (trade name Tofranil)

Tricyclics slow down the reabsorption of catecholamines or serotonin by the presynaptic vesicles, thus allowing them to continue stimulating the postsynaptic neuron.

Monoamine oxidase inhibitors (MAOIs) e.g., phenelzine (trade name Nardil)

Monoamine oxidase (MAO) normally metabolises monoamines and renders them inactive. MAOIs block MAO, thus the monoamines remain longer in the synapse and continue to act on the postsynaptic neuron.

Axon of presynaptic neuron

Postsynaptic neuron

Direction of impulse flow

Vesicles containing neurotransmitter

Synaptic cleft

Axon of presynaptic neuron

Postsynaptic neuron

Direction of impulse flow

The tricyclics are generally more effective than the MAOIs, and produce fewer side-effects. However, the tricyclics can produce dizziness, blurred vision, and dryness of the mouth, and they can impair driving to a dangerous extent. It is not very clear why the various drugs are ineffective with some patients. In general, the tricyclics tend to be more effective with fairly severe forms of depression (Stern, Rush, & Mendels, 1980), perhaps because abnormalities in the levels of monoamines are most likely to be found in severely depressed patients. There can be a high relapse rate with tricyclics unless therapy is continued over a long period of time (Franchini et al., 1997).

It could be argued that the tricyclics and the MAOIs are simply stimulants producing physiological activation, rather than drugs that correct depressed patients' biochemical deficits. However, most of the evidence is inconsistent with that notion. Neither the tricyclics nor the MAOIs have much effect on the mood of normal individuals who do not have biochemical deficits (Cole & Davis, 1975).

A third group of drugs for depression, the selective serotonin re-uptake inhibitors (SSRIs), are specific to serotonin. For example, fluoxetine (trade name Prozac) prevents the re-uptake of serotonin by the presynaptic neuron, so leaving it to have an enhanced effect on the postsynaptic neuron. The SSRIs are about as effective as the tricyclics (Hirschfeld, 1999), but they possess some advantages. Depressed patients taking SSRIs are less likely to suffer from dry mouth and constipation than those taking tricyclics, and it is harder to overdose on SSRIs. However, SSRIs conflict with some other forms of medication.

Drug treatment for the manic phase of bipolar disorder has lagged behind that for major depression. However, lithium carbonate produces rapid improvement in most manic patients, and can delay the onset of depression in patients suffering from bipolar disorder. Lithium carbonate reduces the occurrence of manic and depressed episodes in about 80% of patients with bipolar disorder (Gerbino, Oleshansky, & Gershon, 1978). Before lithium carbonate was introduced, the suicide rate of bipolar disorder patients was about 15%, whereas it is now much lower.

Lithium carbonate can have serious side-effects on the central nervous system, on the cardiovascular system, and on the digestive system, and an overdose can be fatal. Discontinuation of lithium carbonate increases the chances that the symptoms of bipolar disorder will recur, so it tends to be used on a continuous basis. However, the chances of relapse are much less if lithium is taken after the elimination of manic symptoms (Viguera et al., 2000).

In sum, various drugs (especially Prozac) are very effective at reducing patients' levels of depression. However, the drugs affect the symptoms rather than the underlying problems causing the depression. Thus, it is desirable for other forms of therapy to be used alongside chemotherapy to produce rapid recovery.

? It has sometimes been suggested that manic depression is higher among very creative people, and that the manic phase of the disorder can particularly heighten creativity. How might this affect some sufferers' decisions about whether or not to take drug treatment such as lithium carbonate?

Anxiety disorders

Patients suffering from anxiety (e.g., those with generalised anxiety disorder) are often given minor tranquillisers to reduce anxiety and permit normal functioning. At one time, **barbiturates** were the most used form of anti-anxiety drug. They are depressants of the central nervous system, and long-acting barbiturates are effective in reducing anxiety. However, they have various side-effects. These include problems of concentration, lack of co-ordination, and slurred speech. In addition, the barbiturates tend to be addictive. Anxious patients who stop taking barbiturates report numerous symptoms such as delirium, irritability, and increased sweating.

KEY TERM

Barbiturates: drugs that used to be widely used in the treatment of anxiety disorders.

CASE STUDY: VIRGINIA WOOLF

The author Virginia Woolf, who committed suicide in 1941 at the age of 59, was plagued by an intermittent form of depression. This affliction appears to have been bipolar depression, but was accompanied by extreme physical symptoms and psychotic delusions. In her biography of Woolf, Hermione Lee (1997) unravels the series of treatments administered to Woolf between 1895, when she experienced her first breakdown, and the 1930s. Later, Woolf's husband Leonard made detailed notes on her breakdowns (Lee, 1997, pp.78-179):

> In the manic stage she was extremely excited; the mind raced; she talked volubly and, at the height of the attack, incoherently; she had delusions and heard voices . . . During the depressive stage all her thoughts and emotions were the exact opposite . . . she was in the depths of melancholia and despair; she scarcely spoke; refused to eat; refused to believe that she was ill and insisted that her condition was due to her own guilt.

During the period from 1890 to 1930, Woolf consulted more than 12 different doctors, but the treatments barely altered during this time. They tended to consist of milk and meat diets to redress her weight loss; rest to alleviate her agitation; sleep and fresh air to help her regain her energy. Lithium had not yet been discovered as a treatment for manic depression. Instead, bromide, veronal, and chloral, most of which are sedatives, were prescribed. Lee points out that there is great uncertainty about the neuropsychiatric effects of some of these drugs, and Woolf's manic episodes may well have been the result of taking these chemicals.

In what instances might a GP feel justified in prescribing drugs such as Valium or Librium? What does "tolerance" to drugs mean and what are the problems associated with this and the treatment of anxiety disorders? What other forms of treatment would benefit an anxious patient, together with or instead of drugs?

The problems with the barbiturates led to their replacement by the benzodiazepines (e.g., Valium, Librium) in the 1960s. The benzodiazepines are more precise than the barbiturates in their functioning, and so typically produce fewer side-effects. However, they often have sedative effects, with patients reporting drowsiness and lethargy. They can also impair long-term memory. There can be unfortunate withdrawal symptoms when patients stop taking them, and there are potential problems of addiction.

Although it is clear that the benzodiazepines are much safer than the barbiturates, the search has continued for other anti-anxiety drugs that will reduce anxiety without producing the side-effects of previous drugs. One such drug is Buspirone, which has been found to be as effective as the benzodiazepines in the treatment of generalised anxiety disorder (Lader & Scotto, 1998). Buspirone doesn't have the potentially dangerous sedative effects of the benzodiazepines. However, it has been found to reduce vigilance, and it occasionally leads to dizziness or headaches. Of particular importance, problems of dependence or addiction found with the benzodiazepines are absent with Buspirone.

Chemotherapy can be useful in providing rapid reduction of anxiety in patients who are very distressed. However, anti-anxiety drugs are only designed to reduce the symptoms of anxiety, and do not address the underlying problems. Anti-anxiety drugs should generally only be used over fairly short periods of time, and should be used in combination with other forms of therapy.

Schizophrenia

Neuroleptic drugs (drugs that reduce psychotic symptoms but can also produce some of the symptoms of neurological diseases) are often used in the treatment of schizophrenia. Common neuroleptic drugs include the phenothiazines, the butyrophenones, and the thioxanthenes. They reduce the positive symptoms of schizophrenia (e.g., delusions, hallucinations) but have little effect on the negative symptoms (e.g., lack of motivation and emotion, social withdrawal).

KEY TERM

Neuroleptic drugs: drugs that reduce psychotic symptoms but can produce some of the symptoms of neurological diseases.

In spite of the usefulness of neuroleptic drugs, they have serious limitations. Windgassen (1992) found that about half of schizophrenic patients taking neuroleptics reported grogginess or sedation, 18% reported problems with concentration, 16% had problems with salivation, and 16% had blurred vision. More seriously, more than 20% of schizophrenic patients who take neuroleptic drugs for over a year develop the symptoms of tardive dyskinesia—these symptoms include involuntary sucking and chewing, jerky movements of the limbs, and writhing movements of the mouth or face, and the effects can be permanent. In view of these side-effects, neuroleptic drugs are generally given in the smallest possible doses, and there are "drug holidays" during which no drugs are given. Schizophrenic patients are often reluctant to take neuroleptic drugs. As a result, they are sometimes given injections of long-lasting neuroleptics, thus removing the decision whether or not to take a tablet.

> **Ethical issues: Informed consent**
>
> There is a proven link between the use of neuroleptic drugs and the onset of Parkinson's disease, in which the midbrain fails to produce enough dopamine, a chemical that helps to control movement. What ethical issues with regard to informed consent are raised by this fact?

> **Ethical issues: Compulsory medication**
>
> The reduction of the more severe symptoms of schizophrenia has obvious advantages for the carers and families of schizophrenics. Does this mean that patients could or should be given medication without their consent? Are there any differences between the human rights of a schizophrenic person and those of any other patient visiting their doctor? Should the human rights of one person take precedence over those of another person?

There is increasing usage of what are known as atypical anti-psychotic drugs such as clozapine, risperidone, and olanzapine. These drugs have various advantages over the more conventional ones. First, atypical drugs benefit about 85% of schizophrenic patients compared to about 65% of patients given conventional drugs (Awad & Voruganti, 1999). Second, the atypical drugs are of much more use in helping schizophrenic patients suffering mainly from negative symptoms (e.g., lack of motivation; lack of emotion) (Remington & Kapur, 2000). Third, many side-effects of the conventional drugs (especially tardive dyskinesia) are absent with the atypical drugs. On the downside, about 1–2% of schizophrenic patients who take clozapine develop a condition that can be life threatening in which there is a substantial reduction in white blood cells.

The drugs used to treat schizophrenia have the great advantage that schizophrenic patients no longer need to be restrained in straitjackets. However, they have significant disadvantages. First, as we have seen, they have several unfortunate side-effects, although the atypical anti-psychotic drugs have fewer side-effects than the conventional neuroleptic drugs. Second, the drugs basically reduce symptoms, and can't be regarded as providing a cure for schizophrenia.

Evaluation of chemotherapy

On the positive side, chemotherapy often produces rapid, beneficial effects in treating anxiety, depression, and schizophrenia. If we compare chemotherapy against other forms of therapy, then it seems to be especially effective in reducing the symptoms of schizophrenia. Chemotherapy is also of particular value in treating anxious and depressed patients in extreme emotional distress. The reason for this is that chemotherapy can often produce effects more *rapidly* than other forms of therapy.

In addition, chemotherapy has allowed a great number of people to lead relatively normal lives despite underlying disorders. It may prevent suicide during a deeply depressed episode in a person's life and it may also make the world safer for other people (see the Case Study on page 399).

? To what extent should practical concerns take precedence over ethical issues?

Disorder	Drug/group of drugs	How they work	Drawbacks
Depression (major)	Monoamine oxidase inhibitors (MAOIs)	Inhibit oxidation of monoamines (neurotransmitters, including dopamine, serotonin, and nor-adrenaline), so that levels increase	A range of side-effects
	Tricyclics	As MAOIs	Dizziness, blurred vision, dry mouth
	SSRIs (e.g., Prozac)	As MAOIs, but mainly affect levels of serotonin	Preoccupation with suicide and violence
Depression (bipolar)	Lithium carbonate	Anti-mania, but mechanism is imperfectly understood	Side-effects on CNS, cardiovascular, and digestive systems. Overdose can be fatal
Anxiety disorders	Barbiturates	Treat symptoms of anxiety: palpitations, shortness of breath, accelerated heart rate, feeling of choking, nausea, dizziness, etc.	Problems of concentration, lack of co-ordination, slurred speech. Addictive. Withdrawal symptoms include delirium, irritability
	Benzodiazepines (e.g., Valium, Librium)	Have a sedative effect on the CNS	Drowsiness, lethargy, impairments of long-term memory. Withdrawal symptoms and possible addiction
	Buspirone	Affects dopamine receptors in the brain	Doesn't appear to have sedative effect, but other side-effects not yet established
Schizophrenia	Neuroleptic drugs (e.g., phenothiazines butyrophenones, thioxanthenes)	Reduce delusions, hallucinations	Little effect on lack of motivation and emotion, social withdrawal. Some patients report grogginess, sedation, difficulty concentrating, dry mouth, blurred vision
	Atypical anti-psychotic drugs (e.g., clozapine)	As neuroleptics, but with fewer side-effects	Expensive. May produce fatal blood disease in 1-2% of patients

Chemotherapy compares reasonably well against other forms of therapy. For example, Rosenhan and Seligman (1985) compared different forms of therapy in the treatment of schizophrenia, anxiety, and depression, and chemotherapy was about as effective as any other form of therapy with all three disorders. Cognitive therapy provided comparably effective treatment for anxiety and for depression, and family intervention was about as effective as chemotherapy for schizophrenia. In a very large-scale study, Barlow et al. (2000) found that chemotherapy using the tricyclic imipramine was as effective as cognitive-behavioural therapy in reducing the symptoms of panic disorder. However, drug therapy was less effective than cognitive-behavioural therapy at follow-up 6 months after treatment ended.

There are various problems with chemotherapy. First, it tends to take responsibility away from the patient and give it directly to the therapist or psychiatrist. Some people feel that drugs are used to keep patients quiet, i.e., they benefit the institution and society rather than the patient. However, note that the medical profession often effectively takes responsibility away from patients when treating physical illnesses, but few people seem to regard this as a problem!

Second, there is the problem of compliance with treatment. Patients often dislike taking drugs that have serious side-effects, and it is hard for therapists to ensure that the drugs are being taken as and when they should be. There have been tragic results in some cases where schizophrenic patients have stopped taking their medication.

CASE STUDY: CHEMOTHERAPY SAVES LIVES

Novelist blames depression in son's apparent overdose
Danielle Steel says he was manic-depressive

When Nicholas Traina was found dead of an apparent overdose during the weekend, his mother, novelist Danielle Steel, was heartbroken but not entirely surprised. Though her 19-year-old son had a history of drug use, the problem was much deeper: for his entire short life, Traina was tormented by mental illness. "The only time he messed around with drugs was when his medications failed him and he was desperate," Steel told *The Chronicle* in the first interview she has given since her son's death on Saturday. "This was not some wild kid, this was a very sick kid. The awful thing is I knew for years. He was manic-depressive, and wrestled with mental illness all his life. The biggest agony of my life is that for years, no one would listen to me that he was sick until we found a doctor in LA about 4 years ago who gave him amazing medication. He understood because he was manic-depressive, too."

Adapted from an article in the *San Francisco Chronicle*
17 September 1997.

To Dad, girl was Satan and thought he was Messiah when he killed daughter, 6, court told

Paranoid schizophrenic Ron England believed he was the Messiah ridding the world of evil when he murdered his mother and 6-year-old daughter, a psychiatrist says.

Dr Ian Jacques told a coroner's inquest yesterday England still does not believe his daughter, Jenny, and her grandma, Marian Johnston, are dead.

Jacques said England—who'd sworn off medication treating his severe mental illness—was "almost functioning on auto-pilot and getting his instructions (to kill) from television." England called 911 on April 2, 1996, to report he'd killed his mother and daughter at their home in Bowmanville. Marian Johnston, 79, was found slumped on her bed in pyjamas, housecoat and black boots. The former public health nurse, who'd helped England win supervised custody of Jenny over her biological parents, had been stabbed 34 times. On the floor lay Jenny with a knife embedded in her heart. She'd been stabbed 89 times.

Adapted from an article in the *Toronto Sun*.

Third, there is the problem that chemotherapy involves treating the symptoms rather than the underlying reasons. As a result, there is a real danger that the symptoms will reappear when chemotherapy comes to an end, or the patient simply has to take the drugs for life. This is a problem in light of the various side-effects there are with drugs.

Fourth, there are many patients who don't respond to drugs. The precise number varies from drug to drug and from disorder to disorder, but is often about 30–40% of patients treated by chemotherapy. The fact that drugs are not equally effective with all patients raises questions about their usefulness.

> **?** How would you explain the fact that drugs typically don't have the same effect on all people? What other factors might be involved?

General Issues for Evaluating Therapies

In the other two Sections of this chapter we will consider further methods of treatment for mental disorders, but first it is worth considering the basis for evaluating the effectiveness of any therapy, and the main ethical issues that should be considered. These discussions should help you to better understand the issues already touched and to better evaluate these issues as you read on.

How to assess effectiveness

To assess a given form of therapy, it is usual to compare the percentage of clients receiving that therapy who recover with the recovery percentage among clients receiving no therapy or a different form of therapy. There are various problems associated with this way of assessing therapeutic effectiveness:

- There are numerous ways of assessing recovery (e.g., in terms of behaviour or in terms of self-report measures); for example, the goal of therapy for psychodynamic therapists is to resolve internal conflicts, whereas for behaviour therapists it is to change overt behaviour.
- Therapy effective in producing recovery in the short term may or may not be effective in preventing relapse (return of the disorder) in the long term.

> **EXAM HINT**
>
> Use the general issues in therapy as a source of AO2 across the therapies.

? What are the possible reasons why it may be unethical to compare effects between a treated group of depressives (using drugs) and an untreated control group (using a placebo)?

- It is generally unethical to compare the effects of a given form of therapy with those found in a control group of patients denied treatment.
- It is often hard to tell whether any beneficial effects of therapy are due to specific factors (features unique to that form of therapy) or to common factors (e.g., patient expectations, personal qualities of the therapist).
- Account needs to be taken of the so-called placebo effect—the very fact of seeing a therapist can produce beneficial effects (e.g., by making the patient more optimistic) even if the therapist doesn't actually engage in any proper therapy at all (discussed further below).
- Any given form of therapy tends to be given in a different way by different therapists.
- The effectiveness of therapy depends in part on the skills and personal qualities of the therapist as well as on the content of the therapy.
- Some forms of therapy work much better with some kinds of patients than with others—psychodynamic therapy works best with patients who are young, attractive, verbally skilled, intelligent, and successful (Garfield, 1980). (If you take the first letters of young, attractive, and so on, you arrive at YAVIS, which may assist your memory for this list!)
- The **hello-goodbye effect** describes how patients exaggerate their symptoms prior to treatment and exaggerate their recovery afterwards to please their therapist.

? After reading this list, what would you conclude about the feasibility of evaluating the effectiveness of any therapy?

Individual cases

The diagnosis and treatment of a person suffering from, for example, an eating disorder is likely to vary from one individual to another, depending on the person's symptoms, their severity, and the individual case history. The effectiveness of the treatment may therefore hinge on the extent of the therapist's knowledge and understanding of each individual case, rather than on a specific psychological approach to eating disorders.

KEY TERMS

Hello-goodbye effect: the observation that patients tend to exaggerate their unhappiness at the beginning of therapy in order to convince the therapist that they are in genuine need. In contrast, at the end of therapy the reverse may be true; the patient may exaggerate their well-being to show appreciation to the therapist.
Placebo effect: positive responses to a drug or form of therapy based on the patient's beliefs that the drug or therapy will be effective, rather than on the actual make-up of the drug or therapy.

Strupp (1996) argued that the effectiveness of any given form of therapy should be considered from three different perspectives. First, there is the perspective of society including the individual's ability to function in society. Second, there is the client's own perspective including his/her overall subjective well-being. Third, there is the therapist's perspective. This includes relating the client's thinking and behaviour to the theoretical framework of mental disorder underlying the form of therapy used by the therapist. Recovery may vary considerably from one perspective to another.

Control groups

Suppose we find that clients receiving a given form of therapy are no more likely to recover than those in a control group not receiving any systematic therapy. Does this prove that the therapy is totally ineffective? It doesn't, because of the **placebo effect**. This effect has been found in drug research, where it refers to the finding that patients given a neutral substance (e.g., a salt tablet), but told they have been given a strong drug, will often show signs of medical improvement. Thus, the mistaken belief that one has received an effective form of treatment can produce strong beneficial effects. In similar fashion, according to Mair (1992), control clients who are led to expect that they will show improvement may do so:

As a symbolic communication that combats demoralisation by inspiring the patient's hopes for relief, administration of a placebo is a form of psychotherapy. It is therefore not surprising that placebos can provide marked relief in patients who seek psychotherapy.

General studies of therapy

Various studies have used the **meta-analysis** technique to compare the effectiveness of different therapies. Once we have reviewed the various different kinds of therapy in the rest of this chapter, we will consider findings from these comparative studies (see page 425).

Ethical issues in therapy

There are important ethical issues concerning therapy. These are associated with the more general topic of issues in psychological research discussed in Chapter 10, Issues (see pages 451–469). Here we will briefly consider major ethical issues relating to therapy.

Informed consent

It may seem obvious that therapy should only be carried out with the full informed consent of the client. To achieve that, the patient should be fully informed about the various forms of treatment available, about the probability of success of each treatment, about any possible dangers or side-effects, about the right to terminate treatment at any time, and about the likely cost of treatment. Evidence of the value of informed consent was reported by Devine and Fernald (1973). Snake phobics were shown four films of different forms of treatment. Those who were given their preferred form of treatment showed more recovery than those who were not.

There are strong ethical and practical reasons in favour of informed consent. In practice, as is discussed next, there are several reasons why full informed consent is not achieved.

First, the therapist may not have detailed information about the respective benefits and costs of different forms of treatment. In addition, some forms of treatment are very successful with some patients, but cause serious problems with others. These considerations mean that the therapist may be unable to provide the patient with enough information to come to a clear decision.

Second, the client or patient may find it hard to remember the information that he or she has been given by the therapist. Evidence on this issue was obtained by Irwin et al. (1985). They engaged in detailed questioning of patients who had said they understood the benefits and possible side-effects of a form of treatment. In fact, about 75% of them were mistaken, because they had forgotten important information.

Third, many clients cannot provide full informed consent. Examples include young children, those with severe learning difficulties, and schizophrenic patients. As far as schizophrenics are concerned, however, there is evidence (discussed by Davison & Neale, 1996) that they vary considerably in their ability to give informed consent. What typically happens when clients cannot give informed consent is that a guardian or close relative provides it.

Fourth, clients may agree to a form of treatment because of their exaggerated respect for the expertise of the therapist, rather than because of information about the likely benefits and costs of that treatment. This is perhaps especially likely to occur when the client has little or no prior knowledge of different forms of treatment.

Finally, we might consider the difficult problem of informed consent to treatment in cases in which the patient is likely to die without such treatment. The authorities may be in a difficult position with respect to informed consent in such

Do you think that by seeking help in the form of any kind of therapy, clients are in fact expressing hope for the future? Might this contribute to the placebo effect?

Why might informed consent increase the effectiveness of a therapy?

If a relative gives informal consent, might there be a conflict of interest?

KEY TERM

Meta-analysis: an analysis in which all of the findings from many studies relating to a given hypothesis are combined for statistical testing.

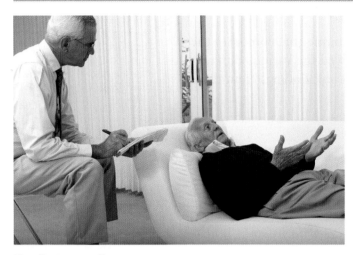

The client–counsellor relationship must be one based on implicit trust, if the former is to feel confident in divulging his or her most intimate details.

cases. Dwyer (2000, personal communication) reports the case of an adult anorexic who refused to give her consent for treatment and subsequently died. The deceased's family took the health authority to court on the basis that they should have treated the patient without her consent.

Confidentiality

Confidentiality is of basic importance in therapy. It is essential if the client is to trust the therapist, and so to feel free to disclose intimate details or his or her life. The law ensures confidentiality in most circumstances. For example, the Police and Criminal Evidence Act (1984) contains within it the requirement that there must be an order signed by a judge before the authorities can consider trying to gain access to a client's confidential records.

MacLeod (1998) pointed out that absolute confidentiality is unusual. For example, cases are discussed with other therapists working in the same place (e.g., a National Health Service Trust). This is done to ensure that clients obtain the best possible treatment, and isn't a matter for great concern. However, sensitive information about a patient is sometimes revealed to others *outside* the organisation for which the therapist works. Some examples are considered next.

Suppose it emerges during therapy that the client is thinking of killing someone against whom he/she has a grudge. If the therapist believes this is a serious threat, then he/she is under an obligation to tell the relevant authorities to ensure that the threat is not carried out. There are two sets of circumstances in which therapists in the United Kingdom have a legal obligation to disclose information about their clients to the relevant authorities. First, when the information is relevant to acts of terrorism. Second, when the information is of relevance to the welfare of children.

Confidentiality and anonymity

Anonymity is an important part of confidentiality. The discussion of case notes at a public lecture or in a published article or book must not involve identifying the client. A breach of this aspect of confidentiality could result in the client or client's relatives taking legal action against the therapist concerned. In situations like these, and with the permission of those involved, clients are usually identified by pseudonyms or initials only.

Effectiveness of Somatic Therapy

Finally, let's return to the question of how effective somatic therapies are. Most forms of somatic therapy (with the exception of psychosurgery) have proved fairly effective. There are common themes running through drug therapy for anxiety, depression, and schizophrenia. First, drugs are usually effective in producing a rapid reduction in symptoms. This can be very valuable, because drugs reduce distress, and may stop patients from attempting suicide. Another reason why drugs are useful with schizophrenia is because they may permit schizophrenic patients to benefit from therapy based on the attainment of insight (e.g., psychodynamic therapy).

Second, nearly all somatic therapies used in therapy have side-effects, and these side-effects can be serious and even dangerous. Third, most somatic therapies reduce the symptoms of a disorder, but don't provide a cure. However, they can form part of a combined therapeutic approach designed to produce a cure. Somatic therapies also have the benefit of requiring little effort on the part of the patient and being more suitable for patients who find it difficult to express their thoughts and feelings.

Somatic therapy emphasises changes in the physiological and biochemical systems, and so it seems especially appropriate to the treatment of disorders involving physiological and/or biochemical abnormalities. A clear example is schizophrenia. Drug therapy is also appropriate when patients are in state of great distress (e.g., anxiety disorders, depression). However, it is sometimes not sufficient on its own. For example, consider panic disorder. As we saw in Chapter 8, Psychopathology, these patients greatly exaggerate the seriousness of their own physiological symptoms. As a result, cognitive-behavioural therapy designed to reduce these exaggerated cognitions can be very effective in combination with chemotherapy (Barlow et al., 2000).

In general terms, somatic therapy is inappropriate for disorders that aren't clearly based on physiological or biochemical abnormalities. For example, cultural values and expectations play an important role in producing eating disorders, and so one might think that somatic therapy is unlikely to be of much relevance. However, genetic factors clearly play a role in the development of most eating disorders, and so somatic therapy may be useful in individual cases.

SECTION SUMMARY
Biological (Somatic) Therapies

❖ Trepanning was an early treatment for mental disorders that was a highly dangerous and ineffective practice.

❖ The main somatic therapies today are:

— Psychosurgery
— Electroconvulsive therapy
— Chemotherapy.

Methods of somatic therapies

❖ Prefrontal lobotomy: This was a method of controlling violent patients pioneered by Moniz in the 1930s. It had major side-effects so the approach is very rarely used today.

❖ Prefrontal leukotomy: This involves inserting fine needles to destroy nerve fibres.

❖ Stereotactic neurosurgery: This is even more refined and can be done under local anaesthesia.

❖ Amygdalotomies and cingulotomies: These have been performed to reduce aggression and curb emotion. There are serious side-effects with amygdalotomies but cingulotomies are used with some success. The ethics of causing permanent brain damage remain questionable.

Psychosurgery

❖ ECT has proved successful in treating depression.

❖ A weak electric current is usually applied to the non-dominant brain hemisphere along with muscle relaxants and an anaesthetic. The patient shows mild twitching and experiences little discomfort.

❖ ECT is used for cases of severe depression with some degree of effectiveness, though it is not seen as a cure.

Electroconvulsive therapy (ECT)

❖ ECT is preferred to drugs in some cases because:

— Some patients respond to ECT but not to drugs.
— ECT is also faster acting.

❖ Improvements may be due to expectations, but sham treatments showed much less improvement.

How appropriate is ECT?

❖ When considering the appropriateness of the treatment it is relevant to consider explanations for how the treatment works:

— ECT may act as a punishment, extinguishing the S-R link for learned maladaptive behaviours. However, sub-convulsive shocks don't appear to change behaviour despite being as unpleasant as shocks that do cause convulsions.
— Associated memory loss may allow some restructuring of disordered thinking, though unilateral ECT leads to minimal memory disruption yet is still effective.
— Levels of noradrenaline and serotonin are reduced, which wouldn't explain why some patients do experience a permanent cure.

❖ Ethical concerns remain because of the direct nature of brain intervention.

Chemotherapy

❖ Depression is treated with:

— MAOIs: increase levels of noradrenaline and serotonin.
— Tricyclics: increase levels of noradrenaline and serotonin. These tend to be more effective with severe depression and have fewer side-effects, though there are still some associated problems.
— SSRIs: affect serotonin levels only.

❖ They all reduce the symptoms of depression.
❖ There are individual differences in effectiveness.
❖ None of these drugs has much effect on the mood of normal individuals, supporting the view that they don't simply cause physiological arousal.
❖ Lithium carbonate reduces the occurrence of manic and depressed episodes in bipolar depressives.
❖ Anxiety disorders:

— These used to be treated by barbiturates until they were replaced by the benzodiazepines, though these often have sedative and addictive effects.
— Buspirone is a new drug with fewer side effects although it can reduce vigilance.

❖ Schizophrenia is treated with:

— Neuroleptics: however, these have little effect on the negative symptoms. Side-effects can be alleviated by "drug holidays". The drug may be given as an injection to ensure it is taken.
— Atypical anti-psychotic drugs: these are increasingly used since they have fewer side effects.

How appropriate is chemotherapy?

❖ There are several problems with chemotherapy:

— It tends to take responsibility away from the patient.
— Patients may not comply with treatment.

— Chemotherapy treats symptoms rather than causes.
— Drugs aren't always effective.

❖ However, chemotherapy has allowed a great number of people to live relatively normal lives.

❖ Effectiveness of any therapy can be assessed by comparing recovery rates of individuals who do or don't receive therapy.

❖ Problems with this are:

— The definition of "recovery" varies
— Patients may still relapse
— It is unethical to withhold treatment
— Effects may be due to common factors
— Each patient has unique symptoms
— Each therapist has unique characteristics
— Patients are self-selected samples
— Some therapies work better for some patients
— Apparent recovery may be due to the hello-goodbye effect.

Assessing the effectiveness of therapies

❖ Therapies can be evaluated from the point of view of society, the individual, and the therapist.

❖ Recovery in control groups may be due to the placebo effect.

❖ Therapy raises various ethical issues.

❖ Informed consent:

— Therapy is normally only carried out with the full informed consent of the client, which enhances its effectiveness.
— However, this isn't always possible because appropriate information isn't available, patients forget the information or can't understand it, and choices are based on the therapist rather than the treatment.

Ethical issues in therapy

See also pages 233–238 of the revision guide.

❖ Confidentiality:

— Absolute confidentiality is unusual.

❖ Somatic therapies are effective for disorders that have a biological basis.

❖ They can produce rapid results and require little effort from the patient, but they have side-effects and are not cures.

The effectiveness of somatic therapies

BEHAVIOURAL THERAPIES

Behavioural therapy was developed during the late 1950s and 1960s. The underlying notions are that most forms of mental illness occur through maladaptive learning, and that the best treatment consists of appropriate new learning or re-education. Behaviour therapists believe that abnormal behaviour develops through conditioning, and that it is through the use of the principles of conditioning that clients can recover. Thus, behavioural therapy is based on the assumption that classical and operant conditioning can change unwanted behaviour into a more desirable pattern. An important feature of behavioural

KEY TERM

Behavioural therapy: forms of clinical therapy based on the learning principles associated with classical and operant conditioning.

What is unwanted behaviour?

The term "unwanted behaviour" leads to questions about who decides which behaviour is disliked, unwanted, or abnormal. Usually the client himself or herself will decide that symptoms (e.g., phobic reactions) need treatment. Some behaviour is so anti-social that everyone agrees it is undesirable. However, it is possible for behaviour that those in authority decide is unacceptable to be labelled as "mental illness". Could the behaviour of rebellious young people, trade union activists, or lonely old people be construed as "ill" and in need of modification? Has this ever happened as far as you know?

Classical conditioning

- Unconditioned stimulus (UCS), e.g., food → causes → reflex response, e.g., salivation.
- Neutral stimulus (NS), e.g., bell → causes → no response.
- NS and UCS are paired in time (they occur at the same time).
- NS (e.g., bell) is now a conditioned stimulus (CS) → which produces → a conditioned response (CR) [a new stimulus-response link is learned, the bell causes salivation].

Operant conditioning

- A behaviour that has a positive effect is more likely to be repeated.
- Positive and negative reinforcement (escape from aversive stimulus) are agreeable.
- Punishment is disagreeable.

Assumptions of the behavioural model

- All behaviour is learned, and maladaptive behaviour is no different.
- This learning can be understood in terms of the principles of conditioning and modelling.
- What was learned can be unlearned, using the same principles.
- The same laws apply to human and non-human animal behaviour.

? How would you use behavioural therapy to address the maladaptive behaviour of compulsive lying?

therapy is its focus on *current* problems and behaviour, and on attempts to remove any symptoms the patient finds troublesome. This contrasts greatly with psychodynamic therapy, where the focus is much more on trying to uncover unresolved conflicts from childhood.

One of the distinguishing features of behavioural therapy is that more than other forms of therapy it is based on the scientific approach. As MacLeod (1998, p.571) pointed out:

> *The behavioural model of disorders and behaviour was a direct application of behavioural principles from experimental psychology, and was closely related to laboratory-based studies of learning (conditioning) which were often carried out on rats. As such, behavioural therapy has been ... closely connected with scientific methodology, both in elaborating the principles of therapy and in evaluating the success of therapy.*

A summary of the key ingredients in classical and operant conditioning are given in the box on the left. Here we will discuss some of the main forms of treatment used by behaviour therapists. After a brief general evaluation, we will deal with three forms of treatment based mainly on classical conditioning, and then consider treatment based on operant conditioning. It has sometimes been argued that the term "behavioural therapy" should be restricted to forms of therapy based on classical conditioning, with the term "behaviour modification" being used to apply to forms of therapy involving operant conditioning. However, what is done here is to use the term "behavioural therapy" in a general way to cover any therapy based on conditioning principles.

General Evaluation of Behavioural Therapy

There are *three* persistent criticisms of behavioural therapy. First, as Kendall and Hammen (1998, p.75) pointed out:

> *Critics have described behavioural therapy as mechanical in its application and as limiting the benefits of treatment to changes in observable behaviour.*

Second, it has been argued that the focus of behaviour therapists on eliminating symptoms is very limited. In particular, psychodynamic therapists claim that the failure to consider the underlying causes of mental illness leads to the danger of **symptom substitution**. Thus, one symptom may be eliminated, but the underlying problems lead to its replacement with another symptom.

Third, there is what is known as the problem of generalisation. The application of behavioural therapy may serve to produce the desired behaviour by the patient in the therapist's room. However, it doesn't necessarily follow that the same behaviour will be produced in other situations.

This 18cm poisonous spider is perhaps more terrifying than the type that would be used in flooding!

Behavioural Therapies Based on Classical Conditioning

Flooding or exposure

According to behaviour therapists, phobic fears (e.g., of spiders) are acquired by means of classical conditioning, in which the phobic stimulus is associated with a painful or aversive stimulus that creates fear. This fear can be reduced by avoiding the phobic stimulus.

One way of breaking the link between the conditioned stimulus (e.g., spider) and fear is by experimental extinction. This can be achieved by a technique known as **flooding** or exposure, in which the client is exposed to an extremely fear-provoking situation. In the case of a spider phobic, the client could either be put in a room full of spiders or asked to imagine being surrounded by dozens of spiders. The client is initially flooded or overwhelmed by fear and anxiety. However, the fear typically starts to subside after some time. If the client can be persuaded to remain in the situation for long enough, there is often a marked reduction in fear.

Why is flooding or exposure effective? We have seen that behaviourists argue that extinction of the conditioned fear response is responsible. However, cognitive therapists (e.g., Salkovskis, 1996) prefer an alternative explanation. According to them, flooding or exposure teaches the patient that there is no objective basis to his/her fears (e.g., the spiders don't actually cause any bodily harm). In everyday life, the phobic person would avoid those stimuli relevant to the phobia, and so would have no chance to learn this.

The main problem with the flooding technique is that it is deliberately designed to produce very high levels of fear. It can, therefore, have a very disturbing effect on the client. If the client feels compelled to bring the session to a premature end, this may teach him/her that avoidance of the phobic stimulus is rewarding, in the sense that it leads to reduced fear. This can make later treatment of the phobic harder.

Systematic desensitisation

Joseph Wolpe (1958) developed an alternative form of behavioural therapy for phobic patients known as **systematic desensitisation**. It is based on **counterconditioning**, and involves the attempt to replace the fear response to phobic stimuli with a new response incompatible with fear. This new response is usually muscle relaxation. Clients are initially given special training in deep

You might consider Mowrer's (1947) two-process theory for phobias, described on page 378.

KEY TERMS

Symptom substitution: when one symptom is eliminated, but the underlying problems lead to its replacement with another symptom.
Flooding: a form of behavioural therapy where a patient is given maximum exposure to a feared stimulus until their fear subsides, thus extinguishing a learned response.
Systematic desensitisation: a form of treatment for phobias, in which the fear response to threatening stimuli is replaced by a different response such as muscle relaxation.
Counterconditioning: in systematic desensitisation, substituting a relaxation response for a fear response to threatening stimuli.

Fear of dogs

If an individual has a fear of dogs, systematic desensitisation could be used to overcome this. The client might have learned their fear in the following way:

- Child is bitten by dog. Unpleasant bite (UCS) → fear (UCR).
- Dog (NS) paired with UCS, becomes CS → fear (now CR).

This can be overcome by associating the dog with a new response—relaxation.

- Dog (CS) → fear (CR).
- Dog paired with new UCS (relaxation) → pleasant feelings (CR).

relaxation until they can rapidly achieve muscle relaxation when instructed to do so.

What happens next is that the client and the therapist together construct what is known as an "anxiety hierarchy", in which the client's feared situations are ordered from the least to the most anxiety-provoking. Thus, for example, a spider phobic might regard one small, stationary spider 5 metres away as only modestly threatening, but a large, rapidly moving spider 1 metre away as highly threatening. The client reaches a state of deep relaxation, and is then asked to imagine (or is confronted by) the least threatening situation in the anxiety hierarchy. The client repeatedly imagines (or is confronted by) this situation until it fails to evoke any anxiety at all, indicating that the counterconditioning has been successful. This process is repeated while working through all of the situations in the anxiety hierarchy until the most anxiety-provoking situation of all is reached.

Aversion therapy

Aversion therapy is used when there are stimulus situations and associated behaviour patterns that are attractive to the client, but which the therapist and the client both regard as undesirable. For example, alcoholics enjoy going to pubs and consuming large amounts of alcohol. **Aversion therapy** involves associating such stimuli and behaviour with a very unpleasant unconditioned stimulus, such as an electric shock. The client thus learns to associate the undesirable behaviour with the electric shock, and a link is formed between the undesirable behaviour and the reflex response to an electric shock.

In the case of alcoholism, what is often done is to require the client to take a sip of alcohol while under the effect of a nausea-inducing drug such as Antabuse. Sipping the drink is followed almost at once by vomiting and/or nausea. In future the smell of alcohol produces a memory of vomiting and should stop drinking. A problem with this approach is that it is all stick and no carrot, and so patients often refuse to continue with treatment. A promising development involves drugs based on tryptophan metabolites. These drugs (which have only been tested in the laboratory so far) make patients feel ill if they have even a small amount of alcohol. However, they also increase serotonin levels, so that patients will have an increased sense of well-being provided that they don't drink. It is hoped that patients will find it easier to continue treatment with these drugs than with previous ones.

Apart from ethical considerations (mentioned earlier), there are two other issues relating to the use of aversion therapy. First, it is not very clear how the

KEY TERM

Aversion therapy: a form of treatment in which undesirable behaviour is eliminated by associating it with severe punishment (classical conditioning).

Aversion therapy

- (UCS) Electric shock → (UCR) fear
- (NS) Pornographic pictures → pleasure

Conditioning: Pornographic pictures associated with electric shock

- (CS) Pornographic pictures → (CR) fear
- (UCS) Vomiting → (UCR) displeasure
- (NS) Alcohol → pleasure

Conditioning: Alcohol associated with vomiting

- (CS) Alcohol → (CR) displeasure

shocks or drugs have their effects. It may be that they make the previously attractive *stimulus* (e.g., sight of alcohol) aversive, or it may be that they inhibit the *behaviour* of drinking. Second, there are doubts about the long-term effectiveness of aversion therapy. It can have dramatic effects in the therapist's office. However, it is often much less effective in the outside world, where no nausea-inducing drug has been taken and it is obvious that no shocks will be given (Comer, 2001).

? People are often sick after drinking too much alcohol. According to aversion therapy this should put them off drinking. Why doesn't this appear to happen?

Behavioural Therapies Based on Operant Conditioning

So far we have focused on forms of behavioural therapy based on classical conditioning. However, much behaviour involves the use of operant conditioning. Therapy using operant conditioning is based on a careful analysis of the maladaptive behaviour of the client and on the reinforcers or rewards maintaining that behaviour. When the therapist has a clear idea of the current patterns of behaviour and their causes, he/she tries to produce environmental changes to increase the rewards for adaptive behaviour and decrease the rewards for maladaptive behaviour.

There are various techniques open to the behaviour therapist using operant conditioning:

- *Extinction*: if a maladaptive behaviour is performed by a patient because it is followed by positive reinforcement, then the incidence of that behaviour can be reduced or extinguished by ensuring the behaviour is no longer followed by reward. Crooks and Stein (1991) discussed an example of extinction involving a 20-year-old woman who picked away at any small spot or blemish on her face until it started bleeding. This compulsive behaviour seemed to be rewarded by the attention she received from her fiancé and from her family. When this behaviour was ignored, but her desirable forms of behaviour received attention, she rapidly stopped exhibiting her compulsive behaviour.
- *Selective punishment*: a specific maladaptive behaviour is punished by means of an aversive stimulus (e.g., electric shock) whenever it occurs; this is part of what is involved in aversion therapy.
- *Selective positive reinforcement*: a specific adaptive behaviour (or "target behaviour") is selected, and positive reinforcement is provided whenever this target behaviour is produced by the patient. This is the approach used by token economies (see next).

? All three of the operant conditioning techniques are limited by ethical considerations. Which of the three presents the most ethical problems? Why do you think this is the case?

Token economies

One important form of therapy based on selective positive reinforcement or reward is the token economy. This is used with institutionalised patients, who are given tokens (e.g., coloured counters) for behaving in appropriate ways. These tokens can later be used to obtain various privileges (e.g., playing snooker; cigarettes). Ayllon and Azrin (1968) carried out a classic study. Female patients who had been hospitalised for an average of 16 years were rewarded with plastic tokens for actions such as making their beds or combing their hair. The tokens were exchanged for pleasant activities such as seeing a film or having an additional visit to the canteen. This token economy was very successful. The number of chores the patients performed each day increased from about five to over 40 when this behaviour was rewarded with tokens.

Paul and Lentz (1977) used a token economy with long-term hospitalised schizophrenic patients. As a result, the patients developed various social and work-related skills, they became better able to look after themselves, and their symptoms were reduced. These findings are all the more impressive in that they were achieved at the same time as there was a substantial reduction in the number of drugs being given to the patients.

More recently, Jordan et al. (2003) used a token economy with a 7-year-old boy suffering from autism who made bomb noises, hit and pushed staff, and yelled verbal comments. He was offered various rewards (e.g., popcorn, playing skittles) if he avoided these kinds of behaviour. As a result of this token economy, there was a significant reduction in his undesirable behaviour.

Evaluation

Token economies have proved moderately effective with groups of patients (e.g., institutionalised schizophrenics) resistant to most forms of therapy. The main problem with token economies is that the beneficial effects they produce are often greatly reduced when good behaviour is no longer followed by the rewards the patients have grown used to receiving. Thus, there is a danger that token economies may produce only token (i.e., minimal) learning. There is no easy answer to this problem. Token economies work because the environment is carefully structured so that good behaviour is consistently rewarded and bad behaviour is not. The outside world is very different, and patients find it hard to *transfer* what they have learned in a token economy to the much less structured environment outside the institution.

One reason for the poor transfer may be that patients have been selectively reinforced in particular situations and therefore would only reproduce the rewarded behaviour in that situation. This is an example of **context-dependent learning**.

A second problem is that the use of external rewards may actually destroy intrinsic motivation. Rewarding people for the absence of negative behaviour, rather than when positive behaviour actually occurs, may not produce a change in the person, because they aren't making a moral decision based on the protection of their own self-esteem, but rather for an external reward.

Third, this form of therapy underestimates the importance of cognitive processes. Although the use of incentives to reward good behaviour may eradicate undesirable behaviour, it may also fail to build a patient's personal autonomy. This will be essential when he or she is faced with choices about how to behave in a given setting.

Fourth, token economies reward patients for socially acceptable behaviour, but they don't allow for variations in patients' capabilities. These may result in fewer tokens being given to the more maladapted individuals because they are more unstable and less able to learn new skills. This might have the undesirable effect of creating a hierarchy in which self-esteem becomes weakened among the more vulnerable people.

Finally, we should consider the ethics of behaviour manipulation. The "desired behaviours" or goals are decided by the institution and may not be acceptable to the patient, given a free choice.

? What does the word "token" refer to in "token economies"?

? What could be done to increase transfer of learning to the outside world?

KEY TERM

Context-dependent learning: recall is better when it occurs in the same context as original learning. May result in learning that some behaviours are appropriate in some contexts and not in others.

Modelling

Modelling is another form of behavioural therapy, based on the principles of vicarious reinforcement and social learning theory. Modelling can also be used in order to treat phobias. A patient watches the therapist experiencing the phobic situation and then imitates the same behaviour. Bandura, Blanchard, and Ritter (1969) found that the therapy was most effective when working with a live example of the feared object (such as a real snake) rather than a symbolic representation. Modelling has been successfully used to help people cope better in social situations and situations they found fearful, such as going to the dentist. They watch other people coping well in such situations and then imitate their behaviour.

Modelling has been extended to wider use as **social skills training**. This is particularly useful in cases of individuals who lack important social skills, such as bullies or autistic children. Goddard and Cross (1987) described a course developed for disruptive pupils that included skills such as listening, apologising, dealing with teasing and bullying, and gaining feedback from video recordings. In all cases long-term benefits were gained by training the parents so that they could continue the programmes at home. Lovaas et al. (1967) trained autistic children in language skills using shaping and positive reinforcement. "Time out" is a technique used to train hyperactive children. When they behave uncontrollably they receive attention which, despite being negative, is positively reinforcing. In order to break this cycle, unacceptable behaviour is treated with time in temporary isolation until they calm down. To be effective this should be accompanied by child-centred attention for good behaviour.

Empirical support for the power of social skills training was provided in a study by Cooke and Apolloni (1976). Children who were excessive shy or solitary were exposed to live models who demonstrated various social skills, such as smiling at others, sharing, initiating positive physical contact, and giving verbal compliments. The study found that the same behaviours did increase in the target children and, in addition, the children showed increases in other positive social behaviours that had not been modelled. Also, the behaviours of untrained children in contact with the target child also showed increases in positive social behaviours.

Modelling works best when the model is similar to the child, for example the model initially acts shy and withdrawn, and when the actions to be imitated are accompanied by some form of commentary that directs the observer's attention to the purposes and benefits of the actions (Asher, Renshaw, & Hymel, 1982).

> **KEY TERMS**
>
> **Modelling:** imitation; a form of learning or therapy based on observing a model and imitating that behaviour.
> **Social skills training:** a form of therapy based on the behavioural approach that involves teaching appropriate social skills by using rewards, modelling, and conditioning.

Effectiveness of Behavioural Therapy

Behavioural therapy is a moderately effective form of therapy. Smith, Glass, and Miller (1980) found that behavioural therapy was as effective as other major forms of therapy. Subsequent reviews of the literature have suggested that behavioural therapy and cognitive-behavioural therapy are usually more effective than psychodynamic therapy (see the next Section).

Behavioural therapy, especially exposure, is often very effective with anxiety disorders. Ost (1989) used

> **EXAM HINT**
>
> In a question on behavioural therapies, you may have to decide which therapies to cover. You could choose two therapies that derive from classical conditioning or two that derive from operant conditioning, or one from each. It is probably wisest to cover one from each in depth as this will offer more scope for AO2, you may then cover one or two more in less detail. Do not cover more than four therapies in this section, or your answer will have breadth but not depth.

one-session exposure on patients with specific phobias, and reported that "90% of the patients obtained a clinically significant improvement . . . which was maintained after an average of 4 years". Exposure therapy has also proved effective in the treatment of social phobia and agoraphobia. Indeed, it is sometimes described as the "gold standard" against which other forms of therapy for anxiety disorders should be compared. For example, Feske and Chambless (1995) found in a meta-analysis of 15 studies of social phobia that exposure on its own was as effective as exposure plus cognitive therapy in producing recovery.

One of the few anxiety disorders for which exposure isn't very effective is obsessive-compulsive disorder. Van Oppen et al. (1995) found that 17% of patients with obsessive-compulsive disorder recovered after exposure therapy, compared with 39% who received cognitive therapy.

The success of some forms of behavioural therapy doesn't depend on the factors claimed by behaviour therapists to be responsible. For example, Wolpe (1958) assumed that systematic desensitisation works because clients learn to link a relaxation response to phobic stimuli. Lick (1975) obtained evidence that this isn't the whole story. He told his clients that he was presenting them with subliminal phobic stimuli (i.e., below the level of conscious awareness) and that repetition of these stimuli reduced their physiological fear reactions. In fact, he didn't present any stimuli, and the feedback about physiological responses was fake! In view of Lick's total failure to follow the "correct" procedures, it would be expected by behaviour therapists that the therapy should have been ineffective. In fact, Lick's "make-believe" procedure was successful in reducing the clients' fear responses to phobic stimuli. Presumably the "make-believe" procedure made the clients think they could control their fear, even though the counter-conditioning emphasised by behaviour therapists didn't occur. It also may be that the relationship between client and therapist is important to recovery, even in behavioural therapies.

Behavioural therapy is most appropriate in the treatment of disorders in which behavioural symptoms are central, and is least appropriate when the key symptoms are internal. For example, specific phobics have the behavioural symptom of avoidance of the phobic stimulus, and behavioural therapy works well with that disorder (Ost, 1989). In contrast, many of the key symptoms of obsessive-compulsive disorder are in the form of internal thoughts and obsessions, and behavioural therapy is no more than modestly effective (van Oppen et al., 1995).

Behavioural therapy is also not very appropriate when dealing with serious disorders having a fairly large genetic component. The prime example here is schizophrenia. Token economies have been successful in modifying the behaviour of schizophrenics in desirable ways, but no form of behavioural therapy has removed the main symptoms of schizophrenia.

> [?] Does the fact that clients in Lick's study experienced a positive outcome override the ethical problems of the deception he used?

> [?] In any therapy, how does one know if effectiveness is due to the personal characteristics of the therapist rather than the therapy itself?

SECTION SUMMARY
Behavioural Therapies

What is behavioural therapy?

❖ Behavioural therapy involves the use of classical and operant conditioning to change unwanted behaviour into something more desirable.

❖ Maladaptive behaviours that were learned can be unlearned.

❖ Therapy focuses on behaviour and symptom removal.
❖ Criticisms of behavioural therapy are:

— Its mechanistic nature
— The problems of symptom substitution and lack of generalisation.

❖ These include flooding, systematic desensitisation, and aversion therapy.
❖ Flooding:

— This aims to break the phobic cycle by demonstrating that there is no basis to the fear, but it may be disturbing and result in increased resistance.

❖ Systematic desensitisation:

— This involves counterconditioning. An anxiety hierarchy is constructed and at each stage the client practises relaxation to learn a new response that is incompatible with fear.

❖ Aversion therapy:

— This involves pairing the undesired behaviour (NS) with a very unpleasant stimulus (UCS) to produce a new response (CR) to the undesired behaviour, and so suppress it.
— This learning may not transfer to the real world.
— However, drugs based on tryptophan metabolites for the treatment of alcoholism are promising.

Therapies based on classical conditioning

❖ These aim to identify how maladaptive behaviours are being reinforced, and to decrease them while increasing reinforcement for adaptive behaviours.
❖ This can be done using:

— Extinction
— Selective punishment
— Selective positive reinforcement: including use of token economies.

Therapies based on operant conditioning

❖ Token economies offer rewards for achieving small behavioural goals:

— They have proved successful but the beneficial effects may disappear when the rewards are no longer given.
— This may be due to the nature of context-dependent learning, or the fact that rewards destroy intrinsic motivation.
— The therapy also underestimates the importance of cognitive processes.
— Variations in patient capabilities and ethics should also be considered.

❖ Modelling therapy is based on vicarious reinforcement and imitation, and has been extended to social skills training, which is effective with, for example, disruptive pupils and autistic children.

See also pages 239–244 of the revision guide.

❖ Research indicates reasonable success for behavioural therapies but such success may be due to expectations and/or therapist variables.
❖ Behavioural therapies are most suitable for disorders where behavioural symptoms are central.

The effectiveness of behavioural therapies

ALTERNATIVES TO BIOLOGICAL AND BEHAVIOURAL THERAPIES

In this Section we will consider two further approaches to the treatment of mental disorders.

Cognitive Therapy

Behavioural therapy focuses on *external* stimuli and responses, and ignores the *internal* cognitive processes (e.g., thoughts, beliefs) happening between stimulus and response. This omission was dealt with in the early 1960s with the introduction of **cognitive therapy**, based on the assumption that successful treatment can involve changing or restructuring clients' cognitions or thinking.

Ellis' rational-emotive therapy (RET)

Albert Ellis (1962) was one of the first therapists to put forward a version of cognitive therapy. He argued that anxiety and depression occur as the end points in a three-point sequence, as illustrated in the diagram below.

According to the A-B-C model shown in this diagram, anxiety and depression don't occur as a direct result of unpleasant events. More precisely, these negative mood states are produced by the irrational thoughts that follow from the occurrence of unpleasant events. The interpretations produced at point B depend on the individual's belief system and in turn determine how much anxiety and/or depression someone will experience.

Ellis (1962) developed **rational-emotive therapy** as a way of removing irrational and self-defeating thoughts and replacing them with more rational and positive ones. As Ellis (1978) pointed out:

> If he [the individual] wants to be minimally disturbable and maximally sane, he'd better substitute for all his absolutistic "It's terribles" two other words which he does not parrot or give lip-service to but which he incisively thinks through and accepts—namely, "Too bad!" or "Tough shit!".

In more technical terms, Ellis argued that individuals who are anxious or depressed should create a point D. This is a dispute belief system that allows them to interpret life's events in ways that do not cause them emotional distress.

Rational-emotive therapy starts with the therapist making patients aware of the self-defeating nature of many of their beliefs. Patients are then encouraged to ask themselves searching questions about these beliefs to discover whether these

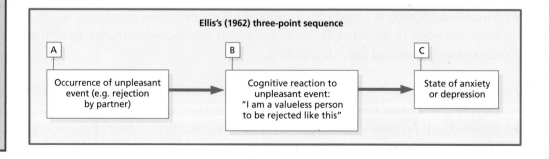

Ellis's (1962) three-point sequence

A — Occurrence of unpleasant event (e.g. rejection by partner) → B — Cognitive reaction to unpleasant event: "I am a valueless person to be rejected like this" → C — State of anxiety or depression beliefs are rational and logical. For example, patients may be told to ask themselves questions such as the following: "Why do I have to be liked by everybody?"; "Why is it so terrible if I can't have my own way all the time?"; "Does it really matter if I am not competent in every way?" After that, patients are taught to replace their faulty and irrational beliefs with more realistic ones (e.g., "It is impossible to be liked by everybody, but most people like me"; "My life can be happy even if I sometimes can't do what I want"; "I will strive to be fairly competent, and accept that perfection cannot be achieved"). The crucial final step is for patients to have *full acceptance* of these new, rational beliefs.

Convincing evidence that anxious patients are much more likely than normals to have irrational beliefs was reported by Newmark et al. (1973). They found that 65% of anxious patients (but only 2% of normals) agreed with the statement, "It is essential that one be loved or approved of by virtually everyone in his community." The statement, "One must be perfectly competent, adequate, and achieving to consider oneself worthwhile", was agreed with by 80% of anxious patients compared with 25% of normals.

■ **Activity:** Devise a situation like the following example and describe how the thoughts, emotions, and behaviour that result from it could be changed.

It is your birthday and you are given a surprise invitation to meet your friends at lunchtime to celebrate. You are disappointed to find that your best friend does not join you and gives no reason or apology.

	Irrational/negative	Rational/positive
Thoughts	He/she is annoyed with you but won't say why	Maybe he/she was under pressure with work, etc.
Emotions	Hurt and upset. Perhaps you aren't friends after all	Disappointed, but sure you'll get together soon to celebrate
Behaviour	Treat him/her with cool detachment next time you meet	Ring him/her to arrange to meet

---

Evaluation of Ellis' approach

Therapists using rational-emotive therapy tend to be much more argumentative than those using client-centred therapy (see page 425), and they show less concern for the sensitivities of their clients. It may well be that which form of therapy is preferable depends on the individual client. For example, rational-emotive therapy is especially effective with clients who feel guilty because of their own perceived inadequacies and who generally impose high demands on themselves (Brandsma, Maultsby, & Welsh, 1978). Rational-emotive therapy seems more suitable for individuals suffering from anxiety or depression than for those with severe thought disorders (Barlow & Durand, 1995).

? Why does rational-emotive therapy appear to be more effective with individuals suffering from anxiety or depression than those who have severe thought disorders?

Beck's cognitive therapy

Probably the most influential cognitive therapist is Aaron Beck. He has developed forms of cognitive therapy for anxiety, but is better known for his work on depression. Beck (1976) argued that therapy for depression should involve uncovering and challenging the negative and unrealistic beliefs of depressed clients. Of great importance is the **cognitive triad**. This consists of negative thoughts which depressed individuals have about themselves, about the world, and about the future (see also page 365). Depressed clients typically regard

KEY TERM

Cognitive triad: negative thoughts about the self, the world, and the future, found in depressed clients.

? Think of an occasion when you felt helpless or worthless. Could you try to reinterpret the situation in a more positive way?

themselves as helpless, worthless, and inadequate. They interpret events in the *world* in an unrealistically negative and defeatist way, and they see the world as posing obstacles that cannot be handled. The final part of the cognitive triad involves depressed individuals seeing the *future* as totally hopeless, because their worthlessness will prevent any improvement occurring in their situation.

According to Beck et al. (1979), the first stage of cognitive therapy involves the therapist and the client agreeing on the nature of the problem and on the goals for therapy. This stage is called collaborative empiricism. The client's negative thoughts are then tested out by the therapist challenging them or by the client engaging in certain forms of behaviour between therapy sessions. It is hoped that the client will come to accept that many of his/her negative thoughts are irrational and unrealistic. For example, a depressed client who argues that people are always avoiding him/her can be asked to keep a diary of specific occasions on which this happens. It is very likely that it happens much less often than the patient imagines.

> **Assumptions of the cognitive model**
> - Maladaptive behaviour is caused by faulty and irrational cognitions.
> - It is the way you think about a problem, rather than the problem itself, that causes mental disorder.
> - Individuals can overcome mental disorders by learning to use more appropriate cognitions.
> - Aim to be positive and rational.

Cognitive therapy: A summary

Cognitive therapists differ among themselves in terms of the approaches they adopt towards their clients. However, the common features were identified by Beck and Weishaar (1989, p.308):

> *Cognitive therapy consists of highly specific learning experiences designed to teach patients (1) to monitor their negative, automatic thoughts (cognitions); (2) to recognise the connections between cognition, affect, and behaviour; (3) to examine the evidence for and against distorted automatic thoughts; (4) to substitute more reality-oriented interpretations for these biased cognitions; and (5) to learn to identify and alter the beliefs that predispose them to distort their experiences.*

Cognitive-behavioural Therapy (CBT)

In recent years, there have been increasing efforts to add some of the more successful features of behavioural therapy to cognitive therapy. This combination is referred to as **cognitive-behavioural therapy**. According to Kendall and Hammen (1998), the four basic assumptions underlying cognitive-behavioural therapy are as follows:

1. Patients typically respond on the basis of their *interpretations* of themselves and the world around them rather than on the basis of what is *actually* the case.
2. Thoughts, behaviour, and feelings are all interrelated and all influence each other. Thus, it would be wrong to identify one of these factors (e.g., behaviour) as being more important than the others.
3. In order for therapeutic interventions to be successful, they need to clarify, and to change, the ways people think about themselves and about the world around them.
4. It is very desirable to try to change both the client's cognitive processes and his/her behaviour, because the benefits of therapy are likely to be greater than when only cognitive processes or behaviour are changed.

KEY TERM

Cognitive behavioural therapy: a development of cognitive therapy where some elements of behavioural therapy (such as a focus on behaviour change) have been added.

We have already considered some of the ways in which cognitive therapists such as Ellis (1962) and Beck (1976) try to restructure the thoughts and beliefs of their clients. They also try to change the behaviour of their clients in a fairly direct fashion, and so can be regarded as cognitive-behavioural therapists. Beck (1976) instructs his clients to monitor and log their thought processes between therapy sessions. He also emphasises the use of homework assignments that require clients to behave in ways in which they were previously unable to behave. A client suffering from a high level of social anxiety might be told to initiate conversations with everyone in his/her office over the following few days. A crucial ingredient in such homework assignments is *hypothesis testing*. Clients typically predict that carrying out their homework assignments will make them feel anxious or depressed, and so they are told to test these predictions. What generally happens is that the clients' hypotheses are shown to be too pessimistic, and this speeds up the rate of recovery.

In what ways might a person's thoughts about themselves influence the way they react in a particular situation?

Stress inoculation therapy

Meichenbaum (e.g., 1977, 1985, 1996) proposed a form of cognitive-behavioural therapy known as stress inoculation therapy. The essence of this form of therapy is to replace negative and irrational thoughts (e.g., "I am totally incompetent") with positive and rational ones (e.g., "I can achieve many things if I try hard enough"). Meichenbaum argued that we should use stress inoculation therapy *before* people become very anxious or depressed rather than afterwards.

There are three main phases to stress inoculation therapy:

1. *Conceptualisation phase*: the therapist discusses the nature of the problem with the individual, together with the individual's perception of how to eliminate it. The individual is encouraged to regard threats and stressors as problems to be solved, and to identify those aspects of the situation that can be changed.
2. *Skills acquisition and rehearsal*: the individual learns various techniques for reducing stress (e.g., relaxation, self-instruction). The essence of self-instruction is that the individual practises several coping self-statements. The self-statements vary across stages of a stressful situation:

   - Preparing for a stressor (e.g., "What do I have to do?")
   - Confronting and handling a stressor (e.g., "Relax and take a slow, deep breath")
   - Coping with the feeling of being overwhelmed (e.g., "Just try to keep fear at a manageable level").

   The self-statements and other coping skills are then gradually rehearsed in real-life situations.
3. *Application and follow-through*: the individual imagines using the stress reduction techniques learned in the second phase in difficult situations, and/or engages in role play of such situations with the therapist. The techniques the individual has learned are applied across increasing levels of stressors.

Research findings

Meichenbaum (1977) compared his stress inoculation therapy against systematic desensitisation (discussed earlier). These methods were applied to individuals who suffered from both snake phobia and rat phobia, but treatment was only provided for one phobia. Both forms of treatment were effective in reducing or eliminating the treated phobia. However, stress inoculation therapy also greatly reduced the non-treated phobia, whereas systematic desensitisation did not. Thus, self-instruction easily generalises to new situations, which makes it more useful than very specific forms of treatment.

Holcomb (1986) compared three forms of therapy for patients with severe stress and anxiety disorders: stress inoculation therapy; stress inoculation therapy + chemotherapy; and chemotherapy. Stress inoculation therapy was more effective than chemotherapy in reducing patients' symptoms of depression, anxiety, and subjective distress. Over the following 3 years, patients in the stress inoculation group had fewer re-admissions with mental disorders than did those in the other two groups.

Meichenbaum (1996) reviewed some of the evidence on stress inoculation therapy. He pointed out that this form of therapy has been used successfully in the treatment of numerous stressors including the following: surgery, military combat, medical illness, divorce, and rape.

Evaluation

Stress inoculation therapy has proved effective in treating stress stemming from numerous causes. In general, stress inoculation therapy compares reasonably well against other forms of therapy when used with individuals whose levels of stress and anxiety are only moderately high. However, stress inoculation therapy is less successful than other forms of therapy with patients suffering from very high levels of anxiety. For example, Sanchez-Canovas (1991) reported that stress inoculation therapy was of only modest usefulness in the treatment of generalised anxiety disorder. Presumably individuals who are extremely anxious find it difficult to use coping self-statements effectively.

Effectiveness of Cognitive and Cognitive-behavioural Therapy

Cognitive therapy and cognitive-behavioural therapy both involve taking full account of the client's own views of the world, no matter how distorted those views might be. If one is trying to produce beneficial change, then it is of value to have clear evidence of the client's present state. There are some advantages of cognitive-behavioural therapy over cognitive therapy, in that many of the symptoms about which clients are concerned are related to their behaviour. As a result, it is reasonable to try to change behaviour *directly*, as well as *indirectly* by changing some of their thoughts and beliefs.

Beck's approach is more developed and sophisticated than that of Ellis. Ellis tends to assume that rather similar irrational beliefs underlie most mental disorders, whereas Beck argues that specific irrational beliefs are associated with each disorder. In spite of the limitations of Ellis's rational-emotive therapy, it is reasonably effective. Engels, Garnefski, and Diekstra (1993) found, across 28 studies, that rational-emotive therapy was as effective as systematic desensitisation and markedly superior to no treatment.

Cognitive-behavioural therapy has proved successful in the treatment of depression and anxiety disorders, and Meichenbaum (1985) has shown its effectiveness in stress reduction (this was discussed in your AS level studies). However, it is of little value in the treatment of disorders that don't involve irrational beliefs. Dobson (1989) reviewed 28 studies of therapy for depression. He concluded that cognitive therapy compared favourably to other forms of psychotherapy in most of the studies. Cognitive-behavioural therapy works well with nearly all anxiety disorders (Eysenck, 1997), but is especially effective with panic disorder. According to Rachman (1993, p.279), "As far as anxiety disorders are concerned, the greatest theoretical and clinical progress has been made in applying cognitive-behavioural therapy (CBT) to the . . . treatment of panic." It is also more effective than behavioural therapy in the treatment of obsessive-compulsive disorder (van Oppen et al., 1995).

Cognitive-behavioural therapy combines the advantages of cognitive therapy and behavioural therapy, and so provides appropriate forms of treatment for a wide range of disorders. As it is also a very inexpensive and cost-effective form of treatment, it is being used increasingly in Britain and the United States as the preferred form of therapy. Cognitive-behavioural therapy has limited appropriateness for the treatment of schizophrenia. However, schizophrenia is a very serious disorder that has proved extremely hard to treat successfully.

> [?] Are there any ethical problems involved in using cost-effectiveness as a criterion for the choice of a preferred form of therapy?

Psychodynamic Therapy

Psychodynamic therapy is based on psychoanalysis, and was introduced by Sigmund Freud at the start of the twentieth century. Some of the principles of psychoanalysis were developed in various ways by Freud's followers such as Carl Jung and Alfred Adler.

> **KEY TERM**
>
> **Repression:** the process of forcing very threatening thoughts and memories out of the conscious mind in Freudian theory; motivated forgetting.

Psychoanalysis

According to Freud, neuroses such as the anxiety disorders occur as a result of conflicts among the three parts of the mind: the ego (rational mind), the id (sexual and other instincts), and the superego (conscience). These conflicts, many of which go back to early childhood, cause the ego to use various defence mechanisms to protect itself (see page 241). The key defence mechanism is repression. **Repression** consists of forcing painful, threatening, or unacceptable thoughts and memories out of consciousness into the unconscious mind. The forces of repression then prevent these thoughts and memories from reappearing in consciousness. The repressed ideas concern impulses or memories that the client could not think about without feeling intense anxiety. Repressed memories mostly refer to childhood, and to the conflicts between the instinctive (e.g., sexual) motives of the child and the restraints imposed by his or her parents. Repression serves the function of reducing the level of anxiety experienced by the client.

According to Freud, adults who experience great personal problems tend to show regression (not

> **Assumptions of the psychodynamic model**
>
> - Much of our behaviour is driven by unconscious motives.
> - Childhood is a critical period in development.
> - Mental disorders arise from unresolved, unconscious conflicts originating in childhood.
> - Resolution occurs through accessing and coming to terms with repressed ideas and conflicts.

Sigmund Freud, 1856–1939.

repression!). Regression involves going backwards through the stages of psychosexual development they went through in childhood (see Chapter 6, Social and Personality Development, for a detailed description of Freud's theory of personality). Children often fixate or spend an unusually long time at a given stage of psychosexual development if it is associated with conflicts or excessive gratification, and regression typically occurs back to a stage at which the person had previously fixated.

Freud argued that the way to cure neurosis was to allow the client to gain access to his/her repressed ideas and conflicts, and to encourage him/her to face up to whatever emerged from the unconscious. He insisted the client should focus on the feelings associated with the repressed ideas, and should not simply regard them unemotionally. Freud used the term **insight** to refer to these processes. The ultimate goal of psychoanalysis is to provide the client with insight. There are great obstacles in the way, because the emergence of very painful ideas and memories into consciousness produces an extremely high level of anxiety. As a result, the attempt to uncover repressed ideas meets much resistance from the client.

Freud (1917, p.289) described some of the forms that resistance can take:

> *The patient attempts to escape by every possible means. First he says nothing comes into his head, then that so much comes into his head that he can't grasp any of it . . . At last he admits that he really cannot say something, he is ashamed to . . . So it goes on, with untold variations.*

Freud and the other psychoanalysts used various methods to uncover repressed ideas, and to permit the client to gain insight into his/her unresolved problems. The three main methods are as follows: hypnosis, free association, and dream analysis.

Hypnosis

The use of hypnosis came first in the history of psychoanalysis. Freud and Breuer (1895) treated a 21-year-old woman called Anna O, who suffered from several neurotic symptoms such as paralysis and nervous coughs (see Case Study on page 240). Hypnosis uncovered a repressed memory of Anna hearing the sound of dance music coming from a nearby house as she was nursing her dying father, and her guilty feeling that she would rather be dancing than looking after her father. Her nervous coughing stopped after that repressed memory came to light.

Freud gradually lost interest in hypnosis, partly because many clients were hard or impossible to hypnotise. Another problem is that people under hypnosis become very suggestible. As a result, little reliance can be placed on the accuracy of what they claim to remember when in the hypnotised state.

Free association

The method of free association is very simple. The client is encouraged to say the first thing that comes

The client is reluctant to say what he or she is really thinking.

into his/her mind. It is hoped that fragments of repressed memories will emerge in the course of free association. However, as we have seen, free association may not prove useful if the client shows resistance, and is reluctant to say what he/she is thinking. On the other hand, the presence of resistance (e.g., an excessively long pause) often provides a strong clue that the client is getting close to some important repressed idea in his/her thinking, and that further probing by the therapist is called for.

Dream analysis

According to Freud, the analysis of dreams provides "the *via regia* [royal road] to the unconscious". He argued that there is a censor in the mind that keeps repressed material out of conscious awareness; this censor is less vigilant during sleep. As a result, repressed ideas from the unconscious are more likely to appear in dreams than in waking thought. These ideas usually emerge in disguised form because of their unacceptable nature. For example, the ideas may be altered by the process of condensation (combining various ideas into a smaller number) or by displacement (shifting emotion from the appropriate object to another one). The best-known examples of displacement involve sexual symbolism, such as someone dreaming about riding a horse rather than having sex.

Freud distinguished between the actual dream (called the **manifest content**) and the underlying repressed ideas (called the **latent content**; see Chapter 4, Biological Rhythms, Sleep, and Dreaming). The unacceptable content of the latent dream is changed into the more acceptable content of the manifest dream. Why do people dream? According to Freud, the main purpose is wish fulfilment: we dream about things that we would like to see happen. Thus, dream analysis can prove useful in making sense of the neurotic client's basic motives.

How plausible is Freud's theory of dreams? A dreamer's major concerns are often expressed in a symbolic fashion rather than directly. For example, patients who are due to have major surgery sometimes dream about standing on an unsteady bridge or falling from a tall ladder, rather than about having an operation (Breger, Hunter, & Lane, 1971). The notion that dream symbols are used to disguise unacceptable ideas has been challenged. Hall (1953) suggested that thinking is simpler and more concrete when we are asleep than when we are awake, and that dream symbols are a useful shorthand way of expressing underlying ideas.

> **Dream analysis**
>
> There are various schools of thought on the significance of dreams and their possible biological function. Freud and Jung believed that dreams signified the thoughts and feelings of the unconscious mind and are therefore necessary to allow the mind to explore them. Others have suggested that dreams perform no concrete function, but this view has been contested by referring to examples of sleep deprivation. Sleep-deprived participants tend to experience an increase in dreaming sleep when they are finally permitted to sleep.
>
> What is your view on the role of dreams? How might psychologists test your views scientifically?

> **EXAM HINT**
>
> When evaluating Freud's theory of dreams you might contrast it with other theories of dreams (see Chapter 4, Biological Rhythms, Sleep, and Dreaming). Some other theories just suggest that dreams are the discarded products of brain activity during sleep and that dreams have no meaning.

> **KEY TERMS**
>
> **Manifest content:** in Freud's theory, the actual or obvious content of a dream.
>
> **Latent content:** in Freud's theory, the underlying meaning of a dream.

Interpretation

Psychoanalysis depends heavily on the therapist's interpretation of what the client says. How, for example, does the therapist know that a girl dreaming about riding a horse is actually thinking about having sex rather than simply about horse-riding? Freud argued that the acid test was the client's reaction to the therapist's proposed interpretation. If the client accepts the accuracy of the interpretation, then it is probably correct. If the client vehemently rejects the therapist's interpretation of a dream, that may simply be resistance by the client's conscious mind to an unacceptable but entirely accurate interpretation.

There is a problem here. The therapist can use either the client's acceptance or denial of the reasonableness of a dream interpretation as supporting evidence that the interpretation is correct! Freud argued that we can regard psychoanalysis as similar to solving a jigsaw puzzle. It may be hard to decide whether a given interpretation is correct, or to decide where to place a particular piece of the puzzle. However, the interpretations of dozens of a client's free associations and dreams should form a coherent picture, just as the pieces of a jigsaw puzzle can only be arranged in one way.

A factor complicating the interpretation of what clients say and do is what Freud referred to as reaction formation. The basic idea is that the ego may transform unacceptable desires into acceptable ones to protect itself. For example, a person who has homosexual tendencies but feels uncomfortable about this may claim to be strongly opposed to homosexuality.

Transference

Freud emphasised the notion that the client should gain access not only to repressed information but also to the feelings that accompanied it. A major factor in ensuring adequate emotional involvement on the client's part is provided by **transference**, which involves the client transferring onto the therapist powerful emotional reactions that were previously directed at his or her own parents (or other highly significant individuals). As Gleitman (1986, p.696) pointed out, transference provides "a kind of emotional reliving of the unresolved problems of the patient's childhood".

A crucial aspect of transference is that the therapist responds in a neutral way to the client's emotional outpourings. The fact that the therapist will not retaliate in any way allows the client freedom to express long-repressed anger or hostility to his or her parents. The neutrality of the therapist helps to make it clear to the client that his/her emotional outbursts stem from repressed memories rather than from the therapeutic situation itself. Transference may also occur simply because the person becomes very frustrated at the neutral reactions and lack of feedback provided by the therapist!

Ego analysis

Karen Horney, Anna Freud, Erik Erikson, and others modified the traditional psychoanalytic approach to therapy in the 1940s and 1950s. Their approach is known as ego analysis. **Ego analysis** is based on the notion that the ego or rational mind is important, and that therapy should focus on strengthening the ego so that it can achieve more gratification. More specifically, ego analysis emphasises the individual's ability to control his/her environment. This contrasts with Freud's emphasis on gratification of the wishes of the id or sexual instinct.

Ego analysis makes use of free association and most of the other techniques associated with psychoanalysis. However, it focuses much more on the patient's *current* social and interpersonal problems than on their childhood experiences. After all, nearly all patients with mental disorders are mainly concerned with life's problems in the here and now. Another difference is that ego analysts regard society as being a positive force in most people's lives, whereas Freud emphasised the ways in which society inhibits individuals.

? Freud developed his theory in the early part of the twentieth century when attitudes to sex and sexuality were very different from today. What effect do you think this might have on the development of psychodynamic therapy?

? How might a therapist help a client strengthen their rational mind by:
(a) changing a negative behaviour pattern when relating to others;
(b) fulfilling a personal ambition?

KEY TERMS

Transference: in psychoanalysis, the transfer of the patient's strong feelings for one or both parents onto the therapist.

Ego analysis: a form of therapy developed from psychoanalysis that focused on strengthening the ego.

Ego analysis has much in common with cognitive therapy, in that the emphasis is on the individual patient developing more positive and constructive views of himself/herself and the problems he/she is facing. However, there is one important difference. The whole focus of cognitive therapy is on arguing—the patient reveals his/her negative self-thoughts and the therapist thinks of arguments for rejecting those thoughts. In contrast, ego analysts claim that the solution lies within the patient—patients who accept all of their thoughts will often discover that they already have thoughts that refute their own negative self-rejecting ones. The point of ego analysis is for the patient to accept all of his/her thoughts including the negative self-rejecting ones. According to ego analysts, patients who use the resources of their own minds to resolve their own problems feel more in control of their own destiny than patients who rely on their therapist to provide answers.

EXAM HINT

Ensure that you can fully explain how ego analysis has derived from Freud's psychoanalysis, and also how the two differ.

Kleinian psychodynamic therapy

Another neo-Freudian approach to therapy is based on Klein's object relations theory. The main focus of this theory is on early relationships and the effects that these relations have on later life. In particular it is how these early relationships, most importantly with one's primary caregiver, affect our ability to relate to others. The emphasis is on significant early figures rather than on the id and ego, and on social rather than biological forces. Adults with emotional problems use the therapy relationship to work through early difficulties, though the emphasis is more on the problems here and now rather than in the past. The therapist seeks to identify consistent relationship problems, and to find ways to improve these.

Kleinian therapy was extended to play therapy. In play therapy children are given the same opportunities as adults to work through their anxieties and repressed feelings. However, as children do not have the verbal skills to do this, play is used as a medium for communication.

Psychodrama

Psychodrama is psychotherapeutic technique developed by J.L. Moreno, who defined it as "the science which explores 'the truth' by dramatic methods" (1972, p.12). More specifically, what happens in psychodrama is that the therapist asks the individual to act our key incidents or roles in his/her presence along with other individuals from a common therapy group (typically about 10–15 in number). Personal issues or problems and their possible solutions are enacted rather than just talked about, and past, present, and future life events can be explored. Psychodrama provides an opportunity to practice new roles safely, to see oneself from the outside, to gain insight, and to change. There is interaction aimed at exploring novel solutions to old problems. The group members share in the drama playing significant others, and at the end of the session they contribute suggestions as how they all learn from the issue that has been addressed.

Some of the strengths of psychodrama were discussed by Casey (2001). First, it allows the individual to live out what Moreno called the Golden Rule—reversing roles and imagining in detail what it would be like to be another person allows the individual to develop empathy (i.e., understanding someone else's experiences) and compassion. Second, psychodrama provides individuals with more perspective about themselves, because there are two levels of experience: (1) the self playing various roles and translating the inner world into action; and (2) the self observing the role play as it proceeds. Third, acting our various roles allows the individual to uncover repressed conflicts and work them through.

Yalom (1975) argued that there are 11 "curative factors" in psychodrama. The most important ones are as follows: instillation of hope, interpersonal learning, group cohesiveness, universality of experiences, imparting of information, altruism, and catharsis (i.e., purifying of the emotions).

There is a reasonable amount of evidence that psychodrama can be useful. For example, it has been found effective in treating individuals with psychosomatic disorders (Karp, 1995). However, some people find it very difficult to expose their inner concerns and conflicts in public, and are emotionally threatened by the experience.

Effectiveness of Psychodynamic Therapy

The first systematic attempt to evaluate the effectiveness of psychoanalysis was reported by Hans J. Eysenck (1952), who reviewed studies in which clients either received psychoanalysis or did not receive any systematic treatment. The figures were striking: 72% of clients with no proper treatment recovered over a period of 2 years (this is known as **spontaneous remission**), compared with only 44% of those receiving psychoanalysis. These findings imply that psychoanalysis is actually bad for you!

> Bergin and H.J. Eysenck each analysed the same data but reached different conclusions. How can you explain this?

The findings reported by H.J. Eysenck (1952) cannot be accepted at face value. He counted clients who dropped out of psychoanalysis as clients for whom therapy had failed. If these clients are excluded, then the recovery rate was 66% for patients receiving psychoanalysis. In addition, there are great doubts as to whether the studies on psychoanalysis and on spontaneous remission were comparable in the severity of the initial disorders and the criteria for recovery. Bergin (1971) considered the same information used by H.J. Eysenck, but used different criteria for recovery. According to his analyses, psychoanalysis produced an 83% success rate, whereas the spontaneous remission rate was only 30%. McNeilly and Howard (1991) re-analysed data from the studies used by H.J. Eysenck. About 50% of the treated patients showed some improvement within 8 weeks compared to only 2% of the untreated patients.

Sloane et al. (1975) carried out a detailed study, mainly on patients with anxiety disorder. Behavioural therapy and ego analysis both produced an 80% improvement rate, which was greater than the 48% found in the waiting-list control group.

However, the three groups didn't differ at the 8-month follow-up, because the control patients had improved considerably. Thus, psychodynamic therapy in the form of ego analysis was as effective as behavioural therapy, and produced more rapid recovery than no treatment.

Psychodynamic therapy is more appropriate for the treatment of some disorders than others. It has proved of value in the treatment of anxiety disorders, depression, and some sexual disorders, but is considerably less effective in the treatment of schizophrenia (Luborsky & Spence, 1978). The central focus of psychodynamic therapy is to permit the client to gain insight into himself or

KEY TERM

Spontaneous remission: recovering from an illness (or experiencing reduced symptoms) as a consequence of the passage of time rather than any treatment.

herself. Patients (such as schizophrenics who are not taking drug therapies) who cannot do this are unsuitable for this form of therapy.

Psychodynamic therapy is most appropriate for some types of individuals. Some of the relevant evidence was discussed by Luborsky and Spence (1978): patients who are better educated benefit more from psychodynamic therapy, perhaps because language skills are so important in therapy. Psychodynamic therapy may not be very appropriate for adults who genuinely had very happy and contented childhoods. If they have very few repressed childhood memories, there is little opportunity for them to gain insight into the meaning of their childhood suffering.

Modern psychodynamic therapies, such as ego analysis and Kleinian therapy, have extended classical approaches in several useful ways such as enabling work to be done with children, and also with groups and over shorter periods of time. In similar fashion, psychodrama has proved useful for those individuals who are able to handle the stress of revealing their innermost thoughts in front of several people.

? Psychodynamic therapies may be best for YAVIS types. Do you remember what this is (see page 400)?

Comparisons Between Therapies: Meta-analysis

Smith et al. (1980) reviewed 475 studies in which the effectiveness of various therapies had been evaluated. In order to be included in the review, each study had

KEY TERM

Client-centred therapy: a form of humanistic therapy introduced by Rogers and designed to increase the client's self-esteem.

Humanistic therapy

The humanistic approach underlies one of the most common approaches to helping people with emotional problems—counselling or **client-centred therapy** (Rogers, 1951, 1959). (This therapy is not mentioned in the A2 specification but we think it is important to outline some of the key points of this approach.)

Humanistic therapy, like the psychoanalytic approach, was designed to change the functioning of the mind. Rogers' starting point for this form of therapy was the concept of self. Individuals often experience problems and seek therapy when there is incongruence (or major discrepancies) between the self-concept and the ideal self. For Rogers (1986) the main assumption lying behind client-centred therapy was:

> The individual has within him or herself, vast resources of self-understanding, for altering his or her self-concept, attitudes and self-directing behaviour, and . . . these resources can be tapped if only a definable climate of facilitative psychological attitudes can be provided

According to Rogers (1951), the way in which the therapist or facilitator behaves towards the client is of key importance in determining the success of treatment. Rogers argued that therapists should be:

- Unconditional in positive regard: this involves the therapist accepting and valuing the client, and avoiding being critical or judgemental.

- Genuine, in the sense of allowing their true feelings and thoughts to emerge.
- Empathic (i.e., understanding the other person's feelings).

Client-centred therapy involves the client discussing his or her self-concept and life goals with the facilitator. The facilitator invites the client to interpret or make sense of his or her experience, and enables the client to do this through unconditional positive regard and empathetic understanding. This increases the client's self-esteem and permits him or her to accept those parts of self into the self-structure that were previously excluded from the self-concept. This allows the client to reduce the discrepancy between his or her self-concept and ideal self. It also allows the client to develop a greater sense of being in control of his or her destiny because the client controls the therapeutic process. Client-centred therapy differs from psychodynamic therapy in that the focus is very much on current concerns and hopes for the future, whereas the emphasis in Freudian psychodynamic therapy is on childhood experiences.

Rogers originally believed that his client-centred therapy was non-directive, in the sense that the therapist did not provide the client with solutions but expected that the client would find his or her own answers. However, Truax (1966) recorded some therapy sessions between Rogers and his clients. What emerged was that Rogers was much more likely to reward or encourage his clients when they produced positive statements and seemed to be making progress. In other words, Rogers was directing the thoughts of his clients much more than he had intended.

to involve a comparison group drawn from the same population, who were treated differently (e.g., untreated). Smith et al. carried out a meta-analysis, which involves combining the data from numerous studies so that an accurate estimate can be made of the effectiveness of each form of treatment. The studies varied considerably. Some involved comparisons between different forms of therapy, whereas others involved comparisons between therapy and no treatment. Several different **outcome measures** were used in many of the studies, ranging from self-report measures to behavioural and physiological measures of various kinds. Altogether, there were 1776 outcome measures from the 475 studies. These 475 studies considered by Smith et al. were unrepresentative of most clinical outcome studies in that more than 50% of the patients receiving treatment were students.

Smith et al. (1980) concluded: "Different types of psychotherapy (verbal or behavioural, psychodynamic, client-centred, or systematic desensitisation) do not produce different types or degrees of benefit." On average, their analyses indicated that a client receiving any systematic form of psychotherapy was better off than 80% of controls in terms of recovery. They reported that the effectiveness of therapy did not depend on its length. As behavioural therapy typically takes much less time than psychodynamic therapy, that is an argument for preferring behavioural therapy. However, Smith et al. also reported that some forms of therapy were especially effective with certain disorders. Cognitive therapy and cognitive-behavioural therapy were most effective with specific phobias, fear, and anxiety. Client-centred therapy worked best with clients having low self-esteem.

The approach adopted by Smith et al. (1980) was limited in a number of ways. First, they failed to include all the existing studies in their review. In addition, they gave equal weight to all studies, regardless of quality. This is serious, because it has been argued (Prioleau, Murdock, & Brody, 1983) that only 32 of the studies considered by Smith et al. were based on sound methods. Second, many of the studies were of dubious relevance to therapy as it is typically carried out. For example, more than 50% of the patients receiving treatment across the 475 studies were students. Third, they deliberately reduce the size of the effects associated with behaviour therapy! They did this because they argued that the outcome measures used by behaviour therapists were less stringent than those used by other therapists.

Rosenhan and Seligman (1995) considered the issue of the most effective forms of therapy for different disorders. Some of their conclusions were as follows:

- *Anxieties, fears, phobias, and panic*: systematic desensitisation, cognitive therapy, and drugs (benzodiazepines) are among the best forms of therapy.
- *Depression*: cognitive therapy, electroconvulsive treatment, and drugs (e.g., Prozac) are all very effective.
- *Schizophrenia*: drugs (neuroleptics such as chlorpromazine) and family intervention (involving communication skills) are effective.

Wampold et al. (1997) carried out a meta-analysis on studies in which two or more forms of therapy had been compared directly, and in which the same

Would it be possible to offer effective therapy if one did not believe in that particular approach?

KEY TERM

Outcome measures: ways of assessing the consequences of different forms of therapy.

KEY STUDY
Matt and Navarro

Matt and Navarro (1997) considered evidence from 63 meta-analyses of the effects of therapy. Across the 28 meta-analyses providing relevant data, the mean effect size was 0.67, meaning that 75% of patients improved more than untreated controls. This is somewhat lower than the figure reported by Smith et al. (1980).

Matt and Navarro also addressed the issue of whether the effects of therapy are due to specific effects or to common effects (e.g., placebo effects). They did this by focusing on 10 meta-analyses in which three types of group were compared:

1. Specific therapy groups, for whom any benefits may depend on specific effects or common effects.
2. Placebo control groups (involving general encouragement but no specific therapy), for whom any benefits are likely to depend on common effects.
3. Waiting-list control groups, for whom no benefits are expected.

The evidence indicated that 57% of placebo control patients did better than the average waiting-list control patient, indicating that common or placebo effects exist. However, 75% of the patients receiving specific therapy did better than the average placebo control patient, indicating that specific effects are almost four times more powerful than common or placebo effects. That may not be the whole story, as is discussed below.

Do different forms of therapy vary in their general effectiveness? Matt and Navarro considered the relevant meta-analyses, and concluded as follows (p.22): "Typically, differences favoured behavioural and cognitive therapy approaches over psychodynamic and client-centred approaches." However, they accepted that it was hard to interpret such differences because there was no standardisation of disorder severity, outcome measures, and so on.

Key study evaluation

A major criticism of Matt and Navarro's research concerns its lack of standardisation. The specific conditions of individual cases are vital in determining the effectiveness of therapy. Linked to this is the timescale used. Regression or relapse would indicate failure of therapy, but this is impossible to discover from Matt and Navarro's study. A much lengthier approach, capable of handling disparate sets of data, with a methodology using detailed case notes and follow-up research would be needed to address this problem.

Accuracy is difficult to determine in meta-analyses, and it would be of value to consider making more use of the case-study-centred approach. The inevitable cost and time implications militate against this more focused type of study. However, if psychologists wish to make any real impact on the effectiveness of therapy, it would make sense to involve clients' own testimonies as valid forms of data, rather than relying only on notes based on second-hand observation. This may not give such a tidy result, but might be an improvement in some ways on the sweeping generalisations that often result from meta-analyses.

Discussion points

1. What are the strengths and weaknesses of meta-analyses as a way of discovering the effectiveness of therapy?
2. How impressed are you by the apparent effectiveness of most forms of therapy revealed by Matt and Navarro?

outcome measures had been applied to patients receiving different forms of therapy. Their findings suggested that the beneficial effects of all forms of therapy are essentially the same. They concluded (p.211):

Why is it that researchers persist in attempts to find treatment differences, when they know that these effects are small in comparison to other effects,

? If this is the case, what do you think should be the most important determinant of treatment choice (e.g., client preference, therapist preference, cost-effectiveness)?

such as therapists' effects . . . or effects of treatment versus no-treatment comparisons?

Evaluation of meta-analyses of therapy

We need to be cautious about interpreting the evidence from meta-analyses, because most of them are limited in various ways. Some of the main problems were identified by Matt and Navarro (1997, p.20; see the Key Study on page 427). First, the studies considered in most meta-analyses are not representative of the ways in which therapy is typically carried out. As a result, it is difficult generalise from the reported findings to typical therapeutic practice. Second, there is too much emphasis on patients with anxiety disorders and on student patients rather than older ones. Third, most meta-analyses focus too much on cognitive and behavioural forms of therapy at the expense of psychodynamic approaches. Fourth, most meta-analyses include too many studies in which the therapists were in training or had little experience and not enough in which the therapists were well established.

Conclusions

In general terms, we have seen that most forms of therapy are of approximately equal effectiveness in treating most mental disorders. However, it is important to note that many of the outcome studies are flawed and inadequate, and that there is some evidence that certain forms of therapy are especially successful with certain disorders (e.g., Rosenhan & Seligman, 1995). In addition, we need to pay close attention to the measure(s) of treatment outcome. For example, chemotherapy and cognitive therapy are both equally effective in producing recovery from depression (e.g., Barber & DeRubeis, 1989). However, chemotherapy is only designed to reduce the symptoms of depression, whereas cognitive therapy or cognitive-behavioural therapy is intended to equip clients with more realistic and positive beliefs about themselves and their situation. As might be expected, patients who have been treated for depression with drug therapy are more likely to relapse into depression in the year following recovery than are patients who received cognitive-behavioural therapy (Barber & DeRubeis, 1989). Thus, cognitive-behavioural therapy can prove more effective than chemotherapy in the long-term.

What conclusions should we draw from the finding that there are only small differences in overall effectiveness of very different forms of therapy? First, the effectiveness of therapy doesn't depend only on the approach to therapy taken by the therapist. As Bergin (1971, p.85) pointed out, "We may say not only that 'therapy works' but that the 'therapist works' and the 'client works'. . . The patient is as much a cause as either the therapist or the technique." So far as therapist qualities are concerned, Najavits and Strupp (1994) found that effective therapists showed more positive behaviours and fewer negative behaviours than did ineffective therapists.

Second, it is tempting to conclude that the reason why most forms of therapy are of equivalent effectiveness is because they all depend heavily on common factors such as the pleasantness and responsiveness of the therapist. However, we shouldn't exaggerate the importance of these common factors. As we have seen, Matt and Navarro (1997) reported that specific effects (i.e., effects specific to a given form of therapy) were four times stronger than common effects. However, Stevens et al. (2000) discovered that matters were more complex. In essence, there were *only* specific treatment effects with severe disorders, but specific and common treatment effects were of equal importance with less severe disorders.

Third, if all forms of therapy are of comparable effectiveness, it makes sense for therapists not to focus exclusively on any given therapy. What has actually happened is that an increasing number of therapists adopt an eclectic approach—what that means is that they are willing to try various forms of therapy when treating a given patient. Some patients respond better to therapy *x* than to therapy *y*, whereas others show the opposite pattern, and so an eclectic approach has much to recommend it.

SECTION SUMMARY
Alternatives to Biological and Behavioural Therapies

❖ Alternative therapies include:

— Cognitive therapy
— Cognitive-behavioural therapy
— Psychodynamic therapy.

What are the alternative therapies?

❖ Cognitive therapy involves changing or restructuring negative irrational beliefs and thoughts into more positive and rational ones.
❖ Its development owes much to the work of Ellis and Beck.
❖ Ellis's rational-emotional therapy:

— This involves challenging the client's self-defeating beliefs and replacing them with more realistic ones.
— Anxious patients do appear to hold more irrational beliefs. RET may be suitable for certain individuals and for certain disorders.

What is cognitive therapy?

❖ Beck's cognitive triad approach:

— This used the concept of the cognitive triad to express the negative beliefs that depressed individuals hold about themselves, the world, and the future.
— Therapy involves collaborative empiricism (joint discussion of the problem and goals) and challenging negative thoughts directly or by setting tasks for the client (e.g., hypothesis testing).

❖ Recently, cognitive therapy has evolved into CBT, which includes elements of behavioural therapy.
❖ The central assumption is that the client's thinking and behaviour both need to change in order to produce the most beneficial effects.

What is cognitive-behavioural therapy (CBT)?

❖ Stress inoculation therapy is a form of CBT. It involves three phases of treatment:

— Conceptualisation
— Skills acquisition and rehearsal
— Application and follow-through.

❖ CBT has been demonstrated as effective with depression and anxiety disorders, especially panic disorder. It is a cost-effective treatment and increasingly popular.

What is psychodynamic therapy?

❖ Various examples of psychodynamic therapy are considered:

— Psychoanalysis and ego analysis
— Kleinian psychodynamic therapy
— Psychodrama.

Psychoanalysis

❖ Psychoanalysis is based on Freud's personality theory:

— Individuals with mental disorders have repressed threatening thoughts and feelings.
— Adults with personal problems regress to earlier stages of psychosexual development, especially to a stage where earlier fixations occurred.
— Neurosis can be cured through insight into repressed ideas but this produces high levels of anxiety.

❖ Various techniques have been used in psychoanalysis:

— Hypnosis: Freud abandoned hypnosis because of problems of suggestion.
— Free association: May be threatened by resistance.
— Dream analysis: Focuses on the latent content. Dreams are wish fulfilment.

❖ Psychoanalysis relies very much on the therapist's interpretations of what the client says, and these interpretations may be wrong.
❖ A client's acceptance or denial of an interpretation is seen as proof of correctness.
❖ Interpretation is further complicated by reaction formation.
❖ Therapy often involves transference, with the client transferring strong emotions towards someone of major significance in his/her life onto the therapist and thus dealing with repressed feelings.

Other psychodynamic therapies

❖ Ego analysis:

— Aims to strengthen the rational mind and focuses more on current social problems.

❖ Psychodrama:

— Involves the individual acting out his/her personal conflicts and problems in public.
— It provides an opportunity to see oneself from the outside and to gain insight.

❖ Kleinian object relations therapy:

— Focuses on early relationships and using the relationship with the therapist to work through early problems.
— Play therapy is an extension of this work.

❖ There has been controversy about the effectiveness of psychoanalysis, but it is generally accepted as reasonably effective:

— It is successful with anxiety disorders, depression, and sexual disorders.
— It is not successful with schizophrenia where patients do not have the ability to be insightful.

❖ Psychodynamic therapy is suitable for articulate individuals and not for those with happy childhoods where repression would not be a factor in their maladjustment.

❖ Modern psychodynamic therapies have extended the approach to children, group work, and to shorter durations.

The effectiveness of psychodynamic therapies

❖ One large-scale meta-analysis suggested:

— Most forms of therapy are about equally effective, with clients being better off than 80% of controls in terms of recovery.
— Length of therapy wasn't important, which suggests that short therapies might as well be used, such as behaviour therapy.
— Therapies were most effective when provided by a therapist who believed strongly in the therapy being used.
— Each form of therapy was more effective with some disorders than with others.

Comparison between therapies

❖ Meta-analysis raises problems, such as the lack of comparability.
❖ In general, most forms of therapy are of equivalent effectiveness.
❖ Some of the beneficial effects of therapy are due to common factors rather than specific factors, but this is more the case with less severe disorders.
❖ Therapeutic success depends on the client and the therapist as well as on the form of therapy itself.
❖ More and more therapists adopt an eclectic approach in which they sample various forms of therapy in order to see which one is most effective with any given patient.

See also pages 245–251 of the revision guide.

FURTHER READING

The topics in this chapter are covered in greater depth by S. Cave (1999) *Therapeutic approaches in psychology* (London: Routledge), written specifically for the AQA A specification. W. Dryden (1996) *Individual therapy: A handbook* (Milton Keynes, UK: Open University Press) contains chapters on all the therapies. There are several good textbooks on abnormal psychology that cover the main therapeutic approaches. They include R.J. Comer (2002) *Fundamentals of abnormal psychology (3rd Edn.)* (New York: Worth), and V.M. Durand and D.H. Barlow (2003) *Essentials of abnormal psychology (3rd Edn.)* (Belmont, CA: Wadsworth).

EXAMPLE EXAMINATION QUESTIONS

You should spend 40 minutes on each of the questions below, which aim to test the material in this chapter. Unlike questions from Unit 4 of the examination, covered in Chapters 2–7 of this book, the questions in the Individual Differences section of the Unit 5 examination, covered in this chapter and Chapter 8, are marked out of 30 and an additional criterion is used in assessment: synopticity. "Synopticity" is defined as your "understanding and critical appreciation of the breadth and range of different theoretical perspectives and/or methodological approaches relevant to any questions" (AQA specification).

1. Discuss issues surrounding the use of biological (somatic) therapies. (30 marks)

2. (a) Describe the use of any **two** biological (somatic) therapies used in the treatment of mental disorders. (15 marks)
   (b) Evaluate these therapies in terms of the issues surrounding their use (e.g., appropriateness and effectiveness). (15 marks)

3. Distinguish between those behavioural therapies based on classical conditioning and those based on operant conditioning. (30 marks)

4. (a) Describe the use and mode of action of **two or more** behavioural therapies based on operant conditioning. (15 marks)
   (b) Justify the use of these therapies in the treatment of psychological disorders. (15 marks)

5. "One of the greatest problems for any patient suffering from mental disorder is the question of how to choose the best and most appropriate therapy." Distinguish between any **two** types of therapies for mental disorders. (30 marks)

6. Discuss the use of **two** therapies that are derived from the psychodynamic **or** cognitive-behavioural models of abnormality. (30 marks)

Examination Tips

Question 1. "Discuss" is an AO1 and AO2 term requiring description plus evaluation. In the specification, likely issues are identified as the appropriateness and effectiveness of such therapies but you might consider other issues as well, such as ethical concerns. It is important that you give equal weight to your description as well as the evaluation in order to access full marks, and that you are aware of the synoptic criteria that are also assessed here.

Question 2. If you consider more than two therapies only the best two will be credited. In part (b) you are specifically required to assess the therapies in terms of issues surrounding their use. It might still be possible to draw comparisons between therapies as long as this was related to an issue such as effectiveness (one therapy is more effective than another in certain situations).

Question 3. "Distinguish between" is an AO1 and AO2 term that requires you to describe behavioural therapies based on classical and operant conditioning for the AO1 marks and then distinguish between them for AO2. The danger will be that you have a great deal to write for AO1 and little for AO2. It will be important to be selective when describing therapies in order to restrict the time spent on this half of the essay. It is possible to make distinctions in terms of effectiveness, ethics, applicability to different patients, research support, and so on. Credit will also be awarded for any similarities that are identified (e.g., lack of distinctiveness). Behavioural therapies as a whole may be contrasted with other approaches.

Question 4. This question is restricted to operant conditioning only. Part (a) requires a description of at least two therapies. There is a depth–breadth trade-off here as increasing breadth (more than two therapies) is likely to incur a cost in terms of depth, and both are needed for top marks. In part (b) you must assess the effectiveness and appropriateness of these therapies and thus justify their use. Synopticity can be demonstrated by reference to other approaches, which may be more or less useful, as well as considering other overarching issues such as ethics and determinism.

Question 5. You are not required to refer to the quotation in your answer but it is there to suggest ways of answering the question. The question allows you to select any therapies for discussion—you might contrast behavioural with psychodynamic approaches, or be more particular in comparing aversion therapy with psychoanalysis. The former approach is likely to be most fruitful because of the breadth of material available. As in question 3 you must take care not to write too much description and therefore fail to attract marks for evaluation.

Question 6. The specification states that you only have to study psychodynamic *or* cognitive-behavioural models of abnormality. Some candidates may find it difficult to achieve a reasonable balance when describing two therapies from one model, knowing one better than the other—as in the case of psychoanalysis and one other example of a psychodynamic therapy. If only one therapy is covered then partial performance penalties will apply for both AO1 and AO2 (maximum of 10 marks each). If only one therapy is evaluated then there are partial performance penalties on AO2.

WEBSITES

http://www.aabt.org/related/related.htm
  Links to behaviour therapy sites on the homepage of the Association for the Advancement of Behavior Therapy.
http://www.antipsychiatry.org/ect.htm
  Arguments against electroconvulsive therapy.
http://neurosurgery.mgh.harvard.edu/functional/Psychosurgery2001.htm
  Article on psychosurgery.
http://www.rcpsych.ac.uk/info/factsheets/pfaccog.asp
  Information and links dedicated to cognitive-behavioural therapy.

PERSPECTIVES

Gender Bias p.435

- Is it justifiable if a theory is based on male behaviour only and then applied to all human behaviour?
- Do any studies just have female participants, or are they all male biased?
- Which is preferable: to regard men and women as being psychologically different, or as the same?

Cultural Bias p.443

- What does the term "culture" mean?
- How can we make comparisons between cultures without being biased by our own cultural assumptions?
- What do psychologists think about the concept of "race"?

Ethical Issues p.451

- How can we balance the needs of the individual against the needs of society?
- Do the ends justify almost any means?
- Should we ban socially sensitive research?

The Use of Non-human Animals p.469

- Is current legislation sufficient to protect non-human animals?
- How can we defend speciesism?
- What are the differences between humans and non-human animals?

Issues

Throughout your studies certain issues have been considered repeatedly: gender, culture, and ethics. In this chapter you have the opportunity to reflect on these issues in relation to your studies so far.

GENDER BIAS

The term "bias" is used to suggest that a person's or society's views are distorted in some systematic way. In psychology, there is evidence that gender is presented in a biased way and this bias leads to a misrepresentation of women. Consider the following example. The performance of participants in psychological research tends to be influenced by the *expectations* of the investigator. Many people still have lower expectations for women than for men. This would lead us to collect data that show poorer task performance in women (for example, on a memory task). Research data are used to formulate theories and these theories may well be gender biased because of the baseline data.

In this Section we will explore different areas and aspects of gender bias, and how this affects psychological knowledge.

Gender Stereotypes

There are many popular (and misleading) stereotypes about the differences between the sexes. For example, it has often been claimed that women are more emotional than men. This was expressed poetically by Alfred, Lord Tennyson:

Man for the sword and for the needle she: Man with the head and woman with the heart.

It is fully accepted that that is a gross oversimplification of reality. However, it is worth mentioning that females typically score significantly higher than males on measures of negative affectivity (a personality dimension relating to the experience of negative emotions such as anxiety and depression) (e.g., Denollet, 2005).

Stereotypes about gender have been fairly common in psychology as well as in society at large. One of the worst offenders was Sigmund Freud. He argued that anatomy is destiny, meaning that there are great psychological differences between men and women because of their anatomical differences. For example, Freud claimed that young girls suffer from "penis envy" when they find out that boys have a penis but they don't (see page 258 for a discussion of this).

The greatest difficulty lies in distinguishing "real" from culturally created gender differences. There are some real differences, or at least that was the

Maccoby and Jacklin (1974) found strong evidence for only four differences between boys' and girls' behaviour and abilities.

Research on sex difference is discussed on page 257.

conclusion reached by Maccoby and Jacklin (1974) in a review of research on sex differences (see Chapter 6, Social and Personality Development). They concluded that there were only four differences between boys and girls for which there was strong evidence. This is a much smaller number of gender differences than would have been predicted by most psychologists. The four differences identified by Maccoby and Jacklin were as follows:

- Girls have greater verbal ability than boys.
- Boys have greater visual and spatial abilities than girls (e.g., arranging blocks in specified patterns).
- Boys have greater arithmetical ability than girls, but this difference only appears at adolescence.
- Girls are less aggressive than boys: this is found in nearly all cultures, and is usually present from about 2 years of age.

Most of these differences are fairly small, and there is much overlap in behaviour between boys and girls. Sex differences in abilities (verbal, visual, spatial, and mathematical) are even smaller now than they were in the early 1970s (Hyde & Linn, 1988). However, there are clear (and increasing) gender differences in academic performance in the UK. For example, findings contained in a 2005 report indicated that girls outperformed boys at A level in 74% of state schools, a difference that probably reflects gender differences in motivation.

As Shaffer (1993) pointed out, there are some differences that were not identified by Maccoby and Jacklin (1974). First, girls show more emotional sensitivity (e.g., they respond more attentively to babies). Second, girls are less vulnerable developmentally than boys and are less likely to suffer from learning disabilities, various language disorders, or hyperactivity. Third, boys tend to be more physically active than girls.

In a large-scale survey of gender stereotypes in 30 different national cultures, Williams and Best (1982) found that there were many similarities across the various cultures. Men were seen as more dominant, aggressive, and autonomous; a more *instrumental role*. Women were more nurturant, deferent, and interested in affiliation; being encouraged to develop an *expressive role*. This suggests some kind of universal, biological basis for gender stereotypes. However, we mustn't assume that any of these differences are always found. Whyte (1978) considered 93 non-industrialised cultures, and found that men dominated their wives in 67% of those cultures. There was equality of the sexes in 30% of the cultures and women dominated their husbands in the remaining 3%. Unsurprisingly, men

Girls are more likely than boys to respond attentively to babies.

were particularly dominant in non-industrialised cultures in which they were better equipped than women to perform tasks vital within that culture (e.g., cultures engaging in frequent warfare; Goldstein, 2001).

Alpha Bias and Beta Bias

If there are real gender differences, how does that affect psychological research? Hare-Mustin and Marecek (1988) considered the issue of gender bias in psychology in detail. Their starting point was that there are two basic forms of gender bias: **alpha bias** and **beta bias**. According to Hare-Mustin and Marecek (p.457), "Alpha bias is the tendency to exaggerate differences; beta bias is the tendency to minimise or ignore differences." They used the term "bias" to refer to an inclination to focus on certain aspects of experience rather than on others.

Febbraro (2003) pointed out that we can see these biases in the work/family literature. Alpha bias is involved when it is argued that women experience much greater work/family stress than men, and so male-dominated structures need to be transformed as a result. Beta bias is involved when it is argued that multiple roles (i.e., parent, spouse, worker) increase the well-being of women in the same way as men.

Alpha bias

Within Western cultures, alpha bias has been more common than beta bias. For example, Freud claimed that children's superego or conscience develops when they identify with the same-sex parent. Girls don't identify with their mother as strongly as boys identify with their father. As a result, Freud argued that girls develop weaker superegos than boys (see Chapter 5, Cognitive Development). However, Freud did admit that "the majority of men are far behind the masculine ideal [in terms of strength of superego]". The evidence doesn't support Freud. Hoffman (1975) discussed studies in which the tendency of children to do what they had been told not to do was assessed. The behaviour of boys and girls did not differ in most of the studies. When there was a sex difference, it was the girls (rather than the boys) who were better at resisting temptation.

The approach adopted by evolutionary psychologists has often been criticised for its alpha bias (see Chapter 7, Evolutionary Explanations of Human Behaviour). According to evolutionary psychologists, evolutionary processes in the development of the human species explain why men tend to be dominant over women, why women typically have much more parental investment than men in their offspring, and why men are more likely to commit adultery. However, there have been major cultural changes over the past 100 years or so, as a result of which it is increasingly argued that the evolutionary perspective shouldn't be used to justify gender differences.

There is some evidence for alpha bias in the diagnosis of mental disorders. Ford and Widiger (1989) argued that histrionic personality disorder (characterised by excessive emotionality) is often regarded as a distortion of stereotypical feminine traits, whereas anti-social personality disorder (characterised by hostility and aggression) is a distortion of stereotypical masculine traits. Therapists were presented with written case studies of histrionic and antisocial personality disorder in which the patient was identified as male or female. Histrionic personality disorder was diagnosed much more frequently

? Why is alpha bias more common than beta bias?

EXAM HINT
You will not be directly examined on gender stereotypes, but it is useful background information for questions on gender bias.

KEY TERMS
Alpha bias: the tendency to exaggerate differences between the sexes.
Beta bias: the tendency to minimise differences between the sexes.

when the patient was female, and anti-social personality disorder was diagnosed more often when the patient was male.

You won't be surprised to discover that the great majority of examples of alpha bias are biased in the direction of favouring males over females. However, there are a few cases in which females are regarded as superior to males. Gilligan (1977, 1982) argued that the morality of care is very important and that women adopt this form of moral reasoning to a greater extent than men. It should be noted that the evidence provides little support for Gilligan's views (e.g., Jaffee & Hyde's, 2000, meta-analysis). However, as Durkin (1995, p.493) pointed out, Gilligan's "critical perspective did serve the purpose of opening up the study of moral development in important ways by broadening conceptions of what morality is and how it should be measured".

There is a final point that needs to be made about alpha bias. Most journals in psychology are much more willing to publish significant findings than non-significant ones. As a result, it is likely that the published literature exaggerates the extent of gender differences in behaviour—researchers finding no gender differences find it difficult to publish their data.

Beta bias

Hare-Mustin and Marecek (1988) argued that beta bias, or the tendency to minimise or ignore sex differences, is less common than alpha bias. They suggested that Bem's (1974) theory of psychological androgyny is an example of beta bias. According to that theory, it is psychologically more healthy to be androgynous (having a mixture of positive masculine and feminine characteristics) than to have only masculine or only feminine characteristics. Individuals who can respond to any situation with either masculine (instrumental) characteristics or feminine (expressive) characteristics are more flexible than an individual who behaves in a more sex-stereotyped way.

There is evidence of beta bias in experimental research, i.e., a tendency to reduce or minimise gender differences. Male and female participants are used in most studies, but there is typically no attempt to analyse the data to see whether there are significant sex differences. It may be possible that sex differences are found in psychological research because researchers ignore the differential treatment of participants. Male experimenters may treat their female participants differently from their male ones. Rosenthal (1966) reported that they were more pleasant, friendly, honest, and encouraging with female than with male participants. Such findings led Rosenthal to conclude: "Male and female subjects may, psychologically, simply not be in the same experiment at all."

This means that, because researchers act as if there are no sex differences, they end up providing evidence that there are such differences. In other words beta bias tends to produce sex differences.

Beta bias in psychological theories

The same reasoning can be applied to some psychological theories that show evidence of beta bias. Kohlberg (1963) put forward a theory of moral development based mainly on studies of moral dilemmas with males as the main actors and with males as participants. He claimed that men tended to be at a higher level of moral development than women (see Chapter 5, Cognitive Development). Kohlberg assumed that there were minimal differences between

How might an experimenter control for this differential treatment of men and women?

How would you measure moral development in a way that is not gender-specific?

men and women in terms of moral thinking (a beta bias) and therefore it would not matter if he used only male participants because this would still represent all people. The outcome is a demonstration of gender differences.

An androcentric view of human nature

The result of beta bias in psychological research is that we end up with a view of human nature that purports to apply to men and women alike, but in fact has a male or **androcentric bias**. This is true of Kohlberg's theory of moral development. It is also true of other areas of research. Asch's (1955) conformity studies involved all male participants. In fact, the same is true of many of the other conformity studies (e.g., Perrin & Spencer, 1980). Psychological theories of conformity are thus based largely on male behaviour. Eagly (1978) found that women may be even more conformist, or at least they are more oriented towards interpersonal goals and therefore *appear* to be more conformist in experimental situations. What is clear is that a failure to attend to gender issues has oversimplified, exaggerated, and/or fudged gender differences!

Facts and Values

The discussion so far has assumed that there are *facts* about gender. A different view is favoured by **social constructionists** such as Gergen (1985). They argue that there are no facts; there are *values* and these determine what are regarded as facts. We construct our reality through shared conversations about the social and physical world. In other words, "scientific knowledge, like all other knowledge, cannot be disinterested or politically neutral" (Hare-Mustin & Marecek, 1988, p.456). Thus we may be "fooled" into believing that our knowledge of gender facts is "real", whereas they are social constructions.

Such facts may have serious repercussions. Burns (1993) provided an example of how society's values can influence the approach taken to studying women. She pointed out (p.103) that a major focus of research on women with learning disabilities is on "sexuality and the issues and concerns surrounding women with learning disabilities becoming pregnant, having babies, being sterilised, using contraception, managing periods and being sexually abused". Thus, such women are seen in a negative way in terms of the possible problems they may cause. As Burns (p.103) concluded, "the consequence of this position is to deny women with learning disabilities a positive identity and role as a woman".

Methodological gender bias

We have already seen that there are various ways in which research on gender differences can be biased and thus invalid. Another way in which findings can be rendered invalid is through **methodological gender bias**, in which the design of the research biases the chances of the researcher obtaining some particular finding. Methodological gender bias is especially likely to be found when the direction of gender differences depends on the precise measures of behaviour that are taken. For example, many researchers have addressed the issue of whether males or females are more aggressive. In one of the most thorough studies, Bjorkqvist et al. (1992) found that boys displayed much more physical aggression than girls, but girls showed significantly more indirect aggression (e.g., gossiping, writing unkind notes) than boys. Armed with that knowledge, you could design a study to show apparently that boys are more aggressive than girls or vice versa!

> **?** Moscovici et al.'s (1969) classic study on minority influence used all female participants. Perhaps if he had used male participants, minority influence would have appeared to be less significant.

> **?** Sherif et al.'s (1961) study of boys at a summer camp involved all boys, and Erikson's (1968) research into lifespan development also involved all male interviews. What other studies used all male or all female participants? How may this have affected the theories derived from the data?

> **KEY TERMS**
>
> **Androcentric bias:** a bias in favour of males. An androcentric theory is based on research data on males and then applied to all human behaviour.
> **Social constructionists:** psychological theorists who assume that our knowledge of ourselves and of others are social constructions, and thus there is no objective reality for research.
> **Methodological gender bias:** designing a study on the effects of gender in a biased way so as to maximise the chances of obtaining the predicted gender differences.

Eagly et al. (1995) carried out a meta-analysis to compare the effectiveness of male and female leaders. They found that there was overall very little difference between male and female leaders, with female leaders being more effective than male leaders in 57% of significant comparisons and male leaders being more effective than female leaders in 43%. The key finding was that female leaders were consistently more effective than males in feminine leader roles (i.e., roles rated as being congenial to women) and male leaders were more effective than females in masculine leader roles (i.e., roles rated as being congenial to men). Thus, the results depended very much on the situation—you could apparently show that men make better leaders if you focused on leadership in the army, but could show that women make better leaders if you focused on leadership among nurses!

In sum, it is important for researchers studying gender differences to make sure that they compare the two sexes in a range of different situations and using various measures of behaviour. If that is not done, then there is a very real risk of methodological gender bias.

> ■ **Activity:** Make a list of value-free factual points about the experience of studying psychology. Now make a second list of value-free factual points about female psychology students. How difficult was it to construct non-judgemental views for either list? To what extent did gender appear to be an issue?

Feminist psychology

Traditional psychology has also sought to explain behaviour in terms of internal causes, such as biological sex differences. This has led to inevitable gender biases in psychological theories. The alternative, social constructionist approach aims to understand behaviour in terms of social processes and thus find a way to greater equality. Feminist psychologists argue that there may be real sex differences but socially determined stereotypes make a far greater contribution to perceived differences.

Feminist psychology takes the view that a prerequisite to any social change with respect to gender roles must be a revision of our "facts" about gender. Whether such facts are true or not, they perpetuate our beliefs about women. Feminist psychology is a branch of psychology that aims to redress the imbalances in psychology.

One way to redress the balance is to use evidence that women may be inferior to provide women with greater support. For example, Eagly (1978)

> ? Pre-menstrual syndrome is described on page 360. In what way is this an example of how female behaviour has been pathologised because it does not fit with male norms for behaviour?

Battered women's syndrome

Bem (1993) used battered women's syndrome as an example of how society constructs frameworks that pathologise women's behaviour. Bem argued that women who live with highly aggressive partners have now been given a means of legal defence in cases where they have killed their partner, often in circumstances where they were not directly provoked—the battered women's syndrome. The recognition of this syndrome allows women to argue that any attack on their partners, whether it was directly provoked or not, was justified by the general treatment they were receiving from their partners over a prolonged period.

However, at the same time, the idea of a "syndrome" turns the woman's behaviour into something that is pathological, i.e., a behaviour that is somehow "sick" ("pathological" means "diseased"). This "sickness" in the woman deflects our attention from the sickness inherent in society that allows some men to feel justified in their behaviour.

Furthermore, feminist lawyers point out that the law itself is androcentric because the concept of self-defence is related to male–male encounters (more usual). If one person attacks another, one can plead self-defence as long as the second person was in immediate danger of serious or deadly injury. This cannot be applied to the battered woman, who usually defends herself at a time other than when she is in immediate danger. Alternatively, it could be argued that as she has not been killed in the past, then she has never actually been in such danger. The law does not allow for a form of self-defence that is not within this male–male context because the law seems to be defined by male interactions.

acknowledged that women may be less effective leaders than men but this knowledge should be used to develop suitable training programmes.

A further way to redress the balance is to become aware of how androcentric theories inevitably lead to the view that female behaviour is abnormal (see the box on the previous page). Bem (1994) argued that in a male-centred world, female differences are transformed into female disadvantages. Bem (1993) used the concept of an "enculturated lens" to suggest that the view of gender that we receive from our culture misshapes how we see men and women. Bem (1993, p.2) suggested that we should make those lenses:

visible rather than invisible, to enable us to look at the culture's gender lenses rather than through them, for it is only when Americans apprehend the more subtle and systemic ways in which the culture reproduces male power that they will finally comprehend the unfinished business of the feminists' agenda.

In sum, there is evidence of gender bias within psychology. However, most of the clearest examples of such bias occurred a long time ago. This suggests that psychologists have become more concerned to avoid gender bias.

Conclusions

There are various biases in theory and research on gender that stand in the way of obtaining an accurate picture of the genuine psychological differences between men and women. Three of the main such biases have been discussed at length in this section: alpha bias, beta bias, and methodological gender bias. While all three biases are matters for concern, the good news is that researchers nowadays are more aware than ever of the existence of these biases and of the need to avoid them. As a result, it is probably true that recent research on gender differences is less affected by these biases.

There is a final important point. Suppose we find that there is a significant difference between males and females on some measure of behaviour. What is almost certainly also the case is that there is a substantial amount of overlap between the sexes on that measure of behaviour. That means that it is nearly always overly simple to state that females outperform males (or vice versa) on some measure.

EXAM HINT

Maximise synopticity by drawing from different areas of psychology to illustrate gender bias.

SECTION SUMMARY
Gender Bias

❖ A bias is a systematic distortion of one's beliefs.
❖ Gender bias is created by gender stereotypes such as Freud's concept of penis envy in girls.
❖ The difficulty lies in distinguishing "real" from culturally created gender differences.
❖ Evidence suggests that there are a small number of real gender differences, confirmed through cross-cultural studies.

What is gender bias?

Alpha bias and beta bias	❖ There are two basic forms of gender bias: alpha bias and beta bias. They have different characteristics.
	❖ Alpha bias:

— The tendency to exaggerate gender differences.
— More common than beta bias in the Western world.
— Freud's theory of moral development is an example of alpha bias.

❖ Beta bias:

— The tendency to minimise or ignore gender differences.
— Bem's theory of androgyny an example of beta bias.
— Tends to produce a view of human nature that is male biased or androcentric.

Beta bias in psychological theories	❖ Kohlberg's theory of moral development:

— Constructed with data from male participants only.
— Assumed that there are minimal gender differences (beta bias) and therefore using male participants only should not matter. The outcome is a demonstration of gender differences.

❖ Conformity theories:

— May be restricted to male behaviour but we have been led to believe that they apply to men and women equally.
— This may oversimplify gender differences and our view of human behaviour.

Social constructionism	❖ A key issue with respect to gender bias is the extent to which values determine facts.
	❖ Social constructionists suggest that facts are socially constructed.
	❖ Such facts may have serious repercussions, for example in the treatment of women with learning disabilities. Whether such facts are true or not, they perpetuate our beliefs about women.

Methodological gender bias	❖ This refers to how the design of research can bias the chances of obtaining a particular finding.
	❖ This can lead to findings that are not valid.

Feminist psychology	❖ This branch of psychology aims to redress the imbalances in psychology.
	❖ This is done by:

— Using evidence that women may be inferior to provide women with greater support, e.g., leadership training.
— Becoming aware of how androcentric theories turn female differences into female disadvantages, as in the case of battered women's syndrome.
— Bem suggested that we should make our "enculturated lenses" visible, and thus overcome the bias created by cultural views.

See also pages 260–262 of the revision guide.

CULTURAL BIAS

Research in psychology has for very many years been dominated by the United States. According to Rosenzweig (1992), 64% of the world's 56,000 researchers in psychology are Americans. Their impact on textbooks in psychology is often even greater. For example, consider Baron and Byrne's (1991) textbook on social psychology. In that book, 94% of the studies referred to were from North America, compared with 2% from Europe, 1% from Australasia, and 3% from the rest of the world. However, North American psychologists do *not* carry all before them. Haggbloom et al. (2002) used various kinds of evidence to identify the greatest psychologists of the twentieth century. Nearly 20% of them (including Freud, Piaget, Pavlov, and Vygotsky) were non-American.

Facts like those just mentioned are of relevance to **cross-cultural psychology**, in which different cultures are studied and compared. What is a culture? According to Smith and Bond (1998, p.39), a **culture** "is a *relatively organised* system of shared meanings". For example, the word "work" has a rather different meaning in the Japanese culture than in others. In Japan, it typically includes going drinking after normal working hours, and sharing in other recreational activities with one's work colleagues. Fiske (2002, p.85) provided a broader definition of culture as "a socially transmitted or socially constructed constellation consisting of such things as practices, competencies, ideas, schemas, symbols, values, norms, institutions, goals, . . . artefacts and modifications of the physical environment".

Most cross-cultural psychology has involved comparisons between different nations or countries. This suffers from the problem that a country is generally not the same as a culture. For example, there are several cultures within a single country such as the United States. Vandello and Cohen (1999) found that the individualistic culture (self-centred approach) applied to most Americans in the Mountain West and the Great Plains, whereas a more collectivistic culture (group-centred approach) applied in the Deep South.

Cultural Differences

It is often assumed that what is true of our culture or country is also true of most other cultures or countries. Many psychologists who carry out studies in the United States or in the United Kingdom make that assumption. However, the assumption is wrong. For example, an attempt was made to repeat the findings of six American studies on an Israeli population similar to that used in the American studies (Amir & Sharon, 1987). There were 64 significant findings in the American studies, only 24 of which were repeated among the Israeli participants. The other 40 findings weren't repeated. In addition, there were six new findings in the Israeli sample that hadn't been obtained in the American studies.

What are the main differences between cultures? Westen (1996, p.679) expressed some of them in vivid terms:

> *By twentieth century Western standards, nearly every human who has ever lived outside the contemporary West is lazy, passive, and lacking in*

Cross-cultural psychology

Cross-cultural psychology is like comparative psychology where different species of animals are studied with the intention of making comparisons with human behaviour, and therefore learning more about the latter. Cultural variation also allows us to observe the effects of different social practices on behaviour.

The Japanese work culture includes the requirement to socialise outside working hours with colleagues.

EXAM HINT

There are many examples of culture bias so do not fall into the descriptive trap. Ensure 50% of your content is AO2 based, by assessing the implications of the culture bias and discussing the changing picture.

KEY TERMS

Cross-cultural psychology: an approach in which different cultures are studied and compared.
Culture: the rules, morals, and methods of interactions specific to a group of people.

Consider evidence for the view that Westerners shun laziness, passivity, and low productivity. Where do these attitudes come from?

industriousness. In contrast, by the standards of most cultures in human history, most Westerners are self-centred and frenetic.

Western culture in general also differs from many others in more fundamental ways, including the ways in which we think of ourselves. As Westen (1996, p.693) pointed out:

The prefix "self-", as in "self-esteem" or "self-representation", did not evolve in the English language until around the time of the Industrial Revolution . . . The contemporary Western view of the person is of a bounded individual, distinct from others, who is defined by more or less idiosyncratic attributes. In contrast, most cultures, particularly the nonliterate tribal societies . . . view the person in her social and familial context, so that the self-concept is far less distinctly bounded.

Evidence consistent with Westen's position was reported by Hofstede (1980; see the Key Study below).

The concept of self and of individual importance is related to societies that are described as **individualist**. Such social groups are contrasted with more **collectivist** cultures where the emphasis is on sharing tasks, belongings, and income. The people in such cultures may live in large family groups and value interdependence. The emphasis is on "we-ness" rather than "I", as illustrated in the text by Nobles (1976; see the Key Study on the next page). Examples of such cultures include Israeli *kibbutzim*, many African cultures, and communes.

Effects of individualism versus collectivism

Throughout this book we have provided examples of how individualist and collectivist culture is related to differences in behaviour. Attributions that are

KEY TERMS

Individualist: a culture that emphasises individuality, individual needs, and independence.

Collectivist: a culture where individuals share tasks, belongings, and income. The people may live in large family groups and value interdependence.

KEY STUDY
Hofstede

Hofstede (1980) carried out a survey of work-related values among workers in a large multinational company. These workers came from 40 different countries. One of the main dimensions that emerged from the survey was that of individualism–collectivism. Individualism involves an emphasis on individual needs and self-development rather than on group needs, whereas collectivism is based on group needs taking precedence over individual ones. The United States had the highest score for individualism of any country, the United Kingdom was third, and France was tenth. Of special interest was Hofstede's finding that individualism correlated +0.82 with modernity as measured by national wealth. This indicates that there is a strong tendency for wealthier countries to be individualistic and self-centred.

Discussion points
1. Why are the people in wealthier countries more individualist than those in poorer countries?
2. What are the advantages and disadvantages of the individualist and collectivist approaches?

KEY STUDY
The extended self: Rethinking the so-called Negro self-concept

Nobles (1976) presents a very strong argument regarding the dominance of psychology by white, Eurocentric attitudes. He suggests that European psychologists have presented a view of humankind that is based on one particular kind of culture and not representative of all people. The European worldview is oriented along the principles of (1) survival of the fittest and (2) control over nature. These, in turn, affect European values and customs. The emphasis on competition, individual rights, independence, and uniqueness is clearly linked to these guiding principles.

On the other hand, if one examines the African worldview, one can readily see differences from the European one. Rather than the survival of the fittest and control over nature, the African worldview is oriented by the principles of (1) survival of the tribe and (2) oneness with nature. Values that are consistent with these guiding principles are co-operation, interdependence, and collective responsibility.

The African self-concept is, by definition, "we" instead of "I". The African philosophic tradition recognises that it is only in terms of one's people that the "individual" becomes conscious of one's own being. It is only through others that one learns one's duties and responsibilities towards oneself and the collective self.

As a result, Nobles describes the traditional African conception of self as an "extended self". Self-awareness or self-conception is not, therefore, limited (as in the Euro-American tradition) to just the cognitive awareness of one's uniqueness, individuality, and historical finiteness. It is, in the African tradition, awareness of self as the awareness of one's historical consciousness (collective spirituality) and the subsequent sense of "we" or being One.

The concept "Negro" refers to African individuals who attempt to deny their Africanity because they are caught in a contradiction between two philosophical systems—the African (black) and Euro-American (white). To be a "Negro" therefore, is to be in a state of philosophical confusion. Nobles further argued that the Negro self-concept is an example of scientific colonialism because (1) data are exported from a foreign community and processed into manufactured goods (articles, books, etc.), (2) the centre of gravity for acquiring knowledge about Negroes is located outside of the Negroes themselves, (3) there is an assumption of unlimited right of access to data, and (4) it is a profitable enterprise.

Discussion points
1. Can you think of an area of psychology that you have studied where this confusion between the European and African tradition has led to a false understanding of human nature?
2. Explain in what way psychology has forced a kind of scientific colonialism on non-Europeans.

made by people from a collectivist culture tend to be contextualised, whereas attributions made by people in individualist cultures tend to be more focused on personal choice. It is also the case that the self-serving bias (accepting credit for success but not blame for failure) is stronger in individualist cultures than in collectivist ones, and that the fundamental attribution error (tendency to attribute others' behaviour to their personality rather than to the situation) is less common in collectivist cultures than in individualist cultures.

Psychological theories of relationship formation and maintenance are also related to individualist versus collectivist cultures (see Chapter 2, Relationships, especially pages 58–60). Altruistic and pro-social behaviour is generally greater in collectivist cultures (see Chapter 3, Pro- and Anti-social Behaviour, pages 105–106). Humanistic theories of motivation include the need for achievement as a motivating factor, but this may relate to individualist cultures only. Gender equality has been found to be more common in individualist cultures, whereas collectivist cultures require more separation of roles, which is often along gender lines.

Theories of adolescence and old age relate to cultural differences (see for example page 289).

The distinction between individualistic and collectivistic cultures is important, but is limited in some ways. First, it is simply not the case that *everyone* in an individualistic culture adopts an individualistic approach or that *everyone* in a collectivistic culture adopts a collectivistic approach. Triandis et al. (2001) estimated that only about 60% of people conform to the dominant culture. Second, Hofstede (1980) assumed that collectivism was the opposite of individualism, but the evidence indicates they are not that different from each other (Gelfand et al., 1996)—it is possible to accept personal responsibility (an individualistic quality) while at the same time obtaining much enjoyment from group activities (a collectivistic quality). Third, just consider the diversity of the various cultures with which you are familiar—it is a great oversimplification to categorise them all as individualistic or collectivistic.

Emic and Etic Constructs

Berry (1969) drew a distinction between emic constructs and etic constructs. **Emic constructs** are specific to a given culture, and so vary from one culture to another. In contrast, **etic constructs** refer to universal factors that hold across all cultures. One useful way to remember this is in terms of the distinction between "phonemics" and "phonetics". Both involve the study of the sounds of words (phonemes) but phonemics is the study of sounds as they contribute to meaning *in a particular language*, whereas phonetics is the study of universal sounds independent of meaning. The notion of the "family" is an example of an etic construct whereas the "nuclear family" (just parents and children) is an emic construct. According to Berry, what has happened fairly often in the history of psychology is that what are actually emic constructs are assumed to be etic constructs.

The study of intelligence can be used to illustrate this point. It has often been argued that the same abilities of problem solving, reasoning, memory, and so on define intelligence in every culture. Berry (1974) disagreed strongly with that view. He favoured a viewpoint known as cultural relativism. According to this viewpoint, the meaning of intelligence is rather different in each culture. For example, as Sternberg (1985, p.53) pointed out:

coordination skills that may be essential to life in a preliterate society (e.g., those motor skills required for shooting a bow and arrow) may be all but irrelevant to intelligent behaviour for most people in a literate and more "developed" society.

Cole et al. (1971) provided further evidence of the emic nature of the concept of intelligence. They asked adult members of the Kpelle tribe in Africa to sort familiar objects into groups. In most Western societies, people would sort the objects into categories (e.g., foods, tools). What the Kpelle tribespeople did was

? Try to generate other examples of emic and etic constructs.

KEY TERMS
Emic constructs: those that vary from one culture to another.
Etic constructs: universal factors that hold across cultures.

to sort them into functional groups (e.g., a knife with an orange, because an orange can be cut by a knife). Thus, what is regarded as intelligent behaviour can differ from one culture to another. By the way, the Kpelle tribespeople showed that they could sort the objects into categories when asked to do so—they did not naturally do this, because they thought it was a stupid way of sorting.

Imposed etic

An **imposed etic** is a technique or theory that is rooted in a researcher's own culture, such as an intelligence test, and then used to study other cultures. Psychologists have studied obedience, moral development, and attachment in various cultures using measures designed within our own culture. This includes measures such as Kohlberg's moral dilemmas (see the Key Study on pages 226–227) and the Strange Situation that was included in your AS level studies. The methods used to diagnose and treat mental disorders are also imposed etics.

The general insensitivity to cultural differences reveals itself in the personality area. Most studies of personality in non-Western cultures have assessed personality by means of translated versions of Western tests rather than by devising new, culture-relevant tests (i.e., they use an imposed etic). Evidence that personality structure may vary from one culture to another was reported by Kuo-shu and Bond (1990). They asked students in Taiwan to describe several people they knew using two sets of adjectives: (1) those found from studies in Western cultures to assess the Big Five personality factors (extraversion, agreeableness, emotional stability, culture, and conscientiousness); and (2) adjectives taken from Chinese newspapers. Kuo-shu Yang and Bond found that five different factors emerged from an analysis of the adjectives taken from the Chinese newspapers: social orientation, expressiveness, competence, self-control, and optimism. There is some agreement between the two sets of factors. For example, the Big Five factor of agreeableness correlated +0.66 with social orientation, and emotional stability correlated +0.55 with competence. However, the overall similarity between the two sets of personality factors was fairly low, suggesting that personality structure in Taiwanese culture differs from that in Western cultures. Thus it is inappropriate to use a Western personality test to assess personality in another culture.

The entire notion of semi-permanent personality traits determining behaviour is less applicable in collectivistic cultures in which it is assumed that individuals will change to fit in with group expectations. For example, Norenzayan et al. (1999) found that people from Western cultures regard personality traits as stable, whereas East Asians regard them as much more flexible and changeable.

Derived etics

Berry (1969) proposed that an alternative method of study might be used, one that is similar to the techniques used by anthropologists. He called this a **derived etic**, where a series of emic studies take place in a local setting conducted by local researchers using local techniques. Such studies can build up a picture of human behaviour in a manner similar to the **ethnographic approach** taken by anthropologists. This is the study of different cultures through the use of comparisons. By making comparisons between cultures we can learn more about a target culture, rather like the way that comparative psychology can enlighten us about human behaviour.

Culture bias in IQ tests is discussed on pages 212–215.

? What social psychological explanations can you give for the results of Kuo-shu Yang and Bond's study?

KEY TERMS

Imposed etic: the use of a technique developed in one culture to study another culture.
Derived etic: using a series of emic studies to build up a picture of a particular culture.
Ethnographic approach: making comparisons between cultures with a view to learning more about a target culture, in a similar way to how comparative psychology can enlighten us about human behaviour.

We can see the above approach in action in the area of diagnosing mental disorders. DSM-IV (APA, 1994), which is American based, focuses mainly on mental disorders that are common in the Western world, although there is a short appendix in DSM on culture-bound syndromes found in other parts of the world. Kleinman and Cohen (1997, p.76) dismissed this appendix as "little more than a sop thrown to cultural psychiatrists and psychiatric anthropologists". They pointed out that detailed work in several non-Western cultures had uncovered many disorders totally ignored by DSM-IV. Here are a few examples:

How might cultural differences in mental disorders affect immigrants?

- *pa-fend* (fear of wind) found in China
- *amafufunyana* (violent behaviour caused by spirit possession) found in South Africa
- brain fag (problems in concentrating and thinking produced by excessive study—one to avoid!) found in West Africa.

Biases in cross-cultural research

One final consideration, in relation to cross-cultural research, is the bias involved when an observer conducts research in a foreign culture. A classic example of such research is the studies conducted by Margaret Mead (1935) where she observed three tribes in New Guinea (see pages 79–80 and 270). Mead concluded that the Mundugumor tribe were all aggressive (masculine quality) regardless of sex. Neither gender gave much attention to child rearing. In contrast the Arapesh were all warm, emotional, and non-aggressive (feminine qualities). Husbands and wives shared everything, including pregnancy: the men took to bed during childbirth! The Tchambuli exhibited a reversal of our own gender roles. Women reared the children but also looked after commerce outside the tribe. The men spent their time in social activities, and were more emotional and artistic.

But how reliable are observations made of individuals in different cultural situations? The greatest problem is the effect that expectations have on what the observer sees. The study of perception tells us this. Perception is a "top-down process": much of what we see (or hear) is incomplete and ambiguous. Therefore, we impose our own meaning to interpret these data. We draw on past experience and expectations. Expectations also influence the categories that are selected and the way that data are recorded.

A further problem for cross-cultural research is that foreign researchers may simply misinterpret the language or cultural practices and draw erroneous inferences. It is also true that they are likely to sample a very small group of individuals within the culture they are studying and this sample may be unrepresentative. Participants aware they are being observed may not behave naturally. For example, concerning another study undertaken by Mead of puberty in Samoa (1928), Freeman (1983) criticised Mead's conclusions, arguing that she may not have established sufficient trust with the Samoan people to expect total honesty from them. One woman in Samoa told Freeman that she had not been honest with Mead about her sexual experiences. Freeman also claimed that Mead was not sufficiently closely involved with the Samoan people and that she saw only what she wanted to see.

Racial Bias

Racial bias is a particularly unpleasant form of cultural bias. Some of the ways in which it manifests itself were discussed by Howitt and Owusu-Bempah (1990). They considered every issue of the *British Journal of Social and Clinical Psychology* between 1962 and 1980. They were dismayed at the way in which Western personality tests such as the 16PF were used inappropriately in non-Western cultures. As they pointed out (p.399), "There were no studies which attempted to explore, for example, the Ghanaian or Chinese personality structures in their own terms rather than through Western eyes." However, as we saw earlier, there have some recent attempts to consider seriously the possibility that personality structure varies from one culture to another.

Owusu-Bempah and Howitt (1994) claimed to have found evidence of racism in the well-known textbook by Atkinson, Atkinson, Smith, and Bem (1993). They pointed out that Atkinson et al. tended to categorise Western cultures together, and to do the same for non-Western ones. This included referring to work on African tribes without bothering to specify which tribe or tribes had been studied. Owusu-Bempah and Howitt (p.165) argued as follows: "The *cumulative* effect of this is the 'naturalness' of white people and their ways of life, and the resultant exclusion . . . of black people and their cultures."

The central point made by Owusu-Bempah and Howitt (1994) was that Atkinson et al. (1993) evaluated other cultures in relation to the technological and cultural achievements of the United States and Europe. In their own words (p.163):

> *Cultures that fall short of this arbitrary Euro-centric standard are frequently described as "primitive", "undeveloped" or, at best, "developing". Religion, morality, community spirit, etc., are ignored in this racist ideological league table.*

In sum, many Western psychologists have written in insensitive ways about cross-cultural differences. Sometimes the mistaken impression may have been given that some cultures are "better" than others rather than simply different. There are certainly grounds for concern, but thankfully any explicit or implicit racism is very much in decline.

Some recent research has focused on trying to reduce racial bias in people taking part in experiments. Plant et al. (2005) used a computerised situation in which white participants pretended they were police officers and decided as rapidly as possible whether to shoot at black and white suspects. There was a greater tendency to shoot at black suspects. However, extensive practice in which race was unrelated to the presence or absence of a gun eliminated that racial bias suggesting that at least some of racial bias can be altered fairly easily.

What do you think is meant by the phrase "in their own terms" when applied to personality structures in different cultures?

Racism in relation to intelligence is considered on page 213.

The Changing Picture

We have seen that there is substantial evidence of cultural bias running through several areas of psychology, and that is obviously a matter of regret. However, it is important to note that the picture is changing fairly rapidly for the better. At least four ways in which psychologists have attempted to reduce or eliminate cultural bias emerge from our earlier discussion. First, far more psychologists are engaged in cross-cultural research based on an acknowledgement that what is the case in one culture may well not be the case in another culture. The distinction between individualistic and collectivistic cultures is oversimplified, but at least it recognises that cultures differ in major ways from each other.

Second, there has been progress within the fields of intelligence and personality. It used to be assumed that intelligence and personality tests devised by Western psychologists could appropriately be used in all other cultures. Very few psychologists believe that any more, and there have been numerous attempts to develop measures that assess more accurately and sensitively the structure of intelligence and personality in each culture studied.

Third, there is progress in the field of diagnosing mental disorders. Early versions of the American DSM system virtually ignored mental disorders that are found mainly or exclusively in non-American cultures. DSM-IV in 1994 acknowledged the inadequacy of that approach, and it seems probable that future version of DSM will move further in the direction of focusing on culture-bound syndromes.

Fourth, the history of psychology contains numerous examples of racial bias, in which some races were regarded as superior to others. This racial bias is now (quite rightly) regarded as totally unacceptable. It has been a gradual process, but nowadays virtually all psychologists accept that races or cultures undoubtedly differ in various ways but that these differences do not in the slightest imply that some are better than others.

SECTION SUMMARY
Cultural Bias

What is cultural bias?

❖ Culture can be defined as a relatively organised system of shared meanings.
❖ There is some tendency to confuse the idea of a cultural group with people living in one country.
❖ Many psychologists in the Western world have ignored important cross-cultural differences.
❖ A major distinction is made between individualist and collectivist cultures, particularly in terms of the self-concept:

— This distinction is important in understanding behaviour, as shown, for example, in studies of attribution and of motivation.
— However, the distinction is limited, because it doesn't apply to everyone within a given culture.

Emic and etic constructs

❖ It is important to distinguish between:

— Emic constructs: specific to a given culture
— Etic constructs: universal.

❖ Intelligence is regarded as an etic construct but there is evidence of it being emic.
❖ Imposed etics:

— Psychologists use tools developed in their own culture to measure behaviour in other cultures.
— Imposed etics include the Strange Situation and Cattell's personality test.
— There is low validity for such studies.

❖ Derived etics:

  — Attempts to offer a solution by taking the findings from a variety of emic studies and making comparisons between cultures
  — Recent developments within the diagnosis of mental disorders are based on derived etics.

❖ Cross-cultural research is hampered by observer bias, and the use of small samples that are often unrepresentative.

❖ Racial bias is a particular example of cultural bias in psychology: *Racial bias*

  — It often involves grouping together quite distinct cultures as in the case of "African tribes".
  — It also leads to evaluations of other cultures in relation to the technological and cultural achievements of the United States and Europe, and the conclusion that other cultures are primitive or undeveloped.
  — Implicit racism is often insensitive and perpetuates erroneous stereotypes.

❖ The good news is that psychological research is increasingly sensitive to potential issues of racial bias, and so this form of bias is in steep decline.

❖ Psychologists are now attempting to reduce cultural bias by: *Reducing cultural bias*

  — Acknowledging cross-cultural differences
  — Developing more accurate measures for assessing personality and intelligence
  — Expanding the field of diagnosing mental disorders
  — Refusing to accept racial bias.

> See also pages 263–266 of the revision guide.

ETHICAL ISSUES

The topic of ethical issues was explored in your AS level studies. It is not our intention to cover the same material again but, instead, to consider some wider ethical issues in relation to what is acceptable in psychological research.

For your reference the British Psychological Society Ethical Guidelines for Research with Human Participants are given on pages 456–457. Before looking at the guidelines you should try the two research activities on the right and the next page to review your familiarity with ethical issues.

> ■ Activity: Ethical issues 1
> List all the ethical issues that you can recall and for each of them write a further two sentences, explaining how a researcher might deal with such issues.

Ethics in Psychological Research

To begin, we will outline some of the issues raised by major studies in psychology.

Milgram

Milgram's (1963, 1974) research on obedience to authority was carried out in the days before most institutions had ethical committees responsible for ensuring the ethical acceptability of all research. He asked his participants to administer very

■ **Activity: Ethical issues 2**

For each of the ethical issues listed below, identify an area in your AS and/or A2 studies that exemplifies the issue, and write a few sentences of commentary (i.e., points that should be considered in relation to the issue). (You can add more examples to the table.)

	Research study to exemplify the issue	Commentary
Deception in a field experiment		
Informed consent in a laboratory experiment		
Confidentiality in a survey		
Right to withdraw in any kind of research study		
Privacy in an observational study		
Protection from harm in a psychology experiment		

When you are answering an examination question on ethical issues, ensure that you discuss a good variety of ethical problems as well as a variety of types of research (rather than just using Milgram and Zimbardo as your examples).

strong (and possibly lethal) electric shocks to someone who was said to suffer from a heart condition. It is very unlikely that an ethical committee would permit an experimenter to carry out the type of research done by Milgram, which explains why very few such studies have been undertaken in recent years.

Milgram's research failed to fulfil some criteria now regarded as very important. First, the participants were deceived about key aspects of the study, such as the fact that the other person didn't actually receive any shocks, and so they didn't give full informed consent. Second, when any of the participants said they wanted to leave the experiment or to stop giving electric shocks, they were told that they had to continue with the experiment. Nowadays it is standard practice to make it clear to participants that they have the right to withdraw from the experiment at any time without providing an explanation. Third, the procedures used by Milgram caused considerable distress to many of the participants. However, Milgram's research did provide us with important insights into obedience to authority.

Zimbardo

Zimbardo's (1973) Stanford prison experiment is another study from many years ago that raises considerable ethical issues. In this study, a mock prison was set up with mock guards and mock prisoners. Some mock guards behaved very aggressively, causing four of the mock prisoners to be released because of "extreme depression, disorganised thinking, uncontrollable crying and fits of rage". Savin (1973) compared Zimbardo to used-car salesmen and others "whose roles tempt them to be as obnoxious as the law allows". He concluded that:

> Professors who . . . deceive, humiliate, and otherwise mistreat their students, are subverting the atmosphere of mutual trust and intellectual honesty without which, as we are fond of telling outsiders who want to meddle in our affairs, neither education nor free inquiry can flourish.

Zimbardo (1973) pointed out that all his participants had signed a formal informed consent form, which indicated that there would be an invasion of

CASE STUDY: DRAWING SANTA CLAUS

Some studies that involve deception of participants can still be regarded as ethically acceptable. One such study was carried out by Solley and Haigh in 1957 (described in Solley & Murphy, 1960). It involved a study on children focusing on a phenomenon resembling "perceptual set". Perceptual set is a bias to perceive a stimulus in a particular way as opposed to any other way, and can arise from external cues (the environment) or internal forces (emotions) which make the individual more sensitive to the stimuli.

In their study, Solley and Haigh asked children aged between 4 and 8 to draw pictures of Santa Claus and his gifts. The children drew their pictures before and after Christmas. Solley and Haigh suggested that emotional set (anticipation of the excitement of Christmas) would lead to increased sensitivity resulting in larger, more elaborate drawings before Christmas, whereas after Christmas, reduced sensitivity would lead to smaller, less detailed drawings. The study indicated that increased sensitivity had indeed affected perceptual organisation.

The children involved in this study were deceived about the real reason for the research. In order to produce natural and realistic results, the children had to be naive about what might be expected of them. However, in this case deception didn't lead to the participants experiencing any form of stress and so could be justified. This study was also ecologically valid, as it generated valuable insights into the effect of perceptual set.

Solley and Haigh's experiment was recently replicated with some Cornish children, with these results. The two larger, more elaborate versions were drawn just before Christmas, but after Christmas they produced the smaller, simple drawings.

privacy, loss of some civil rights, and harassment. However, it could be argued this wasn't *full* informed consent because the participants didn't anticipate how harrowing their experiences were going to be. Zimbardo also noted that day-long debriefing sessions were held with the participants, so that they could understand the moral conflicts being studied. However, Zimbardo failed to protect his participants from physical and mental harm. It was entirely predictable that the mock guards would attack the mock prisoners, because that is exactly what had happened in a pilot study that Zimbardo carried out before the main study.

Asch

A well-known example of research involving deception is the work of Asch (1951, 1956). He gave participants the task of deciding which one of three lines

Zimbardo tried to minimise the after-effects of participation in his Stanford prison experiment by asking the participants to sign an informed consent form before the experiment began. Even so, some of the mock guards became very aggressive during the experiment, and four of the mock prisoners had to be released early.

was equal in length to a standard line. This task was done in groups of between four and 11 people, all but one of whom were "stooge" participants working under instructions from the experimenter. The participants gave their judgements one at a time with the genuine participant giving his/her opinion last. On key trials, all the stooge participants gave the same wrong answer. The aim of the experiment was to see whether the genuine participants would conform to group pressure, which happened on about one-third of the trials. If the participants had been told the experiment was designed to study conformity to group pressure, and that all the other participants were stooges of the experimenter (i.e., they had given full informed consent), then this important study would have been pointless.

Rosenhan

Rosenhan (1973) carried out a controversial study in which eight normal people tried to gain admission to 12 different psychiatric hospitals by complaining of hearing indistinct voices that seemed to be saying "empty", "hollow", and "thud". This led to seven of them being diagnosed as suffering from schizophrenia. After these eight normal people were admitted to psychiatric wards, they all said they felt fine, and that they no longer had any symptoms. However, it took an average of 19 days before they were discharged. In a second study, Rosenhan told the staff at a psychiatric hospital that one or more pseudo-patients (normal individuals pretending to have schizophrenic symptoms) would try to gain admittance to the hospital. No pseudo-patients actually appeared, but 41 genuine patients were judged with great confidence to be pseudo-patients.

These two studies raise several ethical issues. First, in both studies professionals were deliberately misled about the true status of patients (and thus didn't give full informed consent). This deception is no more ethically justified than deception of patients or participants in a study. Second, there is the welfare of the genuine patients in the second study. It would have been possible for a patient who was exhibiting normal behaviour but was actually suffering from a mental disorder to have been mistakenly discharged from psychiatric care.

Ethical Issues with Human Participants

To what extent do ethical guidelines protect participants in psychological research?

According to Kelman (1972, p.993), "Most ethical problems arising in social research can be traced to the subject's power deficiency." More specifically, the experimenter is often a person of fairly high status (such as a university researcher or professor), and he/she has expertise and knowledge about the experimental situation not shared by the participant. When an experiment takes place in the laboratory, the experimenter has the advantage of being on "home ground", and the setting is almost entirely under his/her control. In addition, the acceptance of scientific research as an activity that is valued by society also enhances the position of power enjoyed by the experimenter.

Resolving ethical issues

What can be done to resolve the ethical issues that arise from the fact that participants typically have a power deficiency relative to the experimenter? Of crucial importance is the provision of ethical guidelines that must be followed by all researchers (see the Ethical Guidelines of the British Psychological Society on pages 456–457). Kimmel (1996) compared the ethical codes or guidelines produced by 11 different countries. There are important similarities among the ethical codes produced by the various countries. Most focus on three basic principles:

1. Protection of individuals from physical harm
2. Protection of individuals from psychological harm
3. Confidentiality of the data obtained from individual participants.

There is fairly general agreement that full informed consent and avoidance of deception are important in ensuring that the first two principles are achieved. However, it is sometimes difficult to do this. Small children and patients with certain mental disorders may be unable to provide informed consent, in which case it is usual for a close relative to do so. The notion that deception should always be avoided in psychological research is too stringent, because it ignores the fact that many forms of deception are entirely harmless. For example, some memory researchers are interested in incidental learning, which involves people's ability to remember information they weren't asked to remember. This can only be done by deceiving participants as to the true purpose of the experiment until the memory test is presented.

When is deception justified? There is no simple answer. Various relevant factors need to be taken into account. First, the less potentially damaging the consequences of the deception, the more likely it is to be acceptable. Second, it is easier to justify the use of deception in studies that are important in scientific terms than in those that are trivial. Third, deception is more justifiable when there are no alternative, deception-free ways of studying an issue.

Ethical issues are resolved by ethical committees as well as by the use of ethical guidelines. Nowadays the great majority of universities and research units have their own ethical committees to consider all proposed research, and the same is true of hospitals in which research takes place. Finally, professional organisations in most countries (e.g., the American Psychological Association in America, the British Psychological Society in the UK) will investigate potentially serious ethical issues that arise in the course of research.

Socially Sensitive Research

As we have seen, ethical guidelines focus mainly on the well-being and protection of those who participate in experiments. However, much research raises issues of relevance to society as a whole. As a result, psychologists need to be concerned about broader ethical issues. This is true of nearly all psychological research, but

> **EXAM HINT**
> You should be able to draw from your AS notes on the ethical issues involved in research with human participants, so be prepared for a question on these issues, or on attempts to resolve ethical issues.

> **EXAM HINT**
> This is a new take on ethical issues. Again there are many examples of socially sensitive research so ensure you write enough AO2 by using the arguments for and against the research, and consider the inadequacies of the measures in place such as the ethical guidelines and the social responsibilities of psychologists.

Ethical Principles for Conducting Research with Human Participants

Reproduced from *The Psychologist* (January 1993, 6, 33–35)

1 Introduction

1.1 The principles given below are intended to apply to research with human participants. Principles of conduct in professional practice are to be found in the Society's Code of Conduct and in the advisory documents prepared by the Divisions, Sections and Special Groups of the Society.

1.2 Participants in psychological research should have confidence in the investigators. Good psychological research is possible only if there is mutual respect and confidence between investigators and participants. Psychological investigators are potentially interested in all aspects of human behaviour and conscious experience. However, for ethical reasons, some areas of human experience and behaviour may be beyond the reach of experiment, observation or other form of psychological investigation. Ethical guidelines are necessary to clarify the conditions under which psychological research is acceptable.

1.3 The principles given below supplement for researchers with human participants the general ethical principles of members of the Society as stated in the British Psychological Society's Code of Conduct (1985) and any subsequent amendments to this Code. Members of the British Psychological Society are expected to abide by both the Code of Conduct and the fuller principles expressed here. Members should also draw the principles to the attention of research colleagues who are not members of the Society. Members should encourage colleagues to adopt them and ensure that they are followed by all researchers whom they supervise (e.g. research assistants, postgraduate, undergraduate, A-Level and GCSE students).

1.4 In recent years, there has been an increase in legal actions by members of the general public against professionals for alleged misconduct. Researchers must recognise the possibility of such legal action, if they infringe the rights and dignity of participants in their research.

2 General

2.1 In all circumstances, investigators must consider the ethical implications and psychological consequences for the participants in their research. The essential principle is that the investigation should be considered from the standpoint of all participants; foreseeable threats to their psychological well-being, health, values or dignity should be eliminated. Investigators should recognise that, in our multi-cultural and multi-ethnic society and where investigations involve individuals of different ages, gender and social background, the investigators may not have sufficient knowledge of the implications of an investigation for the participants. It should be borne in mind that the best judges of whether an investigation will cause offence may be members of the population from which the participants in the research are to be drawn.

3 Consent

3.1 Whenever possible, the investigator should inform all participants of the objectives of the investigation. The investigator should inform the participants of all aspects of the research or intervention that might reasonably be expected to influence willingness to participate. The investigator should, normally, explain all other aspects of the research or intervention about which the participants enquire. Failure to make full disclosure prior to obtaining informed consent requires additional safeguards to protect the welfare and dignity of the participants (see Section 4).

3.2 Research with children or with participants who have impairments that will limit understanding and/or communication such that they are unable to give their real consent requires special safeguarding procedures.

3.3 Where possible, the real consent of children and of adults with impairments in understanding or communication should be obtained. In addition, where research involves any persons under sixteen years of age, consent should be obtained from parents or from those in *loco parentis*. If the nature of the research precludes consent being obtained from parents or permission being obtained from teachers, before proceeding with the research, the investigator must obtain approval from an Ethics Committee.

3.4 Where real consent cannot be obtained from adults with impairments in understanding or communication, wherever possible the investigator should consult a person well-placed to appreciate the participant's reaction, such as a member of the person's family, and must obtain the disinterested approval of the research from independent advisors.

3.5 When research is being conducted with detained persons, particular care should be taken over informed consent, paying attention to the special circumstances which may affect the person's ability to give free informed consent.

3.6 Investigators should realise that they are often in a position of authority or influence over participants who may be their students, employees or clients. This relationship must not be allowed to pressurise the participants to take part in, or remain in, an investigation.

3.7 The payment of participants must not be used to induce them to risk harm beyond that which they risk without payment in their normal lifestyle.

3.8 If harm, unusual discomfort, or other negative consequences for the individual's future life might occur, the investigator must obtain the disinterested approval of independent advisors, inform the participants, and obtain informed, real consent from each of them.

3.9 In longitudinal research, consent may need to be obtained on more than one occasion.

4 Deception

4.1 The withholding of information or the misleading of participants is unacceptable if the participants are typically likely to object or show unease once debriefed. Where this is in any doubt, appropriate consultation must precede the investigation. Consultation is best carried out with individuals who share the social and cultural background of the participants in the research, but the advice of ethics committees or experienced and disinterested colleagues may be sufficient.

4.2 Intentional deception of the participants over the purpose and general nature of the investigation should be avoided whenever possible. Participants should never be deliberately misled without extremely strong scientific or medical justification. Even then there should be strict controls and the disinterested approval of independent advisors.

4.3 It may be impossible to study some psychological processes without withholding information about the true object of the study or deliberately misleading the participants. Before conducting such a study, the investigator has a special responsibility to (a) determine that alternative procedures avoiding concealment or deception are not available; (b) ensure that the participants are provided with sufficient information at the earliest stage; and (c) consult appropriately upon the way that the withholding of information or deliberate deception will be received.

5 Debriefing

5.1 In studies where the participants are aware that they have taken part in an investigation, when the data have been collected, the investigator should provide the participants with any necessary information to complete their understanding of the nature of the research. The investigator should discuss with the participants their experience of the research in order to monitor any unforeseen negative effects or misconceptions.

5.2 Debriefing does not provide a justification for unethical aspects of an investigation.

5.3 Some effects which may be produced by an experiment will not be negated by a verbal description following the research. Investigators have a responsibility to ensure that participants receive any necessary debriefing in the form of active intervention before they leave the research setting.

6 Withdrawal from the Investigation

6.1 At the onset of the investigation investigators should make plain to participants their right to withdraw from the research at any time, irrespective of whether or not payment or other inducement has been offered. It is recognised that this may be difficult in certain observational or organisational settings, but nevertheless the investigator must attempt to ensure that participants (including children) know of their right to withdraw. When testing children, avoidance of the testing situation may be taken as evidence of failure to consent to the procedure and should be acknowledged.

6.2 In the light of experience of the investigation, or as a result of debriefing, the participant has the right to withdraw retrospectively any consent given, and to require that their own data, including recordings, be destroyed.

7 Confidentiality

7.1 Subject to the requirements of legislation, including the Data Protection Act, information obtained about a participant during an investigation is confidential unless otherwise agreed in advance. Investigators who are put under pressure to disclose confidential information should draw this point to the attention of those exerting such pressure. Participants in psychological research have a right to expect that information they provide will be treated confidentially and, if published, will not be identifiable as theirs. In the event that confidentiality and/or anonymity cannot be guaranteed, the participant must be warned of this in advance of agreeing to participate.

8 Protection of Participants

8.1 Investigators have a primary responsibility to protect participants from physical and mental harm during the investigation. Normally, the risk of harm must be no greater than in ordinary life, i.e. participants should not be exposed to risks greater than or additional to those encountered in their normal lifestyle. Where the risk of harm is greater than in ordinary life the provisions of 3.8 should apply. Participants

must be asked about any factors in the procedure that might create a risk, such as pre-existing medical conditions, and must be advised of any special action they should take to avoid risk.

8.2 Participants should be informed of procedures for contacting the investigator within a reasonable time period following participation should stress, potential harm, or related questions or concern arise despite the precautions required by these Principles. Where research procedures might result in undesirable consequences for participants, the investigator has the respon-sibility to detect and remove or correct these consequences.

8.3 Where research may involve behaviour or experiences that participants may regard as personal and private the participants must be protected from stress by all appropriate measures, including the assurances that answers to personal questions need not be given. There should be no concealment or deception when seeking information that might encroach on privacy.

8.4 In research involving children, great caution should be exercised when discussing the results with parents, teachers or others in *loco parentis*, since evaluative statements may carry unintended weight.

9 Observational Research

9.1 Studies based upon observation must respect the privacy and pyschological well-being of the individuals studied. Unless those observed give their consent to being observed, observational research is only acceptable in situations where those observed would expect to be observed by strangers. Additionally, particular account should be taken of local cultural values and of the possibility of intruding upon the privacy of individuals who, even while in a normal public space, may believe they are unobserved.

10 Giving Advice

10.1 During research, an investigator may obtain evidence of psychological or physical problems of which a participant is, apparently, unaware. In such a case, the investigator has a responsibility to inform the participant if the investigator believes that by not doing so the participant's future well-being may be endangered.

10.2 If, in the normal course of psychological research, or as a result of problems detected as in 10.1, a participant solicits advice concerning educational, personality, behavioural or health issues, caution should be exercised. If the issue is serious and the investigator is not qualified to offer assistance, the appropriate source of professional advice should be recommended. Further details on the giving of advice will be found in the Society's Code of Conduct.

10.3 In some kinds of investigation the giving of advice is appropriate if this forms an intrinsic part of the research and has been agreed in advance.

11 Colleagues

11.1 Investigators share responsibility for the ethical treatment of research participants with their collaborators, assistants, students and employees. A psychologist who believes that another psychologist or investigator may be conducting research that is not in accordance with the principles above should encourage that investigator to re-evaluate the research.

Reference

The British Psychological Society. (1985). A Code of Conduct for Psychologists. *Bulletin of The British Psychological Society, 38*, 41–43.

See also proposed revisions to this code in *The Psychologist, 5*, 562–563.

Copies of this article may be obtained from The British Psychological Society, St. Andrews House, 48 Princess Road East, Leicester LE1 7DR.

is especially true of socially sensitive research. This was defined by Sieber and Stanley (1988, p.49) as:

studies in which there are potential social consequences or implications either directly for the participants in research or the class of individuals represented by the research.

Socially sensitive research can produce risks for many people other than those directly involved as participants. Among the non-participants at risk, according to Sieber and Stanley, are the following:

- Members of the groups (e.g., racial, religious) to which the participants belong
- People closely associated with the participants (e.g., family, friends)
- The experimenter or experimenters
- The research institution to which the experimenter or experimenters belong.

We can consider a concrete example of non-participants being at risk. McCosker et al. (2001) discussed their research involving interviews with women who had been abused. The interviews were often distressing for the interviewer as well as for the woman being interviewed. In addition, there were transcribers who had the task of typing up what had been said in the interviews. Transcribers often became distressed, and so arrangements had to be made for them to have immediate access to crisis counselling if required.

In their thorough discussion of socially sensitive research, Sieber and Stanley (1988) argued that important ethical concerns can arise with respect to four major aspects of such research:

1. Deciding on the research question or hypothesis to be tested
2. The conduct of research and the treatment of participants
3. The institutional context (e.g., the organisation in which the research is carried out might make unjustified use of the findings)
4. Interpretation and application of research findings, especially the application of findings in ways far removed from the experimenter's intentions.

What are the kinds of problems that can occur in each of these aspects of research? We have already discussed at some length issues relating to the conduct of research and the treatment of participants in your AS book. Accordingly, we will focus on the other three aspects here.

? Which are more important, the interests of the individual or the interests of society as a whole?

Application of findings

The research carried out by psychologists such as John Bowlby and Sir Cyril Burt, among others, had a profound effect on social policy. These studies examined the role of the mother in child care, and the development of IQ, and resulted in policies such as encouraging mothers to stay at home rather than going out to work, and the introduction of the 11-plus examination. The studies posed ethical dilemmas for the researchers because their findings could be used to manipulate human behaviour and life choices, as well as adding to the knowledge base of science.

The research question

The first part of the research process involves deciding on the question or questions that the research is designed to answer. Simply asking certain questions can pose ethical issues. For example, suppose that a researcher asks the question, "Are there racial differences in intelligence?", and decides to answer it in a study. It is likely (but not certain) that he/she assumes that there are racial differences in intelligence, and that this assumption is motivating the research. In similar fashion, most researchers who carry out twin studies to decide the extent to which criminality is inherited probably assume that genetic factors are important. The very fact that this issue is being investigated may cause concern to the relatives of criminals.

Lee (1993) argued that there are three main types of issues raising concerns about sensitivity. First, there are issues that are private or stressful (e.g., sexuality, death). Second, there are issues associated with stigmatisation or fear (e.g., focusing on illegal behaviour). Third, there are issues relating to the presence of political threat (e.g., various controversial topics).

The institutional context

The institutional context can pose ethical issues in at least two ways. First, if the institutional context is perceived to be prestigious or intimidating, it may make the participants feel powerless and thus affect their behaviour. This happened in the work of Milgram (1974), in which he studied obedience to authority in the form of a willingness to administer very strong electric shocks. When the research setting was Yale University, 65% of the participants were fully obedient. This figure dropped to 48% when the setting was a run-down office building. Second, when research is carried out in a company, there can be various ethical problems with respect to the ways in which those running the company use the findings. For example, suppose that a researcher finds that the average stress levels in a company are only moderate. This may lead the company to abandon plans to offer stress counselling to their workers.

Interpretation and application

No one doubts that researchers should be concerned about the ways in which their findings are interpreted and applied. However, we need to distinguish between those uses of research findings that are predictable and those that are not. For example, it was predictable that the National Front and other organisations of the extreme right would use findings of racial differences in intelligence for their own ends. However, researchers studying the effects of sleep deprivation could not reasonably have expected that their findings would be used in brainwashing and cult indoctrination.

Eyewitness testimony

By now, you may have decided that socially sensitive research should be avoided altogether. However, some socially sensitive research is wholly desirable and of real benefit to society. Consider, for example, research on eyewitness testimony (from your AS studies). This research has shown convincingly that the memories of eyewitnesses for events are fragile and easily distorted. An implication is that defendants shouldn't be found guilty solely on the basis of eyewitness identification. However, in the United States in 1973, there were nearly 350 cases in which eyewitness identification was the only evidence of guilt. In 74% of these

Research into sleep deprivation has shown that people are easily confused when under stress from lack of sleep. This apparently innocent finding may have been incorporated into the indoctrination procedures of cults, such as the People's Temple. Over 900 followers of Jim Jones, pictured above with his wife, committed mass suicide in Guyana in 1978.

cases, the defendant was convicted. The problems of relying solely on eyewitness testimony have been shown very clearly now that DNA testing is available. In the United States alone, about 80 people who were found guilty on the basis of eyewitness testimony have been freed on the basis of DNA evidence that proved they had not committed the crime of which they were found guilty.

As a result of psychological research, courts and juries are less impressed by eyewitness testimony than they used to be. However, there was a time when such research was ignored. The Devlin Report on Evidence of Identification in Criminal Cases was published in the United Kingdom in 1976. One of its main conclusions was as follows:

> *The stage seems not yet to have been reached at which the conclusions of psychological research are sufficiently widely accepted or tailored to the needs of the judicial process to become the basis for procedural change.*

Socially sensitive research: Yes or no?

There is some evidence that socially sensitive research (at least in the United States) is more likely than non-sensitive research to be rejected by institutional ethical committees. Ceci, Peters, and Plotkin. (1985) found that the rejection rate was about twice as great. Thus, it seems important to consider arguments for and against socially sensitive research, as we do next.

Defending socially sensitive research

The case in favour of socially sensitive research was made by Scarr (1988, p.56). She argued as follows:

> *Science is in desperate need of good studies that highlight race and gender variables . . . to inform us of what we need to do to help underrepresented people to succeed in this society. Unlike the ostrich, we cannot afford to hide our heads for fear of socially uncomfortable discoveries.*

Scarr made another important point, arguing that there are very good reasons why most ethical guidelines focus much more on the protection of the participants in experiments than on the protection of the groups to which they belong. In essence, researchers can usually predict fairly accurately the direct effects of their experiment on the participants. However, they are unlikely to be able to predict the indirect effects on the groups to which the participants belong until the outcomes of the experiment are known.

McCosker et al. (2001) argued that much socially sensitive research is important and desirable provided that adequate safeguards are built into the research. In their own research, they studied women who had been abused. Those involved in interviewing the participants were very carefully trained in counselling techniques and in developing the ability to detect signs of distress in the participants at an early stage. More generally, much socially sensitive research can be defended provide that the researchers possess the skills and sensitivity to ensure that the well-being of the participants is not adversely affected.

Opposing socially sensitive research

One argument against socially sensitive research is that the very fact that certain socially sensitive issues are being studied by psychologists can suggest to society at large that these issues are real and important. For example, the fact that psychologists have compared the intelligence of different races implies that there are racial differences, and that intelligence exists and can be measured.

Socially sensitive research can be used to justify various forms of discrimination against individuals or groups. In the most extreme cases, the findings of psychological studies have even been used to produce discriminatory changes in the laws and regulations within a given society. Thus, the findings of socially sensitive research can be used to justify new (and often unwarranted) forms of social control.

A case in point occurred in the United States when intelligence tests were developed in the early years of the twentieth century. Between 1910 and 1920, several American states passed laws designed to prevent certain categories of people (including those of low intelligence) from having children. Psychologists often exerted pressure to have these laws passed. For example, the prominent Californian psychologist Lewis Terman (1916) argued as follows: "If we would preserve our state for a class of people worthy to possess it, we must prevent, as far as possible, the propagation of mental degenerates."

As a result of Terman's views, and those of other psychologists, a Californian law of 1918 required all compulsory sterilisations to be approved by a board including "a clinical psychologist holding the degree of PhD". In similar fashion, pressure by psychologists helped to persuade the state of Iowa to legislate in 1913 for "the prevention of the procreation of criminals, rapists, idiots, feeble-minded, imbeciles, lunatics, drunkards, drug fiends, epileptics, syphilitics, moral and sexual perverts, and diseased and degenerate persons".

Few, if any, psychologists nowadays would agree with the introduction of such harsh measures. However, some psychologists in the second half of the twentieth century argued that psychological principles should be used for purposes of social control. For example, B.F. Skinner claimed that we can determine and control people's behaviour by providing the appropriate rewards at the appropriate times: "Operant conditioning shapes behaviour as a sculptor shapes a lump of clay." Skinner (1948), in his novel *Walden Two*, described the use of operant conditioning to create an ideal society. He envisaged a high degree of external control in this society, with children being raised mainly by child rearing professionals, and government being by self-perpetuating committees rather than by elected representatives. In a sense, behavioural methods of treatment for abnormal behaviour do exert this kind of control (see Chapter 9, Treating Mental Disorders).

Overall

We have considered several advantages and disadvantages of socially sensitive research. It is important to strike a balance. The American Psychological Association tried to do this in its *Ethical principles in the conduct of research with human participants* (1982, p.74):

> On one side is an obligation to research participants who may not wish to see derogatory information . . . published about their valued groups. On the other side is an obligation to publish findings one believes relevant to scientific progress, an objective that in the investigator's views will contribute to the eventual understanding and amelioration of social and personal problems.

? Which different groups of people do you think might face prejudice and discrimination because of findings of socially sensitive research?

? Who controls what is acceptable behaviour? Should an individual's behaviour be modified to conform to cultural standards?

Socially Sensitive Research Areas

There are many examples of socially sensitive research areas. Some of the more important ones include race-related research, research on "alternative" sexuality, and research on social and cultural diversity.

A major focus of race-related research in psychology has been on racial differences in intelligence. One of the arguments against permitting such research is that it moves society no nearer the goal of providing good opportunities for all.

Race-related research

The best known (or most notorious) race-related research in psychology has focused on racial differences in intelligence, especially between black and white people in the United States (see Chapter 5, Cognitive Development). Our concern here is with the ethical issues involved. First we will consider the arguments in favour of carrying out such research followed by the arguments against permitting such research to be done.

One of the main arguments in favour of race-related research is that researchers should be free to carry out whatever research seems important to them. If governments start passing laws to prohibit certain kinds of research, then there is a real danger that research will be stopped for political rather than for ethical reasons. What about the ethics of publishing the findings of race-related research that may be used by racists for their own unacceptable purposes? H.J. Eysenck (1981, pp.167–168) argued that:

> it should not be assumed that those who feel that they have a duty to society to make known the results of empirical work are guided by less lofty ethical aspirations than those who hold the opposite view...the obvious social problem produced by the existence of racial and class differences in ability can only be solved, alleviated or attenuated by greater knowledge...it is ethically indefensible to refrain from acquiring such knowledge and making it available to society.

One of the strongest arguments against race-related research into intelligence is that the findings are often based on faulty research methods and are used in unacceptable ways. For example, Goddard (1913) gave intelligence tests to immigrants arriving in New York. He claimed that his findings demonstrated that 87% of Russians, 83% of Jews, 80% of Hungarians, and 79% of Italians were "feeble-minded". Goddard reached this ludicrous conclusion by ignoring the obvious fact that most of these immigrants had a very limited command of the English language.

Subsequent work on immigrant soldiers in the United States seemed to confirm Goddard's findings, while also showing that immigrants from Great Britain and Scandinavia performed better. These various findings were used by the American government in 1924 to introduce national origin quotas to reduce the level of immigration from southern and eastern Europe.

A second argument against much race-related research is that it is almost meaningless given the fact that black and white people in the United States do not

? Is knowing how intelligent you are important to having a happy life?

form biological groups. It is also fairly pointless, because it is impossible to discover for certain precisely why there are race differences in intelligence.

Another argument is that such research doesn't possess any particular scientific interest, in that it offers no prospect of shedding light on the processes and mechanisms involved in intelligence. If it could be shown that all racial differences in intelligence are due to environmental factors, this would tell us nothing about the different problem-solving strategies used by those high and low in intelligence.

Finally, such research has no obvious policy implications. It should be the goal of every society to provide good opportunities for everyone regardless of race, and this is true irrespective of the factors producing racial differences in intelligence.

This poster was produced by the European Youth Campaign Against Racism and the Commission for Racial Equality.

KEY STUDY
Morin

Morin (1977) obtained convincing evidence of heterosexual bias in his review of studies on gays and lesbians published between 1967 and 1974. He found that about 70% of these studies addressed issues such as whether homosexuals are mentally ill, ways in which homosexuality can be identified, and the causes of homosexuality. Focusing on such issues suggests that being homosexual was regarded almost like a disease that needed to be "cured".

This biased approach to research, with its clear implication that gays and lesbians are inferior to heterosexuals, poses serious ethical issues relating to discrimination against gays and lesbians. The American Psychological Association in 1975 took steps to prevent such discrimination by adopting the following resolution:

Homosexuality per se implies no impairment in judgment, stability, reliability, or general social or vocational capabilities. Further, the American Psychological Association urges all mental health professionals to take the lead in removing the stigma of mental illness that has long been associated with homosexual orientations.

Another feature of the research reviewed by Morin (1977) was that 82% of the studies compared gays and/or lesbians against heterosexual individuals. This poses ethical problems, because it misleadingly implies that all gays and lesbians possess the same characteristics that distinguish them from heterosexuals. In fact, of course, gays, lesbians, and heterosexuals are all individuals. Knowing about someone's sexual orientations tells us little or nothing about that person's attitudes, personality, and behaviour.

Discussion points
1. How can alternative sexuality be studied in an ethically acceptable way?
2. Can psychological research change some of the unfortunate and misleading stereotypes that prevail in this area?

Homosexuality and the DSM

The decision to remove homosexuality from the DSM (Diagnostic and Statistical Manual) was taken in the 1970s, and it was finally removed in 1980. Before that, homosexuality was seen as abnormal behaviour that needed to be "cured" like other forms of illness.

The Kurdek and Schmitt study assessed relationship quality in gay, lesbian, married heterosexual, and cohabiting heterosexual couples. The findings supported the liberal humanistic view of an underlying similarity between homosexual and heterosexual relationships.

"Alternative" sexuality

According to Kitzinger and Coyle (1995), research on gays and lesbians has gone through three distinct phases:

1. **Heterosexual bias:** the notion that heterosexuality is more natural than, and superior to, homosexuality (see the Key Study on the previous page).
2. **Liberal humanism:** this is based on the assumption that homosexual and heterosexual couples have an underlying similarity in their relationships.
3. **Liberal humanism plus:** what is added to the liberal humanistic view is an increased recognition of the specific characteristics of gay and lesbian relationships.

Liberal humanism

The second phase of research described by Kitzinger and Coyle (1995) was based on the liberal humanistic approach. This approach rejected the notion that gays and lesbians are inferior to heterosexuals, and accepted that they should be regarded as individuals rather than as members of a group defined by sexual orientation. It was accepted within this approach that homosexuality is as natural and normal as heterosexuality.

Kurdek and Schmitt (1986) carried out a typical study within the liberal humanistic perspective. They compared gay, lesbian, married heterosexual, and heterosexual cohabiting couples. These couples were assessed for relationship quality based on love for their partner, liking of their partner, and relationship satisfaction. The gay, lesbian, and married heterosexual couples all had very similar levels of relationship quality, with heterosexual cohabiting couples being significantly lower. These findings support the view of an underlying similarity between homosexuals and heterosexuals.

The liberal humanist approach is limited rather than ethically dubious, but it does raise ethical issues. It has two major limitations. First, there is an assumption that gays and lesbians conform to heterosexual norms in their attitudes and behaviour. As a result, according to Kitzinger and Coyle (1995, p.67), "Researchers . . . have tended to ignore, distort or pathologise [regard as a disease] those aspects of lesbian and gay relationships which cannot easily be assimilated into heterosexual models." There is an ethical problem here, because it is implicitly assumed that differences between homosexuals and heterosexuals reflect badly on homosexuals.

Second, the approach tends to ignore the difficulties with which gays and lesbians have to contend in terms of the prejudices of society. Some of these difficulties were identified by Kitzinger and Coyle (1995):

Lesbian and gay couples are struggling to build and to maintain relationships in the context of a society which often denies their existence, condemns their sexuality, penalises their partnerships and derides their love for each other.

Liberal humanism plus

The third phase of research on gays and lesbians (liberal humanism plus) is gradually becoming more prominent. This approach accepts the equality of

KEY TERMS

Heterosexual bias: the notion that heterosexuality is more natural than, and preferable to, homosexuality.

Liberal humanism: the view that all people, e.g., gays, lesbians, and heterosexuals, are equal and the ways they conduct relationships are basically similar.

homosexuals and heterosexuals. However, it also recognises that there are some important differences between the relationships of gays and lesbians on the one hand and heterosexuals on the other, based in part on the negative views of gay and lesbian relationships adopted by large sections of society. It is the only approach that manages to avoid most ethical problems.

Social and cultural diversity

We have discussed the importance of ensuring that psychological research is sensitive to ethical issues relating to race and sexuality. Similar issues are raised by research that is concerned with social and/or cultural diversity. Here we will consider research on **ethnic groups**; that is, cultural groups living within a larger society. These ethnic groups can be defined in racial, religious, or other terms. The ethical issues raised by research on ethnic groups will be discussed after their position in society has been covered.

One of the key issues that members of an ethnic group have to address is that of **acculturation strategy**. This has two main aspects:

1. The extent to which they want to retain their original cultural identity and customs
2. The extent to which they seek contact with other groups in society.

As Berry (1997) pointed out, the fact that people have two choices to make (each of which can be for or against) means that there are four major acculturation strategies:

- *Integration*: retaining one's own cultural identity while also seeking contact with other groups.
- *Separation*: retaining one's own cultural identity and avoiding contact with other groups.
- *Assimilation*: losing one's own cultural identity and moving into the larger society.
- *Marginalisation*: relatively little contact with one's own culture or with other cultures.

Most of the research has indicated that members of ethnic groups experience stress as they strive to find the most suitable acculturation strategy. However, the typical finding is that acculturative stress is lowest among those adopting the integration option, and is highest among those who are marginalised (Berry, 1997). As might be expected, acculturative stress is lower when there is a high level of tolerance for diverse ethnic attitudes and behaviour within the larger society.

Why are acculturation strategy and acculturative stress relevant to ethical issues? There are three main reasons. First, the fact that many members of ethnic groups experience acculturative stress means that they are on average more vulnerable psychologically than members of the dominant cultural group.

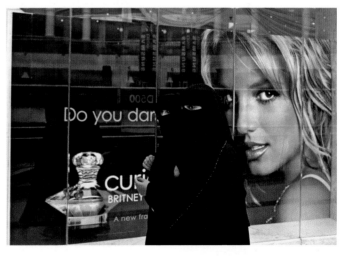

It can be difficult for members of ethnic groups to integrate into a larger society without compromising religious or ethnic beliefs when those beliefs call for them to dress in a way that makes them look different from the majority.

> **?** How might schools encourage integration of different cultures into the curriculum (e.g., by celebrating different cultural festivals)?

> **KEY TERMS**
> **Ethnic groups:** cultural groups (e.g., those defined by race or religion) living within a larger society.
> **Acculturation strategy:** the approach adopted by members of ethnic groups, involving decisions about preserving their own cultural identity and about contact with other cultural groups.

Second, research findings that seem to indicate that members of an ethnic group are inferior to the dominant cultural group may make members of the dominant cultural group less willing to have contact with them. This makes it harder for members of an ethnic group to adopt the integration or assimilation strategies.

Third, research findings that cast an unfavourable light on the members of an ethnic group may make them question their own cultural values. In extreme cases, this can lead to marginalisation and to the stress caused by lacking any stable sense of cultural identity.

In sum, it is important for all investigators to have an awareness of the pressures experienced by many ethnic groups. Investigators then need to ensure that their research (and the findings resulting from it) does not increase those pressures.

Summary

It has sometimes been argued that there are five key concerns of socially sensitive research: implications, uses, public policy, validity, and availability. We have addressed most of these concerns, but it is useful to provide a summary at this point.

1. Implications: much socially sensitive research focuses on one or more group (often vulnerable) within society. The research may seem to have implications for members of that group or those groups who read about the research that has been carried out. For example, as McCosker et al. (2001) pointed out, they have had to pay close attention to the fact that many of the readers of their research on abused women will be women who have found themselves in similar situations. They reported that abused women who read about the research often saw echoes of their own situation in it. That means that researchers must be sensitive to the feelings of members of any groups upon which research is carried out.

2. Uses: researchers who carry out socially sensitive research need to be aware of potential uses of their findings. For example, researchers who focus on alleged racial differences in intelligence may unwittingly lead some members of the public to believe falsely that some racial groups are superior to others. Research on gays and lesbians can also be used in inappropriate ways. Those who have unfavourable opinions of gays and lesbians may use research findings indicating differences between their relationships and those of heterosexuals as confirming their original opinions.

3. Public policy: researchers need to be aware that their findings may be used by policy makers (e.g., politicians) in undesirable ways. For example, it could be argued that Bowlby's research on maternal deprivation had the undesirable effect of encouraging mothers to stay at home throughout most of the childhood of their children. Another example is the unscrupulous use of evidence that blacks have lower tested IQs than whites on average. Some right-wing politicians argued (completely wrongly) that this proved that there was no point in providing special educational programmes for them.

4. Validity: socially sensitive research is often controversial and of interest to the media. That means that it is especially important that researchers who engage in socially sensitive research do everything possible to ensure

? Does the socially sensitive nature of research related to homosexuals mean that it shouldn't be conducted at all?

that their findings are valid. For example, it appears that John Bowlby exaggerated the negative consequences of young children spending some of their time separated from their mother. His somewhat invalid findings probably deterred many mothers who really wanted to go out to work from doing so.

5. Availability: it is important in all research to ensure that information about individuals remains confidential, but it is especially important in socially sensitive research. For example, research that focuses on illegal behaviour (e.g., individuals taking Class A drugs) could lead to the prosecution of the participants unless there is complete confidentiality so that individuals cannot be identified.

SECTION SUMMARY
Ethical Issues

❖ Social influence research provides us with a number of examples where ethical rights were infringed and/or ethical guidelines did not work successfully.

❖ Many well-known studies in psychology (those of Milgram, Zimbardo, Asch, and Rosenhan) pose serious ethical issues such as:

— Deception
— Lack of full informed consent.

❖ Most ethical issues arise because the participants are in a relatively powerless position relative to the experimenter.

❖ The ethical rights of human participants in psychological research are protected by ethical guidelines (though ultimately these are not always successful):

— Participants should be protected from physical and psychological harm.
— The data obtained from participants should be confidential and no information about individual participants should be divulged.
— Participants should give their voluntary informed consent before taking part in an experiment.
— Participants should be told that they have the right to withdraw at any time without giving a reason.
— At the end of the experiment, there should be a debriefing period in which the experiment is discussed fully.

❖ Professional organisations such as the British Psychological Society publish detailed ethical guidelines, and most research institutions have ethical committees.

❖ Socially sensitive research is concerned with studies where there are potential social consequences.

❖ Ethical guidelines focus mainly on protection of the participants. However, it is important with socially sensitive research to consider the protection of groups to which the participants belong and those closely associated with the participants.

What are the ethical issues in psychology?

Resolving ethical issues

What is socially sensitive research?

❖ These broader social issues need to be considered:

— The research question selected: this reflects the researcher's assumptions and may bias the research process from the outset.
— The conduct of the research and treatment of participants.
— The institutional context: this may make the participants feel powerless.
— The interpretation and application of research findings: those running the organisation in which the research takes place may misuse the findings.
— The findings of socially sensitive research may be applied in dubious ways not anticipated by the researcher, or the research may be used to justify new forms of social control.

Is socially sensitive research justified?

❖ On the positive side:

— Socially sensitive research may provide useful information to help minority groups, as in the case of eyewitness testimony.
— Ethical committees do frequently reject research with potentially sensitive social consequences.
— Researchers cannot generally be expected to foresee what they will find or how such findings will be used by others.
— Preventing socially sensitive research can be counterproductive to understanding social inequalities.

❖ On the negative side:

— The findings of socially sensitive research have been used to justify new (and often unwarranted) forms of social control.
— For example, in the past, psychologists have advocated sterilisation for undesirable groups of potential parents, and more recently behaviourists have suggested that psychological research can be applied to social control.
— Such control is exerted through behavioural forms of therapy for mental disorders.

❖ It is important to strike a balance when considering the advantages and disadvantages of socially sensitive research.

Race-related research

❖ This has been defended on the grounds that it is ethically indefensible to refrain from acquiring such knowledge and making it available to society.
❖ Important counterarguments include:

— The fact that such findings may be based on faulty research methods and are used in unacceptable ways.
— Race-related research on intelligence in the United States is almost meaningless, because black and white people don't form distinct biological groups.
— It isn't possible to discover for certain why race differences occur, and the research does not have any obvious policy implications.

"Alternative" sexuality

❖ Early research on "alternative" sexuality suffered from heterosexual bias, tending to regard homosexuality as a disease that needed to be "cured". This was replaced by a liberal humanistic approach.

❖ The limitations to this approach are:

— The inherent assumption that homosexuals conform to heterosexual norms.
— The fact that it ignores the problems created by the prejudice that homosexuals have to contend with.

❖ More recently, an ethically acceptable approach (liberal humanism plus) has evolved.

❖ Research on social and cultural diversity is socially sensitive.
❖ Ethnic groups often experience acculturative stress, which may be resolved through:

Research on social and cultural diversity

— Integration (acculturative stress is lowest among those adopting the integration option)
— Separation
— Assimilation
— Marginalisation (acculturative stress is highest among those who are marginalised).

❖ Acculturative stress makes individuals more vulnerable psychologically.
❖ Research that suggests ethnic minorities are inferior might make members of the dominant cultural group less willing to have contact with them, which makes integration more difficult and may make them question their own cultural values, leading sometimes to marginalisation.
❖ Investigators need to ensure that their research doesn't increase pressures on ethnic minorities.

See also pages 267–274 of the revision guide.

❖ Researchers engaged in socially sensitive studies need to address five concerns: implications, uses, public policy, validity, and availability.

Summary of socially sensitive research

THE USE OF NON-HUMAN ANIMALS

Types of Animal Research

Most research involving non-human animals takes place in laboratories. However, that is by no means the complete picture. Cuthill (1991) considered over 900 research papers, and found that 46% of them were field studies carried out in the wild. About one-third of the field studies were field experiments, meaning that they involved some kind of experimental manipulation. The four most common types of manipulation used in these studies were as follows:

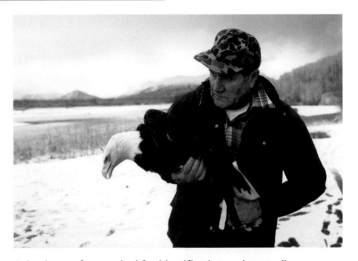

Animals are often marked for identification, or have radio transmitters attached to them, to track and observe them in the wild. This may cause significant stress to the animals being observed and might affect their behaviour and possibly even survival.

1. Dummies: these were mainly stuffed dummy predators; in order to be effective, they need to be realistic, and this means that they cause much distress to animals who encounter them.

2.   Non-trivial handling: tagging or marking of animals so they can be identified subsequently is an example of this; as mentioned already, this can be a stressful procedure.

3.   Playback of recorded signals: these recorded signals are generally realistic; if they are alarm calls, then this can lead to high levels of distress.

4.   Food addition: when the experimenter artificially introduces food into an area, it can cause territorial disputes and fights; it can also lead to undesirable changes in the availability of the animals' normal sources of food supply. Thus food addition can have serious consequences for the animals affected.

■ **Activity:** The use of non-human animals in psychological research.
List studies that you are familiar with that involved non-human animals. Use the headings given below. You may add more.

	Researcher's name(s)	Aims, procedures, findings, and conclusions	Ethical concerns
Laboratory experiment			
Field experiment			
Naturalistic observation			
Correlational study			

Remember, when commenting on non-human animal research, that there are many different kinds of research methods and each has its own ethical limitations.

Animals in Research

We will shortly be considering the kinds of ethical guidelines that have been developed to try to ensure that all animal experimentation is ethically sound. The single most important safeguard is that the experimenter should everything possible to minimise the level of discomfort or suffering experienced by the non-human animals involved in the research. This safeguard needs to be considered in the context of the importance of the research. It is far more acceptable to cause some suffering to non-human animals if the goal of the research is to develop more effective drugs for the treatment of schizophrenia than if the goal is a trivial one (e.g., to enrich a company making cosmetics). In other words, it is very important to carry out a cost–benefit analysis on any proposed research to ensure that the benefits will outweigh (and ideally greatly outweigh) the costs involved.

These safeguards are relevant to what is known as Bateson's decision cube (discussed more fully later). According to Bateson (1986), when considering whether any given experiment on animals is justified, we need to take account of its quality, the suffering that will be involved, and the likelihood of benefit (see page 477).

Animals and medicines

Animal research has been very useful in the medical field, and has led to the saving of millions of human lives. For example, Alexander Fleming discovered penicillin in 1928. However, it was only in 1940 that research on mice showed that penicillin was a very effective antibiotic. Another example concerns kidney dialysis, which is required by about 200,000 people every year in the United States if they are to stay alive. The drug heparin is essential for dialysis, and it has to be extracted from animal tissues, and then tested for safety on anaesthetised animals.

EXAM HINT
This is an emotive issue but writing in an impassioned and personal way will not gain much credit. Instead, make sure you are able to use both the arguments for and against the use of non-human animals.

Animals and psychological research

The benefits of animal research are less clear in psychology than in medicine. However, there are several reasons why psychologists use non-human animals in so many of their experiments.

Research involving physical harm

It is possible (although there are major ethical considerations) to carry out surgical procedures on non-human animals that simply wouldn't be permissible with humans. Gray (1985) discussed animal research designed to identify those parts of the brain associated with anxiety. This animal research stemmed from work on humans, in which it was found that anti-anxiety drugs such as the benzodiazepines and alcohol had 19 separate effects. These findings were compared against those of animal studies in which the effects of septo-hippocampal lesions or cuts were observed. The effects of these lesions were very similar to those of anti-anxiety drugs in humans in 18 out of 19 cases. It is probable that the septo-hippocampal system is involved in anxiety, and so lesions or cuts in it produce the same non-anxious behaviour as anti-anxiety.

Social deprivation

It is possible to expose non-human animals to prolonged periods of social or other forms of deprivation. For example, studies have been carried out on monkeys that weren't allowed to interact with other monkeys for the first few months of life. When monkeys that had been brought up in isolation were brought together, they reacted very aggressively (Harlow & Mears, 1979). Early isolation also produced a virtual absence of a sex life in adulthood. These findings indicate the potentially severe effects of social isolation. In another of Harlow's studies (Harlow & Harlow, 1962), young monkeys were placed with surrogate wire mothers. These wire mothers responded to the young monkeys in various ways (e.g., protruding metal spikes, strong blasts of air). The procedures themselves pose ethical issues, but of more concern are the long-term adverse effects on the monkeys. In the research by Harlow and Harlow, for example, the young monkeys as adults had problems in reproduction and in providing adequate parenting for their offspring.

Heredity and early experiences

The members of many species develop and reproduce over much shorter time periods than do members of the human species. As a result, it is much more feasible to carry out studies focusing on the effects of either heredity or early experience on behaviour in such species. For example, in one study a breeding programme was used to produce rats either reactive or non-reactive to loud noise and bright lights (Eysenck & Broadhurst, 1964). The reactive rats were much more anxious than the non-reactive ones in a wide range of situations. These findings suggest that individual differences in anxiety depend in part on genetic factors.

Simple and complex behaviours

It is generally accepted that the human species is more complex than other species. It may thus be easier to understand the behaviour of other species than that of humans. This makes animal research very useful, provided we assume that other

Monkeys reared in isolation react very aggressively when they are brought together (Harlow & Mears, 1979). This sort of social deprivation would be unacceptable in an experiment on human beings.

Instead of using poison to deter birds from eating crops, a recent programme of research into animal behaviour has led to the development of more effective scarecrows.

species are broadly similar to our own. This line of argument was used by the behaviourists to justify the fact that rats (rather than humans) were used in most of their experiments.

Beneficial non-human animal research

Much animal research is acceptable to nearly everyone because it is clear that the ends justify the means. Malim, Birch, and Wadeley (1992) discussed examples of such animal research. One programme of research was designed to provide us with a better understanding of the behaviour of animals that damage crops. This research led to the development of more effective scarecrows, so that more unpleasant methods of preventing crop damage (e.g., poison) were no longer needed. In this case, animal research actually served to produce a large *reduction* in animal suffering.

Another example of animal research that was almost entirely beneficial in its effects was reported by Simmons (1981). Pigeons were carefully trained by means of operant conditioning to detect life rafts floating on the sea. Pigeons have excellent vision, and so their detection performance was much better than that of helicopter crews: 85% detection compared with only 50%. In this case, animal research has enabled many human lives to be saved.

Psychological examinations of animals can produce benefits for the animals themselves. Examples include wildlife management programmes, efforts to preserve endangered species, and conservation programmes. Of course, these programmes (while of benefit to the animals involved) are primarily used because they help to achieve goals of importance to the humans who initiate them.

Numbers of animals used

Between 1977 and 1989 the numbers of animals used in experiments in the UK reduced considerably.

How many animals are used in psychological research? Thomas and Blackman (1991) answered that question for psychology departments in the United Kingdom in 1977 and 1989. The figure for the earlier year was 8694 animals, whereas it was only 3708 animals in 1989. This dramatic reduction over a 12-year period has almost certainly continued since 1989. Several species were used in psychological research, but about 95% of the total was accounted for by just three species: the mouse, the rat, and the pigeon.

The total figures for animal research of all kinds are declining year by year, but are still very high. According to Mukerjee (1997), about 1.5 million primates, dogs, cats, guinea pigs, rabbits, hamsters, and other similar species are used in laboratories in the United States each year. In addition, however, about 17 million rats, mice, and birds are used in American research every year.

The American Psychological Association released figures in 2005 indicating the scope and nature of psychological research on non-human species. About 7–8% of psychological research involves animals, and about 90% of the animals used in such research are rodents and birds (e.g., rats, mice, pigeons). Monkeys and other primates are used in only 5% of experiments in psychology, and cats and dogs are used only rarely.

Society's Views

In the long run, the ethical principles applied to animal research depend on the views of society at large. However, there are enormous differences of opinion among members of the public. Some people are totally opposed to all animal experiments, whereas others are in favour of animal experiments so long as unnecessary suffering is avoided. In order to obtain some factual information, Furnham and Pinder (1990) gave a questionnaire examining attitudes to animal experimentation to 247 young adults. As might be expected, their average views were not extremely for or against animal research. We will consider the arguments in favour that received good support followed by the arguments against that were well supported.

On the positive side, most young adults agreed with the statements that "Research from animal labs produces great benefits in the lives of both animals and people", and "There should be more animal experimentation in areas of medicine where cures are not yet known (AIDS etc.)", and they disagreed with the statement, "I believe in total abolition of animal experiments". Other studies have indicated that people who are older or less educated tend to be more in favour of animal experiments than those who are younger or better educated (Mukerjee, 1997).

There is a higher level of public support for animal research in the United States than in Europe. However, even in the United States there has been a decline in support. In 1985, 63% of Americans agreed with the statement that "scientists should be allowed to do research that causes pain and injury to animals like dogs and chimpanzees if it produces new information about human health problems". Ten years later, that figure had dropped to 53%. It is not surprising that the views of society have changed over time. As Herzog (1988) pointed out, our moral codes depend on what he referred to as "human psychology". Thus, our particular values, emotions, and beliefs determine our position on ethical issues. Herzog argued that an alternative approach would be one based on "pure reason", but ethical issues don't lend themselves to any simple logical resolution.

On the negative side, most of the young adults surveyed by Furnham and Pinder (1990) agreed that "All lethal experiments on animals of all sorts should be banned", and "There is no justification for the use of animal experimentation in the testing of cosmetics", and they disagreed with the statement that "Fundamental (for no specific purpose) research using animals is valid". In general, females were more opposed than males to animal research, left-wing people were more opposed than right-wing people, and vegetarians were more opposed than non-vegetarians.

? Is the rise of vegetarianism, anti-hunting lobbies, and conservation groups responsible for changing attitudes to the use of animals in research?

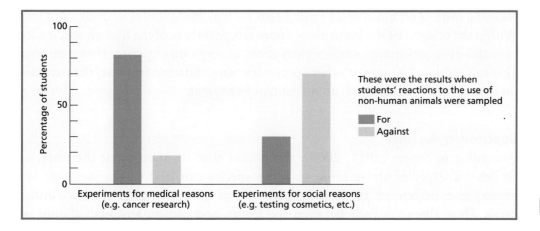

These were the results when students' reactions to the use of non-human animals were sampled

■ For
■ Against

Percentage of students (y-axis: 0, 50, 100)

Experiments for medical reasons (e.g. cancer research)
Experiments for social reasons (e.g. testing cosmetics, etc.)

? What factors might account for these results?

Expert Views

We have just considered the views of society with respect to animal research. There has also been a heated debate among experts on animal research concerning arguments for and against the use of non-human animals in research. A key issue among experts is whether non-human participants deserve (as far as possible) to be as fully protected as humans by ethical guidelines. This issue relates to the notion of **speciesism**, which is "discrimination and exploitation based upon a difference in species" (Ryder, 1990). As we will see, some writers (e.g., Gray, 1991) are in favour of speciesism, whereas others (e.g., Ryder, 1990, 1991; Singer, 1991) are strongly opposed to it.

Speciesism: For

Gray (e.g., 1991) accepted that it is ethically wrong to inflict unnecessary pain on the members of any species. However, he also argued that, "we owe a special duty to members of our own species" (1991, p.197). It is thus acceptable to inflict a fairly high level of suffering on animals to avoid a smaller level of suffering by humans, as is often the case in medical research. However, Gray accepted that there comes a point at which the level of suffering inflicted on animals becomes unacceptable. Gray's major reason for believing in speciesism is that, "It is

likely . . . to be better for lions, tigers, mice, and men if they each put the interests of their conspecifics [members of their own species] ahead of those of members of other species" (p.198). In his opinion, there are powerful evolutionary and biological reasons for this preference, namely that in order to perpetuate one's genes one should place greater value on individuals who are more closely related (the concept of **kin selection**).

It can be argued in favour of speciesism that the human species differs in important ways from other species, and so our needs should come before theirs. For example, the seventeenth-century philosopher René Descartes argued that animals are very much like machines, lacking the soul (with its powers of thinking) that is the supreme human characteristic. Humanistic psychologists argue that a key feature of humans is our need for self-actualisation, which involves full realisation of our potential in all ways. Other species lack this need, focusing instead on much more basic needs such as those for food, drink, and sex. Within the context of the humanistic approach, members of the human species are very different and more complex than those of any other species. However, that also raises ethical issues—if other species are very different from us, then studies on them cannot tell us much about human behaviour.

Speciesism: Against

According to Singer (1991, 2005), the notion that we should put the interests of our own species above those of other species can lead to the idea that we should give preference to the members of our own race over those of other races. Thus, there are links between speciesism and racism, and both should be avoided. However, while he regarded himself as a non-speciesist, Singer was willing to favour the human species over other species in certain circumstances. For example, if he saw a lion fighting a man, he would shoot the lion rather than let the man die. His reasoning was that it is better to save the life of a being that can plan for the future than a being that cannot.

Ryder (1991, p.201) put forward a powerful argument against speciesism. He proposed that speciesism, racism, and sexism all:

> *discriminate unjustly against individuals on irrelevant grounds such as skin colour, physical sexual characteristics and quadrupedality [having four legs]. The infliction of pain or distress upon others without consent is wrong—regardless of their race, sex, or species.*

We are more willing to inflict suffering on species other than our own, and on species for which we feel fear or disgust. Rats are among the most commonly used laboratory animals, but the pet owner in the picture would be as unhappy about inflicting pain on one as she would be about inflicting pain on a puppy or kitten.

Ryder also rejected Gray's argument that speciesism is acceptable because it has biological origins. According to him, what is ethically right should not be based on biology. As Ryder pointed out, "Presumably, Gray would also defend rape, pillage, and murder . . . where these behaviours have 'biological origins'" (p.201).

Those who oppose speciesism tend to argue that the human species is very similar to many other species. The basic point is the following:

> *If animals are close enough to humans that their bodies, brains, and even psyches [minds] are good models for the human condition, then ethical dilemmas must surely arise in using them.*

The argument that humans resemble some other species (e.g., primates) receives support from Darwin's theory of evolution, according to which the human species has evolved out of other species (see Chapter 7, Evolutionary Explanations of Human Behaviour). Of course, many species have evolved in very different ways to the human species, but other primates share about 98–99% of their DNA with humans. More generally, the basic physiology and nervous system of nearly all mammalian species are very similar.

Darwin's (1872) work on emotions is of particular importance to the use of animals in research. He was impressed by the similarities in the expression of emotional states between humans and other species. His findings suggest that it might be unwise to assume that animals experience emotions in very different ways from humans. We cannot be certain, however, because there is no way of knowing for sure the emotional experiences of members of other species.

Dogs, dogs, dogs

An American city council held a public meeting to decide whether they should give the animals kept in the city pound (who had been abandoned by their owners) to scientific research. At the meeting one woman spoke of how her baby's life had been saved by an operation that had been pioneered on dogs. She asked whether the audience would rather save children or dogs, to which they replied "Dogs, dogs, dogs" (Flanagan, 1988).

In terms of human evolution, this response does not bode well for our species. On the other hand the laws of natural selection suggest that those humans with genes that favour their own species will be the ones who survive!

Washoe the chimpanzee was taught to communicate with humans using American Sign Language signs. She still enjoys the company of humans after being part of a study that began in 1966. Have we as humans a responsibility to care for Washoe for the rest of her life, even though she is 40 years old and has a life expectancy of 60 years?

When do the ends justify the means? If we cannot ask an animal directly how much pain it is suffering, is it safe to guess how it feels just from observing the animal's behaviour? Do you know for certain when a cat is in distress?

KEY TERMS

Absolute morality: this is based on the notion that the ends cannot justify the means; some acts are basically immoral regardless of the consequences they produce.
Relative morality: this is based on the notion that the acceptability of any act depends in part on the benefits that it produces; in other words, the ends can justify the means.

Types of morality

It is important to distinguish between **absolute morality** and **relative morality**. Immanuel Kant and other philosophers argued in favour of an absolute morality in which the ends cannot justify the means. In contrast, most people probably agree with the notion of relative morality, according to which the acceptability of actions is judged in terms of the benefits that accrue.

Absolute morality

The notion of an absolute morality may have some appeal, but it tends to be inflexible and unrealistic in practice. For example, the moral principle "Always tell the truth" sounds very reasonable. However, if a madman with a gun demands to know where your mother is, it would make very little sense to adhere to the principle. In similar fashion, consider individuals who have experienced traumatic events such as abuse in early childhood. They may totally understandably be reluctant to reveal the true extent of their suffering when discussing their childhood with other people.

Relative morality

The alternative view that the ends can justify the means is favoured by most psychologists. It was expressed in the following terms by the American Psychological Association Committee on Ethical Standards in Psychological Research: "The general ethical question is whether there is a negative effect upon the dignity and welfare of the participants that the importance of the research does not warrant."

Costs and benefits

The notion that decisions about the use of animals in research should be based on an analysis of the benefits and costs involved is sensible. Suppose, for example, a proposed experiment will inflict considerable pain on several animals. This would surely seem less acceptable if the experiment were designed to produce improved cosmetics than if it were intended to lead to the development of treatment for a dreadful disease affecting humans.

In practice, however, there can be problems. First, it is often impossible to know what the benefits and costs of a piece of research are going to be until after the experiment has been carried out. Second, one person's assessment of the benefits and costs of a piece of research may not agree with someone else's. These issues are discussed further in connection with Bateson's cube on the next page.

Levels of suffering

There is the difficult matter of deciding how much suffering a given experimental procedure inflicts on an animal. As we cannot ask an animal directly what it is experiencing, we have to rely on its behaviour. However, this may be a misleading guide to its feelings. What needs to be done is to find out as much as possible about each species. In spite of the problems involved in assessing animal distress, attempts have been made in several countries such as Australia, Canada, and the Netherlands to develop pain scales. According to this form of assessment, 54% of the animals used in the Netherlands in 1995 suffered minor discomfort, 26% had moderate discomfort, and the remaining 20% suffered severe discomfort.

Ethical Principles

In general terms, most animal researchers subscribe to what are sometimes known as the "three Rs":

? Is it possible to empathise with the suffering experienced by another species?

- *Replacement* of animals by other research methods
- *Reduction* in the number of animals used by means of more advanced statistical techniques
- *Refinement* of experimental procedures to reduce animal suffering.

Use of the three Rs has proved very fruitful. For example, 5000 monkeys a year were used in the Netherlands in the 1970s to produce polio vaccines. During the 1990s, the number was reduced to only 10 monkeys.

The most obvious problem with the use of animals in research is that many of the ethical principles guiding research on human participants cannot be applied. For example, it is impossible for animals to give voluntary informed consent to take part in an experiment, and they cannot be debriefed at the end. Bateson (1986) argued that there are three main criteria that should be taken into account when deciding whether a study on animals is justifiable (this is often known as Bateson's decision cube):

1. The quality of the research: this can be assessed by the funding agency.
2. The amount of animal suffering: this can be assessed from the animal's behaviour and any signs of stress.
3. Likelihood of benefit: this is important, but can be hard to judge accurately.

Animal research of high quality, involving minimal suffering, and with a high probability of benefit is the most justifiable. In contrast, animal research of poor quality, involving considerable suffering, and offering a low probability of benefit is hard to justify.

The limitation with Bateson's approach is that there is no guarantee of assessing any of the three criteria with precision ahead of the research being carried out. So far as research quality is concerned, research that appears in advance to be relatively trivial may actually turn out to be of major importance. So far as animal suffering is concerned, this can only be assessed indirectly since we have no way of determining what any animal is actually experiencing. So far as likelihood of benefit concerned, this typically depends on the precise findings obtained. However, we don't know in advance what findings will be obtained— if we did, there would be no point in carrying out the experiment!

> Field experimenters can disrupt the animal's natural environment. This can continue to be stressful to the animal long after the experiment has finished.

Guidelines

It is very important for psychologists to develop ethical guidelines to protect animals' rights, and to prevent the animals from suffering or being exploited. Most institutions regard the use of animals in research as being such a sensitive matter that it is normal practice for all proposed animal experiments to be carefully considered by an ethical committee. In

> Do you think the things that are considered benefits to human society are fixed, or do they vary across cultures and over time? Do the needs of human societies change over time? How might this affect how we decide whether research is ethically acceptable or not?

the United Kingdom, the Home Office has overall control. Anyone who wants to carry out animal research must have a licence, and inspectors from the Home Office regularly inspect all animal facilities. All research on vertebrates in the United Kingdom is governed by the Animals (Scientific Procedures) Act of 1986. This Act contains numerous safeguards to ensure that vertebrate research is ethically sound.

Investigators in most countries who are planning studies on animals are required to make use of ethical guidelines. For example, here is an extract from the American Psychological Association Guidelines for Ethical Conduct in the Care and Use of Animals:

Psychologists undertake research with animals ". . . with a clear scientific purpose." . . . There should be a reasonable expectation that the research will increase knowledge of the processes underlying the evolution,

---

Research with non-human animals

The British Psychological Society, the professional and regulatory body for psychology in the UK, has published detailed guidance and good practice for psychologists carrying out research work with animals. The full version of the guidelines can be obtained from www.bps.org.uk/documents/Code.pdf.

To summarise, the guidance covers issues such as legislation, choice of species, number of animals, procedures, procurement of animals, final disposal of animals, housing and animal care, final disposal of animals, animals in psychology teaching, the use of animals for therapeutic purposes, and obtaining further information about the care and use of animals in research.

The following points provide a general guide to the sorts of issues that a researcher using animals would have to consider:

- Investigators must be aware of all relevant current legislation. They must comply with all of the laws protecting animals.
- Any investigator who intends to harm or stress animals must consider whether the knowledge to be gained justifies the procedure. Thus trivial experiments should not be carried out on animals even if they will suffer only low levels of harm or stress.
- Account needs to be taken of the differences between species in terms of the pain or discomfort they are likely to experience from a given procedure. If there is any choice, then the members of whichever species will suffer the least should be selected.
- Experiments should be carefully designed in order to minimise the number of animals that are required. Statistical tests that allow several factors to be considered together should be used.
- Experiments should not be carried out on the members of any endangered species. The only exception is if the experiment is part of a conservation programme.
- Investigators need to ensure that they obtain animals from reputable suppliers, and that they are provided with detailed information about their history, including any previous laboratory studies in which they have participated. In addition, investigators should confirm that animals are handled appropriately and with minimal stress during transit.
- Care should be taken with respect to caging conditions. There are clear differences among species in reactions to caging in

isolation and in the effects of high density or crowding. Information on the recommended requirements for the members of the species being caged should be followed.
- Investigators engaged in fieldwork should disturb the animals being studied as little as possible. Breeding and even survival can be markedly affected by simple observations. Marking animals for identification or attaching radio transmitters may stress them, as may their capture and recapture.
- Animal aggression or predation should be studied in the field rather than by means of staged encounters. If it is necessary to make use of staged encounters, then efforts should be made to use models or animals behind glass.
- Care should be taken with studies in which animals are deprived of food or water. Consider the normal eating and drinking habits of the animals being studied, and also to pay attention to their metabolic requirements.
- Investigators should only use procedures causing pain or distress if there are no other ways in which the experiment can be carried out. In such cases, it is illegal for investigators in the United Kingdom to cause pain or distress unless they hold a Home Office licence together with the relevant certificates.
- No surgical or pharmacological procedures can be carried out on vertebrate animals in the United Kingdom unless the investigators have a Home Office licence plus the relevant certificate. Further safeguards are that only experienced staff should perform these procedures, that the investigators should take steps to prevent post-operative infection, and that they know about the technical aspects of anaesthesia.
- It is essential that animals receive adequate care following an operation; this may involve the use of local anaesthetics and/or nursing. It is also essential that there is frequent monitoring of each animal's condition. If an animal suffers severe and enduring pain, then it must be killed using recommended procedures for euthanasia.
- The investigator should obtain a second opinion if he or she is unsure about the condition of any animals involved in an experiment. This second opinion must come from someone who has no direct involvement in the experiment, and is best provided by a qualified veterinarian.

development, maintenance, alteration, control, or biological significance of behaviour, b) increase understanding of the species under study, or c) provide results that benefit the health or welfare of humans or other animals.

Within the United Kingdom, the most important guidelines are those that were issued by the British Psychological Society in 1985. These guidelines state that researchers should "avoid, or at least minimise discomfort to living animals". They represent a systematic attempt to provide a comprehensive set of rules and recommendations to guide the behaviour of any investigators who wish to carry out experiments on non-human participants. The main points of these guidelines are given in the box on the previous page.

SECTION SUMMARY
The Use of Non-human Animals

❖ The benefits of animal research are less clear in psychology than in medicine.

❖ Animals are used in experiments because:

— Some procedures wouldn't be permissible with humans (either those involving physical harm or social deprivation).

— It is easier to use animals, especially to study the effects of heredity, because they reproduce over much shorter time periods than humans, and because it is easier to understand their behaviour.

— Objections aren't raised about some non-human animal research because it benefits non-human animals and/or humans.

❖ The reality is that there has been a great decline in non-human animal research, and a very small proportion of animal research involves primates.

What are the benefits of animal research?

❖ Females, left-wing people, and vegetarians are more opposed to animal experimentation than males, right-wing people, and non-vegetarians.

❖ Most people support animal experimentation in medical research and don't want to see animal experiments abolished.

❖ No set of ethical principles for animal experimentation could possibly satisfy all of these different groups.

❖ There are also cultural and historical differences in attitudes.

Society's views of animal research

❖ This refers to the discrimination and exploitation of another species based on the fact that it is different from our own.

❖ Speciesism can be defended on the grounds that:

— We owe a special duty to our own species, and there are powerful evolutionary reasons for this preference.

— The human species is very different to other species. Humanistic psychologists have emphasised the differences, pointing to aspects of human behaviour such as the drive for self-actualisation. If there are differences then such research is acceptable.

Speciesism

❖ Specieism can be opposed on the grounds that:

— Such differences (between the human species and other species) make the research irrelevant.
— Speciesism resembles racism and sexism, and, like these "isms", discriminates unjustly against individuals on irrelevant grounds.
— Primates and other mammals are similar to the human species in many ways, and thus deserve to be well treated.

Costs and benefits of animal research

❖ The views of most people on animal experimentation are based on relative morality.
❖ However, an analysis based on relative costs and benefits presumes that one can anticipate both of these before conducting the research, and that we can assess levels of suffering.

Ethical principles and guidelines

❖ Ethical principles in relation to non-human animals can be represented by the three Rs:

— Replacement with other methods
— Reduction in numbers
— Refinement of procedures.

❖ One ethical problem is that animals cannot be given the same rights as human participants, such as informed consent.
❖ Bateson's decision cube suggests that researchers should consider:

— The quality of the research
— The amount of suffering
— The likelihood of benefit.

❖ However, all of these factors are difficult to judge accurately in advance of the research.
❖ Ethical committees, ethical guidelines, and the Home Office try to ensure appropriate conduct in non-human animal research.
❖ One should remember that not all studies with non-human animals involve laboratory experimentation.

See also pages 275–279 of the revision guide.

Further Reading

Many of the issues discussed in this chapter are also dealt with in M.W. Eysenck (2000) *Psychology: A student's handbook* (Hove, UK: Psychology Press). There is good coverage of gender issues in R. Unger and M. Crawford (1996) *Women and gender: A feminist psychology (2nd Edn.)* (New York: McGraw-Hill). Cross-cultural research and the issues it raises are discussed in P. Smith and M.H. Bond (1998) *Social psychology across cultures: Analysis and perspectives (2nd Edn)* (New York: Harvester). P. Singer (2005) *In defence of animals: The second wave* (Oxford: Blackwell) covers ethical issues, whereas J.E. Sieber and B. Stanley (1988) Ethical and professional dimensions of socially sensitive research, *American Psychologist*, 43(1), 49–55, offers a consideration of socially sensitive research.

EXAMPLE EXAMINATION QUESTIONS

You should spend 40 minutes on each of the questions below, which aim to test the material in this chapter. Unlike questions from Unit 4 of the examination, covered in Chapters 2–7 of this book, the questions on Perspectives (Unit 5 examination) are marked out of 30 and an additional criterion is used in assessment: synopticity. "Synopticity" is defined as your "understanding and critical appreciation of the breadth and range of different theoretical perspectives and/or methodological approaches relevant to any question" (AQA specification).

1. Describe gender biases in psychological research and assess how these biases may have influenced such research. (30 marks)
2. "Some psychological theories are derived from research studies where there were only American male participants but nevertheless the theory is claimed to apply to all human beings."
   Discuss the extent to which psychological theories are biased in terms of gender **and** culture. (30 marks)
3. Discuss the extent to which cultural bias is a problem in psychological research. (30 marks)
4. Describe and evaluate the special ethical problems faced by psychologists when carrying out socially sensitive research. (30 marks)
5. (a) Describe ethical issues that may arise in psychological investigations using humans. (15 marks)
   (b) Assess how effectively psychologists have dealt with such issues. (15 marks)
6. Critically consider the arguments for **and** against the use of non-human animals in Psychological research. (30 marks)
7. "Both behaviourists and ethologists rely on studies of non-human animals to formulate their theories."
   Discuss the use of non-human animals in psychological research. (30 marks)

Examination Tips

Question 1. The AO1 component of this question requires a description of gender biases. These do not have to be set into the context of psychological research but using actual examples is a means of extending your description, and will be helpful for the AO2 component. "Research" is a term that refers to both theories and/or studies. In order to satisfy the synoptic criteria it will be desirable to select examples across a range of different topics and approaches. For the "assess" (AO2) you need to present an argument about whether these biases are critical to the research mentioned. To what extent do the biases bias our views?

Question 2. The question does not require that you address the quotation but the quotation is intended to be helpful in indicating areas for discussion. It points out that bias in research studies leads to biased theories. "Discuss" is an AO1 and AO2 term; therefore you need to describe biases of both gender and culture in psychological theories, and assess the extent to which psychological theories are biased. A balanced answer will look at examples of both biased and unbiased theories. If you only discuss gender or culture then a partial performance penalty would apply (maximum of 10 marks for AO1 and 10 marks for AO2).

Question 3. This question concerns cultural bias only, though it could be argued that gender groups are a form of cultural group (sharing the same beliefs and so on). "Research" covers theories and studies, thus you can describe instances of cultural bias in research studies only, and/or in theories. The AO2 element requires an evaluation of the extent to which psychological research is biased and, as for question 2, you should present a balanced view. In addition you should consider whether such bias is a problem, for example in the treatment of mental illness or our understanding of intelligence. Synopticity can be achieved by a consideration of research across the specification as well as reference to different approaches and perspectives.

Question 4. The question requires a focus on those ethical problems that are especially difficult in socially sensitive research—though it could be argued that all ethical issues are a problem in socially sensitive research but just simply more so. Reference to examples of socially sensitive research will be an important means of evaluating the ethical problems and how they might be resolved. It is important to maintain a focus on the issue of socially sensitive research otherwise marks will be lost for not answering the question set and just writing a general ethics answer.

Question 5. Part (a) requires a description of ethical issues. For top marks this needs to demonstrate a balance between depth and breadth. Therefore a list of points is unlikely to attract high marks because lists lack detail. Furthermore, if the list comprises ethical guidelines this would be rather limited because the question refers to issues not guidelines, which are means of resolving ethical issues. It may help to use examples as part of your description, and this will increase synopticity. For part (b) you are required to assess the effectiveness of psychologists' attempts to deal with such issues. You are likely to refer to guidelines but will get only minimal credit if you describe these. Such material must be used to construct an argument in answer to the question.

Question 6. You should consider both the strengths and limitations of arguments for the use of non-human animals in psychological research, and do the same for the arguments against their use. Considerations should relate to different kinds of methodologies (providing synopticity) as well as different approaches and also you should examine both appropriateness and ethics. You should ensure that there are equal amounts of description and evaluation in your answer to attract the full range of marks.

Question 7. Again you are not required to address the quotation but it is there to offer some ideas—the notion that non-human animal research comes in many different forms. Reference to different approaches and kinds of research is important for synopticity. The question requires that you both describe the use of non-human animals and assess their use. In a balanced answer this would include consideration of their usefulness as well as the ethical issues such as pain.

WEBSITES

http://www.bps.org.uk/the-society/the-society_home.cfm
British Psychological Society's website, with downloadable Code of Conduct, Ethical Principles, and Guidelines for psychologists.

http://www.apa.org/pi/guide.html
American Psychological Association (APA) Guidelines for Providers of Psychological Services to Ethnic, Linguistic, and Culturally Diverse Populations.

http://www.stonewall.org.uk/
British organisation promoting legal equality and social justice for lesbians, gay men, and bisexuals.

http://www.homeoffice.gov.uk/science-research/animal-testing/
Home Office web pages on animal testing and welfare, including link to the Animals Procedure Committee homepage.

Debates

The synoptic content of this chapter focuses on debates that concern psychologists. A debate is discussion of an issue, usually involving the consideration of different sides of a question. As you are already aware, none of these debates is simply "one *or* the other"—there is nearly always some reasonable middle ground.

FREE WILL AND DETERMINISM

The issue of **free will** versus **determinism** has occupied philosophers and psychologists for centuries. According to those who believe in determinism, people's actions are totally determined by the external and internal forces operating on them. An example of an external force would be the influence of parents when rewarding certain behaviours. An example of an internal force could be hormones influencing the way in which someone behaves.

Those who believe in free will argue that matters are more complicated. Most of them accept that external and internal forces exist. However, they argue that people have free will because each individual is nevertheless able to choose his/her own behaviour within the constraints of these forces. Note that the positions adopted by advocates of determinism and of free will are not that far apart—determinists argue that behaviour is totally controlled by external and internal forces, whereas those favouring free will argue that behaviour is mostly controlled by external and internal forces but with the addition of free will.

The distinction between free will and determinism can be seen if we consider the following question: "Could an individual's behaviour in a given situation have been different if he/she had willed it?" Believers in free will answer that question "Yes". In contrast, advocates of determinism respond "No". Some of the main arguments for and against each of these positions are discussed next.

Determinism

Determinists argue that a proper science of human behaviour is only possible if psychologists adopt a deterministic account, according to which everything that happens has a definite cause. Free will, by definition, doesn't have a definite cause. If free will is taken into account, it becomes impossible to predict human behaviour with any precision. According to some determinists, it is often possible with other sciences to make very accurate predictions from a deterministic position (e.g., forecasting planetary motion). If determinism is regarded as not

---

KEY TERMS

Free will: the notion that we are free to make decisions.
Determinism: the view that all behaviour is caused by factors other than one's own will.

applicable to psychology, then psychology is either a very different science from physics, chemistry, and so on, or it isn't really a science at all.

At this point, we need to distinguish among different types of determinism. Our behaviour is influenced by numerous factors, and theorists differ in terms of the relative importance they attach to each factor. For example, evolutionary psychologists focus on ultimate or fundamental causes of behaviour based on the evolutionary history of the human species. We could call this *evolutionary determinism*. In contrast, most psychologists focus on proximate or immediate causes of behaviour based on the external and/or internal forces operating at any given moment. Behaviourists such as Skinner emphasise external forces in the environment (e.g., rewards and punishments), and we could call this *environmental determinism*. In contrast, Freud emphasised the way in which our behaviour is influenced by internal forces involving conflicts among the ego, id, and superego. He called this *psychic determinism*. Social psychologists emphasise the importance of social forces (e.g., pressures to conform, obedience to authority) in influencing our behaviour—we could call this *social determinism*.

We could go further in identifying different types of determinism. If we tried to produce a complete list of factors influencing our behaviour, it would contain at least the following factors:

- The specific stimuli presented to us
- Our recent experiences (e.g., being stuck in a traffic jam)
- Our genetic make-up
- Our evolutionary history
- Our physiological system
- Our cognitive system (e.g., our perceptions, thoughts, and memories)
- The social environment
- The cultural environment
- Our previous life experiences (including those of childhood)
- Our personal characteristics (including intelligence, personality, and mental health).

Hard vs. soft determinism
Hard determinism

We have seen that there are various types of determinism. At a more general level, we can distinguish between hard determinism and soft determinism. **Hard determinism** as it applies to psychology is based on two key assumptions. First, no action or behaviour is free if it must occur. Second, every human action has antecedent (preceding) causes that ensure that one particular action is performed rather than any other. The conclusion from these assumptions is that all human actions are determined and none of them is free. Those who believe in hard determinism include B.F. Skinner and Sigmund Freud.

Hard determinism has been applied extensively in other sciences (especially physics). It seemed appropriate in the eighteenth and nineteenth centuries when most physicists believed they would eventually be able to make very precise and accurate predictions about everything relevant to physics. However, what happened in the twentieth century suggested they were unduly optimistic. For example, according to chaos theory (Hilborn, 1994), very small changes in initial conditions can produce major changes later on. For example, theoretically the

KEY TERM

Hard determinism: the view that all behaviour is determined and is highly constrained by the current situation and our past experience.

Where do the main approaches in psychology stand on determinism?

The biological approach takes the view that behaviour is determined by internal, biological systems. This is **physiological determinism**. Up to a point physiological determinism is a valid argument. Clearly physiological factors provide explanations of behaviour but do they offer a complete explanation? They may be more applicable to non-human animals where learning has less influence on behaviour. Non-human animals also lack the ability to be self-reflective, as demonstrated by their lack of self-awareness, which is associated with the concept of "will". Without self-awareness and consciousness, can an organism be said to have a will?

The behaviourist approach proposes that all behaviour is learned and can be explained solely in terms of external (environmental) factors. This is **environmental determinism**. Skinner said that freedom was an illusion, maintained only because we are unaware of the environmental causes of behaviour. This gives us an answer to the dilemma: "But I have a personal sense of free will"—the response from behaviourists is that what you experience is an illusion.

The cognitive approach is mechanistic, and any mechanistic explanation is determinist because it suggests that a particular action will result in a predictable result.

The psychoanalytic approach suggests that adult behaviour or personality is predetermined by events in early childhood. This is called **psychic determinism** because the causes of our behaviour are psychological and not freely chosen. Freud, like Skinner, believed that free will was an illusion. Freud believed this was because the actual causes of our behaviour are unconscious and therefore hidden from us.

However, Freud also believed that people have some potential for free will—psychoanalysis is based on the principle that people can change. Freud proposed the principle of "overdetermination", that behaviour has multiple causes some of which are conscious and these would be subject to free will.

The evolutionary approach is highly deterministic. A fundamental assumption of the evolutionary approach (**genetic determinism**) is that physical and psychological characteristics are inherited. This must be so because it is only inherited characteristics that can be naturally selected and passed on to the next generation. This means that the evolutionary approach is a highly deterministic one, though this may be less true as one moves up the evolutionary scale and cultural evolution has a greater effect on behaviour.

The humanistic approach embraces free will. Rogers believed that humans have an innate drive towards positive growth and self-actualisation. Individuals who deny aspects of themselves are unable to do this. If one disowns a part of one's behaviour ("That's not like me to do such a thing") then that behaviour is not part of one's self-concept and therefore cannot be controlled. Your behaviour is then not self-determined. Healthy psychological development and adjustment depend on "owning" all of your behaviour. In this way you are exercising free will, and are able to reach your full potential. In addition to this, the humanistic approach stresses the responsibility each of us has for our own actions. Rather than seeking explanations for our behaviour in terms of other influences, each of us must accept the moral responsibility for our actions. This is a fundamental issue for questions of adult legal responsibilities.

flap of a butterfly's wing in one part of the world could ultimately change the whole weather system in a different part of the world. Such a chain of events doesn't lend itself to prediction, and so we can't show that an approach based on hard determinism is appropriate. More generally, it isn't really possible to test directly the assumptions of hard determinism.

Soft determinism

Many (probably most) psychologists favour an alternative position labelled **soft determinism** by William James. According to this position, it is accepted that all human actions have a cause. However, and this is where soft determinists part company with hard determinists, there is a valid distinction between behaviour highly constrained by the situation (involuntary behaviour) and behaviour only modestly constrained by the situation (voluntary behaviour). For example, a child may apologise for swearing because he/she will be punished if an apology isn't forthcoming (highly constrained behaviour) or because he/she is genuinely upset at causing offence (modestly constrained behaviour). Behaviour is determined in both cases. However, the underlying causes are more obvious when behaviour is highly constrained by situational forces.

Evidence consistent with the views of William James was reported by Westcott (1982). Canadian

KEY TERMS

Physiological determinism: the view that behaviour is determined by internal, bodily systems.
Environmental determinism: the view that all behaviour can be explained solely in terms of the effects of external (environmental) factors.
Psychic determinism: the view that adult behaviour or personality is predetermined by events in early childhood—a mix of biological and experiential factors.
Genetic determinism: the view that animal behaviour is caused by genetic influences; this view underpins evolutionary explanations.
Soft determinism: the notion that we should distinguish between behaviour that is very constrained by the situation (i.e., determined) and behaviour that is only modestly constrained (i.e., less exactly determined).

students indicated how free they felt in various situations. They experienced the greatest feeling of freedom in situations involving an absence of responsibility or release from unpleasant stimulation (e.g., a nagging headache). In contrast, they felt least free in situations in which they had to recognise there were limits on their behaviour (e.g., when they had to curtail their desires to fit their abilities).

Evidence suggesting we don't always know accurately whether our behaviour is voluntary or involuntary was reported by Wegner and Wheatley (1999). Two participants (one genuine and the other a confederate working for the experimenter) placed their fingers on a small square board. When they moved the board, this caused a cursor to move over a screen showing numerous pictures of small objects. The genuine participants thought they had voluntarily decided which object the cursor would stop on (they had heard the name of the object over their headphones just beforehand). In fact, however, the decision had been taken by the confederate—thus, the participants believed their behaviour to be voluntary but it was actually involuntary.

There are various limitations with soft determinism. First, there is excessive reliance on how we subjectively perceive things—the fact that some actions feel voluntary whereas others feel involuntary doesn't mean they are really different. Second, we sometimes make mistakes when deciding whether our behaviour is voluntary or involuntary (e.g., Wegner & Wheatley, 1999). Third, it can be argued that soft determinists want to have their cake and eat it—actions are free if they are voluntary, but those actions are still caused. This could be regarded as a confusing blend of free will and determinism.

Behaviourist and Freudian approaches

Determinism is espoused by more approaches in psychology than is free will. As was mentioned already, the behaviourists and Freud are among those theorists who argue in favour of hard determinism, and so represent the greatest contrast with the views of those believing in free will. We will consider their views here.

Behaviourism

The behaviourists believed especially strongly in determinism. Skinner argued that virtually all of our behaviour is determined by environmental factors. He proposed that we repeat behaviour that is rewarded, and we don't repeat behaviour that isn't rewarded. Other behaviourists argued that we can predict how someone will respond given knowledge of the current stimulus situation and that individual's previous conditioning history.

Skinner (1971) developed his ideas about hard determinism most fully in his book, *Beyond Freedom and Dignity*. He argued that common beliefs about free will and personal moral responsibility (which he called "dignity") were wrong and should be abandoned for the sake of improving society. According to Skinner, the way to change human behaviour is by structuring the environment so that people are rewarded for behaving in desirable ways (i.e., operant conditioning) rather than by focusing on meaningless notions like freedom and dignity.

Bandura (1977, p.27) pointed out a serious limitation with Skinner's approach: "If actions were determined solely by external rewards and punishments, people would behave like weather vanes, constantly shifting in radically different directions to conform to the whims of others." This criticism

---

? How is determinism related to the situation in which a behaviour occurs? Is the behaviour still determined by forces outside our will?

applies more forcefully to the human species than to non-human species, because we are much more likely to act in line with long-term goals.

What is missing from Skinner's approach? Skinner focused excessively on the notion that the external environment determines behaviour. However, our behaviour also determines the external environment—if you don't like a television programme you are watching, you switch to another channel or turn the television off. In addition, our personality helps to determine the environment in which we find ourselves and it also influences our behaviour. Thus, there are multiple determinants of behaviour, but Skinner largely ignored most of them.

Freud

Freud was also a strong believer in hard determinism, claiming that none of our behaviour "just happens" or is due to free will. He even argued that trivial phenomena, such as missing an appointment, calling someone by the wrong name, or humming a particular tune had definite causes within the individual's motivational system. Of particular importance is what is known as the **Freudian slip**—a motivated but involuntary error in which someone says or does something revealing their true desires. Motley et al. (1983) obtained evidence of Freudian slips. Male participants had to say out loud pairs such as *tool—kits*, some of which could be turned into sexually explicit words. When the experimenter was an attractive female, participants tended to make Freudian slips—for example, saying *cool—tits* instead of *tool—kits*. It is difficult to see how we could explain such findings in terms of free will.

Freud's emphasis on determinism and rejection of free will may well owe something to the fact that he focused on individuals suffering from mental disorders (especially anxiety disorders). Such individuals are presumably highly motivated to change their behaviour and eliminate their disorder but are often unable to do so—this seems somewhat difficult to explain if they possess free will. It seems more plausible to assume (as Freud did) that their behaviour is determined by forces they cannot control. Note that one of the distinguishing features of Freud's deterministic approach was his emphasis on *unconscious* forces influencing our behaviour—according to him, we are often unaware of what causes us to behave in certain ways.

Testability

The major problem with determinism (whether soft or not) is that it is not really possible to submit it to a proper test. If it were, then the issue of free will versus determinism would have been settled, and so would no longer exist as an issue! If all behaviour is determined by internal and external forces, then in principle it should be possible to predict behaviour from a knowledge of these causal factors. In fact, we usually only have very limited knowledge of the internal and external forces that might be influencing an individual's behaviour. As a result, it remains no more than an article of faith that human behaviour can eventually be predicted accurately.

Free Will

Most people feel that they possess free will, in the sense that they can freely choose what to do from a number of options. As Dr Samuel Johnson

> Think of a time when you have called someone by the wrong name. Can you think of any underlying reason why you may have made this mistake?

KEY TERM

Freudian slip: a mistake that betrays the concerns of the unconscious mind.

(1709–1784) said to Boswell, "We know our will is free, and there's an end on't." Most people also have feelings of personal responsibility, presumably because they feel that they are in at least partial control of their behaviour. Another argument in favour of free will is that it fits with society's view that people should accept responsibility for their actions and should expect to be punished (e.g., sent to prison) if they break the law.

Humanistic approach

Humanistic psychologists such as Carl Rogers and Abraham Maslow are among those who believe in free will. They argued that people exercise choice in their behaviour, and they denied that people's behaviour is at the mercy of outside forces. Rogers' client-centred therapy is based on the assumption that the client has free will. The therapist is called a "facilitator" precisely because his/her role is to make it easier for the client to exercise free will in such a way as to maximise the rewardingness (reward potential) of the client's life. Humanistic psychologists argue that regarding human behaviour as being determined by external forces is "de-humanising" and incorrect.

Rogers emphasised the notion that we are motivated to minimise the discrepancy between our self-concept and our ideal self (the self-concept we would most like to possess). If we have free will and our behaviour isn't determined by external forces, it might be expected that we would have little difficulty in reducing any discrepancy between our self-concept and ideal self. The fact that there are millions of people with mental disorders who have a substantial discrepancy between the two suggests that free will is often very ineffective in producing highly desired changes or even that it doesn't exist.

Causality

Those who believe in free will have to confront various problems. First, it is hard to provide a precise account of what is meant by free will. If free will has a major influence on human behaviour, it is very important that we define free will precisely. Second, determinism is based on the assumption that all behaviour has one or more causes, and it could be argued that free will implies that behaviour is random and has no cause. However, very few people would want to argue for such an extreme position. Anyone whose behaviour seemed to be random would probably be classified as mentally ill or very stupid! If free will doesn't imply that behaviour has no cause, then we need to know how free will plays a part in causing behaviour.

Third, most sciences are based on the assumption of determinism. It is possible that determinism applies to the natural world but doesn't apply to humans. If that is the case, then there are enormous implications for psychology that have hardly been addressed as yet.

Conclusions

The issue of free will versus determinism has created more heat than light for various reasons. First, it isn't clear that it makes much sense to talk about "free will", because this assumes there is an agent (i.e., the will) that may or may not operate in an unrestrained way. As the philosopher John Locke (1632–1704) pointed out, "We may as properly say that the singing faculty sings and the dancing faculty dances as that the will chooses" (1690/1989).

Second, the issue is philosophical rather than scientific, as it is impossible to design an experiment to decide whether or not free will influences human behaviour. As William James (1890, p.323) put it, "the fact is that the question of free will is insoluble on strictly psychological grounds". Thus, we can never know whether an individual's behaviour in a given situation could have been different if he/she had so willed it.

Third, although those who believe in determinism or free will often seem to have radically different views, there is more common ground between them than generally realised. Regardless of their position on the issue of free will versus determinism, most psychologists accept that heredity, past experience, and the present environment all influence our behaviour. Although some of these factors (such as the environment) are external to the individual, others are internal. Most of these internal factors (such as character or personality) are the results of causal sequences stretching back into the past. The dispute then narrows to the issue of whether a solitary internal factor (variously called free will or self) is somehow immune from the influence of the past.

Fourth, and most important, we can go a step further and argue that there is no real incompatibility between determinism and free will at all. According to determinists, it is possible in principle to show that an individual's actions are caused by a sequence of physical activities in the brain. If free will (e.g., conscious thinking and decision making) forms part of that sequence, it is possible to believe in free will and human responsibility at the same time as holding to a deterministic position. This would not be the case if free will is regarded as an intruder forcing its way into the sequence of physical activities in the brain, but there are no good grounds for adopting this position. Thus, the entire controversy between determinism and free will may be artificial and of less concern to psychologists than has generally been supposed.

The issue of free will versus determinism was considered in detail by Valentine (1992). In spite of the various criticisms of the deterministic position, she came to the following conclusion: "Determinism seems to have the edge in this difficult debate."

> ? How might the notions of free will and determinism be important in a situation where doctors need to decide if a criminal is responsible for his or her own actions?

> ■ **Activity:** In small groups, think of some important decisions you have made or will probably make in the future. Discuss the extent to which they are made using free will. It might be useful to think of them on a scale from 1 to 10, where 1 is free choice and 10 is fully predetermined.

> **EXAM HINT**
>
> Maximise synopticity by drawing from different areas of psychology to illustrate free will and determinism. Select examples to which you can clearly link the arguments for and against free will and determinism.

SECTION SUMMARY
Free Will and Determinism

❖ One way to consider the debate of determinism versus free will is to ask the following question:

— "Could an individual's behaviour in a given situation have been different if he/she had willed it?"

❖ Determinists argue that all human behaviour has a definite cause.

The difference between free will and determinism

❖ The scientific approach is a deterministic one and it used to be thought that, if we allow for free will, then psychology isn't really a science at all. However, even in the physical sciences uncertainty and chaos are now recognised principles.

❖ More psychologists believe in determinism than in free will.

❖ The major problem with determinism is that it isn't possible to submit it to a proper experimental test.

Different types of determinism

— Evolutionary determinism: fundamental causes of behaviour are based on the evolutionary history of the human species.

— Environmental determinism: behaviour is caused by external forces in the environment (e.g., rewards and punishments).

— Psychic determinism: behaviour is influenced by internal forces involving the ego, id, and superego.

— Social determinism: behaviour is influences by social forces (e.g., conformity, obedience to authority).

Hard vs. soft determinism

❖ Hard determinism:

— According to those who favour hard determinism, all human actions are determined and none is free.

— Skinner and Freud are two psychologists who believed in hard determinism.

❖ Soft determinism:

— According to those who advocate soft determinism, some behaviour is highly constrained by the situation (involuntary behaviour), whereas other behaviour is not (voluntary behaviour).

— This permits some adaptability in the definition of determinism.

— Many psychologists believe in soft determinism.

Behaviourist and Freudian approaches

❖ Skinner argued that our behaviour was determined by environmental factors.

❖ This approach can be criticised:

— Bandura argued that humans would not be constant.

— Skinner ignored other determinants of behaviour.

❖ Freud emphasised determinism and rejected free will.

Free will

❖ Most people feel they possess free will, because they feel able to choose freely what to do in most situations.

❖ Humanistic psychologists believe in free will, which is the basis for client-centred therapy.

❖ The belief in free will creates two problems:

— It is hard to provide a precise account of what is meant by free will.

— Most successful sciences are based on the assumption of determinism.

Conclusions

❖ The debate is largely a philosophical one because it cannot be subjected to testing.

❖ Most psychologists accept that heredity, past experience, and the present environment all influence behaviour, and so the key issue is whether there is an internal factor (free will) that also influences behaviour.

❖ The debate may simply be artificial; if free will forms part of physical activities of the brain, it is possible to believe in free will at the same time as holding a deterministic position.

See also pages 286–288 of the revision guide.

REDUCTIONISM

According to Reber (1995), **reductionism** is "the philosophical point of view that complex phenomena are best understood by a componential analysis which breaks the phenomena down into their fundamental, elementary aspects", or "the analysis of complex things into simple constituents" (*Oxford Concise Dictionary*). Within the context of psychology, the term refers to several rather different theoretical approaches. First, there is the belief that the phenomena of psychology can potentially be accounted for within the framework of more basic sciences or disciplines (physiological reductionism). Second, there is the assumption that complex forms of behaviour can be explored by simple experiments (experimental reductionism). Third, there is the notion that the complexities of human cognition can be compared to computer functioning (machine reductionism). Fourth, there is the assumption that human behaviour can be understood with reference to other, less complex species (animal reductionism). Fifth, there is the assumption that human behaviour can be understood in terms of genetic factors (evolutionary reductionism). We will consider each of these forms of reductionism in turn.

? What is the difference between basic disciplines and more basic principles?

Physiological Reductionism

According to physiological reductionism, we need to consider psychology in the light of other scientific disciplines. Of particular importance, all psychological processes are accompanied by physiological processes, and understanding those physiological processes might assist us in understanding human behaviour. Our behaviour is also affected by various social processes (e.g., conformity, the desire to impress others).

Scientific disciplines can be regarded as being organised in a hierarchical way, with the sciences adopting a more global perspective at the top, and the more

KEY TERM

Reductionism: the notion that psychology can ultimately be reduced to more basic sciences such as physiology or biochemistry.

Reductionism: the analysis of complex things into simple constituents.

narrowly focused sciences at the bottom:

- Sociology: the science of groups and societies
- Psychology: the science of human and animal behaviour
- Physiology: the science of the functional working of the healthy body
- Biochemistry: the science of the chemistry of the living organism.

Physiological and psychological explanations

Neurology and biochemistry underlie all behaviour. What happens when a person sees a sunset? The physiological explanation would be that light reflected from the landscape forms an image on the retina, which is converted into a neural signal and transmitted to the brain, and so on. No-one disputes that this is true, and the process is absolutely essential, but does it give a full and adequate explanation of what is going on? A psychological explanation would probably include the personal and social relevance of the experience, which many would argue is of equal (or greater) value.

Reductionists argue that the sciences towards the top of the hierarchy will eventually be replaced by those towards the bottom—if so, it should ultimately be possible to explain psychological phenomena in physiological or biochemical terms.

Physiological reductionism has some advantages. First, it has an immediate appeal. Biochemistry, physiology, psychology, and sociology are all concerned with human functioning, so there is some overlap in their subject matter. This is especially the case with brain imaging, which provides detailed information about activity in different parts of the brain when we are performing some task. There might be an increased understanding of psychology resulting from taking full account of the relevant contributions of other sciences.

Second, biochemistry and physiology can be regarded as more developed than psychology or sociology, since they have more well-established facts and theories.

Third, even those unconvinced of the benefits of reductionism generally accept that psychological theories should be consistent or *compatible* with physiological findings. For example, the findings from brain-imaging research are relevant to cognitive psychologists trying to understand human cognition.

Physiological reductionism has various disadvantages. First, much human behaviour cannot be understood solely in terms of basic biological and physiological processes. Suppose a psychologist wants to predict how a group of people will vote in a forthcoming election. No-one in their right mind would argue that a detailed biochemical and physiological examination of their brains would be of much value! Most psychologists would argue that we need *all* levels of explanation to provide an adequate account of human behaviour.

Second, as Valentine (1992) pointed out, psychology typically describes the *processes* involved in performing some activity (e.g., visual perception), whereas physiology focuses more on the *structures* involved. Thus, psychologists are interested in *how* questions, whereas physiologists are interested in *where* questions.

Third, physiological reductionism hasn't worked very well in practice—very few psychological phenomena have been explained in physiological or biochemical terms.

Fourth, reductionist explanations (such as those provided by physiologists) often contain many irrelevant details from the perspective of psychology. This can make it very hard to identify what is relevant and in a physiological account.

Experimental Reductionism

Most of experimental psychology is based on the assumption that the complexities of human behaviour can be studied effectively in relatively simple experiments—this is known as experimental reductionism. The behaviourists were firmly in favour of experimental reductionism. For example, Skinner carried out studies on rats in which they were placed on their own in so-called "Skinner boxes" that contained little other than a lever to press.

The first advantage of experimental reductionism is that use of the experimental method provides the most scientific (and replicable) evidence we have concerning human behaviour. If we tried to study all the factors influencing human behaviour at the same time, the task would be impossibly complex and the findings uninterpretable. Second, experimental reductionism is the obvious approach to take from the perspective of some theories. For example, the behaviourists argued that learning involves making stimulus–response associations, and experiments involve presenting stimuli and observing responses.

A disadvantage with experimental reductionism is that it omits much that is very important in determining human behaviour. Wachtel (1973) coined the term **implacable experimenter** to describe the typical experimental situation in which the behaviour of the experimenter occurs independently of the participant's behaviour. Since the situation is allowed to influence the participant but the participant isn't allowed to influence the situation, it is likely that the effects of situations on our behaviour are exaggerated. In addition, this approach doesn't permit any of the dynamic interactions between individuals we experience much of the time. A second disadvantage is that the emphasis within experimental reductionism is on factors in the *immediate* situation manipulated by the experimenter. Our behaviour is also influenced by genetic factors, by our present mood, by our childhood experiences, by our present state of health, and so on, but these factors are typically ignored in psychological experiments.

Machine Reductionism

The essence of machine reductionism is that we can understand human thinking and/or behaviour by comparing ourselves with various kinds of machines. An influential form of machine reductionism is found within cognitive psychology—some cognitive psychologists believe there are important similarities between human cognition and computer functioning. For example, computers engage in information processing, and they can store information either briefly (as in human short-term memory) or for long periods of time (as in human long-term memory).

Machine reductionism involving computers has various advantages. First, we can compare the functioning of humans and computers to see how similar they are. If computers don't function like humans, we can reprogramme the computer to improve the similarity between them. For example, the human brain is strongly interconnected, and psychologists have devised computer-based neural or connectionist networks that possess that quality.

A clear disadvantage of machine reductionism is that it omits many factors determining human behaviour. For example, human cognition and behaviour are often strongly influenced by motivational and emotional factors, but a computer's functioning is not influenced by its mood or goals! Another disadvantage is that the human brain is incredibly complex and machine reductionism involves a grossly oversimplified view of its complexity. For example, the number of units in computer neural or connectionist networks is a tiny fraction of the cells in the brain.

> **?** Can you think of some issues within psychology that might lend themselves to a reductionist approach?

> **KEY TERM**
>
> **Implacable experimenter:** the typical laboratory situation in which the experimenter's behaviour is uninfluenced by the participant's behaviour.

Animal Reductionism

The essence of animal reductionism is the assumption that we can understand human behaviour by studying the behaviour of other species regarded as less complex than the human one. This approach is especially associated with the behaviourists. For example, Pavlov carried out studies on dogs and Skinner on rats and pigeons, but they assumed that their findings were fully applicable to humans. Another behaviourist (Clark Hull) argued that all species learn in the same way, but humans typically learn *faster* and more efficiently than other species.

There are various advantages of animal reductionism. First, it can be argued that simple forms of learning (e.g., classical conditioning, operant conditioning) can be studied more directly in other species than in the human one. Our behaviour is influenced by language, by social factors, and by cultural factors, and these may complicate the interpretation of findings. Second, some phenomena initially observed in other species have important implications for humans. For example, Seligman (1975) discovered learned helplessness in dogs, and this led to an enhanced understanding of depression in humans (see Chapter 8, Psychopathology).

What are the disadvantages of animal reductionism? First, the human species is so different from other species that this greatly limits what we learn by studying them. For example, our large neocortex relative to other species equips us with cognitive abilities (e.g., language) that simply don't exist in other species (see Chapter 7, Evolutionary Explanations of Human Behaviour). Second, the findings obtained from studies based on animal reductionism can be very misleading so far as the human species is concerned. Skinner's research on rats revealed that they are motivated to obtain immediate rewards and avoid immediate punishments. However, such research tells us precisely nothing about important aspects of human motivation such as the way our behaviour is influenced by long-term goals (e.g., achieving a good grade in A level Psychology).

Evolutionary Reductionism

According to advocates of evolutionary reductionism, much of the behaviour of the human species can be understood in terms of natural selection. As a result of natural selection, most of our behaviour is adaptive, although there are exceptions because of **genome lag**. Genetic factors are regarded as being of key importance within evolutionary reductionism because natural selection operates on the basis of certain genes or combinations of genes being favoured by any given environment.

One advantage of evolutionary reductionism is that it encourages us to consider genetic factors when trying to understand human behaviour. There are several areas of psychology in which this has proved useful—examples include individual differences in intelligence and factors causing mental disorders such as schizophrenia and bipolar depression. Second, evolutionary psychology has much to contribute to an understanding of differences among species (see Chapter 7, Evolutionary Explanations of Human Behaviour).

The greatest disadvantage with evolutionary reductionism is that it is limited in scope. Natural selection and genetic factors are important, but so are numerous environmental, social, and cultural factors. Another disadvantage is that even

KEY TERM

Genome lag: the notion that some behaviour is not adaptive because genetic changes over thousands of generations have proceeded much slower than changes in our environment.

Where do the main approaches in psychology stand on reductionism?

The biological approach. Reductionism is often equated with **physiological reductionism**, offering explanations of behaviour in terms of physiological mechanisms. The evolutionary approach uses evolutionary reductionism, when reducing behaviour to the effects of genes, as in some explanations of altruism or atypical behaviour.

The behaviourist approach uses a very reductionist vocabulary: stimulus, response, reinforcement, and punishment. These concepts alone are used to explain all behaviour. This is called **environmental reductionism** because it explains behaviour in terms of simple environmental factors. Behaviourists reduce the concept of the mind to behavioural components, i.e., stimulus–response links.

The cognitive approach uses the principle of **machine reductionism**. Information-processing approaches use the analogy of machine systems, and the simple components of such machines, as a means to describe and explain behaviour. More recent computer innovations, such as the Internet and connectionist networks can be described as holist because the network behaves differently from the individual parts that go to make it up. Wundt's early work in the areas of perception and thinking was reductionist, in its attempt to reduce human thought to elementary sensations. In the same way that the chemical elements such as hydrogen and oxygen combine to form complex compounds, the same might be true for sensations

and mental processes. The whole appears to be greater than the sum of its parts.

The *evolutionary approach* derives from Darwin's theory of evolution. Darwin himself didn't know anything about genes, but it emerged after his death that genetic inheritance is of key importance in natural selection. Advocates of this approach argue that we can understand much of human behaviour and differences among species by focusing on evolutionary history.

The *psychoanalytic approach* is reductionist insofar as it relies on a basic set of structures that attempt to simplify a very complex picture. On the other hand, and to complicate things a little (!), Freud used idiographic (i.e., individually based) techniques that aimed to preserve the richness of human experience rather than teasing out simple strands of behaviour.

The *humanistic approach* emerged as a reaction against those dehumanising psychological perspectives that attempted to reduce behaviour to a set of simple elements. Humanistic, or third-force psychologists, feel that holism is the only valid approach to the complete understanding of mind and behaviour.

We should also include experimental reductionism—the use of controlled laboratory studies to gain understanding of similar behaviours in the natural environment. This approach inevitably must reduce a complex behaviour to a simple set of variables that offer the possibility of identifying a cause and an effect.

---

when genetic factors are important, they are nearly always *only* important in interaction with other factors not considered within evolutionary reductionism. For example, someone who inherits the genes for high intelligence will only realise his/her potential provided there is a supportive environment.

Summary of the Advantages and Disadvantages of Reductionism

All forms of reductionism serve the useful function of encouraging us to consider factors that are relevant to an understanding of human behaviour. However, note that these forms of reductionism are not detailed theories in the sense of producing testable hypotheses. What they do is to provide a set of assumptions that can be used to guide theory and research. The various forms of reductionism taken together provide a reasonable basis for understanding human behaviour.

There are three major problems with all forms of reductionism. First, they involve trying to produce simple explanations within psychology, but by so doing they oversimplify. Second, they are all limited in that they focus on certain factors of relevance to an understanding of human behaviour while ignoring many other factors. Third, the available evidence doesn't provide strong support for the reductionist position.

Alternatives to Reductionism

The humanistic approach discussed elsewhere provides one alternative to reductionism. As we have seen, humanistic psychologists such as Maslow and Rogers (see box on page 425) attached great importance to the self-concept,

> **EXAM HINT**
>
> Make sure you link the arguments for and against reductionism to the examples you have selected.

> **KEY TERMS**
>
> **Physiological reductionism:** explanations of complex behaviours in terms of simpler physiological (bodily) changes.
> **Environmental reductionism:** attempting to understand how the natural environment influences our behaviour by studying artificial situations under laboratory conditions.
> **Machine reductionism:** explaining behaviour by analogy with rather simpler machine systems.

and to the efforts by humans to realise their potential by means of self-actualisation. Within this approach, there is no systematic attempt to divide the self up into smaller units, or to identify the physiological processes associated with the self-concept.

Most psychologists argue that the humanistic approach to reductionism is too limited. The refusal of humanistic psychologists to consider any kind of reductionism suggests they don't regard physiological and biological factors as having any real significance. It may be true that each individual's conscious experience is of importance in understanding his/her behaviour. However, it is likely that other factors also need to be taken into account.

Another alternative to reductionism is the **eclectic approach**, in which relevant information is gathered together from various sources and disciplines. Consider, for example, research on the causes of schizophrenia (a serious condition involving hallucinations and loss of contact with reality; Chapter 8, Psychopathology). There is evidence that genetic factors are involved. At the biochemical level, some studies have suggested that schizophrenics tend to be unduly sensitive to the neurotransmitter dopamine (see Davison & Neale, 2001). Other evidence reviewed by Davison and Neale indicates that poor social relationships and adverse life events also play a part in producing schizophrenia (see Chapter 8, Psychopathology).

Reductionists might be tempted to produce a biochemical theory of schizophrenia. However, such an approach would involve ignoring environmental factors such as life events. According to the eclectic approach, a full understanding of schizophrenia involves considering *all* the relevant factors and the ways in which they combine.

The main problem with the eclectic approach is that it is very difficult to combine information from different disciplines into a single theory. For example, how could the concepts of biochemistry be combined with those of life-event research? However, psychology shouldn't ignore valuable information from other disciplines. This can be seen clearly in recent studies involving brain imaging. Observations of physiological processes in the brain by means of PET and MRI scans are increasing our knowledge of human cognition.

<hr>

SECTION SUMMARY
Reductionism

What is reductionism?

- Reductionism in psychology is the notion that psychology can ultimately be reduced down to more basic sciences.
- There are several forms of reductionism including physiological, experimental, machine, animal, and evolutionary reductionism.

Physiological reductionism

- Human behaviour can be understood by looking at other more basic scientific disciplines.
- Advantages include:

  — There is an overlap with psychology and other sciences.
  — Biochemistry and physiology have well established facts and theories.
  — Psychological findings should be compatible with physiological findings.

KEY TERM

Eclectic approach: any approach in psychology that draws on many different perspectives.

- Disadvantages include:

    — Human behaviour cannot be understood solely in terms of biological and physiological processes.
    — Physiology focuses on structures not processes.
    — Physiological reductionism does not work well in practice, and reductionist explanations can contain irrelevant details for psychology.

- Human behaviour can be understood by looking at simple experiments.
- Advantages include:

    Experimental reductionism

    — The experimental method provides the most reliable evidence for human behaviour.
    — It is the obvious approach for some theories.

- Disadvantages include:

    — The typical experimental situation may not reflect real life.
    — The emphasis is on the immediate situation, but other factors can contribute to behaviour.

- Human behaviour can be understood by comparing ourselves with computers.
- Advantages include:

    Machine reductionism

    — We can reprogram a computer to improve similarities between computers and humans.

- Disadvantages include:

    — It omits many other factors such as motivation and emotion.
    — It simplifies the complex human brain.

- Human behaviour can be understood by looking at less complex species.
- Advantages include:

    Animal reductionism

    — Simple forms of learning can be studied more directly in non-human species.
    — Observations in other species can have important implications for humans (e.g., learned helplessness).

- Disadvantages include:

    — The human species is very different from other species.
    — Findings from studies on non-human animals can be misleading in terms of the human species.

- Human behaviour can be understood by looking at genetics.
- Advantages include:

    Evolutionary reductionism

    — Genetics can be useful to understand individual differences.
    — It can contribute to an understanding of differences within species.

- Disadvantages include:

    — It is limited in scope.
    — It doesn't take into account other factors such as environmental support.

Summary of the advantages and disadvantages of reductionism

- Advantages of reductionism as an approach:

  — All forms of reductionism are useful in that they focus our attention on factors relevant to an understanding of human behaviour.
  — They provide assumptions to guide theory and research.

- Disadvantages of reductionism as an approach:

  — All forms of reductionism are oversimplified.
  — They focus on only certain factors of relevance while ignoring others.

Alternatives to reductionism

- The humanistic approach:

  — It may be true (as humanistic psychologists claim) that conscious experience is important but other factors need to be taken into account.

- The eclectic approach:

  — Psychologists should gather together significant and relevant information from various sources and disciplines, as exemplified by explanations of schizophrenia, rather than trying to produce a single theory.

See also pages 289–292 of the revision guide.

PSYCHOLOGY AS SCIENCE

The Nature of "Science"

The appropriate starting point for a discussion of whether psychology is a science is to consider the definition of science. This is difficult to do, because views on the nature of science changed during the course of the twentieth century. According to the traditional view, science has the following features (Eysenck & Keane, 1990):

1. It is objective.
2. This objectivity is ensured by careful observation and experimentation.
3. The knowledge obtained by scientists is turned into law-like generalisations.

The behaviourists were much influenced by a version of this traditional view known as logical positivism. Logical positivists such as Ayer and Carnap argued that the theoretical constructs used in science are meaningful only to the extent that they can be observed. This was very much the position adopted by behaviourists such as Watson and Skinner. As a result, some important concepts within psychology were discarded. For example, Skinner (1990, p.1209) argued as follows: "There is no place in a scientific analysis of behaviour for a mind or self."

There are major problems with the traditional view of science held by the behaviourists and others. As is discussed shortly, the notion that behaviour can be observed objectively has been vigorously attacked. Writers such as Kuhn (1970) have argued that the scientific enterprise has important social and subjective aspects to it. This view was taken to extremes by Feyerabend (1975). He argued that science progresses by a sort of "who-shouts-the-loudest" strategy, in

■ **Activity: Objectivity**

Which of the following would you describe as objective, and why? Discuss your answers in small groups.

- It will probably rain, now that it is spring.
- The life expectancy of a cat is about 15–20 years.
- Deciduous trees all lose their leaves in winter.
- If you eat all that chocolate, you will definitely be sick.

which publicity and visibility count for more than the quality of the research. According to this position, objectivity is essentially irrelevant to the conduct of science.

What about the view that science involves forming law-like generalisations? Suppose we test a given hypothesis several times, and the findings consistently support the hypothesis. Does that prove that the hypothesis is correct? Popper (1969) argued that it doesn't. Generalisations based on what has been found to be in the past may not hold true in the future. Consider Bertrand Russell's example of a turkey forming the generalisation, "Each day I am fed", because for all of its life that has been true.

Law-like generalisations are not always true.

This generalisation provides no certainty that the turkey will be fed tomorrow, and if tomorrow is Christmas Eve it is likely to be proved false!

A New Definition for Science

In view of the fact that the traditional definition of science is inadequate, it is clear that a new definition is needed. This is easier said than done. As Eysenck and Keane (1990, p.5) pointed out, the views of Feyerabend and other twentieth-century philosophers of science "have established the point that the division between science and non-science is by no means as clear cut as used to be believed". However, there is probably reasonable agreement that the following are key features of science:

1. *Controlled observations*: in most sciences (except astronomy and a few others), it is typical for experiments to involve observing the effects of some specific manipulation (e.g., mixing two chemicals together). As applied to psychology, this generally involves observing the effects of some manipulation of the environment on participants' behaviour.
2. *Objectivity*: even if total objectivity is impossible, it is still important for data to be collected in a way as close to objectivity as possible.
3. *Testing theoretical predictions*: Scientific experiments are generally carried out to test the predictions of some theory.
4. *Falsifiability*: the notion that scientific theories can potentially be disproved by evidence.
5. *Replicability*: the findings obtained by researchers need to be replicable or repeatable; it would be hard (or impossible) to base a science on inconsistent findings.
6. *Paradigm*: there is a generally accepted theoretical orientation or paradigm within a science.

Controlled observations

There are numerous ways of carrying out studies in psychology. However, the approach most in accord with the demands of science is the experimental method. With this method, some aspect of the environment is *controlled* (the independent variable) to assess its impact on participants' behaviour (the dependent variable).

Goals of science

What are the goals of science? According to Allport (1947), science has the aims of "understanding, prediction and control above the levels achieved by unaided common sense". Thus, three of the main goals of science are as follows:

1. Prediction
2. Understanding
3. Control.

As we will see shortly, psychologists differ among themselves as to the relative importance of these three goals.

Prediction

Scientists put forward theories, which are general explanations or accounts of certain findings or data. These theories can then be used to generate various hypotheses, which are predictions or expectations of what will happen in given situations. One of the best known theories in psychology is Thorndike's (1911) law of effect, according to which acts that are rewarded or reinforced are "stamped in", whereas those that are punished are "stamped out". This theory has generated numerous hypotheses including, for example, the predicted behaviour of rats that are rewarded for lever pressing or the behaviour of pigeons rewarded for pecking at a disc. The success or otherwise of predictions stemming from a theory is of great importance. Any theory that generates numerous incorrect predictions is seriously flawed.

Understanding

Even if a theory generates a number of accurate predictions, it does not necessarily follow that this will give us a good understanding of what is happening. For example, Craik and Lockhart's (1972) levels-of-processing theory led to the prediction that memory will be better for material that has been processed in terms of its meaning than for material that has not. This prediction has been confirmed experimentally numerous times (as discussed in your AS level studies). However, the precise reasons why it is beneficial to process meaning still remain unclear.

Control

After prediction and understanding have been achieved, it is sometimes possible to move on to control. For example, Thorndike, Skinner, and others predicted (and found) that people tend to repeat behaviour that is followed by reward or positive reinforcement, and the principles of operant conditioning were put forward in an attempt to understand what is going on. It is possible to use reinforcement to control human behaviour, as when parents persuade their children to behave well in return for sweets. Skinner (1948), in his utopian novel *Walden Two*, went further, and argued that it would be possible to create an ideal society by arranging matters so that only socially desirable behaviour was rewarded or reinforced.

Philosophers of science tell us it is impossible to establish causality with certainty. However, the experimental method has the great advantage over other methods that it allows us to have some confidence that the independent variable has influenced the dependent variable.

Objectivity

We have already referred to the importance of data collection or scientific observation as a way of testing hypotheses. According to the traditional view of science, scientific observations are entirely **objective**. However, Popper (1969, 1972) argued that scientific observations are theory-driven rather than objective. His famous lecture demonstration involved telling the audience, "Observe!" Their obvious and immediate retort was, "Observe what?" This demonstration makes the point that no-one ever observes without some idea of what they are looking for. Thus, scientific observation is always driven by hypotheses and theories, and what you observe depends in part on what you expect to see.

We can make this argument more concrete by taking a specific example. There have been thousands of experiments carried out in the Skinner box, in which the number of lever presses produced by a rat in a given period of time is the key behavioural measure. In most studies, the equipment is designed so that each lever press is recorded automatically. This procedure is less objective than might be thought. Lever presses with the rat's right paw, with its left paw, and even with its nose or tail are all recorded as a single lever press, even though the rat's actual behaviour differs considerably. Furthermore, the rat sometimes presses the lever too gently to activate the mechanism, and this isn't counted as a lever press at all.

A more sweeping attack on the notion that data in psychology are objective has been made by social constructionists such as Gergen (1985) and Harré and Secord (1972). Semin (1995, p.545) described their key assumptions as follows:

> *In their view, there are no such things as pure observations. All observations require a prior viewpoint, irrespective of whether these stem from a theoretical perspective, or are due to learning . . . Thus data are socially "manufactured", irrespective of which form these data take.*

Wallach and Wallach (1994) agreed that perfect objectivity cannot be achieved, and that it isn't possible to be certain that the interpretation of someone's behaviour is correct. However, we can be more confident in our interpretation of behaviour if it is supported by other evidence. According to Wallach and Wallach (p.234):

> *When a [participant] presses a lever that ostensibly [i.e., apparently] delivers shocks to another [participant], it may be far from certain that he or she intends to harm this other [participant]. If the [participant] also asserts that this was his or her intention, or it happens that on the experimenter's declaration that the experiment is over, the [participant] proceeds to punch the other [participant] in the nose, then, all else being equal, it seems likely that harm was intended.*

Testing theoretical predictions

It is sensible to design experiments in such a way that they test theoretical predictions. This is because there is in principle an infinite number of experiments that could be carried out, and scientific theories assist in the task of identifying which ones are worthwhile. Science advances when inadequate theories are replaced by ones more consistent with the data.

Falsifiability

An extremely influential view of what distinguishes science from non-science was put forward by Popper (1969). He argued that the hallmark of science is **falsifiability** rather than generalisation from positive instances or findings. Scientists should form theories and hypotheses that can potentially be shown to be untrue by experimental tests. According to Popper, the possibility of falsification is what separates science from religions and pseudo-sciences such as psychoanalysis and Marxism.

Some theories in psychology are falsifiable, whereas others aren't. For example, H.J. Eysenck (1967) put

? Popper argues that we all see the world from our own particular viewpoints or biases. This influences the topic we choose to look at. How can scientists try to avoid bias in their work?

KEY TERM

Falsifiability: the notion that scientific theories can potentially be disproved by evidence; it is the hallmark of science, according to Popper.

Hypothesis testing and falsifiability

Any scientific hypothesis must be open to the possibility of being disproved, i.e., it must be falsifiable. An example that is often quoted is the assertion that "All ravens are black." To test this hypothesis fully, one would have to catch and examine every raven in the world, and even then an albino raven might be on the point of hatching out. Although it may be true that, in most people's experience, ravens are all black, it would only take one albino bird for the whole hypothesis to be shown to be false.

forward a theory, according to which those high in neuroticism (anxiety and depression) should be more physiologically responsive than those low in neuroticism. Numerous studies have tested this theory, with the great majority failing to support it (Fahrenberg, 1992). Thus, the theory has been falsified.

Another example of a theory that is falsifiable is the frustration–aggression hypothesis, according to which frustration leads to aggression and aggression is caused by frustration. There is much research showing that this is a considerable oversimplification of what happens (see Chapter 3, Pro- and Anti-social behaviour).

In contrast, Freud's notion that the mind consists of three parts (ego, superego, and id) is unfalsifiable. It isn't possible to imagine any findings that would disprove such a vague and poorly specified theoretical position. In similar fashion, it is hard to test or to falsify Maslow's (1954) theory of motivation based on a hierarchy of needs. This theory assumes that there are five types of needs arranged in a hierarchical way, from need for survival at the bottom to need for self-actualisation at the top. The problems associated with falsifying this theory may explain why relatively few studies have tested it.

There are also problems of falsifiability with much of evolutionary psychology. According to evolutionary psychology, most of our behaviour should be adaptive because that maximises the chances of reproduction. However, evolutionary psychologists also claim to be able to "explain" behaviour that is *not* adaptive by using the notion of "genome lag", meaning that evolution of the genome has lagged behind environmental changes. Thus, adaptive and maladaptive behaviour can be "explained" after a fashion! More specifically, evolutionary psychologists have provided explanations of various mental disorders such as schizophrenia and depression (see Chapter 8, Psychopathology). However, these explanations are rather speculative and difficult to falsify.

Replicability

It was indicated earlier that **replicability** or repeatability of findings is an important requirement for a subject to be considered as a science. Replicability of findings in psychology varies enormously as a function of the area and type of study being carried out. Replicability tends to be greatest when experiments are conducted in a carefully controlled way, and it tends to be lowest when the experimenter is unable to manipulate the variable or variables of interest.

Clear evidence of replicability is available from studies of operant conditioning. There are characteristic patterns of responding that are found when animals are put into a Skinner box and rewarded on various schedules of reinforcement. For example, there is the fixed interval schedule, in which the animal is rewarded with food for the first response after a given interval of time (e.g., 30 seconds). What nearly always happens is that the animal stops responding immediately after receiving food, because it has learned that no additional food is available at that time. The animal starts to respond again more and more rapidly as the time at which reward will be available approaches.

Replicability tends to be lower when studies are carried out in social psychology, but often remains high when the situation is under good experimental control. For example, there is the Asch situation, in which there is one genuine participant and several participants who are confederates of the experimenter. They are given the task of deciding which of three lines is the same length as

? What are the main obstacles to replicability in human psychology?

? If Skinner and Thorndike's theories are correct, then punishment should always be a deterrent, but this is not always true. What could be the reason for this?

KEY TERM

Replicability: a feature of research, in which the findings of an experiment can be repeated.

another line. The key condition is one in which all the confederates of the experimenter provide the same incorrect decision. Convincing evidence of conformity by the genuine participant has been found in numerous studies in several countries.

Laboratory experiments

Laboratory experiments permit high control and good replicability. In order for psychology to be regarded as a science, we must have confidence in laboratory (and other) experiments as a way of obtaining valid information about human behaviour. But not all psychologists respect the experimental approach as a means to investigate human behaviour. For example, at one extreme Boring (1957) argued as follows: "The application of the experimental method to the problem of mind

Many laboratory-based experiments in psychology show low external validity—that is, their findings do not translate reliably to behaviour outside the laboratory.

is the great outstanding event in the history of the study of mind, an event to which no other is comparable." In contrast, Nick Heather (1976) was very dismissive of laboratory experiments. He argued that they are very artificial, and that all that can be learned from them is how strangers interact in an unusual situation.

Some of the strengths and weaknesses of laboratory research can be made clearer by looking at two kinds of validity. **Internal validity** refers to the validity of research within the context in which it is carried out. For example, if the same experiment is carried out time after time, and the same findings are obtained each time, this would indicate high internal validity. Experiments that can be repeated in this way are high in replicability. **External validity** refers to the validity of the research outside the research situation. Many laboratory experiments are rather low in external validity, meaning that we cannot be confident that what is true in the laboratory is also true of everyday life.

Much psychological research on humans is somewhat lacking in external validity. We spend most of our time actively dealing with our environment, deciding in which situations to put ourselves, and then responding to those situations as seems appropriate. Much of that dynamic interaction is lacking in laboratory research. The experimenter (rather than the participant) determines the situation in which the participant is placed, and what is of interest is the participant's response to that situation. This led Silverman (1977) to argue that the findings obtained from laboratory studies are only likely to generalise to institutions such as prisons, hospitals, or schools.

Paradigm: Kuhn's approach

According to Thomas Kuhn (1962, 1970, 1977), the most essential ingredient in a science is what he called a **paradigm**. This is a general theoretical orientation

■ **Activity:** Construct a brief outline for each of the following:

- An experiment that should show high internal validity
- An experiment that will be unlikely to show high internal validity
- An experiment that is unlikely to show high external validity.

KEY TERMS

Internal validity: the extent to which research findings are genuine and can be regarded as being caused by the independent variable.
External validity: the extent to which findings generalise across populations, locations, measures, and times.
Paradigm: according to Kuhn, a general theoretical orientation that is accepted by most scientists in a given discipline.

Before Copernicus showed that the planets, including the earth, revolved around the sun, all astronomical theories had been based on the paradigm that the earth was the centre of the universe. The complete change in science post-Copernicus is an example of a paradigm shift.

accepted by the great majority of workers in that field of study. With the advance of knowledge, the dominant paradigm in any science will gradually become less adequate. When there is very strong evidence against the current paradigm, it is eventually replaced by another paradigm.

These considerations led Kuhn (1970) to argue that there are three distinct stages in the development of a science:

1. *Pre-science*: there is no generally accepted paradigm, and there is a wide range of opinion about the best theoretical approach to adopt.
2. *Normal science*: there is a generally accepted paradigm, and it accounts for the phenomena regarded as being central to the field. This paradigm influences the experiments carried out, and how the findings are explained. A classic example of normal science is the use of Newtonian mechanics by physicists until the emergence of relativity theory.
3. *Revolutionary science*: when the evidence against the old paradigm reaches a certain point, there is what is known as a paradigm shift. This involves the old paradigm being replaced by a new one. An example of a paradigm shift is the Copernican revolution, in which the old view that the planets and the sun revolve around the earth was replaced by our present view that the earth and the other planets revolve around the sun.

The replacement of an old paradigm by a new one doesn't usually happen in an orderly way. Scientists who support the old paradigm often ignore conflicting evidence, or dismiss it as of little importance. Adherents of the old paradigm resist change for as long as possible, until they can no longer hold out against the onslaught. In other words, social and other pressures lead scientists to stick with paradigms that are clearly inadequate.

Where does psychology fit in?

It is time to return to Kuhn's three stages to consider where psychology fits in. Kuhn (1962) argued that psychology has failed to develop a paradigm, and so remains at the pre-science stage. Various arguments support this point of view. First, there are several general theoretical approaches within psychology (e.g., psychodynamic, behaviourist, humanist, cognitive). As a result, it cannot really be argued that most psychologists support the same paradigm.

Second, psychology is an unusually fragmented discipline. It has connections with several other disciplines, including biology, physiology, biochemistry, neurology, and sociology. Psychologists studying, for example, biochemistry have very little in common with those studying social factors within society. The fragmentation and diversity make it unlikely that agreement can be reached on a common paradigm or general theoretical orientation.

Valentine (1982, 1992) argued for a different position, claiming that behaviourism comes close to being a paradigm. As she pointed out, behaviourism has had a massive influence on psychology through its insistence that psychology is the study of behaviour, and that behaviour should be observed in controlled experiments. It also had a great influence (but one that has declined considerably in recent decades) through its theoretical assumptions that the study of learning is of fundamental importance to psychology, and that learning can be understood in terms of conditioning principles.

It isn't clear that behaviourism is a paradigm. Behaviourism's greatest impact on psychology has been at the methodological level, with its emphasis on studying behaviour. However, a paradigm in Kuhn's sense is more concerned with a general theoretical orientation rather than with methodological issues. Thus, behaviourism doesn't seem to be a paradigm, and Kuhn (1962) was probably correct to place psychology at the pre-science stage. This may not make psychology as different from other sciences as is often assumed. Kuhn's view of normal science, in which nearly all scientists within a discipline are working in harmony using the same paradigm, exaggerates the similarity of perspective found among researchers in physics, chemistry, biology, and so on.

> ■ **Activity: Causes of schizophrenia**
> The competing theories that exist for the causes of schizophrenia could be indicative of a pre-scientific stage in the psychology of mental disorders. Using other sources, research the dominant paradigms that exist in this area, and compare them with other less adequate explanations for schizophrenia. Can we say that psychologists have established a generally accepted explanation for the causes of certain forms of schizophrenia? If so, are these explanations proof of a scientific approach? What do you think are the chances of a competing explanation resulting in a paradigm shift, for example to environmental and/or social causes?

Non-scientific Approaches to Psychology

As we have seen, the behaviourists firmly believed that psychology should be a science, and they tried hard to achieve this. However, other approaches to psychology attach much less emphasis on the notion of psychology as a science. Humanistic psychologists and social constructionists agreed strongly that psychology should not be a science, and social constructionists went further and argued that it cannot be a science.

Humanistic approaches

The humanistic psychologists (e.g., Maslow, Rogers) were fairly strongly opposed to the traditional scientific approach to psychology. According to Maslow (1968, p.13), "The uniqueness of the individual does not fit into what we know of science. Then so much the worse for that conception of science. It, too, will have to endure re-creation."

Maslow and Rogers favoured the use of **phenomenology**, in which individuals report their conscious experiences in as pure and undistorted a way as possible. This approach was justified in the following terms by Rogers (1959):

> *This personal, phenomenological type of study—especially when one reads all of the responses—is far more valuable than the traditional "hard-headed" empirical approach. This kind of study, often scorned by psychologists as being "merely self-reports", actually gives the deepest insight into what the experience has meant.*

KEY TERM

Phenomenology: an approach that emphasises subjective experience as the basis for understanding the world, as opposed to objective, external reality.

It will be remembered that three of the major aims of science are understanding, prediction, and control. The humanistic psychologists emphasised the goal of

SCHOOL IN THE LAST CENTURY.   "TAKE DOWN HIS BREECHES!"

In the past, physical punishment of disobedient children was generally accepted as appropriate. Psychologists today would view it differently, as the social view of physical punishment has undergone drastic changes.

understanding. However, their approach failed to be scientific in part because they attached much less importance to the other two aims of prediction and control.

Social constructionist approaches

Those psychologists who favour **social constructionism** argue that there are no objective data, and that our "knowledge" of ourselves and of the world is based on social constructions. Thus, "What we call facts are simply versions of events which, for various reasons, are presently enjoying wide currency" (Burr, 1997, p.8). Social constructionists have attacked the "so-called objectivity of the 'scientist', disengaged from the cultural and historical circumstances" (Semin, 1995, p.545). According to them, the observations made by psychologists, and the ways those observations are interpreted, are determined in large measure by the cultural and historical forces influencing them. Thus, for example, teachers beating disruptive schoolchildren are now regarded as behaving violently and unacceptably, but the same behaviour was generally tolerated 40 or 50 years ago.

The importance of historical forces was emphasised by Gergen (1973, p.318). According to him, "We must think in terms of a *continuum of historical durability*, with phenomena highly susceptible to historical influence at one extreme and the more stable processes at the other." Behaviourists and other psychologists who favour the scientific approach assume that the historical durability of phenomena is high, whereas social constructionists assume it is often very low.

It follows from what has been said so far that social constructionists believe psychology cannot be a science. How do they think that psychologists should proceed? According to Burr (1997, p.8), "Since there is no ultimate knowledge of human beings that we can call a final truth, what we must do instead is to try to understand where our current ways of understanding have come from." One of the ways in which that can be done is by means of **discourse analysis**, which involves focusing on analysing people's use of language in order to understand how they perceive the world.

Wetherell and Potter (1988) carried out discourse analysis on interviews conducted with white New Zealanders. These interviews dealt with the issue of the teaching of Maori culture in schools. What emerged from this discourse analysis was that many white New Zealanders had racist views, even though they claimed not be racist. They argued in favour of encouraging Maori culture, but emphasised the importance of togetherness (all New Zealanders working co-operatively) and of pragmatic realism (being in touch with the modern world). The hidden message was that fostering Maori culture would have adverse effects on togetherness and pragmatic realism, and so should not be done.

The study by Wetherell and Potter (1988) fails to meet some of the criteria of science identified earlier. More specifically, the interview data weren't obtained under controlled conditions, and there was incomplete objectivity because the data were interpreted in a subjective way by the researchers. In addition, we don't know whether the findings are replicable, and discourse analysis cannot be regarded as falling within a scientific paradigm.

Evaluation

There is some validity in the social constructionist position. However, many psychologists regard it as making exaggerated claims. For example, suppose several people saw a policeman hitting a student hard with a long stick. Regardless of their beliefs, they would probably be able to agree on the basic facts of what had happened. However, there would be much disagreement as to whether the policeman's action was justified or unjustified. In other words, our beliefs may colour our *interpretation* of an action, but they are less likely to influence our *description* of that action.

> **?** What response might a physicist give to the social constructionist view?

Summary and Conclusions

It is hard to decide whether psychology should be regarded as a science. In general terms, psychology possesses many of the features of a science. However, it tends to possess them less clearly and less strongly than other sciences such as physics or chemistry.

On the positive side, much research in psychology involves controlled observations and is designed to test theoretical predictions. In addition, some theoretical approaches in psychology have been successful in achieving the goals of prediction, understanding, and control. Many psychological theories fulfil Popper's criterion of falsifiability, as they have been disproved by experimental studies. The findings of numerous experiments in psychology have been replicated successfully, which is another criterion of a science. However, psychology is very variable with respect to falsifiability and replicability. As we have seen, some theories in psychology are not sufficiently precisely expressed to be falsifiable, and many findings aren't replicable.

On the negative side, there are various legitimate doubts about the scientific nature of psychology. First, at least some of the data obtained are not objective but seem to be influenced by the experimenter's biases, which are determined by his/her social and cultural background. Second, many of the findings obtained from psychological research lack external validity, because they have been obtained under the artificial conditions of the laboratory.

Third, the experimental method can most easily be used when we want to study the effects of the immediate situation on behaviour. However, as was discussed earlier in the chapter, our behaviour is determined by numerous factors in addition to the immediate situation, and most of these factors cannot be manipulated (e.g., childhood experiences, genetic inheritance, our personality). The fact that we cannot control these factors limits the development of psychology as a science. Fourth, Kuhn (1970) is probably correct in arguing that psychology is a pre-science, because it lacks a generally accepted paradigm.

The issue of whether psychology is or isn't a science can have important implications for research funding. The reason is that subjects regarded as sciences generally receive more research funding than those not so regarded. At the end of the 1970s, the main provider of research funding for psychology in Britain was the Social Science Research Council. However, the Conservative government under Margaret Thatcher was not convinced that psychology, economics, and the

> **EXAM HINT**
> You may be asked to consider the arguments for, or the arguments against, each of the debates in psychology, so plan carefully. You need to have a structure for "an arguments for essay" and a structure for "an arguments against essay". Some of the content will be the same but you will need to use the arguments for or against differently depending on whether they are AO1 or AO2.

Phenomenology vs. empiricism

A simplistic example of the difference between the phenomenological school of thought and that of the empiricists (see the next Section) might be approaches to the personality changes that tend to take place during adolescence. Whereas the empiricists would observe and record the reactions (verbal and nonverbal) to a given stimulus such as a list of questions, a phenomenological approach would make observations within the context of the individual adolescent's personal profile, e.g., early childhood memories. The humanist would concentrate on the changes occurring against a backdrop of the whole self. The empiricist would concentrate on the stage of development reached.

other disciplines funded by the Social Science Research Council were really sciences, and it was nearly closed down altogether. What actually happened was that it was renamed the Economic and Social Research Council, and it received less money than before.

In sum, there are good reasons for arguing that psychology is on the way to becoming a science. At present, however, it should probably be regarded as having only some of the features of a science rather than being a fully fledged science.

SECTION SUMMARY
Psychology as Science

What is the definition of "science"?

❖ The traditional view is that science involves the collection of objective data and the drawing of generalisations.
❖ At the opposite extreme some psychologists suggest that objectivity is irrelevant to successful science.
❖ Popper argued that the fundamental scientific belief in testing hypotheses doesn't hold up.
❖ It may be possible to define science as possessing the following features:

— Controlled observations
— Relatively objective data
— Testing theoretical predictions
— Falsifiability
— Replicability of findings
— Use of a paradigm.

Controlled observations

❖ Controlled observations (typically obtained under laboratory conditions using the experimental method) are of key importance.
❖ Science aims to be objective, yet all observations inevitably are influenced by what you expect to see.
❖ According to social constructionists, the observations made by psychologists, and their interpretations of those observations, are determined by cultural forces.

Falsifiability

❖ Popper argued that the hallmark of science is falsifiability (disproving theories and hypotheses by experimental tests).
❖ Not all theories in psychology are falsifiable. Broadbent's filter theory of attention is falsifiable, while Freud's theory of psychoanalysis is not.
❖ In addition to falsifiability, it is important that findings are replicable—if the findings keep changing, there is no basis for developing theories.

Use of a paradigm

❖ Kuhn described three stages in the development of science: pre-science, normal science, and revolutionary science.
❖ Kuhn claimed psychology has failed to develop a paradigm and remains in the pre-science stage.

❖ This is supported by the variety of theoretical approaches within psychology and the fragmented nature of the subject.

❖ Some approaches within psychology, such as behaviourism, may be paradigms. However, behaviourism is largely methodological (concerned with studying behaviour) rather than a general theoretical orientation.

❖ Humanistic psychologists argue that psychology shouldn't be a science:

— They suggest phenomenology as an alternative research approach that provides deep insights through self-reporting.

Non-scientific approaches to psychology

❖ Social constructionists suggest psychology can't be a science:

— They suggest that the historical durability of phenomena is low and thus research and understanding are best served by qualitative research methods such as discourse analysis.

❖ Psychology has some features of a science:

Is psychology a science?

— Controlled observations
— Testing theoretical predictions
— Falsifiability
— Replicability.

❖ However, it doesn't fully possess other features:

— Paradigm
— Objectivity.

See also pages 293–296 of the revision guide.

❖ There are important implications for the funding of research.

NATURE–NURTURE

The so-called "**nature–nurture debate**" in psychology has a long history, stretching back into philosophical debate about the nature of humankind. The term "nature" refers to behaviour that is determined by inherited factors. "Nurture" is the influence of any environmental factors including learning. The debate is sometimes called heredity versus environment.

History of the Nature–Nurture Debate

Philosophers have long recognised that aspects of behaviour are inherited. This was long before the discovery of genes by Mendel in the late nineteenth century. Plato, the Greek philosopher, talked about things being inborn or native to an individual, as contrasting with those characteristics that were acquired through experience. This view of inherited characteristics was referred to as **nativism**.

The opposing philosophical orientation was called **empiricism**. John Locke in the seventeenth century first outlined the view that all newborn babies are alike. They are born with a mind that is like a blank slate (*tabula rasa*) and experience records itself in such a way that each individual becomes a unique being. We inherit nothing and all behaviour is acquired as a consequence of experience.

KEY TERMS

Nature–nurture debate: the question of whether behaviour is determined by inherited factors or by experience (learning). Now increasingly recognised as more than just an either/or question.

Nativism: the view that people's characteristics are inherited.

Empiricism: the view that all behaviour is the consequence of experience. The extreme "nurture" side of the nature–nurture debate.

The term "empiricism" is derived from "empirical" meaning to discover something through one's own senses.

Various implications stem from this divergence of opinion. If behaviour is entirely due to heredity then intervention would have little effect on the development of children. In contrast, if all behaviour is learned through experience then the child's experiences during development are crucial.

Rousseau was an eighteenth-century French philosopher whose work had a major influence on education. He argued that children are noble savages who should be given freedom to follow their innate and positive inclinations. In contrast, the empiricist philosophy suggested that children should be trained in socially acceptable ways. This was the basis for behaviourism and took the view of the child as a passive recipient of instruction.

Nature or Nurture

Consider any area in psychology that you have studied. In what way is behaviour in this area of psychology caused by nature or by nurture?

The use of the term "debate" suggests one must choose between these two opposing views. The nativists and empiricists certainly staunchly supported their different positions but philosophers and psychologists accept that it isn't an either/or question. There are various arguments that demonstrate this, and it can be best seen in the context of understanding the development of intelligence (see also Chapter 5, Cognitive Development).

Examples of the nature–nurture debate in psychology

Perception. To what extent is what we see—for example the perception of depth or visual illusions—an innate aspect of the physical visual system? Or are some aspects of perception learned and therefore different in different cultures?

Language. To what extent are humans "hardwired" to acquire language, or is their ability to use language based on exposure and imitation? If the latter is true, then it should be possible to train non-human animals, which don't have the innate brain mechanisms, to use language.

Aggression. To what extent is violent behaviour an aspect of a person's nature, or is it learned? For example, we might propose that men are more physically aggressive than women because they are innately more aggressive or it may be that, in our society, men are taught to respond more aggressively than women (nurture). The question has important practical applications in the reduction of aggression. If it is down to nature, then drug therapies may offer the best means of prevention.

Chapter 3, Pro- and Anti-social Behaviour, considers anti-social behaviour as well as pro-social behaviour, which may also be due to nature or nurture.

Gender development. Sex is determined by each individual's chromosomes; gender identity and gender role behaviour are largely moulded by society—though there is evidence that biology may play an important role. (See pages 257–266.)

Causes of mental illness. Recent research has found evidence of a genetic basis for many disorders (e.g., schizophrenia). However, the diathesis–stress model suggests that a person's genetic make-up will predispose them to certain disorders but environmental factors (stresses) actually trigger the expression of the disorder. The more susceptible an individual is, the fewer stresses are necessary. This means that neither nature or nurture individually causes dysfunction. The disorder comes about as a result of the interaction of nature with nurture. (See Chapter 8, Psychopathology.)

Diathesis–stress model

KEY TERM

Diathesis–stress model: the notion that psychological disorders occur when there is a genetically determined vulnerability (diathesis) and relevant stressful conditions.

The **diathesis–stress model** is based on a similar argument (see your AS studies and Chapter 8, Psychopathology). The diathesis–stress model proposes that a complete explanation of any mental disorder is likely to involve both a predisposition to the disorder (an inherited susceptibility to become ill) and a stressor triggering the appearance of the symptoms. This model applies to eating disorders, schizophrenia, and other mental disorders where there is clear evidence of a genetic link from studies of twins, yet not everyone with the gene becomes ill. For example, Holland, Sicotte, and Treasure (1988) studied anorexia in identical and non-identical twins. The concordance rate for identical twins was 56% compared with 5% for non-identical twins (who are genetically less similar). This indicates a high inherited factor, but it is not 100%. We can explain this in terms of the psychological factors that trigger the disorder, such as troubled families or stressful life events. This is an example of nature and nurture interacting.

We can also see the diathesis–stress model at work with the inherited metabolic disorder called phenylketonuria (PKU). In PKU, certain proteins are not processed properly, leaving a poisonous substance in the blood that causes brain damage. If the condition is detected early (and all newborns are tested) then the particular proteins can be eliminated from the child's diet and there is no brain damage. The question is whether intellectual impairment, should it occur, would be considered as due to nature or nurture. If the child's environment doesn't contain the proteins, no damage will occur. Therefore, there is an interaction between nature and nurture.

? In the case of anorexia nervosa, can we say whether nature or nurture is the cause of the disorder?

Genotype and phenotype

Those who believe in the importance of heredity draw a distinction between the **genotype** and the **phenotype**. The genotype is an individual's genetic constitution, as determined by the particular set of genes the individual possesses. Your genotype is your biological or genetic *potential* to become what you might become. The phenotype is the observable characteristics of an individual, which result from interaction between the genes he/she possesses (i.e., the individual's genotype) and the environment. Your phenotype is what you actually become as a consequence of the interaction between your biology/genetic make-up and the environment. An example would be hair colour. Your genes determine the colour of your hair, but the fact that you live in a sunny country may mean that your brown hair is bleached in the sun and this produces your blonde phenotype: your observable hair colour, which results from your genetic make-up, and an environmental influence.

As far as intelligence is concerned, we cannot access the genotype. All that can be done is to assess the phenotype by means of administering an intelligence test. This means we never assess inherited abilities except in the context of their environmental expression. There is no such thing as "pure nature".

The concept of nature presumes that we can isolate an individual who has had no interaction with the environment. People often talk of abilities being present at birth but at this time the human infant has already had 9 months-worth of environmental experience. Even before conception the state of the infant is not all "nature", as illustrated by something called the **transgenerational effect**: if a woman has a poor diet during pregnancy her foetus suffers. Perhaps more importantly, if the foetus is female the foetus's eggs for her own children, which are already formed, will be adversely affected. Therefore the next generation will be underdeveloped because of its *grandmother's* poor environment. What may appear to be inherited is in fact environmentally caused.

This all illustrates the practical difficulties in separating nature from nurture. Hebb (1949) suggested that asking the question of "nature or nurture" is like asking whether a field's area is determined more by its length or by its width. Of course, its area depends equally on both length and width. In similar fashion,

KEY TERMS

Genotype: an individual's genetic potential.
Phenotype: the observable characteristics of an individual, resulting from the interaction between genes and the environment.
Transgenerational effect: if a woman has, e.g., a poor diet during pregnancy, her foetus suffers and may be less able to reproduce future generations.

Hebb argued, intelligence depends equally on both heredity and environment. However, while this line of reasoning is valid, we can still reasonably ask whether the areas of different fields vary more because of differences in their lengths or in terms of their widths. In the same way, we can ask whether individual differences in intelligence depend *more* on differences in genetic endowment or on environmental differences. The question is not nature *or* nurture, but which one may contribute more. We will consider research methods shortly.

Expressing inheritance

When psychologists explore the extent to which a characteristic (e.g., intelligence, schizophrenia) is inherited, they use various different techniques.

The **concordance rate** expresses the extent to which two measures are in agreement. For example, suppose that 20 twin pairs are studied in which at least one twin has developed schizophrenia. If there are 18 pairs in which both twins have schizophrenia, then the concordance rate is 18/20 or 90%, indicating a very high level of concordance. We can take things further if we compare concordance rates in monozygotic (identical) twins and dizygotic (non-identical or fraternal) twins.

Monozygotic twins share 100% of their genes, whereas dizygotic twins share only 50%. If genetic factors are important, we would expect monozygotic twins to have a higher concordance rate than dizygotic twins. If genetic factors don't play a role, then there should be no difference in concordance rate between the two types of twins.

We can use information from concordance rates to work out **heritability**. This provides an estimate of the extent to which genetic factors contribute to individual differences in some characteristic within a given population. Heritability of 1.0 would mean that all the variance or variation within a given population was due to genetic factors, and heritability of 0.0 would mean that genetic factors were totally irrelevant.

We can use information about IQ from pairs of monozygotic and dizygotic twins in a similar way. In essence, if individual differences in intelligence depend to some extent on genetic factors, then identical twins should resemble each other more in IQ than should fraternal twins. If environment is all important, then identical twins should be no more similar to each other in IQ than fraternal twins. In either case, the outcome of taking account of the relevant information is an estimate of heritability of intelligence.

The form of interaction

It is often assumed that heredity and environment have *independent* effects. In fact, however, heredity and environment typically *interact* in complex ways. For example, consider intelligence. Genetic factors and environmental factors (e.g., the number of years of education) both influence intelligence but not in an entirely separate way—those with the genes for high intelligence also tend to receive the most years of education. As a result, it is very difficult to disentangle the effects of heredity and environment.

Plomin, DeFries, and Loehlin (1977) identified three different kinds of interaction between heredity and environment:

> **KEY TERMS**
>
> **Concordance rate:** if one twin has a disorder or condition, the likelihood that the other twin also has it.
>
> **Heritability:** the proportion of the variance within a population in some characteristic (e.g., height) that is due to genetic factors.

1. *Passive heredity–environment interaction.* A child's parents shape the environment in which the child grows up. Intelligent, well-educated parents are likely to have a house full of books and prefer to watch certain programmes on television. This environment is related to the parents' genetic make-up and thus the parents' genes are transmitted passively to the child via the environment that the parents create.

2. *Reactive heredity–environment interaction.* Research has shown that adults do not behave in the same way to a beautiful child as to a "plain" one (Burns & Farina, 1992), and that they find it easier to form a relationship with a child who has an easy temperament than with a child who has a difficult one (Thomas & Chess, 1977). The child's inherited characteristics (physical

attractiveness or temperament) create a reaction in others that leads to differences in the child's environment. In this way the child's genetic make-up affects the child's environment.

3. *Active heredity–environment interaction.* As each child interacts with his/her environment, the environment is altered and this in turn affects the behaviour of the individual. Bandura called this **reciprocal determinism** (see page 250). For example, suppose that Mary has just met Juliet. If Mary is friendly to Juliet, she may well be friendly in return. This may then lead to a lasting friendship.

> **Where do the main approaches in psychology stand on nature–nurture?**
>
> The *biological approach* by definition takes a nature position, although, as in the case of phenylketonuria, the environment clearly influences behaviour.
>
> The *behaviourist approach* is entirely on the side of nurture, although the potential for learning is innate.
>
> The *cognitive approach* similarly makes no special claims for nature except insofar as the structure of the mental system is innate. Its development, however, is a response to experience.
>
> The *psychoanalytic approach* combines both nature and nurture in the view that innate, sexual forces are modified by experience to produce adult personality.
>
> The *evolutionary approach* is clearly nativist.
>
> The *humanistic approach* emphasises nurture but holds certain views about the nature of humankind—that it is positive, inclined towards psychological good health, and has the potential for self-actualisation.
>
> The *social constructionist approach* is an example of the nurture approach. We are shaped by social forces.

Theoretical Approaches: Piaget and Evolutionary Psychology

At this point, we will consider in some detail the positions of two different theoretical approaches within psychology to the nature–nurture debate. We will be focusing on Piaget's theory of cognitive development (which has had huge influence on that area of psychology) and on evolutionary psychology (an approach of increasing importance).

Piaget

Piaget's theory of cognitive development is of interest in connection with the nature–nurture debate. In essence, he accepted that nature and nurture are both important. Piaget assumed that nature played a significant in understanding why all children pass through the same stages of cognitive development in the same sequence. According to his theory, innate, maturational changes within the brain account for the sequence of stages. Piaget claimed (with some justification) that children in every culture show the same general pattern of cognitive development, and he attributed that to innate factors.

How does nurture or environment enter the picture in Piaget's theory? First, the speed with which children proceed through the various stages depends on environmental factors. If the environment (e.g., school) facilitates learning, then children's cognitive development will benefit. Second, if there is a mismatch between a current experience and the child's stored knowledge in the form of schemas, this creates a state of *disequilibrium* or lack of balance. This is an uncomfortable state that motivates the child to acquire new knowledge in order to return to a state of equilibrium. Third, the notion of maturation providing the impetus for children to proceed from one stage of cognitive development to the next implies that most children are definitely in a given stage. Piaget accepted to some extent that children's specific learning experiences might influence how well they performed certain tasks. For example, the children of Mexican potters seemed to be at a more advanced stage of cognitive development when tasks involved a ball of clay rather than beakers (Price-Williams et al., 1969).

> **KEY TERM**
>
> **Reciprocal determinism:** Bandura's concept that what one learns is affected by one's characteristics (personality, beliefs, and cognitive abilities). Personality isn't simply determined by the environment, but the individual also shapes the environment.

Evolutionary psychology

Evolutionary psychology is an approach that emphasises nature as the main determinant of behaviour (see Chapter 7, Evolutionary Explanations of Human Behaviour). The essence of this approach was expressed clearly by Pinker (1997, p.42):

> *Natural selection . . . acts by designing the generator of behaviour: the package of information-processing and goal-pursuing mechanisms called the mind. Our minds are designed to generate behaviour that would have been adaptive, on average, in our ancestral environment.*

It follows from this approach that key differences between men and women (e.g., in mate selection; parental investment, in dominance) should be very similar across all cultures. Since changes produced by natural selection typically take thousands of generations to occur, it also follows that key differences between men and women should remain relatively constant *within* any given culture. The assumptions that many aspects of behaviour are the same across all cultures and that there are only small changes in those aspects of behaviour within cultures both involve de-emphasising the importance of environmental factors in determining behaviour. In other words, these assumptions are incorrect.

Another way in which we can see that the emphasis of evolutionary psychologists is almost entirely on nature at the expense of nurture is in their choice of research topics. For example, consider the following topics: patterns in the maintenance and dissolution of relationships; development of intelligence; social development in adolescence; and bystander behaviour. Nearly everyone accepts that environmental factors are extremely important in all these topics, which may explain why most evolutionary psychologists have steered clear of them!

Researching Nature and Nurture

There is no true experimental evidence in nature–nurture research. Nature–nurture studies compare individuals with the same or different genetic make-up to determine the relative contributions of nature and nurture. Identical twins are genetically the same because they come from a single egg—one zygote. Therefore they are called monozygotic. Non-identical twins come from two zygotes— dizygotic. They are genetically as similar as any siblings, except they share a more similar environment than siblings do right from conception.

Twin studies are a form of natural experiment because the independent variable (genetic relatedness) isn't directly controlled by the experimenter, and participants aren't randomly allocated to conditions. It has become clear that, even though identical twins are genetically the same, there are differences from the very moment of conception. This makes it impossible to ever truly investigate the influences of nature versus nurture.

The non-identical nature of identical twins

Recent understanding of genetics has shown us that even cloning will never result in two identical individuals. There are two reasons for this. First of all, due to cell mutation all the cells in a person's body aren't identical. Monozygotic twins may start out as identical cells but as these cells divide and multiply to form the living

Although identical twins are genetically the same, there are still some differences between them.

organism, there is some faulty replication, and this leads to minor but possibly significant differences.

Second, small variations in inherited characteristics and in behaviour create different **micro-environments**. This was the view of Bandura in his concept of reciprocal determinism and is the stance taken by the behavioural geneticist Robert Plomin (1994). In his view each child creates his/her own environment in terms of how they react to others, how they select interactions, what they attend to and so on.

Twins reared apart

In order to conduct research comparing the effects of nature and nurture in identical twins, studies look at the differences between twins who are reared together or apart. Bouchard and McGue (1981) reported a meta-analysis in which the correlation for identical twins brought up apart was +0.72 compared to +0.86 for identical twins brought up together. The difference in the figures indicates that environmental factors are important, but the fairly high correlation for identical twins brought up apart suggests that genetic factors are also important. However, critics point out that identical twins brought up apart have similar environments and it is true that they are often brought up in separate branches of the same family. That means that it is difficult to interpret the findings.

Shared and non-shared environments

Harris (1995) raises the question about why siblings and twins, who are raised in the same environments and who have significant genetic similarity, can turn out so differently. Research indicates that about 50% of the variation in most adult characteristics is due to genetic factors. The rest must be environmental, but this cannot be the shared environment because otherwise twins and siblings would be more similar. Furthermore adopted siblings, who share the same environment, would be more similar than they turn out to be—by adulthood there is minimal resemblance between adopted siblings (Maccoby & Martin, 1983).

What is the "non-shared environment"? It cannot be the micro-environment of the child because this too is related to genetic factors, such as physical looks and temperament. The non-shared environment must be influences outside the child's home. This would explain the fact that twins reared together and twins reared apart show similar correlations in behaviour. The remaining influences are not in the home, i.e., are non-shared, such as peer influences.

> [?] Why do you think that adoption agencies try to match adoptive children with natural homes?

> [?] How do your peers influence your development?

Resolving the Nature–Nurture Controversy

The best solution to the nature–nurture controversy may lie in Gottesman's (1963) concept of a **reaction range**, similar to the concept of susceptibility in the diathesis–stress model. Our genetic make-up limits the range of our potential development in terms of all characteristics: height, intelligence, mental illness, and so on. Actual development is related to our

> **KEY TERMS**
> **Micro-environments:** environments created by individuals through their own behaviour and physical characteristics.
> **Reaction range:** Gottesman's solution to the nature–nurture debate in which genetic make-up (genotype) sets some limit on the range of possible development. Actual development within this range (phenotype) is related to environmental opportunity.

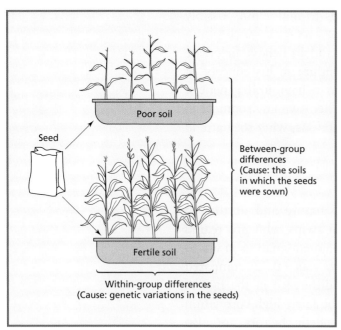

If the same seeds are planted in two different environments there will be large differences in growth between the groups, probably due to rich or poor soil. Within each group there are also differences, and as all the seeds in each group share the same environment, the within-group differences must be due to genetic variation.

environmental opportunities, or lack of them. This is the concept of potential (genotype) versus realised potential (phenotype).

Racial differences

When we consider the question of whether intelligence is more determined by nature or more determined by nurture, there is one particularly significant issue that arises. This is the question of whether certain groups of people ("races") are genetically more intelligent than others. Jensen (1969) produced evidence to demonstrate that, in the United States, black people on average were less intelligent than white people by about 15 points (see page 212). However, this is an average and about 20% of black people have a higher IQ than that of the average white person.

The difficulty with Jensen's argument is that between-group differences can be entirely environmental and not genetic at all. Thus, the differences between two different genetic pools (black and white) could be due to environmental and not genetic differences even though *within* each group genetic factors are important. Consider the following example. If you plant a seed in good soil and provide plenty of sunshine, warmth and food, it thrives. If you plant the identical seed in poor soil with little nourishment it will grow less well. If you plant genetically different seeds in the same soil there will be differences; in this case they are due to nature whereas in the first example the differences are due to nurture. If we compare genetically different groups of people (different racial groups) we must be certain they are sharing the same environment before we attribute the differences to nature, otherwise the differences must be at least in part due to nurture.

Practical and political consequences

The nature–nurture debate has important practical consequences, as suggested earlier. The interactionist view is that intervention is important. For example, if intelligence is entirely inherited then we should test children as early as possible and place them in suitable schools, and occupations, according to their fixed intellect. If intelligence is influenced by environmental factors, then it is critical that children are given enriching experiences wherever possible to enhance their ability. Operation Headstart (see pages 209–211) is an example of the latter kind of programme, whereas psychologists such as Herrnstein and Murray (1994), the authors of *The Bell Curve*, have argued that individual and group differences in intelligence can never be overcome by interventionist programmes, and therefore it makes economic sense to avoid doing this. Furthermore, they argued that the downward spiral in IQ in the United States could be explained by government subsidies for low-income (low-IQ) mothers.

The political element in the nature-nurture issue shouldn't be ignored. In the UK, Cyril Burt's flawed IQ studies were one of the key sources of evidence used to argue in favour of the 11-plus examination and selective placement in secondary schools. (The data were flawed insofar as it later transpired that some of the participants had been invented; see for example Joynson, 1989.) The IQ data suggested that a child's IQ was a fixed quantity and the educational needs of individuals were better served by having two educational streams: one for brighter pupils and one for less academic pupils. The self-fulfilling prophecy tells us that such division will serve to create inequalities even where none existed previously.

? The concept of the self-fulfilling prophecy suggests that expectations can affect development. How is this related to our understanding of nature and nurture?

Conclusions

The most important conclusion with respect to the nature-nurture debate is that heredity *and* environment are *always* both important. Moreover, the two factors interact in complex ways making it difficult to disentangle precisely what each has contributed to an individual's behaviour. The notion that heredity and environment must both be considered is incorporated into the diathesis–stress model that is very popular in accounting for the factors underlying mental disorders. What is starting to happen is that psychologists are focusing on the kinds of interaction that exist with a view to carrying out relevant research to clarify precisely how these interactions occur. Most theoretical approaches (e.g., Piaget's theory of cognitive development) accept the notion of interactions between heredity and environment, but a few (e.g., evolutionary psychology) focus almost exclusively on genetic inheritance.

The most direct way of trying to decide on the relative importance of heredity and environment is to study identical and fraternal twins brought up together or apart. Alas, identical twins are not actually totally identical, and identical twins brought up apart tend to experience similar environments. That means that we lack definitive evidence on which to base any conclusions.

The findings from research (especially on intelligence) have sometimes been misrepresented and exploited for political reasons—sometimes by those carrying out the research! This is deplorable and reflects badly on psychology and on those responsible.

EXAM HINT

To make your answer effective, plan what conclusions you can make about how nature affects nurture, and how nurture affects nature.

SECTION SUMMARY
Nature–Nurture

❖ Nature:

— Refers to inherited characteristics.
— Historically, the nativist position was promoted by Plato and supported by Mendel's discovery of genetic inheritance.

❖ Nurture:

— Refers to the product of experience (environmental influences and learning).
— Empiricism was advocated by philosophers such as Locke, who claimed that at birth we are like a blank slate. We inherit nothing and all behaviour is acquired as a consequence of experience.

❖ Nature and nurture *interact* rather than one or the other determining behaviour.
❖ The cases of phenylketonuria and the diathesis–stress model illustrate this.

The history of the nature–nurture debate

The interaction of nature and nurture

❖ The distinction made between genotype and phenotype shows us that we can never actually access the genotype and therefore are always assessing nature and nurture jointly. This can be seen in the transgenerational effect.

❖ There is no such thing as "pure nature".

❖ The interaction between heredity and environment can be passive, active, and/or reactive.

Theoretical approaches to the nature–nurture debate

❖ Piaget's theory of cognitive development:

— Accepted that both nature and nurture are important.

❖ Evolutionary psychology:

— Emphasises nature as the main determinant of behaviour.

Researching nature and nurture

❖ Nature–nurture influences are often researched using twin studies, and comparing monozygotic and dizygotic twins.

❖ Problems with this research:

— Monozygotic twins are not exactly identical, partly because of small genetic differences and also because they create their own micro-environments.

— The fact that twins who are reared apart often have similar environments further confounds the data.

❖ The non-shared rather than the shared environment has the greater influence.

Resolving the nature–nurture controversy

❖ The concept of a "reaction range" is one way of conceptualising the nature–nurture interaction.

❖ The debate has real-life implications in our understanding of racial differences in IQ. These are very probably not due to genetic factors because the different groups don't share the same environment; therefore differences are largely (or entirely) due to environment.

❖ The contribution of nature and nurture has important practical and political implications for interventionist programmes or schemes that separate individuals on the basis of their innate potential.

❖ The most important conclusion is that nature and nurture are both important.

See also pages 297–301 of the revision guide.

FURTHER READING

The topics in this chapter are covered in greater depth by A. Bell (2001) *Debates in psychology* (London: Routledge), written specifically for the AQA A specification. Debates are also discussed in the classic book by E.R. Valentine (1992) *Conceptual issues in psychology (2nd Edn.)* (London: Routledge), and in M.W. Eysenck (2000) *Psychology: A student's handbook* (Hove, UK: Psychology Press). A useful account of the nature–nurture debate is provided by R. Plomin, J.C. DeFries, and G.E. McClearn (1997) *Behavioural genetics: A primer (3rd Edn.)* (New York: Freeman).

EXAMPLE EXAMINATION QUESTIONS

You should spend 40 minutes on each of the questions below, which aim to test the material in this chapter. Unlike questions from Unit 4 of the examination, covered in Chapters 2–7 of this book, the questions on Perspectives (Unit 5 examination) are marked out of 30 and an additional criterion is used in assessment: synopticity. "Synopticity" is defined as your "understanding and critical appreciation of the breadth and range of different theoretical perspectives and/or methodological approaches relevant to any question" (AQA specification).

1. Describe and critically assess the arguments for and against the existence of determinism in psychology. (30 marks)
2. Describe and analyse how theoretical approaches in psychology have addressed the free will–determinism issue. (30 marks)
3. (a) Outline reductionist approaches in different areas of psychology. (15 marks)
   (b) Critically assess the appropriateness of the reductionist approach in these areas of psychology. (15 marks)
4. Discuss the extent to which reductionism has helped to explain human behaviour. (30 marks)
5. "We might ask whether psychology is a science. We might also ask whether psychologists regard science as an appropriate goal for psychology." Discuss the view that psychology is a science. (30 marks)
6. Discuss the extent to which psychology fits into definitions of science. (30 marks)
7. Discuss the nature–nurture debate in psychology. (30 marks)
8. Critically consider the different views regarding the relationship between nature and nurture in psychology. (30 marks)

Examination Tips

Question 1.   In order to attract good marks in this question you must ensure that you offer equal amounts of description and evaluation. For AO1 you must describe arguments both for and against determinism, using examples across the specification to illustrate the arguments (making your answer synoptic). For AO2 you must consider both the strengths and limitations of each argument (as required by the injunction "critically"), and might use different kinds of arguments in this assessment, such as those regarding ethics, practicality, research evidence, and so on.

Question 2.   This question makes it easy to include synopticity in the answer because you are required to look at different approaches in psychology in terms of how they address the free will–determinism debate. You are not required to describe the theoretical approaches as such, except in so far as to enable you to explain the stance taken by the approach on the debate. For the analysis (AO2) you might consider the implications of the debate within each approach/perspective or you might consider how some approaches have offered means to resolve the debate, such as Bandura's reciprocal determinism. "Analysis" requires breaking the topic down into its constituent parts in order to achieve a greater understanding.

Question 3. In part (a) you should describe different examples of reductionism in psychology, providing a good balance between both breadth and depth in your answer. For part (b) you are required to make a critical assessment (strengths and limitations) of whether such reductionist explanations are appropriate. You are restricted to discussing only those areas mentioned in the first part of your answer.

Question 4. The AO1 element of the essay will be descriptions of reductionism in psychology. The AO2 element is the consideration of how much such explanations have enhanced our understanding of human behaviour. It might be useful to include non-reductionist examples by way of contrast; this will also increase the synoptic content.

Question 5. It is not required that you address the quotation in this question but it is there to give you some ideas of what to discuss. You are invited to debate the question of whether psychology is a science. This requires some consideration of what science is (AO1) and in what way psychology is a science (AO1) followed by an evaluation of whether this is sufficient for psychology to be counted as science and perhaps a further consideration of alternative means of data collection. The AO2 element lies in determining the value of any views presented and/or considering contrasting views. You should endeavour to forge links across the specification as far as possible.

Question 6. A good starting point would be to examine (describe) definitions of science and then assess the extent that psychology can fit in with the criteria identified. You should present arguments both for and against psychology as a science. You might offer further commentary in terms of the question of whether the aims of science are even appropriate for the study of human behaviour and/or non-human animal behaviour. You could also consider the implications of this discussion, for example for research funding.

Question 7. "Discuss" is an AO1 and AO2 term, so you should both describe and evaluate the nature-nurture debate. One problem is likely to be the amount of the material that you could include and therefore selectivity will be important. In order to achieve the right amount of detail and give yourself time for thorough evaluation, you must limit the examples of the debate that you consider. You may approach the essay by considering particular examples of nature and nurture, such as with respect to perception and intelligence, or by considering more general issues such as different kinds of gene–environment interaction.

Question 8. In this essay you should describe contrasting views of nature and nurture, and consider the strengths and weaknesses of these differing views. An example of a strength would be support from research studies or useful practical applications. An example of a weakness would be a logically flawed argument or a socially sensitive issue. Synopticity will be achieved through the breadth of differing views that you consider but you need to restrict this to some extent otherwise you will have insufficient detail in your response.

WEBSITES

http://www.classbrain.com/artread/publish/article_30.shtml
   Nature versus nurture debate.

http://www.trinity.edu/mkearl/socpsy-2.html
   A fantastic website with a plethora interesting facts, links, and resources on
   free will and the nature/nurture debate.

PERSPECTIVES

Approaches in Psychology

What is an approach in psychology? An "approach" is a way of addressing the problem of explaining behaviour. Different psychologists prefer different approaches in the same way that you may be politically liberal whereas someone else is politically conservative. We all find that different things make sense. In terms of psychology, the situation is not as straightforward as in politics, as most people might favour one kind of approach when explaining, say, aggression, whereas they might favour another approach when offering an account of why some individuals develop mental disorders.

No single explanation is "right" and no one explanation is right for every behaviour. Each of them is appropriate in different contexts. They form part of the psychologist's "toolkit". You must choose the psychological explanations that make best sense to you. However, it is important to note that it is *not* necessary to favour one approach over all others when trying to explain behaviour, because they often *all* have something to contribute. For example, there is no single cause of mental disorders such as schizophrenia or depression; instead, several biological and psychological factors all play a role.

"I just love this view of the Firth—does it make you feel as exhilarated?" When psychologists view human behaviour they each have their own perspective.

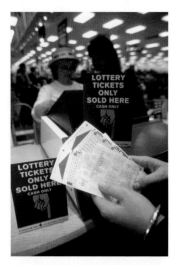

National Lottery tickets. In the following sections of this chapter different approaches are used to explain the target behaviour of lottery addiction.

All of the approaches in this chapter have been discussed elsewhere in this book, so here we will present an overview of the major approaches. You may not be equally familiar with all of them and may therefore just want to concentrate on three or four of them.

In the examination, you will be required to demonstrate your understanding of each approach by using it to explain a particular behaviour. In order to assist you, we have structured the text for each approach in the following way:

- A description of the approach, including some examples of the approach
- An evaluation of the key concepts of the approach
- A description of the methodology adopted by each approach
- An evaluation of the methodology of the approach
- An example of how the approaches question might be answered in the examination. The target behaviour is one provided in the AQA A specimen material:

Lottery addict children

"Britain is producing a generation of child gamblers hooked on the Lottery and fruit machines. Disturbing new research by two eminent academics shows that hundreds of thousands of children—some as young as 11—are now addicted despite the supposed legal restrictions. The findings will fuel warnings from lottery critics that the country is storing up social problems and is likely to trigger pressure for a uniform age limit of 18 on all gambling."

(a) Describe how lottery addition might be explained by **two** different approaches. (6 marks + 6 marks)
(b) Assess **one** of these explanations of lottery addiction in terms of its strengths and weaknesses. (6 marks)
(c) How might lottery addiction be investigated by **one** of these approaches? (6 marks)
(d) Evaluate the use of this method of investigating lottery addiction. (6 marks)

Total for this question: 30 marks

The same target behaviour is used for all the approaches except for the evolutionary approach, as it has no ready explanation for lottery addiction (perhaps because there weren't any lotteries in our ancestral past!).

THE BIOLOGICAL APPROACH

Key Concepts

Biology refers to the study of living organisms. Included within the biological approach are the following:

1. Physiological psychology, which is concerned with the functioning of the body
2. The nativist approach, which is concerned with an individual's genetic nature
3. The medical approach, a term used to describe how mental disorders are explained in the same way that the medical profession explains physical illnesses.

Note that there are some overlaps among these three approaches. For example, researchers within the medical approach often explain mental disorders in terms

EXAM HINT

In the exam you will be required to demonstrate knowledge of two approaches to apply to the stimulus material, which you will have not seen before. It is therefore wise to revise at least four approaches you can draw from.

of genetic factors (the nativist approach), and individual differences at the genetic level may influence physiological processes (physiological psychology).

The *two* key assumptions of this approach are that all behaviour can be explained and understood at the level of the functioning of biological systems, and that both behaviour and experience can be reduced to the functioning of biological systems.

The physiological approach

A **physiological** explanation is one that refers to bodily activity. There are physiological theories about dreaming based solely on brain activities, i.e., the functioning of the central nervous system. It is claimed, using the physiological perspective, that dreams are simply the random electrical activity of the brain during sleep upon which the mind imposes some sense (see pages 155–156). Other physiological explanations make reference to **neurotransmitters** and **synapses**, such as explanations of depression (see page 358).

A further example of a physiological account could be of stress, which would focus on how your heart rate and breathing increase when in the presence of a stressor. Explanations of how the body responds to stress were considered as part of your AS studies. Activity in the autonomic nervous system and endocrine system lead to the production of **hormones** that govern the stress response.

The nativist approach

In the Section on nature and nurture (Chapter 11, Debates), we saw that Plato talked about things being inborn or native to an individual, as contrasted with those characteristics acquired through experience. The nativist approach to understanding behaviour is based on the idea that all behaviour is inherited. The unit of communication between one generation and the next is the **gene**. There is some overlap here with evolutionary psychology (discussed later in the chapter) in that evolutionary psychologists emphasise the importance of genes. However, a key difference is that evolutionary psychologists are mainly interested in extremely long-term evolutionary processes involving natural selection.

The medical approach

The biological or somatic approach to the treatment of mental disorders (see Chapter 9, Treating Mental Disorders) suggests that psychological problems can be treated in the same way as physical problems. The medical model of mental illness assumes that all mental disorders have a physical cause (micro-organisms, genetics, biochemistry, or neuroanatomy). It also assumes that mental illnesses can be described in terms of clusters of symptoms; and symptoms can be

---

KEY TERMS

Physiological: concerning the study of living organisms and their body parts.
Neurotransmitters: chemical substances that are released at the junction between neurons (a synapse) and that affect the transmission of messages in the nervous system.
Synapses: the extremely small gaps between adjacent neurons.
Hormones: chemical substances produced by endocrine glands, and circulated in the blood. They only affect target organs and are produced in large quantities but disappear very quickly.
Gene: a unit of inheritance that forms part of a chromosome. Some characteristics are determined by one gene, whereas for others many genes are involved.

Can psychological problems be treated in the same way as physical problems?

identified, leading to the diagnosis of an illness. Finally, diagnosis leads to appropriate physical treatments (e.g., chemotherapy).

Examples of the biological approach

The biological approach underlies the whole of physiological psychology. You might especially consider how psychologists use the biological approach to explain biological rhythms, sleep and dreaming, motivation, and emotion. You should also contrast such biological explanations with alternative ones such as Freud's account of the purpose of dreams.

Chomsky's account of language acquisition is a biological (nativist) explanation. A number of explanations within developmental psychology are grounded in biology. Piaget's account of cognitive development relies on the notion of maturation or biologically determined stages in development (see Chapter 5, Cognitive Development). This also applies to Piaget's theory of moral development and to some theories of gender development (see Chapter 6, Social and Personality Development).

The evolutionary approach to explaining behaviour (see pages 552–558) is also biological but mostly doesn't involve a focus on physiological processes.

Finally, in your AS studies the study of individual differences included a consideration of the biological (medical) model of abnormality. Chapter 8, Psychopathology, considers biological explanations of schizophrenia, depression, and anxiety disorders; Chapter 9, Treating Mental Disorders, considers biological therapies used in the treatment of mental disorders.

Evaluation of Key Concepts

Below are listed some of the main strengths and weaknesses of the biological approach. Blue words indicate the issue to which the point relates.

Strengths

- Reductionism: Explanations within the biological approach are reductionist, and these explanations have often proved useful. Examples include the activation-synthesis theory of dreaming and theories of schizophrenia that emphasise brain structure and/or brain chemistry.
- Determinism: Advocates of the biological approach have identified important factors (e.g., genes, brain chemistry) that have a substantial impact on human behaviour.
- Individual differences: The biological approach has proved successful in showing that genetic factors play a role in explaining individual differences in intelligence (and in explaining why some individuals are more likely than others to develop certain mental disorders).
- Applications: The biological approach has proved valuable in terms of the use of chemotherapy to treat various mental disorders (e.g., schizophrenia, depression, anxiety). In addition, genetic counselling for prospective parents is an outcome of our understanding of the links between genes and behaviour. For some parents this is an enormous relief where, for example, they carry a genetic susceptibility for a fatal disease. However genetic counselling raises many ethical problems in relation to the concept of "designer babies".

Weaknesses

- Reductionism: The reductionist nature of the biological approach is oversimplified in that we can't obtain a complete understanding of human behaviour by focusing only on biological factors. For example, various psychological, social, and cultural factors influence the development of mental disorders such as depression and anxiety, and these factors are ignored within the biological approach.

- Determinism: Biological explanations are deterministic, and often involve focusing on genetic factors. However, the influence of genetic factors on behaviour is typically *indirect*. For example, Plomin et al. (1990) found in a twin study that genetic factors influence television watching, but it is very difficult to work out *how* genes have this effect!

- Nature–nurture: The biological approach exaggerates the importance of genetic factors in determining behaviour while minimising the importance of environmental factors.

- Biological explanations are more appropriate for some kinds of behaviour (such as vision) than other kinds where higher-order thinking is involved (e.g., emotion; reasoning). However, even vision involves some higher-order mental activity. Therefore, biological explanations on their own are usually inadequate.

Methodology

Researchers within the biological approach use several different methods. Some researchers use physiological measures to increase our understanding of human behaviour. For example, use of the EEG provided evidence for different stages of sleep and showed that there is an association between dreaming and rapid eye movement (REM) sleep (see Chapter 4). Brain-imaging research by Solms (2000) provided support for Freud's dream theory—he found that the motivational system was active during dreaming but the rational parts of the brain were relatively inactive.

As we saw in Chapter 5, a common way of assessing the importance of genetic factors is by studying identical and fraternal twins. If identical twins are more similar than fraternal twins in behaviour (e.g., performance on an intelligence test), this supports the notion that genetic factors are important. Note that it isn't ethically possible to *manipulate* genetic factors in experiments on humans, and so the evidence we have is somewhat indirect.

Advocates of the medical model approach to mental disorders carry out research in which they compare patients with some mental disorder with normal individuals in order to see whether there are any significant differences in bodily functioning or structures. For example, the brain volume of schizophrenics is less than that of normal controls, and schizophrenics also have enlarged ventricles in the brain. There is a problem of interpretation with such findings—do these differences help to cause schizophrenia or are they merely a consequence of being schizophrenic?

Evaluation of Methodology

Below we consider some of the main strengths and weaknesses of the methodology used by researchers within the biological approach. Blue words indicate the issue to which the point relates.

Answering the approaches question

Using the biological approach to explain a behaviour

Lottery addict children

"Britain is producing a generation of child gamblers hooked on the Lottery and fruit machines. Disturbing new research by two eminent academics shows that hundreds of thousands of children—some as young as 11—are now addicted despite the supposed legal restrictions. The findings will fuel warnings from lottery critics that the country is storing up social problems and is likely to trigger pressure for a uniform age limit of 18 on all gambling." (Reproduced from AQA A specimen material.)

In the A level examination you will be required to explain a target behaviour using any approach. The aim of this activity is to offer you, the candidate, the opportunity to express your true understanding of the approach by your ability to use it in a novel situation.

How would you explain lottery addiction in terms of the biological approach? The currency of the biological explanation is brain activity or brain anatomy, nervous impulses and neurotransmitters, hormones, and various organs in the body. A possible explanation could be as follows:

(a) *Why are young people hooked on the lottery and fruit machines? A psychologist might use the biological approach to explain this behaviour. Such a psychologist would explain the behaviour in terms of brain activity and the action of the central and autonomic nervous systems. The psychologist might also mention hormones.*

An answer like this would attract relatively few marks as it does little more than sketch out the possible elements of a biological explanation and has not demonstrated a true understanding of the approach. In order to do this you really need to try to put together an explanation of the target behaviour.

(a) *An explanation of lottery addiction using the biological approach would focus on how biological systems can be used to explain and understand this behaviour. When an individual stands in front of a fruit machine the flashing lights are physiologically arousing, creating a sense of excitement and probably pleasure. Physiological arousal causes the body to produce certain hormones that prepare the person for fight or flight. We can also understand the individual's behaviour in terms of nervous impulses. The eyes watch the pictures on the fruit machine go round and send impulses to the brain where they are interpreted and further messages sent to the hands to press a button at an appropriate moment to stop the machine.*

In the A level examination you will be given an opportunity to evaluate one of your explanations so you can take the opportunity, as below, to indicate in what way the explanation offered in the first part of the question is lacking. This highlights the fact that your explanations may not be satisfactory! They simply need to demonstrate your understanding of the named approach.

(b) *The problem with the biological approach is that for many aspects of behaviour it ignores some of the key elements of behaviour. In this case it is largely a description of what is happening at the level of nerves and hormones and doesn't actually explain anything, for example why the individual is playing the fruit machine or why the individual wants to repeat the behaviour. The behaviourist approach would offer a better account because we can use the idea of reinforcement and partial rewards.*

A suitable methodology for the biological approach

In the examination you will be further asked to suggest how one approach might investigate this phenomenon, and evaluate the use of this method of investigating this phenomenon. As already mentioned the biological approach lends itself to laboratory experiments. Therefore a further response would be to analyse the use of this method. The process of analysis involves identifying the constituent parts of a problem and discussing them. A good student answer might be:

(c) *The biological approach is particularly suitable for experiments because it reduces behaviours to simple components. If we were to conduct an experiment into gambling behaviour we might assess the stress experienced by individuals when playing the fruit machine by using a galvanic skin response. This registers the amount of sweat being produced during an activity and thus is indicative of autonomic arousal because when one is in a state of physiological arousal sweating increases. There are other signs of ANS arousal as well, such as pupil dilation. We might also consider reaction time and see whether this was enhanced during high ANS arousal.*

(d) *The investigation described above could be conducted in a laboratory where conditions are more highly controlled. Or it might be conducted in the field where behaviour might be more naturalistic but, on the negative side, participants' behaviour might be affected by other things in the environment rather than just the fruit machine activity (for example a noisy atmosphere in the pub). Field experiments increase ecological validity at a loss of internal validity for the experiment.*

Strengths

- The various types of experimentation used within the biological approach all have their strengths. For example, physiological studies have added greatly to our understanding of sleep and dreaming by providing an additional source of evidence over and above behaviour. Twin studies have suggested that genetic factors influence much of our behaviour (e.g., intelligence; susceptibility to mental disorders). The fact that chemotherapy is often effective in treating mental disorders (Chapter 9) suggests (but doesn't prove) that physiological processes are involved in mental disorders.

- Nature–nurture: Twin studies (in spite of their limitations) generally provide the best way of trying to determine the role of genetic factors in influencing behaviour, and are used extensively by researchers using the biological approach.

Weaknesses

- Determinism: Researchers within the biological approach generally can't provide convincing deterministic accounts of the ways in which genes influence behaviour—their impact on behaviour is indirect and poorly understood.
- Determinism: Many studies based on the medical model have found biochemical or other differences between patient groups (e.g., schizophrenics) and normal controls. However, it is difficult to provide a clear deterministic account of what is happening because we generally don't know whether the bodily differences help to cause the disorder or whether having the disorder triggers the bodily differences.
- Nature–nurture: Twin studies provide only an indirect way of assessing the importance of genetic factors in determining behaviour. If we find that the behaviour of identical twins is more similar than that of fraternal twins, this may be due (at least in part) to their much greater genetic similarity or to greater similarity in their environments.

> **EXAM HINT**
> Do not give very general answers (e.g., a generic summary of the strengths and weaknesses of the biological method) as you can only achieve marks in the top bands if you fully link your answer to the stimulus.

SECTION SUMMARY
The Biological Approach

Key concepts

❖ There are two key assumptions of the behavioural approach:

— All behaviour can be understood in terms of the functioning of biological systems.
— Both behaviour and experience can be reduced to the functioning of biological systems.

❖ The biological approach includes the following:

— Physiological psychology: behaviour can be explained in terms of bodily activity such as brain activity (e.g., some theories of dreaming), neurotransmitters (e.g., explaining depression), and hormones (e.g., stress).
— The nativist approach: behaviour can be explained in terms of genes and heredity.
— The medical approach: psychological problems can be treated in the same way as physical ones.

❖ The biological approach underlies physiological psychology.

Evaluation of the key concepts

❖ Strengths of the approach include:

— Reductionist explanations, which can facilitate experimental research.
— Genes and brain chemistry have an impact on behaviour.
— Genetics play a role in explaining individual differences in intelligence and mental disorders.
— Various practical applications such as drug therapy for mental illness.

❖ Weaknesses of the approach include:

— An excessive emphasis on biological rather than psychological factors
— The poorly understood connections between genes and behaviour
— The neglect of environmental factors.

Methodology

❖ Researchers within the biological approach use various methods including:

— Physiological techniques
— Twin studies
— Comparisons of bodily functioning in patients with mental disorders and normal individuals.

Evaluation of the methodology

❖ Strengths of the methodology include:

— All these methods are of use.
— The twin-study approach is the best way of assessing the involvement of genetic factors in behaviour.

❖ Weaknesses of the methodology include:

— Problems with deciding whether bodily differences between patients with mental disorders and normals actually play a role in triggering mental disorders.
— Difficulties in interpreting the findings from twin studies.

See also pages 309–311 of the revision guide.

THE BEHAVIOURAL APPROACH

Key Concepts

The essence of the behavioural approach is the assumption that *all* behaviour is learned and that when we are born we are like a blank slate, or *tabula rasa*. Experience and interactions with the environment make us what we are. We become what we become as a result of forming stimulus–response units of behaviour in reaction to the environment. This perspective has been called **environmental determinism** because it suggests that our behaviour is determined by the environments in which we exist.

The second assumption is that all behaviour can be explained in terms of **conditioning theory**: stimulus and response (S–R) links that build up to produce more complex behaviours. In essence, conditioning refers to changing behaviour in the absence of conscious thought, as in saying "I am conditioned to behave in that way".

KEY TERMS

Environmental determinism: the view that all behaviour can be explained solely in terms of the effects of external (environmental) factors.
Conditioning theory: the view that all behaviour can be explained in terms of stimulus–response links.

The third assumption is related to the second one. In essence, Skinner argued in favour of what is known as **equipotentiality**—this is the notion that virtually any response can be conditioned to any stimulus. In other words, it doesn't make any real differences what stimulus–response associations we try to persuade our human or non-human participants to acquire.

The fourth assumption of the basic behaviourist approach is that we need look no further than the behaviours we can observe in order to understand and explain how humans and non-human animals operate. This is why of course it is called "behaviourism"—because the focus is solely on observable behaviour. There is no need to look at what goes on inside the "black box" of the mind (e.g., perception, attention, language, memory, thinking, and so on), it is sufficient to focus *only* on external and observable behaviour. Note, however, that later behaviourists such as Bandura *did* recognise the importance of internal processes (e.g., self-efficacy), so what has been said so far applies mostly to the approach taken by early behaviourists such as Watson and Skinner.

The fifth assumption of the behavioural approach is that humans and non-human animals are only *quantitatively* different, i.e., they differ in terms of having more or less of something rather than differing qualitatively. This means that behaviourists can *generalise* from non-human animals (such as rats and pigeons) to human behaviour. Much behaviourist research is conducted with non-human animals, although that is less the case than it used to be.

It is important to recognise the contrasting perspectives within behaviourism:

Do we really only differ quantitatively from animals?

- **Methodological behaviourism:** the view that that all perspectives use some behaviourist concepts to explain behaviour. This is a mild view of behaviourism—it is the view that the perspective is not a "stand-alone" approach but is part of all explanations.
- **Radical behaviourism:** the view that all behaviour is learned. Skinner was a radical behaviourist but most behaviourists nowadays would take a less radical view.
- **Neo-behaviourism:** this is a newer development and an extension of behaviourism. The best-known example is **social learning theory**, an attempt by Albert Bandura to reformulate learning theory to include a role for cognitive and internal factors. There are three key assumptions in Bandura's social learning theory:

(a) We often learn by observing other people and seeing whether their behaviour is rewarded or punished—thus, there is no need to actually carry out actions oneself for learning to occur. Learning what actions are rewarded or punished by observation alone is known as **vicarious reinforcement.**

(b) Internal factors are important in learning— for example, if we believe we can succeed on some task (i.e., we have high self-efficacy) we are more likely to succeed (Chapter 6, Social and Personality Development).

KEY TERMS

Equipotentiality: the view that essentially any response can be conditioned to any stimulus.
Methodological behaviourism: the view that all psychological perspectives use some behaviourist concepts to explain behaviour.
Radical behaviourism: the view that all behaviour is learned. Skinner was a radical behaviourist.
Neo-behaviourism: an extension of behaviourism to allow for some cognitive factors, e.g., Bandura's social learning theory.
Social learning theory: the theory that behaviour can be explained in terms of both direct and indirect (vicarious) reinforcement; indirect reinforcement and identification lead to imitation.
Vicarious reinforcement: the concept in social learning theory that reinforcement can be received indirectly, by observing another person being reinforced.

(c) The environment influences us but we also influence the environment by our actions—this is known as reciprocal determinism (Chapter 6, Social and Personality Development).

Examples of the behavioural approach

Throughout your AS studies and in this A2 book there have been constant references to behaviourist approaches, learning theory, and social learning theory. We will identify some of the main examples here. At AS level we considered learning theory as an explanation of attachment and also discussed behavioural models of abnormality. At A2, we further considered behavioural explanations of mental disorder and behavioural methods of treatment (see Chapters 8, Psychopathology, and 9, Treating Mental Disorders).

Learning theory was mentioned in Chapter 2, Relationships, when considering the reinforcement theory of interpersonal attraction, and again in Chapter 3, Pro- and Anti-social Behaviour, as an explanation for aggression. Social learning theory is especially carefully explained in Chapter 3.

Both learning theory and social learning theory are important in developmental explanations (Developmental Psychology: Chapters 5 and 6), such as with respect to moral development (Chapter 5, Cognitive Development) and gender development (Chapter 6, Social and Personality Development).

Evaluation of Key Concepts

Below we consider some of the strengths and weaknesses of the behavioural approach. Blue words indicate the issue to which the point relates.

Strengths

- Reductionism: Classical and operant conditioning (both of which are reductionist) form a fundamental part of psychological explanations. Both types of conditioning have been demonstrated in numerous species under very varied conditions.
- Applications: Many successful applications have been derived from the behavioural approach. For example, behaviour therapy is clearly successful for certain mental disorders, such as phobias (see Chapter 9, Treating Mental Disorders). Social skills training is also related to learning theory and may be the best way to teach some individuals how to acquire certain skills (e.g., teaching an autistic child some basic self-care).
- Applications: Learning theory has also been applied to education. Skinner advocated **programmed learning**, a method of teaching whereby the task is broken down into individual "frames" or very small steps. A correct response acts as a reward. The system may be linear (a list of questions) or branching (the programme can "respond" to a student's needs by offering special help with a question the student got wrong). This concept lends itself to computer-mediated learning.

Weaknesses

- Reductionism: The behavioural approach is based on the assumption that conditioning principles operate in similar ways in different species. By so doing, the behaviourists drastically underestimated the differences between species. For example, the fact that humans possess language transforms our

KEY TERM

Programmed learning: a type of learning devised by Skinner and based on operant conditioning, in which tasks are broken down into individual steps or frames.

learning ability. Rats who have learned to press a lever for food reward will keep pressing for a long time after food has stopped being provided. In contrast, most people will stop immediately if told that no more rewards will be given.

- Reductionism: The behaviourists such as Skinner argued that virtually any response could be conditioned in any situation (i.e., equipotentiality). In fact, equipotentiality doesn't exist. For example, Cook and Mineka (1989) found that monkeys learned a fear response to a snake much faster than a fear response to a rabbit (Chapter 7, Evolutionary Explanations of Human Behaviour)—this suggests we are biologically prepared to fear some animals that were dangerous in our ancestral past.

- Determinism: According to Skinner, behaviour is determined almost entirely by external stimuli, especially those signalling rewards and punishments. However, this view exaggerated the importance of *external* or environmental factors and minimised the role of *internal* factors (e.g., goals). Neo-behaviourists such as Bandura have accepted that this view is too limited, and have agreed that the factors determining behaviour include internal factors as well as external ones.

Gamblers will keep playing so long as they think there is money to be won.

- Nature–nurture: The behaviourists assumed that behaviour is determined by learning and environmental factors and largely (or even totally) ignored genetic factors. This assumption has been amply disproved in studies on genetic factors in intelligence (Chapter 5, Cognitive Development), and on the causes of schizophrenia and depression (Chapter 8, Psychopathology).

- Individual differences: The behaviourists assumed that individual differences in behaviour could be explained in terms of differences in conditioning history. However, they never showed this clearly to be the case, because it is very difficult to establish someone's conditioning history over a period of several years. In addition, they failed to acknowledge the role of genetic factors in accounting for individual differences in intelligence and in susceptibility to various mental disorders.

Consistent behaviour is dependent on internal goals, not just rewards.

Methodology

The behaviourists were among the first psychologists to carry out proper laboratory experiments. In these experiments, the emphasis was on controlling the environment by manipulating certain stimuli or independent variables (e.g., presentation of a tone in Pavlov's research on conditioning in dogs) and then observing the participants' behaviour. One way in which control was achieved by using fairly sparse conditions (e.g., in the Skinner box there were bare walls and one lever) so that the participants weren't distracted by irrelevant stimuli. Another example of the research carried out by the behaviourists is Bandura's research on the Bobo doll, in which he presented different groups of children with a model rewarded or punished for behaving aggressively towards the doll (Chapter 3, Pro- and Anti-social Behaviour). Thus, the behaviourists made extensive use of the experimental method in their research.

Another characteristic of most early research carried out by the behaviourists was their use of non-human animals. However, there was a progressive change over time—for example, nearly all of Bandura's research has involved the use of human participants whether children or adults.

Evaluation of Methodology

The various strengths and weaknesses of the methodology used by researchers within the behavioural approach are identified below. Blue words indicate the issue to which the point relates.

Strengths

- Reductionism: The behaviourists made a very important contribution with their use of well-controlled studies using the experimental method. This is the case for studies of classical conditioning (e.g., Pavlov) and of operant conditioning (e.g., Skinner, Bandura). In some ways, the behaviourists' use of the experimental method set the standard for subsequent researchers working within different approaches.
- Reductionism: The experimental approach adopted by the behaviourists was sufficient to ensure that the data obtained were reasonably objective and the findings replicable.
- Determinism: The behaviourists were successful in showing that certain forms of behaviour (e.g., patterns of lever pressing in operant conditioning) are determined mainly by the schedule of reinforcement or reward used by the experimenter.

Weaknesses

- Reductionism: Much of the research carried out by advocates of the behavioural approach lacks external validity in that it doesn't generalise to the real world. For example, the behaviourists assumed that rats (and other species) would return to the place in which they had found food because they had been rewarded or reinforced for going to that place. However, it isn't sensible in rats' natural environment for them to return to a place from which all the food has just been removed, and indeed Gaffan et al. (1983) found that rats avoided a place in which they had previously found food.
- Reductionism: The behaviourist notion that all we need to do is to measure behaviour is very limited. For example, you could persuade someone to say, "The earth is flat", dozens or even hundreds of times if you paid them enough, thus showing that you could control their behaviour. However, that wouldn't alter their internal knowledge that the earth is actually round.
- Determinism: The assumption that behaviour is determined by external stimuli led many behaviourists (e.g., Skinner) to carry out experiments in which other important factors were ignored. However, Bandura recognised that internal factors are also important, as in his research on self-efficacy (Chapter 6, Social and Personality Development).
- Ethics: The use of behaviourist principles to control others (as in some prisons and psychiatric institutions using reward and punishment) can be considered unethical. However, bear in mind that two noted behaviourists (Watson and Skinner) wanted to use conditioning principles to produce a better society.

What other methods of investigation might be suitable for the behavioural approach?

Answering the approaches question

Using the behavioural approach to explain a behaviour

Lottery addict children

"Britain is producing a generation of child gamblers hooked on the Lottery and fruit machines. Disturbing new research by two eminent academics shows that hundreds of thousands of children—some as young as 11—are now addicted despite the supposed legal restrictions. The findings will fuel warnings from lottery critics that the country is storing up social problems and is likely to trigger pressure for a uniform age limit of 18 on all gambling." (Reproduced from AQA A specimen material.)

In the A level examination you will be required to explain a target behaviour using any approach. The aim of this activity is to offer you, the candidate, the opportunity to express your true understanding of the approach by your ability to use it in a novel situation.

How would you explain lottery addiction in terms of the behavioural approach? Any behavioural explanation should involve terms and concepts such as reinforcement, reward, and punishment. You could include social learning theory within your explanation and thus use concepts such as observational learning and vicarious reinforcement. An astute candidate will increase the amount of appropriate material by extending their behavioural explanation to neo-behaviourist accounts, as in the case given here.

(a) *The most likely explanation for gambling behaviour would use the behavioural approach. Behaviourists would argue that the individual who plays the fruit machine experiences some rewards for the behaviour in the form of occasional small amounts of money or even the odd jackpot. Behaviourists have shown that partial reinforcement schedules, as used by fruit machines, create a greater likelihood that a behaviour will be increased than when reinforcement occurs on every trial. It is unlikely that the individual would experience any punishment so the behaviour will not be "stamped out". Such explanations cannot account for lottery addiction because most players never win anything, thus receiving no direct reinforcement. However, the concept of vicarious reinforcement can explain this as put forward by neo-behaviourists—still a behaviourist explanation. The idea of vicarious reinforcement is that, through seeing someone else receiving a reward, this increases the likelihood that you too will repeat the behaviour.*

This is a clear answer that uses behaviourist and neo-behaviourist concepts to explain the target behaviour, thus demonstrating the candidate's understanding of the behavioural approach in psychology. In the examination the candidate might go on to evaluate this approach and should again ensure that the evaluation is related to this particular context and not to behaviourism in general. For example, one might consider in what way this is a rather reductionist explanation of gambling behaviour. One should not overlook the fact that evaluation can consider the strengths of an explanation and the behaviourist account of why people gamble is relatively successful.

A suitable methodology for the behavioural approach

In the examination you will be further asked to suggest how one approach might investigate this phenomenon, and evaluate the use of this method of investigating this phenomenon. The process of analysis involves identifying the constituent parts of a problem and discussing these. A good student answer might be:

(c) *A behaviourist would be likely to test his or her explanation through the use of laboratory experiments because behaviourists believe that only observable behaviours count, and because they feel it is possible to reduce behaviour to simple cause and effect relationships. A behaviourist might investigate the effectiveness of reinforcement schedules by seeing which kind of reinforcement schedule led participants to rate a game more highly. They might also investigate whether people were more likely to play the lottery when there were very large jackpots or rather more jackpots that were smaller.*

The final part of the A level question requires an evaluation of this investigative approach. For example the candidate might write:

(d) *The advantages of the experimental approach are that one can demonstrate cause and effect relationships under highly controlled conditions. This is important in order to be able to exclude any extraneous variables from the investigation. On the negative side, laboratory experiments are low in ecological validity, in other words the results often cannot be generalised to other people and other situations than those used in the experiment. This limits their relevance. A further drawback of the experimental approach is that it focuses on a rather narrow set of factors and therefore may appear to account for a behaviour while in fact it only explains one aspect of this behaviour.*

SECTION SUMMARY
The Behavioural Approach

❖ There are five key assumptions of the behavioural approach:

   — The belief that all behaviour is learned in reaction to our environment (environmental determinism).

Key concepts

— All behaviour can be explained in terms of conditioning theory.
— Any response can be conditioned to any stimulus (equipotentiality).
— The focus of explanation should be on observable behaviour.
— Humans differ quantitatively but not qualitatively from non-human animals.

❖ We should recognise the varieties of behaviourism: methodological and radical behaviourism, and neo-behaviourism (social learning theory). Neo-behaviourists accept that internal factors are important as well as external ones.

❖ The behavioural approach underlies learning theory and social learning theory.

Evaluation of the key concepts

❖ Strengths of the approach include:

— Classical and operant conditioning form a fundamental part of psychological explanations.
— Successful applications such as behavioural therapy and social learning theory have derived from the behavioural approach.
— Learning theory can be applied to education with programmed learning.

❖ Weaknesses of the approach include:

— It is based on the mistaken assumption that humans function in very similar ways to other species.
— It is reductionist: equipotentiality doesn't exist.
— It is deterministic and limits the role of internal factors.
— It ignores the role of genetic factors.
— It doesn't provide an adequate explanation of individual differences.

Methodology

❖ The methodology used by the behaviourists involved:

— Use of the experimental method
— Tight control of the experimental situation
— The emphasis was on observing behaviour
— The early behaviourists mainly used non-human species in their research.

Evaluation of the methodology

❖ Strengths of the methodology include:

— It helped set the standard for subsequent researchers.
— Behaviourists obtained relatively objective data and produced replicable findings.
— They were able to show that certain forms of behaviour are determined by reinforcement or reward.

❖ Weaknesses of the methodology include:

— It has a lack of external validity
— It has an excessive emphasis on behaviour
— It ignores internal factors
— Behaviourist principles can be used in unethical ways.

See also pages 312–314 of the revision guide.

THE PSYCHODYNAMIC APPROACH

Key Concepts

The term "psychodynamic" refers to any explanation that emphasises internal processes of change and development, i.e., the dynamics of behaviour or the forces that drive an individual to behave as he/she does. "Dynamics" are the things *driving* us or a machine to behave in particular ways. The best-known example of a psychodynamic theory is Freud's account of the development of personality. This theory is covered in detail in Chapter 6, Social and Personality Development, as well as in Chapter 5, Cognitive Development, and Chapter 9, Treating Mental Disorders.

Freud's theory and his method of therapy are both called psychoanalysis. The psychoanalytic perspective seeks to explain human development in terms of an interaction between innate drives and early experience. The basic assumption of Freud's approach is that early experience drives us to behave in predictable ways in later life. Childhood is a critical period of development. Infants are born with innate biological drives, e.g., for oral satisfaction. Such drives have a physical (sexual) basis. If these drives are not satisfied this can lead to personality or behavioural problems later in life, because our physical energies (libido) remain attached to these earlier stages and therefore the individual will regress [return] to that stage when experiencing anxiety.

A further key assumption is that *unconscious* forces motivate much of our behaviour. At any time if drives are thwarted or not satisfied, the ego copes by using ego defence mechanisms such as repression (i.e., forcing traumatic memories into the unconscious) and denial (i.e., denying that anxiety-provoking events happened). An individual may express such feelings in dreams and unconsciously motivated behaviours such as Freudian slips (involuntary but motivated errors in speech or behaviour).

Freud described personality dynamics in terms of various structures and stages. He argued that your ego is the conscious and intellectual part of your personality that regulates the id. The id is the primitive, innate part of your personality (concerned with basic motives), and the ego tries to deal with conflicts between the id and the superego. The superego is the moral part learned from parents and society. These parts are hypothetical entities (i.e., they don't physically exist). They develop through the stages of childhood: oral, anal, phallic, latency, and genital.

"Neo-Freudian" psychologists basically agree with the principles of psychoanalysis but have adapted the theory. Neo-Freudians produced psychoanalytic theories that placed less emphasis on biological forces and more on the influences of social and cultural factors. For example, Erik Erikson proposed a stage theory of social development where each stage is marked by a crisis that must be confronted and resolved with the help of other people or else the individual cannot move on (see Chapter 6, Social and Personality Development). Erikson's stages started at age 1 and went through to old age. His perspective maintained some elements of classic psychodynamic theory—the unconscious and the components of personality—but placed greater emphasis on social influences and lifelong development.

Another neo-Freudian approach is ego analysis, which is used in the treatment of patients with mental disorders (Chapter 9, Treating Mental Disorders). While ego analysts agree with much of what Freud had to say, they disagree with him on two key issues. First, ego analysts spend much time in therapy on discussing the patient's current social and interpersonal problems, whereas Freud focused mainly on childhood experiences. Second, ego analysts regard society as basically positive and supportive of the individual. In contrast, Freud sometimes regarded society in a negative way as frustrating the desires of the individual via its impact on the development of the superego.

Examples of the psychodynamic approach

Freud's psychodynamic approach was referred to in your AS studies as an explanation for attachment, and also as a model of abnormality and an explanation for eating disorders. The psychoanalytic perspective was also used to explain obedience—the authoritarian personality represses conflicting thoughts.

In this book, the psychoanalytic perspective was used to explain prejudice and aggression (see Chapter 3, Pro- and Anti-social Behaviour). Freud's theory of dreams was described in Chapter 4, Biological Rhythms, Sleep, and Dreaming. We have already noted Freud's contributions to our understanding of moral development in Chapter 5, Cognitive Development. In addition Chapter 6, Social and Personality Development, includes psychodynamic perspectives on gender development and adolescence. Gould's theory of adult consciousness also has a Freudian basis.

Chapter 8, Individual Differences, refers to Freud's ideas in the explanations of mental disorders and Chapter 9, Treating Mental Disorders, refers to psychoanalysis as a therapy.

Using psychoanalysis to understand why we love monsters

Any approach in psychology can be used to help us understand different behaviours. Here is an example of how the psychoanalytic approach can be used to explain why people appear to be universally drawn to the idea of monsters. Tales of monsters and horror are to be found in a huge range of cultures. There are also instances of remarkable similarity between the legends of otherwise quite distinct cultures. For example, some form of "undead" are to be found in the folklore of cultures as diverse as Haiti (zombies) and central Europe (vampires). This suggests that the idea of monstrous undead must serve a psychological purpose. A psychoanalytic psychologist might suggest that monsters represent the human fear of death and, in overcoming the monsters we can overcome our fear. From a Freudian viewpoint, battling and overcoming monsters may represent the Oedipus complex, in which a monster—symbolising the same-sex parent—attacks but is vanquished (Minsky, 1998).

By considering the historical context of certain films we can see how films may express the anxieties of the time, and help people deal with their, possibly repressed, anxieties. Following the First World War, a number of films such as *The Hunchback of Notre Dame* and *The Phantom of the Opera* featured disfigured heroes. According to Skal (1993) these may have represented society's coming to terms with the mass disfigurement resulting from the war. With the rise of Hitler and the Third Reich, wolves and werewolves became particularly popular monsters, symbolising the marauding, predatory nature of the Nazi threat.

Following the war, with American and European politics dominated by the Cold War, film horror was dominated by alien invasion, symbolic of the threat of war with Russia. Meanwhile horror comics became dominated by images of corpses returning for revenge on the living. Skal draws a link between this and society's collective guilt following the death of 40,000,000 people in the Second World War. *Godzilla*, produced in Japan in 1954, involved a radiation-mutated monster rampaging through Japan burning all in its path, and possibly relates to the devastation caused by the atomic bombs.

In the late 1960s and throughout the 1970s, a major theme in horror was of demonic children. Examples included *Village of the Damned*, *The Omen* series, *Rosemary's Baby*, and *It Lives*. Skal suggested that these films represented society's anxiety following the sexual revolution, and perhaps the horror following the revelation of the effects of Thalidomide, the anti-morning sickness drug that caused babies to be born with missing limbs. More recent trends in horror can also be linked to the anxieties of society. In the 1990s there were a number of films involving computer domination, for example *Terminator*.

From M. Jarvis (2000) *Theoretical approaches in psychology*. London: Routledge Modular Series.

Evaluation of Key Concepts

Below we identify some of the major strengths and weaknesses of the psychodynamic approach. Blue words indicate the issue to which the point relates.

Freud's concepts were quite revolutionary for his time.

Strengths

- Determinism: Freud had a scientific background, and his claim that all behaviour is determined helped to convince sceptics that psychology could aspire to becoming a science.

- In studying psychology, it is important to try to take an unbiased view and reach an informed opinion. There is a tendency to be overcritical about Freud's theories, but remember that the theory was constructed during a different epoch from ours and his concepts were quite revolutionary for their time.

- Freud's ideas have endured—and not just in psychology. They appear in literature and art and everyday life. This testifies to the fact that there must be some important meanings in the theory. Many of these meanings have become such a part of commonplace knowledge that you aren't even aware they are Freudian. For example, when a person says something that appears to have hidden meaning, you might say "That's an unconscious slip". Hall and Lindzey (1970) suggested that the durability of the theory is due to Freud's broad and deep conception of human beings, one that combines the world of reality with make-believe.

- Freud is responsible for introducing certain key concepts to psychology, namely, the recognition that childhood is a critical period of development, and that unconscious sexual (physical) desires influence behaviour. Neither of these notions was recognised in the Victorian society of his formative period. Williams (1987) argued that "psychoanalysis has been society's most influential theory of human behaviour . . . it profoundly altered Western ideas about human nature and changed the way we viewed ourselves and our experience".

- Freud founded developmental psychology and devised a form of therapy unsurpassed for over 80 years. Psychoanalysis has been widely used and adapted, though it tends to be most suitable for literate and wealthy people because of the time and expense involved.

- Jarvis (2000) identified the most significant feature of Freudian theory as the notion that the human personality has more than one aspect: "we reveal this when we say things like 'part of me wants to do it, but part of me is afraid to . . .' ". Freud's introduction of the unconscious permits us to explain how we can be both rational and irrational. This can account for many aspects of our behaviour, such as the fact that people often predict they will behave one way and actually do something quite different.

- Individual differences: Freud put forward what is the first systematic theory of personality (his theory of psychosexual development—see Chapter 6, Social and Personality Development). This is of historical importance, although strangely it was several decades before other psychologists became interested in studying individual differences in personality.

Weaknesses

- Reductionism: Freud produced simple mechanistic explanations of much human behaviour, but these explanations oversimplify a complex reality.
- Determinism: Freud argued strongly in favour of hard determinism (Chapter 11, Debates), claiming that infant behaviour is determined by innate forces, whereas adult behaviour is determined by childhood experiences. However, Freud's theories failed to spell out in much detail how behaviour is determined. For example, Freud claimed that adult mental disorders are determined in large measure by certain childhood experiences, but we aren't told much about *how* events 10, 20, or 30 years ago exert their influence today.
- Much of the theory of psychoanalysis lacks **falsifiability**. For example, it isn't possible to devise an experiment to prove (or disprove) the notion that the mind is divided up into the id, ego, and superego.
- Those parts of Freud's theories that are testable have generally been found to be wrong. For example, Freud emphasised differences between males and females ("anatomy is destiny"), but most of the evidence indicates that males and females are more similar than he believed. This part of Freud's theorising can be criticised as being sexist as well as wrong. For example, Freud argued that fear plays an important part in the development of identification in boys. It follows that boys whose fathers are threatening and hostile should show more identification than boys whose fathers are supportive. In fact, what happens is exactly the opposite (Mussen & Rutherford, 1963). There is also very little evidence for the existence of the Oedipus complex or penis envy (Kline, 1981).

Methodology

Freud focused on the individual, observing particular "cases" in great detail, an **idiographic approach**. This was the approach Freud adopted when engaged in therapy. It has the advantage of providing unique insights into behaviour because of the depth of information collected. For example, his careful analyses of the dreams reported by his patients allowed him to develop a theory of dreams as wish fulfilment that has recently received some support from brain-imaging studies (see Chapter 5, Cognitive Development). However, it may not be justifiable to use *unique* observations to formulate general theories about human behaviour.

In addition to his focus on individual cases, Freud was also a keen observer of human behaviour. For example, he noticed that people often said or did things that were involuntary but that revealed their hidden desires—what became known as Freudian slips (see Chapter 11, Debates). Most of us would probably not have realised the significance of such errors.

Evaluation of Methodology

Below we identify some of the main strengths and weaknesses of the methodology used within the psychodynamic approach.

Strengths

- The main strength of Freud's approach to collecting data was that he studied individual patients over long periods of time, and so developed a reasonably

---

KEY TERMS

Falsifiability: the notion that scientific theories can potentially be disproved by evidence; it is the hallmark of science, according to Popper.

Idiographic approach: an approach that emphasises the uniqueness of the individual.

Answering the approaches question

Using the psychodynamic approach to explain a behaviour

Lottery addict children

"Britain is producing a generation of child gamblers hooked on the Lottery and fruit machines. Disturbing new research by two eminent academics shows that hundreds of thousands of children—some as young as 11—are now addicted despite the supposed legal restrictions. The findings will fuel warnings from lottery critics that the country is storing up social problems and is likely to trigger pressure for a uniform age limit of 18 on all gambling." (Reproduced from AQA A specimen material.)

In the A level examination you will be required to explain a target behaviour using any approach. The aim of this activity is to offer you, the candidate, the opportunity to express your true understanding of the approach by your ability to use it in a novel situation.

How would you explain lottery addiction in terms of the psychodynamic approach? Your response is likely to revolve around unconscious motivations that may be related to early childhood conflicts, and on how the id is motivated by the pleasure principle whereas the ego must restrain the id, leading to inevitable conflict and ego defences. In addition the superego acts as the moral voice. A possible explanation could be as follows:

(a) *The Freudian approach would suggest that gambling behaviour is in some way the expression of unconscious wish fulfilment. The unconscious motivations of the id are regulated by the ego through the reality principle. The conflicts that arise between the id and ego lead to ego defences so that the ego may repress unpleasant thoughts. The superego may also be involved, acting as the moral voice of reason.*

Such an answer would attract relatively few marks as it does little more than identify features of Freud's theory without suggesting in what way these could be used to explain the target behaviour. This suggests that the candidate does not fully understand the psychoanalytic explanation of behaviour because he or she has been unable to use it to actually offer a coherent explanation. A better attempt would be:

(a) *The psychodynamic approach to explaining behaviour takes the view that our behaviour is motivated by unconscious influences of which we are not aware. According to Freud the personality consists of three aspects, the id, which wants immediate satisfaction, the superego that is based on morality and urges restraint, and the ego that has access to reality and can balance the influences of the id and superego. Gambling can be seen as the interaction of the three personality parts. The id wants the prize, the superego says you can't have it as you haven't earned it, so the ego compromises by saying you can gamble for it and have it if you win.*
The psychodynamic approach might further focus on adolescence as a time of identity crisis and this might help explain why gambling becomes

a problem at that time. An adolescent might especially need parental attention during this period and, if both parents are at work, perhaps adolescents are getting less support than they used to so they are more likely to go off the rails.

In the A level examination you will be given an opportunity to evaluate one of your explanations.

(b) *The drawback to psychodynamic explanations is that they lack falsifiability. In other words it would be difficult to test whether this explanation is actually any better than any other explanation. The influence of the id, ego, and superego is a hypothetical concept since none of these actually exist. They only provide a means of conceptualising the problem. However, the idea of unconscious influences has some validity as demonstrated by behaviours such as Freudian slips. Therefore it is possible that gambling is in some way expressing an unconscious desire for more attention especially at this vulnerable time of adolescent identity formation.*

A suitable methodology for the psychodynamic approach

In the examination you will be further asked to suggest how one approach might investigate this phenomenon, and evaluate the use of this method of investigating this phenomenon. The process of analysis involves identifying the constituent parts of a problem and discussing these. A good student answer might be:

(c) *It is likely that a psychoanalytic psychologist would investigate the behaviour described by using the case study approach. This is where one individual is studied intensively over a period of time. Retrospective accounts of their early life are analysed as a means of explaining their current gambling behaviour. A psychoanalytic psychologist would focus on experiences in early life that might have been repressed or led to conflicts. The psychiatrist would do this through free association where the patient just talks about whatever comes into their mind and the psychiatrist encourages their recall. The psychiatrist might also use dream interpretation as a way of understanding the repressed thoughts of the individual. Ultimately the case study could then be used to formulate an explanation for gambling behaviour because the psychiatrist would be able to suggest what past experiences were associated with the current pathological behaviour.*

The final part of the A level question requires the candidate to evaluate the use of this method, again in the context of the target behaviour. The danger, as in the above answers, is omitting to mention gambling behaviour and simply offering an evaluation of the method used in part (c).

full understanding of them and of their underlying motives. This case study approach is still recognised as an important approach to understanding human behaviour.

- Sometimes (as in his analyses of dreams or "Freudian slips"), Freud was able to develop important theories by integrating information obtained from a number of individuals.

Weaknesses

- The individuals studied by Freud were not at all representative. They were mainly middle-class Viennese women suffering from neurotic disorders living in a sexually suppressed culture in the nineteenth century. Freud recorded only one case history of a child (Little Hans) and that study was largely second-hand in that the data were obtained and interpreted retrospectively (after the event).
- It is probable that the evidence Freud obtained from clients during therapy was *contaminated* in the sense that what the patient said was influenced by what Freud had said previously. In addition, Freud may well have used his theoretical preconceptions to produce distorted interpretations of what the patient said.
- Even though Freud only studied individuals with mental disorders in depth, he nevertheless constructed a theory of normal development in his psychosexual theory (Chapter 6, Social and Personality Development). Not surprisingly, this theory was not based on much solid evidence concerning normal development.
- Much of Freud's evidence was basically in the form of *correlations* between certain childhood experiences on the one hand and adult personality or adult mental disorders on the other hand. Correlations can't prove causes, and so these correlations can't show that adult personality (or mental disorder) has been caused by childhood experiences.

SECTION SUMMARY
The Psychodynamic Approach

Key concepts

- ❖ A psychodynamic approach is one that explains the dynamics of behaviour.
- ❖ Freud's psychoanalytic theory identified the forces that motivate personality development and adult behaviour.
- ❖ The key assumptions of Freud's approach are:

— Early experience interacts with innate drives, and this leads us to behave in predictable ways later in life.
— Unconscious forces motivate much of our behaviour, due to ego defences that aim to protect the ego from feelings of anxiety.
— Personality dynamics are related to personality structures (id, ego, and superego) and stages of development (oral, anal, phallic, latency, and genital).

❖ Neo-Freudians adapted the theory as follows:

— They placed more emphasis on social and cultural, rather than biological, factors.
— They developed ego analysis, which looks at current interpersonal problems and regards society as positive.

❖ The psychodynamic approach can help explain attachment, abnormality, prejudice and aggression, theory of dreams, moral development, gender development adolescence, and psychoanalysis as therapy.

❖ Strengths of the approach include:

Evaluation of the key concepts

— Freud's scientific background could help psychology to be seen as a science.
— Freud's theory was revolutionary for its time.
— Freud's ideas have endured.
— Many of Freud's concepts have come into everyday use. Within psychology he changed our views on childhood and the unconscious.
— Freud founded development psychology and psychoanalysis.
— His theory manages to combine both the rational and irrational elements of behaviour.
— Freud put forward the first systematic theory of personality.

❖ Weaknesses of the approach include:

— Freud provided simple mechanistic explanations of behaviour.
— He failed to indicate in detail how behaviour is determined.
— There is a general lack of falsifiability in psychodynamic theory.
— Certain parts of Freud's theory that can be tested have been found to be wrong.

❖ The methodology used within the psychodynamic approach focuses on:

Methodology

— The use of case studies in which individuals are studied in depth
— Observation of human behaviour in everyday life.

❖ Strengths of the methodology include:

Evaluation of the methodology

— The collection of rich and detailed information from individuals
— The development of theories on the basis of acute observation and integrating information.

❖ Weaknesses of the methodology include:

— The study of non-representative individuals
— The difficulty of deciding the extent to which what patients said was unduly influenced by Freud's ideas
— Freud developed a theory of normal development based on a study of individuals with mental disorders.
— The problems of interpreting correlational evidence in which childhood experiences are correlated with adult mental disorders.

See also pages 315–317 of the revision guide.

THE COGNITIVE APPROACH

Key Concepts

The cognitive approach is in some ways at the opposite end of the spectrum to behaviourism. Where behaviourism emphasises external observable events only, the cognitive approach looks at internal, mental explanations of behaviour. The word "cognitive" comes from the Latin word *cognitio* meaning "I apprehend, understand, or know". These are all *internal* processes that involve the mind (brain processes)—processes such as those involved in perception, attention, language, memory, and thinking.

The cognitive approach is based on three main assumptions:

- Behaviour can largely be explained in terms of how the mind (or brain) operates.
- The mind works in a manner that is similar to a computer: inputting, storing, and retrieving data. Cognitive psychologists assume that there is an information-processing system in which information presented to it is altered or transformed. This information-processing system works in an integrated way, meaning that its various parts (e.g., attention, perception, memory) co-operate with each other to understand the environment and behaviour appropriately.
- Psychology is a pure science, based mainly on well-controlled laboratory experiments.

As you can see, the cognitive approach may be the opposite to behaviourism in some ways (e.g., focus on internal vs. external factors), but there are also some similarities. Both approaches are quite reductionist and experimental. The cognitive approach is reductionist in its use of computer analogies, and experimental in its attitudes towards research.

Historical development

Psychology developed properly as a science towards the end of the nineteenth century when Wilhelm Wundt founded the first psychological laboratory at the University of Leipzig in Germany. Wundt can be regarded as a cognitive psychologist. He studied mental processes and wanted to make such research more systematic. Instead of just developing his own ideas (like philosophers), he devised experiments to try to find evidence to support his theories. In this way he made psychology more scientific (seeking objective data on which to formulate theories).

Wundt argued that conscious mental states could be scientifically studied using **introspection**. Wundt's introspection was not a casual affair but a highly practised form of self-examination. He trained psychology students to make observations that were not biased by personal interpretation or previous experience, and used the results to develop a theory of conscious thought. Wundt didn't believe that this perspective could be applied to all aspects of human psychology, but he thought he could identify the elementary sensations and their interrelations, and thus identify the way that human thought was structured.

Wilhelm Wundt, 1832–1920.

KEY TERM

Introspection: examination and observation of one's own mental processes.

The advent of the computer age gave cognitive psychology a new metaphor, and the 1950s and 1960s saw a tremendous rise in cognitive psychology research and the use of cognitive concepts in other areas of psychology, such as social cognition and cognitive-developmental theories. If machines could produce behaviours that were analogous (i.e., similar) to animal behaviours then psychologists might be able to use information-processing concepts to explain the behaviour of living things. Or, to put it another way, cognitive psychologists could explain animal and human behaviour using computer concepts to explain how animals and humans process information. Another important difference from Wundt's approach is that cognitive psychologists over the past 50 years have typically focused on precise measurements of *behaviour* (e.g., time taken to perform a task) rather than on introspection.

The kind of concepts we are talking about are input, output, storage, retrieval, parallel processing, networking, schemas, filters, top-down and bottom-up processing, and so on. The cognitive perspective relies on the computer metaphor or analogy as a means of describing and explaining behaviour. However, the cognitive perspective involves more than the information-processing metaphor. It is a perspective focusing on the way that mental or cognitive processes work. Thus, *any* explanation incorporating mental concepts is using a cognitive perspective. For example, in social psychology (where the relationships between individuals are studied) there is a branch called "social cognition", which focuses on how one's thinking affects social behaviour. In developmental psychology, theorists such as Piaget explained behaviour in terms of mental operations and schemas, and so he has valid claims to be regarded as a cognitive psychologist.

Advancing information technology has inspired cognitive psychologists to draw an analogy between computers and humans, in a bid to understand better how we process information.

Schemas

The concept of **schemas** (or sometimes "schemata") is one of the most important concepts introduced by cognitive psychology. It is the basic unit of our mental processes and is used at various points in this book. What is a schema?

A schema is a cognitive structure that contains knowledge about a thing, including its attributes and the relations among its attributes (Fiske & Taylor, 1991).

Why are schemas so important? The concept of a schema incorporates various critical features of our thought processes:

- A schema doesn't consist of a single dimension but of a cluster of interrelated concepts.
- A schema is derived from an individual's past experience and doesn't directly represent reality. Thus, we can use schemas to explain how people distort information along the lines of their past experience.
- Schemas are also socially determined. They are learned and refined through social exchanges (conversations with other people and from the media).
- There are many different kinds of schema. Schemas about events are called **scripts**. These schemas guide us when performing commonplace activities, such as going to the cinema or to a football match. Role schemas tell us about different roles, and self-schemas embody our self-concept.

> **KEY TERMS**
>
> **Schemas:** organised packets of information stored in long-term memory.
> **Scripts:** sets of schemas that guide people when performing commonplace activities, such as going to a restaurant or catching a bus.

- Schemas are an obvious outcome of our cognitive processes. We need to categorise and summarise the large amounts of information processed in order to generate future behaviour. We are "cognitive misers", meaning that we prefer to minimise the amount of information that we need to store and remember.

You will find the concept of schemas used in Chapter 6, Social and Personality Development; see for example Martin and Halverson's (1987) gender-schema theory (page 265). Piaget also made extensive use of schemas in his theory of cognitive development.

Evaluation of Key Concepts

The main strengths and weaknesses of the cognitive approach are discussed below. Blue words indicate the issue to which the point relates.

Strengths

- Reductionism: As we will see, the functioning of the human brain differs in many ways from that of computers. However, when you consider that the human brain has, over the years, been compared to a catapult, a telephone exchange, and a mill, you may agree that the comparison with computers makes reasonable sense!
- Determinism: The notion that behaviour is determined jointly by external stimuli and by internal processes (e.g., perception, attention, reasoning) is still accepted as important and useful.
- The cognitive approach was very important historically in moving psychology away from the dominance of behaviourism and in the direction of studying mental processes (cognitions).
- Applications: Cognitive psychology has been applied successfully in various ways, including providing advice about the validity of eyewitness testimony, how to improve your memory (useful for examination candidates!), and how to improve performance in situations requiring close attention (e.g., air-traffic control). However, its most useful application is in cognitive therapy, which has benefited the lives of hundreds of thousands of patients with mental disorders (Chapter 9, Treating Mental Disorders).

Weaknesses

- Reductionism: Most theories within cognitive psychology are reductionist in the sense that they involve "decoupling" or separating the cognitive system from the motivational and emotional systems. This is a weakness because motivational and emotional factors have a real influence on human cognition.
- Determinism: The cognitive approach successfully identified some of the factors determining behaviour, but it ignored others (e.g., social and cultural factors, genetic factors).
- Nature–nurture: One of the most puzzling features of the cognitive approach is its failure to consider the role of genetic factors in human cognition. There

is substantial evidence that genetic factors influence individual differences in intelligence (Chapter 5, Cognitive Development). However, this evidence has had very little impact on the cognitive approach, even though cognitive psychologists often study areas of human cognition (e.g., reasoning) much influenced by intelligence!

- Individual differences: There are large individual differences in cognitive processes such as memory, thinking, and reasoning, but most cognitive psychologists ignore these individual differences altogether.

Methodology

Psychologists working within the cognitive approach typically carry out laboratory studies based on the experimental method. In other words, the experimental situation is carefully controlled, and the effects of manipulating aspects of the situation on behaviour are carefully assessed. We can illustrate the strengths and weaknesses of the cognitive approach by considering a fairly typical experiment (Loftus & Palmer, 1974) forming part of the AS psychology course.

In the experiment by Loftus and Palmer (1974) on eyewitness testimony, there were five groups of participants, all of whom watched the same film showing a car accident. After watching the film, they were asked various questions, one of which had a different verb for each group: "About how fast were the cars going when they [hit/smashed/collided/bumped/contacted—the five conditions] each other?" Thus, the aspect of the situation that was manipulated was the precise wording of this crucial question. One week later, all participants were asked whether they had seen any broken glass caused by the accident (in fact, there wasn't any broken glass).

Loftus and Palmer (1974) were interested in two measures of behaviour: (1) the estimated speed of the cars in answer to the crucial question; and (2) whether or not broken glass was reported. Participants in the "smashed" condition reported the highest car speeds, followed in descending order by "collided", "bumped", "hit", and "contacted". Participants in the "smashed" condition were more likely than those in the "hit" condition to report having seen broken glass: 32% vs. 14%, respectively. These findings suggest that eyewitness memory is fragile and easily distorted even when only a *single* word in a sentence is altered.

The study by Loftus and Palmer (1974) shows good experimental control— all five groups of participants were treated identically except for the verb in the crucial question. Thus, we can be confident that group differences in answers to the two questions depend on the precise verb used in the crucial question. However, it can certainly be argued that the experiment lacks mundane realism, since the participants would have less affected emotionally by watching a film than by seeing a car accident in real life. The experiment probably lacked external validity because the participants knew something interesting was going to be shown to them and so were paying full attention to the screen—in real life, eyewitnesses are typically taken by surprise and often fail to pay close attention to the event or incident. However, these differences would *reduce* distortions of memory in the laboratory compared to the real world.

Results from Loftus and Palmer's (1974) study showing how the verb used in the initial description of a car accident affected recall of the incident after one week.

Answering the approaches question

Using the cognitive approach to explain a behaviour

Lottery addict children

"Britain is producing a generation of child gamblers hooked on the Lottery and fruit machines. Disturbing new research by two eminent academics shows that hundreds of thousands of children—some as young as 11—are now addicted despite the supposed legal restrictions. The findings will fuel warnings from lottery critics that the country is storing up social problems and is likely to trigger pressure for a uniform age limit of 18 on all gambling." (Reproduced from AQA A specimen material.)

In the A level examination you will be required to explain a target behaviour using any approach. The aim of this activity is to offer you, the candidate, the opportunity to express your true understanding of the approach by your ability to use it in a novel situation.

How would you explain lottery addiction in terms of the cognitive approach? The key elements of the cognitive approach are that explanations focus on what is going on inside the mind and how cognitions, such as schemas and processing of data, can be used to explain behaviour. Such explanations de-emphasise emotion. A possible explanation could be as follows:

(a) *Addiction can be understood in terms of various theories of cognitive activity. Attribution theory offers one explanation. Addicts typically think of their behaviour as being governed by craving and beyond their voluntary control. However, if they can learn to associate their addiction with situational cues (such as the amusement arcade) then they can stop attributing the behaviour to their internal disposition (I am a gambler) and overcome their addiction.*
The cognitive approach might also use the idea of schemas to explain how we all acquire scripts about behaving in certain situations in certain ways. When you go into an amusement arcade you have a script that tells you what to do. You acquire such scripts from watching things on TV. Without a script you wouldn't know what to do in certain situations, which is why one often feels lost in a foreign city.

This answer is a tricky one for the examiner because the candidate clearly knows something about how attribution theory can explain addiction and has used this knowledge well. It does show an understanding of attribution theory, an example of a cognitive approach. The problem is that in this question you must demonstrate your understanding of the cognitive approach, rather than material you have learned when studying cognitive psychology (i.e., attribution theory). The second paragraph is in some ways better in terms of demonstrating an understanding of the cognitive approach, though perhaps not as successful as the

first. It at least illustrates an attempt to marry understanding of schemas and scripts to gambling addiction rather than just describing a known explanation, as with attribution theory.

A suitable methodology for the cognitive approach

In the examination you will be further asked to suggest how one approach might investigate this phenomenon, and evaluate the use of this method of investigating this phenomenon. The process of analysis involves identifying the constituent parts of a problem and discussing these. A good student answer might be:

(c) *If one wanted to investigate the kind of scripts that adolescents have one might interview people of this age group and ask them to describe what they do when they go into an amusement arcade. It is likely that you would use a fairly unstructured interview technique in order to find out as much as possible. You would start with a set of fixed questions and develop these as you went along in response to the answers that were given. At the end you would have a large amount of data to analyse and this could be done by identifying certain themes that occurred in the different accounts. Your aim would be to synthesise and summarise the data so that you could draw conclusions about the kind of behaviours that typically surrounded gambling addiction in young people.*

This is a reasonable attempt to explain how a cognitive psychologist might investigate gambling behaviour. The description is related to the target behaviour and the candidate has shown an understanding of various aspects of interviewing technique and the qualitative approach to research. The last part of the question requires the candidate to evaluate this methodology again with reference to the target behaviour:

(d) *The advantage of the unstructured interview is that one is able to collect a lot of data and some of this data may be unexpected because the material collected is not restricted by previous expectations about what people think about gambling addiction. One limitation of this method is that the data collected may be biased by the kind of questions the interviewer asks since they make some of the questions up on the spot. This might be a special problem when interviewing teenagers. A further limitation lies in the analysis, which again involves subjective decisions. Objectivity can be increased by triangulating the findings with findings from other research studies as a means of confirming the outcome.*

Evaluation of Methodology

Some of the most important strengths and weaknesses of the methodology used within the cognitive approach are itemised below. Blue words indicate the issue to which the point relates.

Strengths

- The type of experimentation used within the cognitive approach typically involves use of the experimental method. The high level of control obtained produces replicable findings having high internal validity.

- The experimental techniques used by cognitive psychologists have successfully identified important internal processes and structures (e.g., schemas) and have been used widely in other areas of psychology (e.g., social psychology).

- Reductionism: The cognitive approach to experimentation is reductionist in the sense of focusing on basic processes and comparing human cognition to computer functioning. However, it has nevertheless produced many findings that are applicable to the real world. For example, laboratory studies on eyewitness testimony have produced several findings (e.g., distortions of eyewitness memory by subsequent information) that are consistent with what has been found in real-life situations in spite of issues relating to external validity.

Weaknesses

- Reductionism: Cognitive psychologists typically try to study some aspect of human cognition while minimising the impact of emotional and motivational factors on performance. That inevitably means that we obtain only a limited perspective that can lack external validity.

- Reductionism: The previous point indicated one way in which research in cognitive psychology lacks external validity. More generally, participants in most cognitive experiments are well-motivated, undistracted, have no other goals competing with task completion, and know exactly what they are supposed to do with the task stimuli—that doesn't sound much like the real world!

- Individual differences: In most studies carried out by cognitive psychologists, there is no attempt to assess *any* aspects of individual differences (e.g., intelligence, motivation) even though there are large individual differences in performance on most cognitive tasks.

SECTION SUMMARY
The Cognitive Approach

❖ The cognitive approach focuses on internal, mental activity as a means of explaining behaviour. It is based on three key assumptions:

— Behaviour can be explained in terms of how the mind works.
— Behaviour can be understood using information-processing analogies.
— Experimental research is desirable.

❖ The historical development:

— Wundt's early work used introspection as a means of objectively studying mental processes.

Key concepts

— This approach to research was rejected by the behaviourists as too subjective, but the advent of computers offered cognitive psychology a new vocabulary and set of concepts.
— Cognitive explanations are not all based in information processing but share a focus on mental activity.

❖ The word (and concept) "schema" is by now used throughout psychology. It is so pervasive because:

— It is multi-dimensional
— It embodies the influence of expectations and social constructions
— It expresses our tendency for cognitive economy.

Evaluation of the key concepts

❖ Strengths of the approach include:

— The fact that there are important similarities between human and computer functioning
— The emphasis on internal as well as external determinants of behaviour
— The historical importance of cognition
— Applications such as cognitive therapy.

❖ Weaknesses of the approach include:

— Largely ignoring motivational and emotional influences on cognition and behaviour
— Ignoring the role of social and cultural factors
— Neglect of the role of genetic factors in cognition
— Ignoring individual differences.

Methodology

❖ In terms of methodology, the cognitive approach typically involves carrying out laboratory experiments based on the experimental method.

Evaluation of the methodology

❖ Strengths of the methodology include:

— Producing replicable findings with high internal validity
— The identification of important cognitive structures (e.g., schemas)
— Producing some findings that can be applied to the real world.

❖ Weaknesses of the methodology include:

— A limited perspective that can lack external validity
— The artificial nature of the experimental situations used
— The failure in most cognitive research to assess or consider any aspects of individual differences.

See also pages 318–319 of the revision guide.

THE EVOLUTIONARY APPROACH

Key Concepts

Evolution is a fact—to evolve is to change over time. There is clear evidence that groups of animals have changed over time. Charles Darwin's theory of evolution and natural selection is an attempt to offer an explanation for this process of change. The essential principles of this theory are:

- Environments are always changing, or animals move to new environments. Environmental change requires new adaptations for species to survive.
- Living things are constantly changing. This happens partly because of sexual reproduction where two parents create a new individual by combining their genes (although Darwin wasn't aware that there were such things as genes, he knew that the information was transmitted in some way). It also happens through chance **mutations** of the genes. In both cases new traits are produced.
- Competition between individuals for limited resources (such as access to food and/or mates) means that those individuals who possess traits best adapted or suited to the changing environment are more likely to survive to reproduce (it is reproduction rather than survival that matters). Or, to put it another way, those individuals who best "fit" their environment survive (survival of the *fittest*). Or, to put it yet another way, the *genes* of the individuals with these traits are naturally selected. No-one "selects" these individuals with useful traits; they are *naturally* selected.

In order to understand the concept of **natural selection**, consider this example. A cattle or sheep farmer chooses which male and female stock animals have the best characteristics for milk production or for increased reproduction (e.g., giving birth to lots of twins), and mates these individuals. This is selective breeding or artificial selection. In nature, no-one does the selecting—it is natural pressures that do it, hence "natural" selection.

Selective breeding is an artificial way of ensuring that good genes get passed to the next generation.

The end result is that those individuals who possess the physical characteristics and behaviours that are **adaptive**, i.e., help the individual to better fit its environment, are the ones that survive. Those traits that are non-adaptive disappear, as do the individuals with those traits. It should be emphasised that it isn't the individual, but their genes, that disappear. Natural selection takes place at the level of the genes. A classic example of this is the tendency for parents to risk their lives to save their offspring, which can be seen in altruistic behaviour. If altruistic behaviour is inherited then it must in some way promote survival and reproduction. But one would think this can't be true, because an altruistic act involves a risk to the altruist's life. However, if the altruist is risking his/her life to save a genetic relative, then the altruistic behaviour enhances the survival of the individual's genes.

It is important to note that evolutionary psychologists don't assume that *all* forms of behaviour are adaptive. Evolutionary psychologists refer to the **environment of evolutionary adaptation (EEA)**—the period in human evolution during which our genes were shaped and naturally to solve survival problems operating then. This was roughly between 35,000 and 3 million years ago. Non-adaptive forms of behaviour can be explained on the basis of genome lag—it takes thousands of generations

KEY TERMS

Mutations: genetic changes that can then be inherited by any offspring.
Natural selection: the process by which certain traits (and the associated genes) are perpetuated because of the advantage they confer in terms of survival and increased reproduction.
Adaptive: the extent to which a behaviour increases the reproductive potential of an individual and survival of its genes.
Environment of evolutionary adaptation (EEA): the period in human evolution during which our genes were shaped and naturally selected to solve survival problems that were operating at that time (between 35,000 and 3 million years ago).

for non-adaptive forms of behaviour to be eliminated from the human repertoire via natural selection. For example, evolutionary psychologists can use genome lag to explain the stress response. We can't deal effectively with most of today's stressors by increased physiological arousal and "fight or flight", but these reactions were very useful during the time of the environment of evolutionary adaptation.

The concept that altruistic behaviour is adaptive because it promotes the survival of kin wasn't one of Darwin's ideas. In fact, for him, altruism was a paradox. It was sociobiologists such as Hamilton (1964) and Dawkins (1976) who suggested that in addition to natural selection there was kin selection. The principle of kin selection is that any behaviour that promotes the survival of kin will be selected. Darwin's theory of evolution focused on individual fitness. The sociobiologists extended this to include genetic relatives, thus kin selection *includes* the survival of any relatives sharing your genes (inclusive fitness), and the key features of the sociobiological approach were subsequently accepted by evolutionary psychologists.

The evolutionary approach assumes that all behaviour can be explained in terms of genetic determination. **Ethologists** study behaviour to ascertain its function for the individual. They argue that any behaviour must be adaptive in some way (or neutral) otherwise it wouldn't remain in the individual's gene pool. This argument is applied, for example, to mental illnesses (see Chapter 7, Evolutionary Explanations of Human Behaviour). If the genes for mental disorders didn't have some adaptive significance, why would they still be with us? This of course assumes that mental disorders have some genetic basis, and twin studies suggest they do.

The second assumption of the evolutionary approach is that genetically determined traits evolve through natural and kin selection. A behaviour that promotes survival and reproduction of a genetic line will be "selected" and the genes for that trait survive. As the environment changes (or an individual moves to a new environment), new traits are needed to ensure survival. Environmental change and competition exert selective pressure. New genetic combinations produce adaptation and the individual and/or genes best "fitting" the environmental niche will survive (survival of the fittest).

Examples of the evolutionary approach

Chapter 7, Evolutionary Explanations of Human Behaviour, focuses on how evolutionary explanations can be used to understand human reproductive behaviour, the existence of mental disorders, and the evolution of intelligence.

In your AS studies, Bowlby's theory of attachment was an example of the evolutionary approach to explaining behaviour. The adaptive nature of stress was also considered.

In this book, in Chapter 2, Relationships, sociobiology or evolutionary psychology is used as an explanation for the formation of relationships. Evolutionary psychology is also important in understanding pro- and anti-social behaviour (Chapter 3, Pro- and Anti-social Behaviour), moral development (Chapter 5, Cognitive Development), and gender development (Chapter 6, Social

KEY TERM

Ethologists: those who undertake the biological study of animal behaviour, seeking to determine the functional value of behaviours, and tending to rely on naturalistic observation.

and Personality Development). In Chapter 4, Biological Rhythms, Sleep, and Dreaming, an evolutionary theory of sleep is discussed.

Evaluation of Key Concepts

Below are lists of the major strengths and weaknesses of the evolutionary approach. Blue words indicate the issue to which the point relates.

Strengths

- Evolutionary psychology provides a powerful general approach within which to understand human behaviour. As de Waal (2002, p.187) argued, "Evolutionary psychology may serve as the umbrella idea (i.e., an overarching scheme) so desperately needed in the social sciences."
- Determinism: Psychologists have mostly focused on immediate or proximate determinants of behaviour. The notion of evolutionary determinism, with its emphasis on ultimate causes of behaviour, is an important contribution to our understanding of the factors influencing our behaviour.
- Nature–nurture: The evolutionary approach combines effectively with the biological approach—both approaches emphasise the importance of our genetic inheritance, and the evolutionary approach goes beyond that by stressing how our genetic make-up has been determined by natural selection.

Weaknesses

- The theory of evolution offers mainly *ex post facto* (after the fact) evidence. It is hard to know whether a behaviour is actually beneficial, and that is why it remained in a gene pool, or whether it was simply neutral and was never selected against, and thus survived.
- The evolutionary approach is less applicable to human behaviour than to the behaviour of non-human species. This is because our behaviour is more influenced by experience, by conscious thought, and by the culture in which we live.
- Determinism: Human behaviour is influenced by numerous factors, and it is very limited to focus almost exclusively on ultimate causes at the expense of more immediate ones (e.g., the social and cultural context).
- Nature–nurture: Evolutionary psychologists strongly emphasise the role of nature (e.g., natural selection) in determining behaviour but largely ignore important environmental factors.
- Individual differences: Individual differences (e.g., in intelligence, in learning, in susceptibility to mental disorder) are clearly important, but the evolutionary approach has failed to provide an adequate explanation of individual differences.

Methodology

Evolutionary psychologists have tested their theoretical ideas in various ways. First, it is possible to assemble data from numerous cultures to see whether the predicted pattern of behaviour is consistent in all cultures. For example,

Buss (1989) tested the predictions that males should prefer a mate younger than them, whereas females should prefer a mate who has good resources in 37 different cultures (see Chapter 7, Evolutionary Explanations of Human Behaviour).

Second, some predictions of the evolutionary approach can be tested by comparing different species. For example, factors responsible for the evolution of human intelligence and the increased size of the human neocortex have been considered by comparing the living environment (e.g., size of social group) and size of neocortex in primate species (see Chapter 7, Evolutionary Explanations of Human Behaviour).

Third, evolutionary psychologists sometimes carry out experiments to test predictions from their approach. For example, Buunk et al. (1996) tested the predictions that jealousy in men is greater when their partner is physically unfaithful rather than emotionally unfaithful, whereas the opposite is the case in women. Another example concerns laboratory studies on phobias and fears. Such research (e.g., Cook & Mineka, 1989; Tomarken et al., 1989) has shown that humans and other primates are especially sensitive to stimuli (e.g., snakes) that posed much more threat in our ancestral past than they do nowadays (see Chapter 7, Evolutionary Explanations of Human Behaviour)—the implication is that we are biologically prepared to develop fears to such stimuli.

Fourth, evolutionary psychologists sometimes simply study patterns of behaviour that have been observed by others, attempting to interpret them in evolutionary terms. For example, evolutionary psychologists have considered the symptoms of mental disorders such as schizophrenia, depression, and anxiety in order to try to work out what adaptive value these symptoms might have had in our ancestral past.

Evaluation of Methodology

The various strengths and weaknesses of the evolutionary approach are discussed below. Blue words indicate the issue to which the point relates.

Strengths

- One of the main strengths of evolutionary psychology is that several different approaches can be taken to testing its predictions. As we have seen, we can compare behaviour across cultures, we can compare different species, we can carry out experiments in the laboratory, and we can focus on previously obtained patterns of behaviour to assess the validity of the evolutionary approach.
- Reductionism: Following from the first point, evolutionary psychologists claim that we can learn much about human behaviour by studying other species. This claim has some validity, and involves using information about other species typically ignored by advocates of most other approaches within psychology.
- Some of the findings obtained by evolutionary psychologists are most easily interpreted from their theoretical perspective. For example, we acquire fears more readily to objects that used to be dangerous in our ancestral

past than to recently invented objects (e.g., cars) that are much more dangerous.

Weaknesses

- Determinism: Evolutionary psychologists assume that human behaviour depends on ultimate causes based on natural selection. However, it is impossible to *manipulate* these ultimate causes and so the predictions of evolutionary psychology can't be tested directly.

- Determinism: The evidence obtained by evolutionary psychologists is difficult to interpret. For example, comparisons of the living environment and size of neocortex in primate species involve only *correlational* data, and correlations can't be used to establish causes. Many experimental studies (e.g., Buunk et al.'s, 1996, on jealousy) are limited because they are artificial and lacking in external validity. In real life, men and women react very similarly to unfaithfulness by their partners (Harris, 2002), which is very different to the findings from laboratory studies.

- Individual differences: When evolutionary psychologists carry out experiments, they rarely consider individual differences. For example, research on jealousy has sometimes produced evidence of differences between males and females, but there are also substantial differences *within* each sex.

- Much of the evidence used by evolutionary psychologists is weak in the sense that it can be interpreted in several different ways. For example, several theories try to identify the adaptive value originally associated with the symptoms of disorders such as schizophrenia or depression. The absence of strong evidence means that it is very difficult to decide which theories are the most valid.

SECTION SUMMARY
The Evolutionary Approach

❖ Darwin's theory of evolution is an explanation for the process of change in living things. The key principles of this theory are:

Key concepts

— Environmental change requires new adaptation.
— Living things are constantly changing and thus there is the possibility of new characteristics that may be more adaptive.
— Competition means that those best adapted are more likely to survive and reproduce.
— It is the genes for adaptive characteristics that are selected, and this selection takes place naturally.
— Altruistic behaviour is an example of selection at the level of the genes.

❖ Sociobiologists extended evolutionary theory to include the concepts of kin selection and inclusive fitness, and these ideas were then adopted by evolutionary psychologists.

❖ The two main assumptions of the evolutionary approach are that:

— All behaviour can be explained in terms of genetic determinism.
— Genetically determined traits evolve through natural selection and kin selection.

❖ The evolutionary approach focuses on how evolutionary explanations can understand human reproductive behaviour, mental disorders, the evolution of intelligence, attachment, stress, and other human behaviour.

Evaluation of the key concepts

❖ Strengths of the approach include:

— Many aspects of animal behaviour can be explained by the evolutionary approach.
— The evolutionary approach was the first to emphasise ultimate causes of behaviour.
— Its focus on genetic factors helps to explain much behaviour.

❖ Weaknesses of the approach include:

— The evidence is largely *ex post facto* and cannot truly demonstrate cause and effect.
— Evolutionary explanations are highly deterministic.
— The approach is less appropriate for human behaviour than animal behaviour.
— Environmental factors are largely ignored.
— The approach does not provide an adequate explanation for individual differences.

Methodology

❖ In terms of methodology, evolutionary psychologists:

— Compare cultures to test the consistency of behaviour
— Compare different species
— Carry out experiments
— Consider patterns of behaviour (e.g., symptoms exhibited by patients with a given mental disorder) in the attempt to understand how these disorders might have been adaptive in our ancestral past.

Evaluation of the methodology

❖ Strengths of the methodology include:

— There are several useful techniques are available to evolutionary psychologist.
— They have the advantage over most other approaches that they take into account patterns of behaviour in other species when trying to understand humans.
— Findings can be easily interpreted from their theoretical perspective.

❖ Weaknesses of the methodology include:

— The inability to manipulate ultimate causes of behaviour
— The evidence is difficult to interpret
— The neglect of individual differences
— There is an absence of strong evidence.

See also pages 320–322 of the revision guide.

FURTHER READING

The topics in this chapter are covered in greater depth by M. Jarvis (2000) *Theoretical approaches in psychology* (London: Routledge), written specifically for the AQA A specification. A useful general textbook on approaches in psychology is W.E. Glassman (1995) *Approaches to psychology (2nd Edn.)* (Buckingham, UK: Open University Press). For detailed material on particular approaches you might consult the following: L. Slater (2004) *Opening Skinner's box: Great psychological experiments of the twentieth century* (New York: Norton), which gives interesting insights into Skinner's thinking, and P. Thurschwell (2000) *Sigmund Freud* (London: Routledge), which provides a thorough discussion of the value of Freud's contribution to psychology.

EXAMPLE EXAMINATION QUESTIONS

The "approaches" question is different from all the others in the examination. You have about 40 minutes to answer this question and it is worth a total of 30 marks, divided into 5 Units of 6 marks. This gives you the guidance of spending about 6–7 minutes on each Unit (6 minutes for each of the two approaches and 6 minutes for each other part of the question).

This question will be assessed on "synopticity" which is defined as your "understanding and critical appreciation of the breadth and range of different theoretical perspectives and/or methodological approaches relevant to any question" (AQA specification).

In your answer you must be sure that you engage with the stimulus material and do not merely describe and assess an approach and a method of investigation.

1. A farmer's life for me

   "Joe grew up in a town but spent his summers staying with his grandfather on the farm. The summers were always the best times and he felt more at home there, helping his beloved grandfather look after the livestock and the crops. When he was asked about what he wanted to be when he grew up, he said 'a farmer'. This pleased the old man enormously, though he didn't really believe it. When Joe was old enough he moved out to the farm and eventually took it over."

   How might a psychologist explain Joe's desire to become a farmer?

   (a) Describe how the subject presented in the stimulus material might be
       explained by **two** different approaches.   (6 marks + 6 marks)
   (b) Assess **one** of these explanations of the subject presented in the stimulus
       material in terms of its strengths and limitations.   (6 marks)
   (c) How might the subject presented in the stimulus material be investigated
       by **one** of these approaches?   (6 marks)
   (d) Evaluate the use of this method of investigating the subject presented
       in the stimulus material.   (6 marks)

                                                        Total for this question: 30 marks

2. A rock climber

"Sylvia climbs mountains for a hobby. She doesn't walk up them but ropes herself up to ascend sheer faces of rock. It's a hobby that requires skill, patience, and no fear of heights. If you are not a rock climber it is hard to imagine what drives some people to do it."

(a) Describe how the subject presented in the stimulus material might be explained by **two** different approaches. (6 marks + 6 marks)

(b) Assess **one** of these explanations of the subject presented in the stimulus material in terms of its strengths and limitations. (6 marks)

(c) How might the subject presented in the stimulus material be investigated by **one** of these approaches? (6 marks)

(d) Evaluate the use of this method of investigating the subject presented in the stimulus material. (6 marks)

Total for this question: 30 marks

Examination Tips

The question on approaches in psychology is different from all the others set at A2 level. The question will always comprise a piece of stimulus material followed by the same set of four questions. The intention is to assess a candidate's understanding of the synoptic elements of the specification: the approaches and perspectives, the means by which psychologists evaluate their explanations, and the methodologies they use.

Knowledge enables you to solve problems. In mathematics you learn various strategies for solving mathematical problems. What is a "psychological problem"? It is one where you are asked to offer an explanation for a particular behaviour. Having offered an explanation, it is important to determine the value (both positive and negative) of that explanation. This is just what you are asked to do in the approaches question.

> **EXAM HINT**
> Sub-part (c) asks you to outline how one of the approaches might investigate the subject matter presented in the stimulus. An experiment offers a lot more scope than some of the other methods so, if possible, base your answer on the biological or behavioural approach, as these employ scientific methodology.

> **EXAM HINT**
> Make sure you have prepared a list of key concepts for each approach that you can draw from in your answer.

If you were asked to describe the behavioural approach, for example, you could list all sorts of facts that you have memorised. However, by asking you to use the approach to explain a novel behaviour, your real understanding is being assessed. Therefore it is important in this question that you actually engage with the stimulus material and use your knowledge, rather than just describing the behavioural approach and/or outlining theories that you have learned about. You will not receive credit for someone else's theory or study. It is a taxing question but ultimately the question in the study of psychology—given any behaviour, what explanations can we offer as psychologists?

WEBSITES

http://psychclassics.yorku.ca/
  Large collection of articles and links on some of the most influential movements and theories throughout the history of psychology.
http://psychology.about.com/science/psychology/msubindex_beh.htm
  Behavioural psychology links.
http://ahpweb.org/
  Association for Humanistic Psychology homepage.
http://evolution.anthro.univie.ac.at/ishe/
  International Society for Human Ethology home page.
http://www.hud.ac.uk/hip/soccon/soccon.html
  Social constructionism links.

COURSEWORK

- Where does one start with the coursework report?
- What is the project brief and what does it look like?
- What is a psychological journal?
- What is "psychological literature"?
- How do other students present their introduction?
- How do I present the references?
- What items might I have forgotten to include in my report?
- How is the coursework marked?

The Coursework Report

Preparation: Design and Project Brief

Before beginning your study, you must fill in a project brief (see the form on the next page). The mark from this project brief forms part of your final A level mark. The aim of the project brief is to enable your teacher to check that your work is realistically planned and does not breach ethical guidelines. You may draw up a rough version of the project brief first and ask your teacher to comment on it so that you can improve it and maximise your final marks.

It may also be an idea, before starting the study, to consider the contents of the final report. You might write parts of the report beforehand as they may affect some of your design decisions. For example, the literature review may give you additional ideas for design considerations and the choice of statistical test may also influence your choice of method. The details of the report are considered next. Statistical matters are covered in Chapter 14, Statistical Tests.

The Report

Once you have conducted your study, the final stage of the coursework is to write the report. The mark scheme for this report is outlined on page 572. It is the report that gets the marks, so it is especially important to do this carefully. You are again permitted to hand in a rough draft to your teacher and you should take his or her feedback into account when preparing the final draft. You do not have to use a word processor/computer but it makes it much easier when preparing several drafts. It also assists in creating a good overall impression (and should improve your spelling).

The total length for the report should be approximately 2000 words, excluding tables, figures, graphs, and appendices. Reports that are too long will be penalised in sections C1 and H of the mark scheme. This maximum report length is partly for your own benefit (otherwise you might feel that you have to write a great deal to obtain high marks) and also because selectivity is an important skill to practise.

Psychological research

Psychologists publish their research in magazines that are called "journals". The intention of these journal reports is to inform other psychologists of new findings and to give an analysis of what these new findings mean. The journal reports must also provide sufficient detail of the research study so that other psychologists could, if they wanted, replicate the study to confirm the validity of the findings. The report you are going to write follows the format generally used in journal articles, which are also called "papers".

| GCE A2 Psychology A
Unit 6(PYA6) | Project Proposal
Brief Form |

Centre name: _____ **Centre no:** ☐☐☐☐☐

Candidate name: _____ **Candidate no:** ☐☐☐☐

Title of Work: _____ *12 marks in total*

PB1: Identify the aim of the research and state the experimental/alternative hypotheses. *(credited in the report mark scheme)*

PB2: Explain why a directional or a non-directional experimental/alternative hypothesis has been selected. *(1 mark)*

PB3: Identify the chosen research method [experimental, quasi-experimental, natural experiment, survey, observation or correlational research] and [if appropriate] the design used. *(1 mark)*

PB4: Evaluate the advantages and disadvantages of the chosen research method. *(2 marks)*

Project Brief Form continues overleaf

PB5: Identify potential sources of bias in the investigation and any possible confounding variables. *(2 marks)*

PB6: Explain what procedures will be adopted to deal with these. *(2 marks)*

PB7: Select an appropriate level of statistical significance to be reached before the experimental/alternative hypothesis will be retained. *(1 mark)*

PB8: Identify any relevant ethical issues and discuss the steps to be taken to deal with these. *(3 marks)*

Total mark
(12)

Candidates are reminded that in order to fulfil the requirements of the specification they must collect, pool, and analyse their data individually or in groups of 4 or fewer.

They are also reminded that the study described in the Project Brief must be one submitted for the coursework report.

Please note that you should access the AQA website for the official Project Proposal Brief form to fill in. You should not simply copy the form we provide here.

Your report should be divided into the sections outlined next. You can also include a table of contents. The title should be long enough to give the reader a clear idea about the topic under study. "Gender and behaviour" may be too vague, whereas "A study to investigate gender differences in the ways that boys and girls behave in the playground, including pro- and anti-social behaviours" is too lengthy. A suitable title might be "Gender and playground behaviour in primary age children".

Abstract

Invariably a journal article begins with a summary of the main points of the research study. This enables a reader to tell, at a glance, whether the article will be of interest to them. Your abstract should be about 150 words in length (if it is too long you may be penalised on criterion B). You should write this summary in full sentences but stick firmly to the key points. This should begin with the study aims, which might include the hypothesis. Next might be a brief description of the method used in the study, to include the participants and setting, plus the kind of design that was used (e.g., experiment or observation, repeated or independent measures, and so on). If you used named psychological tests or questionnaires, these should be mentioned. The third area to report is the findings. You may describe the findings and/or outline the statistical treatment(s) used, and their significance. Finally record your conclusion, plus any limitations or implications identified.

An example of an abstract is given here:

Craik and Lockhart's level of processing theory predicts that the more deeply a word is processed, the more likely it is to be remembered. This study set out to test this prediction by giving participants material that required different levels of processing: shallow (processing words in terms of case), phonetic (processing words in terms of rhyming), and semantic (processing words in terms of meaning). The study was experimental and a repeated measures design. Twenty female participants completed the questionnaire in silence during a school lesson. Comparisons between semantic and shallow processing were analysed using the Wilcoxon test and found to be significant at the $p < 0.05$ level. This suggests that memory is enhanced by deeper processing, as predicted by levels of processing theory. The theory has useful applications to student revision.

[130 words]

Introduction, aims, and hypothesis

The purpose of this part of the report is to identify the background to your study. The introduction should be about 600 words. Your intention should be to describe background research in such a way that it leads seamlessly into the aims of your study!

The background information is often described as the "psychological *literature*". This refers to the fact that research is published in books and journals. Ideally your introduction should start at a relatively broad level and quickly narrow down to examine two or three particularly relevant pieces of research. Once these studies are described it should seem obvious what the aims of your study are going to be. If you have described research into levels of processing theory it would seem strange to then state that you intend to investigate short-term memory. This is not a logical progression. Equally, if you describe a study and also identify the limitations in the research methodology of that study, it doesn't make sense to say you are intending to follow the same procedures. It would, however, make sense to say that you are going to attempt to conduct a similar study having made certain adjustments in the light of the criticisms mentioned.

An example of an introduction is given here:

Memory is one of the earliest areas to be studied in psychology, starting with Ebbinghaus' (1985/1913) study of forgetting. Other early research focused on the capacity and duration of different memory stores: sensory memory (which is equivalent to the eyes and ears), short-term memory, and long-term memory. Information comes to the sensory memory store through the senses and may either be forgotten or transferred to the STM. From there the memory may be forgotten, either because the memory trace disappears or because the material is displaced by newer material. Verbal rehearsal leads a memory to be transferred to long-term memory. This is called the multi-store model of memory as described by Atkinson and Shiffrin (1968).

Craik and Watkins (1973) found that when participants were asked to remember words from a list they could do this without verbal rehearsal. Instead if they elaborated the words this also led to enhanced recall. This led to levels of processing theory. Craik and Lockhart (1972) suggested that it is the kind of processes that are operating at the time of storing data that determine the extent to which something is remembered. They suggested that it is the depth of processing in terms of elaboration that creates a durable memory.

This theory was tested in an experiment by Craik and Tulving (1975). Participants were shown a list of words (five-letter concrete nouns such as "table") and were asked a question for each word. For each question the answer was "yes" or "no". The questions were one of three types: case (shallow processing), such as "Is the word in capital letters?"; rhyme (phonemic processing), such as "Does the word rhyme with 'able'?"; or sentence (semantic or deep processing), such as "Would the word fit in the sentence 'They met a ___ in the street'?" Craik and Tulving found that those words that had been processed semantically were recalled best and those processed phonemically were recalled second best.

Other research has further investigated how depth of processing can be achieved. For example organisation is a form of elaborative processing. Mandler (1967) showed that organisation alone led to durable memory. Participants were asked to sort 52 word cards into categories. When they had done this repeatedly they were given an unexpected test of memory and they were quite able to recall the words. The more categories they had used, the better their recall. This shows that deeper processing leads to long-term memory.

Another study showed that distinctiveness can also enhance memory. Eysenck and Eysenck (1980) arranged for participants to say words in a non-semantic, distinctive condition (e.g., pronouncing the "b" in "comb") or a non-semantic, non-distinctive condition (e.g., saying the word "comb" normally). There were also semantic distinctive and non-distinctive conditions where the words were also processed for meaning. Recall was almost as good in the non-semantic, distinctive condition as for the semantic conditions. This shows that distinctiveness can be as powerful as meaning in terms of enhancing memory for words.

The *aim of this study* is to replicate the original work by Craik and Tulving as a means of demonstrating the levels of processing theory. The same design will be followed as in the original study where all participants are given three conditions: case, phonemic, and semantic in order to see which condition leads to best recall. The original experiment involved an expected and unexpected test of recall as well, but these will not be included here. In line with the levels of processing theory, we would expect recall to be highest on the semantic condition and lowest on the case condition. Given the fact that previous research has found that the semantic condition is associated with higher memory, a directional hypothesis would be appropriate.

The hypothesis

- Experimental hypothesis 1: Participants recall more words in the semantic condition than in the case condition.
- Null hypothesis: There is no difference in recall between semantic and case conditions.
- Experimental hypothesis 2: Participants recall more words in the semantic condition than in the phonemic condition.
- Null hypothesis: There is no difference in recall between semantic and phonemic conditions.

[660 words]

One point that arises in this example is the issue of references. At the end of the report you are required to provide the full references for any studies cited in the report. The citation style given here is used throughout this textbook, i.e., name (date). It is, however, acceptable to use the following referencing system: name (as cited in Eysenck, 2006). If you use the latter style then, in the reference section, you need only list the full reference for Eysenck plus a list of all articles that you have referred to from this book. (See also page 568.)

A second point regards copying. It is tempting to use passages from a textbook or journal article when reporting the psychological literature. You may feel that the writer of the textbook manages to convey exactly what you want to say, and says it more clearly than you could express it. If you feel you cannot put it into your own words, present the material as a quotation from the textbook. Never copy chunks of material without due credit.

The aims must lead logically from the literature review and act like a buckle in joining the introduction to the hypothesis. The statement of the hypothesis must be clear, unambiguous, and operationalised. (See *Psychology for AS Level* for a discussion of hypotheses.)

Method

Here you are aiming to provide the reader with sufficient detail to replicate your study. This section should cover about 600 words and is typically subdivided into the following sections.

Design

Describe design decisions, such as your choice of method (e.g., experiment or observation, etc.). If it is an experiment then state whether it is a repeated or independent measures design, and the key variables. If it is an observation, you should carefully describe details of your observational techniques. If it is a correlational study, state the covariables.

Participants

State how many people were involved, plus any relevant demographic details such as age, educational background, and gender. Describe where the participants were tested or observed, and how the particular sample was selected (sampling techniques were described in *Psychology for AS Level*). Finally, where appropriate, you should explain how participants were allocated to conditions.

Apparatus/materials

Full details of any questionnaires or other materials should be placed in the appendix section of the report. You should name the measures that you used and say "See Appendix A". If you include a questionnaire, make sure you also include the means of scoring the questionnaire.

If you designed the stimulus material yourself, then you should explain how you did this. For example "we selected a list of 20 four-letter words to use as the words to be remembered. We avoided any unusual or distinctive words. The order of the word list was determined randomly."

Standardised procedures

You may place standardised instructions in the appendix, but in the main body of the report describe clearly and succinctly what you did.

Controls and ethics

You might mention any important controls or ethical decisions that were taken, although some of these have already been included in the project brief.

Results

There are three ways to illustrate your results:

1. *Raw data* are the numbers prior to any analysis. These should be placed in the appendices but a summary might be included in the results section.
2. *Descriptive statistics*, such as the use of measures of central tendency (mean, median, and mode) and/or spread (range or standard deviation), plus graphical representation. Descriptive statistics are vital for getting a feel for the data but don't overdo this. Select suitable methods of displaying your data so that one can see, at a glance, what was found in the study. Ensure that all descriptive statistics are labelled carefully.
3. *Statistical tests*. These enable you to determine whether your findings are significant. You must (a) state what test you are going to use, (b) justify your choice of statistical test, (c) record some details of the test calculations in the appendix, and (d) state the outcome of the statistical test and thus your conclusion regarding the significance of your results. We look at statistical tests and significance in Chapter 14, Statistical Tests.

The AQA A mark scheme (E1) requires the use of appropriate methods. This includes both descriptive and/or statistical tests as appropriate. If statistical tests are not appropriate then you must justify your decision not to use them. The mark scheme (E2) rewards clarity of presentation. (See page 572 for details.)

Discussion

The intention of the discussion section is to interpret the findings in terms of previous research, as mentioned in the introduction or with reference to other research. In addition, this is where the researcher reflects on the strengths and limitations of the study. The discussion section is worth 25% of the overall marks, so spend time getting this right. About 600 words is the right length for this part of the report.

The AQA A mark scheme (F) highlights four areas to include in your discussion. It seems a good idea to follow these clearly by using them as subheadings.

Explanation of findings

You are required to do more than state the significance of your results, which should have been done in the results section. The emphasis here is on an *explanation* of what you found. You might do this by relating your findings to your original aims. You might also note any findings that you did not anticipate.

Relationship to background research

Relate your findings to previous research. This is a reverse of the process at the start where the introduction led logically into the aims. Now you want to link your findings back to previous research. You might refer to studies mentioned in the beginning, although you will get little credit if you simply repeat the same material a second time. You may also wish to mention other research, in the light of your findings. You can refer to theory and/or other research studies.

Limitations and modifications

Select two or three important limitations and state how you might modify the problems. The limitations might refer to sampling procedures, design, lack of controls, procedures, and/or statistical treatments. Ensure that you do more than just state the problem by also explaining in what way it was a problem in this study.

What references did I use?

It saves a great deal of time if you keep a note of all the relevant details of *all* the literature you refer to, cite, or quote from. The information needed for journal articles includes the names and initials of authors, title of article and journal, page numbers, volume and issue numbers, and date of publication. If you used a book, then you need to note the names and initials of authors and/or editors, title of chapter and book, page numbers, edition number, date and place of publication, and name of publisher. If you use material from the internet include the URL and the date you accessed the material.

Page numbers of quotations are also useful.

Try setting up a card-index file, or start a database on your computer, and build it up as you go along.

Implications and suggestions

Could your findings be put to any practical use? Are there any theoretical implications not mentioned earlier? One or two ideas will be sufficient, including suggestions for future research.

References

The reason for full references is to provide the reader with the details of the original article or book if they wish to research the study/theory further themselves. Any named studies or theories in your report must be listed with full details in the reference section of your report. You can follow the same style as used in the reference section of this textbook.

There is an alternative style that is acceptable. This is to state the details of a textbook, and list all the studies you have cited from this book. This means that anyone who would like to follow up one of your references is still able to locate the exact reference and the article.

Appendices

You may include details of materials and/or questionnaires, standardised instructions, raw data, and statistical tests in the appendices. The material in the appendices is not included in the word length for the report.

CHAPTER SUMMARY
The Coursework Report

❖ You must conduct one research study, either on your own or in a small group (four or fewer).

❖ For the study you must individually present a project brief and write a report of not more than 2000 words (not including appendices).

❖ This report follows the format used in journal articles and includes the sections listed below.

❖ Abstract:

— About 150 words, including the basic details of the study: aims, methods, results, and conclusions.

❖ Introduction:

— About 600 words, covering background theory and relevant research, leading logically into the study's aims
— This should not be a general essay but must be relevant and selective.

❖ Aims and hypotheses:

— The aims should explain your area of investigation and justify the direction of the hypothesis.
— Hypotheses should be stated unambiguously (operationalised) and in a way that permits them to be tested. Include both the alternative and the null hypothesis.

❖ Method:

— This section should also be about 600 words.
— The main intention is to provide sufficient detail to permit full replication of your study.
— You should cover design, participants, materials/apparatus, procedures, controls, and ethical considerations. (Stimulus materials, observation checklists, questionnaires, and standardised instructions should be placed in the appendices.)

What are the coursework requirements?

Sections in the coursework report

❖ Results:

— This section should include a summary of the raw data, descriptive statistics, and the interpretation of a statistical test. (Any raw data and calculations should be placed in the appendices.)

• Discussion:

— A discussion of your study should be about 600 words.
— It should include an explanation of the findings, relationship to background research, limitations and modifications, and implications and suggestions.

• The report should also include references and appendices.

FURTHER READING

An example report is included in the *Teacher's Guide* published by AQA. Some useful sources for coursework ideas are C. Flanagan (1998) *Practicals for psychology* (London: Routledge), and McIlveen et al. (2002) *BPS manual of psychology practicals* (Exeter, UK: BPS).

WEBSITES

www/aqa.org.uk
  Access to the AQA A specifications for psychology and other information from the examination board.
www.a-levelpsychology.co.uk
  Psychology Press site with useful exam material and book details. You can also access *A-Level Psychology Online*, a web-based eLearning resource for A-Level Psychology students, which includes sample coursework.

A checklist for your report

Done	Abstract	Drafted	Done
☐	1. Have you stated what you are studying?	☐	☐
	2. Have you mentioned the aim/hypothesis?	☐	☐
	3. Have you described the essentials of the method?	☐	☐
	4. Have you given some details about the participants and where the research was conducted?	☐	☐
	5. What did you discover? Give a statement of your results.	☐	☐
	6. Who cares (seriously!)? What is the importance of your research?	☐	☐

Done	Introduction	Drafted	Done
☐	1. Have you referred to some theory?	☐	☐
	2. Have you described one or two relevant studies but no more than five?	☐	☐
	3. Is the literature logically linked to the aims?	☐	☐

Done	Aims and hypothesis	Drafted	Done
☐	1. Why have you studied this topic? Have you stated your aims?	☐	☐
	2. Have you justified the direction of the hypothesis?	☐	☐
	3. Have you stated an unambiguous alternate hypothesis?	☐	☐
	4. Have you stated whether the hypothesis is directional or non-directional?	☐	☐
	5. Have you stated a null hypothesis?	☐	☐
	6. Have you given the desired level of significance?	☐	☐

Done	Method	Drafted	Done
☐	1. Have you stated the research design?	☐	☐
	2. Have you explained why each design decision was chosen?	☐	☐
	3. If you are conducting an experiment, have you stated the experimental and control conditions?	☐	☐
	4. If you are conducting an observation, have you described the method you used?	☐	☐
	5. Have you stated the IV and DV, or covariables (for a correlational study)?	☐	☐
	6. Have you explained any controls you used? And why?	☐	☐
	7. Have you mentioned ethical considerations?	☐	☐

Continued over

Done	**Method** *continued*	Drafted	Done
☐	8. Have you mentioned all researchers involved?	☐	☐
	9. Have you described the participants and the population from which they were drawn?	☐	☐
	10. Have you stated how the participants were selected and allocated to conditions?	☐	☐
	11. Have you described the design of all apparatus and materials that you used (in the appendix)?	☐	☐
	12. Have you included specimens of apparatus and materials that you used (in the appendix)?	☐	☐
	13. Have you included the "mark schemes" for any tests or questionnaires?	☐	☐
	14. Have you described your exact procedures?	☐	☐
	15. Have you described or included standardised instructions given to subjects?	☐	☐
	16. Have you given sufficient detail for someone else to replicate your study?	☐	☐

Done	**Results**	Drafted	Done
☐	1. Have you given a summary table of raw data (in the appendix)?	☐	☐
	2. Have you provided descriptive statistics for your data (e.g., mean, bar chart, or scattergram)?	☐	☐
	3. Have you labelled axes on graphs, columns on data tables, and given clear titles?	☐	☐
	4. Have you justified your choice (or lack of) statistical test?	☐	☐
	5. Have you included any calculations (in the appendix)?	☐	☐
	6. Does your statement of conclusion contain details of the level of significance, the critical and observed values, degrees of freedom, whether the hypothesis was directional or non-directional, and whether it was accepted or rejected?	☐	☐
	7. Have you stated the conclusion in terms of the original hypothesis?	☐	☐

Done	**Discussion**	Drafted	Done
☐	1. Have you explained your results?	☐	☐
	2. Have you stated what your results mean in relation to your hypothesis?	☐	☐
	3. Do you refer back to your introduction?	☐	☐
	4. Have you compared your results with those of other studies?	☐	☐
	5. What was wrong (or right) about your design and methods?	☐	☐
	6. Are any of the criticisms presented without a good explanation?	☐	☐
	7. How would you improve the study if you were to do it again?	☐	☐
	8. Have you included any ideas for follow-up studies?	☐	☐

Done	**References**	Drafted	Done
☐	1. Have you included all references mentioned?	☐	☐
	2. Have you followed the correct form for presenting references?	☐	☐

Done	**Appendices**	Drafted	Done
☐	1. Are these clearly labelled and well set out?	☐	☐

Done	**Report style**	Drafted	Done
☐	1. Have you checked your spelling?	☐	☐
	2. Is your project in a folder that can be easily opened?	☐	☐
	3. Is your project shorter than 2000 words? If not, then cut it.	☐	☐

Summary of the coursework mark scheme

A1 Implementation: Candidate's contribution

3	By an individual. Original design/adaptation
2	By a small group
1	With teacher support
0	No student input

A2 Implementation: Design decisions

3	Appropriate and competent
2	Appropriate, minor exceptions
1	Weakly applied
0	Inappropriate

B Abstract

3	Covers aims/methods/results/conclusions
2	Fair, lacking clarity or conciseness
1	Poor
0	None or inappropriate

C1 Psychological literature

5	Relevant, carefully selected
4	Relevant, carefully selected but some omissions
3	Lacking selectivity
2	Important omissions
1	Minimal support
0	No support

C2 Aims/hypothesis: Formulation

3	Clear, logical progression
2	Easily testable, quite specific
1	Lacking clarity or difficult to test
0	Incorrect/missing

C3 Aims/hypothesis: Statement

2	Some logical progression
1	Partial/inadequate progression
0	No logical progression

D Reporting of method

4	Full replicatiion
3	Reasonable, sufficient detail for replication
2	Difficult, lacking detail
1	Very difficult, fundamental omissions
0	Replication extremely difficult, information lacking

E1 Results: Techniques

4	Appropriate, fully justified, significance given/explained
3	Substantially appropriate, justification doesn't refer to data
2	Partially appropriate/justified, significance given
1	Minimal use/justification, inappropriate significance
0	Inappropriate/absent

F2 Results: Presentation

4	Precise and clear
3	Precise and clear, with minor exceptions
2	Some deficiencies
1	Serious deficiencies
0	Irrelevant/incorrect

F1 Discussion: Explanation of findings

3	Appropriate, coherent
2	Appropriate, coherent with minor exceptions
1	Inappropriate/lacking coherence
0	None made/irrelevant

F2 Discussion: Background research/theory

3	Thorough discussion
2	Reasonably coherent
1	Limited
0	None/irrelevant/incorrect

F3 Discussion: Limitations and modifications

3	Most mentioned and appropriate
2	Some limitations and modifications
1	Occasional limitations/modifications
0	None/inappropriate

F4 Discussion: Implications and suggestions

3	Appropriate, discussed thoroughly
2	Some, discussed reasonably coherently
1	Occasional/limited
0	None/irrelevant

G References

2	Full
1	Incomplete
0	None

H Report style

3	Concisely written, logical, good quality of language
2	Scientific style and logical structure evident, adequate expression of ideas and language
1	Lacked logical structure and scientific basis, poor expression of ideas and language
0	Little psychological basis

Maximum total is 48 marks + 12 marks for the project brief = 60 marks

COURSEWORK

- What is the difference between descriptive statistics and statistical tests?
- How do I decide whether to use a one-tailed or two-tailed test?
- How do I know if my results are "significant"?
- When can you reject the null hypothesis?
- What level of significance is the most stringent?
- When do you use a test of difference?
- Which difference tests should be used?
- What test should I use if I am investigating an association or correlation between two sets of scores?
- How can I write a justification of this choice?
- What is the difference between the "observed value" and the "critical value"?

Statistical Tests

For your coursework you need to be able to know how to select and use statistical tests and interpret the results of these tests. There are just five tests you need to cover: Mann-Whitney, Wilcoxon, sign, chi-squared, and Spearman's tests. You will not be examined on this material in the AQA A examination.

Descriptive Statistics and Statistical Tests

Descriptive statistics give us convenient and easily understood summaries of what we have found. However, to have a clearer idea of what our findings mean, it is generally necessary to carry out one or more **statistical tests**.

Test of difference, association, or correlation?

The first step in choosing an appropriate statistical test is to decide whether your data were obtained from an experiment in which some aspect of the situation (the independent variable) was manipulated in order to observe its effects on the dependent variable. If so, you need a **test of difference**. On the other hand, if you simply have two observations from each of your participants in a non-experimental design, then you need a **test of association** or **correlation**.

One-tailed or two-tailed test?

In using a statistical test, you need to take account of the alternative hypothesis. If you predicted the direction of any effects (e.g., loud noise will disrupt learning and memory), then you have a **directional hypothesis**, which should be evaluated by a one-tailed test. If you did not predict the direction of any effects (e.g., loud noise will affect learning and memory), then you have a **non-directional hypothesis**, which should be evaluated by a two-tailed test.

KEY TERMS

Statistical tests: various formulae that enable you to analyse and compare data produced in research studies. A statistical test produces a statistic that can then be assessed, using tables of significance, to see if the data fit or do not fit the hypothesis.

Test of difference: a type of statistical test where two sets of data are compared to see if they differ significantly.

Test of association: a type of statistical test where a calculation is made to see how closely pairs of data vary together, i.e., how closely they are associated or correlated.

Correlation: an association that is found between two variables.

Directional hypothesis: a prediction that there will be a difference or correlation between the two variables *and* a statement of the direction of this difference.

Non-directional hypothesis: a prediction that there will be a difference or correlation between two variables, but no statement about the direction of the difference.

Nominal

Ordinal

Interval

Ratio

Level of precision

Another factor to consider when deciding which statistical test to use is the type of data you have obtained. There are four types of data, of increasing levels of precision:

- **Nominal data**: the data consist of the numbers of participants falling into various categories (e.g., fat, thin; men, women).
- **Ordinal data**: the data can be ordered from lowest to highest (e.g., the finishing positions of athletes in a race).
- **Interval data**: the data differ from ordinal data, because the units of measurement are fixed throughout the range; for example, there is the same "distance" between a height of 1.82 metres and 1.70 metres as between a height of 1.70 metres and one of 1.58 metres.
- **Ratio data**: the data have the same characteristics as interval data, with the exception that they have a meaningful zero point; for example, time measurements provide ratio data because the notion of zero time is meaningful, and 10 seconds is twice as long as 5 seconds. The similarities between interval and ratio data are so great that they are sometimes combined and referred to as interval/ratio data.

Statistical Significance

So far we have discussed some of the issues that influence the choice of statistical test. Shortly we will consider how to conduct such tests, but first we should look at the meaning of **statistical significance**. What happens after we have chosen a statistical test, and analysed our data, and want to interpret our findings? We use the results of the test to choose between the following:

- Null hypothesis, which asserts that there is no difference between conditions (e.g., loud noise has no effect on learning)
- Alternative hypothesis (e.g., loud noise disrupts learning).

If the statistical test indicates that there is only a small probability of the difference between conditions (e.g., loud noise vs. no noise) having occurred *if the null hypothesis were true*, then we reject the null hypothesis in favour of the alternative hypothesis.

Why do we focus initially on the null hypothesis rather than the alternative hypothesis? The reason is that the alternative hypothesis is rather imprecise.

KEY TERMS

Nominal data: data consisting of the numbers of participants falling into qualitatively different categories.
Ordinal data: data that can be ordered from smallest to largest.
Interval data: data is measured using units of equal intervals; the intervals reflect a real difference.
Ratio data: as interval data, but with a meaningful zero point.
Statistical significance: the level at which the decision is made to reject the null hypothesis in favour of the experimental hypothesis.

It may state that loud noise will disrupt learning, but it does not indicate the *extent* of the disruption. This imprecision makes it hard to evaluate an alternative hypothesis directly. In contrast, a null hypothesis such as loud noise has no effect on learning *is* precise, and this precision allows us to use statistical tests to decide the probability that it is correct.

Psychologists generally use the 5% (i.e., five out of one hundred, shown as 0.05) level of statistical significance. What this means is that the null hypothesis is rejected (and the alternative hypothesis is accepted) if the probability that the results were due to chance alone is 5% or less. This is often expressed as $p = 0.05$, where p = the probability of the result if the null hypothesis is true. If the statistical test indicates that the findings do not reach the 5% (or $p = 0.05$) level of statistical significance, then we retain the null hypothesis, and reject the alternative hypothesis. The key decision is whether or not to reject the null hypothesis and that is why the 0.05 level of statistical significance is so important. However, our data sometimes indicate that the null hypothesis can be rejected with greater confidence, say, at the 1% (i.e., one out of one hundred, shown as 0.01) level. If the null hypothesis can be rejected at the 1% level, it is customary to state that the findings are highly significant. In general terms, you should state the precise level of statistical significance of your findings, whether it is the 5% level, the 1% level, or whatever.

These procedures may seem easy. In fact, there are two errors that may occur when reaching a conclusion on the basis of the results of a statistical test:

- **Type I error:** we may reject the null hypothesis in favour of the alternative hypothesis even though the findings are actually due to chance; the probability of this happening is given by the level of statistical significance that is selected.
- **Type II error:** we may retain the null hypothesis even though the alternative hypothesis is actually correct.

It would be possible to reduce the likelihood of a Type I error by using a more stringent level of significance. For example, if we used the 1% ($p = 0.01$) level of significance, this would greatly reduce the probability of a Type I error. However, use of a more stringent level of significance increases the probability of a Type II

> **■ Activity: Devising hypotheses**
> Devise suitable null and alternative hypotheses for the following:
>
> - An investigator considers the effect of noise on students' ability to concentrate and complete a word-grid. One group only is subjected to the noise in the form of a distractor, i.e., a television programme.
> - An investigator explores the view that there might be a link between the amount of television children watch and their behaviour at school.

> **From percentage to decimal**
>
> | | |
> |---|---|
> | 10% | = 0.10 |
> | 5% | = 0.05 |
> | 1% | = 0.01 |
> | 2.5% | = 0.025 |
> | 0.01% | = 0.001 |
>
> - To go from decimal to percentage, multiply by 100: move the decimal point two places to the right.
> - To go from percentage to decimal, divide by 100: move the decimal point two places to the left.

KEY TERMS

Type I error: mistakenly rejecting the null hypothesis in favour of the experimental hypothesis when the results are actually due to chance.
Type II error: mistakenly retaining the null hypothesis when the experimental hypothesis is actually correct.

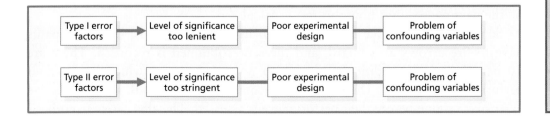

error. We could reduce the probability of a Type II error by using a less stringent level of significance, such as the 10% ($p = 0.10$) level. However, this would increase the probability of a Type I error. These considerations help to make it clear why most psychologists favour the 5% (or $p = 0.05$) level of significance: it allows the probabilities of both Type I and Type II errors to remain reasonably low.

Psychologists generally use the 5% level of significance. However, they would use the 1% or even the 0.1% (i.e., one out of one thousand, shown as 0.001) level of significance if it were very important to avoid making a Type I error. For example, clinical psychologists might require very strong evidence that a new form of therapy was more effective than existing forms of therapy before starting to use it on a regular basis. The 1% or 0.1% level of statistical significance is also used when the alternative hypothesis seems improbable. For example, very few people would accept that telepathy had been proved to exist on the basis of a single study in which the results were only just significant at the 5% level!

Tests of Difference

Here, we will consider those statistical tests that are applicable when we are interested in deciding whether the differences between two conditions or groups are significant. As was discussed in your AS level studies, there are three kinds of design that can be used when we want to compare two conditions:

- The independent groups design, in which each participant is allocated to one and only one condition
- The repeated measures design, in which the same participants are used in both conditions
- The matched participants (matched pairs) design, in which the participants in the two conditions are matched on a one-to-one basis in terms of some variable or variables that might be relevant (e.g., intelligence, age).

When deciding which statistical test to use, it is very important to take account of the particular kind of experimental design that was used.

- If the independent design has been used, then the Mann-Whitney U test is the appropriate test to use.
- If the repeated measures or matched participants design has been used, then the sign test or the Wilcoxon matched pairs signed ranks test is the appropriate test to use.

Mann-Whitney U test

The Mann-Whitney U test can be used when an independent design has been used, and the data are either ordinal or interval. The worked example in the box on the next page shows how this test is calculated.

Suppose that we have two conditions. In both conditions, the participants have to fire arrows at a board, and the score obtained is recorded. There are 10 participants in condition A, in which no training is provided before their performance is assessed. There are 12 participants in condition B, and they receive extensive training before their performance is assessed. The alternative hypothesis

Mann-Whitney U test: A worked example

Alternative hypothesis: Extensive training improves performance

Null hypothesis: Training has no effect on performance

Participant	Condition A	Rank	Participant	Condition B	Rank
1	4	2	1	21	15
2	10	9	2	26	18
3	12	11	3	20	14
4	28	20	4	22	16
5	7	5	5	32	22
6	13	13	6	5	3
7	12	11	7	12	11
8	2	1	8	6	4
9	9	7.5	9	8	6
10	27	19	10	24	17
			11	21	
			12	9	7.5

Smaller sample = condition A

Sum of ranks in smaller sample (T) = 98.5

Number of participants in smaller sample (N_A) = 10

Number of participants in larger sample (N_B) = 12

Formula: $U = N_A N_B + \left(\dfrac{N_A(N_A+1)}{2} \right) - T$

Example: $U = (10 \times 12) + \left(\dfrac{10(10+1)}{2} \right) - 98.5 = 76.5$

Formula for calculating U': $U' = N_A N_B - U$

Example: $U' = (10 \times 12) - 76.5 = 43.5$

Comparing U and U', U' is the smaller value. The calculated value of U' (43.5) is checked against the tabled value for a one-tailed test at 5%.

Table values

	$N_A = 10$
$N_B = 12$	34

Conclusion: As 43.5 is greater than 34, the null hypothesis should be retained—i.e., training has no effect on performance in this task.

The appropriate tables of significance for the Mann-Whitney test can be found on pages 594–595.

is that extensive training would improve performance; in other words, the scores in condition B should be significantly higher than those in condition A.

The first step is to rank all of the scores from both groups together, with a rank of 1 being given to the smallest score, a rank of 2 to the second smallest score, and so on. If there are tied scores, then the mean of the ranks involved is given to each of the tied participants. For example, two participants were tied for the 7th and 8th ranks, and so they both received a rank of 7.5.

The second step is to work out the sum of the ranks in the smaller sample, which is condition A in our example. This value is known as T, and it is 98.5 in the example.

The third step is to calculate U from the formula, in which N_A is the number of participants in the smaller sample and N_B is the number in the larger sample:

$$U = N_A N_B + \left(\frac{N_A(N_A + 1)}{2} \right) - T$$

The fourth step is to calculate U' (U prime):

$$U' = N_A N_B - U$$

The fifth step is to compare U and U', selecting whichever is the smaller value provided that the results are in the correct direction. The smaller value (i.e., 43.5) is then looked up in Table 1 in Appendix A (see bottom table on page 595). Here, we have a one-tailed test, because the alternative hypothesis stated that extensive training would improve performance. With 10 participants in our first condition and 12 in our second condition, the tabled value for significance on a one-tailed test at 0.05 is 34. The observed value must be equal to, or smaller than, the tabled value in order to be significant. As our value of 43.5 is greater than 34, the conclusion is that we retain the null hypothesis. The presence of ties reduces the accuracy of the tables, but the effect is small unless there are several ties.

Sign test

The sign test can be used when a repeated measures or matched participants design has been used, and the data are ordinal. If the data are interval or ratio, then it would be more appropriate to use the Wilcoxon matched pairs signed ranks test. The worked example in the box on the next page illustrates the way in which the sign test is calculated.

Suppose that there were 12 participants in an experiment. In condition A these participants were presented with 20 words to learn in a situation with no noise; learning was followed 5 minutes later by a test of free recall in which they wrote down as many words as they could remember in any order. Condition B involved presenting 20 different words to learn in a situation of loud noise; as in condition A, learning was followed 5 minutes later by a test of free recall. The experimenter predicted that free recall would be higher in the no-noise condition. Thus, there was a directional hypothesis.

In order to calculate the sign test it is necessary first of all to draw up a table like the one in the example, in which each participant's scores in condition A and in condition B are recorded. Each participant whose score in condition A is greater than his or her score in condition B is given a plus sign (+) in the sign column, and each participant whose score in condition B is greater than his or her score in condition A is given a minus sign (−) in the sign column. Each participant whose scores in both conditions are the same receives a 0 sign in the sign column. Such participants are ignored in the subsequent calculations, and they do not contribute to N (the number of paired scores), as they provide no evidence about the direction of any effect.

In the example, there are eight plus signs, two minus signs, and two participants had the same scores in both conditions. If we ignore the two participants with the same scores in both conditions, this gives us N = 10. Now

Sign test: A worked example

Alternative hypothesis: Free recall is better when learning takes place in the absence of noise than in its presence.
Null hypothesis: Free recall is not affected by whether or not noise is present during learning.

Participant	Condition A (no noise)	Condition B (loud noise)	Sign
1	12	8	+
2	10	10	0
3	7	8	−
4	12	11	+
5	8	3	+
6	10	10	0
7	13	7	+
8	8	9	−
9	14	10	+
10	11	9	+
11	15	12	+
12	11	10	+

Number of + signs = 8
Number of − signs = 2
Number of 0 signs = 2
Number of participants with differing scores (N) = 8 + 2 = 10
Number of participants with less frequent sign (S) = 2
Question: Is the value of S in this example the same as or lower than the tabled value for S?

Table values

	5%
N=10	S=1

Conclusion: In this experiment the value of S is higher than the tabled value, when N = 10. The null hypothesis (that noise has no effect on learning and memory) cannot be rejected.

The appropriate table of significance for the sign test can be found on page 596.

all we need to do is to work out the number of these 10 participants having the less frequently occurring sign; this value is known as S. In terms of our example, S = 2. We can refer to the relevant table (Table 2 in Appendix A, see page 596) with N = 10 and S = 2. The obtained value for S must be the same as or lower than the value for S given in the table. The tabled value for a one-tailed test is 1. Thus, our obtained S value of 2 is not significant at the 5% level on a one-tailed test. We therefore conclude that we cannot reject the null hypothesis that noise has no effect on learning and memory.

The sign test is ideal to use if the data are nominal or ordinal as it analyses at a very basic level, e.g., in a race it can tell you that "John beat Peter". It can also be used with interval or ratio data, but, as it only gives a crude analysis, these data would be better applied to the Wilcoxon test, which can give a more sophisticated analysis, e.g., "John beat Peter by 2 seconds."

? Compare this result with that gained from using the Wilcoxon test. How can you explain this apparent contradiction?

Wilcoxon matched pairs signed ranks test

The Wilcoxon matched pairs signed ranks test can be used when a repeated measures or matched participants design has been used, and the data are at least ordinal. This test or the sign test can be used if the data are ordinal or interval. However, the Wilcoxon matched pairs signed ranks test uses more of the information obtained from a study, and so is usually more sensitive and useful than the sign test.

The worked example in the box on the next page uses the data from the sign test. The first step is to place all the data in a table in which each participant's two scores are in the same row. The second step is to subtract the condition B score from the condition A score for each participant. The third step is to omit all the participants whose two scores are the same, i.e., d = 0. The fourth step is to rank all the difference scores obtained in the second step from 1 for the smallest difference, to 2 for the second smallest difference, and so on. For this purpose, ignore the + and − signs, thus taking the absolute size of the difference. The fifth step is to add up the sum of the positive ranks (50 in the example) and separately to add up the sum of the negative ranks (5 in the example). The smaller of these values is T, which in this case is 5. The sixth step is to work out the number of participants whose two scores are not the same, i.e., d ≠ 0. In the example, N = 10.

The obtained value of T must be the same as, or less than, the tabled value (see Table 3 in Appendix A, on page 597) in order for the results to be significant. The tabled value for a one-tailed test and N = 10 is 11 at the 5% level of statistical significance, and it is 5 at the 1% level. Thus, the findings are significant at the 1% level on a one-tailed test. The null hypothesis is rejected in favour of the alternative hypothesis that free recall is better when learning takes place in the absence of noise than in its presence ($p = 0.01$). The presence of ties means that

---

Wilcoxon matched pairs signed ranks test: A worked example

Alternative hypothesis: Free recall is better when learning takes place in the absence of noise than in its presence.
Null hypothesis: Free recall is not affected by whether or not noise is present during learning.

Participant	Condition A (no noise)	Condition B (loud noise)	Difference (d) (A − B)	Rank
1	12	8	4	7.5
2	10	10	0	—
3	7	8	−1	2.5
4	12	11	1	2.5
5	8	3	5	9
6	10	10	0	—
7	13	7	6	10
8	8	9	−1	2.5
9	14	10	4	7.5
10	11	9	2	5
11	15	12	3	6
12	11	10	1	2.5

Sum of positive ranks (7.5 + 2.5 + 9 + 10 + 7.5 + 5 + 6 + 2.5) = 50
Sum of negative ranks (2.5 + 2.5) = 5
Smaller value (5) = T
Number of participants who scored differently in condition A and B, N = 10
Question: For the results to be significant, the value of T must be the same as, or less than, the tabled value.

Table values

	5%	1%
N = 10	11	5

Conclusion: In this experiment T is less than the tabled value at the 5% level and the same as the tabled value at the 1% level of significance, so the null hypothesis is rejected in favour of the alternative hypothesis.

The appropriate table of significance for the Wilcoxon test can be found on page 597.

the tables are not completely accurate, but this does not matter provided that there are only a few ties.

You may be wondering how it is possible for the same data to produce a significant finding on a Wilcoxon test but not on a sign test. Does this indicate that statistics are useless? Not at all. The sign test is insensitive (or lacking in power) because it takes no account of the *size* of each individual's difference in free recall in the two conditions. It is because this information is made use of in the Wilcoxon test that a significant result was obtained using that test. Thus, the Wilcoxon test has more power than the sign test to detect differences between two conditions. This means that the Wilcoxon test is more likely than the sign test to show a significant difference where one exists.

Studies Using Correlational Analysis

In the case of studies using correlational analysis, the data are in the form of two measures of behaviour from each member of a single group of participants. What is often done is to present the data in the form of a **scattergraph** (also known as a scattergram). It is given this name, because it shows the ways in which the scores of individuals are scattered.

Spearman's rho

Suppose that we have scores on two variables from each of our participants, and we want to see whether there is an association or correlation between the two sets of scores. This can be done by using a test known as Spearman's rho, provided that the data are at least ordinal. Spearman's rho or r_s indicates the strength of the association. If r_s is $+1.0$, then there is a perfect positive correlation between the two variables. If r_s is -1.0, then there is a perfect negative correlation between the two variables. If r_s is 0.0, then there is generally no relationship between the two variables. The working of this test is shown in the box on the next page.

An experimenter collects information about the amount of television violence seen in the past month and about the amount of aggressive behaviour exhibited in the past month from 12 participants. She predicts that there will be a positive association between these two variables, i.e., those participants who have seen the most television violence (variable A) will tend to be the most aggressive (variable B). In other words, there is a directional hypothesis.

The first step is to draw up a table in which each participant's scores for the two variables are placed in the same row.

The second step is to rank all the scores for variable A. A rank of 1 is assigned to the smallest score, a rank of 2 to the second smallest score, and so on up to 12. What do we do if there are tied scores? In the example, participants 9 and 12 had the same score for variable A. The ranks that they are competing for are ranks 5 and 6. What is done is to take the average or mean of the ranks at issue: $(5 + 6)/2 = 5.5$.

The third step is to rank all the scores for variable B, with a rank of 1 being assigned to the smallest score. Participants 6, 7, 9, and 11 are all tied, with the ranks at issue being ranks 4, 5, 6, and 7. The mean rank will be $(4 + 5 + 6 + 7)/4 = 5.5$.

A positive correlation:
The taller the player,
the higher the score.

A negative correlation:
The more time spent
playing computer games,
the less time spent
studying.

No correlation:
Where there is no
relationship, variables
are uncorrelated.

KEY TERM

Scattergraph:
two-dimensional representation of all the participants' scores in a correlational study; also known as a scattergram.

Spearman's rho: A worked example

Alternative hypothesis: There is a positive association between amount of television violence watched and aggressive behaviour.

Null hypothesis: There is no association between amount of television violence watched and aggressive behaviour.

Participant	TV violence seen (hours)	Aggressive behaviour (out of 10)	Rank A	Rank B	Difference d	d²
1	17	8	7.5	9	−1.50	2.25
2	6	3	2	2	0.00	0.00
3	23	9	10	10.5	−0.50	0.25
4	17	7	7.5	8	−0.50	0.25
5	2	2	1	1	0.00	0.00
6	20	6	9	5.5	+3.50	12.25
7	12	6	4	5.5	−1.50	2.25
8	31	10	12	12	0.00	0.00
9	14	6	5.5	5.5	0.00	0.00
10	26	9	11	10.5	+0.50	0.25
11	9	6	3	5.5	−2.50	6.25
12	14	4	5.5	3	+2.50	6.25

Sum of squared difference scores $(\Sigma d^2) = 30$

Number of participants $(N) = 12$

Formula: $rho = 1 - \dfrac{(\Sigma d^2 \times 6)}{N(N^2 - 1)}$

Example: $1 - \dfrac{(30 \times 6)}{12(143)} = 1 - 0.105 = +0.895$

Is the value of rho (+0.895) as great as, or greater than the tabled value?

Table values

	0.05 level	0.01 level	0.005 level
N = 12	+0.503	+0.671	+0.727

Conclusion: Null hypothesis rejected in favour of alternative hypothesis, i.e., there is a positive correlation between the amount of television violence watched and aggressive behaviour $(p = 0.005)$.

The appropriate table of significance for the Spearman's rho test can be found on page 598.

The fourth step is to calculate the difference between the two ranks obtained by each individual, with the rank for variable B being subtracted from the rank for variable A. This produces 12 difference (d) scores.

The fifth step is to square all of the d scores obtained in the fourth step. This produces 12 squared difference (d²) scores.

The sixth step is to add up all of the d² scores in order to obtain the sum of the squared difference scores. This is known as Σd^2, and comes to 30 in the example.

The seventh step is to work out the number of participants. In the example, the number of participants (N) is 12.

The eighth step is to calculate rho from the following formula:

$$\text{rho} = 1 - \frac{(\sum d^2 \times 6)}{N(N^2 - 1)}$$

Note that the "6" in the equation is always present, and is a feature of the Spearman's rho formula.

In the example, this becomes

$$1 - \frac{(30 \times 6)}{12(143)} = 1 - 0.105 = +0.895$$

The ninth and final step is to work out the significance of the value of rho by referring the result to the table (see Table 4 in Appendix A, on page 598). The obtained value must be as great as, or greater than, the tabled value. The tabled value for a one-tailed test with N = 12 is +0.503 at the 0.05 level; it is +0.671 at the 0.01 level; and it is +0.727 at the 0.005 level. Thus, it can be concluded that the null hypothesis should be rejected in favour of the alternative hypothesis that there is a positive correlation between the amount of television violence watched and aggressive behaviour ($p = 0.005$).

An important point about Spearman's rho is that the statistical significance of the obtained value of rho depends very heavily on the number of participants. For example, the tabled value for significance at the 0.05 level on a one-tailed test is +0.564 if there are 10 participants. However, it is only +0.306 if there are 30 participants. In practical terms, this means that it is very hard to obtain a significant correlation with Spearman's rho if the number of participants is low.

Why is it a good idea to have a reasonable number of participants in a correlational study?

Test of association

The **chi-squared test** is a test of association. (It is also a test of difference, but it is used as a test of association with which we are concerned here.) It is used when we have nominal data in the form of frequencies, and when each and every observation is independent of all the other observations. For example, suppose that we are interested in the association between eating patterns and cholesterol level. We could divide people into those having a healthy diet with relatively little fat and those having an unhealthy diet. We could also divide them into those having a fairly high level of cholesterol and those having a low level of cholesterol. In essence, the chi-squared test tells us whether membership of a given category on one dimension (e.g., unhealthy diet) is associated with membership of a given category on the other dimension (e.g., high cholesterol level).

In the worked example (see the box on the next page) we will assume that we have data from 186 individuals with an unhealthy diet, and from 128 individuals with a healthy diet. Of those with an unhealthy diet, 116 have a high cholesterol level and 70 have a low cholesterol level. Of those with a healthy diet, 41 have a high cholesterol level and 87 have a low cholesterol level. Our alternative hypothesis is that there is an association between healthiness of diet and low cholesterol level.

The first step is to arrange the frequency data in a 2 × 2 "contingency table" as in the example, with the row and column totals included. The second step is to work out what the four frequencies would be if there were no association at all

KEY TERM

Chi-squared test: a statistical test of association that is used with nominal data in the form of frequencies.

Test of association: Chi-squared test: A worked example

Alternative hypothesis: There is an association between healthiness of diet and low cholesterol level.

Null hypothesis: There is no association between healthiness of diet and low cholesterol level.

Contingency table:

	Healthy diet	Unhealthy diet	Row total
High cholesterol	41	116	157
Low cholesterol	87	70	157
Column total	128	186	314

Expected frequency if there were no association:

Formula: $= \dfrac{\text{row total} \times \text{column total}}{\text{expected frequency}} = \text{overall total}$

	Healthy diet	Unhealthy diet	Row total
High cholesterol	64	93	157
Low cholesterol	64	93	157
Column total	128	186	314

Calculating chi-squared statistic (χ^2):

Formula: $\chi^2 = \sum \dfrac{(|O - E| - \frac{1}{2})^2}{E} = 26.7$

Note: Correction factor $\left(-\frac{1}{2}\right)$ is only used where there are two rows and two columns.

Category	Observed	Expected	$|O-E|$	$\dfrac{(|O-E| - \frac{1}{2})^2}{E}$
Healthy, high cholesterol	41	64	23	7.91
Unhealthy, high cholesterol	116	93	23	5.44
Healthy, low cholesterol	87	64	23	7.91
Unhealthy, low cholesterol	70	93	23	5.44
				26.70

Calculating degrees of freedom:

Formula: (no. of rows − 1) × (no. of columns −1) = degrees of freedom (2 − 1) × (2 − 1) = 1

Compare chi-squared statistic with tabled values:

Table values

	0.025 level	0.005 level	0.0005 level
df = 1	3.84	6.64	10.83

Question: Is the observed chi-squared value of 26.70 and one degree of freedom the same as or greater than the tabled value?

Conclusion: The chi-squared value is greater than the tabled value, so the null hypothesis can be rejected, and the alternative hypothesis, that there is an association between healthiness of diet and cholesterol level, accepted.

The appropriate table of significance for the chi-squared test can be found on page 599.

between diet and cholesterol levels. The expected frequency (by chance alone) in each case is given by the following formula:

$$\text{expected frequency} = \frac{\text{row total} \times \text{column total}}{\text{overall total}}$$

For example, the expected frequency for the number of participants having a healthy diet and high cholesterol is 157×128 divided by 314, which comes to 64. The four expected frequencies (those expected by chance alone) are also shown in the worked example.

The third step is to apply the following formula to the observed (O) and expected (E) frequencies in each of the four categories:

$$\frac{(|O-E|-\frac{1}{2})^2}{E}$$

In the formula, |O − E| means that the difference between the observed and the expected frequency should be taken, and it should then have a + sign put in front of it regardless of the direction of the difference. The correction factor (i.e., $-\frac{1}{2}$) is only used when there are two rows and two columns.

The fourth step is to add together the four values obtained in the third step in order to provide the chi-squared statistic, shown as χ^2. This is $7.91 + 5.44 + 7.91 + 5.44 = 26.70$.

The fifth step is to calculate the number of "degrees of freedom" (*df*). This is given by:

(the number of rows − 1) × (the number of columns − 1)

For this we need to refer back to the contingency table. In the example, this is $1 \times 1 = 1$. Why is there one degree of freedom? Once we know the row and column totals, then only one of the four observed values is free to vary. Thus, for example, knowing that the row totals are 157 and 157, the column totals are 128 and 186, and the number of participants having a healthy diet and high cholesterol is 41, we can complete the entire table. In other words, the number of degrees of freedom corresponds to the number of values that are free to vary.

The sixth step is to compare the tabled values in Table 5 in Appendix A (see page 599) with chi-square = 26.70 and one degree of freedom. The observed value needs to be the same as, or greater than, the tabled value for a one-tailed test in order for the results to be significant.

The tabled value for a one-tailed test with *df* = 1 is 3.84 at the 0.025 level, 6.64 at the 0.005 level, and 10.83 at the 0.0005 level. Thus, we can reject the null hypothesis, and conclude that there is an association between healthiness of diet and cholesterol level ($p = 0.0005$).

It is easy to use the chi-squared test wrongly. According to Robson (1994), "There are probably more inappropriate and incorrect uses of the chi-squared test than of all the other statistical tests put together." In order to avoid using the chi-squared test wrongly, it is important to make use of the following rules:

- Ensure that every observation is independent of every other observation; in other words, each individual should be counted only once and in only *one* category.

> As vertical lines denote absolute values, "|O − E|" is the difference between these values disregarding the sign. Whether it is 3−5 or 5−3, the difference is always a positive number, i.e., 2 in this case.

- Make sure that each observation is included in the appropriate category; it is not permitted to omit some of the observations (e.g., those from individuals with intermediate levels of cholesterol).
- The total sample should exceed 20; otherwise, the chi-squared test as described here is not applicable. More precisely, the minimum expected frequency should be at least 5 in every cell of the table.
- The significance level of a chi-squared test is assessed by consulting the one-tailed values in Table 5 in Appendix A if a specific form of association has been predicted and that form was obtained. However, the two-tailed values should always be consulted if there are more than two categories on either dimension.
- Remember that showing there is an association is not the same as showing that there is a causal effect; for example, the association between a healthy diet and low cholesterol does not demonstrate that a healthy diet *causes* low cholesterol.

Using an Inferential Test for Your Coursework

Choosing a test

The box below summarises the reasons for choosing each test, and thus gives you the necessary information for justifying your choice of test.

Selecting a suitable statistical test

If you wish to see if there is a *difference* between one set of data and another, you need a test of difference. Your choice of test depends on the level of measurement; whether the data are measured at the nominal or ordinal/interval level, and whether the groups of data are independent or related.

If you wish to find out whether pairs of variables are associated or *correlated*, then you need a test of correlation. The test you should use is Spearman's rho or chi-squared test depending on the level of measurement.

	Difference test		Correlational test
Level of measurement	Independent data	Related data (obtained from repeated measures and matched pairs designs)	
Nominal	Chi-squared test	Sign test	Chi-squared test
Ordinal and interval	Mann-Whitney U test	Wilcoxon matched pairs signed ranks	Spearman's rho

Note: this chart deals only with the statistical tests described in this chapter, even though other tests do exist.

Justifying your choice of test

For the purposes of your coursework report you need to explain why you choose a particular test. For example, if you have conducted a study where you are seeking to determine whether there are differences between two independent groups of participants then you might state:

In order to assess the significance of these findings it was necessary to use a statistical test. In this study an appropriate test would be a Mann-Whitney U test because (1) a test of differences was required, (2) the design was independent measures, and (3) the data were at least at an ordinal level.

Calculating the observed value

The next step is to perform the calculations. You may do this with a computer program or you may follow the instructions in this chapter. Either way you must include some details of the calculations in the appendix of your coursework report. The outcome of a statistical test is a number, called the **observed value.**

Using a table of significance

In order to determine whether this observed value is significant we consult an appropriate table of significance. These are located in Appendix A, and instructions about how to use each table are included. A comparison between the **critical value** in the table and your own observed value enables you decide whether you can accept or reject the null hypothesis.

Reporting the result

The final step is to record the outcome of this whole process. You should include the following information in your final statement: details of the level of significance, the critical and observed values, degrees of freedom, whether the hypothesis was directional or non-directional, and whether it was accepted or rejected. For example:

For 10 participants, the critical value for rho is 0.504 at the 5% level of significance ($p < 0.05$, one-tailed). As the observed value of rho is 0.703, this is greater than the critical value and so there is less than a 5% probability that the result is due to chance. The null hypothesis can be rejected and the alternate hypothesis accepted.

> **KEY TERMS**
> **Observed value:** the numerical value calculated when using a statistical test. The observed value is compared with the critical value to determine significance.
> **Critical value:** numerical values found in statistical tables that are used to determine the significance of the observed value produced by a statistical test.

> Descriptive statistics are discussed in *Psychology for AS Level* by the same author.

CHAPTER SUMMARY
Statistical Tests

❖ When we have obtained scores from a group of participants, we can summarise our data using descriptive statistics.

❖ We also can determine the significance of the result(s) using a statistical test.

Descriptive statistics and statistical tests

❖ A test of difference is used when data are obtained from a study in which an independent variable was manipulated to observe its effects.

❖ A test of correlation is used when the data from the study are in the form of scores on two response variables from every participant.

Determining the appropriate statistical test

❖ If the alternative hypothesis predicts the direction of effects (a directional hypothesis), then a one-tailed test should be used.

❖ Otherwise, a two-tailed test should be used (for a non-directional hypothesis).

Levels of precision

❖ There are four types of data of increasing levels of precision:

— Nominal
— Ordinal
— Interval
— Ratio.

Statistical significance

❖ The meaningfulness of research findings is determined through statistical significance.

❖ If the statistical test indicates that there is only a small probability of the difference between conditions (e.g., loud noise vs. no noise) having occurred if the null hypothesis were true, then we reject the null hypothesis in favour of the alternative hypothesis.

❖ Psychologists generally use the 5% level of statistical significance. This produces fairly small probabilities of the following errors:

— Type I error: incorrectly rejecting the null hypothesis in favour of the alternative hypothesis
— Type II error: incorrectly retaining the null hypothesis.

Tests of difference

❖ The Mann-Whitney U test is the appropriate test of difference if an independent design has been used.

❖ The sign test can be used when a repeated measures or matched participants design has been used and the data are nominal or ordinal.

❖ The same is true of the Wilcoxon matched pairs signed ranks test, except that the data must be at least ordinal.

Studies using correlational analysis

❖ Spearman's rho test:

— The correlation between two sets of scores can be calculated by means of Spearman's rho test, provided that the data are at least ordinal.

❖ The chi-squared test:

— This is used when we have nominal data in the form of frequencies, and when each and every observation is independent of all the other observations.
— All the expected frequencies should be five or more.
— Finding an association is not the same as showing the existence of a causal effect.

Using statistical tests in coursework

❖ When using a statistical test in your coursework you must follow five steps:

1. Select a suitable test.
2. Justify the choice of test.
3. Perform the necessary calculations.
4. Consult a table of significance to determine if the observed value is significant.
5. Report the significance of your findings.

FURTHER READING

These topics are covered in greater depth by A. Searle (1999) *Introducing research and data in psychology* (London: Routledge), written specifically for AQA A students. There is detailed but user-friendly coverage of the topics discussed in this Section in H. Coolican (1999) *Research methods and statistics in psychology (3rd Edn.)* (London: Hodder & Stoughton). A shorter version of the Coolican textbook is H. Coolican (1995) *Introduction to research methods and statistics in psychology* (London: Hodder & Stoughton).

APPENDIX A

Tables of Significance

Remember that decisions based on statistical tests are open to error, but if you follow the standard procedures outlined in the chapter on Statistical Tests the potential for errors can be minimised. Try to be as unbiased as possible, and try not to assume too much about the results in advance.

How to Use the Tables

In the Mann-Whitney U test (on pages 594–595), use the smaller value of U and U′ to look up the critical value of U for a one- or two-tailed test, as appropriate, at 0.05, initially (bottom and top tables, page 595). If the tabled value is equal to or less than your value at that level, the null hypothesis is retained; if it is greater than your value, it is rejected and your experimental hypothesis is proved.

In the sign test (on page 596), look up the critical value of S for a one- or two-tailed test, as appropriate, for N, the number of participants with differing scores, at 0.05, initially. If the tabled value is equal to or less than your value at that level, the null hypothesis is retained; if it is greater than your value, it is rejected and your experimental hypothesis is proved.

In the Wilcoxon test (on page 597), look up the critical value of T for a one- or two-tailed test, as appropriate, for N, the number of participants with differing scores, at 0.05, initially. If the tabled value is equal to or less than your value at that level, the null hypothesis is retained; if it is greater than your value, it is rejected and your experimental hypothesis is proved.

In the Spearman's rho test (on page 598), look up the critical value of rs for a one- or two-tailed test, as appropriate, for N, the number of participants, at 0.05, initially. If the tabled value is greater than or equal to your value at that level, the null hypothesis is retained; if it is less than your value, it is rejected and your experimental hypothesis is proved.

In the chi-squared test (on page 599), look up the critical value of chi-squared (also shown as χ^2) for a one- or two-tailed test, as appropriate, for df, the degrees of freedom, at 0.05, initially. If the tabled value is greater than or equal to your value at that level, the null hypothesis is retained; if it is less than your value, it is rejected and your experimental hypothesis is proved.

Table 1: Mann-Whitney U test

Critical values of U for a one-tailed test at 0.005; two-tailed test at 0.01*

N_B \ N_A	1	2	3	4	5	6	7	8	9	10	11	12	13	14	15	16	17	18	19	20
1	—	—	—	—	—	—	—	—	—	—	—	—	—	—	—	—	—	—	—	—
2	—	—	—	—	—	—	—	—	—	—	—	—	—	—	—	—	—	—	0	0
3	—	—	—	—	—	—	—	—	0	0	0	1	1	1	2	2	2	2	3	3
4	—	—	—	—	—	0	0	1	1	2	2	3	3	4	5	5	6	6	7	8
5	—	—	—	—	0	1	1	2	3	4	5	6	7	7	8	9	10	11	12	13
6	—	—	—	0	1	2	3	4	5	6	7	9	10	11	12	13	15	16	17	18
7	—	—	—	0	1	3	4	6	7	9	10	12	13	15	16	18	19	21	22	24
8	—	—	—	1	2	4	6	7	9	11	13	15	17	18	20	22	24	26	28	30
9	—	—	0	1	3	5	7	9	11	13	16	18	20	22	24	27	29	31	33	36
10	—	—	0	2	4	6	9	11	13	16	18	21	24	26	29	31	34	37	39	42
11	—	—	0	2	5	7	10	13	16	18	21	24	27	30	33	36	39	42	45	48
12	—	—	1	3	6	9	12	15	18	21	24	27	31	34	37	41	44	47	51	54
13	—	—	1	3	7	10	13	17	20	24	27	31	34	38	42	45	49	53	56	60
14	—	—	1	4	7	11	15	18	22	26	30	34	38	42	46	50	54	58	63	67
15	—	—	2	5	8	12	16	20	24	29	33	37	42	46	51	55	60	64	69	73
16	—	—	2	5	9	13	18	22	27	31	36	41	45	50	55	60	65	70	74	79
17	—	—	2	6	10	15	19	24	29	34	39	44	49	54	60	65	70	75	81	86
18	—	—	2	6	11	16	21	26	31	37	42	47	53	58	64	70	75	81	87	92
19	—	0	3	7	12	17	22	28	33	39	45	51	56	63	69	74	81	87	93	99
20	—	0	3	8	13	18	24	30	36	42	48	54	60	67	73	79	86	92	99	105

*Dashes in the body of the table indicate that no decision is possible at the stated level of significance.
For any N_A and N_B the observed value of U is significant at a given level of significance if it is *equal* to or *less* than the critical values shown.

Source: R. Runyon and A. Haber (1976), *Fundamentals of behavioural statistics (3rd Edn.)*. Reading, MA: McGraw-Hill, Inc. With the kind permission of the publisher.

Critical values of U for a one-tailed test at 0.01; two-tailed test at 0.02*

N_B \ N_A	1	2	3	4	5	6	7	8	9	10	11	12	13	14	15	16	17	18	19	20
1	—	—	—	—	—	—	—	—	—	—	—	—	—	—	—	—	—	—	—	—
2	—	—	—	—	—	—	—	—	—	—	—	—	0	0	0	0	0	0	1	1
3	—	—	—	—	—	—	0	0	1	1	1	2	2	2	3	3	4	4	4	5
4	—	—	—	—	0	1	1	2	3	3	4	5	5	6	7	7	8	9	9	10
5	—	—	—	0	1	2	3	4	5	6	7	8	9	10	11	12	13	14	15	16
6	—	—	—	1	2	3	4	6	7	8	9	11	12	13	15	16	18	19	20	22
7	—	—	0	1	3	4	6	7	9	11	12	14	16	17	19	21	23	24	26	28
8	—	—	0	2	4	6	7	9	11	13	15	17	20	22	24	26	28	30	32	34
9	—	—	1	3	5	7	9	11	14	16	18	21	23	26	28	31	33	36	38	40
10	—	—	1	3	6	8	11	13	16	19	22	24	27	30	33	36	38	41	44	47
11	—	—	1	4	7	9	12	15	18	22	25	28	31	34	37	41	44	47	50	53
12	—	—	2	5	8	11	14	17	21	24	28	31	35	38	42	46	49	53	56	60
13	—	0	2	5	9	12	16	20	23	27	31	35	39	43	47	51	55	59	63	67
14	—	0	2	6	10	13	17	22	26	30	34	38	43	47	51	56	60	65	69	73
15	—	0	3	7	11	15	19	24	28	33	37	42	47	51	56	61	66	70	75	80
16	—	0	3	7	12	16	21	26	31	36	41	46	51	56	61	66	71	76	82	87
17	—	0	4	8	13	18	23	28	33	38	44	49	55	60	66	71	77	82	88	93
18	—	0	4	9	14	19	24	30	36	41	47	53	59	65	70	76	82	88	94	100
19	—	1	4	9	15	20	26	32	38	44	50	56	63	69	75	82	88	94	101	107
20	—	1	5	10	16	22	28	34	40	47	53	60	67	73	80	87	93	100	107	114

*Dashes in the body of the table indicate that no decision is possible at the stated level of significance.
For any N_A and N_B the observed value of U is significant at a given level of significance if it is *equal* to or *less* than the critical values shown.

Source: R. Runyon and A. Haber (1976), *Fundamentals of behavioural statistics (3rd Edn.)*. Reading, MA: McGraw-Hill, Inc. With the kind permission of the publisher.

Critical values of U for a one-tailed test at 0.025; two-tailed test at 0.05*

N_B	1	2	3	4	5	6	7	8	9	10	11	12	13	14	15	16	17	18	19	20
1	—	—	—	—	—	—	—	—	—	—	—	—	—	—	—	—	—	—	—	—
2	—	—	—	—	—	—	—	0	0	0	0	1	1	1	1	1	2	2	2	2
3	—	—	—	—	0	1	1	2	2	3	3	4	4	5	5	6	6	7	7	8
4	—	—	—	0	1	2	3	4	4	5	6	7	8	9	10	11	11	12	13	13
5	—	—	0	1	2	3	5	6	7	8	9	11	12	13	14	15	17	18	19	20
6	—	—	1	2	3	5	6	8	10	11	13	14	16	17	19	21	22	24	25	27
7	—	—	1	3	5	6	8	10	12	14	16	18	20	22	24	26	28	30	32	34
8	—	0	2	4	6	8	10	13	15	17	19	22	24	26	29	31	34	36	38	41
9	—	0	2	4	7	10	12	15	17	20	23	26	28	31	34	37	39	42	45	48
10	—	0	3	5	8	11	14	17	20	23	26	29	33	36	39	42	45	48	52	55
11	—	0	3	6	9	13	16	19	23	26	30	33	37	40	44	47	51	55	58	62
12	—	1	4	7	11	14	18	22	26	29	33	37	41	45	49	53	57	61	65	69
13	—	1	4	8	12	16	20	24	28	33	37	41	45	50	54	59	63	67	72	76
14	—	1	5	9	13	17	22	26	31	36	40	45	50	55	59	64	67	74	78	83
15	—	1	5	10	14	19	24	29	34	39	44	49	54	59	64	70	75	80	85	90
16	—	1	6	11	15	21	26	31	37	42	47	53	59	64	70	75	81	86	92	98
17	—	2	6	11	17	22	28	34	39	45	51	57	63	67	75	81	87	93	99	105
18	—	2	7	12	18	24	30	36	42	48	55	61	67	74	80	86	93	99	106	112
19	—	2	7	13	19	25	32	38	45	52	58	65	72	78	85	92	99	106	113	119
20	—	2	8	13	20	27	34	41	48	55	62	69	76	83	90	98	105	112	119	127

(N_A across the top)

*Dashes in the body of the table indicate that no decision is possible at the stated level of significance.

For any N_A and N_B the observed value of U is significant at a given level of significance if it is *equal* to or *less* than the critical values shown.

Source: R. Runyon and A. Haber (1976), *Fundamentals of behavioural statistics (3rd Edn.)*. Reading, MA: McGraw-Hill, Inc. With the kind permission of the publisher.

Critical values of U for a one-tailed test at 0.05; two-tailed test at 0.10*

N_B	1	2	3	4	5	6	7	8	9	10	11	12	13	14	15	16	17	18	19	20
1	—	—	—	—	—	—	—	—	—	—	—	—	—	—	—	—	—	—	0	0
2	—	—	—	—	0	0	0	1	1	1	1	2	2	2	3	3	3	4	4	4
3	—	—	0	0	1	2	2	3	3	4	5	5	6	7	7	8	9	9	10	11
4	—	—	0	1	2	3	4	5	6	7	8	9	10	11	12	14	15	16	17	18
5	—	0	1	2	4	5	6	8	9	11	12	13	15	16	18	19	20	22	23	25
6	—	0	2	3	5	7	8	10	12	14	16	17	19	21	23	25	26	28	30	32
7	—	0	2	4	6	8	11	13	15	17	19	21	24	26	28	30	33	35	37	39
8	—	1	3	5	8	10	13	15	18	20	23	26	28	31	33	36	39	41	44	47
9	—	1	3	6	9	12	15	18	21	24	27	30	33	36	39	42	45	48	51	54
10	—	1	4	7	11	14	17	20	24	27	31	34	37	41	44	48	51	55	58	62
11	—	1	5	8	12	16	19	23	27	31	34	38	42	46	50	54	57	61	65	69
12	—	2	5	9	13	17	21	26	30	34	38	42	47	51	55	60	64	68	72	77
13	—	2	6	10	15	19	24	28	33	37	42	47	51	56	61	65	70	75	80	84
14	—	2	7	11	16	21	26	31	36	41	46	51	56	61	66	71	77	82	87	92
15	—	3	7	12	18	23	28	33	39	44	50	55	61	66	72	77	83	88	94	100
16	—	3	8	14	19	25	30	36	42	48	54	60	65	71	77	83	89	95	101	107
17	—	3	9	15	20	26	33	39	45	51	57	64	70	77	83	89	96	102	109	115
18	—	4	9	16	22	28	35	41	48	55	61	68	75	82	88	95	102	109	116	123
19	0	4	10	17	23	30	37	44	51	58	65	72	80	87	94	101	109	116	123	130
20	0	4	11	18	25	32	39	47	54	62	69	77	84	92	100	107	115	123	130	138

(N_A across the top)

*Dashes in the body of the table indicate that no decision is possible at the stated level of significance.

For any N_A and N_B the observed value of U is significant at a given level of significance if it is *equal* to or *less* than the critical values shown.

Source: R. Runyon and A. Haber (1976), *Fundamentals of behavioural statistics (3rd Edn.)*. Reading, MA: McGraw-Hill, Inc. With the kind permission of the publisher.

Table 2: Sign test

N	Level of significance for one-tailed test				
	0.05	0.025	0.01	0.005	0.0005
	Level of significance for two-tailed test				
	0.10	0.05	0.02	0.01	0.001
5	0	—	—	—	—
6	0	0	—	—	—
7	0	0	0	—	—
8	1	0	0	0	—
9	1	1	0	0	—
10	1	1	0	0	—
11	2	1	1	0	0
12	2	2	1	1	0
13	3	2	1	1	0
14	3	2	2	1	0
15	3	3	2	2	1
16	4	3	2	2	1
17	4	4	3	2	1
18	5	4	3	3	1
19	5	4	4	3	2
20	5	5	4	3	2
25	7	7	6	5	4
30	10	9	8	7	5
35	12	11	10	9	7

Calculated S must be *equal* to or *less* than the table (critical) value for significance at the level shown.

Source: F. Clegg (1982), *Simple statistics.* Cambridge University Press. With the kind permission of the publisher.

Table 3: Wilcoxon signed ranks test

Sample size	Levels of significance			
	One-tailed test			
	0.05	0.025	0.01	0.001
	Two-tailed test			
	0.1	0.05	0.02	0.002
$N = 5$	$T \leq 0$			
6	2	0		
7	3	2	0	
8	5	3	1	
9	8	5	3	
10	11	8	5	0
11	13	10	7	1
12	17	13	9	2
13	21	17	12	4
14	25	21	15	6
15	30	25	19	8
16	35	29	23	11
17	41	34	27	14
18	47	40	32	18
19	53	46	37	21
20	60	52	43	26
21	67	58	49	30
22	75	65	55	35
23	83	73	62	40
24	91	81	69	45
25	100	89	76	51
26	110	98	84	58
27	119	107	92	64
28	130	116	101	71
29	141	125	111	78
30	151	137	120	86
31	163	147	130	94
32	175	159	140	103
33	187	170	151	112

Calculated T must be *equal* to or *less* than the table (critical) value for significance at the level shown.

Source: R. Meddis (1975b), *Statistical handbook for non-statisticians*. London: McGraw-Hill. With the kind permission of the publisher.

Table 4: Spearman's rho test

	Level of significance for two-tailed test			
	0.10	0.05	0.02	0.01
	Level of significance for one-tailed test			
	0.05	0.025	0.01	0.005
N = 4	1.000			
5	0.900	1.000	1.000	
6	0.829	0.886	0.943	1.000
7	0.714	0.786	0.893	0.929
8	0.643	0.738	0.833	0.881
9	0.600	0.700	0.783	0.833
10	0.564	0.648	0.745	0.794
11	0.536	0.618	0.709	0.755
12	0.503	0.587	0.671	0.727
13	0.484	0.560	0.648	0.703
14	0.464	0.538	0.566	0.675
15	0.443	0.521	0.604	0.654
16	0.429	0.503	0.582	0.635
17	0.414	0.485	0.566	0.615
18	0.401	0.472	0.550	0.600
19	0.391	0.460	0.535	0.584
20	0.380	0.447	0.520	0.570
21	0.370	0.435	0.508	0.556
22	0.361	0.425	0.496	0.544
23	0.353	0.415	0.486	0.532
24	0.344	0.406	0.476	0.521
25	0.337	0.398	0.466	0.511
26	0.331	0.390	0.457	0.501
27	0.324	0.382	0.448	0.491
28	0.317	0.375	0.440	0.483
29	0.312	0.368	0.433	0.475
30	0.306	0.362	0.425	0.467

For n > 30, the significance of r_s can be tested by using the formula:

$$t = r_s \sqrt{\frac{n-2}{1-r_s^2}} \quad df = n - 2$$

and checking the value of t.

Calculated r_s must *equal* or *exceed* the table (critical) value for significance at the level shown.

Source: J.H. Zhar (1972), Significance testing of the Spearman rank correlation coefficient. *Journal of the American Statistical Association, 67*, 578–580. With the kind permission of the publisher.

Table 5: Chi-squared test

	Level of significance for one-tailed test					
	0.10	0.05	0.025	0.01	0.005	0.0005
	Level of significance for two-tailed test					
df	0.20	0.10	0.05	0.02	0.01	0.001
1	1.64	2.71	3.84	5.41	6.64	10.83
2	3.22	4.60	5.99	7.82	9.21	13.82
3	4.64	6.25	7.82	9.84	11.34	16.27
4	5.99	7.78	9.49	11.67	13.28	18.46
5	7.29	9.24	11.07	13.39	15.09	20.52
6	8.56	10.64	12.59	15.03	16.81	22.46
7	9.80	12.02	14.07	16.62	18.48	24.32
8	11.03	13.36	15.51	18.17	20.09	26.12
9	12.24	14.68	16.92	19.68	21.67	27.88
10	13.44	15.99	18.31	21.16	23.21	29.59
11	14.63	17.28	19.68	22.62	24.72	31.26
12	15.81	18.55	21.03	24.05	26.22	32.91
13	16.98	19.81	22.36	25.47	27.69	34.53
14	18.15	21.06	23.68	26.87	29.14	36.12
15	19.31	22.31	25.00	28.26	30.58	37.70
16	20.46	23.54	26.30	29.63	32.00	39.29
17	21.62	24.77	27.59	31.00	33.41	40.75
18	22.76	25.99	28.87	32.35	34.80	42.31
19	23.90	27.20	30.14	33.69	36.19	43.82
20	25.04	28.41	31.41	35.02	37.57	45.32
21	26.17	29.62	32.67	36.34	38.93	46.80
22	27.30	30.81	33.92	37.66	40.29	48.27
23	28.43	32.01	35.17	38.97	41.64	49.73
24	29.55	33.20	36.42	40.27	42.98	51.18
25	30.68	34.38	37.65	41.57	44.31	52.62
26	31.80	35.56	38.88	42.86	45.64	54.05
27	32.91	36.74	40.11	44.14	46.96	55.48
28	34.03	37.92	41.34	45.42	48.28	56.89
29	35.14	39.09	42.69	46.69	49.59	58.30
30	36.25	40.26	43.77	43.49	50.89	59.70
32	38.47	42.59	46.19	50.49	53.49	62.49
34	40.68	44.90	48.60	53.00	56.06	65.25
36	42.88	47.21	51.00	55.49	58.62	67.99
38	45.08	49.51	53.38	57.97	61.16	70.70
40	47.27	51.81	55.76	60.44	63.69	73.40
44	51.64	56.37	60.48	65.34	68.71	78.75
48	55.99	60.91	65.17	70.20	73.68	84.04
52	60.33	65.42	69.83	75.02	78.62	89.27
56	64.66	69.92	74.47	79.82	83.51	94.46
60	68.97	74.40	79.08	84.58	88.38	99.61

Calculated value of χ^2 must *equal* or *exceed* the table (critical) value for significance at the level shown.

Abridged from R.A. Fisher and F. Yates (1974), *Statistical tables for biological, agricultural and medical research (6th Edn.)*. Harlow, UK: Addison Wesley Longman.

APPENDIX B

Approaches in Psychology: Sample Questions and Answers

By Linda Fletcher (formerly at Brighton, Hove, and Sussex Sixth Form College)

Many students find Section C Perspectives: "Approaches in Psychology" a particularly challenging section of the Unit 5 synoptic paper. It can sometimes be difficult to apply your knowledge of the various approaches to the stimulus material in the question. To help illustrate this, we have provided a sample question and worked answer for each of the five main approaches covered in this book.

The questions are similar to those you might expect to see in the exam; however, in order to emphasise the application of each individual approach, we have amended section (a). This will usually ask you to describe how the behaviour in the stimulus material can be explained by **two** approaches, although these worked answers focus on explaining the behaviour of the **one** approach being addressed.

Please note that although these questions and answers have been written by an experienced A-level teacher, they have not been endorsed by AQA-A.

The Biological Approach

Question

Bungee jumping has become an increasingly popular with the age group 18 to 35. Although more males take part than females, it is not an exclusively male activity.

(a) Describe how one approach might try to explain why such
    people bunjee jump. (6 marks)
(b) Assess this explanation of bungee jumping in terms of its
    strengths and limitations. (6 marks)
(c) How would this approach investigate bungee jumping? (6 marks)
(d) Evaluate the use of this method of investigating bungee jumping. (6 marks)

Answer

(a) The physiological explanation (part of the biological approach) would explain bungee jumping in terms of the functioning of biological systems. One theory concerns the arousal system and suggests there is an optimal level of arousal (OLA), too little and people become bored, too much and they become stressed. People's OLA, however, varies and a group with high OLA, e.g., sensation seekers, would find bungee jumping presented the OLA for them. H. Eysenck's work supports this idea and suggests that there are two main personality types based on biology: introverts with high cortical arousal and extraverts with low cortical arousal. Extraverts seek more arousal and so this group would be more likely to bungee jump. Another part of the nervous system might be activated in bungee jumping releasing neurotransmitters and neuromodulators. This may lead to endorphins being produced, which result in a natural "high". Another aspect of the biological approach is evolutionary theory and in particular mating behaviour. Bungee jumping displays confidence and strength, which can be seen as important traits for females selecting males. This may account for there being more male bungee jumpers than female.

(b) Clearly we are influenced by our physiology and this may have a determining influence on our personality and our choices in life. If a male is tall and slim, he is more likely to choose to play basketball than rugby, but other cognitive factors (parental pressure) may make him choose rugby after all. Similarly peer pressure rather than high OLAs or extraversion may make people bungee jump. Determinist arguments imply people have no choice and so no responsibility for their actions, their biology makes it inevitable that they will bungee jump. This approach does allow for experimental research to take place, arousal can be measured, and extraversion tested (though there are some problems with the validity of these measures), and cause and effect argued. It is a reductionist explanation, reducing complex human behaviour to the action of neurotransmitters etc., and may be useful to some extent (explaining why extraverts are more likely to jump), but it is important not to reject other factors. People may think bungee jumping will improve their confidence or they may do it because their brother did. This explanation also ignores socio-cultural factors, which may explain the recent increase in bungee jumping.

(c) You could investigate this explanation by setting up a quasi-experiment with an independent groups design. Group A would consist of bungee jumpers and group B participants (Ps) who were not. This would be the independent variable. The groups should be similar in terms of gender and age. The dependent variables (DV) would be levels of arousal measured by the Necker cube test or galvanic skin response (GSR) and Eysenck's extraversion test. A Mann-Whitney U test could be used to see if there was a significant difference between the two groups on each of these DVs.

(d) Because this is a quasi-experiment, cause and effect could only be argued cautiously, since lots of variables like past experiences have not been controlled. Some of the control group may just not have had the opportunity to bungee jump for instance. Ps could not be randomly assigned to the two groups. There may also be a problem with the validity of the measurements in that the Necker cube fluctuations are difficult to explain to Ps and also difficult to record accurately. Similarly GSR may be measuring anxiety about the experiment not a general level of arousal and any personality test depends on the honesty of the P when answering the questions. It would also be important that Ps were not aware of the hypothesis so only outline consent would need to be gained beforehand. This means that thorough debriefing should take place afterwards with the option to withdraw data if the P wishes.

632 words in answer

The Behavioural Approach

Question

Tom is 7 years old and whilst he behaves well at school he is disobedient and demanding at home. His parents find it difficult to invite friends round and his sisters resent the time that is spent on him.

(a) Describe how one approach might try to explain Tom's behaviour. (6 marks)

(b) Assess this explanation of Tom's behaviour in terms of its strengths and limitations. (6 marks)

(c) How would this approach investigate behaviour like Tom's? (6 marks)

(d) Evaluate the use of this method of investigating behaviour like Tom's. (6 marks)

Answer

(a) The behaviourist approach might try to explain the starting of Tom's behaviour in terms of Social Learning Theory (SLT). Tom has observed others being rewarded with attention for disobedient behaviour, perhaps on the TV, and has decided to imitate. The behaviour is continued because his parents reacted to his disobedience with attention, which was rewarding or positively reinforced. This developed into a pattern of operant conditioning (OC) whereby positively reinforced behaviour is repeated. His sisters' obvious resentment may also have acted as a reward and reinforced the disobedient behaviour.

(b) The behaviourist explanation of Tom's disobedient behaviour is useful in that there is plenty of evidence from research that behaviour can be learned through OC. However, much of this research has been done on animals (e.g., Skinner's rats) and may not be so appropriate when applied to Tom's human behaviour. Research evidence for SLT has been based on children (e.g., Bandura's Bobo doll), but with humans it is difficult to assess how much of the behaviour may be due to demand characteristics rather than observational learning. The children in this study may have behaved aggressively because they thought that was what the experimenters wanted them to do (demand characteristics). So while behaviourist explanations may have scientific backing, they do ignore the other possibilities that may be the cause; for example a traumatic experience (Tom may have been bullied) or faulty cognitions (Tom thinks being shouted at is a sign of affection). They tend to forget that people talk to each other and this has a marked influence on human behaviour. Therapies based on OC and SLT, however, have proved successful to some extent, which is support for this approach.

(c) Behaviourists would investigate behaviour like Tom's by setting up a laboratory (lab.) experiment. First they would decide whether to look at OC or SLT. For SLT a suitable alternative hypothesis might be that there will be a higher level of disobedient behaviour from those viewing the rewarded or positively reinforced disobedient behaviour. They would collect a sample of children similar in age to Tom (both genders) and bring them to the lab. Participants (Ps) would be randomly assigned to the two groups. The experimenters would show them a video of a child being disobedient.

Some would see the version where the disobedient child is rewarded with attention and another group where s/he is not. The two versions would be the independent variable. The design is independent groups. Next, the children would be assessed for disobedient behaviour with observers using a pre-planned event sampling grid of disobedient behaviours. The assessments would be the dependent variable (DV). The difference in the DV between the two groups would be analysed using the Mann-Whitney U test to see if they were significant and whether the hypothesis could be supported.

(d) Several problems arise with using a lab. experiment. First there are individual differences between the children in the groups (e.g., one group having more disobedient children than the other) so a preliminary test for disobedience is needed, then the children could be matched, turning the design into a matched pairs one. Disobedient behaviour is rather subjective and may be difficult to measure accurately. It may be that having watched the "rewarded" version, children may think they are expected to behave more disobediently and so the experimenters are measuring demand characteristics rather than real effects. The artificial nature of the experiment may also lead to unnatural behaviour. Some qualitative feedback would be useful to clarify this.

There are also ethical problems in that if the hypothesis is correct then the experimenters have caused children to become more disobedient. Informed consent should also be gained from parents, which may be difficult to obtain.

617 words in answer

The Psychodynamic Approach

Question

Kim is very aggressive, but not in a physical way more in a verbal way. At Junior school she upset her friends with blunt comments and later became bitingly sarcastic, which was appreciated by everyone except the person who received the comment.

(a) Describe how **one** approach might try to explain Kim's sarcasm.   (6 marks)
(b) Assess this explanation of Kim's sarcasm in terms of its strengths and limitations.   (6 marks)
(c) How would this approach investigate Kim's sarcasm?   (6 marks)
(d) Evaluate this method of investigating sarcasm.   (6 marks)

Answer

(a) Kim's sarcasm might be explained in terms of her early childhood development. Freud's psychodynamic theory suggests there are five psychosexual stages. Freud would consider Kim's progress through the first, or oral, stage where the life force or libido is focused on the mouth. Specifically the second part of this stage, the oral aggressive part lasting from about 9–18 months, would be the focus. Fixation at this stage leads to an aggressive and dominating character according to Freud so he would suggest that this has happened to Kim. Normally infants tend to put every toy into their mouth at this stage and bite and chew it. If a child is frustrated in this activity then they remain at this stage (fixated) and it becomes part of their adult personality. The combination of biting and frustration shows itself in sarcasm in adults, but also in thumb sucking and nail biting in childhood and later smoking. Erikson might suggest that social factors had lead Kim to develop a sense of mistrust in her first year and so she is hiding her true opinions behind the sarcasm.

(b) One positive aspect to this explanation of Kim's sarcasm is that it considers early childhood as a factor in later development and Freud was the first psychologist to do this, though we all take it for granted now. Erikson's inclusion of social factors as well as sexual ones adds a wider credibility to the explanation of Kim's sarcasm. There is evidence that therapies based on psychodynamic ideas have helped patients. However, these personality theories are notoriously difficult to investigate and so there is not a large body of experimental evidence to support them. Most of the evidence is at best correlational, e.g., a link may be found between Kim's early teething problems and her current sarcasm, but cause and effect could not be accepted since there would be so many uncontrolled variables. Lying behind this explanation of Kim's sarcasm is the idea that libido drives people on. Can Kim's adult behaviour be reduced to a biological drive that has been frustrated in her first year? This seems to oversimplify the case. Much of Freud's theory is untestable and so difficult to falsify, e.g., fixations may occur through overindulgence as well as frustration, which makes for real difficulties in testing experimentally.

(c) Case studies are the way most psychodynamic theorists investigate behaviour. A group of sarcastic people like Kim would be interviewed about their childhood. In addition their parents would be interviewed as the oral is such an early stage and the participants may not recall events before they were 18 months old. Later behaviours like nail biting, thumb sucking, pen chewing, and smoking, which are associated with the oral aggressive personality, would also be investigated using a questionnaire. Psychoanalysis in the form of dream analysis or free association may also be used to see if the early frustration could be uncovered. Together these investigations would result in a detailed report on each person. Then the researcher would look for similarities across the case studies to draw out important factors.

(d) The detailed nature of these case studies and the fact that they look at the whole person are very positive aspects of this type of investigation. Using a group and looking for common factors adds some legitimacy to the research. The lack of a control group, however, makes comparisons less valid in that what they find may be true of non sarcastic people too. The case study reports are very open to researcher bias in terms of what they choose to include and leave out. Ps may also try to aid the researchers by giving the answers they see as being required (demand characteristics) or that they see as making themselves look good (social desirability bias). Researchers would need to clarify beforehand about the publishing of the research to ensure that confidentiality was maintained.

649 words in answer

The Cognitive Approach

Question

Concern has been expressed recently about bodybuilders. About 10% are thought to be suffering from muscle dysmorphia. This involves the person being preoccupied with the idea that they are not muscular enough. They spend hours lifting weights and pay excessive attention to diet, which impairs their social life and causes major distress. They continue this behaviour even when they know it could damage their health.

(a) Describe how **one** approach might try to explain muscle dysmorphia. (6 marks)

(b) Assess this explanation of muscle dysmorphia in terms of its strengths and limitations. (6 marks)

(c) How would this approach investigate muscle dysmorphia? (6 marks)

(d) Evaluate the use of this method of investigating muscle dysmorphia. (6 marks)

Answer

(a) The cognitive explanation would focus on information processing to explain muscle dysmorphia particularly the thinking process. Sufferers have developed maladaptive behaviour because of inappropriate schemas or organised packets of information which they use to view the world. These may have developed through observation, conditioning, or psychodynamic factors. It is the misinterpretation of the evidence that is central to the cognitive approach. The idea that to be respected by others involves a muscular look means that they are accepting the evidence from movies like *Terminator* and ignoring the fact that most heroes from movies are not particularly muscular. Another associated irrational belief is that once they have reached a certain level of muscularity all their social problems will be solved and a new script of interaction patterns will follow. There is a parallel here with unhappy teenage girls thinking they will become popular if they can slim down to a size 8.

(b) There is a large body of scientific evidence to support the existence of inappropriate schema and irrational beliefs (e.g., Beck's work on depression), which could also apply to muscle dysmorphia. Some of it is laboratory experiments and so may lack ecological validity and others like Beck's is based on case studies and so lack generalisability. This explanation is rather reductionist since this approach reduces complex behaviour like muscle dysmorphia to a series of cognitive processes. This mechanistic view of people being like computers ignores the motivational and emotional factors like parental pressure, which may influence how behaviour develops. Muscle dysmorphics may be trying to live up to some unfulfilled parental ideals. In addition the link between cognitions and behaviour is problematic for our behaviour may influence how we think rather than the reverse. One strength of this approach is that it gives a clear indication for therapy in that it is the thinking that has to change (thinking is ignored by most other approaches). Challenging the irrational beliefs of the muscle dysmorphic and changing them may usefully reduce the more extreme behaviours.

(c) One way to investigate muscle dysmorphia using the cognitive approach is to do an independent groups design quasi experiment using a questionnaire to see if there is a difference between muscle dysmorphics and a control group in terms of their thinking about a muscular physique. Questions like:

- Which of the following movie stars do you rate most? Hugh Grant. Arnold Schwarznegger. Tom Cruise. (ring one only)

- On a scale of 1–9, with 9 being most important, where would you place the following features for male attractiveness?

Good sense of humour ☐   Well dressed ☐   Muscular torso ☐   Handsome face ☐

The scoring system would need to look at the relative importance of the questions.

The scores from the two groups could then be compared using a Mann-Whitney U test to see if there is a significant difference between their thinking/schema on this topic. The independent variable is the two groups, muscle dysmorphics and control. The dependent variable is the scores on the test.

(d) When operationalising the independent variable, it would be important that the questionnaire had internal validity and did measure their thinking about muscular physique. Other questions would need to be included to disguise the purpose, otherwise demand characteristics or social desirability might influence the results. Instructions would need to ask participants (Ps) to be as honest as possible. Sample size would need to be at least 20 in each group to reduce individual differences as this is an independent groups design. Whilst this experiment would produce quantitative data there would be a lot of uncontrolled variables like earlier experiences so the results should be used with caution. There are also some ethical concerns in that informing Ps of the purpose of the questionnaire would invalidate the results. Debriefing and offering withdrawal of results might be an acceptable way round this point.

645 words in answer

The Evolutionary Approach

A psychology teacher gave her class a list of animals, objects, and situations and asked the students to rank them in order of how frightening they were. She then collated the lists and discovered that, overall, spiders, snakes, and the dark were the most feared.

(a) Describe how one approach might try to explain these fears.   (6 marks)
(b) Assess this explanation for these fears in terms of its strengths and limitations.   (6 marks)
(c) How would this approach investigate these fears?   (6 marks)
(d) Evaluate the use of this method of investigating these fears.   (6 marks)

Answer

(a) The evolutionary approach might suggest that in earlier times snakes were actually dangerous so people with a fear of them would avoid them whilst people who were not afraid would approach, get bitten, and die. So people with the fear gene would be more likely to survive to reproduce. Darwin called this survival of the fittest, that is those who adapted best to the environment. The same argument can be followed for spiders and a fear of the dark. Those who avoided them were more likely to pass their genes on to the next generation and those who did not, died, so the "not frightened" genes were selected out. This was termed natural selection since it was triggered by the environment. Changes in the environment would lead to different genes being selected. The reason why not all the class had these fears might be explained by suggesting that today in England, spiders, snakes, and the dark are less dangerous than they used to be and so selection out of these traits is not so essential for survival. Another evolutionary explanation might be that a mutation has occurred reintroducing the "not frightened" gene.

(b) Whilst there is plenty of supporting scientific research evidence, this approach may not be the complete answer since people vary considerably and some survive by facing up to the feared object rather than avoiding it. The evidence tends to come from natural experiments and so cause and effect can only be cautiously argued. In fact most of the evidence is ex post facto and hypotheses difficult to test and disprove. Much of the evidence is based on animal research and may not apply to humans. Animal fears may be biologically based, human fears may be cognitively based. This approach has proved very useful in terms of artificial breeding programmes with animals and this supports the theory. In terms of providing therapy for people with extreme fears, it is not at all helpful since it is so deterministic—you cannot change your genes. On the other hand, other therapies can reduce fears, e.g., cognitive therapies, where people talk through their fears, so at best, evolutionary factors are only a partial explanation. Evolutionary theory tends to ignore the fact that people's behaviour is influenced by our ability to communicate and rely on the genome lag argument to explain why people in England are still frightened of spiders when none of our spiders are poisonous.

(c) To investigate fears using the evolutionary approach a correlational analysis could be chosen predicting that there would be a positive correlation between the fear level recorded for the participant (P) and that recorded by the parent. A group of Ps would be required to cover a wide range of fear level. A fear test would be devised, e.g., a galvanic skin response (GSR) to pictures of spiders relative to a non-feared object like a jug. This would be variable A. Variable B would be the parent's test result. Data could be analysed descriptively using a scattergraph with variable A plotted against variable B for parent–child pairs. If the hypothesis is supported, this should show a strong positive correlation. It could also be analysed using inferential statistics (Spearman's rank correlation coefficient).

(d) The advantage of this method is that it generates quantitative data, which can be used to draw graphs, as well as enabling inferential statistics to be performed. The disadvantage lies in the fact that you cannot control all the variables and so must not argue cause and effect. In fact there could be an alternative explanation here. The parents may have provided role models for the children so that the explanation lies with social learning rather than with genes. There may be some problems with the validity of the tests. GSR measures arousal so it may not be fear but surprise that is being measured. It would be important not to inform Ps of the exact nature of the test in case it influenced their behaviour leading to demand characteristics, whereby they support the hypothesis by reacting as required. This raises ethical issues of consent. Ps could be asked in a general way if they will consent to being frightened beforehand.

699 words in answer

REFERENCES

Abbott, T. (2001). *Social and personality development*. London: Routledge.

Abed, R.T., & de Pauw, K.W. (1999). An evolutionary hypothesis for obsessive-compulsive disorder: A psychological immune system? *Behavioural Neurology, 11*, 245–250.

Abele, L.G., & Gilchrist, S. (1977). Homosexual rape and sexual selection in acanthocephalan worms. *Science, 197*, 81–83.

Abernethy, E.M. (1940). The effect of changed environmental conditions upon the results of college examinations. *Journal of Psychology, 10*, 293–301.

Abramowitz, E.S., Baker, A.H., & Fleischer, S.F. (1982). Onset of depressive psychiatric crises and the menstrual cycle. *American Journal of Psychiatry, 139*, 475–478.

Abramson, L.Y., Seligman, M.E., & Teasdale, J. (1978). Learned helplessness in humans: Critique and reformulation. *Journal of Abnormal Psychology, 87*, 49–74.

Ackerman, R., & DeRubeis, R.J. (1991). Is depressive realism real? *Clinical Psychology Review, 10*, 565–584.

Ainsworth, M.D.S., & Bell, S.M. (1970). Attachment, exploration and separation: Illustrated by the behaviour of one-year-olds in a strange situation. *Child Development, 41*, 49–67.

Ainsworth, M.D.S., Blehar, M.C., Waters, E., & Wall, S. (1978). *Patterns of attachment: A psychological study of the strange situation*, Hillsdale, NJ: Lawrence Erlbaum Associates Inc.

Akerstedt, T., & Froberg, J.E. (1976). Interindividual differences in circadian patterns of catecholamine excretion, body temperature, performance, and subjective arousal. *Biological Psychology, 4*, 277–292.

Akerstedt, T. (1977). Inversion of the sleep wakefulness pattern: Effects on circadian variations in psychophysiological activation. *Ergonomics, 20*, 459–474.

Allen, J.P., & Land, D. (1999). Attachment in adolescence. In J. Cassidy & P.R. Shaver (Eds.), *Handbook of attachment theory and research*. New York, NY: Guilford.

Allen, M.G. (1976). Twin studies of affective illness. *Archives of General Psychiatry, 33*, 1476–1478.

Allison, A.C. (1954, February 6). Protection afforded by sickle cell trait against subtertian malarial infection. *British Medical Journal*, 290–294.

Allison, T., & Cicchetti, D.V. (1976). Sleep in mammals: Ecological and constitutional correlates. *Science, 194*, 732–734.

Allport, G.W. (1947). *The use of personal documents in psychological science*. London: Holt, Rinehart, & Winston.

Altman, I., & Taylor, D.A. (1973). *Social penetration theory: The development of interpersonal relationships*. New York: Holt, Rinehart, & Winston.

Amato, P.R. (1983). The helpfulness of urbanites and small town dwellers—A test between two broad theoretical positions. *Australian Journal of Psychology, 35*, 233–243.

Amato, P.R., & Rogers, S.J. (1997). A longitudinal study of marital problems and subsequent divorce. *Journal of Marriage and the Family, 59*, 612–624.

American Diabetes Association (2001). American Diabetes Association clinical practice recommendations 2001. *Diabetes Care, Jan 24*, Suppl. S1–133.

American Psychiatric Association. (1994). *Diagnostic and statistical manual of mental disorders* (4th Edn.). Washington, DC: Author.

American Psychological Association. (1982). *Ethical principles in the conduct of research with human participants*. Washington, DC: American Psychological Association.

Ames, G.J., & Murray, F.B. (1982). When two wrongs make a right: Promoting cognitive change by social conflict. *Developmental Psychology, 18*, 894–897.

Amir, Y., & Sharon, I. (1987). Are social-psychological laws cross-culturally valid? *Journal of Cross-Cultural Psychology, 18*, 383–470.

Anderson, C.A. (1989). Temperature and aggression: Ubiquitous effects of heat on occurrence of human violence. *Psychological Bulletin, 106*, 74–96.

Anderson, C.A., & Bushman, B.J. (2001). Effects of violent video games on aggressive behaviour, aggressive cognition, aggressive affect, physiological arousal, and prosocial behaviour: A meta-analytic review of the scientific literature. *Psychological Science, 12*, 353–359.

Anderson, J.L., Crawford, C.B., Nadeau, J., & Lindberg, T. (1992). Was the Duchess of Windsor right? A cross-cultural review of the socioecology of ideals of female body shape. *Ethology and Sociobiology, 13*, 197–227.

Andersson, M. (1982). Female choice selects for extreme tail length in a widow-bird. *Nature, 299*, 818–820.

Andrews, G. (1988). Stressful life events and anxiety. In R. Noyes, M. Roth & G.D. Burrows (Eds.), *Handbook of anxiety, Vol. 2*. Amsterdam: Elsevier.

Ankney, C.D. (1995). Sex differences in brain size and mental abilities: Comments on R. Lynn and D. Kimura. *Personality and Individual Differences, 18*, 423–424.

Apter, T. (1990). *Altered loves: Mothers and daughters during adolescence*. New York: St. Martin's Press.

Archer, J. (1992). Childhood gender roles: Social context and organisation. In H. McGurk (Ed.), *Childhood social development: Contemporary perspectives*. Hove, UK: Psychology Press.

Archer, R.L. (1979). Role of personality and the social situation. In G.J. Chelune (Ed.), *Self-disclosure*. San Francisco: Jossey-Bass.

Archer, S. (1982). The lower age boundaries of identity development. *Child Development, 53*, 1551–1556.

Argyle, M. (1988). Social relationships. In M. Hewstone, W. Stroebe, J.-P. Codol, & G.M. Stephenson (Eds.), *Introduction to social psychology*. Oxford, UK: Blackwell.

Argyle, M., & Henderson, M. (1984). The rules of friendship. *Journal of Social and Personal Relationships, 1*, 211–237.

Argyle, M., Henderson, M., Bond, M., Iizuka, Y., & Contarello, A. (1986). Cross-cultural variations in relationship rules. *International Journal of Psychology, 21*, 287–315.

Arntz, A., Lavy, E., Vandenberg, G., & Vanrijsoort, S. (1993). Negative beliefs of spider phobics: A psychometric evaluation of the Spider Phobia Beliefs Questionnaire. *Advances in Behaviour Research and Therapy, 15*, 257–277.

Arrindell, W.A., Kwee, M.G., Methorst, G.J., van der Ende, J., Pol, E., & Moritz, B.J. (1989). Perceived parental rearing styles of agoraphobic and socially phobic in-patients. *British Journal of Psychiatry, 155*, 526–535.

Asch, S.E. (1951). Effects of group pressure on the modification and distortion of judgements. In H. Guetzkow (Ed.), *Groups, leadership and men*. Pittsburgh, PA: Carnegie.

Asch, S.E. (1955). Opinions and social pressure. *Scientific American, 193*, 31–35.

Asch, S.E. (1956). Studies of independence and conformity: A minority of one against a unanimous majority. *Psychological Monographs, 70*(Whole no. 416).

Aserinsky, E., & Kleitman, N. (1955). Two types of ocular motility occurring in sleep. *Journal of Applied Physiology, 8*, 1–10.

Asher, S.R., Renshaw, P.D., & Hymel, S. (1982). Peer relations and the development of social skills. In S.G. Moore (Ed.), *The young child: Reviews of research* (Vol. 3, pp. 137–158). Washington, DC: National Association for the Education of Young Children.

Atkinson, R.C., & Shiffrin, R.M. (1968). Human memory: A proposed system and its control processes. In K.W. Spence & J.T. Spence (Eds.), *The psychology of learning and motivation, Vol. 2*. London: Academic Press.

Atkinson, R.L., Atkinson, R.C., Smith, E.E., & Bem, D.J. (1993). *Introduction to psychology* (11th Edn.). New York: Harcourt Brace College Publishers.

Aubry, T., Tefft, B., & Kingsbury, N. (1990). Behavioural and psychological consequences of unemployment in blue-collar couples. *Journal of Community Psychology, 18*, 99–109.

Awad, A.G., & Voruganti, L.N. (1999). Quality of life and new antipsychotics in schizophrenia: Are patients better off? *International Journal of Social Psychiatry, 45*, 268–275.

Ayllon, T., & Azrin, N.H. (1968). *The token economy: A motivational system for therapy and rehabilitation*. New York: Appleton-Century-Crofts.

Baghdoyan, H.A., Spotts, J.L., & Snyder, S.G. (1993). Simultaneous pontine and basal forebrain microinjections of carbachol suppress REM sleep. *Journal of Neuroscience, 13*, 229–242.

Baillargeon, R., & Graber, M. (1988). Evidence of location memory in 8-month-old infants in a nonsearch AB task. *Developmental Psychology, 24*, 502–511.

Bandura, A. (1965). Influences of models' reinforcement contingencies on the acquisition of initiative responses. *Journal of Personality and Social Psychology, 1*, 589–593.

Bandura, A. (1973). *Aggression: A social learning analysis*. Englewood Cliffs, NJ: Prentice-Hall.

Bandura, A. (1977). Self-efficacy: Toward a unifying theory of behavioural change. *Psychological Review, 84*, 191–215.

Bandura, A. (1986). *Social foundations of thought and action: A social cognitive theory*. Englewood Cliffs, NJ: Prentice-Hall.

Bandura, A., Blanchard, E., & Ritter, B. (1969) Relative efficacy of desensitization and modeling approaches for inducing behavioural, affective and attitudinal changes. *Journal of Personality and Social Psychology, 13*, 173–199.

Bandura, A., Ross, D., & Ross, S.A. (1961). Transmission of aggression through imitation of aggressive models. *Journal of Abnormal and Social Psychology, 63*, 575–582.

Bandura, A., Ross, D., & Ross, S.A. (1963). Transmission of aggression through imitation of aggressive models. *Journal of Abnormal and Social Psychology, 66*, 3–11.

Banyard, P., & Hayes, N. (1994). *Psychology: Theory and application*. London: Chapman & Hall.

Baran, S.J., Chase, L.J., & Courtright, J.A. (1979). Television drama as a facilitator of prosocial behaviour—Waltons. *Journal of Broadcasting, 23*, 277–284.

Barber, J.P., & DeRubeis, R.J. (1989). On second thought: Where the action is in cognitive therapy for depression. *Cognitive Therapy and Research, 13*, 441–457.

Barkley, R.A., Ullman, D.G., Otto, L., & Brecht, J.M. (1977). The effects of sex typing and sex appropriateness of modelled behaviour on children's imitation. *Child Development, 48*, 721–725.

Barlow, D.H., & Durand, V.M. (1995). *Abnormal psychology: An integrative approach*. New York: Brooks/Cole.

Barlow, D.H., Gorman, J.M., Shear, M.K., & Woods, S.W. (2000). Cognitive-behavioral therapy, imipramine, or their combination for panic disorder: A randomized controlled trial. *Journal of the American Medical Association, 283*, 2529–2536.

Barnier, G. (1989). L'effet-tuteur dans des situations mettant en jeu des rapports spatiaux chez des enfants de 7–8 ans en interactions dyadiques avec des pairs de 6–7 ans. *European Journal of Psychology of Education, 4*, 385–399.

Baron, R.A. (1977). *Human aggression*. New York: Plenum.

Baron, R.A., & Bell, P.A. (1976). Aggression and heat: The influence of ambient temperature, negative affect, and a cooling drink on physical aggression. *Journal of Personality and Social Psychology, 33*, 245–255.

Baron, R.A., & Byrne, D. (1991). *Social psychology: Understanding human interaction* (6th Edn.). Boston, MA: Allyn & Bacon.

Baron, R.A., & Ransberger, V.M. (1978). Ambient temperature and the occurrence of collective violence: The "long hot summer" revisited. *Journal of Personality and Social Psychology, 36*, 351–360.

Baron, R.A., & Richardson, D.R. (1993). *Human aggression* (2nd Edn.). New York: Plenum.

Baron-Cohen, S., Leslie, A.M., & Frith, U. (1985). Does the autistic child have a "theory of mind"? *Cognition, 21*, 37–46.

Barrett, J.E. (1979). The relationship of life events to the onset of neurotic disorders. In J.E. Barrett (Ed.), *Stress and mental disorder*. New York: Raven Press.

Barry, H., Bacon, M.K., & Child, I.L. (1957). A cross-cultural survey of some sex differences in socialisation. *Journal of Abnormal and Social Psychology, 55*, 327–332.

Bateson, G., Jackson, D.D., Haley, J., & Weakland, J. (1956). Toward a theory of schizophrenia. *Behavioral Science, 1*, 251–264.

Bateson, P. (1986). When to experiment on animals. *New Scientist, 109*, 30–32.

Batson, C.D. (1983). Sociobiology and the role of religion in promoting prosocial behaviour: An alternative view. *Journal of Personality and Social Psychology, 45*, 1380–1385.

Batson, C.D. (1987). Prosocial motivation: Is it ever truly altruistic? In L. Berkowitz (Ed.), *Advances in experimental social psychology, Vol. 20*. New York: Academic Press.

Batson, C.D., Batson, J.G., Slingsby, J.K., Harrell, K.L., Peekna, H.M., & Todd, R.M. (1991). Empathic joy and the empathy-altruism hypothesis. *Journal of Personality and Social Psychology, 61*, 413–426.

Batson, C.D., Cochrane, P.J., Biederman, M.F., Blosser, J.L., Ryan, M.J., & Vogt, B. (1978). Failure to help when in a hurry: Callousness or conflict? *Personality and Social Psychology Bulletin, 4*, 97–101.

Batson, C.D., Duncan, B.D., Ackerman, P., Buckley, T., & Birch, K. (1981). Is empathic emotion a source of altruistic motivation? *Journal of Personality and Social Psychology*, 40, 290–302.

Batson, C.D., Dyck, J.L., Brandt, J.R., Batson, J.G., Powell, A.L., McMaster, M.R., & Griffitt, C. (1988). Five studies testing new egotistic alternatives to the empathy–altruism hypothesis. *Journal of Personality and Social Psychology*, 55, 52–77.

Batson, C.D., & Oleson, K.C. (1991). Current status of the empathy-altruism hypothesis. In M.S. Clark (Ed.), *Review of personality and social psychology, Vol. 12: Prosocial behaviour*. Newbury Park, CA: Sage.

Batson, C.D., O'Quinn, K., Fultz, J., Vanderplas, N., & Isen, A.M. (1983). Influence of self-reported distress and empathy on egoistic versus altruistic motivation to help. *Journal of Personality and Social Psychology*, 45, 706–718.

Baumrind, D. (1991). Effective parenting during early adolescent transition. In P.A. Cowan & E.M. Hetherington (Eds.), *Advances in family research, Vol 2*. Hillsdale, NJ: Erlbaum.

Beck, A.T. (1967). *Depression: Clinical, experimental, and theoretical aspects*. New York: Hoeber.

Beck, A.T. (1976). *Cognitive therapy of the emotional disorders*. New York: New American Library.

Beck, A.T., & Clark, D.A. (1988). Anxiety and depression: An information processing perspective. *Anxiety Research*, 1, 23–36.

Beck, A.T., & Emery, G. (1985). *Anxiety disorders and phobias*. New York: Basic Books.

Beck, A.T., Rush, A.J., Shaw, B.F., & Emery, G. (1979). *Cognitive therapy of depression*. New York: Guilford Press.

Beck, A.T., & Ward, C.H. (1961). Dreams of depressed patients: Characteristic themes in manifest content. *Archives of General Psychiatry*, 5, 462–467.

Beck, A.T., & Weishaar, M.E. (1989). Cognitive therapy. In R.J. Corsini & D. Wedding (Eds.), *Current psychotherapies*. Itacca, IL: Peacock.

Beck, I.L., & Carpenter, P.A. (1986). Cognitive approaches to understanding reading. *American Psychologist*, 41, 1088–1105.

Bee, H. (1994). *Lifespan development*. New York: HarperCollins.

Bee, H. (1995). *The developing child* (7th Edn.). London: HarperCollins.

Behrend, D.A., Harris, L.L., & Cartwright, K.B. (1992). Morphological cues to verb meaning: Verb inflections and the initial mapping of verb meanings. *Journal of Child Language*, 22, 89–106.

Bell, A. (2001). *Debates in psychology*. London: Routledge.

Bem, S.L. (1974). The measurement of psychological androgyny. *Journal of Consulting and Clinical Psychology*, 42, 155–162.

Bem, S.L. (1993). Is there a place in psychology for a feminist analysis of the social context? *Feminism and Psychology*, 3(2), 230–234.

Bem, S.L. (1994, August 17). In a male-centered world, female differences are transformed into female disadvantages. *Chronicle of Higher Education*, B1–B3.

Bennett-Levy, J., & Marteau, T. (1984). Fear of animals: What is prepared? *British Journal of Psychology*, 75, 37–42.

Bentley, E. (2000). *Awareness: Biorhythms, sleep and dreaming*. London: Routledge.

Benton, D. (2001). Micro-nutrient supplementation and the intelligence of children *Neuroscience and Biobehavioral Reviews*, 25, 297–309.

Bergen, D.J., & Williams, J.E. (1991). Sex stereotypes in the United States revisited. *Sex Roles*, 24, 413–423.

Bergin, A.E. (1971). The evaluation of therapeutic outcomes. In A.E. Bergin & S.L. Garfield (Eds.), *Handbook of psychotherapy and behaviour change*. New York: Wiley.

Berk, L.E. (1994). Why children talk to themselves. *Scientific American*, November, 60–65.

Berkowitz, L. (1968). Impulse, aggression and the gun. *Psychology Today*, September, 18–22.

Berkowitz, L. (1989). Frustration–aggression hypothesis: Examination and reformulation. *Psychological Bulletin*, 106, 59–73.

Berkowitz, L., & LePage, A. (1967). Weapons as aggression-eliciting stimuli. *Journal of Personality and Social Psychology*, 7, 202–207.

Berndt, T.J. (1979). Developmental changes in conformity to peers and parents. *Developmental Psychology*, 15, 608–616.

Berrettini, W.H. (2000). Susceptibility loci for bipolar disorder: Overlap with inherited vulnerability to schizophrenia. *Biological Psychiatry*, 47, 245–251.

Berry, D.T.R., & Webb, W.B. (1983). State measures and sleep stages. *Psychological Reports*, 52, 807–812.

Berry, J.W. (1969). On cross-cultural comparability. *International Journal of Psychology*, 4, 119–128.

Berry, J.W. (1974). Radical cultural relativism and the concept of intelligence. In J.W. Berry & P.R. Dasen (Eds.), *Culture and cognition: Readings in cross-cultural psychology*. London: Methuen.

Berry, J.W. (1997). Acculturation strategies. In A. Baum, S. Newman, J. Weinman, R. West, & C. McManus (Eds.), *Cambridge handbook of psychology, health, and medicine*. Cambridge, UK: Cambridge University Press.

Berry, J.W., Poortinga, Y.H., Segall, M.H., & Dasen, P.R. (1992). *Cross-cultural psychology*. Cambridge, UK: Cambridge University Press.

Berscheid, E., & Walster, E.H. (1978). *Interpersonal attraction* (2nd Edn.). Reading, MA: Addison-Wesley.

Bertelsen, B., Harvald, B., & Hauge, M. (1977). A Danish twin study of manic-depressive disorders. *British Journal of Psychiatry*, 130, 330–351.

Bifulco, A., Harris, T., & Brown, G.W. (1992). Mourning or early inadequate care? Re-examining the relationship of maternal loss in childhood with adult depression and anxiety. *Development and Psychopathology*, 4, 433–449.

Binet, A., & Simon, T. (1905). Methodes nouvelles pour le diagnostic du niveau intellectual des anormaux. *L'Annee Psychologique*, 11, 191–244.

Bjorkqvist, K., Lagerspetz, K.M.J., & Kaukiainen, A. (1992). Do girls manipulate and boys fight? Developmental trends regarding direct and indirect aggression. *Aggressive Behavior*, 18, 157–166.

Blake, M.J.F. (1967). Time of day effects on performance on a range of tasks. *Psychonomic Science*, 9, 349–350.

Blakemore, C. (1988). *The mind machine*. London: BBC Publications.

Bloom, J.W. (1998). The ethical practice of web counseling. *British Journal of Guidance and Counselling*, 26, 53–59.

Blumenthal, M., Kahn, R.L., Andrews, F.M., & Head, K.B. (1972). *Justifying violence: The attitudes of American men*. Ann Arbor, MI: Institute for Social Research.

Blumstein, P., & Schwartz, P. (1983). *American couples: Money, work, sex*. New York: Morrow.

Boring, E.G. (1957). *A history of experimental psychology* (2nd Edn.). New York: Appleton-Century-Crofts.

Borsky, P.N. (1969). Cited in Cox, T. (1978). *Stress*. London: Macmillan Press.

Bossard, J. (1932). Residential propinquity as a factor in marriage selection. *American Journal of Sociology*, 38, 219–224.

Bostwick, J.M., & Pankratz, V.S. (2000). Affective disorders and suicide risk: A re-examination. *American Journal of Psychiatry, 157*, 1925–1932.

Bouchard, T.J., Lykken, D.T., McGue, M., Segal, N.L., & Tellegen, A. (1990). Sources of human psychological differences: The Minnesota study of twins reared apart. *Science, 250*, 223–228.

Bouchard, T.J., & McGue, M. (1981). Familial studies of intelligence: A review. *Science, 212*, 1055–1059.

Bower, T.G.R. (1979). *Human development.* San Francisco, CA: W.H. Freeman.

Bower, T.G.R. (1982). *Development in infancy* (2nd Edn.). San Francisco, CA: W.H. Freeman.

Bower, T.G.R., & Wishart, J.G. (1972). The effects of motor skill on object permanence. *Cognition, 1*, 165–172.

Bowlby, J. (1969). *Attachment and love: Vol. 1. Attachment.* London: Hogarth.

Bowlby, J. (1973). *Attachment and loss: Vol. 3.* Harmondsworth, UK: Penguin.

Bradbard, M.R., Martin, C.L., Endsley, R.C., & Halverson, C.F. (1986). Influence of sex stereotypes on children's exploration and memory: A competence versus performance distinction. *Developmental Psychology, 22*, 481–486.

Bradmetz, J. (1999). Precursors of formal thought: A longitudinal study. *British Journal of Developmental Psychology, 17*, 61–81.

Brainerd, C.J. (1983). Modifiability of cognitive development. In S. Meadows (Ed.), *Developing thinking: Approaches to children's cognitive development.* London: Methuen.

Brandsma, J.M., Maultsby, M.C., & Welsh, R. (1978). Self-help techniques in the treatment of alcoholism. Cited in G.T. Wilson & K.D. O'Leary, *Principles of behaviour therapy.* Englewood Cliffs, NJ: Prentice-Hall.

Branwyn, G. (1993). Compu-sex: Erotica for cybernauts. *South Atlantic Quarterly, 92*, 779–791.

Breger, L., Hunter, I., & Lane, R.W. (1971). The effect of stress on dreams. *Psychological Issues, 7*, 1–213.

Brehm, S.S. (1992). *Intimate relationships* (2nd Edn.). New York: McGraw-Hill.

Brickman, P., Rabinowitz, V.C., Karuza, J., Coates, D., Cohn, E., & Kidder, L. (1982). Models of helping and coping. *American Psychologist, 37*, 368–384.

Brigham, J.C. (1971). Ethnic stereotypes. *Psychological Bulletin, 76*, 15–38.

Brodbar-Nemzer, J.Y. (1986). Divorce and group commitment: The case of the Jews. *Journal of Marriage and the Family, 48*, 329–340.

Brody, G.H., & Shaffer, D.R. (1982). Contributions of parents and peers to children's moral socialisation. *Developmental Review, 2*, 31–75.

Brooks-Gunn, J., Klebanov, P., & Duncan, G.J. (1996). Ethnic differences in children's intelligence test scores: Role of economic deprivation, home environment and maternal characteristics *Child Development, 67*, 396–408.

Brown, A. (2000, September 3). Women are promiscuous, naturally. *The Observer.*

Brown, B.B., & Lohr, M.J. (1987). Peer-group affiliation and adolescent self-esteem: An integration of ego-identity and symbolic-interaction theories. *Journal of Personality and Social Psychology, 52*, 47–55.

Brown, G.W. (1989). Depression. In G.W. Brown & T.O. Harris (Eds.), *Life events and illness.* New York: Guilford Press.

Brown, G.W., & Harris, T. (1978). *Social origins of depression.* London: Tavistock.

Brown, J.S., & Burton, R.D. (1978). Diagnostic model for procedural bugs in basic mathematical skills. *Cognitive Science, 2*, 155–192.

Brown, R.C., & Tedeschi, J.T. (1976). Determinants of perceived aggression. *Journal of Social Psychology, 100*, 77–87.

Bruch, M.A., & Heimberg, R.G. (1994). Differences in perceptions of parental and personal between generalized and nongeneralized social phobics. *Journal of Anxiety Disorders, 8*, 155–168.

Brugha, T.S., Bebbington, P.E., Stretch, D.D., MacCarthy, B., & Wykes, T. (1997). *Journal of Clinical Psychiatry, 58*, 298–306.

Bruner, J.S., Olver, R.R., & Greenfield, P.M. (1966). *Studies in cognitive growth.* New York: Wiley.

Brunner, H.G., Nelen, M., Breakefield, X.O., Ropers, H.H., et al. (1993). Abnormal behavior associated with a point mutation in the structural gene for monoamine oxidase. *Science, 262*(5133), 578–580.

Bryant, P. (1995). Jean Piaget. In R. Fuller (Ed.), *Seven pioneers of psychology.* London: Routledge.

Buhrmester, D. (1992). The developmental courses of sibling and peer relationships. In F. Boer & J. Dunn (Eds.), *Children's sibling relationships: Developmental and clinical issues.* Hillsdale, NJ: Lawrence Erlbaum Associates Inc.

Burgess, R.L., & Wallin, P. (1953). Marital happiness of parents and their children's attitudes to them. *American Sociological Review, 18*, 424–431.

Burns, G.L., & Farina, A. (1992). The role of physical attractiveness in adjustment. *Genetic, Social, and General Psychology Monographs, 118*, 157–194.

Burns, J. (1993). Invisible women—women who have learning disabilities. *The Psychologist, 6*, 102–105.

Burnstein, E., Crandall, C., & Kitayama, S. (1994). Some neo-Darwinian roles for altruism: Weighing cues for inclusive fitness as function of the biological importance of the decision. *Journal of Personality and Social Psychology, 67*, 773–789.

Burr, V. (1997). Social constructionism and psychology. *The New Psychologist*, April, 7–12.

Burt, C. (1955). The evidence for the concept of intelligence. *British Journal of Psychology, 25*, 158–177.

Buss, D.M. (1989). Sex differences in human mate preferences: Evolutionary hypotheses tested in 37 cultures. *Behavioral and Brain Sciences, 12*, 1–49.

Buss, D.M. (1999). *Evolutionary psychology: The new science of the mind.* Boston, MA: Allyn & Bacon.

Buss, D.M., Larsen, R.J., Westen, D., & Semmelroth, J. (1992). Sex differences in jealousy: Evolution, physiology and psychology. *Psychological Science, 3*, 251–255.

Bussey, K., & Bandura, A. (1992). Self-regulatory mechanisms governing gender development. *Child Development, 63*, 1236–1250.

Bussey, K., & Bandura, A. (1999). Social cognitive theory of gender development and differentiation. *Psychological Review, 106*, 676–713.

Butcher, J.N., Mineka, S., & Hooley, J.M. (2004). *Abnormal psychology* (12th Edn.). London: Pearson.

Buttolph, M.L., Holland, A.D. (1990). Obsessive-compulsive disorder in pregnancy and childbirth. In M.A. Jenkike, L. Baer, & W.E. Minichiello (Eds.), *Obsessive-compulsive disorders: Theory and management.* Chicago, IL: Year Book Medical Publishers.

Buunk, B.P. (1996). Affiliation, attraction and close relationships. In M. Hewstone, W. Stroebe, & G.M. Stephenson (Eds.), *Introduction to social psychology* (2nd Edn.). Oxford, UK: Blackwell.

Buunk, B.P., Angleitner, A., Oubaid, V., & Buss, D.M. (1996). Sex differences in jealousy in evolutionary and cultural perspective. *Psychological Science, 7*, 359–363.

Buunk, B.P., & VanYperen, N.W. (1991). Referential comparisons, relational comparisons and exchange orientation: Their relation to marital satisfaction. *Personality and Social Psychology Bulletin, 17*, 710–718.

Byrne, D. (1971). *The attraction paradigm*. New York: Academic Press.

Byrne, D., London, O., & Griffitt, W. (1968). The effect of topic importance and attitude similarity–dissimilarity on attraction in an intrastranger design. *Psychonomic Science, 11*, 303–313.

Byrne, R. (1995). *The thinking ape: Evolutionary origins of intelligence*. Oxford: Oxford University Press.

Byrne, R. (2004). The manual skills and cognition that lie behind hominid tool use. In A.E. Russon & D.R. Begun (Eds.), *The evolution of thought: Evolutionary origins of great ape intelligence*. Cambridge: Cambridge University Press.

Byrne, R., & Whiten, A. (1988). *Machiavellian intelligence: Social expertise and the evolution of intellect in monkeys, apes and humans*. Oxford: Oxford University Press.

Caldwell, B., & Bradley, R. (1984). *Home Observation for Measurement of the Environment*. Little Rock, AR: University of Arkansas at Little Rock.

Calhoun, J.B. (1962). Population density and social pathology. *Scientific American*, February, 206.

Campbell, S.S., & Murphy, P.J. (1998). Extraocular circadian phototransduction in humans. *Science, 279*, 396–399.

Capron, C., & Duyne, M. (1989). Assessment of effects of socio-economic status on IQ in a full cross-fostering study. *Nature, 340*, 552–554.

Carmichael, G. (1983). The transition to marriage: Trends in age at first marriage in Australia. Cited in V.J. Callan, C. Gallois, P. Noller, & Y. Kashima (1991). *Social psychology* (2nd Edn.). Sydney: Harcourt Brace Jovanovich.

Carroll, B.J. (1991). Psychopathology and neurobiology of manic-depressive disorders. In B.J. Carroll & J.E. Barrett (Eds.), *Psychopathology and the brain*. New York: Raven Press.

Cartwright, J. (2001). *Evolutionary explanations of human behaviour*. London: Routledge.

Cartwright, R. (1984). Broken dreams: A study on the effects of divorce and separation on dream content. *Journal for the Study of Interpersonal Processes, 47*, 51–59.

Case, R. (1974). Structures and strictures: Some functional limitations on the course of cognitive growth. *Cognitive Psychology, 6*, 544–573.

Case, R. (1985). *Intellectual development*. Orlando, FL: Academic Press.

Case, R. (1992). Neo-Piagetian theories of intellectual development. In H. Beilin & P.B. Pufall (Eds.), *Piaget's theory: Prospects and possibilities*. Hillsdale, NJ: Lawrence Erlbaum Associates Inc.

Casey, P. (2001). Multiple personality disorder. *Primary Care Psychiatry, 7*, 7–11.

Catalano, R., Novaco, R., & McConnell, W. (1997). A model of the net effect of job loss on violence. *Journal of Personality and Social Psychology, 72*, 1440–1447.

Cave, S. (1999). *Therapeutic approaches in psychology*. London: Routledge.

Ceci, S.J. (1991). How much does schooling influence general intelligence and its cognitive components? A reassessment of the evidence. *Developmental Psychology, 27*, 703–722.

Ceci, S.J., Peters, D., & Plotkin, J. (1985). Human subjects review, personal values and the regulation of social science research. *American Psychologist, 40*, 994–1002.

Charlton, A. (1998, January 12). TV violence has little impact on children, study finds. *The Times*, p.5.

Chiara, C., Pompeiano, M., & Tononi, G. (1996). Neuronal gene expression in the waking state: A role for the locus coeruleus. *Science, 274*, 1211–1215.

Child, I.L. (1968). Personality in culture. In E.F. Borgatta & W.W. Lambert (Eds.), *Handbook of personality theory and research*. Chicago, IL: Rand McNally.

Chodorow, N. (1978). *The reproduction of mothering*. Berkeley, CA: University of California Press.

Clark, D.M. (1986). A cognitive approach to panic. *Behaviour Research and Therapy, 24*, 461–470.

Clark, D.M., Salkovskis, P.M., Gelder, M., Koehler, K., Martin, M., Anastasiades, P., Hackman, A., Middleton, H., & Jeavons, A. (1988). Tests of a cognitive theory of panic. In I. Hand & H.-U. Wittchen (Eds.), *Panic and phobias, Vol. 2*. Berlin: Springer.

Clark, M.S. (1984). Record keeping in two types of relationships. *Journal of Personality and Social Psychology, 47*, 549–557.

Clark, M.S., & Mills, J. (1979). Interpersonal attraction in exchange and communal relationships. *Journal of Personality and Social Psychology, 37*, 12–24.

Clark, R.D., & Hatfield, E. (1989). Gender differences in receptivity to sexual offers. *Journal of Psychology and Human Sexuality, 2*, 39–55.

Clarke, D. (2001). *Pro- and anti-social behaviour* (Routledge Modular Series). London: Routledge.

Clegg, F. (1982). *Simple statistics*. Cambridge, UK: Cambridge University Press.

Clutton-Brock, T.H., & Harvey, P.H. (1980). Primates, brains and ecology. *Journal of the Zoological Society of London, 190*, 309–323.

Coenen, A. (2000). The divorce of REM sleep and dreaming. *Behavioral and Brain Sciences, 23*, 922–924.

Cohn, E.G., & Rotton, J. (1997). Assault as a function of time and temperature: A moderator-variable time-series analysis. *Journal of Personality and Social Psychology, 72*, 1322–1334.

Colapinto, J. (2000). *As nature made him*. London: Quartet Books.

Colby, A., & Kohlberg, L. (1987). *The measurement of moral judgement*. Cambridge, UK: Cambridge University Press.

Colby, A., Kohlberg, L., Gibbs, J., & Lieberman, M. (1983). A longitudinal study of moral judgement. *Monographs of the Society for Research in Child Development, 48*(Nos. 1–2, Serial No. 200).

Cole, J.O., & Davis, J.M. (1975). Antidepressant drugs. In A.M. Freedman, H.I. Kaplan & B.J. Saddock (Eds.), *Comprehensive textbook of psychiatry, Vol. 2*. Baltimore, MD: Williams & Williams.

Cole, M., Gay, J., Glick, J., & Sharp, D.W. (1971). *The cultural context of learning and thinking*. New York: Basic Books.

Coleman, J.C. (1974). *Relationships in adolescence*. London: Routledge & Kegan Paul.

Coleman, J.C., & Hendry, L. (1990). *The nature of adolescence*. London: Routledge.

Collaer, M.L., & Hines, M. (1995). Human behavioural sex differences: A role for gonadal hormones during early development. *Psychological Bulletin, 118*, 55–107.

Comer, R.J. (2001). *Abnormal psychology* (4th Edn.). New York: Worth.

Comer. R.J. (2002). *Fundamentals of abnormal psychology* (3rd Edn.). New York: Worth.

Comstock, G., & Paik, H. (1991). *Television and the American child*. San Diego, CA: Academic Press.

Concar, D. (1995). Sex and the symmetrical body. *New Scientist, 146*, 40–44.

Condon, R.G. (1987). *Inuit youth: Growth and change in the Canadian arctic*. New Brunswick, NJ: Rutgers University Press.

Condry, J., & Condry, S. (1976). Sex differences: A study in the eye of the beholder. *Child Development, 47,* 812–819.

Conner, D.B., Knight, D.K., & Cross, D.R. (1997). Mothers' and fathers' scaffolding of their 2-year-olds during problem-solving and literary interactions. *British Journal of Developmental Psychology, 15,* 323–338.

Cook, M., & Mineka, S. (1989). Observational conditioning of fear to fear-relevant versus fear-irrelevant stimuli in rhesus monkeys. *Journal of Abnormal Psychology, 98,* 448–459.

Cooke, T.P., & Apolloni, T. (1976). Developing positive social-emotional behaviors: A study of training and generalization effects. *Journal of Applied Behavior Analysis, 9,* 65–78.

Coolican, H. (1995). *Introduction to research methods and statistics in psychology.* London: Hodder & Stoughton.

Coolican, H. (1999). *Research methods and statistics in psychology* (3rd Edn.). London: Hodder & Stoughton.

Cooper, A. (2000). (Ed.). *Cybersex and sexual compulsivity: The dark side of the force.* New York: Taylor & Francis.

Cooper, A., & Sportolari, L. (1997). Romance in cyberspace: Understanding online attraction. *Journal of Sex Education and Therapy, 22,* 7–14.

Cooper, C. (1998). *Individual differences.* London: Arnold.

Cooper, J., & Mackie, D. (1986). Video games and aggression in children. *Journal of Applied Social Psychology, 16,* 726–744.

Coren, S. (1996). *Sleep thieves.* New York: Free Press.

Cosgrove, G.R., & Ballantine, H.T. (1996). Cingulotomy for psychiatric illness. In P.H. Gildenberg & R. Tasker (Eds.), *A textbook of stereotactic and functional neurosurgery.* Philadelphia, PA: McGraw-Hill.

Cosgrove, G.R., Buchbinder, B.R., & Jiang, H. (1996). Functional magnetic resonance imaging for intracranial navigation. *Neurosurgery Clinics of North America, 7,* 313–324.

Costanzo, P.R., & Shaw, M.E. (1966). Conformity as a function of age level. *Child Development, 37,* 967–975.

Coyne, S.M., Archer, J., & Eslea, M. (2004). Cruel intentions on television and in real life: Can viewing indirect aggression increase viewers' subsequent indirect aggression? *Journal of Experimental Child Psychology, 88,* 234–253.

Craddock, N., & Jones, I. (1999). Genetics of bipolar disorder. *Journal of Medical Genetics, 36,* 585–594.

Craik, F.I., & Watkins, M.J. (1973). The role of rehearsal in short-term memory. *Journal of Verbal Learning and Verbal Behavior, 12,* 599–607.

Craik, F.I.M., & Lockhart, R.S. (1972). Levels of processing: A framework for memory research. *Journal of Verbal Learning and Verbal Behavior, 11,* 671–684.

Craik, F.I.M., & Tulving, E. (1975). Depth of processing and the retention of words in episodic memory. *Journal of Experimental Psychology, 104,* 268–294.

Crick, F., & Mitchison, G. (1983). The function of dream sleep. *Nature, 304,* 111–114.

Crook, J.H. (1964). The evolution of social organisation and visual communication in the weaver birds (Ploceinae). *Behaviour Supplement, 10,* 1–178.

Crook, T., & Eliot, J. (1980). Parental death during childhood and adult depression: A critical review of the literature. *Psychological Bulletin, 87,* 252–259.

Crooks, R.L., & Stein, J. (1991). *Psychology: Science, behaviour and life* (2nd Edn.). London: Harcourt Brace Jovanovich.

Crow, T.J. (2000). Schizophrenia as the price that homo sapiens pay for language: A resolution of the central paradox in the origin of the species. *Brain Research Reviews, 31*(2–3), 118–129.

Csikszentmihalyi, M., & Larson, R. (1984). *Being adolescent: Conflict and growth in the teenage years.* New York: Basic Books.

Cumberbatch, G. (1990). Television advertising and sex role stereotyping: A content analysis [Working paper IV for the Broadcasting Standards Council]. Communications Research Group, Aston University, Birmingham, UK.

Cunningham, M.R. (1986). Measuring the physical in physical attractiveness: Quasi experiments on the sociobiology of female facial beauty. *Journal of Personality and Social Psychology, 50,* 925–935.

Cuthill, I. (1991). Field experiments in animal behaviour. *Animal Behaviour, 42,* 1007–1014.

Czeisler, C.A., Duffy, J.F., Shanahan, T.L., Brown, E.N., Mitchell, J.F., Rimmer, D.W., Ronda, J.M., Silva, E.J., Emens, J.S., Dijk, D.J., & Kronauer, R.E. (1999). Stability, precision, and near 24-hour period of the human circadian pacemaker. *Science, 284,* 2177–2181.

Czeisler, C.A., Moore-Ede, M.C., & Coleman, R.M. (1982). Rotating shift work schedules that disrupt sleep are improved by applying circadian principles. *Science, 217*(4558), 460–463.

Damon, W., & Hart, D. (1988). *Self-understanding in childhood and adolescence.* Cambridge, UK: Cambridge University Press.

Darley, J.M. (1991). Altruism and prosocial behaviour research: Reflections and prospects. In M.S. Clark (Ed.), *Prosocial behaviour: Review of personality and social psychology, Vol. 12.* Newbury Park, CA: Sage.

Darley, J.M., & Latané, B. (1968). Bystander intervention in emergencies: Diffusion of responsibility. *Journal of Personality and Social Psychology, 8,* 377–383.

Darwin, C. (1859). *The origin of species.* London: Macmillan.

Darwin, C. (1871). *The descent of man and selection in relation to sex.* London: John Murray.

Darwin, C. (1872). *The expression of the emotions in man and animals.* London: John Murray.

Davies, N.B., & Lundberg, A. (1984). Food distribution and a variable mating system in the dunnock, *Prunella modularis. Journal of Animal Ecology, 53,* 895–913.

Davis, M.H. (1983). Empathic concern and the muscular dystrophy telethon: Empathy as a multidimensional construct. *Personality and Social Psychology Bulletin, 9,* 223–229.

Davis, S. (1990). Men as success objects and women as sex objects: A study of personal advertisements. *Sex Roles, 23,* 43–50.

Davison, G.C., & Neale, J.M. (1996). *Abnormal psychology* (Rev. 6th Edn.). New York: Wiley.

Davison, G.C., & Neale, J.M. (2001). *Abnormal psychology* (8th Edn.). Chichester, UK: Wiley.

Davison, G.C., & Neale, J.M. (2004). *Abnormal psychology* (9th Edn.). Chichester, UK: Wiley.

Dawkins, R. (1976). *The selfish gene.* Oxford, UK: Oxford University Press.

Dawson, D., & Campbell, S.S. (1991). Time exposure to bright light improves sleep and alertness during simulated night shifts. *Sleep, 14,* 511–516.

Day, R., Nielsen, J.A., Korten, A., Ernberg, G., et al. (1987). Stressful life events preceding the acute onset of schizophrenia: A cross-national study from the World Health Organization. *Culture, Medicine and Psychiatry, 11,* 123–205.

De Waal, F.B.M. (2002). Evolutionary psychology: The wheat and the chaff. *Current Directions in Psychological Science, 11,* 187–191.

Delgado, P.L., Charney, D.S., Price, L.H., Aghajanian, G.K., Landis, H., & Heninger, G.R. (1990). Serotonin function and the mechanism of antidepressant action: Reversal of antidepressant induced remission by rapid depletion of plasma tryptophan. *Archives of General Psychiatry, 47,* 411–418.

Dement, W.C. (1960). The effects of dream deprivation. *Science, 131,* 1705–1707.

Dement, W.C., & Kleitman, N. (1957). The relation of eye movements during sleep to dream activity: An objective method for the study of dreaming. *Journal of Experimental Psychology, 53,* 339–346.

Denollet, J. (2005). DS14: Standard assessment of negative affectivity, social inhibition, and type D personality. *Psychosomatic Medicine, 67,* 89–97.

DeSteno, D., Bartlett, M.Y., Salovey, P., & Braverman, J. (2002). Sex differences in jealousy: Evolutionary mechanism or artifact of measurement? *Journal of Personality and Social Psychology, 83,* 1103–1116.

Deuel, N.R. (1996). Our passionate response to virtual reality. In S.C. Herring (Ed.), *Computer-mediated communication: Linguistic, social and cross-cultural perspectives* (pp. 129–146). Amsterdam: John Benjamins Publishing Company.

Devine, P.A., & Fernald, P.S. (1973). Outcome effects of receiving a preferred, randomly assigned or non-preferred therapy. *Journal of Consulting and Clinical Psychology, 41,* 104–107.

DeVries, R. (2000). Vygotsky, Piaget, and education: A reciprocal assimilation of theories and educational practices. *New Ideas in Psychology, 18,* 187–213.

Dickemann, M. (1979). The ecology of mating systems in hypergynous dowry societies. *Social Science Information, 18,* 163–195.

Dickemann, M. (1985). Human sociobiology: The first decade. *New Scientist, 108,* 38–42.

Diener, E., Suh, E.M., Lucas, R.E., & Smith, H.E. (1999). Subjective well-being: Three decades of progress. *Psychological Bulletin, 125,* 276–302.

DiNardo, P.A., Guzy, L.T., Jenkins, J.A., Bak, R.M., Tomasi, S.F., & Copland, M. (1988). Aetiology and maintenance of dog fears. *Behaviour Research and Therapy, 26,* 241–244.

Dindia, K., & Allen, M. (1992). Sex differences in self-disclosure: A meta-analysis. *Psychological Bulletin, 112,* 106–124.

Dindia, K., & Baxter, L.A. (1987). Maintenance and repair strategies in marital relationships. *Journal of Social and Personal Relationships, 4,* 143–158.

Dobson, K.S. (1989). A meta-analysis of the efficacy of cognitive therapy for depression. *Journal of Consulting and Clinical Psychology, 57,* 414–419.

Doise, W., & Mugny, G. (1984). *The social development of the intellect.* Oxford, UK: Pergamon.

Doise, W., Rijsman, J.B., van Meel, J., Bressers, I., & Pinxten, L. (1981). Sociale markering en cognitieve ontwikkeling. *Pedagogische Studien, 58,* 241–248.

Dollard, J., Doob, L.W., Miller, N.E., Mowrer, O.H., & Sears, R.R. (1939). *Frustration and aggression.* New Haven, CT: Yale University Press.

Donaldson, M. (1978). *Children's minds.* London: Fontana.

Donnerstein, E., & Wilson, D.W. (1976). Effects of noise and perceived control on ongoing and subsequent aggressive behaviour. *Journal of Personality and Social Psychology, 34,* 774–781.

Doob, L.W., & Sears, R.R. (1939). Factors determining substitute behaviour and the overt expression of aggression. *Journal of Abnormal and Social Psychology, 34,* 293–313.

Douvan, E., & Adelson, J. (1966). *The adolescent experience.* New York: Wiley.

Dovidio, J.F., Piliavin, J.A., & Clark, R.D. (1991). The arousal-cost reward model and the process of intervention: A review of the evidence. In M.S. Clark (Ed.), *Review of*

personality and social psychology: Vol. 12. Prosocial behaviour.* New York: Academic Press.

Dryden, W. (1996). *Individual therapy: A handbook.* Milton Keynes, UK: Open University Press.

Duck, S. (1982). *Personal relationships: 4. Dissolving personal relationships.* London: Academic Press.

Duck, S. (1992). *Human relationships* (2nd Edn.). London: Sage.

Duck, S.W. (1994). *Meaningful relationships.* London: Sage.

Duck, S.W., & Pond, K. (1989). Friends, Romans, countrymen: Lend me your retrospective data: Rhetoric and reality in personal relationships. In C. Hendrick (Ed.), *Review of social psychology and personality: Vol. 10. Close relationships* (pp. 3–27). Newbury Park, CA: Sage.

Dunbar, R. (1996). *Grooming, gossip and the evolution of language.* London: Faber & Faber.

Dunbar, R.M. (1998). The social brain hypothesis. *Evolutionary Anthropology, 34,* 178–190.

Dunn, J., & Plomin, R. (1990). *Separate lives: Why siblings are so different.* New York: Basic Books.

Durand, V.M., & Barlow, D.H. (2003). *Essentials of abnormal psychology* (3rd Edn.). Belmont, CA: Wadsworth.

Durkin, K. (1995). *Developmental social psychology: From infancy to old age.* Oxford, UK: Blackwell.

Dworetzsky, J.P. (1996). *Introduction to child development* (6th Edn.). New York: West Publishing Co.

Dwyer, D. (2001). *Interpersonal relations.* London: Routledge.

Eagly, A.H. (1978). Sex differences in influenceability. *Psychological Bulletin, 85,* 86–116.

Eagly, A.H., & Crowley, M. (1986). Gender and helping behaviour: A meta-analytic review of the social psychological literature. *Psychological Bulletin, 100,* 283–308.

Eagly, A.H., Karau, S.J., & Makhijani, M.G. (1995). Gender and the effectiveness of leaders: A meta-analysis. *Psychological Bulletin, 117,* 125–145.

Ebbesen, E.B., Kjos, G.L., & Konecni, V.J. (1976). Spatial ecology: Its effects on the choice of friends and enemies. *Journal of Experimental Social Psychology, 12,* 505–518.

Ebbinghaus, H. (1913). *Memory* (H. Ruyer & C.E. Bussenius, Trans.). New York: Teachers College, Columbia University. (Original work published 1885.)

Eccles, J.S., Midgley, C., Wigfield, A., & Buchanan, C.M. (1993). Development during adolescence: The impact of stage-environment fit on young adolescents' experiences in schools and in families. *American Psychologist, 48,* 90–101.

Egeland, B., Gerhard, D.S., Pauls, D.L., Sussex, J.N., Kidd, K.K., Allen, C.R., Hostetter, A.M., & Housman, D.E. (1987). Bipolar affective disorders linked to DNA markers on chromosome 11. *Nature, 325,* 783–787.

Eisenberg, N., Lennon, R., & Roth, K. (1983). Prosocial development: A longitudinal study. *Developmental Psychology, 19,* 846–855.

Eisenberg, N., Miller, P.A., Shell, R., McNalley, S., & Shea, C. (1991). Prosocial development in adolescence: A longitudinal study. *Developmental Psychology, 27,* 849–857.

Eisenberg, N., & Mussen, P.H. (1989). *The roots of prosocial behaviour in children.* Cambridge, UK: Cambridge University Press.

Eisenberg-Berg, N., & Hand, M. (1979). The relationship of preschoolers' reasoning about prosocial moral conflicts to prosocial behaviour. *Child Development, 50,* 356–363.

Ellis, A. (1962). *Reason and emotion in psychotherapy.* Secaucus, NJ: Prentice-Hall.

Ellis, A. (1978). The basic clinical theory of rational emotive therapy. In A. Ellis & R. Grieger (Eds.), *Handbook of rational emotive therapy.* New York: Springer.

Ellis, S., & Gauvain, M. (1992). Social and cultural influences on children's collaborative interactions. In L.T. Winegar & J. Valsiner (Eds.), *Children's development within social context: Vol. 2. Research and methodology*. Hillsdale, NJ: Lawrence Erlbaum Associates Inc.

Emler, N. (1984). Differential involvement in delinquency: Toward an interpretation in terms of reputation management. In B.A. Maher & W.B. Maher (Eds.). *Progress in Experimental Personality Research, Vol. 13*. New York: Academic Press.

Emler, N., & Reicher, S. (1995). Adolescence and delinquency: The collective management of reputation. *Social Psychology and Society, XIV*.

Emler, N., Reicher, S., & Ross, A. (1987). The social context of delinquent conduct. *Journal of Child Psychology and Psychiatry, 28*, 99–109.

Empson, J.A.C. (1989). *Sleep and dreaming*. London: Faber & Faber.

Engels, G.I., Garnefski, N., & Diekstra, R.F.W. (1993). Efficacy of rational-emotive therapy: A quantitative analysis. *Journal of Consulting and Clinical Psychology, 61*, 1083–1090.

Epstein, S. (1977). Traits are alive and well. In D. Magnusson & N.S. Endler (Eds.), *Perspectives in interactional psychology*. New York: Plenum.

Erickson, M., Sroufe, L.A., & Egeland, B. (1985). The relationship between quality of attachment and behavior problems in preschool in a high-risk sample. In I. Bretherton & E. Waters (Eds.). *Monographs of the Society for Research in Child Development, 50*(1–2, Serial no. 209), 147–186.

Erikson, E.H. (1950). *Childhood and society*. New York: Norton.

Erikson, E.H. (1959). *Identity and life styles: Selected papers*. New York: International Universities Press.

Erikson, E.H. (1963). *Childhood and society* (2nd Edn.). New York: Norton.

Erikson, E.H. (1968). *Identity: Youth and crisis*. New York: Norton.

Erikson, E.H. (1969). *Gandhi's truth: On the origin of militant nonviolence*. New York: W.W. Norton.

Eron, L.D. (1982). Parent–child interaction, television violence, and aggression of children. *American Psychologist, 37*, 197–211.

Eysenck, H.J. (1952). The effects of psychotherapy: An evaluation. *Journal of Consulting Psychology, 16*, 319–324.

Eysenck, H.J. (1967). *The biological basis of personality*. Springfield, IL: C.C. Thomas.

Eysenck, H.J. (1981). *The intelligence controversy: H. J. Eysenck vs. Leon Kamin*. New York: Wiley.

Eysenck, H.J., & Broadhurst, P.L. (1964). Experiments with animals. In H.J. Eysenck (Ed.), *Experiments in motivation*. London: Pergamon Press.

Eysenck, H.J., & Eysenck, M.W. (1989). *Mindwatching: Why we behave the way we do*. London: Prion.

Eysenck, M.W. (1982). *Attention and arousal: Cognition and performance*. Berlin: Springer.

Eysenck, M.W. (1990). *Happiness: Facts and myths*. Hove, UK: Psychology Press.

Eysenck, M.W. (1997). *Anxiety and cognition: A unified theory*. Hove, UK: Psychology Press.

Eysenck, M.W. (2000). *Psychology: A student's handbook*. Hove, UK: Psychology Press.

Eysenck, M.W. (2004). *Psychology: An international perspective*. Hove, UK: Psychology Press.

Eysenck, M.W., & Eysenck, M.C. (1980). Effects of processing depth, distinctiveness, and word frequency on retention. *British Journal of Psychology, 71*, 263–274.

Eysenck, M.W., & Keane, M.T. (1990). *Cognitive psychology: A student's handbook* (2nd Edn.). Hove, UK: Psychology Press.

Eysenck, M.W., & Keane, M.T. (1995). *Cognitive psychology: A student's handbook* (3rd Edn.). Hove, UK: Psychology Press.

Fabes, R.A., Fultz, J., Eisenberg, N., May-Plumlee, T., & Christopher, F.S. (1989). Effects of rewards on children's prosocial motivation: A socialisation study. *Developmental Psychology, 25*, 509–515.

Fagot, B.I. (1985). Beyond the reinforcement principle: Another step toward understanding sex-role development. *Developmental Psychology, 21*, 1097–1104.

Fagot, B.I., & Leinbach, M.D. (1989). The young child's gender schema: Environmental input, internal organisation. *Child Development, 60*, 663–672.

Fahrenberg, J. (1992). Psychophysiology of neuroticism and emotionality. In A. Gale & M.W. Eysenck (Eds.), *Handbook of individual differences: Biological perspectives*. Chichester, UK: Wiley.

Fairchild, H.H. (1988). Creating positive television images. *Applied Social Psychology Annual, 8*, 270–280.

Farde, L., Wiesel, F.A., Stoneelander, S., Halldin, C., Nordstrom, A.L., Hall, H., & Sedvall, G. (1990). D2 dopamine receptors in neuroleptic naive schizophrenic patients: A positron emission tomography study with [C-11] raclopride. *Archives of General Psychiatry, 47*, 213–219.

Febbraro, A.R. (2003). Alpha bias and beta bias in research on labour and love: The case of enhancement versus scarcity. *Feminism & Psychology, 13*, 201–223.

Fellner, C.H., & Marshall, J.R. (1981). Kidney donors revisited. In J.P. Rushton & R.M. Sorrentino (Eds.), *Altruism and helping behaviour*. Hillsdale, NJ: Lawrence Erlbaum Associates Inc.

Feske, U., & Chambless, D.L. (1995). Cognitive behavioural versus exposure only treatment for social phobia: A meta-analysis. *Behavioural Therapy, 26*, 695–720.

Festinger, L., Schachter, S., & Back, K. (1950). *Social pressures in informal groups: A study of a housing community*. New York: Harper.

Feyerabend, P. (1975). *Against method: Outline of an anarchist theory of knowledge*. London: New Left Books.

Fijneman, Y.A., Willemsen, M.E., & Poortinga, Y.H. (1996). Individualism-collectivism: An empirical study of a conceptual issue. *Journal of Cross-Cultural Psychology, 27*, 381–402.

Fincham, F.D., & Bradbury, T.N. (1993). Marital satisfaction, depression, and attributions: A longitudinal analysis. *Journal of Personality and Social Psychology, 64*, 442–452.

Fink, M. (1985). Convulsive therapy: Fifty years of progress. *Convulsive Therapy, 1*, 204–216.

Finlay-Jones, R.A., & Brown, G.W. (1981). Types of stressful life events and the onset of anxiety and depressive disorders. *Psychological Medicine, 11*, 803–815.

Fisher, R.A. (1930). *The genetical theory of natural selection*. Oxford, UK: Clarendon Press.

Fisher, R.A., & Yates, F. (1974). *Statistical tables for biological, agricultural and medical research* (6th Edn.). Harlow, UK: Addison Wesley Longman.

Fiske, A.P. (2002). Using individualism and collectivism to compare cultures—A critique of the validity and measurement of the constructs: Comment on Oyserman et al. (2002). *Psychological Bulletin, 128*, 78–88.

Fiske, S.T. (1993). Social cognition and social perception. *Annual Review of Psychology, 44*, 155–194.

Fiske, S.T., & Taylor, S.E. (1991). *Social cognition* (2nd Edn.). New York: McGraw-Hill.

Flanagan, D. (1988). *Flanagan's version: A spectator's guide to science on the eve of the 21st century*. New York: Knopf.

Floody, O.R. (1968). Hormones and aggression in female animals. In B.B. Suare (Ed.), *Hormones and aggressive behaviour*. New York: Plenum Press.

Flynn, J.R. (1987). Massive IQ gains in 14 nations: What IQ tests really measure. *Psychological Bulletin, 101*, 271–291.

Flynn, J.R. (1994). IQ gains over time. In R.J. Sternberg (Ed.), *Encyclopedia of human intelligence*. New York: Macmillan.

Foa, U.G., & Foa, E.B. (1975). *Resource theory of social exchange*. Morristown, NJ: General Learning Press.

Folkard, S. (1996, September 28). *Daily Express*.

Ford, M.R., & Widiger, T.A. (1989). Sex bias in the diagnosis of histrionic and antisocial personality disorders. *Journal of Consulting and Clinical Psychology, 57*, 301–305.

Forman, E.A., & Cazden, C.B. (1985). Exploring Vygotskian perspectives in education: The cognitive value of peer interaction. In J.V. Wertsch (Ed.), *Culture, communication, and cognition: Vygotskian perspectives*. Cambridge, UK: Cambridge University Press.

Fox, K. (2005). Evolution, alienation and gossip: The role of mobile telecommunications in the 21st. century. Retrieved from sirc.org/publik/gossip.shtml

Franchini, L., Gasperini, M., Perez, J., Smeraldi, E., & Zanardi, R. (1997). A double-blind study of long-term treatment with sertraline or fluvoxamine for prevention of highly recurrent unipolar depression. *Journal of Clinical Psychiatry, 58*, 104–107.

Francks, C., DeLisi, L.E., Shaw, S.H., Fisher, S.E., Richardson, A.J., Stein, J.F., & Monaco, A.P. (2003). Parent-of-origin effects on handedness and schizophrenia susceptibility on chromosome 2p12q11. *Human Molecular Genetics, 12*, 3225–3230.

Franz, C., Weinberger, J., Kremen, W., & Jacobs, R. (1996). *Childhood antecedents of dysphoria in adults: A 36-year longitudinal study*. Unpublished manuscript, Williams College.

Franzoi, S.L. (1996). *Social psychology*. Madison, MI: Brown & Benchmark.

Freedman, J.L. (1973). The effects of population density on humans. In J.T. Fawcett (Ed.), *Psychological perspectives on population*. New York: Basic Books.

Freeman, D. (1983). *Margaret Mead and Samoa: The making and unmaking of an anthropological myth*. Cambridge, MA: Harvard University Press.

Freud, A. (1946). *The ego and the mechanisms of defence*. London: Hogarth Press.

Freud, S. (1900). *The interpretation of dreams* (J. Strachey, Trans.). London: Allen & Unwin.

Freud, S. (1917). Introductory lectures on psychoanalysis. In J. Strachey (Ed.), *The complete psychological works, Vol. 16*. New York: Norton.

Freud, S. (1921). Essay on theory of sexuality. *The standard edition of the complete psychological works*. Trans. and Ed. James Strachey. London: Hogarth.

Freud, S. (1933). *New introductory lectures in psychoanalysis*. New York: Norton.

Freud, S., & Breuer, J. (1895). Studies on hysteria. In J. Strachey (Ed.), *The complete psychological works, Vol. 2*. New York: Norton.

Friedrich, L.K., & Stein, A.H. (1973). Aggressive and pro-social television programmes and the natural behaviour of pre-school children. *Monographs of the Society for Research in Child Development, 38*, 1–64.

Frith, C.D. (1992). *The cognitive neuropsychology of schizophrenia*. Hove, UK: Psychology Press.

Frueh, T., & McGhee, P.E. (1975). Traditional sex-role development and the amount of time spent watching television. *Developmental Psychology, 11*, 109.

Fuligni, A.J., & Eccles, J.S. (1993). Perceived parent–child relationships and early adolescents' orientation toward peers. *Developmental Psychology, 29*(4), 622–632.

Furnham, A., & Pinder, A. (1990). Young people's attitudes to experimentation on animals. *The Psychologist, 3*, 444–448.

Fyer, A.J., Mannuzza, S., Chapman, T.F., Liebowitz, M.R., & Klein, D.F. (1993). A direct-interview family study of social phobia. *Archives of General Psychiatry, 50*, 286–293.

Fyer, A.J., Mannuzza, S., Gallops, M.S., Martin, L.Y., et al. (1990). Familial transmission of simple phobias and fears: A preliminary report. *Archives of General Psychiatry, 47*(3), 252–256.

Gaertner, S.L., & Dovidio, J.F. (1977). The subtlety of white racism, arousal, and helping behaviour. *Journal of Personality and Social Psychology, 35*, 691–707.

Gaffan, E.A., Hansel, M., & Smith, L. (1983). Does reward depletion influence spatial memory performance? *Learning and Motivation, 14*, 58–74.

Garfield, S.L. (1980). *Psychotherapy: An eclectic approach*. New York: Wiley.

Gauze, C.M. (1994). *Talking to Mom about friendship: What do mothers know?* Paper presented at the meeting of the Society for Research on Adolescence, San Diego, CA.

Gavey, N. (1992). Technologies and effects of heterosexual coercion. *Feminism and Psychology, 2*, 325–351.

Gelfand, M.J., Triandis, H.C., & Chan, D.K.-S. (1996). Individualism versus collectivism or versus authoritarianism? *European Journal of Social Psychology, 26*, 397–410.

Gerbino, L., Oleshansky, M., & Gershon, S. (1978). Clinical use and mode of action of lithium. In M.A. Lipton, A. DiMascio, & F.K. Killam (Eds.), *Psychopharmacology: A generation of progress*. New York: Raven Press.

Gerbner, G., & Gross, L. (1976). The scary world of TV's heavy viewer. *Psychology Today, 9*, 41–45.

Gergen, K.J. (1973). Social psychology as history. *Journal of Personality and Social Psychology, 26*, 309–320.

Gergen, K.J. (1985). Social constructionist inquiry: Context and implications. In K.J. Gergen & K.E. Davis (Eds.), *The social construction of the person*. New York: Springer-Verlag.

Gergen, K.J. (1997). Social psychology as social construction: The emerging vision. In C. McGarty & A. Haslam (Eds.), *The message of social psychology*. Oxford, UK: Blackwell.

Gergen, K.J., Morse, S.J., & Gergen, M.M. (1980). Behaviour exchange in cross-cultural perspective. In H.C. Triandis & W.W. Lambert (Eds.), *Handbook of cross-cultural psychology: Vol. 5. Social psychology*. Boston, MA: Allyn & Bacon.

Gerlsman, C., Emmelkamp, P.M.G., & Arrindell, W.A. (1990). Anxiety, depression, and perception of early parenting: A meta-analysis. *Clinical Psychology Review, 10*, 251–277.

Germain, M.A., Nielsen, T.A., Zadra, A., & Montplaisir, J. (2000). The prevalence of typical dream themes challenges the specificity of the threat simulation theory. *Behavioral and Brain Sciences, 23*, 940–941.

Gershon, E.S. (1990). Genetics. In F.K. Goodwin & K.R. Jamison (Eds.), *Manic-depressive illness*. Oxford, UK: Oxford University Press.

Geschwind, N., & Galaburda, A.M. (1985). Cerebral lateralisation: Biological mechanisms, associations and pathology: I. A hypothesis and a program for research. *Archives of Neurology, 42*, 428–459.

Gilligan, C. (1977). In a different voice: Women's conceptions of the self and of morality. *Harvard Educational Review, 47*, 481–517.

Gilligan, C. (1982). *In a different voice: Psychological theory and women's development*. Cambridge, MA: Harvard University Press.

Gilligan, C., & Attanucci, J. (1988). Two moral orientations: Gender differences and similarities. *Merrill-Palmer Quarterly, 34*, 223–237.

Gilligan, C., & Wiggins, G. (1987). The origins of morality in early childhood relationships. In J. Kagan & S. Lamb (Eds.), *The emergence of morality in young children*. Chicago, IL: University of Chicago Press.

Gjedde, A., & Wong, D.F. (1987). Positron tomographic quantitation of neuroreceptors in human brain in vivo with special reference to the D2 dopamine receptors in caudate nucleus. *Neurosurgical Review, 10*, 9.

Glass, D.C., Singer, J.E., & Friedman, L.W. (1969). Psychic cost of adaptation to an environmental stressor. *Journal of Personality and Social Psychology, 12*, 200–210.

Glassman, W.E. (1995). *Approaches to psychology* (2nd Edn.). Buckingham, UK: Open University Press.

Gleitman, H. (1986). *Psychology* (2nd Edn.). London: Norton.

Goddard, H.H. (1913). *Feeble-mindedness: Its causes and consequences*. New York: Macmillan.

Goddard, S.J., & Cross, J. (1987). A social skills training approach to dealing with disruptive behaviour in a primary school. *Maladjustment and Therapeutic Education, 5*(3), 24–29.

Goldstein, J.S. (2001). *War and gender: How gender shapes the war system and vice versa*. Cambridge, UK: Cambridge University Press.

Goldwyn, E. (1979, May 24). The fight to be male. *Listener*, 709–712.

Golombok, S., & Hines, M. (2002). Sex differences in social behaviour. In P.K. Smith & C.H. Hart (Eds.), *Blackwell handbook of childhood social development*. Oxford, UK: Blackwell.

Goodall, J. (1978). Chimp killings: Is it the man in them? *Science News, 113*, 276.

Goodwin, R. (1995). Personal relationships across cultures. *The Psychologist, 8*, 73–75.

Goodwin, R. (1999). *Social relationships across cultures*. London: Routledge.

Gottesman, I.I. (1963). Heritability of personality: A demonstration. *Psychological Monographs, 77*(Whole No. 572).

Gottesman, I.I. (1991). *Schizophrenia genesis: The origins of madness*. New York: W.H. Freeman.

Gottesman, I.I., & Bertelsen, A. (1989). Dual mating studies in psychiatry: Offspring of inpatients with examples from reactive (psychogenic) psychoses. *International Review of Psychiatry, 1*, 287–296.

Gottfried, A.W. (1984). Home environment and early cognitive development: Integration, meta-analyses, and conclusions. In A.W. Gottfried (Ed.), *Home environment and early cognitive development: Longitudinal research*. Orlando, FL: Academic Press.

Grammer, K., & Thornhill, R. (1994). Human (*Homo sapiens*) facial attractiveness and sexual selection: The role of symmetry and averageness. *Journal of Comparative Psychology, 108*, 233–242.

Gray, J.A. (1985). A whole and its parts: Behaviour, the brain, cognition and emotion. *Bulletin of the British Psychological Society, 38*, 99–112.

Gray, J.A. (1991). On the morality of speciesism. *The Psychologist, 14*, 196–198.

Graziano, W.G., Jensen-Campbell, L.A., & Hair, E.C. (1996). Perceiving interpersonal conflict and reacting to it: The case for agreeableness. *Journal of Personality and Social Psychology, 70*, 820–835.

Gredler, M. (1992). *Learning and instruction theory into practice*. New York: Macmillan Publishing Company.

Green, S. (1994). *Principles of biopsychology*. Hove, UK: Psychology Press.

Greenfield, P.M. (1984). *Mind and media: The effect of television, video games and computers*. Aylesbury, UK: Fontana.

Grier, J.W., & Burk, T. (1992). *Biology of animal behaviour* (2nd Edn.). Oxford, UK: W.C. Brown.

Griffit, W.B., & Guay, P. (1969). 'Object' evaluation and conditioned affect. *Journal of Experimental Research in Psychology, 4*, 1–8.

Griffiths, M. (1997). Video games and aggression. *The Psychologist, 10*, 397–401.

Griffiths, M.D. (1999). All but connected (online relationships). *Psychology Post, 17*, 6–7.

Griffiths, M.D. (2000). Cyberaffairs. *Psychology Review, 7*, 28–31.

Griffiths, M.D., & Hunt, N. (1995). Computer game playing in adolescence: Prevalence and demographic indicators. *Journal of Community and Applied Psychology, 5*, 189–193.

Gross, R. (1996). *Psychology: The science of mind and behaviour* (3rd Edn.). London: Hodder & Stoughton.

Gunter, B., & McAleer, J.L. (1990). *Children and television: The one-eyed monster?* London: Routledge.

Gunter, B., & McAleer, J. (1997). *Children and television* (2nd Edn.). London: Routledge.

Gupta, U., & Singh, P. (1982). Exploratory studies in love and liking and types of marriages. *Indian Journal of Applied Psychology, 19*, 92–97.

Gwinner, E. (1986). Circannual rhythms in the control of avian rhythms. *Advances in the Study of Behaviour, 16*, 191–228.

Hackmann, A., Clark, D.M., & McManus, F. (2000). Recurrent images and early memories in social phobia. *Behaviour Research and Therapy, 38*, 601–610.

Haggbloom, S.J., Warnick, R., Warnick, J.E., Jones, V.K., Yarbrough, G.L., Russell T.M., Borecky, C.M., McGahhey, R., Powell, J.L., Beavers, J., & Monte, E. (2002). The 100 most eminent psychologists of the 20th century. *Review of General Psychology, 6*, 139–152.

Hajek, P., & Belcher, M. (1991). Dreams of absent-minded transgression: An empirical study of a cognitive withdrawal symptom. *Journal of Abnormal Psychology, 100*, 487–491.

Halbreich, U., Endicott, J., Schacht, S., & Nee, J. (1982). The diversity of premenstrual changes as reflected in the Premenstrual Assessment Form. *Acta Psychiatrica Scandinavica, 65*, 46–65.

Hall, C., & van de Castle, R. (1966). *The content analysis of dreams*. New York: McGraw-Hill.

Hall, C.S. (1953). A cognitive theory of dream symbols. *Journal of General Psychology, 48*, 169–186.

Hall, C.S., & Lindzey, G. (1970). *Theories of personality*. London: Wiley.

Hall, C.S., Lindzey, G., & Campbell, J.B. (1997). *Theories of personality*. New York: John Wiley.

Hall, C.T. (2001). Breast cancer risk greater for women on night shifts. http://www.mindfully.org/Health/Cancer-Women-Nightshift.htm

Hall, G.S. (1904). *Adolescence*. New York: Appleton-Century-Crofts.

Halliday, T., & Arnold, S.J. (1987). Multiple mating by females: A perspective from quantitative genetics. *Animal Behaviour, 35*, 939–941.

Hamilton, W.D. (1964). The genetical evolution of social behaviour: I and II. *Journal of Theoretical Biology, 7*, 1–52.

Hamilton, W.D., & Zuk, M. (1982). Heritable true fitness and bright birds: A role for parasites? *Science, 218*, 384–387.

Hammen, C.L. (1991). The generation of stress in the course of unipolar depression. *Journal of Abnormal Psychology, 100*, 555–561.

Hampson, S.E. (1988). *The construction of personality: An introduction* (2nd Edn.). London: Routledge.

Harcourt, A.H. (1992). Coalitions and alliances: Are primates more complex than non-primates? In A.H. Harcourt & F. de Wall (Eds.), *Coalitions and alliances in humans and other animals*. Oxford: Oxford University Press.

Hardyck, C.D., & Petrinovich, L.F. (1970). Subvocal speech and comprehension level as a function of the difficulty level of reading material. *Journal of Verbal Learning and Verbal Behavior, 9*, 647–652.

Hare-Mustin, R.T., & Maracek, J. (1988). The meaning of difference: Gender theory, post-modernism and psychology. *American Psychologist, 43*, 455–464.

Hargreaves, D. (1967). *Social relations in a secondary school*. London: Routledge & Kegan Paul.

Harlow, H.F., & Harlow, M.K. (1962). Social deprivation in monkeys. *Scientific American, 207*, 136.

Harlow, H.F., & Mears, C. (1979). *The human model: Primate perspectives*. Washington, DC: Winston.

Harré, R., & Secord, P. (1972). *The explanation of social behaviour*. Oxford, UK: Basil Blackwell.

Harris, C.R. (2002). Sexual and romantic jealousy in heterosexual and homosexual adults. *Psychological Science, 13*, 7–12.

Harris, E.L., Noyes, R., Crowe, R.R., & Chaudhry, D.R. (1983). Family study of agoraphobia: Report of a pilot study. *Archives of General Psychiatry, 40*, 1061–1064.

Harris, T.O. (1997). Adult attachment processes and psychotherapy: A commentary on Bartholomew and Birtschnell. *British Journal of Medical Psychology, 70*, 281–290.

Harris, W.H. (1995, June). *The opportunity for romantic love among hunter-gatherers*. Paper presented at the annual convention of the Human Behavior and Evolution Society, Santa Barbara, CA.

Harrison, Y., & Horne, J.A. (2000). The impact of sleep deprivation on decision making: A review. *Journal of Experimental Psychology: Applied, 6*, 236–249.

Harry, J. (1983). Gay male and lesbian relationships. In E. Macklin & R. Rubin (Eds.), *Contemporary families and alternative lifestyles: Handbook on research and theory*. London: Sage.

Harter, S., & Monsour, A. (1992). Developmental analysis of conflict caused by opposing attributes in the adolescent self-portrait. *Developmental Psychology, 28*, 251–260.

Hartmann, E.L. (1973). *The functions of sleep*. New Haven, CT: Yale University Press.

Hatfield, E., Utne, M.K., & Traupmann, J. (1979). Equity theory and intimate relationships. In R.L. Burgess & T.L. Huston (Eds.), *Exchange theory in developing relationships*. New York: Academic Press.

Hawkins, L.H., & Armstrong-Esther, C.A. (1978, May 4). Circadian rhythms and night shift working in nurses. *Nursing Times*, 49–52.

Hayes, N. (1993). *Principles of social psychology*. Hove, UK: Psychology Press.

Hayes, N. (1994). *Foundations of psychology: An introductory text*. London: Routledge.

Hazan, C., & Shaver, P.R. (1987). Romantic love conceptualised as an attachment process. *Journal of Personality and Social Psychology, 52*, 511–524.

Hearold, S. (1986). A synthesis of 1043 effects of television on social behaviour. In G. Comstock (Ed.), *Public communication and behaviour, Vol. 1*. Orlando, FL: Academic Press.

Heather, N. (1976). *Radical perspectives in psychology*. London: Methuen.

Hebb, D.O. (1949). *Organisation of behavior*. New York: Wiley.

Hebb, D.O. (1958). *A textbook of psychology*. Philadelphia: W.B. Saunders.

Henderson, J. (2001). *Development of thinking*. London: Routledge.

Henderson, J.J.A., & Anglin, J.M. (2003). Facial attractiveness predicts longevity. *Evolution and Human Behavior, 24*, 351–356.

Hennigan, K.M., Del Rosario, M.L., Cook, T.D., & Calder, B.J. (1982). Impact of the introduction of television on crime in the United States: Empirical findings and theoretical implications. *Journal of Personality and Social Psychology, 42*, 461–477.

Hergenhahn, B.R., & Olson, M.H. (1999). *An introduction to theories of personality* (5th. Edn.). New York: Prentice-Hall.

Herman, D., & Green, J. (1991). *Madness: A study guide*. London: BBC Education.

Herrnstein, R.J., & Murray, C.A. (1994). *The bell curve: Intelligence and class structure in American life*. New York: Free Press.

Herzog, H.A. (1988). The moral status of mice. *The American Psychologist, 43*, 473–474.

Hewstone, M., & Stroebe, W. (2001). *Introduction to social psychology* (3rd Edn.). Oxford, UK: Blackwell.

Hilborn, R.C. (1994). *Chaos and nonlinear dynamics*. Oxford, UK: Oxford University Press.

Hill, D. (2000, February 27). *The Observer*.

Hill, K., & Kaplan, H. (1988). Tradeoffs in male and female reproductive strategies among the Ache: Part 1. In L. Betzig, M. Borgerhoff Mulder, & P. Turke (Eds.), *Human reproductive behaviour: A Darwinian perspective*. Cambridge: Cambridge University Press.

Hirschfeld, R.M. (1999). Efficacy of SSRIs and newer antidepressants in severe depression: Comparison with TCAs. *Journal of Clinical Psychiatry, 60*, 326–335.

Hirschman, C., & Teerawitchitchainan, B. (2003). Cultural and socioeconomic influences on divorce during modernisation: Southeast Asia, 1940s to 1960s. *Population and Development Review, 29*, 215–253.

Hobson, J.A. (1988). *The dreaming brain*. New York: Basic Books.

Hobson, J.A. (1994). Sleep and dreaming. In A.M. Colman (Ed.), *Companion encyclopedia of psychology, Vol. 1*. London: Routledge.

Hobson, J.A., & McCarley, R.W. (1977). The brain as a dream state generator: An activation-synthesis hypothesis of the dream process. *American Journal of Psychiatry, 134*, 1335–1348.

Hobson, J.A., Pace-Schott, E.F., & Stickgold, R. (2000). Dreaming and the brain: Toward a cognitive neuroscience of conscious states. *Behavioral and Brain Sciences, 23*, 793–842.

Hodgkinson, P.E. (1987). Responding to inpatient suicide. *British Journal of Medical Psychology, 60*, 387–392.

Hoffman, M.L. (1970). Moral development. In P.H. Mussen (Ed.), *Carmichael's manual of child psychology, Vol. 2*. New York: Wiley.

Hoffman, M.L. (1975). Altruistic behaviour and the parent–child relationship. *Journal of Personality and Social Psychology, 31*, 937–943.

Hoffman, M.L. (1988). Moral development. In M.H. Bornstein & M. E. Lamb (Eds.), *Developmental psychology: An advanced textbook*. Hillsdale, NJ: Lawrence Erlbaum Associates Inc.

Hofling, C.K. (1974). *Textbook of psychiatry for medical practice*. Philadelphia, PA: Lippincott.

Hofstede, G. (1980). *Culture's consequences: International differences in work-related values*. Beverly Hills, CA: Sage.

Hogg, M.A., & Vaughan, G.M. (2002). *Social psychology* (3rd Edn.). Harlow, UK: Prentice Hall.

Holcomb, W.R. (1986). Stress inoculation therapy with anxiety and stress disorders of acute psychiatric inpatients. *Journal of Clinical Psychology, 42*, 864–872.

Holland, A.J., Sicotte, N., & Treasure, J. (1988). Anorexia nervosa: Evidence for a genetic basis. *Journal of Psychosomatic Research, 32*, 561–572.

Holmes, T.H., & Rahe, R.H. (1967). The social readjustment rating scale. *Journal of Psychosomatic Research, 11*, 213–218.

Hooley, J.M., & Hiller, J.B. (2000). Personality and expressed emotion. *Journal of Abnormal Psychology, 109*, 40–44.

Hooley, J.M., Orley, J., & Teasdale, J.D. (1986). Levels of expressed emotion and relapse in depressed patients. *British Journal of Psychiatry, 148*, 642–647.

Horn, J.M. (1983). The Texas adoption project: Adopted children and their intellectual resemblance to biological and adoptive parents. *Child Development, 54*, 268–275.

Horne, J. (1988). *Why do we sleep? The functions of sleep in humans and other mammals*. Oxford, UK: Oxford University Press.

Horne, J. (2001). State of the art: sleep. *The Psychologist, 14*, 302–306.

Horne, J.A., & Minard, A. (1985). Sleep and sleepiness following a behaviourally "active" day. *Ergonomics, 28*, 567–575.

Howard, J.A., Blumstein, P., & Schwartz, P. (1987). Social evolutionary theories? Some observations on preferences in human mate selection. *Journal of Personality and Social Psychology, 53*, 194–200.

Howe, C., Tolmie, A., & Rodgers, C. (1992). The acquisition of conceptual knowledge in science by primary school children: Group interaction and the understanding of motion down an incline. *British Journal of Developmental Psychology, 10*, 113–130.

Howitt, D., & Owusu-Bempah, J. (1990). Racism in a British journal? *The Psychologist, 3*, 396–400.

Howland, R.H., & Thase, M.E. (1991). Biological studies of dysthymia. *Biological Psychiatry, 30*, 283–304.

Hsu, F. (1981). *Americans and Chinese: Passage to difference* (3rd Edn.). Honolulu, HI: University Press of Honolulu.

Hüber-Weidman, H. (1976). *Sleep, sleep disturbances and sleep deprivation*. Cologne, Germany: Kiepenheuser & Witsch.

Hudson, J.L., & Rapee, R.M. (2000). The origins of social phobia. *Behavior Modification, 24*, 102–129.

Huesmann, L.R., & Eron, L.D. (1986). *Television and the aggressive child: A cross-national comparison*. Hillsdale, NJ: Lawrence Erlbaum Associates Inc.

Huesmann, L.R., Lagerspetz, K., & Eron, L.D. (1984). Intervening variables in the TV violence–aggression relation: Evidence from two countries. *Developmental Psychology, 20*, 746–775.

Hughes, M. (1975). *Egocentrism in preschool children*. Unpublished PhD thesis, University of Edinburgh, UK.

Humphreys, P. (2001). *Exam success in AQA A psychology*. London: Routledge.

Huston, A.C. (1985). The development of sex typing: Themes from recent research. *Developmental Review, 5*, 1–17.

Huston, T.L., Ruggiero, M., Conner, R., & Geis, G. (1981). Bystander intervention into crime: A study based on naturally-occurring episodes. *Social Psychology Quarterly, 44*, 14–23.

Hyde, J.S., & Linn, M.C. (1988). Gender differences in verbal ability: A meta-analysis. *Psychological Bulletin, 104*, 53–69.

Imperato-McGinley, J., Guerro, L., Gautier, T., & Peterson, R.E. (1974). Steroid 5–reductase deficiency in man: An inherited form of male pseudohermaphroditism. *Science, 186*, 1213–1216.

Ingram, N. (2004, April 26–28). Schizophrenia: Destiny in your genes? *Psychology Review, 10*.

Inhelder, B., & Piaget, J. (1958). *The growth of logical thinking from childhood to adolescence*. New York: Basic Books.

Irwin, A.R., & Gross, A.M. (1995). Cognitive tempo, violent video games, and aggressive behaviour in young boys. *Journal of Family Violence, 10*, 337–350.

Irwin, M., Lovitz, A., Marder, S.R., Mintz, J., Winslade, W.J., Van Putten, T., & Mills, M.J. (1985). Psychotic patients understanding of informed consent. *American Journal of Psychiatry, 142*, 1351–1354.

Jacobs, P.A., Brunton, M., & Melville, M.M. (1965). Aggressive behaviour, mental abnormality and XXY male. *Nature, 208*, 1351–1352.

Jaffee, S., & Hyde, J.S. (2000). Gender differences in moral orientation: A meta-analysis. *Psychological Bulletin, 126*, 703–726.

James, W. (1890). *Principles of psychology*. New York: Holt.

Janicak, P.G., Davis, J.M, Gibbons, R.D., Ericksen, S., Chang, S., & Gallagher, P. (1985). Efficacy of ECT: A meta-analysis. *American Journal of Psychiatry, 142*, 297–302.

Jarvis, M. (2000). *Theoretical approaches in psychology*. London: Routledge.

Jarvis, M. (2001). *Angles on child psychology*. Cheltenham, UK: Stanley Thornes.

Jensen, A.R. (1969). How much can we boost IQ and scholastic achievement? *Harvard Educational Review, 39*, 1–123.

Jerison, H.J. (1973). *Evolution of the brain and intelligence*. New York: Academic Press.

Johnson, F.L., & Aries, E.J. (1983). Conversational patterns among same-sex pairs of late-adolescent close friends. *Journal of Genetic Psychology, 142*, 225–238.

Johnson, S.C., Pinkston, J.B., Bigler, E.D., & Blatter, D.D. (1996). Corpus callosum morphology in normal controls and traumatic brain injury: Sex differences, mechanisms of injury, and neuropsychological correlates. *Neuropsychology, 10*, 408–415.

Johnston, J., & Ettema, J. (1986). Using television to best advantage: Research for prosocial television. In J. Bryant & D. Zillman (Eds.), *Perspectives on media effects*. Hillsdale, NJ: Lawrence Erlbaum Associates Inc.

Johnston, J., & Ettema, J.S. (1982). *Positive image: Breaking stereotypes with children's television*. Beverly Hills, CA: Sage.

Jones, E. (1953). *Sigmund Freud: Life and Work, Vol. 1*. London: Hogarth.

Jones, M.C. (1925). A laboratory study of fear: The case of Peter. *Pedagogical Seminary, 31*, 308–315.

Jordan, S., McLaughlin, T.F., Weber, K.P., Derby, K.M., Barretto, A., Williams, R.L., & Luiten, L. (2003). The effects of work then play in combination with a token economy on the frequency of inappropriate behaviours for an elementary school child with autism. *Internal Journal of Special Education, 18*, 31–36.

Joseph, J. (2003). *The gene illusion: Genetic research in psychiatry and psychology under the microscope*. Ross-on-Wye: PCCS Books.

Josephson, W.L. (1987). Television violence and children's aggression: Testing the priming, social script, and disinhibition predictions. *Journal of Personality and Social Psychology, 53*, 882–890.

Jouvet, M. (1967). Mechanisms of the states of sleep: A neuropharmological approach. *Research Publications of the Association for the Research in Nervous and Mental Disorders, 45,* 86–126.

Joynson, R.B. (1989). *The Burt affair.* London: Routledge.

Kalat, J.W. (1998). *Biological psychology.* Pacific Grove, CA: Brooks/Cole Publishing Co.

Kamin, L. (1981). *The intelligence controversy: H.J. Eysenck vs. Leon Kamin.* New York: Wiley.

Kandel, D.B. (1978). Similarity in real-life adolescent friendship pairs. *Journal of Personality and Social Psychology, 36,* 306–312.

Karney, B.R., & Bradbury, T.N. (1995). The longitudinal course of marital quality and stability: A review of theory, method, and research. *Psychological Bulletin, 118,* 3–34.

Karp, M. (1995). An introduction to psychodrama counselling. *Journal of the British Association of Counselling, 6,* 294–298.

Kavanagh, D.J. (1992). Recent developments in expressed emotion and schizophrenia. *British Journal of Psychiatry, 160,* 601–620.

Kelly, T.L., Neri, D.F., D. Grill, P.D. Ryman, Hunt, P.D., Dijk, D.-J., Shanahan, T.L., & Czeisler, C. (1999). Nonentrained circadian rhythms of melatonin in submariners scheduled to an 18-hour day. *Journal of Biological Rhythms, 14,* 190–196.

Kelman, H.C. (1972). The rights of the subject in social research: An analysis in terms of relative power and legitimacy. *American Psychologist, 27,* 989–1016.

Kendall, P.C., & Hammen, C. (1998). *Abnormal psychology* (2nd Edn.). Boston, MA: Houghton Mifflin.

Kendler, K.S. (1995). Adversity, stress and psychopathology: A psychiatric genetic perspective. *International Journal of Method in Psychiatric Research, 5,* 163–170.

Kendler, K.S., Karkowski, L.M., & Prescott, C.A. (1999). Fears and phobias: Reliability and heritability. *Psychological Medicine, 29,* 539–553.

Kerckhoff, A.C., & Davis, K.E. (1962). Value consensus and need complementarity in mate selection. *American Sociological Review, 27,* 295–303.

Kety, S.S. (1975). Biochemistry of the major psychoses. In A. Freedman, H. Kaplan, & B. Sadock (Eds.), *Comprehensive textbook of psychiatry.* Baltimore, MD: Williams & Wilkins.

Keuthen, N. (1980). *Subjective probability estimation and somatic structures in phobic individuals.* Unpublished manuscript, State University of New York at Stony Brook.

Kimmel, A.J. (1996). *Ethical issues in behavioural research.* Oxford: Blackwell.

Kimura, D. (1992). Sex differences in the brain. *Scientific American, 10,* 26–31.

Kimura, D. (2002). Sex hormones influence human cognitive pattern. *Human Ethology and Evolutionary Psychology, 23(suppl. 4),* 67–77.

Kirchler, E., Pombeni, M.L., & Palmonari, A. (1991). Sweet sixteen . . . Adolescents' problems and the peer group as a source of support. *European Journal of Psychology and Education, 6,* 393–410.

Kitsantas, A. (2000). The role of self-regulation strategies and self-efficacy perceptions in successful weight loss maintenance. *Psychology and Health, 15,* 811–820.

Kitzinger, C., & Coyle, A. (1995). Lesbian and gay couples: Speaking of difference. *The Psychologist, 8,* 64–69.

Klein, H.J., Wesson, M.J., Hollenbeck, J.R., & Alge, B.J. (1999). Goal commitment and the goal-setting process: Conceptual clarification and empirical synthesis. *Journal of Applied Psychology, 84,* 885–896.

Klein, K.E., Wegman, H.M., & Hunt, B.I. (1972). Desynchronisation of body temperature and performance circadian rhythm as a result of outgoing and homegoing transmeridian flights. *Aerospace Medicine, 43,* 119–132.

Kleiner, L., & Marshall, W.L. (1987). The role of interpersonal problems in the development of agoraphobia with panic attacks. *Journal of Anxiety Disorders, 1,* 313–323.

Kleinman, A., & Cohen, A. (1997, March). Psychiatry's global challenge. *Scientific American,* pp. 74–77.

Kleinmuntz, B. (1974). *Essentials of abnormal psychology.* New York: Harper & Row.

Kline, P. (1981). *Fact and fantasy in Freudian theory.* London: Methuen.

Kline, P., & Storey, R. (1977). A factor analytic study of the anal character. *British Journal of Social and Clinical Psychology, 16,* 317–328.

Kluger, M.J. (1991). Fever: Role of pyrogens and cryogens. *Physiological Reviews, 71,* 93–127.

Kohlberg, L. (1963). Development of children's orientations toward a moral order. *Vita Humana, 6,* 11–36.

Kohlberg, L. (1966). A cognitive-development analysis of children's sex-role concepts and attitudes. In E.E. Maccoby (Ed.), *The development of sex differences.* Stanford, CA: Stanford University Press.

Kohlberg, L. (1969). Stage and sequence: The cognitive-developmental approach to socialisation. In D.A. Goslin (Ed.), *Handbook of socialisation theory and practice.* Skokie, IL: Rand McNally.

Kohlberg, L. (1975). The cognitive-developmental approach to moral education. *Phi Delta Kappan,* June, 670–677.

Kohlberg, L. (1976). Moral stages and moralization. In T. Likona (Ed.), *Moral development and behaviour.* New York: Holt, Rinehart & Winston.

Kohlberg, L. (1981). *Essays on moral development: Vol. 1. The philosophy of moral development.* San Francisco: Harper & Row.

Kroger, J. (1996). *Identity in adolescence.* London: Routledge.

Kuhn, T.S. (1962). *The structure of scientific revolutions.* Chicago, IL: Chicago University Press.

Kuhn, T.S. (1970). *The structure of scientific revolutions* (2nd Edn.). Chicago, IL: Chicago University Press.

Kuhn, T.S. (1977). *The essential tension: Selected studies in scientific tradition and change.* Chicago, IL: Chicago University Press.

Kuo-shu, Y., & Bond, M.H. (1990). Exploring implicit personality theories with indigenous or imported constructs: The Chinese case. *Journal of Personality and Social Psychology, 58,* 1087–1095.

Kurdek, L.A. (1994). The nature and correlates of relationship quality in gay, lesbian, and heterosexual cohabiting couples: A test of the individual difference, interdependence, and discrepancy models. In B. Greene & G.M. Herek (Eds.), *Lesbian and gay psychology: Theory, research and clinical applications.* London: Sage.

Kurdek, L.A., & Schmitt, J.P. (1986). Relationship quality of partners in heterosexual married, heterosexual cohabiting, and gay and lesbian relationships. *Journal of Personality and Social Psychology, 51,* 711–720.

LaBerge, S., Greenleaf, W., & Kedzierski, B. (1983). Physiological responses to dreamed sexual activity during lucid REM sleep. *Psychophysiology, 20,* 454–455.

Lack, D. (1968). *Ecological adaptations for breeding in birds.* London: Methuen.

Lader, M.H., & Mathews, A. (1968). A physiological model of phobic anxiety and desensitisation. *Behaviour Research and Therapy, 6,* 411–421.

Lader, M., & Scotto, J.C. (1998). A multicentre double-blind comparison of hydroxyzine, buspirone and placebo in patients with generalized anxiety disorder. *Psychopharmacology, 139*, 402–406.

Lalljee, M. (1981). Attribution theory and the analysis of explanations. In C. Antaki (Ed.), *The psychology of ordinary explanations of social behaviour*. London: Academic Press.

Lam, R.W., Tam, E.M., Shiah, I.S., Yatham, L.N., & Zis, A.P. (2000). Effects of light therapy on suicidal ideation in patients with winter depression. *Journal of Clinical Psychiatry, 61*, 30–32.

Langlois, J.H., Roggman, L.A., & Musselman, L. (1994). What is average and what is not average about attractive faces. *Psychological Science, 5*, 214–220.

Langlois J.J., Kalakanis, L., Rubenstein, A.J., Larson, A., Hallam, M., & Smoot, M. (2000). Maxims or myths of beauty? A meta-analytic and theoretical review. *Psychological Review, 126*, 390–423.

Larson, R.W., & Lampman-Petraitis, C. (1989). Daily emotional states as reported by children and adolescents. *Child Development, 60*, 1250–1260.

Larson, R.W., Richards, M.H., Moneta, G., Holmbeck, G., & Duckett, E. (1996). Changes in adolescents' daily interactions with their families from ages 10 to 18: Disengagement and transformation. *Developmental Psychology, 32*, 744–754.

Latané, B., & Darley, J.M. (1970). *The unresponsive bystander: Why doesn't he help?* Englewood Cliffs, NJ: Prentice-Hall.

Lee, H. (1997). *Virginia Woolf*. London: Vintage.

Lee, L. (1984). Sequences in separation: A framework for investigating endings of the personal (romantic) relationship. *Journal of Social and Personal Relationships, 1*, 49–74.

Lee, R.M. (1993). *Doing research on sensitive topics*. London: Sage.

Lempers, J. D., & Clark-Lempers, D. S. (1993). A functional comparison of same-sex and opposite-sex friendships during adolescence. *Journal of Adolescent Research, 8*, 89–108.

Levine, R., Sato, S., Hashimoto, T., & Verma, J. (1995). Love and marriage in eleven cultures. *Journal of Cross-Cultural Psychology, 26*, 554–571.

Levinger, G. (1976). A social psychological perspective on marital dissolution. *Journal of Social Issues, 32*, 21–47.

Levinger, G. (1980). Toward the analysis of close relationships. *Journal of Experimental Social Psychology, 16*, 510–544.

Lewinsohn, P.M. (1974). A behavioural approach to depression. In R.J. Friedman & M.M. Katz (Eds.), *The psychology of depression: Contemporary theory and research*. Washington, DC: Winston-Wiley.

Lewinsohn, P.M, Joiner, T.E., Jr., & Rohde, P. (2001). Evaluation of cognitive diathesis–stress models in predicting major depressive disorder in adolescents. *Journal of Abnormal Psychology, 110*, 203–215.

Lewinsohn, P.M., Steimetz, J.L., Larsen, D.W., & Franklin, J. (1981). Depression related cognitions: Antecedent or consequences? *Journal of Abnormal Psychology, 90*, 213–219.

Leyens, J.-P., Camino, L., Parke, R.D., & Berkowitz, L. (1975). Effects of movie violence on aggression in a field setting as a function of group dominance and cohesion. *Journal of Personality and Social Psychology, 32*, 346–360.

Lick, J. (1975). Expectancy, false galvanic skin response feedback and systematic desensitisation in the modification of phobic behaviour. *Journal of Consulting and Clinical Psychology, 43*, 557–567.

Lidz, T., Cornelison, A.R., & Fleck, S. (1965). *Schizophrenia and family*. New York: International Universities Press.

Light, P., Buckingham, N., & Robbins, A.H. (1979). The conservation task as an interactional setting. *British Journal of Educational Psychology, 49*, 304–310.

Light, P., Littleton, K., Messer, D., & Joiner, R. (1994). Social and communicative processes in computer-based problem solving. *European Journal of Psychology of Education, 9*, 93–109.

Locke, J. (1690/1989). *An essay concerning human understanding*. (P.H. Nidditch, Ed.). Oxford, UK: Clarendon.

Loehlin, J.C., Horn, J.M., & Willerman, L. (1989). Modeling IQ change: Evidence from the Texas Adoption Project. *Child Development, 60*, 893–904.

Loehlin, J.C., & Nichols, R.C. (1976). *Heredity, environment and personality*. Austin, TX: University of Texas Press.

Loftus, E.F., & Palmer, J.C. (1974). Reconstruction of automobile destruction: An example of the interaction between language and memory. *Journal of Verbal Learning and Verbal Behavior, 13*, 585–589.

Loo, C.M. (1979). The effects of spatial density on the social behaviour of children. *Journal of Applied Social Research, 2*, 372–381.

Lorenz, K.Z. (1966). *On aggression*. New York: Harcourt, Brace & World.

Lott, B.E. (1994). *Women's lives: Theories and variations in gender learning*. Pacific Grove, CA: Brooks Cole.

Lovaas, O.I., Freitas, L., Nelson, K., & Whalen, C. (1967). The establishment of imitation and its use for development of complex behaviour in schizophrenic children. *Behaviour Research and Therapy, 5*, 171–181.

Lovelace, V., & Huston, A.C. (1982). Can television teach prosocial behaviour? *Prevention in Human Services, 2*, 93–106.

Luborsky, L., & Spence, D.P. (1978). Quantitative research on psychoanalytic therapy. In S.L. Garfield & A.E. Bergin (Eds.), *Handbook of psychotherapy and behaviour change: An empirical analysis* (2nd Edn.). New York: Wiley.

Lucas, A., Morley, R., Cole, T.J., Lister, G., & Leeson, P.C. (1992). Breast milk and subsequent intelligence quotient in children born preterm. *Lancet, 339*(8788), 261–264.

Luce, G.G., & Segal, J. (1966). *Sleep*. New York: Coward, McCann & Geoghegan.

Lugaressi, E., Medori, R., Montagna, P., Baruzzi, A., Cortelli, P., Lugaressi, A., Tinuper, A., Zucconi, M., & Gambetti, P. (1986). Fatal familial insomnia and dysautonomia in the selective degeneration of thalamic nuclei. *New England Journal of Medicine, 315*, 997–1003.

Lund, M. (1985). The development of investment and commitment scales for predicting continuity of personal relationships. *Journal of Social and Personal Relationships, 2*, 3–23.

Ma, H.K. (1988). The Chinese perspective on moral judgement development. *International Journal of Psychology, 23*, 201–227.

Maccoby, E.E., & Jacklin, C.N. (1974). *The psychology of sex differences*. Stanford, CA: Stanford University Press.

Maccoby, E.E., & Martin, J.A. (1983). Socialisation in the context of the family: Parent–child interaction. In P.H. Mussein (Ed.), *Carmichael's manual of child psychology: Vol. 4. Socialisation, personality and social development*. New York: Wiley.

Mackintosh, N.J. (1986). The biology of intelligence? *British Journal of Psychology, 77*, 1–18.

MacLean, P.D. (1982). On the origin and progressive evolution of the triune brain. In E. Armstrong & D. Falk (Eds.), *Primate brain evolution*. New York: Plenum Press.

MacLeod, A. (1998). Abnormal psychology. In M.W. Eysenck (Ed.), *Psychology: An integrated approach*. Harlow, UK: Addison Wesley Longman.

Mair, K. (1992). The myth of therapist expertise. In W. Dryden & C. Feltham (Eds.), *Psychotherapy and its discontents*. Buckingham, UK: Open University Press.

Malim, T., Birch, A., & Wadeley, A. (1992). *Perspectives in psychology*. London: Macmillan.

Mandler, G. (1967). Organisation and memory. In K.W. Spence & J.T. Spence (Eds.), *Advances in research and theory: Vol. 1. The psychology of learning and motivation:* London: Academic Press.

Marcia, J. (1966). Development and validation of ego-identity status. *Journal of Personality and Social Psychology, 3*, 551–558.

Marcia, J.E. (1967). Ego-identity status: Relationship to change in self-esteem, "general maladjustment", and authoritarianism. *Journal of Personality, 35*, 118–133.

Marcia, J. (1976). Identity six years after: A follow-up study. *Journal of Youth and Adolescence, 5*, 145–160.

Marcia, J. (1980). Identity in adolescence. In J. Adelson (Ed.), *Handbook of adolescent psychology*. New York: Wiley.

Markus, H.R., & Kitayama, S. (1991). Culture and the self: Implications for cognition, emotion, and motivation. *Psychological Review, 98*, 224–253.

Marsh, H.W. (1989). Age and sex effects in multiple dimensions of self-concept: A replication and extension. *Australian Journal of Psychology, 37*, 197–204.

Marsh, P., Rosser, E., & Harré, R. (1978). *The rules of disorder*. London: Routledge & Kegan Paul.

Martin, C.L., & Halverson, C.F. (1983). The effects of sex-typing schemas on young children's memory. *Child Development, 54*, 563–574.

Martin, C.L., & Halverson, C.F. (1987). The roles of cognition in sex role acquisition. In D.B. Carter (Ed.), *Current conceptions of sex roles and sex typing: Theory and research*. New York: Praeger.

Maslow, A.H. (1954). *Motivation and personality*. New York: Harper.

Maslow, A.H. (1968). *Toward a psychology of being* (2nd Edn.). New York: Van Nostrand.

Masters, J.C., Ford, M.E., Arend, R., Grotevant, H.D., & Clark, L.V. (1979). Modelling and labelling as integrated determinants of children's sex-typed imitative behaviour. *Child Development, 50*, 364–371.

Mathalon, D.H., Ford, J.M., Turken, U., Gray, M., Whitfield, S., Kalba, S., Faustman, W.O., Colrain, I., & Glover, G. (2001). Self-monitoring deficits in schizophrenia: ERP and fMRI evidence. *International Journal of Psychophysiology, 41*, 203.

Mathes, E.W., Adams, H.E., & Davies, R.M. (1985). Jealousy: Loss of relationship rewards, loss of self-esteem, depression, anxiety, and anger. *Journal of Personality and Social Psychology, 48*, 1552–1561.

Mathews, A., & Mackintosh, B. (2000). Induced emotional interpretation bias and anxiety. *Journal of Abnormal Psychology, 109*, 602–615.

Matt, G.E., & Navarro, A.M. (1997). What meta-analyses have and have not taught us about psychotherapy effects: A review and future directions. *Clinical Psychology Review, 17*, 1–32.

Maynard Smith, J. (1964). Group selection and kin selection. *Nature, 201*, 1145–1147.

McCain, B., Gabrielli, W.F., Bentler, P.M., & Mednick, S.A. (1980). Rearing, social class, education, and criminality: A multiple indicator model. *Journal of Abnormal Psychology, 90*, 354–364.

McCartney, K., Harris, M. J., & Bernieri, F. (1981). Growing up and growing apart: A developmental meta-analysis of twin studies. *Psychological Bulletin, 107*, 226–237.

McClintock, M.K. (1971). Menstrual synchrony and suppression. *Nature, 229*, 244.

McConaghy, M.J. (1979). Gender permanence and the genital basis of gender: Stages in the development of constancy of gender identity. *Child Development, 50*, 1223–1226.

McCosker, H., Barnard, A., & Gerber, R. (2001). Undertaking sensitive research: Issues and strategies meeting the safety needs of all participants. *Forum: Qualitative Social Research*, [On-line Journal], 2(1). Available at: http://www.qualitative-research.net/fqs-texte/1-01/1-01mccoskereetal-e.htm

McCrae, R.R., & Costa, P.T. (1990). *Personality in adulthood*. New York: Guilford Press.

McGarrigle, J., & Donaldson, M. (1974). Conservation accidents. *Cognition, 3*, 341–350.

McGinnies, E. (1949). Emotionality and perceptual defence. *Psychological Review, 56*, 244–251.

McGue, M., Brown, S., & Lykken, D.T. (1992). Personality stability and change in early adulthood: A behavioural genetic analysis. *Developmental Psychology, 29*, 96–109.

McGuffin, P., Katz, R., Watkins, S., & Rutherford, J. (1996). A hospital-based twin register of the heritability of DSM-IV unipolar depression. *Archives of General Psychiatry, 53*, 129–136.

McGuigan, F.J. (1966). Covert oral behaviour and auditory hallucinations. *Psychophysiology, 3*, 421–428.

McGuire, P.K., Silbersweig, D.A., Wright, I., Murray, R.M., Frackowiak, R.S.J., & Frith, C.D. (1996). The neural correlates of inner speech and auditory verbal imagery in schizophrenia: Relationship to auditory verbal hallucinations. *British Journal of Psychiatry, 169*, 148–159.

McIlveen, R., & Gross, R. (1996). *Biopsychology*. London: Hodder & Stoughton.

McIlveen, R., Higgins, L., & Wadeley, A. (1992). *BPS manual of psychology practicals*. Leicester, UK: BPS Books.

McKenna, K., & Yael, A. (1999). The computers that bind: Relationship formation on the internet. *Dissertation Abstracts International Section A: Humanities and Social Sciences, 59*, 2236.

McNeilly, C.L., & Howard, K.I. (1991). The effects of psychotherapy: A re-evaluation based on dosage. *Psychotherapy Research, 1*, 74–78.

Mead, M. (1928). *Coming of age in Samoa*. New York: Morrow.

Mead, M. (1935). *Sex and temperament in three primitive societies*. New York: Morrow.

Meadows, S. (1986). *Understanding child development*. London: Routledge.

Meadows, S. (1994). Cognitive development. In A.M. Colman (Ed.), *Companion encyclopedia of psychology, Vol. 2*. London: Routledge.

Meddis, R. (1975a). On the function of sleep. *Animal Behaviour, 23*, 676–691.

Meddis, R. (1975b). *Statistical handbook for non-statisticians*. London: McGraw-Hill.

Meddis, R. (1979). The evolution and function of sleep. In D.A. Oakley & H.C. Plotkin (Eds.), *Brain, behaviour and evolution*. London: Methuen.

Meddis, R., Pearson, A.J.D., & Langford, G. (1973). An extreme case of healthy insomnia. *Electroencephalography and Clinical Neurophysiology, 35*, 213–224.

Mednick, S.A., & Schulsinger, F. (1968). Some premorbid characteristics related to breakdown in children with schizophrenic mothers. *Journal of Psychiatric Research, 6*, 267–291.

Medori, R., Montagna, P., Tritschler, H.J., LeBlanc, A., Cortelli, P., Tinuper, P., Lugaressi, E., & Gambetti, P. (1992). Fatal familial insomnia: A second kindred with mutation of prion protein gene at codon 178. *Neurology, 42*, 669–670.

Meichenbaum, D. (1977). *Cognitive-behaviour modification: An integrative approach.* New York: Plenum Press.

Meichenbaum, D. (1985). *Stress inoculation training.* New York: Pergamon.

Meichenbaum, D. (1996). Stress inoculation training for coping with stressors. *The Clinical Psychologist, 49*, 4–7.

Meilman, P.W. (1979). Cross-sectional age changes in ego identity status during adolescence. *Developmental Psychology, 15*, 230–231.

Meltzoff, A.N. (1988). Imitation of televised models by infants. *Child Development, 59*, 1221–1229.

Menzies, R.G., & Clarke, J.C. (1993). The aetiology of childhood water phobia. *Behaviour Research and Therapy, 31*, 499–501.

Menzies, R.G., & Clarke, J.C. (1994). Retrospective studies of the origins of phobias: A review. *Anxiety, Stress, and Coping, 7*, 305–318.

Merckelbach, H., de Jong, P.J., Muris, P., & van den Hout, M.A. (1996). The etiology of specific phobias: A review. *Clinical Psychology Review, 16*, 337–361.

Michaels, J.W., Acock, A.C., & Edwards, J.N. (1986). Social exchange and equity determinants of relationship commitment. *Journal of Social and Personal Relationships, 3*, 161–175.

Midlarsky, E., & Bryan, J.H. (1972). Affect expressions and children's imitative altruism. *Journal of Experimental Research in Personality, 6*, 195–203.

Miles, L.E.M., Raynal, D.M., & Wilson, M.A. (1977). Blind man living in normal society has circadian rhythms of 24.9 hours. *Science, 198*, 421–423.

Milgram, S. (1963). Behavioural study of obedience. *Journal of Abnormal and Social Psychology, 67*, 371–378.

Milgram, S. (1974). *Obedience to authority: An experimental view.* New York: Harper & Row.

Miller, G. (1996). Sexual selection in human evolution. In C. Crawford & D.L. Krebs (Eds.), *Evolution and human behaviour.* Mahwah, NJ: Lawrence Erlbaum Associates Inc.

Miller, G.A. (1966). *Psychology: The science of mental life.* Harmondsworth, UK: Penguin.

Miller, G.F. (1998). How mate choice shaped human nature: A review of sexual selection and human evolution. In C. Crawford (Ed.), *Handbook of evolutionary psychology.* Mahwah, NJ: Lawrence Erlbaum Associates Inc.

Miller, J.G. (1994). Cultural diversity in the morality of caring: Individually oriented versus duty-based interpersonal moral codes. *Cross-Cultural Research, 28*, 3–39.

Miller, J.G., & Bersoff, D.M. (1994). Cultural influences on the moral status of reciprocity and the discounting of endogenous motivation. *Personality and Social Psychology Bulletin, 20*, 592–602.

Miller, J.G., & Bersoff, D.M. (1998). The role of liking in perceptions of the moral responsibility to help: A cultural perspective. *Journal of Experimental Social Psychology, 34*, 443–469.

Miller, J.G., Bersoff, D.M., & Harwood, R.L. (1990). Perception of social responsibilities in India and the United States: Moral imperatives or personal decisions? *Journal of Personality and Social Psychology, 58*, 33–47.

Miller, L.J. (2002). Postpartum depression. *Journal of the American Medical Association, 287*, 762–765.

Miller, N.E. (1941). The frustration–aggression hypothesis. *Psychological Review, 48*, 337–342.

Miller, P.H. (1993). *Theories of developmental psychology* (3rd Edn.). New York: Freeman.

Mineka, S., Davidson, M., Cook, M., & Kuir, R. (1984). Observational conditioning of snake fear in rhesus monkeys. *Journal of Abnormal Psychology, 93*, 355–372.

Minsky, R. (1998). *Psychoanalysis and culture.* Cambridge, UK: Polity Press.

Mischel, W. (1968). *Personality and assessment.* New York: Wiley.

Mischel, W. (1993). *Introduction to personality* (5th Edn.). Fort Worth, TX: Harcourt Brace.

Mischel, W., & Peake, P.K. (1982). Beyond déjà vu in the search for cross-situational consistency. *Psychological Review, 89*, 730–755.

Mischler, E.G., & Waxler, N.E. (1968). Interaction in families: An experimental study of family processes and schizophrenia. In A. Smith (Ed.), *Childhood schizophrenia.* New York: Wiley.

Moghaddam, F.M. (1998). *Social psychology: Exploring universals across cultures.* New York: W.H. Freeman.

Moghaddam, F.M., Taylor, D.M., & Wright, S.C. (1993). *Social psychology in cross-cultural perspective.* New York: W.H. Freeman.

Money, J., & Ehrhardt, A.A. (1972). *Man and woman, boy and girl.* Baltimore, MD: John Hopkins University Press.

Monk, T.H., & Folkard, S. (1983). Circadian rhythms and shiftwork. In R. Hockey (Ed.), *Stress and fatigue in human performance.* Chichester, UK: Wiley.

Montemayor, R., McKenry, P.C., & Julian, T. (1993). Men in midlife and the quality of father-adolescent communication. *New Directions in Child Development, 62*, 59–72.

Moore, C., & Frye, D. (1986). The effect of the experimenter's intention on the child's understanding of conservation. *Cognition, 22*, 283–298.

Moore-Ede, M. (1993). *The 24-hour society.* Reading, MA: Addison-Wesley.

Moore-Ede, M., Sulzman, F., & Fuller, C. (1982). *The clocks that time us: Physiology of the circadian timing system.* Cambridge, MA: Harvard University Press.

Moreland, R.L., & Beach, S.R. (1992). Exposure effects in the classroom—The development of affinity among students. *Journal of Experimental Social Psychology, 28*, 255–276.

Moreno, J.L. (1972). *Psychodrama, Vols. 1–3.* New York: Beacon Press.

Morgan, E. (1995). Measuring time with a biological clock. *Biological Sciences Review, 7*, 2–5.

Morin, S.F. (1977). Heterosexual bias in psychological research on lesbianism and male sexuality. *American Psychologist, 32*, 629–637.

Moruzzi, G., & Magoun, H.W. (1949). Brain stem reticular formation and activation of the EEG. *Electroencephalography and Clinical Neurophysiology, 1*, 455–473.

Moscovici, S., Lage, E., & Naffrenchoux, M. (1969). Influence of a consistent minority on the responses of a majority in a colour perception task. *Sociometry, 32*, 365–380.

Moss, E. (1992). The socioaffective context of joint cognitive activity. In L.T. Winegar & J. Valsiner (Eds.), *Children's development within social context: Vol. 2. Research and methodology.* Hillsdale, NJ: Lawrence Erlbaum Associates Inc.

Motley M.T., Baars, B.J., & Camden, C.T. (1983). Experimental verbal slip studies: A review and an editing model of language encoding. *Communication Monographs, 50*, 79–101.

Motluck, A. (1999). When too much sex is exhausting. *New Scientist, 2181*, 8.

Mowrer, O.H. (1947). On the dual nature of learning: A re-interpretation of "conditioning" and "problem-solving". *Harvard Educational Review, 17,* 102–148.

Møller, A.P. (1990). Effects of a haematophagous mite on the barn swallow *Hirundo rustica*: A test of the Hamilton and Zuk hypothesis. *Evolution, 44,* 771–784.

Mukerjee, M. (1997). Trends in animal research. *Scientific American,* February, 70–77.

Mukherjee, S., Sackeim, H.A., & Schnur, D.B. (1994). Electroconvulsive therapy of acute manic episodes: A review of fifty years' experience. *American Journal of Psychiatry, 151,* 169–176.

Mulac, A., Bradac, J.J., & Mann, S.K. (1985). Male/female language differences and attributional consequences in children's television. *Human Communication Research, 11*(4), 481–506.

Munro, G., & Adams, G.R. (1977). Mothers, infants and pointing: A study of gesture. In H.R. Schaffer (Ed.), *Studies in mother–infant interaction*. London: Academic Press.

Munroe, R.H., Shimmin, H.S., & Munroe, R.L. (1984). Gender understanding and sex-role preferences in four cultures. *Developmental Psychology, 20,* 673–682.

Murray, S.L., & Holmes, J.G. (1993). Seeing virtues in faults: Negativity and the transformation of interpersonal narratives in close relationships. *Journal of Personality and Social Psychology, 65,* 707–722.

Murstein, B.I. (1972). Physical attractiveness and marital choice. *Journal of Personality and Social Psychology, 22,* 8–12.

Murstein, B.I., & Christy, P. (1976). Physical attractiveness and marriage adjustment in middle-aged couples. *Journal of Personality and Social Psychology, 34,* 537–542.

Murstein, B.I., MacDonald, M.G., & Cerreto, M. (1977). A theory and investigation of the effects of exchange-orientation on marriage and friendship. *Journal of Marriage and the Family, 39,* 543–548.

Mussen, P.H., & Rutherford, E. (1963). Parent–child relations and parental personality in relation to young children's sex-role preferences. *Child Development, 34,* 589–607.

Myers, L.B., & Brewin, C.R. (1994). Recall of early experiences and the repressive coping style. *Journal of Abnormal Psychology, 103,* 288–292.

Nadler, A. (1986). Help seeking as a cultural phenomenon—Differences between city and kibbutz dwellers. *Journal of Personality and Social Psychology, 51,* 976–982.

Nadler, A. (1993). Help-seeking behaviour: Psychological costs and instrumental benefits. In M.S. Clark (Ed.), *Prosocial behaviour*. Newbury Park, CA: Sage.

Naitoh, P. (1975). Sleep stage deprivation and total sleep loss: Effects on sleep behaviour. *Psychophysiology, 12,* 141–146.

Najavits, L.M., & Strupp, H.H. (1994). Differences in the effectiveness of psychodynamic therapists: A process–outcome study. *Psychotherapy, 31,* 114–123.

National Sleep Foundation (2001). Less fun, less sleep, more work: An American Portrait. March 21. www.sleepfoundation.org

Nesse, M., & Williams, C. (1995). *Evolution and healing: The new science of Darwinian medicine*. London: Weidenfeld & Nicolson.

Nesse, R.M. (2000). Is depression an adaptation? *Archives of General Psychiatry, 57,* 14–20.

Newcomb, T.M. (1961). *The acquaintance process*. New York: Holt, Rinehart & Winston.

Newmark, C.S., Frerking, R.A., Cook, L., & Newmark, L. (1973). Endorsement of Ellis' irrational beliefs as a function of psychopathology. *Journal of Clinical Psychology, 29,* 300–302.

Nobles, W.W. (1976). Extended self: Rethinking the so-called Negro self-concept. *Journal of Black Psychology, 2,* 99–105.

Nolen-Hoeksma, S., Girgus, J.S., & Seligman, M.E.P. (1992). Predictors and consequences of childhood depressive symptoms: A 5-year longitudinal study. *Journal of Abnormal Psychology, 101,* 405–422.

Norenzayan, A., Choi, I., & Nisbett, R.E. (1999). Eastern and Western perceptions of causality for social behaviour: Lay theories about personalities and situations. In D.A. Prentice & D.T. Miller (Eds.), *Cultural divides: Understanding and overcoming group conflict*. New York: Russell Sage Foundation.

Noyes, R., Crowe, R.R., Harris, E.L., Hamra, B.J., McChesney, C.M., & Chaudry, D.R. (1986). Relationship between panic disorder and agoraphobia: A family study. *Archives of General Psychiatry, 43,* 227–232.

O'Connor, J. (1980). Intermediate-size transposition and children's operational level. *Developmental Psychology, 16,* 588–596.

Offer, D., Ostrov, E., Howard, K.I., & Atkinson, R. (1988). *The teenage world: Adolescents' self-image in ten countries*. New York: Plenum Press.

Ost, L.G. (1985). Mode of acquisition of phobias. *Acta Universitatis Uppsaliensis, 529,* 1–45.

Ost, L.G. (1989). *Blood phobia: A specific phobia subtype in DSM-IV*. Paper requested by the Simple Phobia subcommittee of the DSM-IV Anxiety Disorders Work Group.

Oswald, I. (1980). *Sleep* (4th Edn.). Harmondsworth, UK: Penguin Books.

Owusu-Bempah J., & Howitt, D. (1994). Racism and the psychological textbook. *The Psychologist, 7,* 163–166.

Pahl, J.J., Swayze, V.W., & Andreasen, N.C. (1990). Diagnostic advances in anatomical and functional brain imaging in schizophrenia. In A. Kales, C.N. Stefanis, & J.A. Talbot (Eds.), *Recent advances in schizophrenia*. New York: Springer-Verlag.

Palincsar, A.S., & Brown, A.L. (1984). Reciprocal teaching of comprehension-fostering and comprehension-monitoring activities. *Cognition and Instruction, 1,* 117–175.

Palinkas, L., Reed, H.L., Reedy, K.R., van Do, N., Case, H.S., & Finney, N.S. (2001). Circannual pattern of hypothalamic-pituitary-thyroid (HPT) function and mood during extended Antarctic residence. *Psychoneuroendocrinology, 26,* 421–431.

Palmonari, A., Pombeni, M.L., & Kirchler, E. (1989). Peer groups and evolution of the self-system in adolescence. *European Journal of Psychology of Education, 4,* 3–15.

Parke, R.D. (1977). Some effects of punishment on children's behaviour: Revisited. In E.M. Hetherington & R.D. Parke (Eds.), *Contemporary readings in child psychology*. New York: McGraw-Hill.

Parker, S.T., & Gibson, K.R. (1979). A developmental model for the evolution of language and intelligence in early hominids. *Behavioural and Brain Sciences, 2,* 367–408.

Parks, M.R., & Floyd, K. (1996). Making friends in cyberspace. *Journal of Communication, 46,* 80–97.

Pascual-Leone, J. (1984). Attentional, dialectic, and mental effort. In M.L. Commons, F.A. Richards, & C. Armon (Eds.), *Beyond formal operations*. New York: Plenum.

Pastore, N. (1952). The role of arbitrariness in the frustration–aggression hypothesis. *Journal of Abnormal and Social Psychology, 47,* 728–731.

Patterson, G.R., DeBaryshe, B.D., & Ramsey, E. (1989). A developmental perspective on antisocial behaviour. *The American Psychologist, 44,* 329–335.

Paul, G.L., & Lentz, R.J. (1977). *Psychosocial treatment of chronic mental patients: Milieu versus social learning programs.* Cambridge, MA: Harvard University Press.

Pengelley, E.T., & Fisher, K.C. (1957). Onset and cessation of hibernation under constant temperature and light in the golden-mantled ground squirrel, *Citellus lateralis, Nature, 180*, 1371–1372.

Peplau, L.A. (1991). Lesbian and gay relationships. In J.C. Gonsiorek & J. Dweinrich (Eds.), *Homosexuality: Research implications for public policy.* Newbury Park, CA: Sage.

Perrin, S., & Spencer, C. (1980). The Asch effect: A child of its time. *Bulletin of the British Psychological Society, 33*, 405–406.

Perry, D.G., & Bussey, K. (1979). The social learning theory of sex differences: Imitation is alive and well. *Journal of Personality and Social Psychology, 37*, 1699–1712.

Peters, M. (1995). Race, evolution, and behaviour: Rushton, J.P. Aggressive Behavior, 21, 463–468.

Peterson, J.L., & Zill, N. (1986). Marital disruption, parent-child relationships and behaviour problems in children. *Journal of Marriage and the Family, 48*, 295.

Pettit, G.S., Bates, J.E., Dodge, K.A., & Meece, D.W. (1999). The impact of after-school peer contact on early adolescent externalising problems is moderated by parental monitoring, perceived neighbourhood safety, and prior adjustment. *Child Development, 70*, 768–778.

Piaget, J. (1932). *The moral judgement of the child.* Harmondsworth, UK: Penguin.

Piaget, J. (1967). *The child's conception of the world.* Totowa, NJ: Littlefield, Adams.

Piaget, J. (1970). Piaget's theory. In J. Mussen (Ed.), *Carmichael's manual of child psychology, Vol. 1.* New York: Basic Books.

Piaget, J., & Szeminska, A. (1952). *The child's conception of number.* London: Routledge & Kegan Paul.

Piliavin, I.M., Rodin, J., & Piliavin, J.A. (1969). Good samaritarianism: An underground phenomenon? *Journal of Personality and Social Psychology, 13*, 289–299.

Piliavin, J.A., Dovidio, J.F., Gaertner, S.L., & Clark, R.D. (1981). *Emergency intervention.* New York: Academic Press.

Pilleri, G. (1979). The blind Indus dolphin, *Platanista indi, Endeavour, 3*, 48–56.

Pinel, J.P.J. (2003). *Biopsychology* (5th Edn.). Boston, MA: Allyn & Bacon.

Pinker, S. (1997). *How the mind works.* New York: Norton.

Plant, E.A., Peruche, B.M., & Butz, D.A. (2005). Eliminating automatic racial bias: Making race non-diagnostic for responses to criminal suspects. *Journal of Experimental Social Psychology, 41*, 141–156.

Plomin, R. (1988). The nature and nurture of cognitive abilities. In R.J. Sternberg (Ed.), *Advances in the psychology of human intelligence, Vol. 4.* Hillsdale, NJ: Lawrence Erlbaum Associates Inc.

Plomin, R. (1990). The role of inheritance in behaviour. *Science, 248*, 183–188.

Plomin, R. (1994). *Genetics and experience: The interplay between nature and nurture.* Thousand Oaks, CA: Sage.

Plomin, R., Corley, R., DeFries, J.C., & Fulker, D.W. (1990). Individual differences in television viewing in early childhood: Nature as well as nurture. *Psychological Science, 1*, 371–377.

Plomin, R., DeFries J.C., & Loehlin, J.C. (1977). Genotype–environment interaction and correlation in the analysis of human behavior. *Psychological Bulletin, 84*, 309–322.

Plomin, R., DeFries, J.C., & McClearn, G.E. (1997). *Behavioural genetics: A primer* (3rd Edn.). New York: Freeman.

Polimeni, J., & Reiss, J. (2002). How shamanism and group selection may reveal the origins of schizophrenia. *Medical Hypotheses, 58*, 244–248.

Popper, K.R. (1969). *Conjectures and refutations.* London: Routledge & Kegan Paul.

Popper, K.R. (1972). *Objective knowledge.* Oxford, UK: Oxford University Press.

Postmes, T., & Spears, R. (1998). Deindividuation and anti-normative behaviour: A meta-analysis. *Psychology Bulletin, 123*, 238–259.

Price, J.S., Sloman, L., Gardner, R., & Rohde, P. (1994). The social competition hypothesis of depression. *British Journal of Psychiatry, 164*, 309–315.

Price-Williams, D., Gordon, W., & Ramirez, M. (1969). Skill and conservation: A study of pottery-making children. *Developmental Psychology, 1*, 769.

Prioleau, L., Murdock, M., & Brody, N. (1983). An analysis of psychotherapy versus placebo studies. *Behavior and Brain Sciences, 6*, 273–310.

Przybyla, D.P.J. (1985). *The facilitating effects of exposure to erotica on male prosocial behaviour.* Doctoral dissertation, State University of New York at Albany.

Quay, L.C. (1971). Language, dialect, reinforcement, and the intelligence test performance of Negro children. *Child Development, 42*, 5–15.

Rabbie, J.M., & Horwitz, M. (1960). Arousal of ingroup–outgroup bias by a chance win or loss. *Journal of Personality and Social Psychology, 13*, 269–277.

Rachman, S.J. (1993). A critique of cognitive therapy for anxiety disorders. *Behaviour Research and Therapy, 24*, 274–288.

Rachman, S.J., & de Silva, P. (1978). Abnormal and normal obsessions. *Behaviour Research and Therapy, 16*, 233–238.

Raine, A., Buchsbaum, M., & LaCasse, L. (1997). Brain abnormalities in murderers indicated by positron emission tomography. *Biological Psychiatry, 42*, 495–508.

Ramey, C.T. (1993). A rejoinder to Spitz's critique of the Abecedarian experiment. *Intelligence, 17*, 25–30.

Ramey, C.T., Campbell, F.A., & Ramey, S.L. (1999). Early intervention: Successful pathways to improving intellectual development. *Developmental Neuropsychology, 16*, 385–392.

Rampello, L., Nicoletti, F., & Nicoletti, F. (2000). Dopamine and depression: Therapeutic implications. *CNS Drugs, 13*, 35–45.

Reber, A.S. (1995). *Dictionary of psychology.* London: Penguin.

Rechtschaffen, A., Gilliland, M., Bergmann, B., & Winter, J. (1983). Physiological correlates of prolonged sleep deprivation in rats. *Science, 221*, 182–184.

Reicher, S., & Emler, N. (1986). The management of delinquent reputations. In H. Beloff (Ed.), *Getting into life.* London: Methuen.

Reid, E. (1999). Hierarchy and power. Social control in cyberspace. In M. Smith & P. Kollock (Eds.), *Communities in cyberspace.* London: Routledge.

Reinberg, R. (1967). *Eclairement et cycle menstruel de la femme.* Rapport au Colloque International du CRNS, la photorégulation de la reproduction chez les oiseaux et les mammifères, Montpelier, France.

Remington, G., & Kapur, S. (2000). Atypical antipsychotics: Are some more atypical than others? *Psychopharmacology, 148*, 3–15.

Rey, J.M., & Walter, G. (1997). Half a century of ECT use in young people. *American Journal of Psychiatry, 154*, 595–602.

Ridley, M. (1993). *The red queen*. London: Viking.

Ridley, M. (1996). *Evolution* (2nd Edn.). Cambridge, MA: Blackwell Science.

Rifkin, S. (1995). The evolution of primate intelligence. *Harvard Undergraduate Society for Neuroscience*, 1–10.

Robson, C. (1994). *Experimental design and statistics in psychology* (3rd Edn.). Harmondsworth, UK: Penguin.

Rodin, J., Solomon, S.K., & Metcalf, J. (1978). Role of control in mediating perceptions of density. *Journal of Personality and Social Psychology, 36*, 988–999.

Rogers, C.R. (1951). *Client-centred therapy*. Boston, MA: Houghton Mifflin.

Rogers, C.R. (1959). A theory of therapy, personality, and interpersonal relationships as developed in the client-centred framework. In S. Koch (Ed.), *Psychology: A study of a science*. New York: McGraw-Hill.

Rogers, C.R. (1986). Client-centred therapy. In I. Kutash & A. Wolf (Eds.), *Psychotherapist's casebook*. San Francisco: Jossey-Bass.

Rose, S.A., & Blank, M. (1974). The potency of context in children's cognition: An illustration through conservation. *Child Development, 45*, 499–502.

Rosekrans, M.A., & Hartup, W.W. (1967). Imitative influences of consistent and inconsistent response consequences to a model on aggressive behaviour in children. *Journal of Personality and Social Psychology, 7*, 429–434.

Rosenhan, D.L. (1970). The natural socialisation of altruistic autonomy. In J. Macaulay & L. Berkowitz (Eds.), *The uncommon child*. New York: Plenum Press.

Rosenhan, D.L. (1973). On being sane in insane places. *Science, 179*, 250–258.

Rosenhan, D.L., & Seligman, M.E.P. (1985). *Abnormal psychology*. New York: Norton.

Rosenhan, D.L., & Seligman, M.E.P. (1989). *Abnormal psychology* (2nd Edn.). London: Norton.

Rosenhan, D.L., & Seligman, M.E.P. (1995). *Abnormal psychology* (3rd Edn.). New York: Norton.

Rosenkoetter, L.I. (1999). The television situation comedy and children's prosocial behaviour. *Journal of Applied Social Psychology, 29*, 979–993.

Rosenthal, D. (1963). *The Genain quadruplets: A case study and theoretical analysis of heredity and environment in schizophrenia*. New York: Basic Books.

Rosenthal, R. (1966). *Experimenter effects in behavioural research*. New York: Appleton-Century-Crofts.

Rosenzweig, M.R. (1992). Psychological science around the world. *The American Psychologist, 47*, 718–722.

Ruback, R.B., & Pandey, J. (1991). Crowding, perceived control, and relative power—An analysis of households in India. *Journal of Applied Social Psychology, 21*, 315–344.

Rubin, K.H., & Trotter, K.T. (1977). Kohlberg's moral judgement scale: Some methodological considerations. *Developmental Psychology, 13*, 535–536.

Rubin, Z. (1970). Measurement of romantic love. *Journal of Personality and Social Psychology, 16*, 265–273.

Rubin, Z. (1973). *Liking and loving: An invitation to social psychology*. New York: Holt, Rinehart & Winston.

Rubinstein, S., & Caballero, B. (2000). Is Miss America an undernourished role model? *Journal of the American Medical Association, 283*, 1569.

Ruble, D.N., Balaban, T., & Cooper, J. (1981). Gender constancy and the effects of sex-typed televised toy commercials. *Child Development, 52*, 667–673.

Rumbaugh, D.M., Savage-Rumbaugh, E.S., & Washburn, D.A. (1996). Toward a new look on primate learning and behaviour: Complex learning and emergent processes in comparative perspective. *Japanese Psychological Research, 38*, 113–125.

Runyon, R., & Haber, A. (1976). *Fundamentals of behavioural statistics* (3rd Edn.). Reading, MA: McGraw-Hill.

Rusbult, C.E. (1980). Commitment and satisfaction in romantic associations: A test of the investment model. *Journal of Experimental Social Psychology, 16*, 172–186.

Rusbult, C.E., Zembrodt, I., & Iwaniszek, J. (1986). The impact of gender and sex-role orientation on responses to dissatisfaction in close relationships. *Sex Roles, 15*, 1–20.

Rushton, J.P. (1988). Race differences in behaviour–A review and evolutionary analysis. *Personality and Individual Differences, 9*, 1009–1024.

Rushton, J.P. (1991). Cranial capacity correlated with race, rank, and sex among military personnel. *Behavior Genetics, 21*, 596.

Rushton, J.P. (1992). Cranial capacity related to sex, rank, and race in a stratified random sample of 6,325 United States military personnel. *Intelligence, 16*, 401–413.

Rushton, J.P., & Ankney, C.D. (1995). Brain size matters: A reply. *Canadian Journal of Experimental Psychology, 49*, 562–569.

Russell, M.J., Switz, G.M., & Thompson, K. (1980). Olfactory influences on the human menstrual cycle. *Pharmacology, Biochemistry and Behaviour, 13*, 737–738.

Rutter, M., Graham, P., Chadwick, D.F.D., & Yule, W. (1976). Adolescent turmoil: Fact or fiction. *Journal of Child Psychology and Psychiatry, 17*, 35–56.

Ryan, R.M., & Lynch, J.H. (1989). Emotional autonomy versus detachment: Revisiting the vicissitudes of adolescence and young adulthood. *Child Development, 60*, 340–356.

Ryder, R. (1990). *Animal revolution: Changing attitudes towards speciesism*. Oxford, UK: Blackwell.

Ryder, R. (1991). Sentientism: A comment on Gray and Singer. *The Psychologist, 14*, 201.

Rymer, R. (1993). *Genie: Escape from a silent childhood*. London: Michael Joseph.

Sackheim, H.A., Nordlie, J.W., & Gur, R.C. (1993). Effects of stimulus intensity and electrode replacement on the efficacy of the effects of electroconvulsive therapy. *New England Journal of Medicine, 328*, 839–846.

Sacks, O. (1995). *An anthropologist on Mars*. London: Picador.

Sagotsky, G., Wood-Schneider, M., & Konop, M. (1981). Learning to co-operate: Effects of modelling and direct instructions. *Child Development, 52*, 1037–1042.

Salamon, S. (1977). Family bonds and friendship bonds: Japan and West Germany. *Journal of Marriage and the Family, 39*, 807–820.

Salkovskis, P.M. (1996). The cognitive approach to anxiety: Threat beliefs, safety-seeking behaviour, and the special case of health anxiety and obsessions. In P.M. Salkovskis (Ed.), *Frontiers of cognitive therapy*. New York: Guilford.

Salomon, G., & Globerson, T. (1989). When groups do not function the way they ought to. *International Journal of Educational Research, 13*, 89–99.

Salovey, P. (Ed.). (1991). *The psychology of jealousy and envy*. New York: Guilford Press.

Sameroff, A.J., Bartko, W.T., Baldwin, A., Baldwin, C., & Seifer, R. (1998). Family and social influences on the development of child competence. *Families, Risk, and Competence*, 161–185.

Sameroff, A.J., Seifer, R., Baldwin, A., & Baldwin, C. (1993). Stability of intelligence from preschool to adolescence: The influence of social and family risk factors. *Child Development, 64*, 80–97.

Sameroff, A.J., Seifer, R., Barocas, R., Zax, M., & Greenspan, S. (1987). Intelligence quotient scores of 4-year-old children: Social-environmental risk factors. *Paediatrics, 79*, 343–350.

Samuel, J., & Bryant, P. (1984). Asking only one question in the conservation experiment. *Journal of Child Psychology and Psychiatry, 25*(2), 315–318.

Sanchez-Canovas, J. (1991). *La medida del afrontamiento. Paracticas para el estudio de las diferencias individuales y situacionales.* Valencia: Universidad de Valencia.

Santrock, J.W. (1975). Moral structure: The interrelations of moral behaviour, moral judgement, and moral affect. *Journal of Genetic Psychology, 127,* 201–213.

Sarason, I.G., Smith, R.E., & Diener, E. (1975). Personality research: Components of variance attributable to the person and the situation. *Journal of Personality and Social Psychology, 32,* 199–204.

Sasse, G., Müller, H., Chakraborty, R., & Ott, J. (1994). Estimating the frequency of non-paternity in Switzerland. *Human Heredity, 44*(6), 337–342.

Savin, H.B. (1973). Professors and psychological researchers: Conflicting values in conflicting roles. *Cognition, 2,* 147–149.

Scarr, S. (1988). Race and gender as psychological variables. *The American Psychologist, 43,* 56–59.

Schachter, S., & Singer, J.E. (1962). Cognitive, social, and physiological determinants of an emotional state. *Psychological Review, 69,* 379–399.

Schochat, T., Luboshitzky, R., & Lavie, P. (1997). Nocturnal melatonin onset is phase locked to the primary sleep gate. *American Journal of Physiology, 273,* R364–R370.

Schwartz, W., Recht, L., & Lew, R. (1995, October 29). Three time zones and you're out. *New Scientist.*

Searle, A. (1999). *Introducing research and data in psychology.* London: Routledge.

Seidman, L.J. (1983). Schizophrenia and brain dysfunction: An integration of recent neurodiagnostic findings. *Psychological Bulletin, 94,* 195–238.

Seitz, V. (1990). Intervention programs for impoverished children: A comparison of educational and family support models. *Annals of Child Development: A Research Annual, 7,* 73–103.

Seligman, M.E.P. (1970). On the generality of the laws of learning. *Psychological Review, 77,* 406–418.

Seligman, M.E.P. (1971). Phobias and preparedness. *Behavior Therapy, 2,* 307–320.

Seligman, M.E.P. (1975). *Helplessness: On depression, development and death.* San Francisco, CA: W.H. Freeman.

Semin, G.R. (1995). Social constructionism. In A.S.R. Manstead, M. Hewstone, S.T. Fiske, M.A. Hogg, H.T. Reis, & G.R. Semin (Eds.), *The Blackwell encyclopaedia of social psychology.* Oxford, UK: Blackwell.

Serbin, L.A., Powlishta, K.K., & Gulko, J. (1993). The development of sex-typing in middle childhood. *Monographs of Society for Research in Child Development, 58,* 1–74.

Serpell, R.S. (1979). How specific are perceptual skills? A cross-cultural study of pattern reproduction. *British Journal of Psychology, 70,* 365–380.

Serpell, R. (1982). Measures of perception, skills, and intelligence. In W.W. Hartup (Ed.), *Review of child development research.* Chicago, IL: University of Chicago Press.

Shaffer, D.R. (1993). *Developmental psychology: Childhood and adolescence* (3rd Edn.). Pacific Grove, CA: Brooks/Cole.

Shapiro, C.M., Bortz, R., Mitchell, D., Bartel, P., & Jooste, P. (1981). Slow-wave sleep: A recovery period after exercise. *Science, 214,* 1253–1254.

Shaver, J.P., & Strong, W. (1976). *Facing value decisions Rationale-building for teachers.* Belmont, CA: Wadsworth.

Shaver, P.R., Wu, S., & Schwartz, J.C. (1991). Cross-cultural similarities and differences in emotion and its representation: A prototype approach. In M.C. Clark (Ed.), *Review of personality and social psychology, Vol. 13.* Beverly Hills, CA: Sage.

Sherif, M., Harvey, O.J., White, B.J., Hood, W.R., & Sherif, C.W. (1961). *Intergroup conflict and co-operation: The robber's cave experiment.* Norman, OK: University of Oklahoma.

Short, R., & Potts, M. (1999). *Ever since Adam and Eve: The evolution of human sexuality.* Cambridge, UK: Cambridge University Press.

Shotland, R.L., & Straw, M.K. (1976). Bystander response to an assault: When a man attacks a woman. *Journal of Personality and Social Psychology, 34,* 990–999.

Shweder, R.A., Mahapatra, M., & Miller, J.G. (1990). Culture and moral development. In J. Stigler, R.A. Shweder, & G. Herdt (Eds.), *Cultural psychology: Essays in comparative human development* (pp. 130–204). New York: Cambridge University Press.

Sieber, J.E., & Stanley, B. (1988). Ethical and professional dimensions of socially sensitive research. *The American Psychologist, 43*(1), 49–55.

Siffre, M. (1975). Six months alone in a cave. *National Geographic,* March, 426–435.

Silver, R., LeSauter, J., Tresco, P.A., & Lehman, M.N. (1996). A diffusible coupling signal from the transplanted suprachiasmatic nucleus controlling circadian locomotor rhythms. *Nature, 382*(6594), 810–813.

Silverman, I. (1977). *The human subject in the psychological laboratory.* Oxford, UK: Pergamon.

Simmel, G. (1971). *On individuality and social forms.* Chicago, IL: University of Chicago Press.

Simmons, J.V. (1981). *Project Sea Hunt: A report on prototype development and tests* [Tech. Rep. No. 746]. San Diego, CA: Naval Ocean System Center.

Simmons, R.G., Burgeson, R., Carlton-Ford, S., & Blyth, D.A. (1987). The impact of cumulative changes in early adolescence. *Child Development, 58,* 1220–1234.

Singer, P. (1991). Speciesism, morality and biology: A response to Jeffrey Gray. *The Psychologist, 14,* 199–200.

Singer, P. (2005). *In defence of animals: The second wave.* Oxford, UK: Blackwell.

Singh, D. (2002). Female mate value at a glance: Relationship of waist-to-hip ratio to health, fecundity and attractiveness. *Neuroendocrinology Letters, 23*(Suppl 4), 81–91.

Skal, D. (1993). *The monster show: A cultural history of horror.* London: Plexus.

Skeels, H. M., & Dye, H. A. (1939). A study of the effects of differential stimulation in mentally retarded children. *Proceedings of the American Association of Mental Deficiency, 44,* 114–136.

Skinner, B.F. (1948). *Walden two.* New York: Macmillan.

Skinner, B.F. (1971). *Beyond freedom and dignity.* New York: Knopf.

Skinner, B.F. (1990). Can psychology be a science of mind? *American Psychologist, 45,* 1206–1210.

Skre, I., Onstad, S., Torgersen, S., Lygren, S., & Kringlen, E. (1993). A twin study of DSM-III-R anxiety disorders. *Acta Psychiatrica Scandinavica, 88,* 85–92.

Slaby, R.G., & Frey, K.S. (1975). Development of gender constancy and selective attention to same-sex models. *Child Development, 46,* 849–856.

Slater, L. (2004). *Opening Skinner's box: Great psychological experiments of the twentieth century.* New York: Norton.

Sloane, R.B., Staples, F.R., Cristol, A.H., Yorkston, N.J., & Whipple, K. (1975). *Psychotherapy versus behaviour therapy.* Cambridge, MA: Harvard University Press.

Smetana, J.G. (1988). Adolescents' and parents' concepts of parental authority. *Child Development, 59,* 321–335.

Smith, K., & Crawford, S. (1986). Suicidal behavior among "normal" high school students. *Suicide and Life Threatening Behavior, 16*, 313–325.

Smith, K.A., Clifford, E.M., Hockney, R.A, & Clark, D.M. (1997). Effect of tryptophan depletion on mood in male and female volunteers: A pilot study. *Human Psychopharmacology, Clinical and Experimental, 12*, 111–117.

Smith, K.D., Keating, J.P., & Stotland, E. (1989). Altruism reconsidered: The effect of denying feedback on a victim's status to empathic witnesses. *Journal of Personality and Social Psychology, 57*, 641–650.

Smith, M.L., Glass, G.V., & Miller, T.I. (1980). *The benefits of psychotherapy*. Baltimore, MD: John Hopkins Press.

Smith, N.V., & Tsimpli, I.-M. (1991). Linguistic modularity? A case-study of a "savant" linguist. *Lingua, 84*, 315–351.

Smith, P., & Bond, M.H. (1998). *Social psychology across cultures: Analysis and perspectives* (2nd Edn.). New York: Harvester.

Smith, R.L. (1984). Human sperm competition. In R.L. Smith (Ed.), *Sperm competition and the evolution of animal mating systems*. Orlando, FL: Academic Press.

Snarey, J.R. (1985). Cross-cultural universality of social-moral development: A critical review of Kohlbergian research. *Psychological Bulletin, 97*, 202–232.

Solley, C.M., & Murphy, G. (1960). *Development of the perceptual world*. New York: Basic Books.

Solms, M. (2000). Dreaming and REM sleep are controlled by different brain mechanisms. *Behavioral and Brain Sciences, 23*, 843–850.

Sprafkin, J.N., Liebert, R.M., & Poulos, R.W. (1975). Effects of a pro-social televised example on children's helping. *Journal of Experimental Child Psychology, 20*, 119–126.

Sroufe, L.A., Bennett, C., Englund, M., & Urban, J. (1993). The significance of gender boundaries in preadolescence: Contemporary correlates and antecedents of boundary violation and maintenance. *Child Development, 64*, 455–466.

Stajkovic, A.D., & Luthans, F. (1998). Self-efficacy and work-related performance: A meta-analysis. *Psychological Bulletin, 124*, 240–261.

Stanford, C.B. (1999). *The hunting apes*. Princeton, NJ: Princeton University Press.

Stangor, C., & Ruble, D.N. (1989). Differential influences of gender schemata and gender constancy on children's information processing and behaviour. Social Cognition, 7, 353–372.

Stern, S.L., Rush, J., & Mendels, J. (1980). Toward a rational pharmacotherapy of depression. *American Journal of Psychiatry, 137*, 545–552.

Stern, W.C., & Morgane, P.J. (1974). Theoretical view of REM sleep function: Maintenance of catecholamine systems in the central nervous system. *Behavioural Biology, 11*, 1–32.

Sternberg, R.J. (1985). *Beyond IQ: A triarchic theory of human intelligence*. Cambridge, UK: Cambridge University Press.

Sternberg, R.J. (1986). A triangular theory of love. *Psychological Review, 93*, 119–135.

Sternberg, R.J. (1994). Intelligence and cognitive styles. In A.M. Colman (Ed.), *Companion encyclopedia of psychology, Vol. 1*. London: Routledge.

Sternberg, R.J. (1998). *Cupid's arrow: The course of love through time*. Cambridge, UK: Cambridge University Press.

Sternberg, R.J. (2003, April). The other three Rs: Part two, reasoning. *APA Monitor*.

Sternberg, R.J., & Ben-Zeev, T. (2001). *Complex cognition: The psychology of human thought*. Oxford, UK: Oxford University Press.

Sternberg, R.J., & Grajek, S. (1984). The nature of love. *Journal of Personality and Social Psychology, 47*, 312–329.

Sternberg, R.J., Grigorenko, E.L., Ngorosho, D., Tantufuye, E., Mbise, A., Nokes, C., Jukes, M., & Bundy, D.A. (2002). Assessing intellectual potential in rural Tanzanian school children. *Intelligence, 30*, 141–162.

Stevens, A., & Price, J. (1996). *Evolutionary psychiatry*. London: Routledge.

Stevens, A., & Price, J. (2000). *Evolutionary psychiatry* (2nd Edn.). London: Routledge.

Stevens, S., Hynan, M.T., & Allen, M. (2000). A meta-analysis of common factor and specific treatment effects across the outcome domains of the phase model of psychotherapy. *Clinical Psychology: Science and Practice, 7*, 273–290.

Stevenson, M.R., & Black, K.N. (1988). Paternal absence and sex-role development: A meta-analysis. *Child Development, 59*, 793–814.

Stewart, K. (1998, February 15). *The Davis Enterprise*.

Stewart, R. (1997). Evolution of the human brain. http://homepage.mac.com/binck/reports/bevolution/ breport:html

Stirling, J.D., & Hellewell, J.S.E. (1999). *Psychopathology*. London: Routledge.

Stirling, J.D., & Hellewell, J.S.E. (2000). *Psychopathology*. London: Routledge.

Stopa, L., & Clark, D.M. (1993). Cognitive processes in social phobia. *Behaviour Research and Therapy, 31*, 255–267.

Strassberg, D.S., & Holtz, S. (2003). An experimental study of women's internet personal ads. *Archives of Sexual Behavior, 32*, 253–264.

Strupp, H.H. (1996). The tripartite model and the Consumer Reports study. *American Psychologist, 51*, 1017–1024.

Suddath, R.L., Christison, G.W., Torrey, E.F., Casanova, M.F., & Weinberger, D.R. (1990). Anatomical abnormalities in the brains of monozygotic twins discordant for schizophrenia. *New England Journal of Medicine, 322*, 789–794.

Sue, D., Sue, D., & Sue, S. (1994). *Understanding abnormal behaviour*. Boston, MA: Houghton Mifflin.

Sullivan, P.F., Neale, M.C., & Kendler, K.S. (2000). Genetic epidemiology of major depression: Review and meta-analysis. *American Journal of Psychiatry, 157*, 1552–1562.

Susser, E., Neugebauer, R., Hoek, H., Brown, A., Lin, S., Labovitz, D., & Gorman, J. (1996). Schizophrenia after prenatal famine: Further evidence. *Developmental Psychobiology, 29*, 25–31.

Taylor, S.E., Klein, L.C., Lewis, B.P., Gruenewald, T.L., Gurung, R.A.R., & Updegraff, J.A. (2000). Biobehavioural responses to stress in females: Tend-and-befriend, not fight-or-flight. *Psychological Review, 107*, 411–429.

Terman, L.M. (1916). *The measurement of intelligence*. Boston, MA: Houghton-Mifflin.

Terman, M. (1988). On the question of mechanism in phototherapy for seasonal affective disorder: Considerations of clinical efficacy and epidemiology. *Journal of Biological Rhythms, 3*, 155–172.

Teuting, P., Rosen, S., & Hirschfeld, R. (1981). *Special report on depression research* [NIMH-DHHS Publication No. 81–1085]. Washington, DC.

Thase, M.E., Rush, A.J., Howland, R.H., Kornstein, S.G., et al. (2002). Double-blind switch study of sertraline treatment of antidepressant-resistant chronic depression. *Archives of General Psychiatry, 59*, 233–239.

Thibaut, J.W., & Kelley, H.H. (1959). *The social psychology of groups*. New York: Wiley.

Thomas, A., & Chess, S. (1977). *Temperament and development*. New York: Brunner/Mazel.

Thomas, J., & Blackman, D. (1991). Are animal experiments on the way out? *The Psychologist, 4*, 208–212.

Thomas, M.H., Horton, R.W., Lippincott, E.C., & Drabman, R.S. (1977). Desensitisation to portrayals of real-life aggression as a function of exposure to television violence. *Journal of Personality and Social Psychology, 35*, 450–458.

Thorndike, E.L. (1911). *Animal intelligence: Experimental studies.* New York: MacMillan.

Thornhill, R., & Gangestad, S. (1999). Facial attractiveness. *Trends in Cognitive Sciences, 3*, 452–460.

Thurschwell, P. (2000). *Sigmund Freud.* London: Routledge.

Tienari, P. (1991). Interaction between genetic vulnerability and family environment: The Finnish adoptive family study of schizophrenia. *Acta Psychiatrica Scandinavica, 84*, 460–465.

Tolstedt, B.E., & Stokes, J.P. (1984). Self-disclosure, intimacy, and the depenetration process. *Journal of Personality and Social Psychology, 46*, 84–90.

Tomarken, A.J., Mineka, S., & Cook, M. (1989). Fear-relevant associations and covariation bias. *Journal of Abnormal Psychology, 98*, 381–394.

Tomlinson-Keasey, C., Eisert, D.C., Kahle, L.R., Hardy-Brown, K., & Keasey, B. (1979). The structure of concrete-operational thought. *Child Development, 57*, 1454–1463.

Tomlinson-Keasey, C., & Keasey, C.B. (1974). The mediating role of cognitive development in moral judgement. *Child Development, 45*, 291–298.

Tonay, V. (2003). *Every dream interpreted.* London: Collins & Brown Ltd.

Torgersen, S. (1983). Genetic factors in anxiety disorders. *Archives of General Psychiatry, 40*, 1085–1089.

Torrey, E.F. (1987). Psychiatric survivors and non-survivors. *Psychiatric Services, 48*, 143.

Torrey, E.F. (1992). Are we overestimating the genetic contribution to schizophrenia? *Schizophrenia Bulletin, 18*, 159–170.

Towhey, J.C. (1979). Sex-role stereotyping and individual differences in liking for the physically attractive. *Social Psychology Quarterly, 42*, 285–289.

Triandis, H.C. (1994). *Culture and social behaviour.* New York: McGraw-Hill.

Triandis, H.C., Carnevale, P., Gelfand, M., Robert, C., Wasti, A., Probst, T.M., Kashima, E.S., Dragonas, T., Chan, D., Chen, X.P., Kim, U., Kim, K., de Dreu, C., van de Vliert, E., Iwao, S., Ohbuchi, K., & Schmitz, P. (2001). Culture, personality and deception in intercultural management negotiations. *International Journal of Cross-Cultural Management, 1*, 73–90.

Trivers, R.L. (1971). The evolution of reciprocal altruism. *Quarterly Review of Biology, 46*, 35–57.

Trivers, R.L. (1972). Parental investment and sexual selection. In B. Campbell (Ed.), *Sexual selection and the descent of man, 1871–1971.* Chicago, IL: Aldine.

Truax, C.B. (1966). Therapist empathy, genuineness, and warmth and patient therapeutic outcome. *Journal of Consulting Psychology, 30*, 395–401.

Turkheimer, E., Haley, A., Waldron, M., D'Onofrio, B., & Gottesman, I.I. (2003). Socioeconomic status modifies heritability of IQ in young children. *Psychological Science, 14*, 623–628.

Turkle, S. (1995). *Life on the screen: Identity in the age of the internet.* New York: Simon and Schuster.

Turner, R.J., & Wagonfeld, M.O. (1967). Occupational mobility and schizophrenia. *American Sociological Review, 32*, 104–113.

Unger, R., & Crawford, M. (1996). *Women and gender: A feminist psychology* (2nd Edn.). New York: McGraw-Hill.

US Bureau of the Census (1992). *Poverty in the United States: 1992.* Washington, DC: US Government Printing Office.

US Congress, Office of Technology Assessment. (1991). *Biological rhythms: Implications for the worker* [OTA-BA-463]. Washington, DC: US Government Printing Office.

Valentine, E.R. (1982). *Conceptual issues in psychology.* London: Routledge.

Valentine, E.R. (1992). *Conceptual issues in psychology* (2nd Edn.). London: Routledge.

Van Kammen, D.P., Docherty, J.P., & Bunney, W.E. (1982). Prediction of early relapse after pimozide discontinuation by response to d-amphetamine during pimozide treatment. *Biological Psychiatry, 17*, 223–242.

Van Oppen, P., de Haan, E., van Balkom, A.J.L.M., Spinhoven, P., Hoogduin, K., & van Dyck, R. (1995). Cognitive therapy and exposure in vivo in the treatment of obsessive-compulsive disorder. *Behaviour Research and Therapy, 33*, 379–390.

Van Schie, E.G.M., & Wiegman, O. (1997). Children and videogames: Leisure activities, aggression, social integration, and school performance. *Journal of Applied Social Psychology, 27*, 1175–1194.

Vandello, J.A., & Cohen, D. (1999). Patterns of individualism and collectivism across the United States. *Journal of Personality and Social Psychology, 77*, 279–292.

Vassilas, C.A., & Morgan, H.G. (1997). Suicide in Avon. *British Journal of Psychiatry, 170*, 453–455.

Veitch, R., & Griffitt, W. (1976). Good news, bad news: Affective and interpersonal effects. *Journal of Applied Social Psychology, 6*, 69–75.

Verburg, K., Griez, E., Meijer, J., & Pols, H. (1995). Respiratory disorders as a possible predisposing factor for panic disorder. *Journal of Affective Disorders, 33*, 129–134.

Viguera, A.C., Nonacs, R., Cohen, L.S., Tondo, L., Murray, A., & Baldessarini, R.J. (2000). Risk of recurrence of bipolar disorder in pregnant and nonpregnant women after discontinuing lithium maintenance. *American Journal of Psychiatry, 157*, 179–184.

Virkkunen, M., Nuutila, A., Goodwin, F.K., & Linnoila, M. (1987). Cerebrospinal fluid monamine metabolite levels in male arsonists. *Archives of General Psychiatry, 44*, 241–247.

Vygotsky, L.S. (1976). Play and its role in the mental development of the child. In J.S. Bruner, A. Jolly, & K. Sylva (Eds.), *Play.* Harmondsworth, UK: Penguin.

Vygotsky, L.S. (1978). *Mind in society: The development of higher psychological processes.* Cambridge, MA: MIT Press.

Vygotsky, L.S. (1981). The genesis of higher mental functions. In J.V. Wertsch (Ed.), *The concept of activity in Soviet psychology.* Armonk, NY: Sharpe, Inc. (Original work published 1930).

Wachtel, P. (1973). Psychodynamics, behaviour therapy and the implacable experimenter: An inquiry into the consitency of personality. *Journal of Abnormal Psychology, 82*, 324–334.

Wahlberg, K.E., Lynne, L.C., Oja, H., Keskitalo, P., et al. (1997). Gene-environment interaction in vulnerability to schizophrenia: Findings from the Finnish adoptive family study of schizophrenia. *American Journal of Psychiatry, 154*, 355–262.

Walker, E.F., Savoie, T., & Davis, D. (1994). Neuromotor precursors of schizophrenia. *Schizophrenia Bulletin, 20*, 441–451.

Walker, L.J. (1999). Seedy world: Sexual scandal is rife in the grain store. *New Scientist, 2181*, 12.

Walker, L.J., de Vries, B., & Trevethan, S.D. (1987). Moral stages and moral orientations in real-life and hypothetical dilemmas. *Child Development, 58*, 842–858.

Wallace, P. (1999). *The psychology of the internet.* Cambridge, UK: Cambridge University Press.

Wallach, L., & Wallach, M.A. (1994). Gergen versus the mainstream: Are hypotheses in social psychology subject to empirical test? *Journal of Personality and Social Psychology, 67*, 233–242.

Walster, E., Aronson, V., Abrahams, D., & Rottman, L. (1966). The importance of physical attractiveness in dating behaviour. *Journal of Personality and Social Psychology, 4*, 508–516.

Walster, E., & Walster, G.W. (1969). *A new look at love*. Reading, MA: Addison Wesley.

Walster, E., Walster, G.W., & Berscheid, E. (1978). *Equity: Theory and research*. Boston, MA: Allyn & Bacon.

Walters, R.H., & Thomas, L. (1963). Enhancement of punitiveness by visual and audiovisual displays. *Canadian Journal of Psychology, 16*, 244–255.

Wampold, B.E., Mondin, G.W., Moody, M., Stich, F., Benson, K., & Ahn, H. (1997). A meta-analysis of outcome studies comparing bona fide psychotherapies: Empirically, "All must have prizes". *Psychological Bulletin, 122*, 203–215.

Wason, P.C., & Shapiro, D. (1971). Natural and contrived experience in reasoning problems. *Quarterly Journal of Experimental Psychology, 23*, 63–71.

Waterman, A.S. (1982). Identity development from adolescence to adulthood: An extension of theory and review of research. *Developmental Psychology, 18*, 341–348.

Waterman, A.S. (1985). Identity in the context of adolescent psychology. *New directions for child development, 30*, 5–24.

Waterman, C.K., & Waterman, A.S. (1975). Fathers and sons: A study of ego identity across two generations. *Journal of Youth and Adolescence, 4*, 331–338.

Watson, J.B., & Rayner, R. (1920). Conditioned emotional reactions. *Journal of Experimental Psychology, 3*, 1–14.

Watson, P.J., & Andrews, P.W. (2002). Toward a revised evolutionary adaptationist analysis of depression: The social navigation hypothesis. *Journal of Affective Disorders, 72*, 1–14.

Webb, W.B. (1982). Sleep and biological rhythms. In W.B. Webb (Ed.), *Biological rhythms, sleep and performance*. Chichester, UK: John Wiley & Sons.

Webb, W.B., & Bonnet, M.H. (1978). The sleep of "morning" and "evening" types. *Biological Psychology, 7* (1–2), 29–35.

Webb, W.B., & Cartwright, R.D. (1978). Sleep and dreams. *Annual Review of Psychology, 29*, 223–252.

Wegner, D.M., & Wheatley, T. (1999). Apparent mental causation: Sources of the experience of will. *American Psychologist, 54*, 480–492.

Weinreich, P. (1979). Ethnicity and adolescent identity conflicts. In S. Khan (Ed.), *Minority families in Britain*. London: Macmillan.

Weissman, M.M., Klerman, G.L., & Paykel, E.S. (1971). Clinical evaluation of hostility in depression. *American Journal of Psychiatry, 39*, 1397–1403.

Wender, P.H., Kety, S.S., Rosenthal, D., Schulsinger, F., Ortmann, J., & Lunde, I. (1986). Psychiatric disorders in the biological and adoptive families of adopted individuals with affective disorders. *Archives of General Psychiatry, 43*, 923–929.

Werner, C., & Parmalee, P. (1979). Similarity of activity preferences among friends: Those who play together, stay together. *Social Psychology Quarterly, 42*, 62–66.

Wertsch, J.V., McNamee, G.D., Mclane, J.B., & Budwig, N.A. (1980). The adult–child dyad as a problem-solving system. *Child Development, 51*, 1215–1221.

Westcott, M.R. (1982). Quantitative and qualitative aspects of experienced freedom. *Journal of Mind and Behavior, 3*, 99–126.

Westen, D. (1996). *Psychology: Mind, brain, and culture*. New York: Wiley.

Westen, D., & Gabbard, G.O. (1999). Psychoanalytic approaches to personality. In L.A. Pervin & O.P. John (Eds), *Handbook of personality: Theory and research*. New York: Guilford Press.

Wetherell, M., & Potter, J. (1988). Discourse analysis and the identification of interpretive repertoires. In C. Antaki (Ed.), *Analysing everyday explanation: A casebook of methods*. London: Sage.

Wever, R. (1979). *Circadian rhythms system of man: Results of experiments under temporal isolation*. New York: Springer.

Wheeler, L.R. (1932). The intelligence of East Tennessee children. *Journal of Educational Psychology, 23*, 351–370.

Wheeler, L.R. (1942). A comparative study of the intelligence of East Tennessee mountain children. *Journal of Educational Psychology, 33*, 321–334.

Wheldall, K., & Poborca, B. (1980). Conservation without conversation: An alternative, non-verbal paradigm for assessing conservation of liquid quantity. *British Journal of Psychology, 71*, 117–134.

Whiting, B.B., & Whiting, J.W. (1975). *Children of six countries: A psychological analysis*. Cambridge, MA: Harvard University Press.

Whyte, M.K. (1978). *The status of women in preindustrial societies*. Princeton, NJ: Princeton University Press.

Wiegman, O., Kuttschreuter, M., & Baarda, B. (1992). A longitudinal study of the effects of television viewing on aggressive and prosocial behaviours. *British Journal of Social Psychology, 31*, 147–164.

Wilkinson, R.T. (1969). Sleep deprivation: Performance tests for partial and selective sleep deprivation. In L.A. Abt & J.R. Reiss (Eds.), *Progress in clinical psychology*. New York: Grune & Stratton.

Willerman, L. (1979). *The psychology of individual and group differences*. San Francisco, CA: W.H. Freeman.

Willerman, L., Schultz, R., Rutledge, J.N., & Bigler, E.D. (1991). *In vivo* brain size and intelligence. *Intelligence, 15*, 223–228.

Williams, J.E., & Best, D.L. (1982). *Measuring sex stereotypes: A thirty nations study*. London: Sage.

Williams, J.E., & Best, D.L. (1990). *Measuring sex stereotypes: A multination study*. Newbury Park, CA: Sage.

Williams, J.E., & Best, D.L. (1992). Psychological factors associated with cross-cultural differences in individualism-collectivism. In S. Iwawaki, Y. Kashima, & K. Leung (Eds.), *Innovations in cross-cultural psychology*. Amsterdam: Swets & Zeitlinger.

Williams, J.H. (1987). *Psychology of women* (3rd Edn.). London: W.W. Norton & Co.

Williams, L.M. (1994). Recall of childhood trauma: A prospective study of women's memories of child sexual abuse. *Journal of Consulting and Clinical Psychology, 62*, 1167–1176.

Williams, R.L. (1972). *The BITCH Test (Black Intelligence Test of Cultural Homogeneity)*. St. Louis, MI: Washington University.

Williams, T.M. (Ed.). (1986). *The impact of television: A national experiment in three communities*. New York: Academic Press.

Wilson, E.O. (1975). *Sociobiology: The new synthesis*. Cambridge, UK: Harvard University Press.

Winch, R.F. (1958). *Mate selections: A study of complementary needs*. New York: Harper.

Windgassen, K. (1992). Treatment with neuroleptics: The patient's perspective. *Acta Psychiatrica Scandinavica, 86*, 405–410.

Winson, H. (1997). The relationship of dissociative conditions to sleep and dreaming. In S. Krispner & S.M. Powers (Eds.), *Broken images, broken selves: Dissociative narratives in clinical practice.* Bristol, PA: Brunner/Mazel.

Wirz-Justice, A., Graw, P., Krauchi, K., Sarrafzadeh, A., English, J., Arendt, J., & Sand, L. (1996). "Natural" light treatment of seasonal affective disorder. *Journal of Affective Disorders, 37,* 109–120.

Wolpe, J. (1958). *Psychotherapy by reciprocal inhibition.* New York: Pergamon Press.

Wood, D.J., Bruner, J.S., & Ross, G. (1976). The role of tutoring in problem solving. *Journal of Child Psychology and Psychiatry, 17,* 89–100.

Wood, J.T., & Duck, S. (Eds.). (1995). *Understanding relationships: Off the beaten track.* Thousand Oaks, CA: Sage.

Wood, W., & Eagly, A.H. (2002). A cross-cultural analysis of the behaviour of women and men: Implications for the origins of sex differences. *Psychological Bulletin, 128,* 699–727.

Wood, W., Wong, F.Y., & Chachere, J.G. (1991). Effects of media violence on viewers' aggression in unconstrained social interaction. *Psychological Bulletin, 109,* 371–383.

Wright, P., Takei, N., Rifkin, L., Murray, R.M., & Shaw, P.C. (1999). Seasonality, prenatal influenza exposure, and schizophrenia. In E.S. Susser, A.S. Brown, & J.M. Gorman (Eds.), *Prenatral exposures in schizophrenia.* Washington, DC: American Psychiatric Press.

Yalom, I.D. (1975). *The theory and practice of group psychotherapy* (2nd Edn.). New York: Basic Books.

Yeates, K.O., MacPhee, D., Campbell, F.A., & Ramey, C.T. (1983). Maternal IQ and home environment as determinants of early childhood intellectual competence: A developmental analysis. *Developmental Psychology, 19,* 731–739.

Yelsma, P., & Athappily, K. (1988). Marital satisfaction and communication practices: Comparisons among Indian and American couples. *Journal of Comparative Family Studies, 19,* 37–54.

Young, K. (1999). *Cyber-disorders: The mental illness concern for the millennium.* Paper presented at the 108th annual meeting of the American Psychological Association, Boston, MA.

Young, W.C., Goy, R.W., & Phoenix, C.H. (1964). Hormones and sexual behaviour. *Science, 143,* 212–219.

Zaadstra, B.M., Seidell, J.C., Vannoord, P.A.H., Tevelde, E.R., Habbema, J.D.F., Vrieswijk, B., & Karbaat, J. (1993). Fat and female fecundity: Prospective study of effect of body-fat distribution on conception rates. *British Medical Journal, 306,* 484–487.

Zahavi, A. (1977). The cost of honesty (further remarks on the handicap principle). *Journal of Theoretical Biology, 67,* 603–605.

Zahn-Waxler, C., Radke-Yarrow, M., & King, R.A. (1979). Child rearing and children's prosocial initiations toward victims of distress. *Child Development, 50,* 319–330.

Zhar, J.H. (1972). Significance testing of the Spearman rank correlation coefficient. *Journal of the American Statistical Association, 67,* 578–580.

Zigler, E., & Muenchow, S. (1992). *Head Start: The inside story of America's most successful educational experiment.* New York: Basic Books.

Zigler, E.F., Abelson, W.D., & Seitz, V. (1973). Motivational factors in the performance of economically disadvantaged children on the Peabody Picture Vocabulary Test. *Child Development, 44,* 294–303.

Zillmann, D. (1979). *Hostility and aggression.* Hillsdale, NJ: Lawrence Erlbaum Associates Inc.

Zillmann, D., Johnson, R.C., & Day, K.D. (1974). Attribution of apparent arousal and proficiency of recovery from sympathetic activation affecting excitation transfer to aggressive behaviour. *Journal of Experimental Social Psychology, 10,* 503–515.

Zimbardo, P.G. (1973). On the ethics of intervention in human psychological research: With special reference to the Stanford prison experiment. *Cognition, 2,* 243–256.

AUTHOR INDEX

SUBJECT INDEX

ILLUSTRATION CREDITS

CHAPTER 1

Page 15: Marking allocation for AQA specification has been reproduced by kind permission of the Assessment and Qualifications Alliance.

CHAPTER 2

Page 26 (top left): © Frank Trapper/CORBIS. Page 26 (top right): © Royalty-Free/CORBIS. Page 26 (bottom left): © Baverel/Lefranc/ CORBIS KIPA. Page 26 (bottom right): © Royalty-Free/CORBIS. Page 28: Popperfoto. Page 29: © Royalty-Free/CORBIS. Page 33: © Royalty-Free/ CORBIS. Page 34: © Cortes Jody Anthony/CORBIS SYGMA. Page 37: © Royalty-Free/CORBIS. Page 40: © Leland Bobbé/CORBIS. Page 45: © Yang Liu/CORBIS. Page 50: © Patrik Giardino/CORBIS. Page 54: © Royalty-Free/CORBIS. Page 59: © Michael S. Yamashita/CORBIS. Page 62: © Maggie Hallahan/CORBIS. Page 64: © Tim McGuire/CORBIS.

CHAPTER 3

Page 76 (top): © Royalty-Free/ CORBIS. Page 76 (bottom): Reproduced by kind permission of Professor Albert Bandura. Page 81: © Philip James Corwin/CORBIS. Page 83: © Reuters/CORBIS. Page 84 (top): © Owen Franken/CORBIS. Page 84 (bottom): © Darren Staples/Reuters/CORBIS. Page 86: © Steve Prezant/CORBIS. Page 88: © John Atashian/CORBIS. Page 95: © Ariel Skelley/CORBIS. Page 96: © Kim Kyung-Hoon/Reuters/CORBIS. Page 100: © Tom Stewart/CORBIS. Page 103: © Royalty-Free/CORBIS. Page 116: © Bureau L.A. Collection/CORBIS. Page 118: © William Gottlieb/CORBIS.

CHAPTER 4

Page 126: © Crack Palinggi/Reuters/ CORBIS. Page 127 (top): Reproduced with permission from Evie Bentley (2000), *Awareness: Biorythms, sleep and dreaming*. London: Routledge.

Page 133: © Najlah Feanny/CORBIS. Page 134: © Najlah Feanny/CORBIS SABA. Page 140: Reprinted from W.C. Dement and N. Kleitman (1957), Cyclic variations in EEG during sleep and their relations to eye movements, body motility and dreaming. *Clinical Neurophysiology*, 9, 673–690. Copyright © 1957, with permission from the International Federation of Clinical Neurophysiology. Page 143: © Anne W. Krause/CORBIS. Page 145: © Tom Stewart/CORBIS. Page 148: © George Hall/CORBIS. Page 152: Alan Hobson/Science Photo Library. Page 155: © Bettmann/ CORBIS.

CHAPTER 5

Page 168 (top): © Bettmann/CORBIS. Page 168 (bottom): © Roy Botterell/ CORBIS. Page 169: © LWA-Dann Tardif/CORBIS. Page 171: Photos by Peter Willatts. Reproduced with permission. Page 186: © Laura Dwight/CORBIS. Page 187: © Ronnie Kaufman/CORBIS. Page 188: © Craig Hammell/CORBIS. Page 190: © Ken Kaminesky/CORBIS. Page 191: © LWA-Dann Tardif/CORBIS. Page 193: © Royalty-Free/CORBIS. Page 194: © Ted Horowitz/CORBIS. Page 195: © Robert Maass/CORBIS. Page 202: © Francoise de Mulder/CORBIS. Page 203: © Cydney Conger/CORBIS. Page 205: © Norbert Schaefer/CORBIS. Page 210: Adapted from A.J. Sameroff, R. Seifer, A. Baldwin, and C. Baldwin (1993). Stability of intelligence from preschool to adolescence: The influence of social and family risk factors. *Child Development*, 64, 80–97. Page 213: © Royalty-Free/CORBIS. Page 219: © Royalty-Free/CORBIS. Page 221: © Amet Jean Pierre/CORBIS SYGMA. Page 222: © Alexandra Winkler/ Reuters/CORBIS. Page 227: Adapted from A. Colby, L. Kohlberg, J. Gibbs, and M. Lieberman (1983). A longitudinal study of moral judgment. *Monographs of the Society for Research in Child Development*, 48,

(Nos. 1–2, serial no. 200). Page 232: © Ariel Skelley/CORBIS.

CHAPTER 6

Page 240: © Hulton-Deutsch Collection/CORBIS. Page 245: Popperfoto. Page 248: © Royalty-Free/ CORBIS. Page 249: Reproduced by kind permission of Professor Albert Bandura. Page 251 (left): © Owen Franken/CORBIS. Page 251 (right): © Baumgartner Olivia/CORBIS SYGMA. Page 258: © Philip Gould/CORBIS. Page 259: © Tim Pannell/CORBIS. Page 260: © Royalty-Free/CORBIS. Page 262: © Jim Zuckerman/CORBIS. Page 264: © Ronnie Kaufman/CORBIS. Page 269: © Royalty-Free/CORBIS. Page 272: © Lynsey Addario/CORBIS. Page 285: © Ariel Skelley/CORBIS. Page 290: © Charles & Josette Lenars/ CORBIS.

CHAPTER 7

Page 299: © Matthias Kulka/CORBIS. Page 300: © Yann Arthus-Bertrand/CORBIS. Page 301 © Tim Davis/CORBIS. Page 303: Popperfoto. Page 304: © Bob Krist/CORBIS. Page 305: © Royalty-Free/CORBIS. Page 307: © Marcello Calandrini/CORBIS. Page 309: Figure from "Human sperm competition" in *Sperm competition and the evolution of animal mating systems* by Robert L. Smith, copyright © 1984 Academic Press, reproduced with permission from Elsevier. Page 321: © Bettmann/CORBIS. Page 328 (top): Adapted from J.M. Fuster (1989). *The prefrontal cortex (2nd Ed.)*. New York: Raven Press. Page 329: Adapted from A.S. Romer (1962). *The vertebrate body*. PA: W.B. Saunders Co. Page 330: Reproduced with permission from *The Times*. Copyright © The Times London, June 18 1999. Page 332: © Gallo Images/CORBIS.

CHAPTER 8

Page 343: © Royalty-Free/CORBIS. Page 345: © Bill Ross/CORBIS. Page 357: © David Turnley/CORBIS.